16

*Readings in
the Psychology of
Human Growth
and Development*

Readings in the Psychology of Human Growth and Development

WARREN R. BALLER
UNIVERSITY OF NEBRASKA

Holt, Rinehart and Winston, Inc.
NEW YORK

Preface

THIS BOOK OF READINGS WAS PLANNED TO serve as a companion-piece to *The Psychology of Human Growth and Development* by Warren R. Baller and Don C. Charles. It therefore contains a substantial number of the publications which are drawn upon—of necessity only briefly—for the conclusions set forth in the textbook. The writer shares the belief of many instructors that courses in psychology can be improved considerably by introducing students to such material, and a satisfactory book of readings solves the problem of their accessibility.

An alternative function of the *Readings* is as an independent basic textbook. One of its features in particular should facilitate such use. There is in most of the chapters an introductory reading chosen in part for its value in orienting the student to the problems with which the chapter as a whole deals. Thus, stu-

v

dents having a limited acquaintance with the areas covered by the chapters have the way cleared for their better understanding of the more technical readings that follow the opening selection. Additional enhancement of the *Readings'* usefulness as a textbook is provided by the orienting introductions to chapters and by statements that serve as transitions from one part of the *Readings* to another.

In addition to the comparatively easy introductory selections, there is, in most of the chapters, some reading that will challenge and, it is hoped, arouse the interest of the more capable students. In this way, both the more sophisticated student and the relatively unsophisticated one should find some readings suited to their abilities and interests.

The *Readings* follow the textbook, *The Psychology of Human Growth and Development,* in being divided into four main parts. Part One, "Orientation to the Study of Human Behavior and Development," is intended (1) to acquaint the student with the objectives of psychology and the importance of knowledge of human development in a psychology for teachers; (2) to provide some *basic ideas* that can be developed and expanded by the student as he proceeds through the book and that will further emphasize the relevance of the material to his training as a teacher; and (3) to demonstrate at the outset the dependence that sound knowledge of human development has on the use of the scientific method. Part Two, "The Bio-social Foundations of Human Behavior," includes in its several chapters selections dealing with the prenatal origins of behavior and the roles of perception, emotion, motivation, and cultural experience in the producing and shaping of individual behavior. The five chapters of Part Three, "Development and Adjustment," present many of the facts of physical, mental, verbal, and social development and also consider certain of their implications for personality development and adjustment. Part Four, "Personality and the School's Role in Its Development," consists of two chapters, Fourteen and Fifteen. The readings in Chapter Fourteen should help the student correlate many of the principles and concepts that have been developed in the preceding chapters and especially to relate his ideas about personality development to the organizing function of the self-concept. Chapter Fifteen confronts the practical question of how a teacher can apply effectively his knowledge of human growth and development to the experiences of the school. Several important aspects of this major responsibility of the teacher are dealt with in this concluding chapter.

Many persons have in one way or another assisted the editor in his preparation of this book. Certainly, without the generous cooperation of the authors of the selections and their publishers, and many instances of their *special* help, this volume could not have been produced. The editor can only hope that a sincere *thank you* and the credit lines that appear with the readings will convey at least in part his gratitude to all concerned.

The editor wishes also to acknowledge his indebtedness to present and former members of the Department of Educational Psychology and Measurements of the University of Nebraska, upon whose experience in the teaching of educational psychology he could draw in his planning of this book. Especially in this regard is he grateful to Dr. Charles O. Neidt, until recently Chairman of the Department, and to Dr. Dean A. Worcester, also former Chairman of the Department, now of the University of Arizona.

Particularly helpful in the preparation of the *Readings* were some other persons closely associated with the editor. They are James Beaird, William Jensen, John Lawson, Ebert L. Miller, George Pinckney, David Raulston, Douglas Sjogren, and Dr. Howard E. Tempero, all of the Department of Educational Psychology and Measurements of the University of Nebraska, and Dr. Martin J. Maehr, of the Department of Psychology, Concordia Senior College, Fort Wayne, Indiana.

In the preparation of a book there are innumerable details that only able secretaries and typists can handle well. For their competent assistance with the manuscript, I wish to thank Miss Diane Ankerstar, Mrs. Elsa Peck, Mrs. Joyce Sjogren, Mrs. Sheryl Oberg Snyder, Miss Carolene Steuck, Miss Lorraine Sysel, and Mrs. Sally Wagner.

Lincoln, Nebraska   W. R. B.
December 1961

Contents

PART

ONE

↑

Orientation to the Study of Human Behavior and Development

The purpose of Part One is to afford the student an *overview* of the psychology of human development. The nine selections that comprise the three chapters of Part One contribute different—but related—views of the domain of psychology and especially that part of the domain that relates to the study of the growth and development of *persons*.

CHAPTER

ONE

▲

A Teacher's Need for Psychology

THE PURPOSE OF THIS CHAPTER IS TO ANSWER several main questions about psychology. The answers to these questions will also help explain the purpose of this book of readings.

What is psychology and with what kinds of problems does it deal? Where does educational psychology fit into this picture? Finally, what specifically is the psychology of human development and how does it relate to educational psychology?

An overly simplified definition of psychology is to call it a study of *behavior*. This definition needs to be qualified by the assertion that many kinds of behavior are *not* any part of psychology's subject matter. "The absorption of food by the digestive system of the organism" (to cite an example from Leonard Carmichael's discussion) is behavior, but not of the kinds with which

3

psychology deals. What a person does and thinks, what his feelings, hopes, fears, and attitudes are; these *are* the kinds of behavior that constitute psychology's subject matter. So considered, psychology is defined by Carmichael as *"the science which deals with the facts and events arising out of the interaction between a creature and its environment by means of receptors, nervous system and effectors."*

The reader will get additional insights into what psychology tries to do from Carmichael's description of its domain as a science and his account of certain fundamental differences among psychologists as to how best to define and investigate its problems. For much of his professional life Carmichael has been directly associated with developments in psychology as author of numerous publications and as member of the faculty in psychology at Princeton University, Brown University, the University of Rochester, and Tufts University. Since 1953 he has been Secretary and administrative head of the Smithsonian Institute.

What has psychology to offer for the prediction and control of behavior? Is there substantial evidence that psychology can help solve many of the puzzles about human behavior that take the form of "if this—then what?" Can it, in other words, help us relate antecedent conditions and behavioral consequences? Carl R. Rogers, of the University of Wisconsin, has given an affirmative answer in the form of a dozen illustrations of the kinds of situations in which psychology has much to offer regarding the prediction and control of behavior. The fact that Rogers in this discussion chose to focus his attention on the educational implications of psychology's advances as a science makes this article all the more important to the reader whose professional responsibilities are—or will soon be—in the domain of teaching.

The article by Arthur P. Coladarci of Stanford University has a close and logical relationship to the one which precedes it. "The teacher's task," says Coladarci, "can be seen as one of manipulating the learning situation in such a way that the *predicted* behavior changes actually do occur." But Coladarci finds that in many situations confronting teachers the right manipulations are not easily determined. Hence, "The teacher . . . *must be an active, continuous inquirer into the validity of his own procedures."*

Coladarci describes the relationship that must exist between the teacher and the educational psychologist for this vital, continuous inquiry to be sustained: the type of inquiry out of which comes better understanding of learning and the methods best suited to the effective influencing of learning.

Finally, Harold E. Jones, an acknowledged leader in human growth studies, underscores the importance of the recognition on the part of educators and teachers that it is *persons* who go to school, "not just an equipment for learning, not just memories, minds or intellects." This being the truth—that those we instruct and guide in school are persons (individuals)—it follows that teachers, educational psychologists, and researchers in child growth and development have a common task of sizeable proportions and far-reaching significance. It is the task of combining the best knowledge available about child growth and development with improved methods of studying children as individuals to the end that what we do in school will constitute *teaching of persons.* Jones, prior to his death in 1960, was for twenty-five years Director of the Institute of Human Development (formerly the Institute of Child Welfare), University of California at Berkeley.

───▶ **Leonard Carmichael**

What Modern Psychology
Tries to Do

From *Basic Psychology*, by Leonard Carmichael. © Copyright 1957 by Leonard Carmichael. Reprinted and abridged by permission of Random House Inc.

The vast structure of modern science which includes psychology is itself one of the greatest intellectual triumphs of what we commonly call man's *mind*. Psychology is that part of this structure which studies human and animal behavior, consciously known experience, and indeed all the phenomena that are basic to the idea of mind itself. Scientific psychology in a general sense is thus dedicated to the investigation of the characteristics and causes of the actions of living organisms which take place in varying external conditions. It studies human activities such as those involved in the successful mastery of school subjects, the acquisition of athletic skills, the development of fears, the capacity to sell products and services, artistic creation and the maintenance of socially approved ideals.

In the case of the human being, the psychologist begins his study with an investigation of the behavior that characterizes the infant before birth. He considers the altogether marvelous series of growth changes by which this relatively helpless, non-social, biological organism becomes an effective adult person capable of living a somewhat independent existence in society and ordering his own life with some real freedom in terms of the circumstances and traditions of the society of which he is a part.

To present an over-all view of basic scientific psychology, it is necessary to examine the actions of real, modern, normal and, by way of illustration, abnormal human beings. The point of view here presented deals with some of the observed facts and the generalizations of psychology. To try to approach the problems of the control of one's self or of others today without some knowledge of psychology may be as illogical as would be an attempt to learn how to cure human physical illness without first gaining an understanding of the physiology and anatomy of the normal human body, or how to try to invent a new type of color television without some knowledge of physics.

The reader, therefore, who may be impatient to find some particular application of psychology which he believes may be of value to him is urged not to judge the usefulness of psychology in increasing his understanding of himself or of other people by an isolated segment of the subject. Whoever wishes to gain the values that come from a knowledge of psychology can best achieve this end by first of all acquiring, in outline, at least, a knowledge of the general structure of present-day scientific psychology.

Fundamentally, scientific psychology deals with the interaction between a living organism and the world in which that organism exists. Every creature is continually being acted upon by the surrounding world, its environment, and as a consequence of its own bodily make-up the individual in turn acts upon this environment. Sometimes this process is direct and obvious and sometimes it is involved and even completely hidden from casual observations.

The special interplay between the living individual and his surroundings, which includes both personal experience such as thoughts, and observable behavior such as acts of skill, has been summarized in the single phrase, *mental life*. Many of the chemical and physical relationships between the body and its surrounding world, such as the absorption of food by the digestive system of the organism and the taking up of oxygen by the blood although "organism-environment reactions," do not belong to the specific field of psychological study.

What is meant by mental life may be further clarified by considering the anatomical structures of the living body which are especially concerned in the activities upon which people universally base their opinions concerning an individual's mental make-up. In the higher animals and man these activities are dependent on a complex living system which has been termed the *response mechanism*.

The structures which make up this mechanism are those parts of the body which are most directly concerned in the interaction between the individual and the world in which he lives . . . Changes in the external physical energies of the environment (such as light or radiant energy, that is, visual *stimuli*) act upon certain of the individual's sense organs (or *receptors*). Following this stimulation of the receptors, activity is started in the *nervous system*, which includes the brain as its most important part. The human organs by means of which response is carried out are technically called *effectors*. There are two classes of effectors in the human body, muscles and glands. An example of effector action following stimulation which involves a gland rather than a muscle is the secretion of saliva by the salivary glands of the mouth at the sight or smell of a squeezed lemon. The result of stimulus-induced activity in an effector which accomplishes something for the organism as a whole is called a *response* or *reaction*.

Modern psychological investigation has been able to show that the relationship between stimulation and response . . . is fundamental in understanding mental life. This field may thus be defined as follows: *Psychology is the science which deals with the facts and events arising out of the interaction between a creature and its environment by means of receptors, nervous system and effectors.*

A central problem of psychology can thus be said to be the exact description and scientific explanation of the development of the adaptive responses made by organisms to stimuli. The stimuli, or certain variable aspects of limited groups of all the stimuli acting upon the organism, also are as accurately measured as possible in scientific psychological investigations.

Hundreds of specific and humanly important questions face the psychologist. He must try to analyze them and deal with them in as general terms as possible. He thus comes to face questions such as: How do human beings learn? What is day dreaming? How do men and women develop lasting forms of social life? How do people communicate with each other? What is the nature of emotion? All of these human problems already have been experimentally investigated and can now be quite accurately dealt with. Others are still imperfectly understood and are beyond the present but always advancing frontiers of scientific psychology.

The time has come when a well-educated person who is willing to be ignorant of what psychology is like is on unstable ground. He may be almost as out of date as he would be if he accepted the other view of Heraclitus that all of physics is based upon an element of universal fire.

In considering mental life it is well to know that in the past its subject matter has been considered in relation to so-called *schools of psychology*. This point of view is not emphasized as much today as formerly. Psychology as a science has come to embrace a general conceptual framework which is not easily set off in parts as related to schools of thought.

At least the names of the principal schools of psychology, however, are still a part of the general knowledge of psychology.

Psychologists who emphasize the study of introspectively known conscious experience are called *Introspective Psychologists*. Those introspective psychologists who try to analyze the content of thought and experience into mental elements were said to be members of the Structural School. The word, "were" is used here because this point of view has few adherents now. These structuralists did not study the structure of the body but rather the structure or make-up of conscious experience itself. One type of structural psychology was called *Existential*. It was so called because it limited its study to describable aspects of present experience. It is not related to current European philosophical Existentialism.

Those who considered that some important psychological processes were not given in the mental structures of sensations, images or other contents of consciousness were called *Imageless Thought Psychologists*. They were interested in the processes which steer or direct (as in the case of persisting mental attitudes or "sets") many processes of thought. Sometimes these processes were found to be conscious and sometimes non-conscious. The term *Phenomenology* is given to the study of the "raw" phenomena of conscious experience just as they occur in immediate experience and without analysis. Historically some types of Phenomenology and Imageless Thought Psychology are not unrelated.

Many American psychologists early rebelled against psychology as the exclusive study of the structure or function of conscious experience. They thought of the evolution of biological forms and of the part that intelligence, emotion and related mental processes play in the adaptive life of all mammals including man. This point of view in its early days still emphasized consciousness and the use of introspection in its studies. Those who advocated it came to be called the *American Functional School*. Gradually under the direction of many experimental students and especially because of the intensive study of animal psychology, the consideration of adaptive bodily behavior for its own sake became one of the principal objectives or even the only subject matter of psychology. In this *Behaviorism* a positive claim is made that psychology need not deal at all directly with introspectively known conscious experiences but should only study responses and the factors which underlie them. A type of "purposeful behaviorism" or *Hormic Behaviorism* also has developed which has some affinity with vitalism in biology in that it assumes that behavior fits a plan or purpose beyond that of the person himself.

Gestalt Psychology is so called from the German word for form, shape or pattern. This psychology studies the behavior of children and animals as well as perception and the other topics of introspective psychology. Its main emphasis is on the fact that the forms of mental life, as considered in behavior and in experiences, are to be studied as organized wholes. In a sense it was a revolt against the excessive tendency of many psychologists to try so hard to take apart experience and behavior that the products of their analysis had little value either as science or in the applied knowledge in everyday life. The Gestalt psychologist saw total pattern as much more than the sum of parts put together by association or in any other way.

A point of view that developed in part out of Gestalt psychology is *Psychological Field Theory*. In this way of looking at psychology the idea of life space as including the person and his environment is emphasized. This point of view is very inclusive and has been applied with especial success in considering those aspects of social behavior that are related to *Group Dynamics*. In much of this work man is considered as existing in a field of forces like the fields of force in physics and his behavior is described as a result of the valences and vectors of the field. The field is dynamic and involves positive and negative forces and the interposition of barriers between the individual and his goals.

Many psychological facts are revealed and emphasized by one or the other of the "schools" mentioned above. Far from championing any school, this book rather tries to approach the study of mental life as nearly as possible from a general scientific point of view, but with special reference to physiological facts. Within this frame of reference, it is possible to consider some aspects of the kind of mental life that give man at his best a unique place in all creation and his dignity as a free individual in an achieving society.

BRANCHES OF PSYCHOLOGY

Today psychology is divided into various sections. Human psychology is one name customarily given to the study of mental life of the normal adult human being. This study is distinct from each of the special fields given below, *but there is no one of the other branches of psychology which does not contribute to the scientific understanding of basic adult psychology.*

Developmental or child psychology is the branch of psychology which deals with the origin and growth of mental life before birth, in the infant, the child, the adolescent and the aged. More and more it becomes obvious that adult human mental processes have their origin in childhood and in some instances even in the active fetal period of behavioral life.

Comparative or animal psychology is a separate division of psychology. Animals and indeed plants respond to stimuli in certain ways which make it possible to consider their behavior as part of psychology. The study of the behavior of organisms below man is also important in its own right. Above all, this study is helpful in understanding normal human psychology. Controlled observations of a kind impossible in man can be made on animals. Certain mental processes such as some but not all of those basic in learning appear in especially clear-cut ways in animals, because they are not complicated by language or man's socially determined conventions. Care must be taken, however, never to assume because a process has a certain form in an animal below man that it necessarily has the same form in man. Such assumptions must be directly verified before they can be accepted.

Physiological psychology takes as its special field of study the structures and functions of the response mechanism. This branch of psychology considers the anatomy and the physiology of the structures of the living body which underlie mental life. The study is undertaken not because the psychologist, as psychologist, is concerned with knowing more about the nervous system for its own sake, but because a knowledge of the nervous system helps him understand normal and certain abnormal mental processes. Continuous reference is made to physiological psychology, because, after all, everything that a human individual does, be it writing a sonnet, or solving a differential equation, is dependent on the way in which the living brain and muscles of that particular living organism work in the situation in which the organism is at that time.

Abnormal psychology is another subdivision of the field. The problems investigated in this division may be considered under two general categories. The first is that which studies the retardation of mental development and the second is that which takes as its subject matter mental illness, the disturbed behavior of poorly adjusted people and the disorders of mental life that occur in individuals who were not previously mentally retarded.

The study of exceptionally slow mental development has shown that some children do not grow up normally in so far as some of their psychological processes are concerned. Such individuals are, in popular speech, referred to as idiots, feeble-minded or retarded individuals. The careful and sympathetic psychological study of such unfortunate individuals not only assists in securing proper treatment for them, but when their growth is contrasted with those who grow normally, helpful facts are disclosed about the development of normal mental processes.

In the elaborate investigations of individuals whose mental development is retarded that are carried out in special hospitals and training schools, some facts have been discovered concerning emotional life and the learning process. This knowledge has made possible a more skillful and humane treatment of such atypical human beings, and also a more complete understanding of normal growth of mental capacities has been achieved. Some so-called feeble-minded children suffer from forms of mental illness that can be cured and great care must be used by physicians and psychologists in diagnosing and treating such patients.

The study of mental illness itself, as we have pointed out, is a special field in psychology and also in medicine. Individuals who have previously been able to meet the problems of adjustment to the world in which they live and then become more or less incompetent to do so present a special problem not only to the scientist and physician, but to the business executive, the humanitarian and the taxpayer. Many abnormal mental conditions are transient. Some, unfortunately, are relatively permanent. Certain mental illnesses have their causes in obvious and known changes in the nervous system; others depend upon much more subtle and still undescribed microscopic cellular and sub-cellular alterations in the brain of the sort similar to those which underlie the normal processes of emotional reaction and habit formation.

The psychologist is interested in mental abnormality for its own sake and also because a knowledge of mental deviations throws much light upon many of the psychological reactions of relatively normal men and women.

Clinical psychology is the name now given to that part of psychology which concerns itself with patients or clients who are mentally ill or who need help in adjusting themselves to their environments. Clinical psychologists often work with psychiatrists, psychiatric social workers and nurses in special teams. The training of the clinical psychologist in experimental method and in statistics often helps him in undertaking research on problems related to mental illness. He also is an expert in the use of various types of tests that help in the objective assessment of intelligence and other personality characteristics.

Mental hygiene is the name given to an organized effort to forestall mental ill health by appropriate preventive measures. When the first signs of mental illness appear, it is sometimes, although as yet not always, possible to halt the further development of such illness by taking proper precautions. The importance of doing everything possible in this preventive field will be at once obvious because of the human suffering involved and when it is remembered that about half of the hospital beds of the United States are devoted to those who are mentally ill.

The study of psychiatry, abnormal psychology, mental retardation and mental hygiene is related to general, experimental and physiological psychology in many ways, but these subjects also have important methods and techniques of their own. In general the study of deviation from "the normal process" involves the study of individual cases. The use of the case method in psychology has thus been given very special consideration, particularly in recent years. Case-study techniques are now quite well standardized and to some extent very specialized. . . . Generalizations based upon the proper evaluations of case studies form an important part in all modern considerations of general psychology.

Social psychology studies those aspects of the mental life of individuals which are immediately and in a derivative way determined by the activities of other individuals. The collective action of groups of people, each of whom is so influenced, is also studied by this branch of psychology. Most speaking and writing are, therefore, in part subjects for consideration by social psychology because these actions are almost wholly socially determined. Those human judgments which are generally called moral and ethical are also largely socially determined. As the individual develops from babyhood to adult life, he comes more and more to be a real part of the group of individuals into whose membership he is evolving. No matter what his lot in life may be, sometimes he leads and sometimes he follows. In all this activity a growing knowledge of the beliefs and actions, not only of his contemporaries, but also of individuals long dead, comes, through the use of printed books and other forms of communication, to influence his behavior in many obvious and in many subtle ways. Thus, what are called social institutions, such as the law and religion, influence the individual and in turn such institutions are influenced by each generation of individuals.

While social psychology is a special field of psychology, it is also a part of the subject that cannot be neglected by one who would understand any normal adult mental life. Many of the differences between the Australian aborigine and the New York club man are phenomena for the study of social psychology. The development and characteristics of the human personality are largely related to social experiences.

Social psychology has developed many special techniques of investigation. One of the most interesting of these methods is opinion sampling or opinion surveying. This technique is used to determine existing attitudes in scientifically selected samples of the populations that are being studied. Historically some of these methods were first developed to solve specific psychological problems, but now they are used in efforts to predict the outcome of elections, the characteristics of buyers' preferences and in many other useful ways. Attitude scales are also used in more specific studies of group tendencies in regard to controversial matters. It is not possible to think of man's mental life as wholly biologically determined because its "form" and special "content" come largely from social education and indoctrination.

Applied psychology, human engineering and educational psychology are, in a sense, not divisions of psychology, but are rather names given to studies of selected psychological areas which have been developed or adapted so that they can be used in the solution of problems which involve the prediction or the control of human behavior in special situations. Some of the social psychological techniques just considered are methods of applied psychology.

One of the most important fields of practical life in which psychology has been applied is education. The process of human learning in school and college demands, among other things, that each of those who are to be educated should be understood as individuals. This means that the procedures necessary to bring about the modification of performance in a pupil's sentence structure, in his use of a metal lathe or in his ideas about truth be comprehended scientifically. More and more it becomes obvious that the results of the subtle and important process of education should be accurately measured if the work of education as a whole is to be maintained at a high level of efficiency. Education thus involves human reactions of almost every sort studied by psychologists. Hence, in recent years practically all teachers have recognized the importance of knowing something of the fundamental psychological processes which underlie their humanly important profession.

No science is complete, and this is especially true of psychology. And yet, as has been indicated, it is now true that a knowledge of the facts and principles which have already been firmly established in psychology can at this time be of use to any individual who wishes to understand himself and others. A real knowledge of psychology cannot fail to help any man, woman or child meet the complex problems of adjustment which are demanded of everyone in modern civilized life.

—▶ **Carl R. Rogers**

Implications of Recent Advances in Prediction and Control of Behavior

From *Teachers College Record*, 1956, 57:316–322. Reprinted and abridged by permission.

The science of psychology, in spite of its immaturities and its brashness, has advanced mightily in recent decades. From a concern with observation and measurement, it has moved toward becoming an "if-then" science. By this I mean it has become more concerned with the discernment and discovery of lawful relationships such as that *if* certain conditions exist, *then* certain behaviors will predictably follow.

I believe that few people are aware of the breadth, depth, and extent of the advances in psychology and the behavioral sciences, and still fewer seem to be aware of the profound social, political, economic, ethical, philosophical, and educational problems posed by these advances. In this discussion I should like to focus on the educational implications of these advances in the science of psychology (which inevitably will involve me in some concern with the philosophical implications as well) and to review a few selected examples of what I mean by the increased ability of psychology to understand and predict or control behavior. Each illustration I will give is supported by reasonably rigorous and adequate research, though like all scientific findings, each is open to modification or correction through more exact or imaginative future studies.

What, then, are some of the behaviors or learnings for which we now know how to supply the antecedent conditions?

We know how to set up the conditions under which many members of a group will report judgments which are contrary to the evidence of their senses. They will, for example, report that Figure A covers a larger area than Figure B, when the evidence of their senses *plainly* indicates that the reverse is true. Experiments by Asch [6],* later refined and improved by Crutchfield [18] show that when a person is led to believe that everyone else in the group sees B as larger than A, then he has a strong tendency to go along with this judgment, and in many instances does so with a real belief in his false report.

We know a great deal about how to establish conditions which will influence consumer responses and/or public opinion. I refer you to the advertisements in any magazine, or to the TV program, "The $64,000 Question," and the sales of the sponsor's lipsticks.

We know how to influence the buying behavior of individuals by setting up conditions which provide satisfaction for needs of which they are unconscious, but which we have been able to determine. It has been shown that some women who do not buy instant coffee because of "a dislike for its flavor" actually dislike it at a subconscious level because it is associated in their minds

---

* Numbers in brackets refer to the References at the end of each chapter.

with laziness, spend-thrift qualities, and being a poor house-keeper. [25] This type of study has led to sales campaigns based upon appealing to the unconscious motives of the individual—his unknown sexual, aggressive, or dependent desires.

We know how to predict which members of an organization will be troublesome and delinquent. On the basis of a paper and pencil test, Gough [24] has predicted which department store employees will be unreliable and dishonest or otherwise difficult. He freely states that it is quite possible to identify, with a good deal of accuracy, the potential troublemakers of any organized group.

This ability to identify troublemakers is only an extension of the knowledge we have about prediction in other fields—predicting which individual is most likely to become a good salesman, or typesetter, or physician, or student in college.

We know how to provide conditions in a work group, whether in industry or in education, which will be followed by increased productivity, originality, and morale. Conversely we know how to provide the conditions which lead to low productivity and low morale. Studies by Coch and French [11], and by Katz, Maccoby, and Morse [31] show in general that when workers in industry participate in planning and decisions, and when they are not supervised in a suspicious or authoritarian way, production and morale increase. The reverse conditions produce a reverse effect. A study reported by Corey [16] indicates that when the leader of a teacher group acts in a manner which is understanding, and which facilitates participation, the group is more productive in making and carrying through plans.

We know how to provide the conditions of leadership which will be followed by personality growth in the members of the group, as well as by increased productivity and improved group spirit. Richard [41], in his experience as manager of an industrial plant, and Gordon [23], in his study of leadership of a workshop, have shown that where the leader or leaders hold the attitudes customarily thought of as therapeutic, the results are good. In other words, if the leader is understanding, accept-ant, and permissive toward his group and also acceptant of his own feelings in the situation, then the members of the group show evidence of personality growth and function more effectively and with better spirit.

We know how to provide the psychological conditions in the classroom which will result not only in the usual learning of academic content, but in improved personal adjustment as well. Studies by Asch [5] and Faw [19] show that if the attitudes of the teacher are similar to those described above for the leader, and hence responsible participation by the student is permitted and encouraged, then academic learning proceeds about as usual as measured by conventional tests, and personal growth and adjustment improve significantly.

We know how to provide an interpersonal relationship with qualities such that it enables the individual to meet stress with more serenity, less anxiety. Thetford [50], in an experiment with group therapy, and Faw [20], in a recent study of teacher-pupil relationships in the classroom, came to similar conclusions, though using very different methods and instruments. When individuals—clients or students—have experienced for a time a relationship of warmth, understanding, and acceptance, they are able to meet stress situations with less physiological upset and quicker recovery of physiological balance (Thetford) and are less upset psychologically by the stress. [Faw]

We know the attitudes which, if provided by a counselor or a therapist, will be predictably followed by certain constructive personality and behavior changes in the client. Studies which in recent years have been completed in the field of psychotherapy justify this statement. [42, 43, 45] The findings from these studies may be very briefly summarized in the following terms:

If the therapist provides a relationship in which he is (*a*) genuine, internally consistent; (*b*) acceptant, prizing the client as a person of worth; (*c*) empathically understanding of the client's private world; then the client becomes (*a*) more realistic in his self-perceptions; (*b*) more confident and self-directing; (*c*) more positively valued by himself; (*d*) less likely to repress elements of his experience, (*e*) more mature, socialized, and adaptive in his behavior; (*f*) more like the healthy, integrated, well-functioning person in his personality structure.

It is obvious that the essence of these findings in the field of therapy is closely related to the three previous illustrations.

We now know how, I believe, to disintegrate a man's personality structure, dissolving his self-confidence, destroying the concept he has of himself, and making him completely dependent upon another. This example has not been, so far as I know, verified by objective research. I make this statement after having studied, as far as one is able, the methods used in preparing prisoners for confession in various purge trials in Russia, and the brainwashing procedures applied in Communist China. It seems rather evident that these methods use many of the principles of psychotherapy, but use them in reverse fashion to bring about the disintegration of the autonomous personality, rather than integration. In a curious and abhorrent way this tends to validate the principles of psychotherapy mentioned above, because it indicates that the lawfulness of the process of therapy may be used to build or destroy personality.

We know how to provide psychological conditions which will produce vivid hallucinations and other abnormal reactions in the thoroughly normal individual in the waking state. This knowledge came about as the unexpected by-product of research at McGill University. [8] It was discovered that if all channels of sensory stimulation are cut off or muffled, abnormal reactions follow. If healthy subjects lie relatively motionless, to reduce kinaesthetic stimuli, with eyes shielded by translucent goggles which do not permit perception, with hearing largely stifled by foam-rubber pillows as well as by being in a quiet cubicle, and with tactile sensations reduced by cuffs over the hands, then hallucinations and ideation bearing some resemblance to that of the psychotic occur within forty-eight hours in many of these subjects. What the results would be if the sensory stifling were continued longer is not known.

We know how to influence psychological moods, attitudes, and behaviors through drugs. For this illustration we have stepped over into the rapidly developing borderline area between chemistry and psychology. From "truth serum," to the chemotherapy now practiced in psychiatric wards, to drugs for the normal citizen there are many ways of changing psychological states. We may take a drug to mobilize our energy to cram for an exam, or a drug to allay our anxiety about the exam. Drugs have reportedly been given to soldiers before a battle to eliminate fear. While much is still unknown in this field, Dr. Skinner of Harvard states that "In the not-too-distant future, the motivational and emotional conditions of normal life will probably be maintained in any desired state through the use of drugs." [47]

We know the psychological conditions of family life which, if established in a home, will tend to produce emotionally secure children with many socially valuable characteristics. Here we go to a very different field, that of personality development in children, for our example. We can measure the attitudes and emotional climate which parents are creating for their children, and from these measurements we can predict that Home A will in all probability produce children who will grow somewhat brighter over the years, will be emotionally secure, original, relatively unexcitable; who will be liked by their peers, likely to be leaders, and well-adjusted to adults. On the other hand we can predict that Home B will be likely to produce emotional, excitable children, with little emotional control, and with less of originality than the children from Home A. The studies done by Baldwin and others [7] at the Fels Research Institute are the basis for these statements. Home A is the home in which the parents' attitudes and behaviors cluster in what the investigators have termed the "democratic" category, and parental attitudes and behaviors in Home B cluster in what they term the "actively rejectant" group.

My purpose in the above examples has been to point up the wide-ranging power, the very diverse potentialities for control and prediction, which psychological knowledge is giving us. When we project ourselves into the future, and try to imagine the further developments which will inevitably come, the prospect arouses uneasiness. Small wonder that Dr. Robert Oppenheimer, in speaking of the points of similarity between his own profession, physics, and the profession of psychology, says that one of these points "is the extent to which our progress will create profound problems of decision in the public domain. The physicists have been quite noisy about their contributions in the last decade. The time may well come—as psychology acquires a sound objective corpus of knowledge about human behavior and feeling—when the powers of control thus made available will pose far graver problems than any the physicists have posed."[1]

Inherent in this development of the psychological or behavioral sciences are, I believe, two profound questions for educators. They are: How do educators propose to use these rapidly increasing potentialities for influencing and altering human learning and human behavior? How shall we prepare students to live in a world where the possibilities for such control of human behavior exist?

I shall not attempt to answer either of these questions, but shall only comment on each one. As to how educators propose to use this accumulating knowledge, I believe it is clear that it will depend entirely on their philosophy of education, as that philosophy is operationally defined in action. We are rapidly acquiring the knowledge and the skills which will enable us to turn out passive followers or independent citizens. Many teachers and educators, if we take account of their actions rather than their words, have the former as their goal. They will be able to implement this purpose much more adequately in the future. On the other hand, if the aim is to turn out self-directing, inquiring minds which will form their own judgments as to the truth, then knowledge exists which can facilitate this purpose also. It will be up to the educators, and even more broadly, up to the community, to choose the direction in which we shall go.

With regard to how we shall prepare students to live in this fearsome future world, I believe some of the research I have cited suggests possible answers.

---

1 From a speech to the American Psychological Association, San Francisco, September 5, 1955.

In the investigation by Crutchfield [18], it was found that about one-third of the responses made by a group of individuals were strongly influenced by the majority opinion, even when that majority opinion was clearly false. However, not all individuals were equally influenced. Some persons were swayed on almost every item by what they thought to be a solid group opinion, but others were influenced scarcely at all. They "called the shots as they saw them," regardless of what others might think.

When Crutchfield analyzed the personality characteristics of these two groups on the basis of extensive personality assessment, the differences were sharp. The conforming group, who were swayed by the majority opinion, tended to be individuals who had little understanding of themselves, were defensive, had to put up a good "front." They were rigid, moralistic, and had great respect for authority. They were somewhat anxious, guilty, suggestible, and unable to tolerate ambiguity. They lacked self-confidence, were vacillating, and tended to become confused under stress.

The independent group, on the other hand, were active, effective, persuasive leaders. They were individuals in whom others felt confidence, and they had confidence in themselves. They were natural, unaffected, non-defensive, and expressive. They were unconventional and adventurous.

To generalize somewhat speculatively from Crutchfield's study to some of the others, I believe it may be tentatively said that the individuals who may be most easily "managed" through the psychological know-how I have tried to sketch in this paper are those who are passive, rigid, insecure, and authoritarian. On the other hand, those who resist being "managed," who are able to deal intelligently with these possible influences, are confident, open, secure, independent, and spontaneous.

But here again we face an exciting fact. The individuals who were not overwhelmed by the majority opinion in Crutchfield's experiment bear a very strong resemblance to individuals produced in a democratic home atmosphere, to workers who have developed in a group-centered industrial situation, to students who have been exposed to an acceptant teacher-pupil relationship, to clients who have experienced a warm and empathic relationship in therapy. In other words, we already know to a considerable degree how to provide the conditions in which such individuals develop. And though the reverse evidence is not quite so clear, I believe it may be said that in large measure we also know how to provide the conditions in which the passive, insecure followers develop.

What I have been trying to say is that the growing body of knowledge in the behavioral sciences gives to our modern culture an astonishing power of choice. We know how to influence and mold behavior and personality in a great many significant ways. We also have available the choice of whether to set the conditions which develop a suggestible, submissive, unsure individual who can be easily influenced to behave in any way that "we" think wise, or the conditions which will develop an open, adaptive, independent, free-thinking, self-respecting individual. It is this latter person who will perhaps be able to use with intelligence and sensitivity to human values the enormous powers which the physical and behavioral sciences are putting at his disposal. The issue of what choice to make in this regard constitutes, I believe, the challenge of tomorrow both for education and for our whole culture.

──▶ **Arthur P. Coladarci**

The Relevancy of Educational Psychology

From *Educational Leadership*, 1956, 13:489–492. Reprinted and abridged by permission.

The relevancy of an applied area depends in part upon the definition of the process, institution, or event to which it is applied. The contribution that can be made by *educational* psychology is partially a function of the particular meaning invested in "education." This statement is not merely the usual innocuous preface to an extended discussion. Indeed, it is our major thesis. Too many teachers and administrators have thought of educational psychology as consisting only of an ordered catalogue of educational prescriptions, which, together with those provided by the other foundational fields in education, "tell" the teacher "how to teach" and the administrator "how to administer." The fallacy lies not only in the much too complimentary respect for the status of our knowledge in these areas but, more fundamentally, in the conception of education as a collection of successful recipes—the teacher or administrator is a person who has been armed with a bag-of-tricks into which he reaches for a decision regarding any given specific professional problem. Although this unfortunate orientation becomes an increasingly less frequent one, it still exists and may be partially attributable to the turn-of-the-century efforts to make education "scientific" by attempting to make it merely more *factual*. [48]

If one, however, thinks of the nature of the educator's role in another way, educational psychology, and education generally, become more powerful, exciting and rigorous. The conception we have in mind can be described by beginning with a rather coarse but generally acceptable definition of the educator's role: to help the learner change his behavior in specified desirable directions. Although the definition is too ambiguous for detailed analysis, it serves to point out the two basic factors involved: a *process* ("behavior change") and a *criterion* ("specified desirable directions"). Suppose that the educator has clearly specified what he means by "desirable" behavior changes in the form of operationally stated educational goals. [51] It appears, now, that the focal task for the teacher is to so interact with his pupils, and to so arrange the conditions and materials, that these pupils will change in the hoped-for ways. Put in these terms, the teacher's task can be seen as one of manipulating the learning situation in such a way that the *predicted* behavior changes actually do occur. If, at this point, the educational psychologist could say that we now know which manipulations will produce the desired changes, no problem would exist—we have only to apply the correct recipe. However, educational psychology cannot do this. Any particular combination of teacher-pupil-class-group-community-available materials, etc., is somewhat different from any other combination. There is no general prescription that can be considered to be clearly valid for particular cases. The teacher, then, *must be an active, continuous inquirer into the validity of his own procedures.* As Corey puts it:

> Most of the study of what should be kept in the schools and what should go and what should be added must be done in hundreds of thousands of classrooms and thousands of American communities. The studies must be understood by those who may have to change the way they do things as a result of the studies. Our schools cannot keep up with the life they are supposed to sustain and improve unless teachers, pupils, supervisors, administrators, and school patrons continuously examine what they are doing. Singly and in groups, they must use their imagination creatively and constructively to identify the practices that must be changed to meet the needs and demands of modern life, courageously to try out those practices that give better promise, and methodically and systematically gather evidence to test their worth. [17]

At the risk of belaboring the point, let us put it in somewhat different form before considering the relevancy of educational psychology. The educator's decisions about methods, materials, and curricular procedures should be thought of as *hypotheses* regarding the way in which the desired behavior changes can be brought about. These hypotheses must be *tested* continuously by inquiring into the degree to which the predicted behavior changes actually occurred. This view has been referred to elsewhere by the writer [12] as "teaching behavior defined as the-testing-of-hypotheses behavior." The crucial element is *tentativeness*; ideas and decisions about method and curriculum are to be held hypothetically, continuously tested, and continuously revised if necessary.

Contribution of Educational Psychology

Given this conception of the educator's role, how can educational psychology be brought to bear on it in helpful ways? The contribution can be broken down into two related categories. First, educational psychology, as a body of information and an arena of research activity, can help in the generation of the educational hypotheses. Intelligent hypotheses are not chosen randomly nor are they found full-blown. An intelligent hypothesizer thinks along the lines of the following model: *"On the basis of the best information now available to me,* I hypothesize that this procedure will produce this result."* To translate this into the context of education, we might say, for instance: *"On the basis of what I now know* about individual differences and the reading process, I hypothesize that this kind of grouping-for-reading will lead to the kind of pupil progress in reading that I would like to bring about."

Educational psychology, as a source of information, contributes to the "on-the-basis-of-what-I-now-know" portion of the statement. It helps provide information on which to base hypotheses for particular purposes and particular children.

A second kind of contribution which educational psychology can make is that of helping teachers and administrators to acquire the attitudes and skills necessary to intelligent hypothesizing and the testing of hypotheses.

Generally, what is involved is learning such skills as how to interpret data intelligently, how to observe accurately, how to avoid common logical fallacies in making inferences, how to make adequate decisions regarding what data should be gathered, ways in which data can be gathered and recorded, etc. Educational psychology, of course, has many additional and somewhat unique values for the educator. We have chosen to overlook those in this discussion since they are covered comprehensively and in detail in the available published literature. Those who are interested are invited to examine the published reports of a committee organized by the Executive Committee of the National Society of College Teachers of Education. The first report [35] discussed the ways in which educational psychology relates to curriculum development; the second [4] considers the nature of educational psychology and its general place in teacher education; the third [36] gives detailed attention to the ways in which specific areas of educational psychology can be helpful to the prospective teacher; the last report [37] describes present practices and developments in the teaching of educational psychology.

It is appropriate, in this case, that the final comment should be cautionary as well as benedictory. The writer has stated his position as though there are no responsible competing alternatives to it. Any dogmatic flavor in the statement is more a consequence of brevity than of intent. Many persons will hold that such a conception of education as we have presented here is both impractical and not valuable. Our response would be that the orientation is at least practical in the sense that many, many educators have learned to behave as inquirers; the orientation appears to be valuable in that where one finds such an educator he usually finds him to be valued by his colleagues, ego-involved in his profession, and able to criticize his procedures rationally. In short, such educators do exist and they appear to make the profession a better one by their membership in it.

——▶ **Harold E. Jones**

The Educational Psychology
of Persons

From *Journal of Educational Psychology*, 1946, 37:513–526. Reprinted and abridged by permission of Warwick & York, Inc.

If we are sometimes perplexed as to the field covered by educational psychology, we can look back to a time when it had very definite boundaries. A quarter century ago it was bounded on the east by Thorndike and on the west by Judd. For all to see, its Principia were in Judd's vigorous writings and in Thorndike's three volumes, which spread before the fascinated student a feast of wisdom about original nature, learning, and individual differences. It is no accident that for many years, following this lead, the subject-matter of educational psychology was drawn very largely from two allied branches: differential psychology and the experimental psychology of learning. For two decades the great preponderance of new research dealt either with aptitudes and attainments, or with studies of verbal learning or of classroom techniques for imparting specific knowledges and skills.

But science, which Vannevar Bush has described as the endless frontier, cannot be static and still remain science. Even though the individual student may sometimes be as stationary as the bottom man on a totem pole, educational psychology as a whole moves forward not only within the field to which it was originally devoted, but also into new topical areas. These newer topics are closely associated with developmental psychology, with social psychology and personality.

It would be a mistake to regard such changes as an about-face, a denial of former goals, or a conversion to a new faith. There have, to be sure, been over-reactions against earlier fields of interest; there have been crusading attempts to devalue measurement and scientific experiment, and to elevate the 'whole child' into a position of awe and mystery. The advocates of children's needs, of the child-centered school, or of self-expression or self-activity have sometimes carried these reasonable concepts into a sphere of hallelujah which seems foreign to the more sober purposes of science.

But these are phenomena of exploit, marked by emotional rejection or affirmation and by a kind of enthusiastic confusionism. We are concerned here not with the squeaks in the machinery, but with the more lasting products of its operation. To use an organic rather than a mechanical analogy, we may say that educational psychology, like other sciences, has been subject to growth, with aspects both of differentiation and of integration . . . the differentiation of new problems and methods, going beyond our initial preoccupation with individual differences and learning, and the integration of new with earlier achievements.

These growth changes are organically appropriate. We may also call them logical, for we would all concede that the purpose of educational psychology is to assist in the process of education, and this process obviously entails not merely technical learning, not merely the mental ability and educational readiness to learn, but also the personal motivation to learn, the control of maladjustive interferences with learning, and the personal traits which make possible the use of learning in socially desirable ways.

From earlier years we can point to many solid accomplishments which bear on the efficient classification of school children, on techniques of learning and teaching, on the measurements of skills and the prediction of readiness to acquire skills. But it is now realized more clearly than before that this is not enough, for we are more concerned with the implications of the fact that 'persons' go to school, not just an equipment for learning, not just memories, minds or intellects.

The Person in the Educational Process

There is, of course, no lack of evidence as to the importance of the person in the educational process. Some of this evidence has been summarized by Gordon Allport in his illuminating discussion of "The Ego in Contemporary Psychology." [2] Allport points out the role of ego involvement, or what we might more simply term the personal stake, in learning, memory, judgment, attitudes, and beliefs. An example is the relationship between learning and the affective tone of the material learned. It is common knowldge that pleasantly toned materials are in general easier to learn than those which are affectively neutral. Unpleasantly toned materials on the other hand may be either easy or hard to learn. They are likely to be hard if the unpleasantness carries an ego reference, if it involves the learner as a person and leads to a feeling of personal uneasiness, infringement or guilt.

Thus, although we can predict for groups, we cannot safely predict for individuals the relative difficulty of things to be learned. We must take into account not only the average difficulty value of the material, but also the learner as a person. Although this seems too obvious to be stressed, Allport observes that in the Yearbook on Learning [34] which the National Society for the Study of Education published only four years ago, "One searches its four hundred sixty-three pages in vain for any mention of the ego, and almost in vain for any recognition of interest. True, one finds occasional remarks to the effect that 'the teacher who neglects the simple but powerful word of praise does so at her pedagogical peril,' but the potential significance of such remarks for learning theory seems lost to view." [3]

Growth Trends in Educational Psychology

To observe the actual trend with regard to some of these topics, I have made a rough classification of the research reports in the *Psychological Abstracts,* including all of those which seemed to be conceived with reference to the psychology of education, whether they were in that section of the *Abstracts* or were noted in cross-reference. Account was taken only of empirical studies, not including discussions, summaries or announcements, without data, of a new test or rating scale.

Of these research reports in 1929, approximately forty-five per cent dealt with aptitudes, prognosis or achievement. Only six per cent dealt with personality . . . in terms of a broad concern with personal characteristics, including nonintellectual traits, or in terms of a concern with social relationships, motivation, or adjustment. Ten years later, in the last year before the war, fourteen per cent dealt with personality, and in a more recent count, for the present year, this has increased to twenty-two per cent, while studies of educational achievement and prognosis have diminished slightly.

Thus we seem to have some indication of a trend, and this is also shown by our textbooks in educational psychology, although sometimes in less marked form, for textbooks often have a cultural lag of several years behind scientific practice. Starch's *Educational Psychology* [49], perhaps the best in the field in 1919, contained practically nothing about personality or child development. This is also true of Pintner's [38], appearing ten years later. Jordan [29], in 1942, makes the observation that "most of the desirable outcomes of all education are encompassed in the one of a well-balanced personality—it is the problem of educational psychology to bring about this end." About thirteen per cent of Jordan's volume appears to deal with personality, about ten per cent with interests and motivation, about eight per cent more with growth, and the remainder with topics of more classical repute.

But we also have examples, in very good circulation, of texts which show a somewhat more marked change of emphasis. Gates' *Psychology for Students of Education* [21], in its first, 1922, edition contained about fifteen per cent of what might be termed child development materials . . . growth, personality, children's interests and attitudes, emotional and social development. In the 1930 edition this had grown to thirty per cent, and by 1942, in an edition by Gates and collaborators [22], to forty-five per cent. Similarly, Pressey's *Psychology and the New Education* [39, 40] contained in 1933 about thirty per cent of child development materials, and in 1944, forty-five per cent.

LIMITATIONS IN CURRENT TRENDS

Thus it is apparent that many teachers in training are today learning much more about non-intellectual aspects of behavior than was the case a few years ago. But we should not neglect to observe that even those studies which emphasize an interest in personality do not necessarily illustrate a concern with persons as individuals. They are more likely to deal with personality traits in the abstract, and with the analysis of trait relationships. Often they exhibit a preoccupation with applying the techniques of measurement to elusive and complex variables, such as 'neurotic tendency' or 'dominance' or 'introversion.' When, in this manner, a well defined and significant personality characteristic is reliably and validly measured we can only feel gratification at the successful extension of scientific method. But too often what we find is a mere numeralization, to use Kantor's phrase, with the neglect of essential features because they are not numeralizable.[1]

---

[1] Kantor adds (what should be more obvious to us now than twenty years ago, because there are so many examples of it) that to numeralize or quantify badly conceived variables "can only lead to results which are increasingly precise in their misguidance." [30]

When the educational psychologist does speak of persons, in what context does he use this term? Usually, it appears, in a context of sampling. Not persons as having individual personalities, not cases with case histories, but statistical cases, units to be assembled into distributions, tallied in correlation plots, or punched into IBM cards. All of these are useful operations, no doubt foreshadowed as necessary when man began to learn to count.

Scientific Hazards

One recalls a discussion by James Marshall [32] entitled "Plato, Buddha, and President Hutchins," in which he presents the problem of neurotic scholarship: the neurotic scholar being one who sees daring in an asterisk and finds immortal security in a footnote. We would not substitute this conception of careful research, or reresearch, for more genuinely adventurous enterprise, but we are justified in looking most judicially through our bifocals at studies which have 'purposes' and 'techniques' too far out of balance.

Gardner Murphy [33] has described the danger to any science whose methods are developed entirely in advance of its problems, so that the experimenter sees only those phases of a problem for which a method is already at hand. The danger is one of congealing research into a few self-limiting sectors. But there is also a danger, which is by far more to be regarded in the study of personality, of letting our purposes and aspirations so far outrun our techniques that we become complacent in the use of intuition and of other primitive ways of knowing, and neglectful of verifying the things we think we know.

If this is the case, the question may be raised as to whether educational psychology, in becoming more personalistic, may not be in danger of losing or weakening its standards as a science.

Allport has been our most eloquent American advocate of the view that since "every mental function is imbedded in a personal life," and since "each personality is a law unto itself," the primary goal of the psychology of personality must be to understand the individual forms of mental life. [1] The comparison of one person with another in respect to their common traits is considered to be only a secondary goal.

Idiographic research of this nature, directed at "understanding some particular event in nature or society," or the unique individual case, is contrasted with nomothetic studies which are directly concerned only with universal phenomena and general laws. Now, the uniqueness of the individual personality, and the influence of unique personal factors upon every aspect of the educational process, are general principles. But the way in which these personal factors operate in any given case, as distinguished from any other case, is a specific matter—important for guidance, for education, but not a prime preoccupation for the scientist. Skaggs has observed that if we carry Allport's doctrine to its extreme there would be as many psychologies as there are individuals. "Whenever a new baby is born a new psychology would have to be written. When it died it would be put aside as of no further interest because this was a unique person." [46]

And yet the teacher, as well as the therapist, must study persons as individuals because the art of teaching as well as of therapy demands individual understanding and individual treatment. In studying persons, we have a choice of relatively more scientific and relatively less scientific methods. The former, we would agree, involve the appropriate use of systematic and standardized techniques of assessment. They involve predictions from these assessments, on the basis of statistical probability. The less scientific approaches consist of interpretation in which data, more or less explicitly known, are combined in what may be called clinical inferences.

Sarbin has noted that these interpretative processes can be described in one of two ways: "Either they are statistical predictions, made in an informal, subjective, and uncontrolled way, or else they are purely verbal manipulations, unverifiable, and akin to magic." [44] In the former case, they represent an early step in scientific procedure, or perhaps we should say a pre-scientific method which we must all practice when we wish to take account of factors which are not precisely measured or not explicitly formulated, and of relationships and probabilities which are guessed at or 'hunched' at but not exactly known. In the latter case, however, in which Sarbin describes inferences as akin to magic, the procedure is anti-scientific and belongs in the addled region of lore, primitive intuition, and superstition.

THE CASE STUDY AS A TRAINING DEVICE

If it is the task of the teacher to know something about his pupils as persons, then it is also the task of the educational psychologist to acquaint the teacher with the best methods for doing this . . . with methods for measuring abilities, for observing behavior, for interviewing, and for synthesizing these and other approaches. The individual case study is an indispensable aid in this area of instruction. Whether or not it is in itself a contribution to science, we can agree that it is a contribution to teacher-training.

During the past five or six years a number of case reports[2] have been published for this purpose, and to an increasing extent textbooks now draw upon case studies in order to present concrete examples of individual behavior in life situations. In its proper sphere as an educational device, the case study offers an important supplement to our standard textbooks, and should (to offer one opinion) make up from a quarter to a half of the reading assignments in educational psychology.

FIELD METHODS

The further point must now be made that teachers should learn to study persons not merely through the eyes of psychologists who write case studies, but through their own eyes. In many institutions students have little opportunity to acquire, through field experience, techniques of case study. Practice-teaching of subject-matter is demanded, but not practice in learning about and understanding children.

This major weakness in training teachers was one of the principal concerns of the Teacher Education Commission, of which I had the privilege of being a member, and which has recently finished a nation-wide coöperative program directed toward the

---

[2] See, for example, references 9 and 28.

location of problems in teacher-training and the development of methods for dealing with these problems. One part of this program involved the establishment of the Child Development Collaboration Center at the University of Chicago, where teachers in training, teachers, and professional consultants could work together in conferences, study groups, and workshops, making use of materials which have been assembled from various child research centers. Another part of our Commission's program was in the development of methods of child study which could be practiced by teachers in training. An example of this is presented in some detail in the book published by the Commission, *Helping Teachers to Understand Children*. [13]

In one of the school systems coöperating with the Commission, an intensive program was carried on for several years, beginning with a meeting of a group of teachers with a psychologist. The teachers were asked to present problems for discussion. Their problems were of this nature:

"What would you do with a child who steals?" "How would you handle lazy children?" "What are the ways to stop so much inattention?" Such questions, typical of what psychologists are often asked by worried and overworked teachers, suggest a failure to understand the relation between behavior and a pupil's earlier experiences, his developmental status, his aspirations. They suggest that teachers are primarily concerned not with understanding behavior, but with obtaining ready-made techniques for controlling and disciplining pupils. The comment seems justified that "Perhaps the most disconcerting thing about these questions was that the teachers seemed to expect answers to them . . ." [14], in terms of standard general procedures which would be applicable to any child showing the problem mentioned. This demand of teachers for authoritative prescriptions in managing children is probably related to the fact, as Burling has pointed out, that the classroom teacher is 'officially' placed in a position to wield authority. "She is backed by the state law and the attendance officer and behind them is the State Reform School. It takes a person with a very deeply rooted respect for personality not to succumb to the temptation of this position and to use authority in inappropriate situations." [10]

If we think of this, as Burling has suggested, as an occupational hazard of teachers, we need to take special steps in teacher selection and in teacher-training to avoid overdevelopment of the drive to dominate, rather than of the drive to understand.

These comments are not offered in a spirit of unsympathetic criticism of teachers. If they are deficient in understanding children, or lacking in a psychological approach to behavior problems, must we not attribute these shortcomings in large part to our own failure, as educators of teachers, to give them an effective orientation toward children?

In the particular school system just mentioned, cumulative records had been maintained, for a number of years, containing descriptions of individual children. As a first step in a program of in-service training, the teachers decided to make a study of these records, in consultation with a representative of the Commission. The result of this study was the realization that these records, although cumulative and often voluminous, contained very little objective information about any child. As a rule, they set forth general impressions, without specific evidence. Moreover, these impressions were heavily weighted with value judgments—appraisals of behavior as good or bad, as attractive or disagreeable. If the child's family was mentioned, it was likely to be in terms of social standing, with little or no information about psychological factors. A good deal was said about the child's achievement, his success or failure as a scholar, but very little of a definite nature about his characteristics as a person.

It was then decided to undertake a cooperative child study program. Study groups were set up, which worked together in collecting developmental records and observational data, and which discussed these records with the Commission's consultant. From the teacher's own evaluation of this program, after a three-year period, it was quite apparent that they had gained new attitudes and new ways of thinking about children. They were more alert to motivational factors in family relationships, and to interpersonal relationships in the classroom. They were more aware of the nature and significance of individual differences, not merely in abilities but also in aspirations, not merely in mental growth but also in physical and physiological maturing.

"The impact of the culture, enlisting the influences of social status upon developing personalities became better understood. The school itself became seen as an arena of important social interaction among children." [15]

Such changes could hardly occur without some corresponding changes in teaching methods and in the emotional climate of the classroom. Teachers came to rely less upon threats and admonition, and more upon ingenuity in developing cooperative procedures. Less time was needed for discipline, more time was free for understanding and working with the individual. The implications of this extend, of course, to the curriculum and also to school administration, for it is idle to expect progress in teacher-child relationships if these are submerged in large classes. The educational situation represented by Mark Hopkins at one end of a log is no longer within our present scheme of things. The delicate balance of teacher and pupil on opposite ends of the log is replaced by the concept of a teacher pulling a load—a teaching load, composed, it would seem, of an inert aggregate of pupil units in average daily attendance.

A Proposal for Undergraduate and Graduate Training

The brief account that I have just given is of a program of in-service training designed to combat this concept and to make up, in some respects, for deficiencies in the pre-service education of teachers. The deficiencies are to a large extent a matter of curricular inertia, due to the preservation of vested interests in course programs. The most important vested interest, in this connection, is the standard beginning course in educational psychology. We think it is a good course; in a study by Jensen, from the testimony of three thousand students educational psychology was regarded as the most valuable part of their program. [26] Since this course was established some thirty or forty years ago, we have witnessed the rise of new courses: in child development and in personality. Each of these is now busily engaged in setting up its own vested interest, with its own secure spot in the catalogue, its own textbooks, its own personnel.

I have no quarrel with any of these parts of the curriculum, except this: that they are parts, not too well integrated, and that the individual child they discuss is rarely treated in an integrated way as a person.

Some years ago, Yerkes, reporting on the Yale Anthropoid Station, proudly announced that the Station then possessed fourteen chimpanzees which were born in captivity and whose life histories were known. For biological inquiry, this life history was regarded as the distinctive resource of the Yale station. Yerkes went on to state: "Within a few years there will not—or at least need not—be an individual in the colony whose ancestry, birth date, developmental and experimental history are not matters of reliable record and steadily increasing value." [52]

I once proposed that every leading department of psychology should have as part of its equipment a well-organized cumulative record upon a sample of children studied from infancy. [27] A student who has a year or two years to devote to a dissertation might then be working with a known sample of cases, and upon a problem bearing a significant relation to other problems of development. The problem might be normative, experimental, clinical, or represent a combination of methods. If longitudinal records are valuable, perhaps for many purposes indispensable, in the study of chimpanzees, should we not also enter a claim for their importance in normal human psychology and especially in educational psychology—not merely for research in child institutes, but more widely for the training and research of graduate students in psychology and education.

Through such a course of study we might expect to develop a generation of students who are more at home with the biological and other disciplines which cooperatively study development, and who are also more at home with the individual child as a person.

REFERENCES

1. ALLPORT, G. W., *Personality: A Psychological Interpretation*, New York: Holt, Rinehart and Winston, Inc., 1937, Chapter 20.
2. ———, "The Ego in Contemporary Psychology," *Psychological Review*, 1943, 50:451–478.

3. ———, "The Ego in Contemporary Psychology," *Psychological Review*, 1943, 50:465.

4. ANDERSON, G. L., "Educational Psychology and Teacher Education," *Journal of Educational Psychology*, 1949, 40:257–294.

5. ASCH, M. J., "Non-directive Teaching in Psychology: A Study," *Psychological Monographs*, 1951, 65:4, 24.

6. ASCH, S. E., *Social Psychology*, Englewood Cliffs, N.J.: Prentice-Hall, Inc., 1952, pp. 450–83.

7. BALDWIN, A. L., KALHORN, J., & BREESE, F. H., "Patterns of Parent Behavior," *Psychological Monographs*, No. 268, 1945, 58:1–75, No. 3.

8. BESTON, W. H., HERON, W., & SCOTT, T. H., "Effects of Decreased Variation in the Sensory Environment," *Canadian Journal of Psychology*, 1954, 8:70–76.

9. BLOS, P., *The Adolescent Personality*, New York: Appleton-Century-Crofts, Inc., 1941, p. 517.

10. BURLING, T., "Psychiatry and Education" in *Psychiatry and the War*, Springfield, Ill.: Charles C Thomas, publisher, 1943, p. 159.

11. COCH, L., & FRENCH, JR., J. R. P. "Overcoming Resistance to Change," *Human Relations*, 1948, 1:512–32.

12. COLADARCI, A. P., "Are Educational Researchers Prepared to Do Meaningful Research?," *California Journal of Educational Research*, 1954, 5:3–6.

13. COMMISSION ON TEACHER EDUCATION, Helping Teachers to Understand Children, Washington, D.C.: *American Council on Education*, 1945, p. 468.

14. ———, *op. cit.*, p. 2.

15. ———, *op. cit.*, p. 399.

16. COREY, S. M., *Action Research to Improve School Practices*. New York: Bureau of Publications, Teachers College, Columbia University, 1953, pp. 47–61.

17. ———, *op. cit.*, p. viii.

18. CRUTCHFIELD, R. S., "Conformity and Character," *American Psychologist*, 1955, 10:191–98.

19. FAW, V. E., "A Psychotherapeutic Method of Teaching Psychology," *American Psychologist*, 1949, 4:104–9.

20. ———, "Evaluation of Student-Centered Teaching." Unpublished manuscript.

21. GATES, A. I., *Psychology for Students of Education*, New York: The Macmillan Co., 1930, p. 612.

22. ———, JERSILD, A. T., McCONNELL, T. R., & CHALLMAN, R. C., *Psychology for Students of Education*, New York: The Macmillan Co., 1942, p. 805.

23. GORDON, T., *Group-Centered Leadership*, Boston: Houghton Mifflin Company, 1955, Chapters 6–11.

24. GOUGH, H. E., & PETERSON, D. R., "The Identification and Measurement of Predispositional Factors in Crime and Delinquency," *Journal of Consulting Psychology*, 1952, 16:207–12.

25. HAIRE, M., "Protective Techniques in Marketing Research," *Journal of Marketing*, April 1950, 14:649–56.

26. JENSEN, H. T., "Three Thousand Students Evaluate an Education Course," *The Education Forum*, 1943, 7:127–32.

27. JONES, H. E., *Development in Adolescence*, New York: Appleton-Century-Crofts, Inc., 1943, p. 166.

28. ———, *The Growth Study as a Psychological Method*, Society for Research in Child Development, Washington, D.C.: National Research Council, 1935, p. 7.

29. JORDAN, A. M., *Educational Psychology*, New York: Holt, Rinehart and Winston, Inc., 1942, p. 597.

30. KANTOR, J. R., "Current Trends in Psychological Theory," *Psychological Bulletin*, 1941, 39:29–65.

31. KATZ, D., MACCOBY, N., & MORSE, N. C., *Productivity, Supervision, and Morale in an Office Situation*, Part I. Ann Arbor Survey Research Center, University of Michigan, 1950.

32. MARSHALL, J., "Plato, Buddha, and President Hutchins," *Harper's Magazine*, 1941, 183:27–35.

33. MURPHY, G., "The Research Task of Social Psychology," *Journal of Social Psychology*, 1939, 10:107–20.

34. NATIONAL SOCIETY FOR THE STUDY OF EDUCATION, *The Psychology of Learning*, Forty-first Yearbook, Pt. 2, Bloomington, Ill.: Public School Publishing Co., 1942, p. 502.

35. NATIONAL SOCIETY OF COLLEGE TEACHERS OF EDUCATION, "The Psychological Basis of the Modern Curriculum," *Journal of Educational Psychology*, 1948, 39:129–69.

36. ———, "Educational Psychology for Teachers," *Journal of Educational Psychology*, 1950, 41:321–72.

37. ———, "Current Practices and Innovations in the Teaching of Educational Psychology," *Journal of Educational Psychology*, 1952, 43:1–30.

38. PINTNER, R., *Educational Psychology*, New York: Holt, Rinehart and Winston, Inc., 1929, p. 378.

39. PRESSEY, S. L., *Psychology and the New Education*, New York: Harper and Brothers, 1933, p. 594.

40. ——— & ROBINSON, F. P., *Psychology and the New Education*, Harper & Brothers, 1944, p. 654.

41. RICHARD, J., in *Group-Centered Leadership* by Thomas Gordon, Boston: Houghton Mifflin Company, 1955, Chapters 12 and 13.

42. ROGERS, C. R., *Client-Centered Therapy*, Boston: Houghton Mifflin Company, 1951.

43. ———— & DYMOND, ROSALIND F., editors, *Psychotherapy and Personality Change*, Chicago: University of Chicago Press, 1954.

44. SARBIN, T. R., "The Logic of Prediction in Psychology," *Psychological Review*, 1944, 51:210–28.

45. SEEMAN, J., & RASKIN, N. J., "Research Perspectives in Client-Centered Therapy," in O. H. Mowrer, ed., *Psychotherapy: Theory and Research,* New York: Ronald Press, 1953, Chapter 9.

46. SKAGGS, E. B., "Personalistic Psychology as a Science," *Psychological Review*, 1945, 52:234–38.

47. SKINNER, B. F., "The Control of Human Behavior," Paper presented to the New York Academy of Sciences, April 18, 1955, and published in the transactions of that body, pp. 547–51.

48. SMITH, B. O., "Science of Education," in W. S. Monroe, ed., *Encyclopedia of Educational Research,* New York: The Macmillan Co., 1950, pp. 1145–52.

49. STARCH, D., *Educational Psychology,* New York: The Macmillan Co., 1919, p. 473.

50. THETFORD, W. N., "An Objective Measure of Frustration Tolerance in Evaluating Psychotherapy," in W. Wolff, ed., *Success in Psychotherapy,* New York: Grune & Stratton, Inc., 1952, Chapter 2.

51. TRAVERS, R. M. W., *Educational Measurement,* New York: The Macmillan Co., 1955, pp. 19–36.

52. YERKES, R. M., "Yale Laboratories of Primate Biology, Incorporated," *Science*, 1935, 82:618–20.

CHAPTER

TWO

↑

Basic Ideas in Understanding
Children and Youth

"A PERSON MAY HAVE ACQUIRED CONSIDER-
able understanding of psychology as a body of facts and principles
without becoming any better prepared to understand the individuals he lives with and works with." This statement, taken from
the textbook (Baller and Charles) to which these *Readings* are
related, supports the central idea expressed by Jones in the preceding chapter. "Persons go to school," said Jones.

The present chapter consists of readings that furnish ideas
basic to the understanding of persons—*the actual boys and girls*
who put the real test to our abilities to counsel and instruct. The
readings of this chapter not only present basic concepts of human
behavior; one of them—the second one—also suggests ways in
which teachers and prospective teachers can sharpen their insights into child behavior by engaging in systematic study of
actual individuals.

During the past twenty years a program of child study developed by Daniel A. Prescott has enrolled well over fifty thousand teachers and other school personnel. Some of the basic assumptions that underlie the plan and methods of the child-study program are stated and briefly examined in the discussion by Prescott. Prescott is Director of the Institute for Child Study, at the University of Maryland.

In the second of the readings of this chapter Horace B. English, until his death in 1961, Professor of Educational Psychology at Ohio State University, describes a method that teachers and their professional colleagues can employ to improve their knowledge of human behavior and their ability to understand individuals. The method has much in common with that which is used in Prescott's child-study program. While the plan of study as described by English is especially well adapted to the needs and situations of in-service teachers, there is reason to believe that, with some modifications, it could be incorporated into pre-service courses with highly beneficial results.

"To understand children, we must understand their ways of growth. This is why we need a science of child development to interpret the more mysterious meanings of child behavior." How could the function of child and adolescent psychology be better expressed? The quoted sentences represent the ideas of the late Dr. Arnold Gesell, who organized and for thirty-eight years directed the well-known Yale Clinic in Child Development —now known as the Gesell Institute in Child Development. Not only does Gesell's discussion make clear some basic ideas about child growth and development . . . it also provides an effective transition from the present chapter to the next which further considers the nature of psychology as a science.

——▶ **Daniel A. Prescott**

Basic Assumptions in Child Study

From *The Child in the Educative Process*, by Daniel A. Prescott. Copyright © 1957 by McGraw-Hill Book Company, Inc. Reprinted and abridged by permission.

The Control of Human Behavior

Many people in the United States of America are badly frightened during these middle decades of the twentieth century. But it may well be that they are scared by the wrong facts. The most dangerous fact of our time is probably not that we know enough to blow our whole civilization to smithereens with hydrogen and uranium bombs, but that ruthless, empirically directed dictator groups have learned enough about human motivation and behavior to control the actions both of individuals and of masses of people. They deliberately produce fear, hatred, suspicion, and anxiety—the symptoms of mental ill health—as means of motivating and controlling children and youth. They withhold information and experience and substitute the reiteration of the big lie as a means of controlling the ideas of young people, thus warping and limiting their development. They plant informers in school classes and on school faculties. Through these informers they collect unfavorable bits of information about teachers in order to blackmail them into becoming communicators of propaganda and violating the friendship and mutual trust of professional colleagues, thus perverting human relationships and demeaning human dignity.

The only way a person can retain his sanity and self-respect under such stress is to rationalize his situation as that of participating in a great crusade for human good against terrible forces of evil. And this is exactly what happens to many people. I saw it happening in Czechoslovakia during a period in 1948 when I was in that country.[1] We should be very thoroughly frightened that, through the possession and use of knowledge about how to control human behavior, ruthless individuals and groups are able to seize and hold power within any social group or institution, within communities and nations, perhaps throughout the world. It is very disturbing to have seen the beginning of the use of similar techniques in our own country.

Science and the Determination of Goals

In the United States we possess a great deal more valid scientific knowledge about human development, motivation, and behavior than any totalitarian country possesses. But the possession of knowledge does not guarantee its use in wholesome ways for the benefit of all. The purposes which scientific knowledge can serve do not inhere in the knowledge itself. They depend rather upon the philosophical, religious, and social assumptions about the meaning of life and about the nature of valid human self-realization that are held by the person, the group, or the nation that uses the knowledge. It is, therefore, obligatory for us to understand the assumptions that underlie our use of scientific information.

The child-study program about which this book[2] is written is based upon a series of religious and philosophical assumptions, social values, and scientific axioms. All of us who, as consultants, guide the operation of this program with teachers or parents, believe that it is the right of every human being to initiate and develop his own assumptions about the meaning of life and the nature of human destiny and to derive his own social values therefrom; for this reason, we do not try to convince others that our own assumptions represent ultimate truth. But we also believe that in working with others it is only fair to reveal to them the basic assumptions by which we are living and the values we are seeking to enhance. From our point of view, the child-study

---

[1] See Daniel A. Prescott, "Two Months Behind the Iron Curtain," *Bull. Elemen. Principals Assn.*, 1949, 29, 30–40.

[2] Daniel A. Prescott, *The Child in the Educative Process*, New York: McGraw-Hill Book Company, Inc., 1957.

program is an attempt to use scientific knowledge and the scientific method to enhance the values for which we stand. But we grant the right of any teacher or parent to reject any of these assumptions or values, and, therefore, we insist that participation in the program must be completely voluntary in every school and community.

The plan of this discussion is first to present succinct statements of the religious, philosophical, and ethical assumptions, the social values, and the scientific axioms upon which the program rests. Then we shall examine briefly the reasons why they may be considered valid and mention a few of their implications.

Sources of Values

Religious, Philosophical, and Ethical Assumptions

The assumptions from which our child-study program derives its values are the following:

1. *Every human being is valuable,* regardless of his age, sex, race, creed, cultural background, social status, capacities, knowledge, or state of emotional adjustment. An individual's *value inheres in the fact that he is a living human being with potentialities to be realized.*

2. *Every human being has the right to strive for those conditions of living,* learning, and action, for *those relationships* with other human beings, *and for those experiences, which are necessary and appropriate to the achievement of his optimum development* as a person and *to his optimum usefulness within society,* providing always that these conditions, relationships, and experiences are at the same time consistent with the welfare and optimum development of other human beings. It is the proper function of all social institutions and of every individual to assist each person to achieve optimum development and usefulness.

3. *Whatever promotes wholesome development is moral; whatever blocks or prevents optimum development is evil.*

4. *Every human being has the right to be treated at all times in ways that show respect for his dignity and permit him to re-*

tain respect for himself as a person. This is an essential condition to optimum development.

5. *The Golden Rule is the soundest ethical principle against which to evaluate the behavior of individuals, the programs of social institutions, and the policies of nations.* To love other human beings as one loves oneself, and to treat others as one would wish to be treated under similar circumstances ought to be fundamental goals constantly sought by members of the educational profession.

Social Assumptions

The social assumptions and values upon which the child-study program rests are derived from the philosophical and ethical assumptions stated above and from the traditions of our American society. They are:

1. It is axiomatic that *every child, inevitably and properly, internalizes the culture* of the family, the social groups, the community and the nation *into which he is born. Society thus gives each individual a large portion of his interpretation of reality. The school's task is to facilitate,* to correct, and to supplement the internalizations that the child is acquiring outside the school. At the same time *the school must accept, respect, and value every individual,* even when circumstances have caused him to internalize inappropriate ideas, attitudes, or action patterns. This is especially important because of the great cultural diversity that exists within the United States.

2. *Every individual has certain rights, which may not be abridged.* The Constitution and the common law seek to guarantee these rights. *Every individual must be made aware of these rights and must be taught to value and to defend them — for* himself and for others.

3. *The democratic process is the best procedure yet worked out for carrying on the decision making that is a part of all social living and* at the same time *safeguarding and guaranteeing to each individual the conditions necessary to self-realization.* The democratic process is defined as that process in which each individual affected actually participates in making all the decisions

that determine his conditions of life, of work, and of further development.

4. *Each individual must be* reared in such a manner that he is *capable and desirous of assuming the responsibilities that go with freedom to make* basic *choices* about the conduct of his own life and to participate in decisions about the conduct of government. Only responsible citizens can maintain and develop so complex a society as the current Western European-American one. Only free individuals can achieve optimum self-realization within this context of social responsibility.

5. *The scientific method is the best process yet devised for using the mind* to distinguish facts from fallacies, to discover relationships between known facts and to work out the implications of facts for action. Members of the educational profession should be trained consciously to use the scientific method when making judgments about what to expect from and how to deal with their pupils. Many young people will understand and adopt it, too, if they observe it daily in operation as the fundamental way their teachers approach their problems.

Scientific Assumptions

Integrating information from the dozen or more sciences that study human beings yields certain fundamental views about how children and youth develop and why they behave as they do. The group of axioms given below supplies a core of general concepts to guide the more explicit study of individuals. They are:

1. *Behavior is caused and is meaningful.* It is the resultant of the tensions set up by a series of forces operating within and upon the individual. The behavior that emerges usually makes sense when viewed through the eyes of the behaver.

2. *The causes which underlie behavior are always multiple.* Some of them are physical—within the body or acting upon the body. Some are relationships of love or hatred, of friendship or antagonism, with other individuals. Some are cultural, depending upon ideas, habits, and attitudes taken in from the family and the community or pressed upon the individual by the operation of various social institutions. Some grow out of participation

in group activities with persons of the same maturity level. Still others grow out of the individual's own interpretations of his accumulating experiences, as he defines values, strives toward goals, and works out defenses against frustrations and limiting circumstances.

3. *Each individual is an indivisible unit.* The forces that shape him do not merely accumulate to produce a human being. Rather they interact. Consequently, one cannot take the individual apart, figuratively speaking, and deal with only one aspect of his dynamic make-up at a time. The whole will participate in and be influenced by all educative experiences.

4. *The human individual develops. No child or youth was born as he is or necessarily destined to become what he is. As the body grows and becomes more elaborate, new capacities* for experiencing, for learning, and for action *emerge. As experiences accumulate, more and more meanings and feelings are differentiated.* In other words, it is the interaction between the organism and its environment over a period of time that develops the individual personality. Hence *the developing individual must reintegrate,* or reunify, *himself from time to time at successively higher and higher levels of complexity both of structure and of meaning.* With successive reintegrations additional capacities emerge—capacities to remember, to perceive, to discriminate, to relate, to understand, to value, to plan and to act. This process of making successive reintegrations does not end with physical "maturity," but can continue to occur as experience adds new knowledge and understanding and as realized goals, related to fundamental values, open vistas of new goals and of long-term possibilities.

5. *Every human individual is a dynamic energy system, not just a machine acted upon from without.* The living oneness that is a human being develops self-awareness, concepts of and about himself, and a dynamic need to become, to realize his potentialities. This self-conscious personality becomes able to distinguish the direction of his own evolution, to envisage goals of his own, to discern and to create beauty, to discriminate between right and wrong and to choose the right, to find meaning and hope not only for his own life but also for that of mankind. This dynamic organization of energy that is *a human being is po-*

tentially a self-actualizing unity. It emerges from the interaction of organism with world and society. But it always has the potentiality of going on from where it is, to participate in shaping its own further destiny, together with that of the society of which it is a part, and even that of mankind.

6. Dynamic *self-actualization is made possible* to an individual ✓ *by* the existence of *an organizing core of meanings (values) at the center of the personality. These meanings govern the interaction between the individual and the succession of situations in which he finds himself.* They influence what he perceives each situation to be and to imply for him. They determine what he feels in each situation. They evoke criteria (desired goals and permitted means) against which the various behavior alternatives must be measured. Consequently, they regulate the individual's flow of behavior from situation to situation. Of course, this organizing core of meanings is built up gradually by experience and is modifiable at any time during life when the individual reintegrates himself. Usually it becomes quite strongly established during infancy, childhood and youth. The development of this core of meanings should be a major concern of education. Its modification and reintegration are the chief tasks of therapy, when it has led to ineffective or inappropriate behavior.

7. *Each individual is different from every other.* The same basic forces and processes operate to shape all human beings and are available to all for self-realization. But these forces and processes vary both qualitatively and quantitatively from person to person. Consequently, an individual can be understood and intelligently assisted in his self-actualization only if one has very explicit information about him. The information needed concerns his circumstances and experiences in life and the meanings and accompanying feelings that these experiences have engendered in him. These meanings and feelings are often discernible from systematic accumulations of objective descriptions of his behavior.

The Gist of It

The five religio-philosophical and ethical assumptions presented above affirm the value of all human life and the nurturing respect and love that it should command from all of us, regardless of the background and circumstances in which this life is found. The five social assumptions and values affirm that society is made for and by man, to assist his development; man is not made to enhance society at the expense of his development. But inasmuch as all members of society are interdependent, the welfare of all must be protected and the participation of all must be guaranteed, whether in the carrying out of responsibilities or in the reaching of decisions. The seven scientific axioms show that, although man is shaped by the world with which he interacts, he also becomes dynamic and builds his own destiny and, to some extent, that of society and the world.

Together these three sets of statements constitute a sort of biosocial philosophy of human relations and education. In this philosophy man is not only the apex of the evolutionary process, but a creature with special value or significance in the universe. He is not a blindly operating machine but a creative being. Man appears to be, at one and the same time, the partial fulfillment of a great creative dynamic in the universe and a participant in the creative process.

—→ **Horace B. English**

A Dynamic Study of Children

From *Child Development*, by Horace B. English. Copyright, 1951, by Holt, Rinehart and Winston, Inc., pp. 15–31. Reprinted and abridged by permission.

"First Catch Your Hare"

Few of you are so unfortunate, one hopes, as to study child psychology in a region where there are no children. There is, therefore, much to be said for the idea that "the way to begin is to begin"—just pick a child and start in studying him. Experience shows, however, that there are a few principles which should be brought to your attention, not as rigid prescriptions but as suggestive guide lines.

First of all, the child selected should usually *not* be a "problem child." Of course, every child presents a problem to the teacher who has any imagination. But the term *problem child* has become something of a technical term for a badly adjusted child in need of specialized psychological treatment.

Your first need is to learn to deal with "normal" children. Most of your problems—and your most important ones—will be *normal* problems. It would be one of the worst possible results of a study of child psychology to get in the habit of trying to find something "abnormal" in every puzzling bit of behavior, or of seeing a "problem child" beneath every curly head.

There is another and eminently practical reason, moreover, why it is wise to select a typical child. When we are asked why this child is being picked for study, we must be able to say with complete honesty that he is chosen because he is just an ordinary, everyday specimen.

Making Contact with the School

In most cases you should begin by a preliminary visit to the school. It is true, as we have insisted, that the child's school behavior cannot be fully understood in terms of only what happens in the classroom, but it is equally true that much that happens at home is unintelligible without an understanding of what is happening to the child in school.

There is a very practical reason, also, for starting with the school. We obviously need the cooperation of parents, and the investigation of Johnny will seem less mysterious if presented as a school project rather than a "case study."[1]

---

[1] As a matter of fact, you would probably do well not to get in the habit of talking about your "case study." Educated parents may look for too much, uneducated ones are likely to be made to feel rather uncomfortable; too many of them have had experience with relief case workers. For similar reasons it is better not to make much mention of psychology. People are apt to expect miracles of anything called psychology but also to be unduly skeptical of more mundane findings. "Child study" is a fairly accurate statement of our purposes and is less likely to be misunderstood.

As a rule, then, your instructor will have broached the matter to the principal for you. Nonetheless, your first step is to present yourself to the principal and obtain his explicit permission to begin observation in his school. You must remember that the principal is legally and morally responsible for the conduct of school matters; it is only fair that he be kept fully informed of what is going on. Your call at his office, even if you should get no instructions and no information, is an elementary professional courtesy.

Because, however, she stands so much closer to the child, the cooperation of the classroom teacher is even more vital. One of the student's first obligations is thus to insure that the teacher understands the purposes of the investigation and is prepared to forward it. Many teachers, especially older ones, tend to feel a little on the defensive when their classes are being visited by students who are full of enthusiasm for new ways. It has been my experience that it helps to emphasize that your purpose is not so much to observe the class routine as it is to observe the individual child, that you are not at all interested for the time being in methods of teaching but only in the behavior of the child. Nor does it do any harm to show that you realize you are making extra work for the teacher and shall be very grateful for any help extended.

Making Initial Contacts with the Home

If there is a sound tradition of friendly parent-teacher relations in the community, there should be no difficulty about an occasional visit to the child's home. The exact approach to the parents will have to depend on how one is introduced by the school. In general, it is to be hoped that the observer will have the way prepared for him by the principal of the school.

Should you make an appointment or should you go unannounced to your first interview? Middle-class housewives—and most of your subjects will come from middle-class homes—are likely to be embarrassed if a "visitor" comes unannounced. They prefer to go to a lot of wholly unnecessary trouble to have things "looking nice." You, of course, would much prefer to see a normal or everyday situation, but the choice is not yours. Moreover, the mother will talk more freely when she is confident of the appearance of the house and of herself; for your first visit that is more important than seeing the usual routine of the home. If, then, the family has a telephone, it is generally best to try to make an appointment. If you can wangle an invitation in general terms ("Any afternoon this week except Thursday"), so much the better.

In all cases you must remember that you occupy a rather delicate position. In the first place you are inevitably a representative both of the college and of the school. You have thus an opportunity to learn how to conduct yourself in a professional and tactful manner. In seeking your first appointment, for example, you should put yourself at the parents' disposal rather than seek your own convenience. We know, of course, that students, no less than the parents, have other appointments to meet. But in arranging for a mutually convenient meeting, you can manage to convey the impression that the parent's convenience has first consideration—as, indeed, it should have.

If the general plan has been outlined to the parent by the school, you should not elaborate much upon the statements already made. You can say quite simply that you are taking a course in child study in preparation for teaching, that the college considers a better understanding of children of great importance for effective teaching and has sought an opportunity for each prospective teacher to become thoroughly familiar with a typical, normal child. This child has been selected, not because he is a problem in school but simply because he represents the kind of child you will have to deal with when you become a teacher.

At this point it is generally well to allow the parent to ask questions. These questions should be answered frankly and directly. If the parents do not ask any questions, you might continue somewhat as follows: "Naturally it is impossible to understand a child without knowing how he has developed, so I should like to have you tell me something about his earlier years. And one thing that we certainly need to understand, better than teachers usually do, is how the child acts with his brothers and sisters around home." You would like permission, therefore, to come home from school with the child some day and notice how he acts there.

You should admit smilingly that neither the school nor the parent is likely to be very greatly enlightened by your study of the child. You will, of course, be quite glad to discuss with the mother anything that you find, but you are, after all, just a beginner in this field, and the purpose of this study is mainly your own improvement. You hardly expect to discover anything that the mother does not already know. As some slight return, however, for any bother you occasion, you will be happy to act as a "sitter" some evening while the parents are away.[2] And you may also indicate that if the parents are willing, you would like to take the child with you to a concert or motion picture or some such treat to see how he reacts there.

You should not volunteer any estimate of how much of the parent's time you will take, but if you are asked you should say: "Why, of course, I shall take only such time as you find it possible to give me. However, there seems to be no need, unless something unusual should develop, to take up more than an hour, or perhaps two hours at the most. I should like to be around the home somewhat longer just playing or talking with Suzanne, but I should certainly not expect to take up very much of your time in any direct way."

Be careful at this time to ask no questions about the parents themselves; the first approach should concern the child. When you are on a more familiar footing it may (or may not) be possible to ask a few questions about the family situation.

Just because some of the above directions take the form of direct quotation, you are not to make a prepared talk along these lines! There could be no greater mistake than to memorize these words and deliver them as a mechanical speech.

On the contrary it is desirable to get the *parent* to talk freely to you. It does no harm to let the conversation range very widely —even to "cabbages and kings." You will be at once learning something about the child's home and parents and cultivating an easy relationship. And, be assured, the conversation will presently come back to the child or can be very gently steered back.[3]

---

[2] Need it be pointed out that this is a chance not merely to repay the parents but to further your study of the child!

[3] In the exceptional case where this is not true, it is likely to be symptomatic of the relationship between parent and child.

Only one thing is essential: a simple, friendly, unassuming approach. Most parents will be cooperative and quite understanding of your mission. A few will be suspicious and doubtful at the start, but they will readily accept you if you are friendly and tactful. Only a very small number will prove so uncooperative that it is advisable to start over with another family.

Contact with the Child

The approach to the child can be made with the utmost simplicity. Children, of course, are very curious, but their curiosity as a rule is easily satisfied. In general, the best thing is just to make a plain statement: "I am studying to become a teacher (or to make myself a better teacher), and so I want to know children better. You see, if I am to be a good teacher I have to know what children are like." This simple statement seldom fails to satisfy the child, and it has the merit of being direct—and, strangely enough, true. If, however, the child has any further questions, these can be answered frankly and with similar simplicity. If the child asks, "Why pick on me?" answer that the teacher had suggested that he was a perfectly "regular" sort of a child to become acquainted with. If the child wants to know what you are going to do, say that you will come around and play with him sometimes, get acquainted with his father and mother, find out about his health when he was a little boy and things like that. Suggest that perhaps you and he will go to a movie sometime or that you may take him to a concert or a museum (or something that will seem attractive). Do not offer to help him with his schoolwork; if he asks whether you will, say that you might look over some of his schoolwork sometime to see how he is getting on. This aspect, however, should not be emphasized. You will be surprised to find how readily children accept this whole proceeding, especially where several in the same room have what they are likely to call "My college girl."

To emphasize the necessity for sympathy and understanding of the child's feelings, we adapt from Teagarden eleven rules for the guidance of case workers which you will do well to ponder and observe. Lest you be worried about having to memorize them, Teagarden and I hasten to add that they are only a code of good sense.

(1) Remember that the child may be uncomfortable. Make the situation as easy for him as possible. Unless you are so old that it makes you feel uncomfortable to do so, you should have the child call you by your first name. You are not at this time, see, to act the teacher.

(2) Be kindly but objective—not effusive.

(3) Don't talk too much. Get the child to talk.

(4) Don't "talk down" to the child.

(5) Don't ask questions until rapport has been established.

(6) Don't try to get too much the first time.

(7) Don't follow any outline or interviewing device woodenly.

(8) Don't take notes obviously.

(9) Don't show shock at anything the child tells you. (If he "tries you out" with obscenity, let him see you know what he is up to and are unimpressed.)

(10) Don't try to handle problems that require expert handling in a particular field.

(11) Don't betray confidences. You should repeat what you hear only where by doing so you may actually be giving help or protection. The child should never be allowed to feel imposed on.[4]

Planning Observation

Limiting the Field

There is practically no limit to the number of things which can be observed about any child of any age. A detailed and exhaustive study of a child's family relationships alone would take many weeks to complete. And even then it would be necessary to check every conclusion against further observations in order to insure that the study was based on permanent attitudes rather than chance occurrences. For a brief study such as you are about to make, it is especially necessary to discover as soon as possible what are likely to be the most important factors in the life of the child under observation.

It is impossible, however, to set up a rigid list of the "most

---

4 Modified from Florence M. Teagarden, *Child Psychology for Professional Workers*, rev. ed., Englewood, N.J.: Prentice-Hall, Inc., 1946, p. 337.

important factors." What is most significant for one child may have very little significance for another. We can, however, make certain rather general suggestions.

One of the most important areas to explore is the child's relationships with other people, especially members of the immediate family. Unfortunately, you will not have much opportunity to observe such relationships because of the limits of your study and prohibitory social conventions. A child's relations with his teacher are much more accessible and open to observation; and, so, in general, are the influences of schoolmates and neighborhood friends. In some cases a certain child may identify himself with a person not in the immediate family; his relations with that person are of prime importance.

Anything that makes the child a little different is always interesting and important: differences in physical size or appearance, in racial stock, in culture, in interests, in religion. You should be particularly alert to discover anything in the child's behavior that is unusual or that is personally characteristic.

Your preliminary observations, then, and your early interviews will provide you with certain "information" and, unless you are different from most persons, with certain rather vague impressions. These should be neither accepted nor rejected at this time. Instead, they should be "put on ice."

First-impressions Record

For this purpose, it may be well to follow a suggestion I owe to Dr. Fritz Redl and write out a fairly detailed thumbnail sketch of the child very early in your relation with him—say after your second observation. Tell what you saw and heard, what seemed likely to you to be his chief characteristics, his chief problems, his probable background, and—here you must be honest—how you felt toward the child. If he seems unattractive, don't be afraid that you are telling on yourself if you say so. While you should not lose contact with reality and write a merely imaginary sketch, you are encouraged *for just this once* to give way to your "hunches." This *first-impressions* record should be put aside and *not referred to again* until after the case history is finally written. Then—and then only—bring out your *first-impressions* record and compare it with the conclusions of your study. This should be done in writing, and both the original note and the comparison included in the appendix to your study.

A word of warning. If, for just this once, you are encouraged to "let yourself go" in these initial "hunches," you are not thereby encouraged to take them seriously. Or perhaps I should urge that you be seriously skeptical of them. Too frequently we see only those things in another person's behavior that are in accord with our initial impressions. This is especially true when we have written down impressions, for then anything that contradicts the impressions means that "we were wrong." It may amuse as well as interest you to observe how readily you spring to your own defense, but you won't catch yourself unless you are constantly on the alert to do so. My purpose in having you commit your first impressions to writing is to have you become sufficiently aware of them that you will also beware! Don't let them blind you. Moreover, the accuracy or inaccuracy of your first impressions, as shown by the comparison in your appendix, is no indication of the excellence of your case study. The first impressions of even experienced personnel workers, psychiatrists, and psychologists are open to error.

If, however, your final conclusions are to be sound, your tentative conclusions must be checked and rechecked *continuously*. We speak of "final" conclusions only because all human enterprises must have an end sometime. Otherwise, quite clearly what is called your "final" conclusion is only the last in a series of tentative conclusions. In the next section is outlined a method of checking these conclusions which is much less formidable than its title indicates.

Getting Preliminary Hypotheses

The great physicist Michael Faraday was once asked to observe an experiment. "Before we begin," he responded, "just what am I expected to see?" He knew better than to believe himself capable of detecting, offhand and without guidance, the essential features of a complicated machine.

Now you are about to begin observing the most complicated "machine" on earth. You, too, need the guidance of certain preliminary hypotheses. Faraday, please note, hoped to get his preliminary hypothesis from someone who already understood something of the problem. And we believe that you, too, are likely to make progress more quickly in the early stages if you turn to the persons who know the child. Accordingly, after a brief visit to the class merely to acquaint yourself with the object of your investigation, you should talk with parent or teacher.

Certain precautions, however, are very important if you are to get off on the right foot. We have already noted that you will gain friendly rapport with an "interviewee" in proportion as you succeed in getting him or her to talk freely. Such free conversation also serves your purpose of learning what seem to be the child's outstanding characteristics and qualities. You should not, therefore, attempt to dominate the interview. Instead, cultivate the art of listening. If it is possible, avoid direct questioning and elicit the interviewee's spontaneous remarks. To keep him going and to show your interest, it is occasionally wise to say something which indicates your understanding, putting the matter in question form: "Do you mean that Harold seemed very happy when his sister was born?" Or you may somewhat direct the trend by such a question as: "He got over the measles rather easily?" Usually it will not be long before the interviewee has revealed his or her own major understandings of the child.

Now these understandings must be taken very tentatively. Suppose you are having your first interview with the child's teacher, who tells you that Robert seems to be neither a leader nor a follower but cooperates with his playmates and sometimes leads, other times follows. This statement, *carefully and duly ascribed to its author,* may be entered in your notes as a tentative hypothesis. Very tentative, in fact, for your next interview may be with a former teacher who was very enthusiastic about Robert and tells you that in her class Robert was always a leader.

Your next observation may be of Robert on the playground. It is tempting to plan to spend your time in confirming or rejecting the tentative hypothesis that you may have set up with respect to Robert's leadership. Since, however, this is your first direct observation of Robert on the playground you should not spend all your time in this way. In the first place, perhaps we hear a little too much about leadership in child study; it is an important characteristic but not the only one. In any case, the

question of leadership cannot be solved unless it is seen in relationship to other variable factors, for example, health. Thus, if
you were thinking only of how much Robert leads, it would be
quite possible that you would fail to note that he hangs back and
does not initiate activities because he is out of breath or suddenly
very tired; these are the characteristics of a child somewhat lacking in health or physical vigor.

In other words, at this stage, your observations should be directed *by the behavior you are witnessing* rather than by any
preconceived questions you have formulated. Note *what* the
child has been doing, *with whom* he is doing it, and *how* in general he seems to conduct himself. Note also the reactions of
other children or adults to him and how he reacts to them.

In both these preliminary approaches—that is, in the first interview and in the first direct observations—make sure that you are
seeing and hearing correctly what the other person or the child
is saying and doing. The observation needs to be very concrete,
very objective and factual, very precise. Any appraisal or judgment not only may be, but should be, rather vague and indefinite.
Yet out of all this there should emerge certain *tentative* hypotheses.

Keeping an Open Mind

At this point there is grave danger of taking these hypotheses
too seriously. First, even when they are correct, they may be
stated in too general a form.

And secondly, there is the question of the correctness of the
hypothesis. The behavior may not have been correctly observed
or interpreted, or the behavior may not be typical. For these
reasons, you will do better to frame your hypotheses in the form
of *questions* instead of statements or conclusions. All of us are
too prone to take direct statements as conclusions and read them
into all our further observations, whereas the questions serve to
remind us that the issue is still open.

Using Hypotheses to Direct Observation

But, in order that they take on a definite enough form to guide
your observing, your hypotheses should be put in writing—early

in your work with the child. *Before and after* each observation you should look over your notes, notice what seems *on the way* to confirmation, what seems disproved, which hypotheses need modification.

This part of scientific method seems time-consuming and is often neglected. Actually it is time-saving, since it enables you to get a greater wealth of really usable fact from your observations. The greatest vice of most child-study observation is *aimlessness*, dependence upon mere impressionism. Scientific observation is pointed, intensive search, not aimless gazing. Even in the first two or three observations you are not just looking around purposelessly; you are searching for your starting points. Hence I lay down one of the few rigid rules contained in this guide: Before beginning an observation period, formulate definitely the one or two questions or hypotheses with which your observation is to be particularly concerned. Ask yourself—in advance—what kinds of behavior will throw light on the hypothesis. After the observation is finished, report with respect to these questions (*a*) what you found, (*b*) what you did not find, and (*c*) what you should look for another time. All this must be very concrete and specific.

Should one ignore facts that do not bear on the hypothesis? By no means! Whatever else you observe and report is an "extra dividend." The *rule* given above is rigid, but *you* should be flexible and adaptable and sensitive to all sorts of child behavior. The whole situation may become radically unfavorable to finding out anything about the kind of behavior you had planned to study. A rapid change of plan is then called for. But there should still be a plan, a real search, not just aimless gazing.

KEEPING THE RECORDS

Adequate records are essential if your case study is to be acceptable, but they have a wider value. To an extent often not realized, the attempt to put fleeting observations in words clarifies them and brings out their significance.

And be sure your record is complete. The Big Four of sound

journalism apply here as well. Make clear *who* is the source of your information. If it was your own direct observation, let that be clear. If you are reporting what someone told you, be crystal clear as to just who told you what. The methods and circumstances of gathering the information must be given. If you observed the event, it is not too difficult to tell *how* you observed it. But if you are retelling something you learned secondhand, you have a double obligation. You must report how you got the information from your informant; and you must tell how your informant got it—if you can. Finally, tell where and when the event occurred.

As a double-check, you should always indicate when you wrote the report.

Taking Notes

While observing the child in class, you can generally take notes freely. In interviewing the teacher you will be expected to take notes. Many parents, on the other hand, are made nervous if you bring out a pencil and notebook. When you have become well acquainted with them, or when certain objective facts are being given (such as the date of Harold's attack of measles), you might ask permission to jot down a memo. If anyone seems concerned about your taking notes and asks for an explanation, you will find it best to say frankly that you are making notes merely to help you think things through afterward. It is obvious that only rarely may you write down things in the child's presence, though in case of need you can tell the child you are writing yourself a reminder of something to do.

If you have been unable to take notes during the observation, write them as soon as possible thereafter. In every instance record the time (day and hour), the circumstances of the observation, the place, the purpose you had in mind in making the observation, and the time elapsing between observation and writing.

Field Notes

The notes you thus take on the spot or write down immediately afterward are known as *Field Notes* and should be included in the appendix of your final report to the instructor. *Unless they are very illegible or untidy, they need not be copied.* It is desirable, however, that they be uniform in size and in plan. We suggest that you use full 8½ × 11 paper. This can be conveniently folded in half or quarter for "on-the-spot" notes and still fit in with the rest of your written or typed report. Make sure that the field notes are uniform in size and securely fastened together, so that they do not get out of order.

THE DISTINCTION BETWEEN FACT AND INTERPRETATION

While it is impossible to keep the human or personal element out of your observations, it must be your constant effort to reduce it to a minimum. This implies that you must distinguish what actually happened (observed fact) from how the fact impressed you (interpretation or meaning of the fact).

For present purposes we may think of observed fact as a percept—something seen, heard, smelled, touched, or tasted. As a rough criterion, whatever an actor directly conveys is observable. If he strides up and down, we actually observe a "nervous manner." Similarly we can observe a child's "happy smile" or "puzzled frown." These are the basic materials of observation.

In reacting to such "facts," however, we almost invariably indulge in a certain amount of interpretation. Several levels of interpretation may be usefully distinguished.

Consider the following statements:

(1) He replied, when his mother spoke to him, in a very cross tone. (2) He was irritated by the interruption to his work. (3) Besides that, his mother tends to nag him quite a lot and that makes him snappy in his replies. (4) This habit of making cross replies is getting to be general; he might be described as a cross or surly boy. (5) No wonder he is unpopular.

A Scale of Closeness to the Immediate Facts

The first statement is reasonably factual. You observed a cross tone—although it may be difficult to state what, in physical terms, a cross tone is.

The second statement goes somewhat beyond the bare fact; it

is obviously an interpretation or explanation of the fact. But the explanation is stated in terms of the immediate setting of the event and is necessary if the event is to have any meaning. We may call this a *meaning* or *context* interpretation. Unless it is obvious, it should always be given as a part of the observation. Without it the bare fact would be too bare.

The third statement goes beyond the immediate situation; it is an *appraisal* in terms of quite a number of facts which have previously been observed and in the light of quite a complex psychological theory. (The hypothesis that a nagging mother leads to snappy replies seems so self-evidently true that we forget that it is only an hypothesis or theory.)

The fourth statement even more obviously goes beyond the immediate facts. It implies enough observations to warrant a judgment that the behavior in question is habitual or characteristic. This may be called generalization from the facts.[5] And once more we see a theory as to cause-and-effect relationships.

The last statement involves us in another theory and obviously implies moral and social evaluation as well.

We have here, then, a sort of scale of closeness to the immediate facts of experience: first, *observed fact;* second, fact plus immediate *context* or meaning; third, *appraisal* of the fact; fourth, *generalization* from the fact; fifth, *evaluation.*

Now perhaps all of this is justifiable. In a full study of an individual we have to come to rather far-reaching judgments; that, in a sense, is what the study is for. But most of this interpretation has no place in what purports to be a record of *factual observation.* The field notes should therefore give only a minimum of interpretation; any interpretation we do make should be clearly distinguished from the facts, and its tentative nature made clear.

Particularly troublesome is that form of interpretation which consists in attributing some "trait" of character or personality to the child—as in (4) above, where the child is said to be "surly."

---

[5] Generalization *from* the facts must be distinguished from generalization *of* the facts. The latter may be illustrated by such statements as: "He answered crossly every time his mother spoke to him the entire afternoon." Generalization of the facts is not interpretation at all but simply a short way of stating them.

Since "traits" are always a matter of inference and not of observed fact, they have no place in a factual report.

Such trait descriptions, moreover, cover up our lack of full knowledge. A child is said to have shown "strong will" because for hours he refused a half stick of gum when he had asked for a whole piece. But saying this was "strong will" merely says he persisted in his refusal. It does not tell us *why*. It does not give us a clue as to how often or cunningly he was tempted with the half stick. It does not tell us what he gained from the refusal.

Compare the usefulness of these two reports:

1. Chester is very quick tempered, as was seen in the way he acted when his sister jogged his elbow while he was working on a model airplane.

2. While Chester was working on a model airplane, his sister accidentally jogged his elbow. He was instantly angry and pushed her away. [Of course, the model is fragile and very dear to him and his sister did endanger it. Yet I wondered whether that was the whole story. Does she pester him a lot? Or what is his relation to her? Does he think she is mother's pet just because she is young and rather doll-like? Does he feel that he must defend his possessions against her? I shall have to watch closely for indications that will bring out this. I wonder whether his mother has insight and objectivity enough to know. I think I shall not ask her directly, but she may have some evidence for me.]

The writer of the second report is looking for facts, the writer of the first found a ready-made conclusion.

Secondhand Information

You will note also that the writer of the second note considers getting some secondhand information—in this instance, from the mother. That, of course, is quite legitimate, provided we know what we are doing.

In the first place, what people *say* about a child is a fact, even when what is said is untrue. We simply have two sets of facts: what the reporter says and the way things really are. Get both into the record if you can.

The *way* people talk about a child, the tones and the facial expressions, the turn of phrase—all these are observable facts, however difficult they may be to set down on paper or to interpret. And they are important facts, too, for they may influence the child or others in the child's environment; they may be indicators of attitudes toward the child. However uncertain the interpretation, such facts should be reported; when correlated with other data, they may later assume significance.

Field notes, then, represent an attempt to capture fleeting events and commit them to paper before they are forgotten. We seek a maximum of accuracy and completeness rather than that ordered design which marks a work of art. Abbreviations may be used freely; full sentences are unnecessary; form and logical order give way here to the order of reality, even though that order may seem to us to be disorder. There is an art in making observations, but in their *recording* we should try for photographic and phonographic reproduction, ignoring considerations of style. The place for literary art is in the final report.

—▶ **Arnold Gesell**

The Miracle of Growth[1]

From *Studies in Child Development,* by Arnold Gesell. Copyright 1948 by Arnold Gesell. Reprinted by permission of Harper & Brothers.

The task of science is to make the world we live in more intelligible. This world is filled with knowable realities. At one extreme is the Atom; at another is the Child. In the Miracle of Growth these two extremes meet.

There are two kinds of nuclei—the nucleus of the physical atom and the nucleus of the living cell. Each contains energies derived from the cosmos through ageless processes of evolution. An atom

[1] Address delivered at the inauguration of an exhibit portraying "The Miracle of Growth" at The Museum of Science and Industry, Chicago, August 6, 1947.

can be pictured as a tiny solar system, composed of a central nucleus surrounded by electrons. In comparison, the fertilized human egg cell is transcendently complex, for its organic nucleus initiates the most miraculous chain reaction known to science— a cycle of growth in which a minute globule of protoplasm becomes an embryo, the embryo a fetus, the fetus an infant, the infant a child, the child a youth, the youth an adult, and the adult a parent.

With parenthood, another cycle of growth is liberated. And so it comes to pass that children, mothers, fathers, preparents, and grandparents can all behold the miracles of growth.

The exhibit which has been prepared with such imagination for your great museum is impressive, because it portrays the pageant of child development in full perspective. The central figure properly is the mother, who bears the child. But we are reminded that the child as an individual is equally derived from the nuclear chromosomes of a father. The incontrovertible importance of sound inheritance is made clear to all who wish to ponder.

Science is probing deeper and deeper into the mechanisms of heredity which underlie both the bodily and the mental growth of the human infant. Biochemists are identifying the genetic substances in the nucleus and cytoplasm of the growing cell. They have even begun to picture the possible shapes of the individual genes which determine the basic events of the drama of growth. By latest report, the genes may be likened to a curious double comb with a long row of protein teeth on one side and a row of nucleotides on the other. Simply arrange the teeth of these combs in appropriate sizes and sequences, and they will play a developmental melody. In a suitable environment, as a pushbutton exhibit may indicate, there will come to life a brown-eyed or a blue-eyed baby who reaches out for a rattle at six months, stands on his feet at one year, talks at two, and cuts his sixth-year molar at six. You see, it is indeed a prodigious chain reaction which deserves every possible insight that science and wisdom can bestow.

Accordingly, the experimental embryologist has brought the problems of organic growth into the laboratory where he is systematically analyzing the mechanisms of development. With the aid of microscope, staining methods, and recording devices, he boldly explores the growth processes of tadpole, salamander, sea urchin. He manipulates the conditions of growth to determine the effect of surgical and environmental alterations. He modifies the temperature and the nutriment of the organism, or he bombards it with X-rays to ascertain the developmental forces at work. He transplants tissue from one part of the organism to another part, or even transfers tissue from one species to another—all for the purpose of probing more deeply into the concealed miracles of growth. He transplants a regenerating amphibian tail into the eye chamber of a frog larva and discovers that the potential tail transforms into a crystalline lens, a man-made miracle, based however on natural law.

In a growing system the components are in a state of labile equilibrium. One component has the capacity to *induce*, probably by some bio-electric mechanism, a new shape or arrangement in another component. The latent energy of the genes issues into patterned forms.

The medical scientist is especially interested in the harmonies and disharmonies of growth—disharmonies like cancer, and developmental anomalies such as retrolental fibroplasia which may blind the eyes of a human infant too prematurely born. Not without reason, the investigation of the physiology of development has become a major occupation of the life sciences. This investigation embraces plant and animal, human and subhuman, normal and abnormal manifestations.

Do all these varied laboratory studies throw light on the nature and needs of child development? Indeed they do, because we may be sure that the profoundest laws of development are universal and apply alike to the growth of tissues, to the growth of organs, of functions, and of human behavior.

From the standpoint of development, body and mind are indivisible. The child comes by his mind as he comes by his body, through the organizing processes of growth. Consider, for example, the embryology of *eyes and hands and brain*. These three are inseparably interlinked, both somatically and psychologically. As early at the fifth week after conception (the embryo is but ¼ inch in length), the eyes emerge as optic cups, the hands as limb buds, the brain as rudimentary cerebral hemispheres. The growing cells multiply at an extraordinary rate. Cells invade the diminutive limb buds and cause them to elongate. The outer segment assumes the shape of a paddle. Five lobes appear on the edge of the paddle, which in another month transforms into a five-fingered hand. Muscles and tendons attach themselves to the skeleton of arm and hand. Nerve fibers penetrate the muscular tissue. Nerve endings ramify into the joints. End organs by the thousands establish themselves in the sensitive skin. Thus the hand becomes a patterned structure, elaborately connected with the central nervous system, including the brain. Presently, some of the structures are ripe enough to react. Arms and fingers make their first spontaneous movements. About the third month of gestation the eyeballs move in their sockets beneath fused lids, the fingers flex, open and close. These are patterned movements, embryonic behavior patterns. The mind has begun to grow.

There are six hundred paired muscles with billions of contractile fibrils in the human fetus. The fibrils are supplied by multibillions of neuron fibrils. The growing mind is part and parcel of this vast network of living filaments. The mind grows because tissue grows. Neurons have prodigious powers of growth. They multiply at a rapid rate in the embryonic and fetal period when the foundations of behavior are laid. The 5-months-old fetus is already in possession of the final quota of twelve or more billions of nerve cells which make up the nervous system. These cells continue to grow and to organize throughout the cycle of growth.

One may think of the child's mind as a marvelous fabric—a growing, functional fabric. Functionally the mind consists of propensities and patterns of behavior. If you should ask whether a newborn baby has a mind, the baby might well answer, "Look at my behavior patterns and watch them grow."

Note how *eyes and hands and brain* co-ordinate during the first year of life. The newborn baby can breathe, can suckle, can sleep. In the early weeks his hands remain fisted most of the time, but presently he opens his eyes and begins his psychological conquest of the physical world. He seeks the light of the window.

At the age of 2 months, his eyes follow a moving person. At 3 months, he can look at his own hand which is now opening. At 4 months he can pick up a tiny object with his eyes, but not yet with his hands. At 6 months he can pick it up on sight. His grasp at first is crude and pawlike, but at 10 months he extends his index finger and picks up a crumb on his highchair tray by a precise pincer prehension. This extension of the index finger is an important event in the story of growth. It represents a refinement and specialization of the child's action system.

At this age the New Haven infant, and I believe also the Chicago infant, is under an irrepressible compulsion to poke and to pry and to probe. He uses his index finger as though it were a tool. He uses it as an awl to thrust, as a lever to push. His prehension and manipulation are no longer pawlike. He has made a neurological advance toward adult levels of skill, and he is discovering the mysteries of container and contained, and of the third dimension. He continues to progress from one level of skill to another, not altogether because of specific training or instruction, but primarily because he is richly endowed with natural powers of growth, which bring eyes, hands, nerve cells into increasingly complex co-ordinations.

By the age of one year his brain has sufficiently matured so that he is capable of inhibiting his grasp and of exercising voluntary release. Give him a dozen cubes. He picks them up one by one and then drops them one by one to exercise this newfound power of release. He disposes the cubes in random array, but at 18 months he uses them as though they were building stones and erects a tower of three blocks. At 2 years he builds horizontally, arranging the blocks into a wall. At 3 years he can rearrange the three blocks to construct a bridge. This is a lawful sequence determined by the intrinsic growth of the relationships between eyes and hands and brain.

Similar sequences determine the later progressions of behavior. The 3-year-old can draw a circle; the 4-year-old a square. The 5-year-old uses eyes and hands to mold objects with clay. The 6-year-old can use a pencil or crayon as a tool, printing capital letters. Seven-year-old boys begin to use hammer and saw; girls color and cut out paper dolls. The 8-year-old draws action figures in good proportion, and puts perspective into his drawings. The 10-year-old can build complex structures with an erector set, and he uses handwriting as a tool with freedom and facility.

This sketchy summary of the eye-hand-brain relationships indicates that the progressions of child development are governed by a ground plan. Growth is a step-by-step miracle—a gradual and not a sudden apocalypse. Each step is made possible only by the step that preceded. First the blade, then the ear; after that the full corn in the ear. As with a plant, so with a child. His mind grows by natural stages. The eyes take the lead, the hands follow. The baby grasps with his palm before he grasps with his finger tips. He creeps before he walks, cries before he laughs, babbles before he talks, builds a tower before a wall, a wall before a bridge, draws a circle before a square, a square before a diamond. Such sequences are part of the order of Nature.

With the aid of motion-picture cameras, our Clinic has documented thousands of behavior patterns and pattern phases at thirty-four age levels from the period of fetal infancy through the first ten years of life. These voluminous records show that although no two individuals are exactly alike, all normal children tend to follow a general ground plan of growth which is characteristic of the species or of a cultural group. Every child, therefore, has a unique pattern of growth, but that pattern is a variant of a basic ground plan.

The ground plan is determined by the genes. Environmental factors support, inflect, and modify, but they do not generate the progressions of development. It can be said with scientific assurance that when the infant enters the world, he is already an individual with growth potentialities which are distinctively his own. He comes into his racial inheritance through processes of maturation governed by the genes. He comes into his social inheritance through processes of acculturation. These two processes operate and interact in close conjunction, but maturation is so fundamental that it cannot be transcended.

We have been studying a pair of duplicate twins over a period of twenty years. Beginning with infancy and with the help of the cinema, we have identified numerous similarities and differences which demonstrate the basic role of maturation, in shaping the individuality of behavior even in extremely similar twins. If you are reluctant to acknowledge the importance of genes, you may say, "This is all very well for such physical reactions as walking, stair climbing, block building, writing, drawing, and motor performance. But does it apply to emotions, to morals, to personality, and to the spiritual aspects of childhood?"

Our studies show that the higher psychical manifestations of child life also are profoundly subject to laws of development. The foundation and the framework of human personality are laid down in the first ten years of life by processes of growth which continue with new intensity throughout the teens.

Psychically, the child inherits nothing fully formed. Each and every part of his nature has to grow—his sense of self, his fears, his affections, and his curiosities, his feelings toward mother, father, playmates, sex, his judgments of good and bad, of ugly and beautiful, his respect for truth and property, his sense of humor, his ideas about life and death, crime, war, races, nature, and deity. All of his sentiments, concepts, and attitudes are products of growth and experience. They are patterned modes of behavior which are obedient to the same lawful sequences which determine the patterning of posture, locomotion, prehension, and the acts of skill mediated by eyes, hands, and brain.

The culture, through home and school, through religion, art, and recreation, leaves its imprint on the growing child. The culture directs and guides; it helps to organize his goals and his conduct, but always he must do his own growing. In his growth he passes through recurrent stages of transition, disequilibrium and recurrent equilibrium. He does not mount at one bound to the higher ethical levels. His development takes a spiral course. With each turn of the spiral, the level of his maturity rises. We can have faith in the constructive essence of growth.

We must not lose faith if at the age of 2½ years, the child grabs a toy from his playmate; if at 4 years he calls names and brags and boasts and tells tall tales; if at 6 years he suddenly becomes aggressive in word and action. We do all that we can to divert his behavior into desirable channels, but we must recognize the nature of his immaturity. He is not necessarily depraved if at 6 years he appropriates something which does not belong to him. At this time he has a weak sense of ownership, even with respect to his own property, and he may give away his best possessions. He is in a stage of transition where values are not yet established.

But at 7 and 8 years of age he rapidly develops a sense of fairness, of honesty. He begins to think in terms of right and wrong as well as of good and bad. At 10 years he becomes interested in social problems and develops an embryonic civic as well as personal conscience. He may even discuss problems of racial minorities, gangsters, crime, labor and management, black markets. It is a golden period for planting liberalizing ideas and attitudes.

All this is part of the miracle of growth. For the laws of growth apply to all aspects of the child's nature. The child grows as a unit throughout the entire cycle of development. He comes into the world with distinctive potentialities of growth which are part of his inalienable rights. Very naturally, he manifests a spirit of liberty which has its deepmost roots in the biological impulsion toward optimal growth.

Growth, therefore, becomes a philosophical concept when applied to the affairs of human culture. Just as the Darwinian concept of racial evolution transformed our outlook upon human institutions, so the new biological doctrines of growth have vast social implications—implications for child guidance, for mental diagnosis, for health supervision, for the conduct of education, and for the very arrangements of our ways of living. In the light of modern science, we cannot define a system of ethics or of mental hygiene without acknowledging the relativities of growth.

To understand children, we must understand their ways of growth. This is why we need a science of child development to interpret the more mysterious meanings of child behavior. This is why the clinical science of pediatrics is becoming more and more concerned with the diagnosis and the supervision of child development. American pediatrics is embarking on a program of developmental protection which will embrace all children in their early years. It is altogether fitting that the present exhibit of the physical, the dental, and the mental development of the child should have been prepared under the auspices of a department of pediatrics in a university school of medicine.

At the moment, the physical sciences—physics and chemistry—hold the stage. This is inevitable because the immediate fate of mankind depends upon how the explosive fruits of these sciences are used. But when peace is assured, the life sciences as well as the physical sciences will hold the stage, and both together will be constructively addressed to the betterment of human relationships, and to the preservation of family life.

After all, do we need to draw a sharp distinction between the physical, the biological sciences, or for that matter, between science and the humanities? All nature is unitary. I think it enhances the significance of the Exhibit on Child Development that it will be housed in a comprehensive Museum of Science and Industry, where the visitor can see the triumphs of engineering and the remarkable products of our technological age side by side with medical and biological exhibits which portray the nature of the creative, inventive man who, with eyes, hands, and brain, brought a civilization into being.

But this civilization will come to ruin if man cannot preserve his mental and spiritual health. We need a more profound knowledge of child development to teach us the limitations of the human nervous system under the impacts of a technological culture.

This knowledge will come not only from direct studies of infant and child, but from the converging contributions of all the natural and life sciences. As governments and communities become more responsible for the support of science, there should be an increasing focalization of research upon the child and upon the family which is the fundamental unit of our social structure. Already our citizens are becoming more science minded with respect to their human relationships and to the problems of child care and education. They doubt the efficacy of mere indoctrination and authoritarian discipline. Sensing the dignity and worth of individuality even in the infant, they sense likewise the growth mechanisms which determine the mind and morals of the child as he advances toward maturity.

Knowing something of the beauty and relentless precision of engines and machines, modern man is ready for new realistic insights into the mechanisms of development, mechanisms which are as exacting as the laws of gravitation. The task of science is to increase the intelligibility of the lawful factors which make man what he is, and what he might be. Such intelligibility leads to tolerance among grown men, and to humaneness between adult and child. With science and yet more science, the race may hope to attain higher orders of morality and subjugate the lingering wickedness which a million years of evolution have not abolished.

A science of man which recognizes the dignity of the individual infant, accordingly, could become a creative force in the atomic age. It would heighten and multiply human values. It would diffuse mutual understanding.

In a more sincerely sustained effort to understand children, men and women of maturity will better comprehend themselves and their fellows. Thus we might slowly acquire those moral techniques which are necessary for the control of a technological culture, and which also are necessary for an answer to the age-old prayer in which we ask to be delivered from evil.

To sum up in a sentence, we cannot conserve the mental health of children, we cannot make democracy a genuine folkway, unless we bring into the homes of the people a *developmental philosophy* of child care rooted in scientific research.

CHAPTER
THREE

▲
|

*Scientific Method
in Psychology*

THE SUBJECT MATTER OF PSYCHOLOGY HAS
evolved in the main from scientific studies of behavior. No
amount of speculation, resort to logic, or appeal to authority
would ever result in dependable knowledge about man and his
actions. Only as the scientific method has been brought to bear
on the problems of psychology has it been possible to develop a
body of principles and trustworthy concepts.

What is the scientific method? Not all that a student will want
to know about it is to be found in the two readings that comprise this chapter. These readings do, however, furnish a good
basis for our understanding of (1) the general aims and methods
of science as applied to the study of human behavior and (2) the
rather more specific methods employed in a highly important
kind of inquiry into human behavior and development, namely,
longitudinal study.

In the first of the readings in this chapter, Clarence W. Brown and Edwin E. Ghiselli, both of the University of California, point out that there are four fundamental questions that a scientist asks as he investigates a given phenomenon. He asks whether the experience he has of the phenomenon is real and permanent rather than illusory and transitory. He asks about the incidence and magnitude of the phenomenon. He then asks what is behind the facts which he has observed—he must systematically probe beyond the facts in search of plausible answers to the question, "Why is it so?" Finally, he asks what the conditions are that account for the phenomenon. The student will find in this discussion of the general aims and methods of science considerable clarification of the respective roles of facts, prediction, scientific controls, symbolization, description, and explanation in the conduct of scientific investigations. Each has a definite function to perform in man's search for truth about puzzling phenomena.

The second of the two readings in this chapter is one part of a pour-part book which Leland H. Stott prepared (especially for students) as a guide to the longitudinal study of individual development. When the reader examines the evaluative methods and considers the total operation involved in a broad-spectrum, longitudinal study of an individual, he can begin to visualize the magnitude of the fact-finding involved in certain of the long-term human growth studies reported later in this book. Stott is Leader of the Longitudinal Research Program at Merrill-Palmer Institute.

Many of the researches that are presented in later chapters exhibit the features of the scientific method discussed by Brown and Ghiselli. Many of them have made use of the kinds of data-gathering procedures described by Stott; some—the third reading in Chapter Nine, and the second, third and the fourth readings in Chapter Ten—are especially good examples of longitudinal study.

The student will do well to bear in mind that the longitudinal method of study—highly valuable as it is—is just one among a number of important methods used in the scientific study of human growth, development, and behavior. Another is the *experimental method;* it is well illustrated in the reading by Hebb in Chapter Six. Also, there are methods that are basically *correlational;* the first and second readings in Chapter Thirteen make good presentations of this methodological procedure. A method described as *ecological* (the study of individuals in their "natural habitat") is illustrated in the third reading of Chapter Eight. The student should find especially interesting the contrast of this last-mentioned method with the *clinical method,* briefly but helpfully mentioned by Stott in the present chapter.

The point of the foregoing paragraph is that a number of quite different methodological procedures have been employed by different scientists, respectively, in their study of human behavior and development. Each has its particular appropriateness and all have in them the essential features of the scientific method. To note the various procedures and to compare them as they appear in various chapters of this book should enhance the value of the ideas contained in the present chapter.

──▶ **Clarence W. Brown and
Edwin E. Ghiselli**

The Major Methods
of Science

From *Scientific Method in Psychology,* by Clarence W. Brown and Edwin E. Ghiselli. Copyright, 1955, by McGraw-Hill Book Company, Inc. Reprinted and abridged by permission.

In an earlier discussion [in *Scientific Method in Psychology*] it was pointed out that science can be interpreted as a very general method composed of many important but less general procedures. Some of these procedures deserve separate treatment because they form the solid core of the scientific method. They consist of symbolization, description, explanation, and theorizing.

Symbolization as a Method of Science

The Meaning of Symbolizing

Symbolization has to do with translating experience into symbols. Experience is fleeting; it is here, then gone. There is little time for pondering its nature while its sensory components are still manifest. If we are to deal with an experience after its disappearance, some change caused by the experience must be carried over in time and must be of such a nature that it can be re-aroused in memory and manipulated by means of various thought processes. This is accomplished through symbols or words. Experiences are given names. Every event, and every characteristic of every event, is given a symbol or word-tag by which it is known from that time forward.

Language is stressed in symbolization because it is the most widely used type of sign. It is not sufficient for all purposes, however, and an investigator may need to adopt or invent some other forms of symbolization. Two other systems of signs that are of great service are mathematics and symbolic logic.

The Characteristic of Correspondence in Symbolizing

The most important characteristic of symbolization concerns the degree of accuracy with which the symbols represent the facts they stand for. The objective in science is to develop symbols which can accurately substitute for the particular aspects of the events we want to represent; that is, to devise symbols so there will be some form of correspondence between the world of events, on the one hand, and the system of symbols, on the other.

Symbolizing in Science

We find that symbolization contributes to the scientist's work in two very significant ways; namely, (a) it makes possible a permanent record of experience, and (b) it furnishes a vehicle or mechanism for the rational manipulation of past experience.

It will be recalled that the manipulation of symbols in thinking is one of the essential procedures in science. The scientist, by mentally manipulating the word that stands for an event, is doing the next best thing to manipulating the event itself. In fact, dealing with an event in thought by manipulating its word meanings is in some respects superior to manipulating the event as an experience. The actual experienced event occupies a single precise point in time and space; the recalled event does not, and can therefore be manipulated indefinitely without respect to temporal and spatial contexts.

The Demands to Be Met by Symbolization

It will help us to understand what we should expect from symbolization as a method of science if we briefly review three characteristics of natural phenomena that set the demands that must be met by a successful system of symbols.

The tremendous complexity of natural phenomena sets the most severe demand. There is no apparent limitation to the extent to which natural phenomena can be subdivided and differentiated. To be successful, our system of symbolization must have unlimited possibilities in regard to the number of signs it can supply.

A second demand to be met by our system of symbols is referable to the characteristic of change. Never is the "same" event exactly the same. It is merely treated as constant in order to fulfill some particular purpose. Our system of symbols must be flexible enough to accommodate itself to changes in meanings occurring in time.

A third characteristic is summed up in the word relationship. Not only is an object found to be divisible into parts, and the object and its parts found to undergo continuous change, but the object and its subdivisions are found to be related in very complex ways with each other and with other objects and their subdivisions. We must make our symbols accurately express the nature and degree of these relationships.

Deficiency of Words as Symbols of Natural Phenomena

Keeping in mind the foregoing demands placed upon symbolization, let us consider the handicap under which we are working in trying to force natural phenomena into the system of signs called language—a system that we have poorly mastered even at best. We need not question the fact that language is one of the most valuable tools that man has invented, but there is need for questioning man's failure to make a more accurate use of the language he possesses. In meeting the demand for increased numbers of meanings, we have not exploited language to the fullest. We have been content to allow the same word to do double duty —actually, many times more than double duty. We also have been negligent in another way; we have assigned the same meaning to more than one word. Certainly, when we are in need of accurate representation of such a tremendous number of meanings, it is most inefficient to use the same word to stand for several meanings and to make several words function as representatives of the same meaning.

Language is deficient in representing changes in time. In many instances natural phenomena change faster than the words with which we describe them. Much of our language is still in the "horse-and-buggy" era. In fact, we persist in refusing to accept the innovations that crowd in upon us, and even ridicule the individual who dares to "coin" a new word.

Language, in the strict meaning of the term, is most deficient in regard to the symbolization of relationships. Here there is a severe limitation on the number of words that are available, so the scientist has had to look elsewhere to find a more exact and comprehensive system. This he has found in the symbolization of mathematics. Seldom does a scientist nowadays rely solely upon words for representing the relationships he wishes to describe. Numbers and their relationships are now a prime necessity in science.

Science has demonstrated through its use of mathematics and tabular and pictorial techniques that meanings can be represented with precision. It likewise has improved the precision of its descriptions through a more careful use of language as a vehicle for meanings. We are not expected to invent a new term every time we encounter difficulty in expression. It can be expected, however, that we shall exercise increasingly greater care in the selection of the words we use.

DESCRIPTION AS A METHOD OF SCIENCE

The Meaning of Description

As already noted, the function of symbolization is to assign word meanings to experiences of natural phenomena. But word meanings left as isolated events serve no useful purpose. Description is a systematic attempt to symbolize the obvious relationships that are found among the natural phenomena under study. By manipulating the name-tags, description creates a word picture of the orders that are readily observable among the phenomena. The organizations and relationships dealt with are of a simple nature. An important feature of the new meanings formed in description is that the characteristics and relationships evolved can be readily traced to sensory experiences and involve little or no abstraction from these experiences.

Description serves a bookkeeping function. Through description, an account of the experience is put in a more or less permanent written form. With the written record available, we are able to examine the data at will. The written record does not consist merely of a listing of symbols; rather, the patterns and arrangement experienced in the data are recorded. It is then that description as a simple rational process comes into play.

Description as Classification

Classification has to do with the discovery of relatively stable associations among properties or characteristics and with the symbolizing of these associations. Events or processes that have the same characteristics are grouped together and these groups or categories are given names. The tendency is to make the classificatory categories as specific and precise as possible. Highly abstract classes which tend to go far beyond the empirical facts are not considered description.

The classification assigned a given event or process is to be considered as somewhat tentative in nature. Classificatory schemes gradually undergo change as more and more knowledge is gained about the events or processes being classified.

Description as Seriating

A second form of description is called simple ordering or seriating. Seriating requires more knowledge about the events than does classification. It requires not only that some common characteristic be known but that this characteristic be known to exist in degrees or amounts, or be arrangeable on some form of continuum in a consistent way. Then the characteristic being described is a magnitude and is measurable, and a basis is available for accurately determining differences between the objects or events and thus a more precise classification scheme can be developed.

Description as Correlation

A third application of description is called correlation. In examining a group of objects it is sometimes noted that two different characteristics are associated in such a way that when one is present the other is present and when one is absent the other is also absent. The two characteristics are said to occur concomitantly and such a relationship is referred to as correlation.

It will be noted that, in general, the correlation form of description goes somewhat beyond classification and seriating; that is, the facts are first classified and arranged in order of magnitude before an attempt is made to correlate them.

In the forms of description discussed above, it is to be remembered that the feature or characteristic used as a basis for classifying, seriating, or correlating must be discoverable in the facts or events themselves. What actually can be observed or what can be empirically demonstrated becomes the basis on which the description proceeds. No recourse is made to knowledge that lies beyond the events or to inferences or theories that transcend the knowledge gained directly from the events.

EXPLANATION AS A METHOD OF SCIENCE

The Meaning of Explanation

As already stated, one of the fundamental objectives of science is to find the reasons for the occurrence of events. The scarcity of facts may compel us to resort to higher-order conceptual meanings in order to account for the phenomena we are studying. In searching for the possible conditions giving rise to an event, we are trying to answer the question: Why is it so? Explanation is the fundamental method through which we discover the answer to this type of question.

Explanation proceeds to the discovery of higher-order meanings by means of the manipulation of concepts. Symbolization, then, is necessary for explanation. The sensed experiences and the meanings derived from them must be symbolically represented in verbal or other form and thus made available for mental manipulation.

Explanation involves abstraction. Conceptual meanings depend upon the process of abstraction. As we attempt to create new patterns and relationships among the facts, reasoning takes us further and further away from the factual meanings of description to meanings at higher and higher levels of abstraction and generalization. Meanings in the form of postulated entities, processes, or relations, which the scientist conceptually invents to account for his results, are called logical constructs.

At higher levels of abstraction, explanation becomes theorizing. When an explanation effects a pattern of logical constructs as a conceptual framework into which all the facts relevant to some phenomenon can be fitted, it is usually called a theory.

Explanation and Description

There is general agreement that there is no sharp dividing line between description and explanation. Explanation begins where description leaves off. Both have the fundamental function of discovering the meanings of experienced events through the manipulation of symbols. The primary feature that distinguishes the two is the relative amount of conceptualizing involved. As already pointed out, the purpose of description is to discover the meanings that are observable in the sensed data themselves. The manipulation of the data is done in ways that issue directly from an observation of the facts available to experience. In explanation, the meanings are less observable in the data and are discovered through some process of mental manipulation of the data. The meanings derived at the descriptive level are further manipulated in explanation in an attempt to discover additional meanings.

Compared to the meanings of description, the meanings of explanation are more flexible, that is, they can be more easily changed to suit the purposes of the investigator. As a consequence, the meanings of explanation are more controversial. Procedures of mental manipulation are private to each thinker, and it is often difficult to get these manipulatory processes sufficiently similar in two or more individuals to achieve correspondence in the final meanings devised. In the experiencing of concepts, individuals do not see eye to eye as readily as in the experiencing of percepts.

The meanings of explanation are subject to less control than the meanings of description. Being removed by several steps from the empirical facts, explanatory meanings also are further removed from the controlling influence of experience.

Compared to descriptive meanings, explanations are more tentative in nature. In general, an explanation contains so much meaning that is guessed that it must be accepted only as a possible truth. As it receives verification through logic and experience it can be expressed as a probable truth, and sometimes the degree of probability can be accurately stated, depending on the amount and accuracy of the empirical data available.

The Purposes Served by Explanation

Explanation is directed toward increasing our understanding of natural phenomena. It is like description in that it results in the formation of classificatory schemes into which sensed data may be meaningfully organized, but the schemes of explanation are not readily observable in the data and depend primarily upon the reasoning processes.

Explanation enables us to carry knowledge forward. Explanation reveals the gaps existing in our understanding and sets about to devise the necessary conditions that will bridge these gaps. Explanations built on past experiences make easier the understanding of present and future experiences. Knowledge from the past has to be put on trial. Through postulation, this knowledge is modified and formed into explanation, which then is subjected to empirical testing. Knowledge is then carried forward in time through explanation and is thus used in the gaining of further knowldege.

THEORIZING AS A METHOD OF SCIENCE

In his attempt to understand nature, man has never been content with merely gathering and ordering existential facts. He seems always to have a burning curiosity to discover some supposed "final explanation." An examination of the explanations that he has conjured up to account for his behavior will show that he has run the full gamut of the explanatory continuum, from the factual at one end to the highly imaginary at the other. What he has lacked in fact he has readily made up with fiction.

Older Fallacious Theories of Behavior

One of the earlier explanations of the behavior of the feeble-minded and insane is illustrative of the prescientific theories man has held. The early diagnosticians believed that a mentally deficient person was possessed of an evil spirit or of a good spirit, according to the nature of his behavior. If the diagnosis was of an evil spirit, all manner of exorcisms, magic rituals, physical punishments, and the like were practiced in an effort to banish the supposed demon. More fortunate was the person who was judged possessed of a saintly spirit, as he was considered a messenger of the Deity, and his every want was administered to by those who curried his favor.

Current Fallacious Theories of Behavior

Modern man has not freed himself of the use of imaginary entities in his attempts to account for his behavior. Modern pixies, however, are not always personified, and they are more abstract in nature. But they are still products of the imagination constructed to serve as ready answers for difficult questions, and often serve in the same uncritical way as did the pixies of earlier generations. For many individuals, these modern pixies satisfactorily account for behavior, and, after all, that is their function.

One of the current overworked pixies of uncritical psychological thinking is *human nature*. This concept has had wide application in the explanation of group behavior. For example, war is a form of social behavior that has never been adequately explained. It can readily be dismissed from the minds of some thinkers, however, by being attributed to human nature. The *unconscious* is another modern pixy of questionable repute, seemingly charged with about every function that the human individual possesses.

To characterize concepts such as these as modern pixies is to bring into relief their uncritical use as end explanations of human response. It is to level criticism against those users of concepts who, when they announce that a given concept is applicable to some behavior, consider that thereby they have fully accounted for that behavior. We do not suggest that their concepts are entirely useless to psychology. Rather, we wish to indicate the need for clearer thinking with regard to the manner in which their concepts are formulated, interpreted, and used.

Scientific Pixies

A scientist devises theories to understand better that which he observes. He does not engage in theorizing merely to satisfy some intellectual curiosity. By the use of logical reasoning he deduces and formulates from present knowledge postulates through which common features and relationships or underlying principles and laws can be discovered, thereby rendering more understandable the phenomena he is investigating. He devises a rule that states the common conditons of a group of events, and then under this rule he subsumes the new event to be explained. This step of bringing forward knowledge in the form of hypotheses to be verified is an essential step in his program to discover truth. He makes progress because the insufficiency of old explanations stimulates him to evolve new hypotheses. These, in turn, lead to new modes of experiment and analysis and thus to the discovery of additional knowledge.

Scientific Compared with Nonscientific Pixies

It is interesting to note that the pixies of the scientist and the nonscientist are alike in one point; namely, they are born of the imagination—they are beyond apprehension by the senses.

More important for our consideration are the points on which the pixies of the scientist differ from those of the nonscientist. To begin with, scientific theories are not personified. They are not imaginary people, big or little, good or evil. They do not have the characteristics of people. They do not have desires, feelings, or intentions. They do not have to be placated as do the gods of primitive tribes.

Scientific Theories Stem from Facts

Although a theory involves entities or constructs that are not observable, the propositions through which the theory was devised stem from facts. The scientist defines his theories very carefully, assigning them the characteristics that they have in order that they may explain the observed events. He is aware that they are products of his imagination which he projects into reality. The nonscientist is usually unaware of the linkages through which his pixies have evolved from empirical situations.

To the scientist, a theory is a tool of research. It is not an end in itself but a means to further understanding, a form of lever by means of which he can pry loose more facts. A theory to him is something to be tested. It provides various postulates, and from these postulates the scientist is able to devise theorems for empirical testing.

A scientific theory has a predictive character through which the scientist seeks to improve his control over new phenomena. The pixies of the nonscientist offer hindsight, not foresight. They are conjured up to account for past events and are used by the witch doctor and his modern counterparts as portents of the future. They are unpredictable.

The scientist controls his theory. He keeps it subservient to his problems and purposes and makes it work for him. In many respects the pixies of the nonscientist control him much as the rabbit's foot controls the behavior of the superstitious person. They function to stifle and channelize thought, facilitating the acceptance of stereotypes, and discouraging the entertainment of new ideas.

—→ **Leland H. Stott**

Appraising Developmental Status

From *The Longitudinal Study of Individual Development* (Part II), 1955. Reprinted and abridged by permission of the author and The Merrill-Palmer Institute.

INTRODUCTION: ASPECTS OF DEVELOPMENT STUDIED

In our study of an individual child our first objective is to build up an abstract picture of the stage of development he has reached at a particular point in time. We want that picture to be as complete as possible. We really want an answer to certain questions which are of concern to parents, teachers, and others who deal directly with children.

This problem of portraying developmental status in its various aspects is complex and difficult. Since developmental change in a young individual is always in the forward direction, toward adult status and maturity, and since our objective is to portray the particular stage of progress attained at a particular point in time, it is obvious that measurement is indicated, and that the results of measurement must be expressed in quantitative terms.

The measurement problem, however, varies with the particular aspect to be appraised. Physical growth, as we have defined it, is by its very nature quantitative. Thus the measurement problem in regard to growth status (height and weight) is relatively simple. Standard scales and precise measuring instruments are readily available. Growth status can be expressed directly in objective, standard measurement units.

But when we are dealing with less quantitative aspects of biological development, those in which maturation plays a major role, the problem is much more involved. It is a problem, first, of observing systematically the fact of qualitative change, and then of devising quantitative indexes to represent these qualitative changes.

The measurement problem in relation to certain functional aspects of development is even more difficult, and from the point of view of precision and reliability is less adequately dealt with. In general we can only approximate a picture of a child's developmental status, for with the devices and techniques available only a limited and "spotty" view is possible. In certain aspects of development the methods and instruments at hand are so crude as to render the outcome quite hazy, and sometimes distorted.

Nevertheless, even with such measuring techniques as are available, it is possible to present a picture, incomplete and hazy as it may be, of the developmental status of a child, from which important insights may be gained regarding the rates and patterning of his development. It is our present purpose, therefore, to describe certain of these techniques and measuring devices.

Physical Growth: Height and Weight

Gross physical growth presents no special measurement problem, for there are standard measuring units and precision instruments which can be applied directly. The child is weighed in terms of pounds or kilograms, and his stature is measured in terms of inches or centimeters. At this naïve level of analysis of gross physical growth each successive assessment of status differs only quantitatively from the one preceding it, and the change is expressed simply as the addition of more of the same quantitative units.

However, a statement of crude measurement values by itself has no meaning. It is only when such measures are seen in relation to standards of reference that they become meaningful. The standard, or reference point, in the case of a quantitative measurement is usually some index of central tendency, such as the arithmetical mean or the median for the population of which the child is a member. A measure of variability within the population is also essential for adequate appraisal of an individual child.

For example: A child, Jane (408)[1] at 5 years of age was 42.4 inches tall and weighed 44.5 pounds. Without further information these objective measurements fail to give us a physical picture of this child. However, when we learn that the mean height of the group of 5-year-old girls of which Jane is a member is 42.5 inches, and that these girls weigh on the average 39.5 pounds, Jane's measurements begin to take on meaning. We see her then as quite a "plump" child whose height is about that of most of the girls of her peer group. When we learn, further, that while her height places her at the 50th percentile, her weight gives her a percentile rank of 95 among girls of her height, we can then say that only five girls of her height in 100 would be heavier than she.

The Concept of Maturity Indicators

The evaluation of maturational status presents quite a different problem. It is obviously impossible to gain access to most of the maturational processes that are under way in a growing child, for most of them are internal and thus hidden from direct observation. The fact that maturation does take place within the various

---

[1] Throughout this book the developmental record of Jane and her family (No. 408), selected from the files of Merrill-Palmer Longitudinal Studies, is used to demonstrate the use of the various scales, graphing techniques, and devices. Jane is the youngest of three children, of whom the others are Albert and Edward, respectively 10 and 6 years of age when Jane was born in 1931. Longitudinal records were kept on each of the three children from birth. Jane was a very bright child. She experienced certain "adjustment difficulties" in early childhood, but by wise care and handling she developed into an attractive and effective young woman. The family is fairly representative of urban, professional, middle-class families of the 1920's and 1930's. They suffered the effects of the "boom" and depression of that period, but came through without serious dislocation.

organs and organ systems has generally been inferred on the basis of the observed functional level. Estimates of maturational level reached are made on the same indirect basis. The various stages of maturation in the nervous system have been studied and charted through microscopic examinations of nonliving nervous tissue, and thus the reality of the maturational process in the growing human nervous system has been established. However, the maturational status of most of the body systems cannot be directly evaluated in terms of present techniques.

A notable exception is the roentgenological study of the skeleton. By means of X-ray it is possible to observe the exact status of the ossification process and other qualitative changes in certain portions of the skeleton. The problem here is to arrive at quantitative indexes to the various phases of the process of qualitative change.

A resolution of this problem has been achieved in the concept of the *maturity indicator,* which grew out of the study of bone anatomy and growth. In the intensive examination of many series of X-ray films of the wrist and ankle bones of children it was possible to identify certain qualitatively different stages of development. These stages or features were found to be fixed in order of appearance and universal in occurrence, though the time interval between the stages is highly variable from individual to individual. Since the order of appearance of these features is invariable, each in turn can be taken as an indicator of a bone developmental status more advanced than the one preceding it. These features are therefore called maturity indicators.

In recent years the concept of the maturity indicator has broadened to include any clearly defined stage of development, either of a function or of a structure or body part. Dr. Idell Pyle describes maturity indicators, in an unpublished statement, as ". . . features of a body part, secretory products of the cells of a part, or specialized forms of behavior which appear in a fixed or universal order to mark the progress of a child toward young maturity, or the progress of an adult toward senescence. They are strictly ontogenetic in nature, i.e., they appear in human beings around the world in an order which is universal but at a speed which is characteristic of the child or adult in question." A maturity indicator, then, is an identifiable point or stage in the development of a structure or a function which occupies a fixed position in a series.

The appraisal of status in skeletal development. Series of maturity indicators, fixed in order of appearance, were first established in the maturation of the skeletal system. In order to convert such an invariable sequence of unique features into a quantitative scale, the average chronological age at which each feature made its appearance was noted. This average age for each indicator was designated as its *age equivalent*. Thus the series of maturity indicators, each with its age equivalent, constitutes a scale for appraising maturational status in the skeletal system. The status of a particular child's bone development is represented by the average age equivalent of the various maturity indicators identified in his X-ray plates. This average is expressed as his *skeletal age*.

This procedure of assessing skeletal age, involving the direct observation of developmental stages, is technical in nature, requiring a knowledge of bone anatomy and an understanding of the nature of the intricate processes of bone maturation, as well as training and experience in the reading and interpretation of bone X-ray plates.

A rough estimate of a child's status, however, may be obtained through a relatively simple procedure that requires less technical skill. It involves the identification of a maturity indicator that appears in the development of all bones and is relatively easy to identify in the X-ray film. This indicator, the *onset of ossification,* is really "maturity indicator number one" in the series for each center of ossification.

To identify this feature, the X-ray films taken at a given age are carefully examined. An ossification center can usually be found which is at or near the point of onset. Having located such a center, the next step is to refer to Greulich and Pyle's atlas of skeletal maturation [9], to identify the center by number.

In Tables 1 and 2 are listed the centers of ossification to be found in the wrist, each with its number as indicated in the *Atlas*. In Table 1 these centers are arranged in the time order in which onset of ossification appears in boys. The order is some-

TABLE 1

Onset of Ossification in 28 Ossification Centers of Hand
and Wrist: Boys

No. (Greulich and Pyle)	Order of Appearance (Based on Mean Age)	Ossification Center	Mean Age at Appearance (Years-Months)	Standard Deviation (Months)
1	1	Capitate	0– 2	2
2	2	Hamate	0– 3	2
3	3	Distal radius	1– 1	5
4	4	Proximal 3d finger	1– 4	4
5	4	Proximal 2d finger	1– 4	4
6	5	Proximal 4th finger	1– 5	5
7	6	Metacarpal II	1– 6	5
8	7	Distal 1st finger	1– 7	7
9	8	Metacarpal III	1– 8	5
11	9	Proximal 5th finger	1– 9	5
10	10	Metacarpal IV	1–11	6
12	11	Middle 3d finger	2– 0	6
13	11	Middle 4th finger	2– 0	6
14	12	Metacarpal V	2– 2	7
15	12	Middle 2d finger	2– 2	6
17	13	Distal 3d finger	2– 4	6
18	13	Distal 4th finger	2– 4	6
16	14	Triquetral	2– 6	16
19	15	Metacarpal I	2– 8	9
20	15	Proximal 1st finger	2– 8	7
21	16	Distal 5th finger	3– 1	9
22	16	Distal 2d finger	3– 1	8
23	17	Middle 5th finger	3– 3	10
24	18	Lunate	3– 6	19
27	19	Navicular	5– 6	15
25	20	Greater multangular	5– 7	19
26	21	Lesser multangular	5– 9	15
28	22	Distal ulna	6–10	14

Adapted from Table 1, Nelson. [16, p. 22] These norms represent a composite of published data from the Fels Research Institute [22], and unpublished data from the Brush Foundation, Western Reserve University, and the Harvard School of Public Health. (The unpublished data will be included in the new edition of the Greulich and Pyle *Atlas* [9] to be published by the Stanford University Press in 1955 or 1956.)

what different in girls, as shown in Table 2. The mean age at onset in each center, and the standard deviation in months are also given. The mean age or age equivalent of the particular center which, in the child's X-ray film, has been judged to be at the point of onset may be taken as the approximate skeletal age for the child at the time the X-ray film was made.

There are thus two procedures for estimating the developmental status of the skeletal system in quantitative terms. The first, and most reliable of the two, is to assess all the bones and centers of ossification shown in the available X-ray films taken at a given time in terms of the sequences of maturity indicators established for those centers. The mean age equivalent of the various maturity indicators identified is an *index of status*. This method cannot be used by an untrained person.

The second procedure for estimating skeletal age, that of identifying centers at the point of onset of ossification, is relatively simple and may be undertaken by a student with minimum training. Such estimates are, however, less reliable than those made on the basis of a complete skeletal assessment. Moreover, this simpler procedure can be used only with X-ray plates taken during the first six or seven years of the child's life.

A comparison of assessments obtained by these two methods is provided by the X-ray record of Stark (379).[2] A complete assessment of all the bones of his hand and wrist at chronological age 36 months indicated a skeletal age of 40 months. This X ray (at CA 36 months) happened to coincide with onset of ossification in three centers, the distal second finger, the distal fifth finger, and the lunate. (See Table 1.) The mean ages at which onset of ossification occurs in these bones are 37, 37, and 42 months. In terms of these indicators a skeletal age of about 39 months would be the best estimate. It corresponds quite closely to the estimate based on a total assessment. Thus Stark at 3 years of age was slightly ahead of schedule (3 months accelerated) in skeletal development, but still well within the normal range.

Dental developmental status. Dentition as a process of de-

---

[2] Stark, a child of Family 379 of the Merrill-Palmer Longitudinal Studies, proved to be a more suitable illustration for this purpose than Jane, whose record is used elsewhere in this book.

TABLE 2

ONSET OF OSSIFICATION IN 28 OSSIFICATION CENTERS OF HAND AND
WRIST: GIRLS*

No. (Greulich and Pyle)	Order of Appearance (Based on Mean Age)	Ossification Center	Mean Age at Appearance (Years-Months)	Standard Deviation (Months)
1	1	Capitate	0– 2	2
2	1	Hamate	0– 2	2
3	2	Distal radius	0–10	4
4	2	Proximal 3d finger	0–10	3
5	3	Proximal 2d finger	0–11	3
6	3	Proximal 4th finger	0–11	3
7	4	Metacarpal II	1– 0	3
8	4	Distal 1st finger	1– 0	4
9	5	Metacarpal III	1– 1	3
11	6	Proximal 5th finger	1– 2	4
10	7	Metacarpal IV	1– 3	4
12	7	Middle 3d finger	1– 3	5
13	7	Middle 4th finger	1– 3	5
14	8	Metacarpal V	1– 4	5
15	8	Middle 2d finger	1– 4	5
17	9	Distal 3d finger	1– 6	4
18	9	Distal 4th finger	1– 6	15
19	9	Metacarpal I	1– 6	5
20	10	Proximal 1st finger	1– 8	5
16	11	Triquetral	1– 9	14
23	12	Middle 5th finger	1–10	7
21	13	Distal 5th finger	1–11	6
22	13	Distal 2d finger	1–11	6
24	14	Lunate	2–10	13
25	15	Greater multangular	3–11	14
26	16	Lesser multangular	4– 1	12
27	17	Navicular	4– 3	12
28	18	Distal ulna	5– 9	13

* See footnote, Table 1.

velopment is also manifested in a series of stages or changes which are essentially qualitative in nature and may be observed directly. A child's teeth erupt in a fairly definite ordinal sequence which may be regarded as a series of maturity indicators. The usual ages at eruption may be used as a rough age equivalents scale for assessing status in dentition. For example, the appearance in a child's mouth of his first permanent molar is a maturity indicator. Since the average age at which this tooth (the "six-year molar") appears is about 6 years, the child's "dental age" may be estimated as 6, regardless of his chronological age.

For ready identification the teeth, both deciduous and permanent, are designated by name and also by number or letter. Figure 1 shows diagramatically the arrangement of the teeth in the jaws, as well as the number or letter designation and the name of each tooth. They are numbered or lettered beginning with the two

TABLE 3

ERUPTION OF TEETH AS MATURITY INDICATORS
OF DENTAL DEVELOPMENT

Tooth	Number or Letter Designation		Expected Age at Eruption
	Upper	Lower	
Deciduous			(Months)
Medial incisor	I	a	6– 8
Lateral Incisor	II	b	8–10
First molar	IV	d	12–16
Cuspid or canine	III	c	16–20
Second molar	V	e	20–24
Permanent			(Years)
First molar	6	F	6
Medial incisor	1	A	7
Lateral incisor	2	B	8
First bicuspid or premolar	4	D	10
Cuspid or canine	3	C	11
Second bicuspid or premolar	5	E	11
Second molar	7	G	12
Third molar	8	H	15–21

teeth in front in each jaw, then proceeding to the observer's left and right with with identical numbers above and letters below for corresponding teeth.

These numbers and letters, it must be noted, simply indicate *position* of the teeth in the jaws. In most instances they do not correspond to the order of eruption. In Table 3 the deciduous

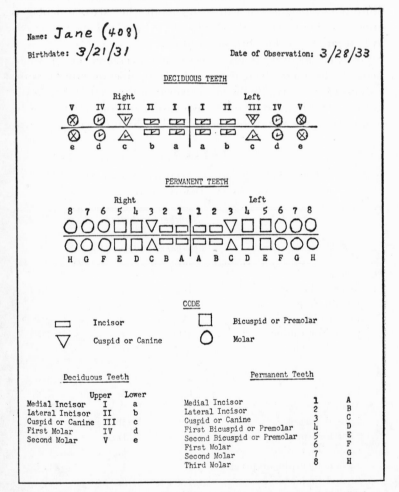

Fig. 1. Showing arrangement and number and letter designations of the deciduous and permanent teeth.

and permanent teeth are listed in the *order* of their expected eruption. [24] Corresponding teeth in the upper and lower jaws are indicated as having the same eruption age equivalents.

The validity of an appraisal of status in dentition at any particular pont in the child's life depends directly upon the degree of accuracy with which the eruption dates are known. Owing to the relatively wide variability in age at which the various teeth appear, the age equivalents may be taken to represent only a crude developmental scale.

The last entry on Jane's (408) dental record was made when she was exactly 2 years old. That record is checked on the form (Fig. 1). The cross marks indicate the particular deciduous teeth not yet erupted at that time. It will be noted that, of the four cuspids (III and c), one, the upper left, had not yet erupted. Since the expected chronological age at which these four teeth are expected to appear is 16 to 20 months (Table 3), it would seem that a fair estimate of Jane's dental age at that time (CA 24 months) would be 18 months.

Posture

That children vary considerably in general body posture is a matter of common observation. [23] The general assumption is that there is an inherent relationship between posture, and body bearing in general, and health and well-being. "The child who is well nourished and rosy cheeked, who is alert and vigorous in play, is likely to be the child who holds his body well poised or balanced. The child who is thin, pale, listless, and 'always tired' is likely to be the child who stands in a slouchy, drooping position such as is commonly called the 'fatigue posture'." [8]

Posture has its developmental aspect in that certain postural conditions are somewhat more common, or more pronounced on the average, at certain chronological ages than at later ages, as body proportions change and shifts in alignment and centers of gravity occur. For example, the degree of lumbar lordosis increases on the average between the ages or 2 and 12 years, then decreases during adolescence. Knock-knee, on the other hand, tends gradually to decrease through ages 2 to 12 years. [3, 4]

However, these age trends seem not to be sufficiently consistent to justify the formulation of a postural development scale in terms of age norms. The effort has been, rather, to set up evaluative scales in terms of which a child's posture at any point in his development can be appraised. A child has good "balance" in standing posture, for example, when the center of gravity of each body segment (head, neck, trunk, legs) lies directly above its supporting base. "Total balance is maintained with a minimum of expenditure of energy by balancing each movable body part securely on its own supporting base, so that the pull of gravity on it serves only to hold it firmly in line with the rest of the body." [14] When these conditions are not maintained, muscular energy must be expended in counteracting the pull of gravity upon individual body segments in the effort to achieve an overall balance.

Rating scales have also been devised for evaluating a child's posture in terms of such postural defects[3] as knock-knee, pronation of feet, hyperextension of knees, lumbar lordosis, and "slump back." [25] Each of these scales consists of a selection of four to six nude photographs (posture pictures) representing degrees of the postural condition from a minimum to an extreme degree. The selections were made from some 1,400 photographs, lateral and rear views, of children between the ages of 2 and 12 years. These scales were found to be fairly reliable in use. They can be used in direct observations of children or with posture pictures comparable with the standard or scale pictures. The degree of a given "defect" seen in the child is compared with the standard picture series. The number of the picture in the standard series which most closely corresponds to the child's condition becomes the child's rating score for the posture variable concerned.

Figure 2 shows silhouette drawings of the lateral and rear pos-

---

[3] The word "defect" as used here seems appropriate only in the sense of an imperfection of posture which may or may not be partially or completely overcome in the process of development. Limited degrees of such "defects" are characteristic of children in certain stages of their development. They are a function of immaturity, just as are deficiencies in physical strength or skill or imperfections in speech. However, when such a condition is present to a degree beyond the normal range it may justifiably be regarded as a defect in the sense of "not normal."

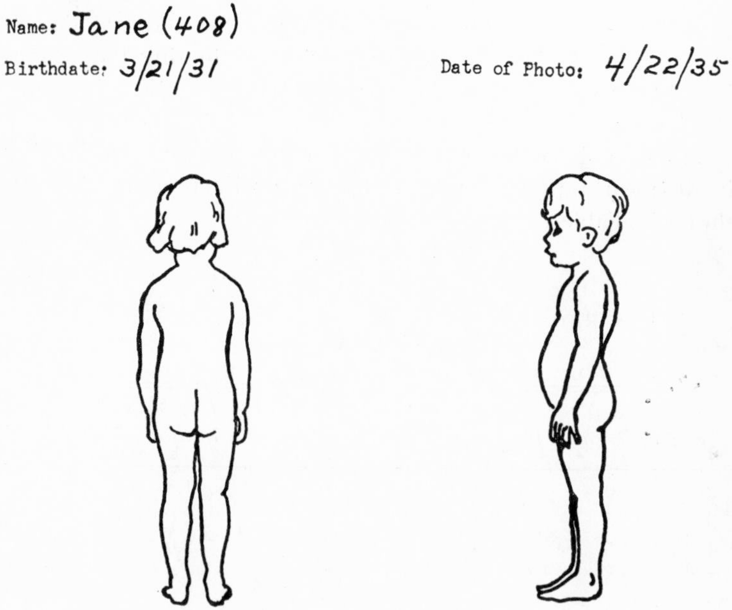

Name: *Jane (408)*

Birthdate: 3/21/31   Date of Photo: 4/22/35

Fig. 2. Silhouette tracings from posture photographs taken at age 4 years, 1 month.

ture pictures of Jane (408) at 4 years of age. From these pictures ratings on the five postural variables were made by comparing Jane's pictures with the standard rating series, with these results:

Knock-knee 2
Pronation of feet 1
Hyperextension of knees 2
Lumbar lordosis 2
Slump back 2

Since a quantitative rating score or measurement has little meaning by itself, some sort of standard is essential for its interpretation. Two possibilities suggest themselves for use here. First, we can look at the total scale and note the position of our child's rating on the scale. The scale for knock-knee ranges from 1 to 6. Jane's position is therefore second from the minimum end and fourth from the maximum end of the scale. On a 4-point scale for pronation she was in first position, and on the remaining three scales in second position. In other words, her postural defects were minimal. However, this method of evaluating the ratings is subject to error because it ignores the actual distribution of children's placements on the scale.

The second and more satisfactory basis for interpretation lies in the mean ratings found for children of different ages [25], as shown in Table 4.

TABLE 4

MEAN RATINGS ON FIVE POSTURAL VARIABLES IN CHILDREN
AGED 2 TO 12 YEARS*

Age	Knock-knee	Pronation	Hyperextension of Knees	Lumbar Lordosis	Slump Back
2	4.0	3.0	1.0	1.5	1.5
3	4.5	2.5	1.0	2.0	2.0
4	3.5	2.0	1.5	2.0	2.0
5	2.5	2.0	1.5	2.0	2.0
6	2.5	2.0	1.5	2.5	2.0
7	2.5	2.0	1.0	2.5	1.5
8	2.5	2.5	1.0	3.0	1.5
9	2.0	2.5	1.0	3.0	1.5
10	2.0	2.0	1.0	3.0	1.5
11	2.5	2.0	1.0	3.5	1.5
12	2.5	2.0	1.0	3.0	1.5

* These values are approximations read from the graphs of Robinow, Leonard, and Anderson [25, p. 661].

In terms of these mean ratings Jane's posture was in general quite typical for her age. According to Robinow, Leonard, and Anderson [25] the tendency to knock-knee is strongest in the preschool years. Jane, however, showed less tendency to knock-knee than is common in 4-year-olds. At that age the mean rating is approximately 3.5 on a 6-point scale, while Jane's rating was 2.0. On pronation of feet Jane's rating was 1.0 as compared with a mean rating of 2.0 for 4-year-olds. Her other ratings were at or near the mean for her age. The low correlation of certain of these ratings with chronological age lends some justification for referring to these conditions as "postural defects."

The Appraisal of Behavioral Development

Our focus now shifts from biological growth and maturation to the functioning and behavior of the whole individual. It must be recognized, however, that development in functional facility is based fundamentally upon the biological development of the body structures involved. Learning in its broad sense has been described as development due to the exercise of the structures made ready for functioning through maturation. This exercise, this practice of a new function, undoubtedly brings about changes in the structures involved, as well as in function per se. Structure and function are inseparable. In the living organism each is a manifestation of the other.

The evaluation of developmental status in functioning presents, again, difficult problems of measurement and quantification. The human being is characterized by a great complexity and endless variety of functions, and thus far only a beginning has been made in devising techniques for appraising these functions.

The development of certain specialized functions, for example, hand grip, or typing proficiency, or the high jump, may be measured directly in terms of standard units, because such development consists merely of quantitative changes, through learning, in a function already present, or in some specific attribute of that function, such as speed. Functions of this sort are special learned skills superimposed upon basic universal human functions. They are ontogenetic in nature, as contrasted with the basic phylogenetic functions in the development of which maturation plays a significant role.

The eating function. Eating is one such function. The ability to take and manage foods and to deal with eating situations of increasing complexity is a function of the total organism which is essential to the satisfaction of a biological need. The specific nature of the need itself changes with age, as do the physiological pattern and the overt behavioral pattern of the eating function. These changes are largely qualitative in nature. That is, each stage in the development of the function constitutes something new in the situation, rather than merely "more of what was there before." [23]

Table 5 presents a tentative sequence of stages in the development of the eating function.[4] These stages, it will be observed, are qualitatively different one from another. They appear to meet fairly well the requirements of a series of indicator stages. Tentative age equivalents are also given. These mean ages represent summarizations of clinical observations, without benefit of actual records. They should therefore be regarded as tentative until confirmed and until measures of variability have been added by means of systematic observation and recording.

TABLE 5

Tentative Progress Indicators of Development of Ability to Manage Increasingly Complex Foods and Feeding Situations

Stage	Behavior	Age Expected
		(Months)
Liquid feeding	Sucking, swallowing liquids only	1
Augmented liquid feeding	Able to swallow puréed food as easily as milk	3
Infant solids feeding	Capable of reducing lumps by chewing	8
Solids feeding (table food)	Capable of chewing and swallowing table food with family	14
		(Years)
Young mature eating	Can serve and feed self	3

To use this scale (Table 5) for appraising a child's status in the eating function, it is necessary either to have access to records of diet and descriptions of eating behavior for the particular time in the child's life in which one is interested, or to make first-hand observations of eating behavior and inquiries regarding his

---

4 This sequence of indicators was arrived at jointly by Dr. Charles G. Jennings, Consultant in Pediatrics, and Mary E. Sweeny, former Assistant Director and Head of the Physical Growth Department, Merrill-Palmer School.

diet and pattern of food intake. These data may then be referred to the scale and an approximate age equivalent of the child's level of development in this function may be arrived at.

Developmental status in bladder control. Another "developmental task" with which children in our culture are early confronted is the achievement of sphincter control. The perfection of this function, like others, must await the adequate preparation of the structures involved through maturation. This fact is too frequently not recognized by parents, who through lack of understanding often exert undue pressure on the child, sometimes with unfortunate results.

As a rule this function develops gradually. Sometimes the developmental curve is quite irregular, indicating very erratic performance. This irregularity is probably due more to adult interference than to anything inherent in the processes of development. [4, 20]

No maturity indicators have been suggested for evaluating status in this function. Qualitative changes would be extremely

TABLE 6

AVERAGE NUMBER OF DRY NIGHTS PER MONTH AT DIFFERENT
CHRONOLOGICAL AGES

Chronological Age (Months)	Average Number Dry Nights per Month	
	Boys ($N = 49$)	Girls ($N = 43$)
26–28	18.2	23.2
29–31	21.0	23.5
32–34	20.6	25.7
35–37	23.9	27.8
38–40	26.5	28.6
41–43	27.5	28.9
44–46	28.5	29.2
47–49	29.2	29.3
50–52	28.6	29.9
53–55	29.1	29.6
56–58	28.4	30.0
59–61	30.0	30.0

difficult to differentiate. However, a tentative "quantitative" scale has been set up for this purpose. Table 6 gives a tentative picture of the development of bladder control for boys and for girls in terms of the average number of "dry nights" per month for given chronological ages. These results were obtained from a short longitudinal study of the records of 49 boys and 43 girls for the age range 26 to 61 months. The figures are tentative and subject to check, since the records were not in every instance complete and the number of cases was small. Moreover, the values are averages, and variability within the group was wide. It will be observed that the boys were on the average consistently behind the girls in the development of this function.

Each chronological age for which an "average performance" (mean number of dry nights) was obtained may be taken as the age equivalent for that particular level of performance. A tentative developmental age scale for bladder control is thus derived (Table 7). Although these values are tentative, they may be used

TABLE 7

TENTATIVE AGE EQUIVALENTS, FOR BOYS AND FOR GIRLS, OF DIFFERENT
MEAN NUMBERS OF DRY NIGHTS PER MONTH

Number Dry Nights per Month	Age Equivalents (Months)	
	Boys	Girls
18	26	21
19	28	23
20	30	24.5
21	32	26
22	34	27
23	35	28.5
24	36	30
25	37	31.5
26	38	33
27	40	35
28	44	37
29	50	42
30	66	60

for an approximate assessment of a child's status in the development of this function.

Jane (408), for example, was 3 years, 10 months of age before she was able to achieve a record of 28 dry nights out of 30, the average achievement of 3-year-old girls (Table 6).

The locomotor function. Another scale of progress indicators upon which some preliminary work has been done is designed for the appraisal of locomotor development. Here again the search was for qualitatively different stages which are clearly observable and identifiable, and which cannot be bypassed by the child in achieving normal adult status in the function of walking.

A number of careful studies of walking development have been made. [2, 4, 10] In none, however, has the purpose been to establish an invariable, universal sequence of stages. For instance, in all these studies crawling was listed as a stage in locomotor development, but in no case was it important to the study that not all children crawl in learning to walk, or that crawling may precede or follow "pulling to stand" or taking independent steps. Accordingly, only those stages likely to meet the criteria of a maturity indicator were selected from the lists of stages suggested by these investigators. The following three stages seemed to represent such an invariable sequence.

    I. Rolling over from supine to prone position.
   II. The independent sit-up.
  III. The independent walk on a level plane.

In order to test this sequence and to identify other possible stages that might be included, an investigation was initiated at Merrill-Palmer in September, 1952, which involved the participation of more than 100 mothers of young babies. These mothers kept records of the locomotor development of their babies on a specially prepared, illustrated form.

A preliminary analysis of the data bearing on the three listed stages in locomotor development clearly suggests the possibility of differentiating four distinct phases in the child's achievement and perfecting of each indicator stage. A generalized description of these phases follows.

A. *Attempting*. The child shows signs of readiness for the particular act (indicator) in behavior which suggests that he is *trying* to accomplish it. (For example, he appears to be trying to turn over from back to stomach.)

B. *Nodal phase. First success* in accomplishing the feat.

C. *Practicing phase*. The feat is performed over and over. The pattern has some organization, but it is not easily accomplished.

D. *Integrated phase*. The pattern is smoothly organized and easily performed, apparently without conscious direction. It has become *automatized and integrated to further purpose*. (Child sits up now, not as end in itself, but in order to reach an object or to pull himself to stand, etc.)

The data at hand also permitted the designation of approximate age equivalents for each of the four main indicator stages with its four phases. Table 8 gives a brief description of each of these stages and phases, with its age equivalent in weeks. This tabulation provides a tentative scale for appraising locomotor developmental status in an individual child.

Obviously this scale has utility only during the first two or three years of the child's life. At any point during this early period, however, careful observation of a child while he is engaged in active, free play, along perhaps with a discussion of his locomotor behavior with the mother, should provide sufficient data for assessing his status in terms of these locomotor maturity indicators.

Jane (408), for example, was not walking in a "grown-up fashion" (stage III-D) until she was approximately 2 years (100 weeks) old, as nearly as can be determined from the available record. Assuming that the appraisal is correct, Jane was unusually slow in attaining this level of performance, for at CA 100 weeks her locomotor age was 60 weeks.

The "Higher" Functions

The modes of functioning which we have attempted to appraise thus far are usually thought of as physical in nature. They obviously involve whole organ systems and the gross musculature of the body. Those now to be discussed are more "psycholog-

TABLE 8

PROGRESS INDICATORS IN THE DEVELOPMENT OF LOCOMOTION*

Indicator and Phase	Age Expected (Weeks)
I. Rollover from supine to prone	
A. While on back, raises head as if trying to roll over	8
B. First success in rolling over	21
C. Rollover not easy, *repeats* it over and over	24
D. Rollover easy, automatic, apparently without conscious direction in order to accomplish further purpose (to reach a toy, etc.)	25
II. Independent sit-up	
A. Pushes self up from stomach, apparently trying to sit up	11
B. First success in pushing self from stomach to sitting position	34
C. Practices feat over and over—not easily accomplished	35
D. Act of sitting up well organized and easily accomplished with attention apparently on some further purpose (as using hands to reach for object)	37
III. Independent walk	
A. Pulls self to stand, tries to take independent steps	36
B. First success with few independent steps	51
C. Persistently practices walking alone	54
D. Walks in grownup fashion, apparently without conscious direction, *with purpose* of going somewhere or doing something	60

* Adapted from research on locomotor development at the Merrill-Palmer School conducted by Leland H. Stott with the assistance of Marian K. Lampard, Research Assistant. (To be reported.)

ical" in nature and less obviously physical. They tend to be peculiar to man, and thus to set him apart from other species. Actually, however, these "higher" functions are no less physical than ingesting food or walking. Clearly, every form of actitivy, from sucking to abstract thinking, is a function of the physical organism.

In the following pages only those forms and attributes of psychological functioning for which some method or methods of appraising developmental status can be suggested to the student are discussed.

Speech Development

Learning the use of vocal speech as a means of communication is one of the major achievements of childhood. Two main sorts of learning are involved. The child must learn, first, the common meanings that the many patterns and combinations of vocal sounds have come to possess in his culture, so that he can understand the spoken language. Second, he must master an extensive repertory of the complex muscular coordinations involved in producing these vocal sounds. This task is complex and difficult. A number of organs and structures are involved, including the lips, tongue, and throat muscles, as well as the larynx and lungs.

Many studies of the various aspects of speech development have been reported in the literature. [6, 12, 13, 17, 18, 19, 26] Careful observations have been made of the earliest vocal sounds of infants, of their crying, and of their later random vocalizations. The results of these observations indicate that in this early stage the child probably produces all the sounds that constitute the various languages of man. However, the child apparently begins soon to drop many of these seemingly random and unorganized vocal sounds and to retain the constituent sounds of the language of his particular culture. At this stage, though these sounds are not organized or integrated into meaningful words, the child often takes on, in his vocalizations, some of the inflections and voice modulations characteristic of the speech to which he is daily exposed. He is also inclined to hit upon certain syllables such as "da" or "ba" and to repeat them

TABLE 9

Progress Indicators of Speech Development*

Indicators—Stages of Speech Development	Age Expected (Months)
Prespeech vocalizations	
Most vowel sounds and some consonants, such as "h," "g," and "k"	4
All language sounds in random vocalizations	8
Babbling stage. Sounds not common to language of child's culture drop out. Repeats certain sounds over and over ("da da da"—"ga ga ga," etc.). Apparently enjoys sound of own vocalizations	10
Imitation of a few spoken words	10
Speech	
Single word sentences stage; "give" (pointing to object) "ball," etc.	12
Generalized meaning of nouns, e.g., "da-da" refers to any man	12
Understands an assortment of action words—"drink," "go," "bye-bye," etc.	12
Early sentence stage. Two or three words (noun, verb, adverb, or adjective; no prepositions or pronouns; "Da-da, bye-bye," etc.)	18
Understands simple sentences, e.g., "Where is the ball?" "Give Mother the spoon," "Want to go bye-bye?" etc.	18
Short sentence stage. Sentences of three or four words; an excess of nouns; lack of articles, prepositions, etc.	24
Comprehends simple requests and is able to carry them out, e.g., "Give me the kitty," "Put the spoon in the cup," etc. (Stanford-Binet test)	24
Question asking or "why?" stage. (Mainly for pleasure of asking)	36
Complete sentence stage. Sentences of six to eight words; virtually all parts of speech present	48
Counts three objects (Stanford Binet)	60
Knows the meaning of "three," "nine," "five," "ten," "seven"	72
Has command of virtually every form of sentence structure	72
Knows meaning of "morning," "afternoon," "night," "summer," "winter" (Stanford-Binet)	78

* The items of this "scale" have been gathered from the writings of a number of investigators: Chen [6], McCarthy [12], Nice [17], Shirley [26], and Terman and Merrill. [28]

over and over, as if he enjoyed the sound of his own babbling. Out of these babblings emerge words with meaning.

The findings of various investigators of speech development provide the material for a scale of progress indicators or stages in the development of speech, together with approximate age equivalents (Table 9). Although many of these items represent qualitatively different stages in speech development, the scale as a whole does not represent an irreversible and universal series of maturity indicators. Further research is needed for the identification of such a series. Nevertheless, the scale in its present form serves as a tool for evaluating developmental status in the function of speech.

In terms of this scale, Jane (408) at age 2½ years had a speech facility equal to that expected of a child of 3½ years. David (235), on a slower schedule in speech development, at age 3 years was at the stage characteristic of a child of 2½ years.

Social Development

The life task of achieving the ability to get along harmoniously and creatively with one's fellows is of extreme importance from many points of view, especially in our complex modern world. Yet it is a facet of human development for which measures or means of appraisal are relatively inadequate. Perhaps one reason for this state of affairs is that we are dealing, not with a specific function like walking or talking, but rather with a sort of pervasive quality of behavior in relation to others which determines one's general acceptability and harmonious interaction with others.

There is no doubt that the maturational process is basic to the development of this quality. The facility with which the young child is able to function in relation to others depends basically upon his stage of maturation. Under ordinary circumstances the baby who has reached a certain age is likely to respond to the smiling face and the voice of an adult, to withdraw from strangers at another age, and to play cooperatively with other children at a considerably older age. Thus there appears to be something of a generalized pattern or orderly sequence in social development, particularly during early childhood.

A number of students of child development have studied the

developmental changes in the social behavior of children. [10] From their observations it is possible to list approximately in the order and age equivalent of their appearance a number of such behavior items (Table 10).

TABLE 10

PROGRESS INDICATORS OF SOCIAL DEVELOPMENT*

Behavior Item	Age Expected
	(Weeks)
Responds to smiling and talking	6
Knows mother	12
Shows marked interest in father	14
Is sober with strangers	16
Withdraws from strangers	32
Responds to "bye-bye"	40
Responds to inhibitory words	52
Plays pat-a-cake	52
Waves "bye-bye"	52
	(Years, Months)
Is no longer shy toward strangers	1–3
Enjoys imitation of adult activities (smoking, etc.)	1–3
Is interested in and treats another child like an object rather than a person	1–6
Plays alone	1–6
Brings things (slippers, etc.) to adult (Father)	1–6
Shows beginning of concept of private ownership	1–9
Wishes to participate in household activities	1–9
Has much interest in and watches other children	2
Begins parallel play	2
Is dependent and passive in relation to adults	2
Is shy toward strangers	2
Is not sociable; lacks social interest	2–3
Is ritualistic in behavior	2–6
Is imperious, domineering	2–6
Begins to resist adult influence; wants to be independent	2–6
Is self-assertive; difficult to handle	2–6
Is in conflict with children of own age	2–6
Refuses to share toys; ignores requests	2–6
Begins to accept suggestions	3
Has "we" feeling with mother	3

T A B L E 1 0 (continued)

PROGRESS INDICATORS OF SOCIAL DEVELOPMENT*

Behavior Item	Age Expected
	(Years, Months)
Likes to relive babyhood	3
Is independent of mother at nursery school	3
Tends to establish social contacts with adults	3
Shows imitative, "me, too" tendency	3
Begins strong friendships with peer associates, with discrimination against others in group	3–6
Is assertive, boastful	4
Has definite preference for peer mates	4
Tries to gain attention; shows off	4
Tends to be obedient, cooperative; desires to please	5
Seeks approval, avoids disapproval of adults	5
Shows preference for children of his own age	5
Shows protective, mothering attitude toward younger sibling	5
Is sensitive to parents' and others' moods, facial expressions	6
Has strong desire to be with father and do things together (especially true of boys)	6
Insists on being "first" in everything with peers	6
Bosses, teases younger siblings	6
Has rich capacity to "pretend" in social play	6
	(Years)
Shows compliance in family relations	7
Desires to be "good"	7
Begins to discriminate between sexes	7
Forms close friendships with one of same sex; the age of "bosom pals"	8
Sex cleavage is definite; girls giggle, whisper; boys wrestle, "rough house"	9
The age of "clubs"	9
Sex differences are pronounced: girls show more poise, more folk wisdom, more interest in family, marriage, etc., and in their own personal appearance	10

* The items in this table were selected by the author from the results of several investigators and observers. These studies are summarized by Hurlock [10, pp. 287–389].

These indicators do not meet the criteria of a maturity indicator, for many of them are not universal in appearance, nor is
the order of sequence fixed. Nevertheless, they are helpful in
evaluating a child's developmental status in social facility.

On this scale, as judged in terms of social behavior items found
in her record, Jane (408) at age 2½ years was very near the stage
characteristic of that age. She was exhibiting the common "im-
perious and domineering" behavior and a tendency to resist
adult influence. Her mother reported that Jane was "dictatorial
and rebellious when I urged food," and that she was "very demanding and strident lately." Her nursery school teachers at
about the same time rated her "sociability with other children"
at a level characteristic of a child of 3 years. (This rating in
"sociability" is discussed in a later section. See personality ratings.)

Emotional Behavior and Development

Careful observations have been made of the emotional behavior of infants and young children. During this early developmental period, when the maturational processes are pre-
eminent and conditions are more subject to control, the picture
is relatively clear. Some attempts have been made to investigate
adult emotionality in the laboratory, but the possibilities here
are limited. Our greatest insights have come from the clinical
approach. In the clinical setting real emotional problems of individuals with widely varying backgrounds and experiences are
worked through. The clinician must in each case understand and
deal with a total, unique emotional situation. Through such clinical experience there has come a growing realization of the importance of understanding and respecting the child's point of
view, his "private meanings," his individual strivings and frustrations, his own "self-image," and his attitudes toward himself in
relation to others and the total situation, if we are to foster his
emotional development.

In our studies of individual children the purpose is to approximate as nearly as possible a "clinical" understanding of the
child's characteristic emotional behavior patterns, and to arrive
at an estimate of his level of development in emotional be-

havior. Observations, at first hand and recorded, of the child at school, in the home, and as he interacts with his peers and with the adults in his daily life are the primary sources of data for this understanding and evaluation.

Psychoanalytic stages. For an adequate assessment of developmental status in emotionality some sort of scale or sequence of stages is necessary, as with other aspects of development. Again, as with other generalized qualities of behavior, no completely satisfactory series of indicators has been established, though several formulations have been proposed. Probably the best known of these is the series of stages postulated by Freud.

These Freudian periods in psychosexual development [7], adopted by many psychologists as the basic framework of personality development, are the oral, the anal, the genital or phallic, the latency, and the puberal periods. Briefly stated, the underlying theory is that through the basic metabolic and other processes in the living organism certain tensions are built up. For example, as the supply of nutrients in the body becomes depleted, tension increases to the point of sheer discomfort. This discomfort is experienced as hunger. The taking of food gives gratification, or release from tension. The continual seeking for release from tension, and for gratifications of all sorts, requires energy. This energy Freud called "libido," or libidinal energy.

During early infancy, the oral period, the taking of food through nursing at the breast and being made comfortable by this process are the totality of life. They make life endurable. Thus all release from tension and all gratification come from, or are associated with, oral activity. When gratification through nursing is not forthcoming, when tension has mounted, feelings of frustration are experienced and anxiety and the sense of insecurity arise. With gratification come pleasure and a sense of security. This period, when emotional experience, either pleasurable or otherwise, centers around infantile oral activity, lasts to about the end of the first year.

The second period, the anal phase, corresponds roughly to the second and third years of life. The onset of this period does not mean the cessation of the activities and satisfactions of the oral period, which continue through life. It means, rather, that in order to conform to social demands attention must now be turned to new activities. By this time the child is able to move about and explore his world. His interests in the world around him are expanding, and at the same time new demands are made upon him. For example, society's attitudes toward cleanliness require him to gain control of his bowel and bladder functions. Since the eliminative functions pertain to and directly involve his own body and its feelings, they are "closer" to him than are any other activities in the sense that they involve tension and release from tension, frustration, and gratification. The attitudes and feelings of those about the child have much to do with the kinds of feeling reactions and adjustments he is able to make during this period of concentration upon eliminative activities and the anal area.

By the time the child has reached the age of 3 years, oral pleasures are no longer predominant in his life. He is well along in achieving bowel and bladder control, so that concentration upon anal activities has also lessened. His curiosity about and interest in the world and people are also expanding. This interest inevitably leads to questioning about sexuality and reproduction. According to psychoanalytic theory, the child at about this age tends to become especially attached emotionally to the parent of the opposite sex, and this attachment is erotically tinged. Little boys feel themselves to be the rivals of their fathers for the love of their mothers, and girls likewise become their mothers' rivals in love. These feelings, we are told, are often associated with wishes for the death of the rival.

The outcome of this "Oedipus complex" is the repression of the guilt-arousing wishes, along with all childish associations and memories of the period. Psychoanalytic theory thus purports to account for the common lack of memory of childhood experiences.

The fourth, or latency, period in psychosexual development occurs approximately between the ages of 6 and 10 years. It is described as relatively quiescent, as compared with the three preceding periods. The child's interest in his immediate body processes and gratifications, and in his parents as sources of satisfaction and security, becomes less intense. Much of the responsibility for his guidance and development is delegated to the school, often with a feeling of relief on the parents' part. Such a parental attitude tends to foster the developing interest in peer groups, gangs, and secret societies.

With the onset of puberal changes the child experiences a period of physiological instability—a period of transition from childhood to early adulthood. Again, during this period, there is much preoccupation with the body and its changes. A step-up in interest in the opposite sex and many other changes in feelings and attitudes make this period an extremely important one developmentally.

These five periods—the oral, the anal, the genital, the latency, and the puberal—may be taken in broad outline to represent emotional development. Theoretically, at least, they are directly related to specific stages in the maturation of the organism. The oral period is one of infantile helplessness. The anal period begins as the child, through the maturation of body structures, begins to overcome his helplessness, to operate with some degree of independence, and thus to have shifted to himself some measure of responsibility for his independent acts. Thus, he must begin now to conform to the cleanliness requirements of society by gaining control of his hitherto involuntary eliminative processes. The demands of society force upon him a preoccupation with anal functions during the period when maturation is in process of bringing the body and neural structures involved to a stage of development in which voluntary control is possible.

The maturational basis for the early phallic period, however, is not so clear. Perhaps general maturation of the child's organ systems, particularly of the brain cortex and the neuromuscular systems, makes possible a shift from conscious efforts to control the eliminative processes, and a preoccupation with them, to an increased interest in his parents and their relationships with each other and with him. Hence the development of the Oedipus situation, with its tensions and conflicts.

The latency period begins with the end of this stressful period. Controls have been achieved, the pressure is off, and considerable independence has been gained. The child's tensions and gratifications are no longer so largely determined by the functions of the alimentary canal and his intense relationships with his parents. They come now largely from a physically active life in an interesting world of things and people outside his home and family situation.

The maturational and growth changes that characterize the puberal period are quite dramatic. They furnish an obvious basis for the many changes in interests and activities which take place during this period. The implications of puberal changes for emotional development and adjustment are profound.

Bridges' developmental sequences. From the point of view of practical usefulness as a scale for assessing the attained level of emotional development in a given child, the phases of psychosexual development based on psychoanalytic theory leave much to be desired. There is need for much more specific behavioral indicators of progress.

Perhaps the nearest approach to a useful series of developmental stages for the first two years of life comes from an investigation by Bridges. [5] In this study, based on observations of the emotional behavior from birth of 62 children, a careful record was made in each case of the response and the environmental conditions that preceded it. One result of the study was a generalized description of emotional development in terms of four kinds of change, as follows:

1. Intense emotional responses become less frequent.
2. The reaction to any given stimulus becomes more specific.
3. Emotional responses are transferred from one situation to another which did not originally evoke them.
4. Emotional responses gradually become more differentiated.

In relation to the fourth aspect of change, differentiation, Bridges described, with approximate timing, the sequence that takes place from birth to 2 years of age (Fig. 3). From the beginning, it was found, certain kinds of stimulation give rise to a generalized, overall *excitement*, which Bridges regards as the original emotion. Children who are thus excited are described in terms of suddenly tensed muscles, quickened breath, jerky, kicking leg movements, and wide open eyes gazing into the dis-

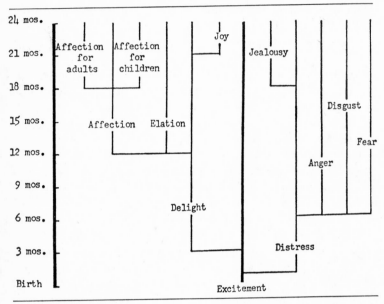

Fig. 3. The early development of emotions. (After Bridges, *Emotional Development in Early Infancy*. [5, p. 340]

tance. This pattern was found to persist throughout the first two years of life.*

Mental Development

In this section we shall be concerned with a function that has an even more pervasive quality, namely, with mental functioning and the nature of intelligence.

We human beings meet the various situations and problems of life with varying degrees of effectiveness and facility. Everyone finds himself adequate in some situations and inadequate in others, depending upon a number of factors. There are wide variations in the effectiveness with which individuals meet the same or similar situations. In other words, there is an overall, variable quality of general functioning—the quality of effectiveness or adequacy of personal functioning.

---

    * Editor's note: The remainder of this section on Bridges' *Development Sequence* has been omitted and the reader is invited to see the first reading in Chapter 7, for Bridges' discussion.

More specifically, the concern here is the methods and means available for appraising personal functioning at a particular time, in terms of its adequacy and effectiveness. Such an appraisal is the purpose for which the so-called intelligence tests were constructed. When a child performs effectively in an intelligence test situation we say he acted intelligently, and a relatively high IQ or "mental age" or other rating in intelligence is assigned to him. Similarly, when in daily life we see an individual meet a particularly difficult situation in an adequate and effective manner we regard him as a capable, clever, intelligent person.

The nature of intelligence.   Intelligence, then, is not a thing, not an entity. Rather, it is a general quality or characteristic of personal activity. This attribute of functioning (intelligence) has been described in many different ways. It has been variously defined. Binet, father of the intelligence test movement, stressed the importance of such factors as the ability to give attention and to sustain it sufficiently to achieve certain ends, and to make appropriate adaptations to everyday situations. Thorndike stated that intelligence was demonstrated in the individual's "ability to make good responses from the standpoint of truth or fact." Some psychologists have stressed the importance of the ability to learn, while others, along with Binet, emphasize the ability to adjust adequately to new situations. Terman [28] who has played perhaps the most important role in the development of intelligence testing, states that a person "is intelligent in propotrion to his ability to carry on abstract thinking." Munn [15] is also inclined to limit use of the term to the more strictly "mental" activities by defining intelligence as "flexibility or versatility in the use of symbolic processes."

Stoddard [27] is somewhat more analytical in his approach to the problem of intelligence. He postulates seven "attributes of intelligence" which, according to his own analysis, actually turn out not to be attributes of intelligence at all. The first three, namely, "difficulty," "complexity," and "abstractness," are really attributes of the tasks or problems set for the individual whose intelligence is being assessed, and in terms of which the proficiency level of his performance is gauged. "Other things being equal," Stoddard would say, the more difficult, the more complex, the more abstract the problems a child is able to solve, the higher his level of intelligence. Four other attributes analyzed by Stoddard, "economy of effort," "adaptiveness to goal," "social value," and "emergence of originals," do not describe the problem to be solved or the task to be performed, but have to do with the quality of the child's performance in solving them. The child's behavior may be described as "economical" if he spends less time than others of his group in solving a problem. It may also be described as being well in line with ("adapted to") the goal set for him, or as being acceptable behavior in terms of "social values," or it may show the rare quality of originality. "Other things being equal," the higher the child's behavior rates in terms of these qualities, the more intelligent he is.

Taken together, the "attributes of intelligence" postulated by Stoddard constitute a set of criteria for evaluating the overall effectiveness or adequacy with which an individual in a test situation meets the problems and performs the tasks presented to him. That is, they are really not separate "attributes" characterizing an entity called "intelligence."

On examining the various other conceptions of "intelligence" one finds a common feature in all of them. All are concerned directly or indirectly with general effectiveness of behavior. Binet, in his efforts to measure "memory," "attention," and "adaptation," was actually concerned with individual differences in the effectiveness or adequacy of meeting life situations. Other things being equal, the better the memory and the longer the attention span the more adequate in general will be the performance. Certainly, the greater one's facility in abstract thinking, the greater one's "flexiblity or versatility in the use of symbolic processess," and the more readily one is able to learn new patterns of behavior and thinking, the more adequate and effective one is in meeting life's situations.

In summary, "intelligence" is most accurately conceived, not as a thing, or an entity, or even as an "innate capacity" or ability, but rather as a general quality of personal functioning—that is, adequacy and effectiveness in meeting life situations. The more effectively one characteristically meets life situations at any stage in his overall development, the "brighter," the "smarter," the more "intelligent" he is judged to be.

Factors determining personal effectiveness. The next question of interest to us is: What are the factors that determine personal effectiveness in meeting everyday situations? The answer is not simple. Every individual undoubtedly would present a unique pattern if all the factors of heredity and experience which determine his level of personal effectiveness were known. However, certain generalized factors are quite obviously related to this personal attribute. [21] One of these is the particular repertory of readily available, learned patterns of response one possesses; that is, one's skills, manual, mental, and social. The greater one's facility for relating positively to others, the less likely is one to mishandle a social situation and the more likely is one to meet it adequately.

A second common factor is one's habitual approach to a task or a problem situation. One's effectiveness in dealing with the situation depends to some extent upon whether, after appraisal of the situation, one is able to come immediately and vigorously to grips with it or approaches it with evasions and "stalling."

One's habitual emotional patterns may also constitute an important conditioning factor. Emotionality can be either an impeding or a facilitating factor in relation to personal adequacy. One of the lessons from common experience is that thought and rational behavior are incompatible with "emotional upset." On the other hand, the stirred up physiological aspect of an emotional experience makes readily available extra amounts of physical energy which can be mobilized for a more energetic and effective attack upon certain kinds of problem situations.

Perhaps more basic than the factors already mentioned is the general level of effective physical energy which is characteristic of an individual. Children living in impoverished homes on deficient diets have been found to be not only smaller in stature and lighter than average, but also generally to do poorly in school work, which depends upon mental alertness. When whole milk was added to the diets of these same children a significant improvement was noted, in both their physical condition and their school performance. Effective personal functioning in our society makes heavy demands upon physical energy.

Innate potentiality and its measurement. The basic and indispensable factor upon which adequacy and effective functioning depends is the innate potentiality for development in functional facility with which the individual begins life. Obviously it is only within the limits of this innate capacity that the various skills, understandings, and effective habits of approach to problems can be acquired from daily contact and interaction with the environment.

This potentiality is established by the union of the germ cells at conception. The particular combination of hereditary determiners brought together at that time apparently controls the rate and patterning of development and thus determines the structural nature of the brain and the total organism and its functional limitations. This inherent potentiality is the factor psychologists call "native ability" or "native intelligence"; it is the factor intelligence tests are designed to measure.

The approach to measuring potentiality is necessarily indirect, since it cannot be observed or measured directly. The tester can only draw inferences regarding the nature or magnitude of a child's inherent potentiality from the way he functions in the test situation. His performance is in terms of behavior patterns and items of information previously learned. However, theoretically the test items (the tasks and problems presented to the child) are of such a nature as to be equally familiar in the environment of all to whom the test is administered. Accordingly, differences in performance between children of the same age are presumed to be due largely to differences in inherent "capacity" or potentiality.

In the construction and validation of intelligence tests various methods have been followed. The usual procedure has been to place each test item at the level in the age equivalents scale at which 50 per cent of the children of that chronological age were able to "pass" it. Thus it was found in the 1937 revision of the Stanford-Binet test that 50 per cent of 7-year-old children could repeat correctly five digits read by the examiner at the rate of one per second. This test of immediate memory for five digits was therefore placed at the 7-year level in the scale. The main objective was to achieve such an arrangement of the test items throughout the whole scale that the mean mental age of an unselected group of children of any given chronological age would turn out to be equivalent to their chronological age. The individual mental ages of the group would be expected to distribute themselves normally about this mean. The environmental factor is presumed to be controlled, and so these differences in mental age are interpreted as representing real differences in inherent mental capacity. In so far as the test is valid, those who are able to function only at a low level of effectiveness possess a relatively low innate capacity, those who function at a high level are high in the innate factor, since by the nature of the test material environmental opportunity is equalized for all. To the extent to which the environmental factor is not thus controlled the test is not a valid instrument for the assessment of inherent capacity for mental development, which is basically essential to functional adequacy and effectiveness in meeting life situations.

Thus the mental developmental status of an individual child can be appraised in terms of mental age by use of intelligence tests. Our young subject, Jane (408), for example, was tested each year at a time near her birthday throughout the developmental period. At approximately 5 years of age (59 months), she was able to pass all test items on the Stanford-Binet test (1917 revision) at the 6-year level. Her first failures were on tests at the 7-year level. She was not able to tie a bowknot sufficiently well or to state the essential difference between a stone and an egg, or between wood and glass. Even at the 8-year level she was able to define words sufficiently well to pass the item. Thus the high point of her performance was in language. The test results gave Jane a mental age of 80 months when her CA was only 59 months; her IQ was 136.

Jane's high level of functioning is a direct reflection of her high native developmental potential. A study of her record shows that other factors were also conducive to functional adequacy. Certainly she was physically well nourished. Both home and school environments had provided favorable conditions for acquiring skills, manual and social. Her habitual approach to tasks like those encountered in an intelligence test was positive and direct. There is no evidence of emotional interference at the time this test was given. Accordingly, Jane was able to function at a high level of facility in relation to her age.

Personality Evaluation

The idea of the "whole child" as an integrated functioning unit is a valid concept. We all recognize the essential unity, the integratedness, of the person. We know that the organism functions as a whole. Even in an act of skill in which only a small muscle system carries out the act, or when a problem in mental arithmetic is solved, the whole organism, the whole person, is involved.

But to study or to understand that person as a whole, as he behaves and functions, is another matter. The aspects of his integrated functioning are unlimited, and the possible points of view from which such functioning might be seen and interpreted are infinite. From our perspective we can observe and know only limited aspects of the whole person's functioning. A further complication, as pointed out earlier, is the developmental changes that are constantly in process. That is, the whole child at one time is not the same as the whole child at another time.

Nevertheless, even with our observational limitations and despite constant change, we do experience certain attributes that characterize an individual and certain qualities of his functioning that persist through time. These qualites, in unique combination, constitute his individuality and characterize him as a personality.

The term "personality" refers particularly to the "individuality" of a person, the fact that he is different from every other person. Thus in describing a personality use is made of adjectives and adverbs. Such words as tall, beautiful, fat, stooped, petite, homely, are descriptive of the person, of his personal attributes. Such words as effectively, slowly, hostile, submissive, kind, forceful, are more descriptive of behavior—of manner, of functioning, particularly in relation to others.

Just as life means change, so a personality changes. The girl who is "pleasingly plump" at 18 years becomes "plain fat" in middle age. The sickly, "skinny" child of 5 years later makes the college football team. Behavioral qualities too are subject to change with development. Timidity in childhood can be and often is largely overcome. Many of our attitudes change in quality with education and other experience, sometimes radically. Saul of Tarsus, for example, after his conversion abandoned his hostile and aggressive behavior against the Christians and himself become an ardent supporter of the cause.

Nevertheless, however much certain personal characteristics may change with age, however radically the behavior pattern may change, there are certain inherent qualities of personality that remain. The growing organism operates within its natural limits. Its particular developmental pattern is inherently determined. Organismic structure, with certain qualities of behavior which the developmental pattern of that structure imposes, is genetic in origin and persists throughout life. There is something basically unchanged in the physical aspect of the plump girl who becomes the fat woman. As to the persistence of behavioral qualities, Allport [1] says there are "dispositions that are almost unchanged from infancy throughout life (disposition saturated with a constant emotional quality, with a peculiar pattern of mood, alertness, intensity, or tonus)." These "dispositions," according to Allport, make up what we call "temperament," which is inherent and genetically determined. Such are the qualities that largely constitute the individuality of the person. Even in instances of radical change in behavior the inherent qualities remain. The brilliant, intense, vehement Saul of Tarsus who persecuted the Christians became the brilliant, intense, vehement Paul the Apostle of Jesus. The essential qualities of his behavior did not change, even though the behavior pattern per se changed radically.

In our study of personality, then, our focus will be upon the core of the personality—upon those attributes and behavioral qualities which persist and which uniquely pattern themselves to give the person his individuality and make him different from every other person. Our purpose is to "see" as much of the "whole child" as possible through an evaluation of certain aspects of his personality in terms of a number of specific personal attributes and certain qualities of his total functioning at a given point in his developmental history.

Certain qualities of functioning and the problems involved in their evaluation have been discussed; namely, emotionality, sociality, and the pervasive behavioral quality we call "intelligence"—the quality of adequacy and effectiveness of functioning in daily life. These are all aspects of personality. We shall now discuss the problem of evaluating certain other qualities which, along with those already considered and many others, in their unique patterning, make up "a personality."

The rating method. The problem of measuring or quantitatively appraising personality characteristics has been attacked from a number of angles. No method thus far devised is entirely satisfactory from the point of view of precision. The instruments at best are crude. One method much used is the rating scale. The shortcomings of the rating method are many and are freely recognized by the devisers and users of the method. However, in our studies of individual children this method lends itself best to our situation.

The rating scale is a device designed to facilitate the summarizing quantification, and uniform recording of previously made observations. Ratings, therefore, can be no more meaningful or valid than the observations on which they are based are adequate and accurate. Ratings always reflect to a greater or less extent the biases and limitations peculiar to the rater. Nevertheless, in spite of its inaccuracies and limitations, the rating scale in many situations is the best available device.

Many forms and varieties of rating scales are in use. The device here presented is relatively simple in use, though the construction of such a scale is a laborious and time-consuming process, involving the cooperation of many persons and the statistical treatment of data. Briefly, the method of construction was as follows: First, for each trait or quality to be rated a list of statements was compiled, descriptive of behavior expressive of the trait; these statements were those frequently used by nursery school teachers in their characterizations of the children in their care. These statements were then submitted to each of several competent judges, with the instruction that they be sorted into eleven groups, in terms of the expressed degree or "strength" of the quality in question. The median placement of a given statement by the group of judges on this 11-point judgmental scale became its "scale value." Thus each statement was assigned a position on the scale in terms of its numerical scale value.

A set of rating scales, the Merrill-Palmer Personality Rating

Scales,[5] was thus constructed, designed to measure the following composite personal attributes and behavioral qualities of nursery school children: Physical Attractiveness; Attractiveness of Personality; Tendency to Face Reality; Independence of Adult Affection and Attention; Respect for Property Rights; Response to Authority; Compliance with Routine; Ascendance-Submission; Sociability with Other Children.

In use, the statements on these scales are read with a particular child in mind, and those items that seem best to fit the child and his behavior are checked. The mean scale value of the checked items is the child's rating score on the scale.

These nine traits are simply those selected from a countless number of possible variables as having special relevance to the nursery school child and situation. They are not regarded, in any sense, as portraying the child's total personality. However, an analysis of the ratings on a particular child in relation to the ratings of other children may reveal something of his individuality of patterning in personality characteristics.

Jane (408), as rated at 5 years of age on the scale "Independence of Adult Affection and Attention" by her nursery school teacher, had a score of 71.4, the percentile rank of which is 60 (Fig. 4). Thus she was judged to be slightly above average in "independence," since approximately 60 per cent of the children of her group were rated lower on the scale than she. Thus the raw rating score, meaningless of and in itself, takes on meaning when converted into a percentile value. (Jane's ratings on the other eight scales and the pattern they present are discussed in a later section.)

Ratings of this type, in terms of arbitrarily defined traits and

---

5 These scales were constructed mainly by Rachel Stutsman Ball. The research that produced the scales is described in the monograph by Roberts and Ball. [24] However, the interest of the Merrill-Palmer School in the problem of studying personality began much earlier. The first of a series of studies, initiated by Helen Thompson Woolley, was published in 1925. [32] Her approach at that time was essentially the same as the one we use today. Thus, the individual child was studied as a member of a family; both his family background and personal development were studied. He was studied as a physical organism in process of growing and maturing and as a developing total personality, in which mental, social, emotional, and physical factors were concerned.

The Merrill-Palmer School
71 East Ferry Avenue
Detroit, Michigan

PERSONALITY RATING

SCHEDULE 4

Date 5/26/36

Name Jane (408) Rated by N. S. Teacher

Directions for Rating:

Check only those statements which you feel are really true of the child. Do not guess if you are not reasonably sure. A few true statements are better than many half-true ones.

INDEPENDENCE OF ADULT AFFECTION OR ATTENTION

(✓)...60......Perfectly natural in the presence of adults.
(....)..............Always conscious of adult's presence.
(✓)...80......Matter of fact in his relations with adults.
(....)..............Has defiant attitude toward adults.
(....)..............Avoids adults as much as possible.
(....)..............Insists that a specific adult assist him.
(✓)...38......Has great admiration for particular adults (hero worship).
(✓)...96......Independent of adult in overcoming difficulties.
(....)..............Dependent upon adult to solve difficulties.
(✓)...98......Independent of adult in having ideas about or planning work or play activities.
(....)..............Dependent upon adult for ideas and plans for work or play.
(....)..............Seeks adult aid at every move.
(✓)..104.....Resents aid from adults.
(✓)...86......Pays no attention to visitors.
(....)..............Makes friendly advances toward visitors.
(....)..............Acts silly in presence of visitors or newcomers.
(....)..............Presence of parent (underline: father, mother) upsets the child's regular routine.
(✓)...77......Leaves parent (underline: father, mother) in a matter-of-fact manner.
(....)..............Is emotionally upset upon leaving parents (underline: father, mother).
(✓)...24......Bids for attention from adults.
(....)..............Cries often to secure adult attention.
(....)..............Does his best only when praised by adults.
(✓)...92......Not dependent upon praise from adult to do his best.
(....)..............Seems worried that adults will not like him.
(....)..............Expects adults to feel sorry when he is not good.
(....)..............Forms adult attachments often.
(....)..............Craves and definitely seeks affection from adults.
(✓)...30......Craves affection from adults but is afraid to show it.
(....)..............Asks for physical demonstration of affection from adults.
(....)..............Gives physical demonstration of affection.
(....)..............Shows affection toward adults.
(....)..............Usually affectionate but bursts occasionally into "I hate you."
(....)..............Resents affection from adults.

Score = 71.4
P = 60

Fig. 4.

group norms, naturally fall short of revealing the "real person." Completely to know the personality of another, in all its intricacies, will probably forever remain an impossibility. Even to approach an adequate understanding of a child one must first gain an understanding of one's self and be able to accept one's self, with all the feelings and prejudices that are part of the self. Then, through repeated experiences and with the child in an atmosphere that encourages spontaneity, one can gain an approach to an understanding. [11]

One can learn something of the child's feelings about himself; about how he sees himself in relation to others and to his external world; and to what extent his concept of himself and his pattern of attitudes toward himself correspond to those of others regarding him. Such insights are usually not amenable to recording on fixed rating scales. The student should therefore try to portray in his own way and in his own words such insights into the child's world as he may have gained from his personal involvement with the child. It is interesting to note the ways in which these personal insights correspond to or harmonize with ratings based on more objective observations of behavior, and to observe the extent to which the two views are divergent and incompatible.

Presenting an Integrated Picture of Developmental Status

In our review of the methods devised for appraising developmental status we have noted some of the common measurement problems. The methods presented appear to be the most appropriate and adaptable to the problem of studying the developmental status and developmental history of an individual child.

Our present problem is that of bringing together and integrating these various measurements, scores, and ratings in ways best suited to show their relatedness and relative significance. Each individual is unique in the exact patterning of his development. Though there are fixed sequences of developmental changes, and these uniform processes result in many uniformities in human beings, the relative timing and rates of development are highly individualistic, and in this respect no two individuals are alike. Thus our problem is to portray as adequately as possible, with the methods at our disposal, the status or level attained at a particular point in the child's life in as many aspects of development as possible, and in a way that will reveal his uniqueness, his individuality.

The profile method.   The methods for accomplishing this objective of presenting an integrated picture leave much to be desired. Perhaps the "profile," with its variations, is most effective.

The simple profile is merely a graphic representation of the stages of the various aspects of development, of levels of achievement, or of measured amounts or degrees of any personal quality possessed by an individual, at any particular time. These various levels are always expressed in relation to norms or standards previously established, and in terms of a common scale unit. The profile itself may be in the form of a line connecting the points on the common scale representing the various levels of development or adjustment being portrayed; or the attained level for each aspect may be represented by a bar of proper length, without implication of a connection or relationship between these aspects. The latter type of profile representation is often called a "bar diagram."

Physical growth status.   Figure 5 is a simple bar diagram representing status in physical growth and maturation. Developmental age is the common scale unit used in this figure. The variables included are height, weight, skeletal development, and "size."

Figure 5 gives a fairly clear picture of Jane in her bodily aspects as a 5-year-old child. In height she was just average for her age (CA, 5; height age, 5). Her weight, however, was unusual; she had attained a weight age usual for girls of 6 years, 2 months (CA, 5; WA, 6–2). Her body size (Wetzel Developmental level)[6] reflects the relationship between her height, which was average, and her weight, which was above average. A large child in terms

---

[6] Body size is determined by use of the Wetzel Grid [29, 30, 31], a device for plotting height and weight in relation to each other throughout the growth period. The Grid is discussed more fully as a device for plotting *developmental progress* in a later section.

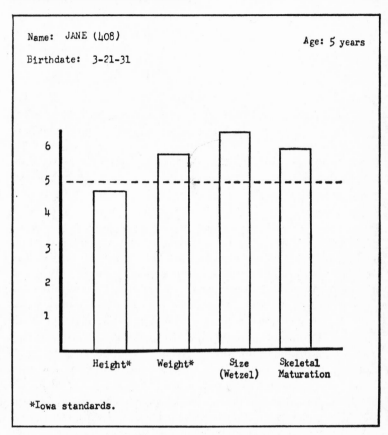

Name: JANE (408)   Age: 5 years

Birthdate: 3-21-31

Fig. 5. Profile of physical developmental levels.

of body volume, her Wetzel developmental level was 6 years, 6 months. The assessment of her bone X-ray films taken at age 5 years also reflects an accelerated rate of development. Her skeletal age was 6 years.

Developmental level in functional areas.   Methods for measuring or otherwise appraising developmental level in a number of functional areas have been described. These functions ranged from the relatively specific, such as locomotion, to the broad area of relating to and interacting with other individuals which we call "social behavior." In each instance we were concerned with an attribute or quality of the function, namely, the proficiency or adequacy of performance. Walking status is evaluated in terms of the degree of proficiency attained in that function. So also are talking, eating, elimination control, and social behavior. The problem of appraising intelligence was also viewed as the evaluation of this quality in relation to general personal functioning. Briefly, the quality or "dimension" in terms of which all these areas of functioning, from the specific function of walking to functioning in general, are evaluated is proficiency, adequacy, effectiveness. Accordingly, these related areas are grouped together graphically for comparison.

Since locomotion as a basic function has in most cases reached maturity before the age of 5 years, the record of Jane (408) with respect to these developmental aspects was examined at the 2½-year level. Figure 6, showing her developmental status at that age, presents a good example of extreme unevenness in development. In walking, as we have seen, she was considerably below the level of performance expected of a child of 30 months; her performance was about like that of a child of 17 months. Her tendency toward overweight may have had something to do with her slow locomotor development. In striking contrast was her level of performance in speech. At age 30 months she was performing at the 42-month level in this respect, almost a year in advance of normal expectations. In terms of age equivalents, then, her development in walking and talking at age 2½ was a full two years apart. Her record in regard to the eating function is inadequate, but the available evidence suggests that she was at or near the average for her age.

The contrast between Jane's developmental level in social facility and in general personal adequacy (intelligence) is again rather striking, though the total picture is consistent. Her size and body build, along with her relatively low level in locomotor ability, were undoubtedly a handicap to her social functioning among her peers at age 2½ years. Statements in her record upon which her rating in social development was partly based were: "Jane seems lost in a large group. Some negativism appearing"; and "Jane is very demanding and strident lately; ego very conspicuous." On the other hand, verbal facility is regarded as one

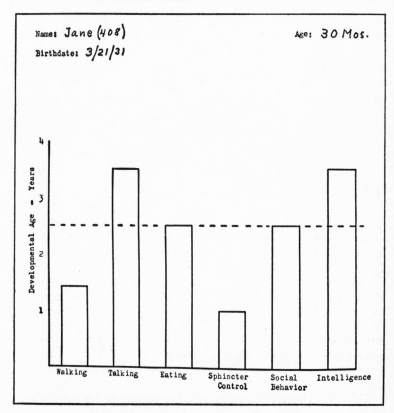

Name: Jane (408)   Age: 30 Mos.
Birthdate: 3/21/31

Fig. 6. Profile of functional developmental levels.

of the most valid indicators of general intelligence, and it is therefore in line with expectations for her level of speech development and in intelligence to be approximately the same.

The personality profile.   We have noted that many personality traits are in general expressions of inherent constitutional structure and organization. Undoubtedly there are other such traits that arise from constitutional nature in interaction with environmental factors early in the child's life. There is some evidence, for example, that deprivation in relation to the baby's needs for food when hungry and for "mothering" may give rise to a pervasive insecurity, or to some other personality tendency, depending upon the inherent temperamental pattern of the child. These traits tend to persist throughout life and in their patterning constitute individuality. Certain other traits have more nearly the nature of behavior patterns, attitudes, feelings, and opinions, and are more subject to change with development, experience, and education.

TABLE 11

RATINGS OF JANE (408) ON NINE MERRILL-PALMER PERSONALITY
RATING SCALES

Trait	Score	Percentile
Physical Attractiveness	76.0	70
Attractiveness of Personality	83.1	90
Tendency to Face Reality	86.4	90
Independence of Adult Affection and Attention	71.4	60
Respect for Property Rights	77.6	50
Response to Authority	31.3	60
Compliance with Routine	88.3	80
Ascendance-Submission	82.9	90
Sociability with Other Children	84.2	80

The nine Merrill-Palmer Personality Rating Scales mentioned earlier, with the possible exception of those for rating Sociability with Other Children and Respect for Property Rights, appear to represent lasting personality characteristics. The concept of developmental status in relation to these variables therefore has relatively little meaning. Accordingly, the term "level of adjustment" will be used instead with reference to these personality ratings.

The total rating (percentile score) by itself does not "tell the whole story" revealed by the rating sheet. An examination of the specific behavior items checked by the rater gives more insight into the nature of the child's behavior trends. For example, according to the items checked for Jane on "independence," she was "perfectly natural in the presence of adults," was "matter of fact" in her relations with them, and was "not dependent upon praise" from them in order "to do her best." Furthermore, she was "independent of adults in having ideas and plans for work or play" and in "overcoming difficulties." She was even seen to "resent aid from adults." Her independence was further shown by the fact that she could leave her parents "in a matter-of-fact manner" and tended to pay "no attention to visitors." But this ease and independence in her relations with her teachers and parents did not mean that she had no need for the attention and affection of the adults in her life, or that they were of no importance to her. She had "great admiration for particular adults," and made bids for their attention. She was also checked as craving "affection from adults but is afraid to show it." The overall impression is one of a little girl who actually worked to impress her teachers and to gain their high regard and their attention by being capable of operating on her own and thus being independent of their help.

In Table 11 are given Jane's ratings at age 5 years on the nine scales, all by the same nursery school teacher. The raw score and the percentile rank for each trait are listed. Figure 7, a bar-type profile representation of the percentile ratings shown in Table 11, indicates clearly that Jane, a very intelligent girl, was regarded highly by her teacher. In "attractiveness of personality," "tendency to face reality," "compliance with routine," and "ascendance" she was rated as high or higher than 80 per cent of her peers. In the analysis of her rating in independence it was observed that the good opinion of her teachers was important to her, and that she sought it by making herself competent to meet high standards of performance. The higher ratings shown in the profile are consistent with this description of Jane's behavior trends.

Figure 8 brings together the various aspects of Jane's status as a social being at age 5 years. The rating on posture is an approximation, based on the ratings of the five postural variables ("defects") described earlier. It is fairly clear that poor posture was not a handicap to her at that early age. Her slightly better than average posture was probably a factor in her favorable rating in "physical attractiveness." The variable "Social Adjustment

(Adults)" represents a combination of the percentile ratings on "Response to Authority" and "Compliance with Routine." "Sociability with Other Children" is a measure of her social adjustment in relation to her peer group. Again, the overall picture is

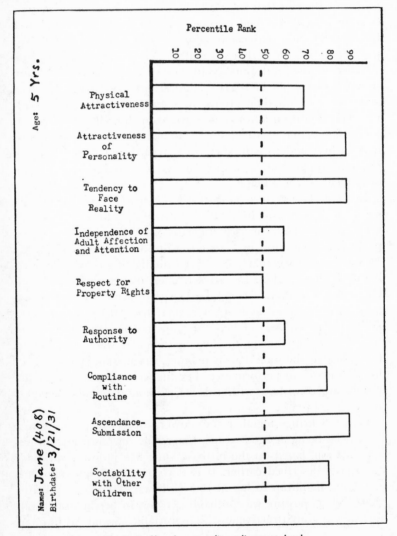

Fig. 7. Profile of personality adjustment levels.

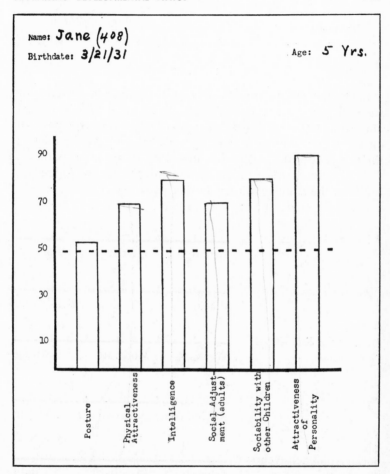

Fig. 8. Summary profile of physical, mental, and social aspects of personality.

that of a child highly endowed with desirable attributes. Even with her extreme weight and large physique she was rated by her teacher well above the median in "Physical Attractiveness." This rating was made when Jane was 5 years old, after 30 months in the nursery school.

The behavior profile. Another selection of attributes or qualities of personal functioning, most of which would be likely to persist through time and therefore characterize an individual, are

Name: Jane (408)   Date: 3/23/36
Birthdate: 3/21/31   Age at Rating: 5–0

INSTRUCTIONS

Let each horizontal line below represent the various degrees or strengths of the particular behavior tendency indicated at the end of the line. In each instance the optimal or most desirable position on the rating continuum would be somewhere near the middle, the two ends of the line representing the less favorable extremes.

Place a dot on each line at a point which, in your judgment, indicates the child's position on that particular scale.

Make a "profile" by drawing lines connecting the dots.

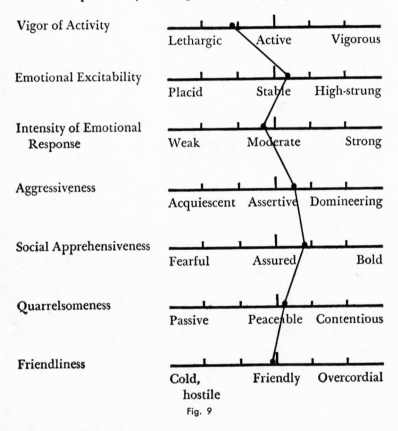

Vigor of Activity
    Lethargic   Active   Vigorous

Emotional Excitability
    Placid   Stable   High-strung

Intensity of Emotional Response
    Weak   Moderate   Strong

Aggressiveness
    Acquiescent   Assertive   Domineering

Social Apprehensiveness
    Fearful   Assured   Bold

Quarrelsomeness
    Passive   Peaceable   Contentious

Friendliness
    Cold, hostile   Friendly   Overcordial

Fig. 9

the seven variables constituting the "Behavior Profile" (Fig. 9).

This device, a multiple rating scale of the graphic type, when completed constitutes a profile in and of itself. The rating task is therefore quite different from that involved in the "personality ratings." In this device each of the seven horizontal lines represents a trait continuum. The center point on each line represents subjectively the most desirable, or optimum, position, while either end represents an undesirable extreme. The range between the second and fourth marked points represents roughly the desirable range.

Jane's profile (Fig. 9) at about age 5 years places her generally within the optimal range with respect to the particular behavior tendencies included in the profile. Her most extreme rating was in vigor of activity; she was judged as tending to be "lethargic" rather than vigorous. This rating is consistent with other notations about her and with her size and weight. Otherwise she was judged to be stable emotionally and to express her emotions with a moderate degree of intensity. She was rated as healthily assertive, assured in social situations, peaceable, and friendly. Once more, the overall picture is that of a highly favored child.

REFERENCES

1. ALLPORT, G. W., *Personality: A Psychological Interpretation*, New York: Holt, Rinehart and Winston, Inc., 1937, p. 53.

2. BAYLEY, NANCY, "The Development of Motor Abilities During the First Three Years," *Monographs of the Society for Research in Child Development*, 1935, 1, 3.

3. BEAL, V. A., *et al.*, "Nutritional Studies of Children Living at Home," *American Journal of Diseases of Children*, 1945, 70:216.

4. BRECKENRIDGE, MARION E., & VINCENT, E. L., *Child Development: Physical and Psychological Growth Through the School Years*, 3rd ed. rev., Philadelphia: W. B. Saunders Co., 1955.

5. BRIDGES, KATHERINE M. B., "Emotional Development in Early Infancy," *Child Development*, 1932, 3:324–341.

6. CHEN, H. P., & IRWIN, O. C., "Infant Speech Vowel and Consonant Types," *Journal of Speech Disorders*, 1946, 11:127–138.

7. ENGLISH, O. S., & PEARSON, G. H. J., *Emotional Problems of Living*, New York: W. W. Norton and Co., Inc., 1945, pp. 15–291.

8. *Good Posture in the Little Child,* Washington, D.C.: Federal Security Agency, Social Security Administration, Children's Bureau Publication 219, p. 1.

9. GREULICH, W. W., & PYLE, I. S., *A Roentgenological Atlas of Skeletal Maturation in Hand and Wrist,* Stanford: Stanford University Press, 1950, p. 150.

10. HURLOCK, ELIZABETH B., *Child Development,* New York: McGraw-Hill Book Company, Inc., 1950, pp. 287–389.

11. JERSILD, A. T., *Child Psychology,* 4th ed., Englewood Cliffs, N.J.: Prentice-Hall, Inc., 1954, pp. 14–21.

12. McCARTHY, DOROTHEA A., *The Language of the Preschool Child,* Minneapolis: University of Minnesota Press, 1930.

13. ———, "Language Development," in L. Carmichael, ed., *A Handbook of Child Psychology,* Worcester: Clark University Press, 1933, 329–373.

14. METHENY, E., *Body Dynamics,* New York: McGraw-Hill Book Company, Inc., 1952, pp. 108–109.

15. MUNN, N. L., *Psychology,* New York: Houghton Mifflin Company, 1946, p. 411.

16. NELSON, W. E., *Textbook of Pediatrics,* 6th ed., Philadelphia: W. B. Saunders Company, 1954.

17. NICE, M. M., "Length of Sentences as a Criterion of A Child's Progress in Speech," *Journal of Educational Psychology,* 1925, 16:370–379.

18. ———, "An Analysis of the Conversations of Children and Adults," *Child Development,* 1932, 3:240–246.

19. ———, "A Child's Attainment of the Sentence," *Journal of Genetic Psychology,* 1933, 42:216–224.

20. PHELPS, W. M., & KIPHUTH, J. H., *The Diagnosis and Treatment of Postural Defects,* Springfield, Ill.: Charles C. Thomas, 1932.

21. PRESSEY, S. L., & ROBINSON, F. P., *Psychology and the New Education,* rev. ed., New York: Harper and Brothers, 1933.

22. PYLE, I. S., & SONTAG, L. W., "Variability in Onset of Ossification in Epiphyses and Short Bones of the Extremities," *American Journal of Roentgenology,* 1943, 49:796.

23. RAND, W., SWEENEY, M. E., & VINCENT, E. L. (revised by M. E. Breckenridge & M. N. Murphy), *Growth and Development of the Young Child,* 5th ed. rev., Philadelphia: W. P. Saunders Co., 1953, pp. 154–162, 175–187.

24. ROBERTS, K. E., & BALL, R. S., "A Study of Personality in Young Children by Means of a Series of Rating Scales," *Journal of Genetic Psychology,* 1938, 52:79–149.

25. ROBINOW, M., LEONARD, M. L., & ANDERSON, M., "A New Approach to the Quantitative Analysis of Children's Posture," *Journal of Pediatrics,* 1943, 22:655–663.

26. SHIRLEY, MARY M., "Common Content in the Speech of Preschool Children," *Child Development,* 1938, 9:333–346.

27. STODDARD, G. D., *The Meaning of Intelligence,* New York: The Macmillan Co., 1943.

28. TERMAN, L. M., & MERRILL, MAUD A., *Measuring Intelligence,* New York: Houghton Mifflin Company, 1937.

29. WETZEL, N. C., "Assessing Physical Fitness in Children. I. Case Demonstration of Failing Growth and the Determination of "Par" by the Grid Method; II. Simple Malnutrition: A Problem of Failing Growth and Development; III. The Components of Physical Status and Physical Progress and their Evaluation," *Journal of Pediatrics,* 1943, 22:82–110, 208–225, 329, 361.

30. ———, "Physical Fitness in Terms of Physique Development and Basal Metabolism," *Journal of the American Medical Association,* 1941, 116:1187–1195.

31. ———, "The Baby Grid: An Application of the Grid Technique to Growth and Development in Infants," *Journal of Pediatrics,* 1946, 29:439–454.

32. WOOLLEY, HELEN T., "Peter: The Beginnings of the Juvenile Court Problem," *Pedagogical Seminary and Journal of Genetic Psychology,* 1925, 32:569–598.

▲

PART TWO

The Bio-social Foundations of Human Behavior

What are the basic factors and conditions that impart to the individual his particular style of life? To what extent are his behavioral traits predetermined by his genetic inheritance? In what measure are they the product of the way in which he is brought up—a product of the shaping influence of his social-cultural surroundings? Different versions of these questions have occupied for considerable time (and continue to occupy) the attention of researchers in the behavioral sciences.

There are other important questions about the conditions that underlie the behavior of the individual. We would expect that a person's actions would be governed considerably by the way he sees his world and the view he has of himself as he tries to relate to his world. But there are numerous "unknowns" about the manner in which the individual acquires his view of his world and himself. From what sorts of processes and occurrences are the meanings of things and events derived by him? What are the facts about the role that his "inner life" plays in moulding, motivating, and giving color to his behavior?

The next five chapters deal with the kinds of problems about which such questions arise. The readings in these chapters have been selected for the contributions they make to an understanding of the distinguishable, but closely interwoven, influences that broadly speaking are the *causes* of behavior.

CHAPTER

FOUR

↑

*Prenatal Origins
of Behavior*

THE HUMAN ORGANISM IS AT CONCEPTION A creature with a unique growth potential and developmental design. It is, therefore, not enough that we acquire a satisfactory understanding of human development beginning at birth; we must also learn the facts about how life begins and how the individual develops before birth.

Many misconceptions are held concerning prenatal origins of behavior. These misconceptions range from pseudo-sophisticated ideas about how chromosomal inheritance dominates the unfolding pattern of an individual's life (or the opposite extreme of virtually ignoring nature's part in the organism's development) to a variety of old wives' tales about how behavioral tendencies are impressed on the individual before birth by certain practices and experiences of the mother. Teachers have the opportunity

149

and responsibility to encourage children and youth to seek the truth regarding life before birth and to learn to recognize untruths and part-truths.

Researches by biochemists, geneticists, medical specialists, and others are constantly providing new insights into the prenatal growth and development of the individual. The readings in this chapter show some of the advances of knowledge in this domain.

In the first reading, C. H. Waddington, Professor of Animal Genetics, University of Edinburgh, Scotland, describes certain things scientists have done to unlock the secrets of the human cell. To a considerable extent his description deals with the puzzling question of how cells become differentiated into the specialized tissues that constitute a human organism. What is the explanation for the remarkable fact that in the process of differentiation cells are organized? What is the principle of organization? Professor Waddington's answers are clear and informative.

Herbert Thoms, M.D., Professor Emeritus at Yale University, and Bruce Blevin present a comprehensive and an intriguing account of life before birth. They point out that every pregnancy is "wonderfully like every other," but also that "every pregnancy is a little different." They make it clear that individual patterns of growth and development are evident even before birth.

How does heredity operate? What is the role chromosomes and genes play in heredity? How do heredity and environment share in producing the characteristics of the human individual? Such is the range of topics pertaining to hereditary influences on growth that Marian E. Breckenridge and E. Lee Vincent discuss in the final reading of the chapter. Of special importance to the reader are the authors' comments on radiation influences, the Rh factor, and the evidence regarding the number of chromosomes an individual receives from each of his parents. All these points involve relatively new research evidence. Professor Breckenridge is a member of the staff in Physical Growth and Nutrition, Merrill Palmer Institute. Vincent is Professor of Human Development and Behavior, Chatham College.

——▶ C. H. Waddington
How Do Cells Differentiate?

From *Scientific American*, September, 1953. Reprinted by permission.

How is it that a single fertilized egg, a tiny blob of apparently formless protoplasm, can become a man—with eyes, ears, arms, legs, heart and brain? How from one generalized cell do we get the myriad of different specialized cells that make a human body? This puzzle, differentiation, is of course one of the great questions of biology. The process of differentiation has always seemed particularly mysterious because there are so few phenomena in the non-living world that might give us clues as to how it takes place. In the inanimate realm we do not often come across a situation in which parts of a single mass of material gradually diverge from one another and become completely distinct in character. Yet in all living things, except perhaps the viruses, differentiation is a basic law of nature.

For half a century biologists have been searching for the answers to this question by two main methods of attack: the modern sciences of embryology and genetics. On one hand they have been investigating directly by experiment how the embryo develops, and on the other they have studied how the genes control the processes of development. Let us start with the embryological approach.

The problem was bogged down for a long time in a debate between two theories first described by Aristotle in the fourth century B.C. One school argued that the newly fertilized egg contains all the organs of the animal in miniature, and that these preformed parts merely grow and enlarge to produce the adult. The second view, supported by Aristotle, was that the organs are formed only gradually by interaction among simple parts or constituents of the egg. Aristotle called this process "epigenesis," and epigenetics is still an appropriate name for the embryological approach to the problem.

When modern investigators began to experiment on animal embryos, they seemed to find support for both of the ancient theories. They cut an egg of a simple animal in half, or removed a part of the egg, and let the remaining part develop. In some types of animals, the fragment of egg developed into an adult with certain parts missing, which suggested that the egg contained

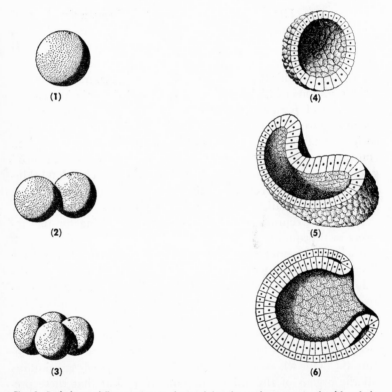

(1)

(2)

(3)

(4)

(5)

(6)

Fig. 1. Prelude to differentiation is depicted by the early stages in the life of the marine animal Amphioxus. In drawing (1) is the fertilized egg. In (2) the egg has divided into two cells. In (3) the two cells have divided into four. In (4) after more divisions, the cells are marshaled into a hollow ball called the blastula. In (5) one side of the blastula has begun to turn inward. In (6) the cells form a cup called the gastrula. The hole at the right of the gastrula is the blastopore.

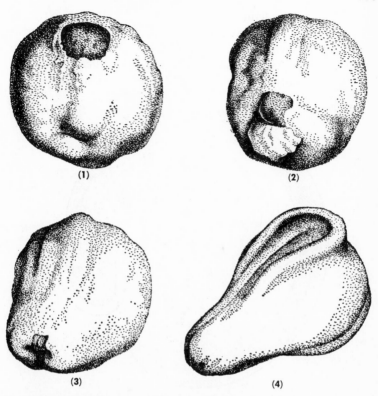

Fig. 2. Organizer is demonstrated by grafting a piece of the blastopore region from one newt's embryo into another. In drawing (1) the original blastopore is at the bottom; the graft is at the dark spot at the top. In (2) and (3) the graft rolls into the interior of the embryo. In (4) the horseshoe-shaped structure is the rudiment of the central nervous system induced by the graft.

preformed and rather rigidly localized rudiments of the adult organs. On the other hand, in other cases a complete and normal adult grew from the amputated egg. It was clear that epigenetic interactions must have taken place in these eggs.

The first experimenter to carry out a controlled study of such interactions was the German embryologist Hans Spemann, of the little Black Forest town of Freiburg. He operated on early embryos of the common newt. As the eggs of this animal develop, the first visible structure to appear is a small depression, called the blastopore, which eventually will become the main part of the intestine. Spemann cut out the region of the blastopore from one egg and grafted it into a second egg in a different position. There it not only continued to develop but influenced the cells

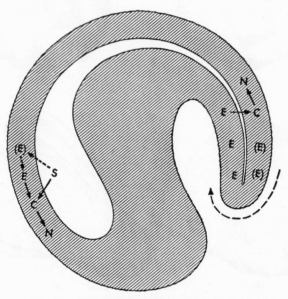

Fig. 3. Two hypotheses of organizer action are illustrated by this cross section of a newt's embryo. At the right is the organizer region. Tissue containing an inducing substance in an inactive form labeled (E) moves into the interior of the embryo. There (E) becomes an active form E, which reacts with the competent tissue C and causes it to become the nervous tissue N. At the left is a diagram showing how a chemical substance S might produce nervous tissue either directly by acting on C or indirectly by causing (E) to be converted into E.

surrounding it. They then became the main organs of the embryo, *e.g.*, the central nervous system and the rudiments of the spinal column.

Here was a clear-cut case of exactly the kind of interaction suggested by the epigenetic theory. Spemann called the blastopore region the "organizer" of the embryo. Soon organizers very similar to the one he had discovered in his salamander were found in many other classes of vertebrate animals. Such organizers were found to be responsible for the formation not only of the main embryonic axis but of many secondary organs which arise rather later: the ear, the nose, the lens of the eye, and so on. Sometimes the organizer region is relatively sharply demarcated and precisely localized. In other eggs it may be more diffuse, and the interactions may take place in a graded way, one end of the region being more powerful than the other. But in either case, the development of organs is determined by the interaction between some dominant part of the egg and its more receptive surroundings.

Now an organ has two aspects. It consists in the first place of specific types of tissue, which can come into being only by differentiation of the cells. But further than that, the tissues in an organ are arranged in certain relations to one another that give the organ its characteristic shape. Of course in the last analysis the shape of an organ presumably is an expression of the nature of the tissues composing it, but it is convenient to make a rough distinction between the formation of specific tissues and the molding of these tissues into organic structures. Most recent work has concentrated on the first of these problems: the nature of the chemical processes by which the embryonic cells become differentiated.

It was natural to suppose at first that the organizer could act only as a living entity. But in 1932 it was discovered that an organizer is able to influence its surroundings even after it has been killed! This discovery was made simultaneously in the newt embryo by a group of German workers including Johannes Holtfreter (who is now at the University of Rochester) and in the chick embryo by myself at Cambridge University. It seemed that we might be on the verge of a critically important advance: that the influence of the organizer on development might be traced to some chemical substance which could be extracted from it. Several groups of workers tried to identify the substance, but their hopes were too optimistic and their picture of the situation too simple. The trouble is not in finding a substance that will act like the organizer in inducing cellular differentiation but that *too many*

substances will do just that. Within a year or two Joseph Need-
ham, Jean Brachet and I had proved conclusively that methylene
blue, a substance which cannot by any stretch of the imagination
be supposed to exist in the normal embryo, will bring about the
formation of nerve tissue when injected into the embryo. It seems
useless to look for some master substance in the cells which will
give us the key to the understanding of differentiation. The place
to study differentiation is in the reacting tissue, which actually
carries out the differentiation. Only during a certain period of
development is this tissue able to react to the organizer stimulus;
it is then said to be "competent." The way to a deeper insight
into the nature of development is through a fuller understanding
of competence.

It is here that the hereditary genes come into the picture. In
all likelihood the competence of the cell for differentiation is a
complex state of affairs, involving many different chemical systems. We know that there are many genes in the nucleus of a
cell and that each gene controls the formation of one or more
of the substances produced as the cell develops. Thus the set of
gene-controlled processes must be the system of reactions involved
in the state of competence.

The most obvious question to ask is: What is the nature of each
individual gene recation? But, before considering that, there is
another point which may be almost as important and is perhaps
easier to approach. We are dealing with a complex system of reactions, one starting from each gene, and finishing up with all
the numerous constituents of an adult tissue. Do any general features characterize the system as a whole?

There is one important general feature. An adult animal consists of a number of different organs and tissues which are sharply
bounded off from one another. The liver does not merge gradually into the pancreas and that into some other organ. Cells
develop into one type or the other; they do not form graded
intermediates. Further, there is a strong tendency for these normal end-products to be produced even if conditions during development have been somewhat abnormal. We can, for instance, cut
pieces out of the embryo or cause other experimental alterations,
and the embryo will still produce a normal adult.

This means that development must be organized into a number of distinct systems. One system of processes will bring about the development of, say, the nervous tissue. A different system will produce liver or kidney or some other tissue of the body. Moreover, each system must be stabilized in some way so that it gives its normal end-product even if it has to go by an unusual way to get there.

This shows us the kinds of facts we have to account for. One of the great tasks for embryology in the immediate future is to explore the ways in which systems with properties of this kind can arise. There are several different ways by which we could seek to account for the fact that development is channeled into separate, distinct pathways. For instance, if the product of the reaction itself makes the reaction go faster—that is to say, if the processes are autocatalytic—it is easy to see that once a process has begun to form a particular product, that product will encourage the process to go still further in the same direction, and thus exclude any other possible product. Similarly, if the product of one reaction inhibits the progress of some other reaction, then as soon as the first process gets under way it will tend to prevent the second from occurring. Common sense is enough to offer certain general suggestions of this kind, but we badly need a thorough theoretical study of the various conceivable types of interaction between processes. Beyond that, we need an experimental analysis of developmental processes, aimed at discovering which of the theoretical possibilities are realized in practice.

For the self-regulating feature of the embryo's development, we can find models in the field of engineering: automatic ships' compasses, automatic pilots and other feedback mechanisms for which the name of cybernetics has recently become fashionable. In cell differentiation we must be dealing with chemical cybernetic systems. The properties of biological enzymes should make it possible for such systems to be built up in several different ways, but we still know remarkably little about them. Very probably much of the work required to understand these systems will be done on systems of isolated chemical substances which may at first sight seem to have little or nothing to do with embryology.

I have found it helpful to make a mechanical picture of the

set of differentiation systems, each of which leads to one definite end-result and is balanced internally by some sort of cybernetic mechanism. Let us imagine the cells as a group of balls perched on the top of a slope. On this slope we may suppose there is a radiating system of valleys. As each ball rolls down, it must pass into one valley or another. Once it has started down a given valley, its fate (the end-product it will become) is determined, for it

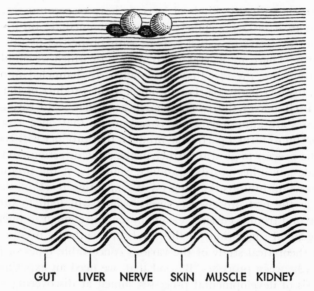

GUT   LIVER   NERVE   SKIN   MUSCLE   KIDNEY

Fig. 4. Epigenetic landscape is an abstract representation of differentiation. The balls roll down the slope into one or another valley leading to a specialized organ of the adult.

will be very unlikely to roll over the intervening hill into another valley, and even if some abnormal condition temporarily pushes it part way up the bank, it will tend, like a bobsled, to slide back to the bottom of its chute and continue its normal course. I have used the name "epigenetic landscape" for this picture of the developing system.

Our other principal task is a detailed study of the chemical processes that go on in a cell as it moves from its embryonic beginnings to its final differentiated state. When it was discovered that many substances could act like the organizer to induce differentiations, most people argued that they must be acting in a secondary way. Suppose that all the cells of the embryo contain some substance which can induce the formation of, for instance, nervous tissue. Suppose further that in most cases this substance is concealed or inactivated, but that it can be liberated by certain types of cell metabolism. Then one would expect that the organizer gets its peculiar properties from its specific metabolism. Following this line of thought, several groups of investigators have measured the metabolism of the organizer against that of other regions of the egg. They have duly found that the organizer has certain special metabolic characteristics, and it is quite clear that these are essentially involved in its developmental activity. For instance, in the eggs of the sea urchin the fundamental developmental system consists of two gradients of activity, one of which is most powerful at the upper end of the egg, the other at the lower end. The thing that varies along these gradients is the intensity of processes of cellular metabolism, and on these variations depends the differentiation of the parts of the egg.

Eggs and embryos are, of course, exceedingly small things, and the technical difficulty of studying the metabolism of parts of the egg is very large indeed. Some subtle types of supersensitive apparatus have been worked out which enable one to operate with minute quantities of material. One of the most refined is the well-known Cartesian diver. This old toy, which apparently has nothing to do with the French philosopher Descartes, after whom it is named, is a tiny vessel of thin glass with an open neck. In this neck a drop of oil is placed and the whole thing is immersed in a flask of water. As the diver sinks below the water surface, the pressure of water from above forces down the oil drop, compresses the air in the vessel into a smaller volume and so makes the glass bubble sink further. It can be made to float at a predetermined level, however, by adjusting the atmospheric pressure on the surface of the water in the flask. If now we have inside the stabilized diver a small piece of tissue which is using up oxygen or giving out carbon dioxide, this will alter the volume of the gas inside the diver and thus affect its buoyancy. This change

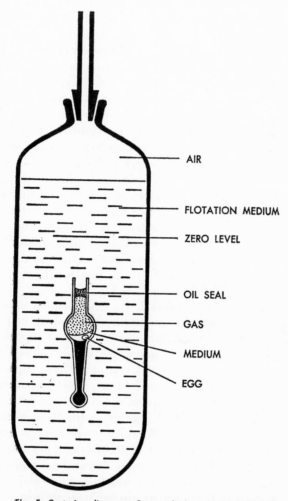

AIR

FLOTATION MEDIUM

ZERO LEVEL

OIL SEAL

GAS

MEDIUM

EGG

Fig. 5. Cartesian diver was first applied to the study of cell respiration by K. U. Linderstrom-Lang at the Carlsberg Laboratories in Copenhagen. Minute quantities of gas absorbed or given off by egg in vessel affect the buoyancy of the diver in the flotation medium.

can be measured by altering the atmospheric pressure until the diver just floats at its original level. The apparatus provides an exceedingly sensitive method of measuring minute changes in gas volume; with it one can measure respirations which involve as little as one millionth of a cubic centimeter of gas.

With such instruments we have acquired in the last few years a large amount of information about the respiration of various parts of the egg and other aspects of metabolism which are technically easy to measure. Unfortunately these processes are not always the kinds that seem most likely to lead to an understanding of cell differentiation. Differentiated cells probably are distinguished from one another principally by their protein constituents. We still know exceedingly little about how proteins are formed, and biochemical investigation of protein production in embryos has not yet made much progress.

Like so many projects in biology, this investigation may turn largely on finding a suitable experimental material. The whole of embryology suffers at present from operating too much in terms of complex entities. Instead of considering the development of nervous tissue or liver tissue, each of which contains many substances, we must be able to investigate the development of some single substance. Again, instead of thinking in terms of transplanting lumps of material from one part of the embryo to the other, we shall have to start experimenting on the constituents of a single cell. We have as yet no good material in which we can follow quantitatively the synthesis of some specific protein and investigate the effect of various conditions on this process.

The genetic study of development is not open to this reproach. In genetics we can easily study one kind of unit involved in development, namely the gene. One of the most important things that has been going on in genetics recently is the attempt to connect individual genes with the specific single substances for whose production they are responsible. In microorganisms such as yeasts or fungi, which have a very simple body and a somewhat simpler biochemical sysem than more complicated animals, a change in a single gene often produces an obvious alteration in only one chemical constituent. Frequently this constituent is an enzyme, that is to say, one of the biological catalysts on which the function-ing of the cell depends. It is probable, indeed, that all genes exert their influence through enzymes, and data from microorganisms suggest that each gene has an effect on a particular enzyme. If this is so, it would be logical to suppose that the gene manufac-tures the enzyme. It is not by any means certain that the matter is really as simple as all that. There may be several steps between the gene and the enzyme, in which case a number of different substances would be involved. We should then be dealing with a chemical system not very different from the one discussed in connection with the competence of embryonic tissues.

From the point of view of cell differentiation, however, this work in microbiology is not so helpful as one might think. The microorganisms are the very creatures that show the least amount of differentiation. Genes exercise their control, it is generally be-lieved, by interacting in different ways with different regions of the cytoplasm in the egg. In microorganisms there is little or no specialization of different regions of cytoplasm, so we cannot hope to get from them any direct information about this fundamental relationship between genes and cytoplasm.

We have, however, found some valuable indirect clues. It has been known for some time that a strain of yeast growing in a sugar solution will often develop the ability to ferment that type of sugar although it could not do so originally. It forms what is known as an adaptive enzyme for doing so. Biochemists and genet-icists have learned that in general a strain of yeast can form an adaptive enzyme to a particular sugar only if it has a hereditary capacity to do so. In other words, the forming of an adaptive enzyme depends on the presence of the appropriate gene. This gene must, however, be activated by the presence of the sugar. The situation is an extraordinary parallel to what we imagine must happen when specific genes are activated in certain cyto-plasmic regions of the egg. Since each adaptive enzyme is a specific protein, we have here an opportunity to study quantitatively the physical and chemical factors involved in protein synthesis. Sir Cyril Hinshelwood at Oxford University, Sol Spiegelman at the University of Illinois, Jacques Monod in Paris and others are already pursuing this line of inquiry.

From this protein study has come the stimulating suggestion that between the gene and the final enzyme there may be intermediates which, once formed, can reproduce themselves, for some time at least, even if the gene that produced them is removed. Several authors recently have come to the conclusion, some rather hastily, that they had evidence for the existence of such substances, and they have given them a variety of names—plasmagenes, cytogenes and so on. In several cases further investigation showed either that the evidence was not as good as had been thought or that the suggested plasmagenes were actually foreign virus particles or something of a similar nature. In a certain number of cases, however, there is fairly convincing evidence for the existence of plasmagene-like bodies. One of the best known is found in the little Paramecium. In this single-celled organism the cell develops certain substances which can be recognized by the fact that they stimulate the production of specific antibodies when they are injected into rabbits. The development of each substance is controlled by a corresponding plasmagene. The plasmagenes again are under the control of nuclear genes, and the nucleus itself is influenced by the condition of the cytoplasm of the cell. The cytoplasmic state can be altered by growing the animals at different temperatures or by changing their environment in other ways. Each cytoplasmic condition activates a certain gene to manufacture its corresponding plasmagene, and that in turn produces the final cell constituent.

It seems likely that something similar goes on in embryonic development. The different regions of the egg can be supposed to activate particular groups of genes in the nuclei which enter them; the activated genes then control the differentiation of cells. The first step in this will be the production of immediate gene products which may or may not be endowed with the power of self-reproduction, like plasmagenes. The Belgian embryologist Brachet has argued that certain minute particles which can be discovered in cells, the so-called microsomes, are the actual plasmagenes. These particles, just barely visible under ordinary microscopes, can be separated from the rest of the cell by ultracentrifugation. Brachet supposes that they are the immediate agents of protein synthesis in the cytoplasm, operating under the ulti-

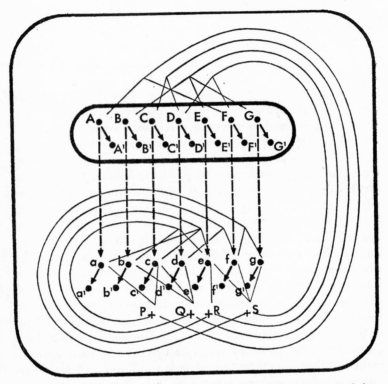

Fig. 6. Developmental system within the cell must be an elaborate network of chemical interactions. The genes in the nucleus (A, B, C, etc.) not only form replicas of themselves (A^1, B^1, C^1, etc.) for the next division of the cell but also must produce "immediate gene products" (a, b, c, etc.). These may or may not be "plasmagenes," able to form duplicates of themselves (a^1, b^1, c^1, etc.). They must interact, however, to produce the cell proteins (P, Q, R, etc.). These in turn condition the activities of both the gene products and the genes.

mate control of the nuclear genes. There is as yet no absolutely convincing proof of this. We badly need to develop techniques for investigating more thoroughly the relation between these microsomes and the nucleus, for instance by isolating the microsomes from one cell and transplanting them into another whose development would normally be different.

The gene-plasmagene and gene-microsome story is the place at which the two sciences of genetics and embryology are coming together most closely. It also introduces the last pair of actors in our account. These are the two nucleic acids, usually known as DNA (desoxyribonucleic acid) and RNA (ribonucleic acid). They are always present in those parts of the cell most deeply involved in the production of new substances, and it seems most probable that nucleic acid of one kind or the other is essential for the production of any protein. There seems to be no doubt that DNA, a constituent of the chromosomes that house the genes, must be in some way closely connected with the genes themselves, which contain protein. RNA always occurs in high concentration in any region of cytoplasm in which rapid synthesis of proteins is proceeding. The microsomes, for instance, contain large quantities of RNA but little or no DNA. According to one present theory, the DNA-containing chromosomes manufacture RNA, which passes out of the nucleus into the cytoplasm and there becomes attached to the microsomes and takes part in the synthesis of the cellular proteins.

Here again we are standing on the challenging frontier of unexplored territory. We may flatter ourselves that we are converging on the secret of differentiation from all sides, but the advances we have made so far do more to reveal the extent of the area still to be explored than to provide satisfying explanations. The older surgical methods of experimental embryology and the general genetical studies have given us some clues as to the over-all nature of the system we are dealing with. But they emphasize, on the one hand, the need for developing a broad picture of it and, on the other, the importance of getting down to concrete chemical detail. Thus every part of the advancing front of knowledge must look for support to every other, and the order of the day all along the line must be to press on.

──▶ **Herbert Thoms, M.D., and
Bruce Blevin, Jr.**

Life Before Birth

From *McCall's Magazine*, February, 1958. Reprinted and abridged by permission.

If a baby were to go on growing as rapidly after his birth as he did during his last month before birth, he would weigh something like one hundred and sixty pounds on his first birthday. Yet the last month is the slowest of all his nine months of prenatal development. In the first month alone this tiny organism increases to nearly ten thousand times its initial size. In the first three months it progresses from a simple roundish dot to an infinitely complicated human form—unfinished, to be sure, but recognizably a baby-to-be, like an artist's advanced sketch for a detailed drawing.

The total journey from a speck of watery material to a seven-pound, nineteen-inch-long human being takes 267 days and is a marvel of refinement. One change prepares the way for the next, and the plan, for all its subtlety, is marked by an incredible accuracy, both in running true to form and in staying on schedule.

Speed, subtlety, accuracy—they characterize this growth process. But it is the over-all transformation that really staggers the imagination; this is the unbelievable manner in which one's own, and everybody's, biography begins.

Conception starts the first of the 267 days. The female egg is joined by the male sperm, and immediately the forty-six chromosomes in the nucleus of this completed cell begin to churn about as if they had been electrified, a prelude to the first cell division. The particle of jellylike stuff, the fertilized egg, slightly more substantial than a drop of water, is approximately as big as the dots over the "i's" in this type face, but it seems to deserve some name more dignified than "egg." For it is not going to become a chicken or a hamster or, for that matter, just any human being. It is going to be a particular child of a particular family, the John J. Smith family, let's say.

The Smith children's genetic characteristics have been determined by the great family trees spreading back on both their father's and their mother's sides. If this Smith baby is going to be a boy, the particular chromosome that decides the question has already been acquired from the sperm. If this Smith boy is going to inherit, say, his maternal grandmother's aptitude for music, that too, along with all his other inherited characteristics, is physically present within the roundish droplet's form.

As the cell divides (splitting into two, the two becoming four, and so on) the egg continues to float, as it did before and during conception, down the hollow interior of one of the two Fallopian tubes on its way to the womb, a two-inch journey that takes at least three or four days.

By the time it reaches the womb the egg is usually in about its sixteen-cell stage. It is more complicated than it was at first, but it is not much larger. It drifts with ease through the tube opening, which is about as big as a hairbrush bristle. Even at this early date there are two markedly different kinds of cells. One type divides faster than the other. The prolific cells and their fast-dividing offspring surround the slow-dividing cells, forming an infinitely delicate casing around them, a protective layer one cell thick. The egg has turned into a tiny ball covered by a transparent membrane considerably less substantial than a single layer of our multilayered skin. Not only do the outer cells multiply faster but they are flat, in contrast to the plump, roundish inner cells. Since both the flat and the round cells are such recent descendants of the same original, this differentiation is a particularly mysterious development.

From the fourth to the sixth or seventh day the egg-ball floats in the warm, dark, three-inch-deep, fluid-filled womb cavity, and during that time a liquid appears and collects at the center of the ball. The best guess is that the liquid is a secretion from the flat outer cells. The egg-ball slowly expands as the fluid gathers, like a miniature balloon swelling to the size of a pinhead. The fluid, as it accumulates, pushes the plump cells away from the center to one of the poles of the tiny globe. There, just inside the shell-like protective covering, they form a small colony.

A week has elapsed. The egg-ball with its liquid center is perhaps twice as big as the original egg. By this time the velvety lining of the womb, a tissue not unlike the lining of the throat, has become extraordinarily soft and thick, as it does once every twenty-eight days (shortly before menstruation, ordinarily) during the mother's childbearing years.

Until now the egg has been passive, unable to move under its own power. But on the seventh day (or in some cases as early as the end of the sixth), as it drifts against the womb lining, almost invariably at some point in the upper portion, it begins to burrow into the soft, succulent material. It seems absurd to speak of "aggressiveness" on the part of a simple speck of cells, but the contrast between the burrowing action and the ovum's previous helplessness is striking. The flat, outer-layer cells dig into the mother's tissue, scattering some of the cells of the tissue right and left, destroying others, opening up some hairlike capillaries and releasing the blood inside them, perhaps breaking through the walls of one of the many secretory gland pockets with which the lining is endowed. In a matter of hours the egg-ball has completely embedded itself. The hole it has made closes over it, separating it from the womb cavity. The womb's lining tissue now surrounds it on every side.

Its immediate problem is food. It needs some way to get at the mother's blood around it. It sprouts tiny projections called "villi" all over its surface. There are close to a thousand fast-growing villi; like minute plant roots, they dip into the infinitesimal pools of blood and absorb by osmosis the oxygen, minerals, carbohydrates, proteins and fats the blood contains.

All these events have taken place before the mother knows she is pregnant; the chances are that she will not find out about it before the twenty-first day at the earliest. But already profound changes are taking place in her body. The first thing the mother notices, apart from the absence of her usual menstrual flow, is likely to be a feeling of tightening or stretching in her breasts. She may also feel unreasonably sleepy. Or perhaps nauseated, although more than half the women pregnant for the first time do not have "morning sickness." Her appetite may very well change in one direction or another; she may not feel like eating, or she may be hungry practically all the time.

Her state of mind is sure to be influenced in some direction and to some degree. Many women find pregnancy pleasant. Women who are ordinarily somewhat anxious may feel calm and relaxed; sometimes listless women blossom into energetic enthusiasm. Others have just the opposite experience—they feel depressed, doubtful or unsettled.

Once its villi have begun to absorb food, the egg-ball grows quickly and causes a noticeable lump on the inner surface of the womb lining. The hair-like projections branch out in every direction and start to develop their own blood vessels, which will greatly add to their efficiency as food carriers. Some of them, reaching farther than the rest, push almost all the way through the lining, a depth of nearly three-quarters of an inch, toward the womb's outer muscular wall; their function is to anchor the embryo.

Inside the fluid-filled sphere, meanwhile, the colony of cells has formed itself into two tiny sacs, the yolk sac and the amnion. They are touching each other, and since they both are soft, the area of contact is a small, roundish (or slightly oval), flat place. This junction, a layer of yolk-sac cells flattened against a layer of amnion cells, now takes the spotlight. For the two layers interact upon each other, and before long they produce between themselves a third layer. A three-layered disk has been created. The rest of the yolk sac will not be important in the future. The amnion, on the other hand, remains a key structure until delivery. But the three-layered disk has the star part, for the tiny oval is about to transform itself into the embryo.

Each of the disk's layers will provide the baby-to-be with cell material for specific kinds of tissues. One layer is the source for the cells that will form its nervous system, skin, hair, finger and toenails, the enamel of its teeth and the linings of its nose and throat. The middle layer will supply cells for the baby's muscles, bones and cartilage, blood and blood vessels, kidneys and tooth dentine (the inner part of the tooth beneath the surface enamel). The third layer will provide the digestive tract and most of the respiratory system.

About the nineteenth or twentieth day the smooth disk develops a groovelike crease down one of its oval surfaces, and ridges arise on either side of the depression. The ridges converge at one of its ends; that is to be the head end of the embryo. As the ridges rise along the length of the groove and fold toward each other, the disk becomes partly tubular and crescent-shaped. The outside curve of its semicircular form in time will become the baby's backbone. Within just a few days, in fact, near the middle of that curve, the first suggestion of the spinal column will appear, along with brain matter starting to fill the hollow formed by the meeting of the ridges at the head end. Small buds, the first hint of arms and legs, are due shortly. By the twenty-first day a rudimentary heart has formed. Ten days later it has started to beat.

The embryo is connected with the villi-covered casing of the sphere by a thread of cells, an outgrowth from one end of the middle layer of the three-layer disk. (In time the thread will lengthen from its present small fraction of an inch into a dull white rope twenty-two inches long—the twisted, coiling umbilical cord.)

The amniotic sac, like the egg-ball, is filled with a clear liquid, 98 per cent water, in which the embryo floats and is free to grow without restraint or interference. The temperature of the amniotic fluid, and consequently of the embryo, seldom varies by as much as one degree. The water serves furthermore as an effective shock absorber. For the time being the sac is very small and contains only a thimbleful or two of fluid. But by the last weeks of the pregnancy, when it will have expanded to fill most of the enormously enlarged womb, it will contain at least a quart of liquid in addition to the fetus—and two quarts are by no means uncommon.

The most radical changes in form—from egg to egg-ball, from three-layered disk to tubular crescent—are past. From now on the embryo quickly takes on a babyish appearance and looks like a miniature of what it is going to be. By the end of the second month it is only one inch long from head to rump and weighs a minor fraction of an ounce, but the head has facelike characteristics—a nose, mouth, ears and a suggestion of what will become eye sockets. (It bears no real resemblance to an adult fish, a reptile, or anything, in fact, except a baby.)

In every major respect the embryo is formed by the end of the third month. (In honor of that, its formal name from now on is "fetus.") It is only three inches long and about one ounce in weight, but it has the general form and structure of a baby; while they are not yet operating except in a tentative, practice way, its various body systems show plainly what they are soon to become. Its eyes and eyelids are formed. Its sexual organs are present. For the next six months, while the fetus grows to baby size, its ability to function as a newborn will develop gradually, and to a large extent by actually functioning in an anticipatory way inside the womb. Its heart has already been beating for as long as two months, gaining muscular strength. Its arms and legs are now complete, down to fingernails and toenails, and the fetus has started to move them—its first movement of this kind, although the activity is too feeble at the outset to be felt by the mother. The fetus has begun to swallow small amounts of the amniotic fluid, a beginning exercise not only in swallowing but in something like breathing. It is now just practice, using the liquid as a substitute for air. Until birth and the first gasp of air the fetus gets all the oxygen it needs, along with its food, from the blood flowing into its body through the umbilical cord.

Commonest among superstitions about pregnancy is the ancient myth that the things a pregnant woman sees, thinks or hears can affect her child. The superstition is false because the umbilical cord is the only connection between mother and fetus, and the umbilical cord contains no nerves. Since the nervous systems are entirely separate, nothing the mother thinks or perceives can affect her offspring. And there is a certain irony in the fact that those who believe this are particularly likely to worry about it toward the later months of their pregnancies—long after the fetus is fully formed.

Like its nervous system, the fetus's circulatory system is completely independent from its mother's. The fetus manufactures all its own blood. Molecules of material pass from one blood stream to the other—the traffic goes both ways, from mother to fetus and vice versa—but the bloods never mix. The mother does not supply blood to the fetus, and nothing like a transfusion from mother to fetus is possible.

The two blood streams simply exchange materials. The transfer takes place inside a most remarkable organ which develops during the pregnancy and is then destroyed in the birth process. It is called the placenta. Inside the placenta the two blood streams are intimately associated, although they never actually meet. There the materials in the mother's blood, on the way to the fetal blood stream, are filtered through a cellular barrier—a screen so finely meshed that only the smallest molecules can pass through it. The placenta sits against the wall of the womb in the midst of the lining tissues and is connected to the fetus by the umbilical cord. It is shaped like a cookie or flat cake, which is what the Latin "placenta" means, and it becomes pretty big— five or six inches in diameter and an inch or so in thickness. Most of this bulk is made up of villi—the same villi we saw before, but larger now and fully equipped with blood vessels. These blood vessels run back to the blood vessels in the umbilical cord; and the vessels in the cord, after passing through the fetus's navel, join the veins and arteries inside the small body, making one continuous supply line. The rest of the placenta's bulk consists of the mother's blood vessels and tissues, which intermesh with the villi in a compact, complicated pattern.

The villi, packed in close profusion inside the structure, expose an incredible total of food-absorbing tissue to the mother's blood—fifteen square meters, an area as large as a nine-by-twelve-foot rug. The fetus is a parasite; the placenta breathes and digests on its behalf.

The placenta is such an efficient filter, and the food it allows into the fetal blood stream is so nearly all usable, that there are almost no fetal waste products. Small amounts of urine are discharged into the amniotic fluid, which is constantly in the process of renewal. (It is almost completely changed on the average of every three hours.) But the fetus's bowels do not move. Some waste material accumulates in them, but so slowly that the amount is negligible even by the end of the full pregnancy.

Toward the latter part of the fourth month, the mother feels the fetus moving. The sensation is at first very faint, so tentative that she often wonders if it isn't just her imagination. And from her first intimation of the new life weeks may elapse before the flexing of the fetus's arms and legs becomes unmistakably strong.

It has been moving for as long as a month, of course, before the mother feels this activity. Of its new attainments its increased stature (six inches) and weight (six ounces) are perhaps the most impressive. Its eyebrows and eyelashes have appeared. Its skin has become less translucent and more pink. Now for the first time the fetus's heartbeat is strong enough to be heard by the doctor when he places his stethoscope against the mother's abdomen. The fetal heart beats about 136 times a minute, almost twice as fast as its mother's heart. The fetus has reached one additional milestone in its prenatal life—its skeleton can be X-rayed. Until now the soft, gristlelike bones have been too much like the other tissues to show up under X-ray examination.

As the fetus grows, stretching and squirming, strengthening muscles, the mother's uterus continues to rise out of the pelvis into the abdominal cavity. By the end of the sixth month when the the fetus is a foot long, weighs about a pound and a half, and is beginning to turn into a fatter, more babyish shape, the top of the uterus is at the level of the mother's navel.

The fetus can hiccup, move its facial muscles and feel pressure. We know experimentally that it is able to sneeze, and that it may be able to do something like hear. At any rate, a number of fetuses have seemed to squirm in response to the noise of a tuning fork placed against their mother's abdomens. But they may have felt the fork's vibrations rather than heard its musical note. The fetus's lifetime complement of twelve billion nerve cells are formed, but as a system they do not function as well as they soon will. That's part of the reason why its eyes, which are almost fully developed, are at best only sensitive to light.

That dramatic gain in strength is in full swing. The fetus is continuing to practice arm and leg movements, but now it can also stretch its body and move its head from side to side as well as up and down. It is still swallowing fluid, and its chest muscles, in preparation for breathing air, grow stronger every day. Before it swallows, the fetus first sucks the fluid into its mouth—rehearsing the reflex action that after birth will provide food. In fact, sucking is probably the thing the fetus does best. It may very well be sucking its thumb, as many babies do before they are born; it is making sucking motions more or less constantly.

By the end of the eighth month the fetus has grown another

five inches and weighs four and a half pounds. The womb, which began as a three-inch-long, compact muscular sac, has stretched out to an amazing sixteen-inch diameter.

If the fetus is not already in a head-down position in the womb, it is almost surely about to revolve to assume it; in close to ninety-five out of one hundred births the baby's head presents itself first. Some time after the middle of the ninth month—at least among women pregnant for the first time—the steady rise of the uterus reverses itself. The head of the fetus descends farther into the pelvis, and the top of the womb sinks to a slightly lower level.

Toward the end of the ninth month, or on about the 252nd day, the fetus is ready to be born. It is, to use the technical word, "mature"—meaning that the baby's chances for survival when the birth takes place are as good as they will ever be. If the baby were to be delivered immediately, to put it another way, it would be early but not premature. The 267-day figure is only a statistical average, and fifteen-day variations either way are commonplace. In fact, out of one hundred normal births only four will hit this average day-of-arrival right on the nose.

The mature fetus today usually weighs something between six and seven pounds; it is close to nineteen inches tall. Most of the time it is quiet, but by now when it thrusts its arms or legs the movements are really powerful. If the doctor places the palm of his hand over the womb, the fetus is likely to answer with a series of soft but well-defined blows of protest.

Its arms are folded and its thighs are drawn up against its stomach, a most compact position and one that not only fits the oval womb but takes up the least possible space. This small but complete human being's life, in the most literal sense, lies ahead. Any day now he will face his first great ordeal, the process of being born. Everything for him is still to come. And yet no one would deny his experience already has been a truly marvelous one.

⟶ **Marian E. Breckenridge
and E. Lee Vincent**

Influences on Growth: Heredity

From *Child Development* (4th ed.), by Marian E. Breckenridge and E. Lee Vincent. Philadelphia: W. B. Saunders Company, 1960; pp. 59–74. Reprinted and abridged by permission.

The moment of conception when the parent cells fuse and when, therefore, a unique biologic pattern is fixed, is the most important moment in the life of a child. At that time a pattern for future growth and development of the individual is set. To what extent and in what direction a child's potentialities will be realized will depend upon his environment. Certain potentials may be partially or entirely repressed. A potential genius may become a moron because of a birth injury. Early rheumatic fever may injure the heart of one who otherwise could have been an outstanding athlete. These two influences of heredity and environment are so closely interlocked that one cannot be considered separately from the other.

The dynamic relationship between these two factors may be seen by the influence which a child's genetic endowment may have upon his use of the environment. Given the same environment and all other factors being constant, a child with a higher intellectual endowment will tend to exploit his environment more completely than one with smaller potential. Thus a very bright child may learn more from a meager environment than a less gifted child may learn from richer surroundings.

In view of observed facts, there is no doubt that some individuals with certain genetic combinations are more liable to certain diseases, such as tuberculosis, diabetes or certain mental diseases. However, an individual who springs from a family in which there is a history of such a disease is not necessarily doomed to have that disease. Tuberculosis is not a hereditary disease; it is caused by the tubercle bacillus. Whether an individual acquires the disease depends upon (a) exposure to the bacillus, (b) his genetic makeup, and (c) his health and nutrition. Some people inherit a high resistance; others inherit so little resistance that they cannot be protected by the best of environments; most people fall between. Certain types of mental illness develop because of the impact of certain kinds of environment upon a consitutionally weak nervous system. This was indicated during World War II when the stresses and strains of warfare were too much for some of the men and they became mentally ill. It must be remembered that, on the other hand, there are certain types of exposure to nervous strain which will eventually break down the best psychologic constitution.

How Heredity Operates

In the nucleus of the fertilized egg are found units which comprise the heredity of the individual and in which lie his potentialities for development. These are the 46 chromosomes, formerly thought to be 48 in number. [51] These chromosomes, of deoxyribonucleoproteins, are arranged in pairs, with twenty-three different kinds as to shape, size, etc. In each of these chromosomes there are a number of small substances, called genes, the bearers of heredity, which are arranged in a linear sequence along the length of the chromosome. [17] Each gene has its own place in this chain; and each has its distinct function in inheritance.

Genes do not act independently; they react one with another and with the environment to affect development. Each body characteristic as, for example, body build requires the action of many genes which serve as the chemical mechanism that makes a trait possible. These genes affect one another and, in turn, are affected by the medium in which they exist. Genes are believed to operate in much the same fashion as enzymes in the digestive tract, namely, through influencing chemical processes. A chemical reaction is dependent not only upon the reactive substances, but also upon the solution in which they are placed. So it is with genes. They operate by interacting (a) one with another, (b) with the cytoplasm of the cell, (c) with the chemical products of gene activity and (d) with materials obtained from the environment outside the organism. In this complex organization the alteration of one gene may so disturb the reactions within the cell that the

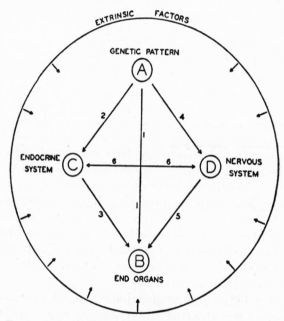

Fig. 1. Pathways through which genetic factors may influence the growth, development or "constitutional pattern" of an individual. Diagram illustrates the fact that genetic factors may influence the growth and development of the body directly (A–B) or may cause constitutional differences in the endocrine (A–C–B) or nervous system (A-D-B). Extrinsic factors, such as nutritional deficiencies or disease, may exert an influence at any time during prenatal or postnatal life. (Wilkins, L.: *The Diagnosis and Treatment of Endocrine Disorders in Childhood and Adolescence.* Charles C. Thomas, Publisher.)

course of development of a particular trait may be changed. Modification or defectiveness of a part of the body may be due to modification or imperfection of the genes cooperating to produce that part. [6, 9, 10, 34, 49] In influencing the development or constitutional pattern of an individual, genes, interacting with extrinsic factors, may have a direct effect or an indirect one through their effect upon endocrine glands or the nervous system. See Figure 1.

EFFECT OF PRENATAL ENVIRONMENT ON DEVELOPMENT

It has been stated above that the immediate environment within the body influences the action of the genes. The normal course of development as set by them can be altered by changes in the environment of the child in the uterus.[1] Some contributing factors may be maternal dietary inadequacies [5], viral infections [1] as, for example, German measles during the first six to ten weeks of pregnancy. [16, 24, 30] A child whose mother has had German measles in early pregnancy may have congenital defects. The virus evidently affects the young developing tissues of the brain, eyes, ears or heart. Such malformations, however, are rare.

Maternal health during pregnancy is also important. Passamanick, Lilienfeld and co-workers have found an association between the frequency of abnormalities of prenatal and paranatal periods and the frequency of cerebral palsy [26], epilepsy [27], mental deficiency [38], reading disorders [21], and behavior disorders as reported by teachers. [47]

Radiation [42, 60] is another important influence, as is the Rh factor. Rh factors, so named because they were first discovered in the blood of a rhesus monkey, may produce an incompatibility in the blood of mother and child. They are inherited. When a mother who has no Rh factor (Rh negative) has a baby who has Rh factors (Rh positive), a substance from the baby stimulates the formation of a substance in the mother which, in time, may act upon the blood cells of the baby and prevent them from distributing sufficient oxygen. Thus, through deprivation of oxygen, development may be altered. Mental deficiency may result if the deprivation of oxygen, which is so necessary for brain

---

1 See Breckenridge and Murphy [5], pp. 104–108 and Masland, et al. [30] Patten [39] discusses varying developmental mechanisms which may be involved. Fraser, et al. [11], discuss genetic and environmental factors in cleft palate.

tissue activity, should occur when the brain is in a critical stage of development. However, two studies of infants recovering without motor nerve damage from erythroblastosis fetalis [8, 12] indicate that impairment of intelligence is slight. In one study the IQ was 11.8 and in the other 6.13 points lower than their unaffected siblings. Sensitization of the infant with ensuing anoxia seldom happens to a first child. Even though about one in every twelve pregnancies involves an Rh-negative mother and an Rh-positive baby, the Rh disease has been found to appear in no more than about one in every 150 to 200 full-term deliveries. [49] With present knowledge and safeguards which can be taken, an Rh-negative woman and an RH-positive man need not hesitate to marry and have children.

The Mechanics of Inheritance

The child receives from his parents a uniquely new combination of parental genes, a combination of the genes which the parents themselves received when they were conceived (see Fig. 2). Occasionally a new characteristic appears in a family line due to a basic biologic phenomenon, mutation. A mutation results in the sudden origin of a gene with biologic properties which are different from those possessed by the original gene. Such mutations are rarely for the better. It is believed that, on the average, each individual may have received at least one mutant gene from one or the other parent. [34] The most important cause of mutations is radiation, which comes from four chief sources to which man is exposed, namely (a) cosmic rays, (b) radiation from decomposition of naturally occurring radioactive isotopes, (c) x-rays used for diagnosis and therapy, and (d) radiation from peacetime and military applications of atomic energy. To limit the mutation rate, it has been estimated that the average accumulated dosage of radiation to the gonads should not exceed 10 roentgen from conception to 30 years of age. [31, 32]

Genes are not changed by alterations in the body cells of the parents. The fact that a father has several college degrees in itself does not affect the inherited mental capacity of his children.

Figure 2 shows that the child receives forty-six chromosomes, half from each of his parents. The particular twenty-three chro-

mosomes which he receives from either parent may come from
either or both grandparents on that side of the family. The child,
therefore, may have certain traits in common with one or both of
his parents; in others, he may resemble one of his grandparents,
or he may be different from his immediate family. What he is like
depends upon the particular assortment of chromosomes he receives. Because of the numerous possibilities of chromosome combinations, it is not surprising that children of the same family
are different, that one sister may be dark while another is blonde,
that a brother may have curly hair while his sister's hair is

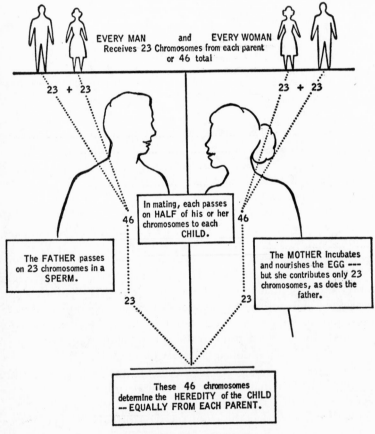

Fig. 2. The pattern of heredity.

straight. Only in the case of identical twins do children have the same genetic constitution and are, therefore, genetically alike.

The matched chromosomes contain a series of genes. Each gene in one of a pair of chromosomes is paired with a gene in the other chromosome. These genes perform the same function, either in a similar or dissimilar manner. If the genes in a pair are similar in their performance, the characteristic influenced by them will appear, provided no other pair of genes interferes. If they are dissimilar, the different influences of the two genes may blend to produce an intermediate characteristic or one gene may conceal the effect of the other. A gene which produces a certain characteristic in the presence of another gene is said to be dominant; the concealed one, recessive. The recessive factor remains intact and may be passed on to a child in the next generation. If, in the succeeding generation, this recessive is paired with a like recessive, its influence will become evident. The probability of appearance of a trait in a family that carries that trait can be determined mathematically. [52]

Services for analyzing pedigrees are available in many places. Individuals can be given information regarding the possibility and probability of the appearance of certain undesirable traits in their children. Reed [43] lists heredity clinics in the United States and Canada where genetic counseling is available. For a discussion of techniques used in analyzing hereditary characteristics in man see Neel and Schull. [34]

Some characteristics are associated with the sex of an individual, namely the sex-linked and sex-influenced. Sex-linked characteristics—for example, color blindness and hemophilia—are produced by genes carried by the chromosomes responsible for determining sex. Specifically, the genes involved are those found in the nonhomologous segments of the X-chromosome. [34] Such characteristics appear more often in men than in women. They rarely appear in both father and son. (Color blindness, for example, occurs in about 5 to 9 per cent in males and is about twenty times as rare in females. Hemophilia is practically unknown in women.) [52] They are transmitted from a man through his daughter to some of her sons. Sex-influenced characteristics are those which are expressed differently in the two sexes. Among these are the secondary sex characteristics which are controlled by secretions of the endocrine glands and baldness with its higher frequency in males.

Errors in metabolism sometimes occur. Examples of genetic metabolic errors are found in the disorders associated with the metabolism of two amino acids, namely phenylalanine and tyrosine. [23] One of these is phenylketonuria [59], which has both physical and psychologic characteristics. A concept of a partial genetic block in the ability of an organism to carry out specific steps in metabolism has been described to explain differences in individual nutritional needs. Such a block may increase the body's need for some nutritional factor or factors and may explain to a considerable degree why each individual possesses a characteristic and distinctive metabolic pattern. [56, 58]

Characteristics Influenced by Heredity

Sex of the child is basically determined by the genes of a special pair of chromosomes. In the female the two chromosomes are alike (XX); in the male they are different (XY). Every ovum that is ready to be fertilized contains one X. Some sperms contain X; some sperms contain Y. If an X-bearing sperm fertilizes the ovum, the new organism will be a girl. If a Y-bearing sperm fertilizes the ovum, the new organism will be a boy. It is, therefore, the father who unknowingly determines whether his child will be a girl or a boy.

The characteristics which are accepted as due almost exclusively to heredity are color of eyes and hair, blood types, form of features, structure of body and many physical peculiarities. Differences in health and vigor, mentality, behavior, susceptibility and immunity to various diseases including dental caries, color of skin, stoutness or slenderness are considered to be due either to a goodly portion of both or a relatively small dose of heredity and a large dose of environment. They have been found to be the traits more readily affected by their surroundings than those enumerated as due almost exclusively to heredity. While we never inherit criminality as a full-fledged behavior pattern, life patterns set by heredity help to determine whether behavior will be "social" or "anti-social." Some people become criminals not because of a particularly bad environment but because of internal instabilities that prevent them from making a satisfactory adjustment to the requirements of life. Most criminality, however, is thought to be environmentally determined.

EFFECT OF HEREDITY UPON INTELLIGENCE

There have been many studies of the effect of heredity and of environment upon the development of intelligence and personality.[2] Studies [35, 50] of pairs of identical twins reared separately and of identical twins reared together as contrasted to pairs of fraternal (nonidentical) twins reared together have led to the conclusion that environment does modify those characteristics described as intelligence, personality, and educational achievement.

One study [50] confirms the long-accepted clinical opinion that emotional warmth and security are of great importance in developing the best of the intellectual potential in own as well as in adopted children.[3]

Environment probably cannot, however, change this potential by more than a certain amount in either a good or a bad direction. [13, 33, 40, 50] It appears that as far as intelligence is concerned heredity seems to set the stage for the major level of intelligence. An idiot cannot be made normal, although his functioning level can be improved. A low normal child cannot be trained into a genius. The greatest IQ gains recorded in any study are in the neighborhood of 20 to 30 points. This amount is of great significance since it can mean all the difference between successful functioning in life and failure. But if one sets these changes in terms of 100 IQ as average, even a change of 30 points still leaves 70 points which heredity claims for its own.

EFFECT OF HEREDITY UPON PERSONALITY AND BEHAVIOR

In the area of personality and behavior the dynamic relationship of heredity and environment again is evident.

---

[2] See Ausubel [2], pp. 54–55, 74–79, 597 ff.

[3] For a discussion of emotional factors in intellectual activities see Russell [48], pp. 347–349. He also discussed the closeness of the relationship between emotion and thinking in Chapter 6.

The importance of heredity has been demonstrated in many studies. Direct evidence comes from family histories of diseases such as epilepsy [25], phenylketonuria, ametria [29], studies of intelligence [35], and the functioning of the autonomic system. [20] Indirect sources of evidence are many, including (a) consistent individual differences of newborns in areas such as activity, irritability and reaction to stress; (b) the meaningful relationships between various personality traits and variability in endocrine or autonomic functioning; and (c) correlations between body type and temperament, neurotic and psychotic trends, and hormonal and autonomic functioning. It is suggested that this is not a simple type of inheritance but rather polygenic. For elaboration and references see Ausubel. [2]

It seems evident that heredity may influence personality and behavior through its effect upon the metabolic processes of the body since the genes can be thought of as potent physiochemical activators. Williams [57] states that man inherits a distinct "metabolic personality" which can affect almost every aspect of behavior and social relationships.

Studies of identical twins [35, 50] are generally interpreted as indicating that hereditary-constitutional factors are of considerable, if not of predominant, importance in determining the general direction or core of personality pattern. There is not such clear agreement about the development of specific personality traits. The tendency on the part of the growing child to show himself as a certain kind of person and then, in spite of rather marked environmental changes, to be true to this pattern as time goes on has been corroborated in several types of studies. In summarizing these studies, Jersild [19] notes that this persistence of personality characteristics is an important fact whether it is attributable to gene-heredity or stems from environmental factors which affect the child in very early life.

Martin and Stendler [28] have also called attention to this persistence of personality trend and have discussed it as a possible constitutional difference in emotionality. Their conclusion, after careful review of the literature, agrees with that of many writers, namely, that: "It is not really the physical characteristic alone that determines that the child shall be dominant or assertive or easy-going. It is the significance and value which his society places upon that physical characteristic which become the crucial determinant." This social-cultural influence upon personality development has been emphasized by many other writers [7, 28] in recent years.

Thus we see in the nature-nurture discussions differences in emphasis but general agreement that gene inheritance, the early family environment, and the social-cultural impact all have a part to play in determining the pattern and direction of personality development.

IMPLICATIONS FOR CHILD DEVELOPMENT

Earlier we discussed the importance of recognizing individual differences in children in planning for them as individuals and in groups. In this chapter we have seen that the interplay of heredity and environment produced these differences. A look at heredity offers us one explanation for children's selective response to their environment. All children have certain needs for growth. All children do not meet these needs in the same way. Children will differ in the kinds and amounts of food they need for optimal growth. They will differ in sleep and activity requirements and in sensitivity to emotional stimuli. There can, therefore, be no program which is standardized in detail for all children in the home or school. It is to be remembered that children in the same family do not generally have exactly the same genetic makeup, so their response to the home environment will differ. Also the environment for each child in the family will be somewhat different, either because of time and the changes which come with it, or because of differences in relationships.

Checking on the hereditary ledger should not result in a laissez-faire policy. It should give one a basis on which to operate. Environment is a strong factor to be remembered. As Todd once said, "The adult physical pattern is the outcome of growth along lines determined by heredity but enhanced, dwarfed, warped, or mutilated in its expression by the influence of environment in the adventure of life." [55] The same can be said for psychologic growth.

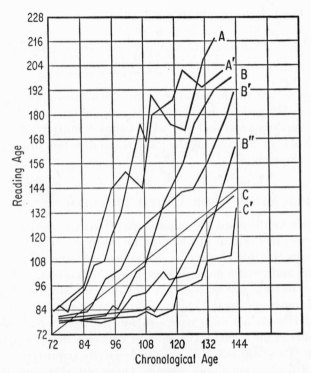

Fig. 3. Growth curves showing familial resemblance in Reading Age for children of three families. Compare A with A', B, B' and B'', and C with C'. (From Olson, W. C., and Hughes, B. O.: Concepts of Growth—Their Significance to Teachers, Child Educ., Oct., 1944, p. 8.)

INFLUENCE OF THE INTERACTION OF HEREDITY AND ENVIRONMENT ON GROWTH PATTERNS

Various longitudinal growth studies[4] provide evidence that children of the same family tend to show a notable similarity in their patterns of growth.[5]

4 Studies at the University of Michigan, Fels Institute for Research, and Brush Foundation.

5 See Bayley [3] and Ausubel [2], pp. 600–601.

Olson and Hughes [37] have studied growth curves in reading for forty-six pairs of siblings. The growth curves in Figure 3 are samples of sibling curves which represent high, intermediate and low achievement. A and A′ are brothers born twenty-five months apart. B, B′ and B″ are three brothers born at intervals of twenty-seven and twenty-five months and C and C′ are brothers born at an interval of thirty-six months apart. Their reading ages are plotted against their chronologic ages. The rate and level of achievement for A and A′ and C and C′ are strikingly similar. B and B′ cling together but B″ drops behind for several years.

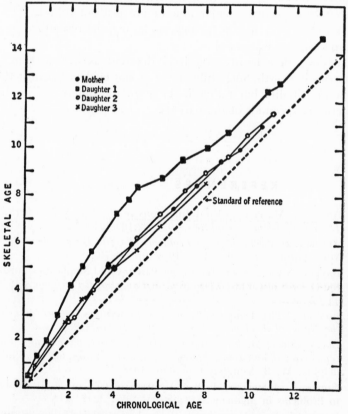

Fig. 4. Curves of skeletal age of mother and three daughters, indicating advanced skeletal maturation for all.

However, he is approaching them toward the end of the record.

In physical growth there also is evidence of similarities in families. Similar growth patterns in height [4], in bone development [15, 45] and in tooth decay [22], and similar speed of maturing [14, 18, 41, 44, 53, 54] have been seen in families. There are slow-maturing and fast-maturing families. Similarities in the growth of a mother and three daughters are shown in Figure 4 on fast schedules. They are all advanced in skeletal development.

Knowing the father and mother of a child may help in the interpretation of his health status and growth. There are some children who, in spite of the best environments, are underweight, perhaps have poor muscular tone or are just not robust. When such a child is seen with his parents he may be recognized as a "chip off the old block." [46]

Members of a family may have different as well as similar patterns of growth. Such differences are not evidence against the force of heredity but rather in favor of the differences in the genetic backgrounds of the parents.

REFERENCES

1. ADAMS, J. M., et al., "Viral Infections in the Embryo," American Journal of Diseased Children, 1956, 92:109–114.

2. AUSUBEL, D. P., Theory and Problems of Child Development, New York: Grune & Stratton, Inc., 1958, pp. 74–79.

3. BAYLEY, NANCY, "Some Increasing Parent-Child Similarities during the Growth of Children," Journal of Educational Psychology, 1946, 45:433–461.

4. BOAS, F., "The Tempo of Growth of Fraternities," Proceedings of the National Academy of Science, 1935, 21:413–418.

5. BRECKENRIDGE, M. E., & MURPHY, M. N., Rand, Sweeny and Vincent's Growth and Development of the Young Child, 6th ed., Philadelphia: W. B. Saunders Company, 1958.

6. CHILDS, B., & SIDBURY, T. B., "A Survey of Genetics as It Applies to Problems in Medicine," Pediatrics, 1957, 20:177–218.

7. DAVIS, W. A., & HAVIGHURST, R. J., Father of the Man, Boston: Houghton Mifflin Company, 1947.

8. DAY, R., & HAINES, M. S., "Intelligence Quotient of Children Recovered from Erythroblastosis Fetalis since the Introduction of Exchange Transfusion," *Pediatrics,* 1954, 13:333–338.

9. DODSON, E. O., *Genetics, The Modern Science of Heredity,* Philadelphia: W. B. Saunders Company, 1956.

10. FRASER, F. C., "Recent Advances in Genetics in Pediatrics," *Journal of Pediatrics,* 1958, 52:734–757.

11. ———, *et al.,* "Experimental Production of Congenital Cleft Palate: Genetic and Environmental Factors," *Pediatrics,* 1957, 19:782–871.

12. GERVER, J. M., & DAY, R., "Intelligence Quotient of Children Who Have Recovered from Erythroblastosis Fetalis," *Journal of Pediatrics,* 1950, 36:342–345.

13. GOODENOUGH, FLORENCE L., "Can We Influence Mental Growth? A Critique of Recent Experiment," *Educational Record Supplement,* January, 1940.

14. GOULD, H. N., & GOULD, M. R., "Age of First Menstruation in Mothers and Daughters," *Journal of the American Medical Association,* 1932, 98:1349–1352.

15. HEWITT, D., "Some Familial Correlations in Height, Weight and Skeletal Maturity," *Annals of Human Genetics,* 1957, 22:26–35.

16. INGALLS, T. H., "German Measles and German Measles in Pregnancy," *American Journal of Diseased Children,* 1957, 93:555–558.

17. INGRAM, V. M., "How Do Genes Act?" *Scientific American,* January, 1958.

18. JACOBSEN, A. W., & MACKLIN, N. T., "Hereditary Sexual Precocity; A Report of a Family with 27 Affected Members," *Pediatrics,* 1952, 9:682–695.

19. JERSILD, A. T., *Child Psychology,* 4th ed., Englewood, N.J.: Prentice-Hall, Inc., 1954.

20. JOST, H., & SONTAG, L. W., "The Genetic Factor in Autonomic Nervous System Function," *Psychosomatic Medicine,* 1944, 6:308–310.

21. KAWI, A. A., & PASAMANICK, B., "Association of Factors of Pregnancy with Reading Disorders in Childhood," *Journal of the American Medical Association,* 1958, 166:1420–1423.

22. KLEIN, H., "The Family and Dental Disease. Dental Disease (D. M. F.) Experience in Parents and Offspring," *Journal of the American Dental Association,* 1946, 33:735–743.

23. KRETCHMER, N., & ETZWILER, D. D., "Disorders Associated with the Metabolism of Phenylalanine and Tyrosine," *Pediatrics,* 1958, 21:445–475.

24. Krugman, S., & Ward, R., "The Rubella Problem. Clinical Aspects, Risk of Fetal Abnormality and Methods of Prevention," Journal of Pediatrics, 1954, 44:489–498.

25. Lennox, W. G., "The Heredity of Epilepsy as Told by Relatives and Twins," Journal of the American Medical Association, 1951, 146:529–536.

26. Lilienfeld, A. M., & Parkhurst, E., "Study of the Association of Factors of Pregnancy and Parturition with the Development of Cerebral Palsy," American Journal of Hygiene, 1951, 53:262–282.

27. Lilienfeld, A. M., & Pasamanick, B., "Association of Maternal and Fetal Factors with Development of Epilepsy: I. Abnormalities in Prenatal and Paranatal Periods," Journal of the American Medical Association, 1954, 155:719–724.

28. Martin, W. E., & Stendler, C. B., Child Behavior and Development, rev. ed., New York: Harcourt, Brace and World, Inc., 1959.

29. Masland, R. L., "The Prevention of Mental Retardation," American Journal of Diseased Children, 1958, 95 Part II:3–105.

30. ———, Sarason, S. R., & Gladwin, T., Mental Subnormality, New York: Basic Books, Inc., 1958.

31. Medical Research Council, The Hazards to Man of Nuclear and Allied Radiations, London: Her Majesty's Stationery Office, 1956.

32. National Academy of Sciences-National Research Council, The Biological Effect of Atomic Radiation: Summary Reports from a Study by the Academy, Washington, D. C.: National Academy of Sciences-National Research Council, 1956.

33. National Society for the Study of Education, Intelligence, Its Nature and Nurture, The Thirty-Ninth Yearbook. Part I. Comparative and Critical Exposition. Part II. Original Studies and Experiments, Bloomington, Ill.: Public School Publishing Company, 1940.

34. Neel, J. V., & Schull, W. J., Human Heredity, Chicago: University of Chicago Press, 1950.

35. Newman, H. H., Freeman, F., & Holzinger, K., Twins. A Study in Heredity and Environment, Chicago: University of Chicago Press, 1937.

36. Olson, W. C., Child Development, 2nd ed., Boston: D. C. Heath & Company, 1959.

37. ———, & Hughes, B. O., "Concepts of Growth—Their Significance to Teachers," Childhood Education, 1944, 21:53–63.

38. Pasamanick, B., & Lilienfeld, A. M., "Association of Maternal and Fetal Factors with Development of Mental Deficiency: Abnormalities of Prenatal and Paranatal Periods," Journal of the American Medical Association, 1955, 159:155–160.

39. PATTEN, B. M., "Varying Developmental Mechanisms in Teratology," *Pediatrics,* 1957. 19:734–748.

40. PENROSE, L. S., *The Biology of Mental Defect,* New York: Grune & Stratton, Inc., 1949.

41. PETRI, E., "Untersuchungen zur Erbbedingtheit der Menarche," *Z. Morph. Anthr.,* 1935, 33:43–48.

42. PLUMMER, G., "Anomalies Occurring in Children Exposed in Utero to the Atomic Bomb in Hiroshima," *Pediatrics,* 1952, 10:687–693.

43. REED, S. C., *Counseling in Medical Genetics,* Philadelphia: W. B. Saunders Company, 1955.

44. REYMERT, M. L., & HOST, H., "Further Data Concerning the Normal Variability of the Menstrual Cycle During Adolescence and Factors Associated with Age of Menarche," *Child Development,* 1947, 18:169–179.

45. REYNOLDS, E. L., "Degree of Kinship and Pattern of Ossification; Longitudinal X-ray Study of Appearance Pattern of Ossification Centers in Children of Different Kinship Groups," *American Journal of Physical Anthropology,* 1943, 1:405–416.

46. ————, & SONTAG, L. W., "The Fels Composite Sheet. II. Variations in Growth Patterns in Health and Disease," *Journal of Pediatrics,* 1945, 26:336–352.

47. ROGERS, M. E., LILIENFELD, A. M., & PASAMANICK, B., *Prenatal and Paranatal Factors in the Development of Childhood Behavior Disorders,* Baltimore, Md.: The Johns Hopkins University School of Hygiene and Public Health, 1955.

48. RUSSELL, D. H., *Children's Thinking,* Boston: Ginn and Company, 1956.

49. SCHEINFELD, A., *The New You and Heredity,* Philadelphia: J. B. Lippincott Company, 1950.

50. SKODAK, M., & SKEELS, H. M., "A Final Follow-up Study of One Hundred Adopted Children," *Journal of Genetic Psychology,* 1949, 75:85–125.

51. STERN, C., "The Chromosomes of Man, in Symposium of Genetics in Medical Research," *Journal of Medical Education,* 1959, 34:310–314.

52. ————, *Principles of Human Genetics,* San Francisco: W. H. Freeman and Company, 1950.

53. TALBOT, N. B., SOBEL, E. H., MCARTHUR, J. W., & CRAWFORD, J. D., *Functional Endocrinology from Birth through Adolescence,* Cambridge: Harvard University Press, 1952.

54. TANNER, J. M., *Growth at Adolescence,* Springfield, Ill.: Charles C. Thomas, 1955.

55. TODD, T. W., "Anthropology and Growth," *Science*, 1935, 81:259–263.

56. WILLIAMS, R. J., *Biochemical Individuality*, New York: John Wiley & Sons, Inc., 1956.

57. ————, *The Human Frontier*, New York: Harcourt, Brace and World, Inc., 1946.

58. ————, *et al.*, "The Concept of Genetotrophic Disease," *Lancet*, 1950, 1:287–289.

59. WRIGHT, S. W., "Phenylketonuria," *Journal of the American Medical Association*, 1957, 165:2079–2083.

60. YAMAZAKI, I. N., *et al.*, "Outcome of Pregnancy in Women Exposed to the Atomic Bomb in Nagasaki," *American Journal of Diseased Children*, 1954, 87:448–463.

CHAPTER

FIVE

↑

*Perception and the Beginning
of Self-awareness*

NOT MANY WEEKS AFTER A BABY'S ADVENT
into this world he begins to manifest an interest in finding the
meaning in things and occurrences around him. The buzzing and
flickering confusion that has surrounded him gradually gives way
to the beginnings of an awareness of interruptions and recur-
rences of sensations and of meaningful relationships among them.
Thus it is with every individual as he enters upon the lifelong
process of "structuring" his world and, in time, of structuring an
impression of himself.

The observation and identification of objects and happenings
in one's world—the attaching of significance to them—this, in
essence, is perception. As we shall note in the readings of this
chapter, perception is an amazingly complex process. There is
much about its explanation that challenges the best efforts of

researchers; there is much about it that deserves the most thought-ful consideration of teachers and others who would try to under-stand the way individuals view their world and themselves.

To the question, "why do things look as they do?" is it suf-ficient to reply, "because that's the way they are"? The discussion by William H. Ittelson, of Brooklyn College, in the first reading will make it quite apparent that so simple an answer is anything but adequate. Ittelson's explanation of the role of the individual's experience in the formation of his perceptions and the related role of his expectations provides a good basis for beginning the study of perception.

The way an individual's world looks to him—how he perceives the objects and events in it—furnishes much of the basis for his decisions and his actions. With the mounting research evidence that points to nonsensory components in perception as well as strictly sensory components, the person who hopes to understand people's judgments and actions must achieve broad perspective in his study of these phenomena. An interesting and highly informa-tive discussion of perceptual determinants that have no material existence is that of A. Irving Hallowell in the second reading of this chapter. Hallowell is Professor of Anthropology, University of Pennsylvania.

The experiment by Jerome S. Bruner and Cecile C. Goodman, of Harvard University, is especially notable for the impetus it has given to studies of the influence of an individual's values upon his perceptions. The experiment was focused on the role of *accentuation*—the tendency for objects to be perceptually more vivid to the individual as they possess, for him, greater amounts of social value. The evidence that such a relationship holds sug-gests important modifications in older explanations of perception.

Finally, in the selection from L. Joseph Stone and Joseph Church the question is confronted of how the infant progresses from his initial, nonperceiving responses to his surroundings, through the beginning stages of awareness of objects and activi-ties, and onward toward the discovery of himself as a separate and—for him at least—highly significant entity. Professors Stone and Church are members of the staff of the Department of Child Study, Vassar College.

There is much ground to be covered between the moments in self-discovery described by Stone and Church and the individual's arrival at an enduring self-concept as presented in Chapter Fourteen of this book. But the reader will benefit from anticipating the relationship that obtains between the kinds of experiences Stone and Church describe and those that are central to the discussion in Chapter Fourteen.

——▶ **William H. Ittelson**

The Involuntary Bet

From *Vogue*, March 15, 1952, pp. 76–77, 127. Copyright © 1952 The Condé Nast Publications Inc. Reprinted by permission.

How and why do we see the people and things around us? Trying to answer this question—technically called the study of perception—may seem at first glance to be a trivial task. But understanding this simple fact, perhaps just because it is one of the most universal and basic of human experiences, is by no means simple. Ask yourself, for example, why the chair across the room looks the way it does. And does it look the same to someone else? If not, how can either of you know what it really is like? Or how can you ever come to any sort of agreement or decision about the chair? It is just such questions as these that psychologists studying perception are trying to answer. And while they may seem trivial when asked about a chair, their importance is obvious if we ask them of more complicated perceptions, such as those of the men about a conference table in the United Nations.

Of all the work being done in the study of perception today, beyond any doubt the most fascinating is that of a scientist in Hanover, New Hampshire, Adelbert Ames, Junior, who is today actively collaborating with some of the members of the psychology department at Princeton University in designing new experiments and extending our understanding of this important no-man's-land, the psychology of perception. In commenting on Ames's work, Dr. Allan Gregg, vice-president of the Rockefeller Foundation, has said, as quoted in a recent book, *The Rockefeller Foundation,* by R. B. Fosdick, "I think Ames will be rediscovered in future years as often as anyone the Medical Sciences Division has aided."

Ames believes that his experiments, four of which are described on these pages, show that every perception we have, even of the chair across the room, is essentially an "involuntary bet." These bets are based on the probabilities each of us has learned through previous experiences with similar situations. To the extent that several people have had similar experiences, they will tend to make the same bets, to see the same things. If they have had different experiences, they will tend to see things differently. And since every perception is basically a bet, it can, like any bet, be wrong on occasion. The only way we can tell if any particular perception, any one bet, is right or wrong is by acting on it. If we are successful, the bet was "right." If we fail, it was "wrong."

1. *The Three Chairs* experiment, from the outside, looks like a big, black box, about the size of two large office desks placed one on top of the other. Along one side of this box are three small peepholes through which one can look into the interior of the box. Looking through each of these peepholes, the observer sees what appears to be the same chair, dimly illuminated inside the completely dark box. The chair seems to be made of heavy wires, but otherwise it looks like an ordinary, solid, well-built chair. The seat is flat, the legs and back are straight, and it sits squarely on the floor. After the observer has noted this through each of the peepholes, he walks to the back of the box, which is open so that he can see what is really inside. To his amazement, he discovers that only one of these objects actually is a wire chair. The other two resemble nothing more than weird wire cobwebs. In each

case, what the observer sees does not correspond to what is really there. The three-dimensional "chairness" which he experiences does not exist in the physical objects at which he is looking. After finding out what is actually in the box, the observer can go back and look through the peepholes again. *He still sees the same solid wire chairs* (Fig. 1).

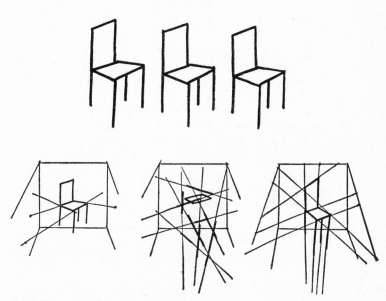

Fig. 1. Upper: Chairs as they appeared to the viewer. Lower: As they actually were made.

2. *The Leaf Room* experiment, as its name suggests, consists of a small room, the inside of which is completely covered with leaves. An observer looks into this room carefully, is allowed to examine it and even to walk in it. He then looks at it while wearing a specially designed pair of aniseikonic glasses which have the peculiar property of altering some of the visual indications he is receiving while not affecting others. Now the room assumes weird and fantastic shapes. The leaves and walls change size and shape and appear to move mysteriously under their own power. The observer becomes confused, bewildered. When asked to walk into the room, he may become terrorized and remain frozen to his seat.

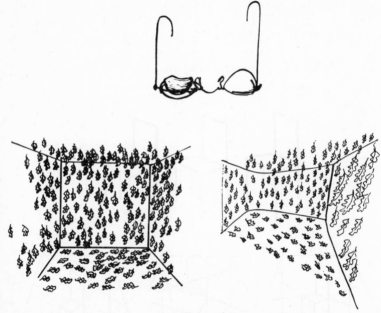

Fig. 2. Leaf room (left), distorted by glasses into nightmare (right).

Even if he does enter the room, he does so hesitatingly. He can not walk steadily. He is unable to touch objects when he reaches for them. He can not very well describe the room because it seems always to be changing.

For most people this experience is quite disturbing and even frightening. It is frequently described as a "nightmare." Sometimes, if the observer looks at an ordinary, familiar room, instead of the "leaf room," the glasses have little or no effect, and the experience is not at all disturbing. Occasionally, an observer seems to enjoy wearing the glasses even in the "leaf room," but this reaction is most often seen in children. For children, wearing the glasses is better than a party. They laugh and squeal as they go through experiences which terrify many adults. They not only do not mind, but they seem actually to delight in having their own world turned topsy-turvy.

It is interesting that in this demonstration, as in everyday life, no matter how confusing the situation may be, no matter how extreme the conflicts, most people manage to make some decision, to arrive at what seems to be the "best bet" under the circumstances (Fig. 2).

3. *The Distorted Room* is a model, about the size of a large packing case, of a crazily built room. The floor slopes down, the ceiling slopes up, and back wall slopes away. All the walls are different sizes and shapes. But this peculiar room has one important property—from one *point of view* it looks like an ordinary rectangular room. The observer is shown the room in detail before he looks at it from the viewing position. He examines its construction, shape, and size carefully until he becomes quite

Fig. 3. Distorted room (left); the illusion of normalcy (right).

familiar with it. No attempt is made to fool him; on the contrary, every effort is made to have him learn all that he can about the room. When the observer is satisfied that he knows the room thoroughly, he sits at the viewing point. The room now appears to be perfectly rectangular while familiar objects, such as a pair of hands, appear distorted. He experiences a conflict between what he sees and what he knows, accompanied by a sense of confusion and uncertainty. Now the observer is given a pointer and told to hit a spot on one of the side walls as if he were swatting a fly. He confidently swings but misses, wildly smashing the pointer into the back wall (Fig. 3).

No matter how much a person knows about the true shape of the room, when asked to do something in it, he acts, not on what he *knows,* but rather on what he *sees.* It would seem, therefore, that the bets we make, which determine what we see, are really guesses as to the probable results of acting in the particular situation. We can check our perceptions, find out if our bets are right or wrong, only through action.

In life's constant sequence of checking by acting, the role of failure, of unsuccessful action, is as important as that of success. Success can only confirm what we already know, while failure points out our inadequacies and opens up opportunities for change and development toward greater adequacy. The over-protected child is a familiar example of a person denied this opportunity by never being allowed to experience the consequences of his own actions.

The way a person reacts to a failure is an indication of that person's potentialities for development and growth. In the distorted room, for example, initial failure in "swatting the fly" quickly makes the observer much more able to act in the room than he ever would have been if he just sat and looked at it. But different people react quite differently. Most observers keep on trying after the first failure, some with grim determination, some with nervous embarrassment, and a few with real, wholehearted enjoyment. At the other extreme are those who refuse to try again at all. A few observers have been known to throw the pointer down and stalk from the experimental room in a fury.

4. *The Rotating Trapezoid* consists of a trapezoidal piece of sheet metal or cardboard, with holes cut in it and shadows painted on it to give the appearance of a window. It is mounted on a rod connected to a motor which rotates it continuously about a vertical axis. When an observer views this device, however, he does not see a rotating trapezoid, but instead an oscillating rectangular window, swinging back and forth through an arc of about 100 degrees. A particularly interesting effect can be seen if a solid tube is inserted in the window through one of the openings. Part of the time the tube and the window appear to be swinging in opposite directions so that at one point they seem to hit head on. Different observers see different things when this

happens. Some see the tube remain absolutely rigid and appear to cut its way through the window frame. To others, the tube seems to be flexible, so that it appears to stretch out and bend around the window. Here is an important laboratory proof that when different people make different "bets" about the same situation they experience that situation differently. *They literally live in different worlds* (Fig. 4).

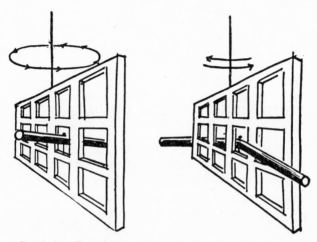

Fig. 4. Actually a revolving object: the illusion (right) an oscillating object.

In one especially interesting experiment using the rotating trapezoid, observers were shown and allowed to feel a steel tube and told that it would be put on the window. They were later shown and handed a rubber tube and told the same thing. Actually a third, wood tube was placed in the window both times. Most observers, however, saw the "steel" tube remain rigid and cut through the window while they saw the "rubber" tube stretch and bend around. Since they had had very little experience in situations like this, the bets they made were quite tentative and easily changed by suggestion or "propaganda."

Such bets are essentially predictions of the results of future actions, based on the probabilities learned from acting in the past. This means that people can pick out of a welter of conflicting possibilities those actions that have the highest probability of being successful. And when we recognize that people never act in a vacuum, that they always act for some purpose of greater or lesser value to them, we can see that the study of perception may eventually help increase our understanding of basic human values.

──────▶ A. Irving Hallowell

Cultural Factors in the Structuralization of Perception

From *Social Psychology at the Crossroads*, by John Rohrer and Muzafer Sherif, editors. New York: Harper & Brothers, 1951; pp. 178–190. Reprinted and abridged by permission.

BELIEF AND PERCEPTION

I shall attempt to demonstrate, by reference to the Northern Ojibwa how entities that have *no* tangible or material existence may become perceptual objects in the actual experience of individuals. That is to say, the reality of what to outsiders are only symbolically mediated and concretely elaborated images may receive perceptual support through the experiences of individuals for whom such entities are reified in an established system of traditional beliefs. Under these conditions it is even predictable, I think, that some persons will not only report perceptual experiences involving such entities, but will *act* as if they belonged in the category of tangible or material objects.

From a descriptive point of view the belief system of the Northern Ojibwa includes several different classes of non-human "spiritual" entities, i.e., orders of sentient beings that are not classed as *Anicinabek* (men-Indians). It will be unnecessary to describe these in detail here since the major point I wish to make is that the Ojibwa themselves distinguish between these orders of being with respect to the manner in which they become manifest to *Anicinabek*. Their most characteristic manifestation is in dreams and the generic term *pawaganak* may be translated as "dream visitors." Furthermore, *pawaganak* become closely associated with an individual in so far as they function as his guardian spirits. He obtains these guardian spirits in the dreams of his puberty fast and he does not expect these particular *pawaganak* to manifest themselves to him in any other way. In short, the Ojibwa does not *expect* to perceive them under the same circumstances as the objects and events of daily life. By cultural definition *pawaganak* are "perceivable" only in the "inner world" of dreams. But if a man is a conjurer, he may call some of his guardian spirits to his conjuring tent where they become audible to other persons. Consequently, it is particularly interesting to note that there is one reified being, the High God, who never becomes the guardian spirit of an individual, nor appears as a "dream visitor," nor becomes an object of perception even in the conjuring tent. The existence of this being is a matter of faith. By cultural definition the High God is not a perceptible object in any context. If any Indian reported that he had seen or heard *kadabendjiget,* his veracity would be challenged, or he might be thought "crazy."

Now in addition to these types of spiritual beings, there is another category of special interest. The Ojibwa believe in the existence of certain animals of exceptionally large size, despite the fact that animals of this type are seldom seen. Among others, there are Big Turtles, Big Snakes, Big Frogs, and Thunder Birds. Although these large animals are classed by the Ojibwa with the other fauna of their habitat, in only one or two cases are there actual species of animals of the same family that differ markedly in size. One example would be the Turtles. In this case, there exists one species of large turtle—along with smaller ones that are called the "younger brothers" of *mikinak*. Considered as a class, therefore, the "big" animals are "mythical" animals from our point of view. What is of special interest, even if confusing to us, is that there is a "mythical" *mikinak,* too. I call attention to this because it is likewise paradoxical that the faunal counterpart of this "mythical" turtle is very rare and seldom *seen* whereas the reified *mikinak* has been *heard* by everyone. For along with other *pawaganak* he speaks, and even sings, in the conjuring tent. [9] In this conjuring rite a small structure is built which conceals the conjurer. He has the power to invoke the *pawaganak* who happens to be among his guardian spirits. They manifest themselves audibly to the Indians who sit on the ground, outside the tent. These *pawaganak* talk and sing like human beings and the dogma is that it is not the conjurer's voice that you hear. From the standpoint of perceptual experience, therefore, the conjuring rite is a device whereby spiritual entities become reified through sound as the sensory medium. Since *mikinak* always has something to say in a conjuring performance, he becomes a familiar figure to everyone. On the other hand, his actual faunal counterpart is scarcely ever seen.

As I have already pointed out, Thunder Birds, Great Snakes, and Great Frogs have no faunal counterparts. But since they are classified with the fauna of the region in the conceptual scheme of the Ojibwa, it follows, logically enough, that these animals *may* be heard, seen, or some other evidence of their "actual" existence be perceived by any one, even though rarely. Rarity of observation is irrelevant to the conviction that animals of this category actually exist.

Among the large animals, Thunder Birds are familiar to everyone because thunder is their cry. They are put in the avian category, moreover, for a very good reason. Their cries are only heard from late spring until early fall, so it is said that they belong in the same class with the Summer Birds who migrate north at this time and leave the country before winter sets in. As a matter of fact, I once compared the meteorological facts on record regarding the occurrence of thunder with the facts on bird migration to this region and there is an almost perfect correlation. [10] So the reification of Thunder Birds like the Great Turtle of the conjuring tent is actually supported by auditory experience, but in a different context. On the other hand, although Thunder Birds may appear to an individual in dreams, they are *rarely* seen. Some years ago there was a man who claimed to have seen *pinesi* (a Thunder Bird) "with his own eyes" when he was about twelve years old. During a severe thunderstorm, he ran out of his tent and there on the rocks lay a strange bird. He ran back to get his parents but when they arrived, the bird had disappeared. He was sure it was *pinesi* but his elders were skeptical because it is almost unheard of to *see* a Thunder Bird. Sometime later the veracity of the boy's experience was clinched when a man who had dreamed of *pinesi* verified the boy's description.

In the case of Big Snakes, Big Frogs, and certain other animals of the same category who are believed to be terrestrial in habitat, it is thought that there are relatively few of them about. And since they are never sought out, like other animals, it is not expected that they will be frequently observed. But there is always the possibility that these animals, or their tracks, may be seen in the most literal sense.

Thus Maman, the best hunter of the Little Grand Rapids Band, a man of high intelligence and vivid imagination as judged both from common sense observation and his Rorschach record,[1] told me he saw one of the Great Snakes when he was hunting moose up a small creek that runs into Family Lake. He was so surprised, he said, that he did not shoot. The creature was moving into the water. He saw the head, which looked something like that of a deer, but without horns. The snake was white around the chin. I asked him about the diameter of the body. "It was as big around as that" he said, pointing to a stove pipe. He said he saw as much of the snake as the diagonal distance across the cabin in which we were sitting at the time, which was about 15-16 feet. The Great Snake moved in a straight path, not this way and that, as the smaller snakes do. I also have another eye-witness account of a Great Snake seen by my informant Chief Berens and his two sons when they were on a hunting trip. Both these accounts document the fact that culturally reified images may, under given conditions, become directive factors in the perceptions of the individual. But these cultural constituents of perception may have much deeper implications than these relatively simple instances demonstrate. For in any given situation they may also evoke deep-seated attitudes and emotions that precipitate action. Cognitive and motivational factors become in-

---

[1] He had an extraordinary number of M's; not only more than any other subject, but excellent in quality..

extricably linked. Great Frogs, for instance, are greatly feared, so
that no one wishes to meet one. On one occasion when four Indians were crossing Lake Winnipeg in a canoe and landed on an
island where they expected to spend the night, one of them discovered what he interpreted as tracks of a Great Frog. His companions examined the tracks and agreed. All of these men became
stricken with fear so although night was approaching and they
had a considerable distance to paddle, nevertheless, they felt
compelled to leave the island at once.

What I should like to stress in this example is the fact that all
of these men were excellent hunters and were accustomed to differentiate the tracks of the various animals that inhabit this
region. Yet *all* of them agreed that the marks they saw indicated
traces of a Great Frog. Hence the significant thing to be noted
is the depth of the affect associated with the conceptualization
of Great Frogs. Once this was touched off, it was impossible for
any of them to examine the tracks on the beach in the *unemo-
tional* way the tracks of the ordinary fur-bearing animal or a
moose or deer would be inspected. And then fear, in turn, made
it inevitable that they should leave the island with the greatest
haste, since the whole perceptual situation became meaningfully
structured in terms of flight. The psychological field in which
these Indians were behaving, although culturally constituted, was
much more complex than the accounts I have cited in the case
of the Great Snakes. Furthermore, the conduct of these men
would be completely *unintelligible,* if viewed or analyzed in
terms of the "objective" situation alone. Their belief in and attitude toward Great Frogs alone give it meaning and explain
their overt conduct.[2] It is a concrete exemplification of the general assertion of MacLeod that: "Purely fictitious objects, events

2 Donald W. MacKinnon in his chapter on Motivation in Boring, E. G.,
Langfeld, H. S., and Weld, H. D., *Introduction to Psychology,* New York: 1939,
p. 159, stresses the need for distinguishing the physical situation, i.e., the environment "considered as having independent real existence" from the psychological field, viz., "the situation as it exists psychologically for the individual." "The psychological field," he goes on to say, "is not to be equated merely
to what is consciously perceived or known but rather to everything that at
the moment determines the behavior of an individual." In the case described
there was no "fearful object" in the situation, objectively viewed; the source
of fear was in the *psychological field.*

and relationships can be just as truly determinants of our behavior as are those which are anchored in physical reality." [18]

As a final example, I wish to discuss another case in which I
happen to have a more detailed personal account of the experience of an Indian who "met" and took flight from a cannibal
giant—a *Windigo*. A belief in such monsters is an integral part
of Northern Ojibwa culture. There are two categories of *Windigowak*. The first comprises actual persons who have turned into
cannibals. In this discussion, I am not concerned with *Windigowak* of this class. The second category consists of mythical
cannibal giants who may be found roaming the country, especially
in the spring, avid for human flesh. They are conceptualized as
horrible in appearance, they have hearts of ice and every time
they call out they get taller so that to hear the shouts of a *windigo*
is enough to make one shudder with fear. Only a few such shouts
and he is taller than the towering spruce which are so characteristic a feature of the landscape.

Both categories of *windigowak* are the focus of a considerable
number of anecdotes. For just as it was considered necessary to
kill actual persons who had turned into cannibals, there are
parallel anecdotes which relate the heroic battles between human beings and monster mythical cannibals. Besides anecdotes
of this sort there are those told in the first person by individuals
who have heard the blood-curdling shouts of a *windigo* in the
bush, or by those who have seen the tracks of such a creature.
The following anecdote of this class is of particular interest with
reference to the total structuralization and functioning of perception since Adam Big Mouth became convinced that a *windigo*
was close by, although he never saw him, and only toward the
end of the anecdote is there any reference to a shout. The circumstances under which an objectively innocuous situation became perceived as an extremely dangerous one can best be conveyed in Adam's own words:

Once in the spring of the year, I was hunting muskrats. The
lake was still frozen, only the river was open, but there was lots
of ice along the shore. When it began to get dark I put ashore and
made a fire close to the water edge to cook my supper. While I
was sitting there I *heard* someone passing across the river. I could

hear the branches cracking. I went to my canoe and jumped in. I paddled as hard as I could to get away from the *noise*. Where the river got a little wider I came to a point that has lots of poplars growing on it. I was paddling quite a distance from the shore when I came opposite to this point. Just then I *heard a sound* as if something was passing through the air. A big stick had been thrown out at me but it did not strike me. I kept on going and paddled towards the other side again. But he went back and headed me off in that direction. This was in the spring of the year when the nights are not so long. He kept after me all night. I was scared to go ashore. Towards morning I reached a place where there is a high rock. I camped there and when it was light I went to set a bear trap. Later that day I came back to the river again. I started out again in my canoe. Late in the evening, after the sun had set, there was a place where I had to portage my canoe over to a lake. I left my canoe and went to see whether the lake was open. There were some open places so I went back to get my canoe. Then I *heard* him again. I carried my canoe over to the lake—it was a big one—and paddled off as fast as I could. When I got to the other end of the lake it was almost daylight. I did not *hear* him while I was traveling. I went ashore and made a fire. After this I *heard* something again. I was scared. "How am I going to get away from him," I thought. I decided to make for the other side of an island in the lake. I was sitting by my canoe and I *heard* him coming closer. I was mad now. He had chased me long enough. I said to myself, "The number of my days has been given me already!" So I picked up my axe and my gun and went in the direction of the *sounds I had heard*. As soon as I got closer to him he made a break for it. I could *hear* him crashing through the trees. Between the shore and the island there was a place where the water was not frozen. He was headed in this diretcion. I kept after him. I could *hear* him on the weak ice. Then he fell in and I *heard* a teriffic yell. I turned back then and I can't say whether he managed to get out or not. I killed some ducks and went back to my canoe. I was getting pretty weak by this time so I made for a camp I thought was close by. But the people had left. I found out later that they had *heard* him and were so scared that they moved away.

In the foregoing anecdote there are thirteen references to *hearing* the *windigo*. Auditory stimuli alone appear to have been the chief *physical* source of the subject's interpretation of the initial presence of a *windigo* and all his *subsequent* overt behavior. In principle, therefore, there is some analogy to a linguistic situation although, in speech sounds, there is a very high order of patterning. But in principle a succession of sounds is heard which, although they are physical stimuli, become significant to the perceiver because they also convey a conventional *meaning*. This meaning is only understood because the perceiver has undergone a learning process which makes the meaning intelligible. And intelligibility in linguistically conveyed meanings always involves concepts. Analogously, the sounds heard by Adam "meant" *windigo* to him. But this was only possible because cannibal monsters were among the traditionally reified concepts and imagery of his culture. Furthermore, just as a word or a sentence may induce an affective response, or immediately define a situation as dangerous and thus call forth appropriate conduct, such was the case here. Once the situation became perceptually structuralized in this way, subsequent sounds likewise became meaningful in terms of the same pattern. I should also like to stress the fact that, at the time, a premise for action became established in terms of which Adam's behavior becomes thoroughly intelligible. It is important to recognize this because we see exemplified in this case, too, the integral relation between perception and action that is characteristic of all organisms. In actual life situations, perceptual responses never occur in a behavioral vacuum. Considered in cross-cultural perspective I think we may say that, in addition to enabling man to adapt himself to a world of physical objects and events, like other animals, perception in our species enables human beings to adjust to a realm of culturally constituted objects as psychologically "real" as other orders of phenomena. Consequently, motivation and appropriate conduct must be judged with reference to a culturally constituted order of reality. Adam's behavior, therefore, was highly appropriate in his own frame of reference.

But there is another side to this coin which may, at first, seem paradoxical. Perception in man may be said to have acquired an overlaid *social* function. For is it not true, that in the light of the foregoing material, perception serves such a function to the extent that it is one of the chief psychological means whereby belief in reified images and concepts as integral parts of a cultural order of reality, are *substantiated* in the experience of individuals? It is through the activity of the same sensory modalities that always have been considered sufficiently reliable in bringing us into contact with the "reality" of the outer world that the "reality" of objects that have their roots in man's inner world are reinforced.

PERSONALITY FACTORS AND PERCEPTION

Part of the psychological interest of Adam Big Mouth's experience with a *windigo* lies in the fact that he himself was responsible for the perceptual structuralization of *this particular situation*. Another Indian in the same objective situation and belonging to the same cultural group may, or may not, have perceived a *windigo*. Consequently, it is inaccurate and misleading, I believe, to speak of cultural *determinism* in such a case. It is for this reason that I have deliberately referred to culturally constituted factors in perception, when speaking of individuals. This leads to a more general question. While given a belief in giant cannibals, it may be predicted that *some* Ojibwa Indians will report perceptual experiences which offer tangible evidence for the actual existence of *windigowak,* are there not selective factors that determine which particular individuals have these experiences under given conditions? I am sure that everyone agrees that there are such factors even though it may be difficult to identify them and to demonstrate their relevance in a given instance. Let us call them idiosyncratic or personal determinants.

Is there any evidence for the operation of such determinants in the case of Adam Big Mouth? I think that there is some evidence, although I do not have sufficient details to push it too far. (a) Adam's father was a very powerful medicine man. (b) He was also one of those who was reported to have *killed* mythical cannibals. (c) Adam was the man who told me more anecdotes about cannibals than anyone else. (d) When he was a small boy Adam had also seen a *windigo* a short distance from where his family was camping. He reported this to his father. (e) Adam's Rorschach record is characterized by the fact that out of a total of thirteen responses he gave a whole answer to each card. This was always his first answer and he responded with considerable rapidity. Furthermore, in his immediate interpretation of each successive blot as a whole Adam was almost unique in my series. And when I add that his wholes were not particularly good ones, I believe that the relevance of his Rorschach performance to his responses in the situation narrated is even more fully evident. His rapid but not too accurate structuralization of an ambiguous situation gave free play to the influence of traditional belief as well as personal determinants.

Although Adam was a conjurer and medicine man too, he did not enjoy the reputation of his father. One might guess that all this indicates that Adam wished to be like his father and to have his power but he had never succeeded in his inner striving for identification. I also suspect that the anecdote I have narrated might be psychologically interpreted to mean that although Adam unconsciously wished to be able to face a *windigo* and kill it as his father had done, he was not quite up to it. He did not have the courage of his father. Nevertheless, he managed to escape from the *windigo* alive. At first he was terrified; ultimately he regained his courage for he says: "I was mad now. He had chased me long enough." So at that point he starts off in the direction of the *windigo* and the *windigo* becomes pursued and falls through the ice! In the end, Adam became a kind of hero to himself, which satisfied an inner need. From the personal angle, therefore, it matters little whether his account is strictly accurate. It is quite possible that he may have elaborated it as time went on. But taken at its face value, his experience not only illustrates cultural factors in the structuralization of perception but, at the same time, personal needs as directive factors in perception.

Another case that illustrates the integral functioning of cultural and idiosyncratic variables has quite a different setting than the one just described. It will serve to demonstrate the importance of directive factors in perception in the area of interpersonal relations among a nonliterate people. On the face of it the facts look very simple. An old man named Kiwetin (North Wind) told me that a married woman who was his neighbor was using sorcery against him. He had been sick and Catherine, he said, was back of it.

From a cultural point of view, therefore, we have a belief in sorcery to consider and the general attitudes it engenders among a people who are convinced of its reality. On the personal side we have to ask: Why did Kiwetin think that Catherine was responsible? Was it simply because she had the reputation of being a witch or were there selective factors of a more idiosyncratic nature rooted in the psychodynamics of his personality? Since I do not have all the necessary facts in this case, including any personal impressions of Catherine, whom I never met, my main purpose in discussing it at all is to use it as a sort of paradigm. I want to call attention to some of the possibilities that the investigation of the role of perception in interpersonal relations affords in a primitive society.

A belief in sorcery, of course, is based on the assumption that human individuals may possess, and exercise at will, malevolent powers against other individuals. Such a belief is found in many human societies. Among the Ojibwa there are certain provincial features that must also be understood. (a) Typically, men rather than women are thought to possess powers of sorcery. If women have magic power they use it principally to protect themselves and their children. (b) Power that can be used malevolently comes from the same sources of power that can be used benevolently, such as curing people who are ill. These sources are the *pawaganak*, already referred to. They are a man's guardian spirits. They confer certain powers upon him and stand ready to do his bidding. (c) Since such powers are acquired in a lonely vigil at puberty, no one can tell how much power another individual has, or whether it enables him to do evil or not. (d) Sorcery, by cultural definition is always practiced covertly. No one ever admits he possesses evil power, or that he has acted malevolently, except under circumstances I need not go into here. The only really tangible evidence of the practice of sorcery is that in some cases of illness, believed to be due to malevolent action of this kind, a special kind of doctor removes an object from the body of the patient—a piece of hair, a quill, a sharp piece of bone.

Among the Ojibwa there are certain obvious psychological consequences of a belief in sorcery. Men in particular are wary of one another; they cannot fully trust each other. For sorcery is always a potential threat to the central value of these people—*pimadazi-*

win—Life, in the sense of longevity and freedom from illness and misfortune. Interpersonal relations are affectively toned by suspicions that may arise from the manner, tone, facial expression, gestures, attitudes, and conduct of persons with whom an individual is associated in daily life. There is always a latent anxiety that can be easily aroused because sorcery is believed to exist and may threaten *pimadaziwin*. If I fall ill my anxiety increases, because someone may have bewitched me. In consequence I am highly motivated to reflect upon the whole matter, my purpose being to discover *who* it might be. To arrive at a satisfactory answer I have to have some evidence on the basis of which I can make a judgment. So I appeal to the "evidence of my senses." Where else, indeed, could I turn?

The chief point I want to emphasize is the important psychological fact that the Ojibwa have to pick out sorcerers for themselves. With reference to our central topic we may ask: What kind of perceptual evidence becomes important in the identification of a particular sorcerer? And what kind of directive factors influence perception? The situation would be quite different, of course, in a society where there was a cultural definition of the traits of sorcerers or even where ordeals of a public nature were customary so that an accused individual could be put to some test. Where ordeals exist, everyone can see for himself whether an accused sorcerer passes the test or fails. But among the Ojibwa sorcery itself is not only covert. If I am sick I may privately make up my mind who is responsible and take whatever measures I see fit. If I have any power myself, I may sorcerize my enemy covertly in turn. This is the essence of the situation. So it is easy to see how in this sort of socio-psychological field it is inevitable that projective mechanisms will operate with the utmost freedom. There are culturally constituted barriers to any kind of reality testing.

Returning now to the particular case I mentioned, there are several facts to be noted which seem to me to have special importance. In the first place, Catherine, although I never saw her, was, from all accounts, an unusual woman. She was even notorious. She was large in size, terrifically dynamic for an Indian woman, and she had had many husbands. Besides this, many Indians were convinced that she had a knowledge of sorcery which, in itself, made her unusual. Kiwetin at the time of which I speak was a widower, living by himself. I had gone to see him because he had once been active in the *Midewiwin* whose major function was curative. He was a medicine man reputed to have considerable power. How did Kiwetin arrive at the conclusion that *Catherine* was using sorcery against him? In the first place he had been sick. Since he did not respond at once to the medicine used, his suspicions became aroused. Someone must be using malevolent power against him. But why Catherine? What struck me so forcibly when Kiwetin told me his story was the kind of evidence he regarded as decisive. It was the woman's *outward display of amiability and kindness toward him* that made him think she had malevolent intentions. She smiled pleasantly at him. But he knew this was put on. "It was only on her face, not in her mind," he said. She also had invited him into her house to have something to eat. But he always refused. She might put something in his food. The selection of outward amiability as evidence of covert malevolence in this instance is not unique. I have heard the same thing in one or two other cases. On one occasion when I heard a rumor that one old man was a very wicked sorcerer, I naïvely said, "But he is such a nice old man." "That's just it," my informant said, "That's why you have to watch him." I do not wish to create the impression that outward amiability among the Ojibwa is *institutionalized* as indicative of malevolent intentions. This is far from being the case. What is interesting is the fact that what might be supposed to be a universal expression of positive attitudes in interpersonal relations may be perceived as having a completely negative meaning. How far it would be possible to institutionalize a negative appraisal of *all* expressions of kindness and amiability in any culture is a nice question. In the case of Catherine, I may add, I think there is good reason to believe that, in reality, there was no actual malevolence involved.

This leads us to a consideration of directive factors of a purely idiosyncratic nature that may have been responsible for Kiwetin's "choice" of a witch. What finally clinched the whole matter for Kiwetin was the fact that, in a dream, one of his *pawagan* informed him that Catherine was responsible for his illness. This suggests that unconscious as well as conscious forces were operating in the same direction. This fact is of importance because, as I pointed out in the beginning, men, rather than women, are the chief manipulators of malevolent power. So why choose a woman? My hypothesis would be that Kiwetin's choice of Catherine was involved with his basic psychosexual adjustment. His interpretation of the whole situation was a projection on his part which served as an effective personal defense against Catherine, whom he could not help seeing and being aware of constantly since she was his neighbor. At the conscious level, therefore, he made use of a belief well-entrenched in his culture, backed up, of course, by the "evidence of his senses," to build up a rationalization that enabled him to avoid her and condemn her. Unconsciously, I have no doubt, he was fearful of women and Catherine in particular, while at the same time he was attracted to her.

In this case, therefore, we find perception linked to complex personal needs which influence it selectively. At the same time we see another instance in which perception served a social function in so far as it helped to corroborate the belief that witches, even if unusual, existed. Faced with the same personal problem, in some other culture, Kiwetin would have had to make use of some other means of rationalization. Defense mechanisms and perception are universal processes in human adjustment. Culturally available means are local and variable. But in the whole adjustment process the central role which perception plays is evident. Perception is made the basis of judgment, decision, action. Abstractly stated, this is an old axiom in psychology. A case such as the foregoing suggests that the kind of judgments made, the nature of the decisions arrived at, and the consequences in terms of motivation and conduct are related to both cultural and idiosyncratic variables. Consequently, the dynamics of perception are not entirely clear if we do not approach the whole problem in a fashion that enables us to take account of non-sensory as well as sensory determinants.

An inclusive approach such as is now being more systematically pursued than formerly, and which stresses functional factors, is directly relevant to a deeper understanding of the role of cultural factors in the structuralization of perception and even necessary for the explanation of concrete behavior in cross-cultural perspective.

——→ **Jerome S. Bruner
and Cecile C. Goodman**

Value and Need as Organizing Factors in Perception[1]

From *Journal of Abnormal and Social Psychology*, 1947, 42:33–44. Reprinted and abridged by permission. The reader will find a review of the related literature by referring to the original source.

Throughout the history of modern psychology, until very recent times, perception has been treated as though the perceiver were a passive recording instrument of rather complex design. One might, in most experiments, describe him in much the same graphical terms as one uses to describe the latest piece of recording apparatus obtainable from Stoelting or the American Optical Company. Such psychology, practiced as it were *in vitro*, has fallen short of clarifying the nature of *perception* in everyday life much as did the old nerve-muscle psychophysiology fall short of explaining *behavior* in everyday life. Both have been monumentally useful—in their place. The names of Weber, Fechner, Wundt, Titchener, Hecht, and Crozier are safely ensconced in any respectable psychological hall of fame. But their work, like the work of the nerve-muscle men, is only a beginning.

For, as Professor Thurstone [28] has put it, "In these days when we insist so frequently on the interdependence of all aspects of personality, it would be difficult to maintain that any of these functions, such as perception, is isolated from the rest of the dynamical system that constitutes the person." The problem is, indeed, to understand how the process of perception is affected by other concurrent mental functions and how these functions in

---

1 The writers are greatly indebted to Pauline B. Hahn and Dr. Leo J. Postman for invaluable assistance and advice.

their turn are affected by the operation of perceptual processes. Given a dark room and a highly motivated subject, one has no difficulty in demonstrating Korte's Laws of phenomenal movement. Lead the subject from the dark room to the market place and then find out what it is he sees moving and under what conditions, and Korte's Laws, though still valid, describe the situation about as well as the Laws of Color Mixture describe one's feelings before an El Greco canvas.

It is the contention of this paper that such perceptual phenomena are as scientifically measurable in terms of appropriate metrics as such more hallowed phenomena as flicker fusion, constancy or tonal attributes. But let us pause first to construct a sketchy terminology. Let us, in what ensues, distinguish heuristically between two types of perceptual determinants. These we shall call *autochthonous* and *behavioral*. Under the former we group those properties of the nervous system, highly predictable, which account for phenomena like simple pair formation, closure, and contrast, or at another level, tonal masking, difference and summation tones, flicker fusion, paradoxical cold, and binaural beats. Given ideal "dark-room" conditions and no compelling distractions, the "average" organism responds to set physical stimuli in these relatively fixed ways. Autochthonous determinants, in brief, reflect directly the *characteristic* electrochemical properties of sensory end organs and nervous tissue.

Under the category of *behavioral* determinants we group those active, adaptive functions of the organism which lead to the governance and control of all higher-level functions, including perception: the laws of learning and motivation, such personality dynamics as repression, the operation of quasi-temperamental characteristics like introversion and extraversion, social needs and attitudes, and so on. Underlying these behavioral determinants, doubtless, are a host of physiological mechanisms. But we can hardly wait until we understand these before tackling experimentally the role of behavioral determinants in perception. The physiology of Weber's Law is still more or less obscure, yet the enunciation of it has been recognizably useful—even to the physiologist for whom it has been a challenge to discovery.

The organism exists in a world of more or less ambiguously

organized sensory stimulation. What the organism sees, what is *actually there* perceptually represents some sort of compromise between what is presented by autochthonous processes and what is selected by behavioral ones. Such selection, we know, is determined not only by learning, as already indicated, but also by motivational factors such as have been indicated for hunger by Sanford [24, 25] and Levine, Chein, and Murphy. [17] The selective process in perception we shall refer to as a *perceptual hypothesis,* using the term with Krechevsky [14], to denote a systematic response tendency. Such an hypothesis may be set into operation by a need, by the requirements of learning a task, or by any internally or externally imposed demands on the organism. If a given perceptual hypothesis is rewarded by leading to food, water, love, fame, or what not, it will become *fixated;* and the experimental literature, notably the work of Ellson [7] and Leeper [16], indicates that the fixation of "sensory conditioning" is very resistant to extinction. As fixation takes place, the perceptual hypothesis grows stronger not only in the sense of growing more frequent in the presence of certain types of stimulation, but also more perceptually *accentuated.* Perceptual objects which are habitually selected become more vivid, have greater clarity or greater brightness or greater apparent size.

Two other systematic matters must concern us before we turn to the experiments. One has to do with perceptual *compromise,* the other with perceptual *equivocality.* Frequently, alternative hypotheses operate: a quick glimpse of a man in gray on a European battlefield may leave us in doubt as to whether he is a civilian or a Wehrmacht infantryman. Almost inevitably one or the other hypothesis prevails, and the field is perceived as either one or the other. But in spite of the dominance of a single hypothesis in perception, *compromise* also occurs. Using Ansbacher's experiments [2] as an example, a group of small paper squares is seen both in terms of number and in terms of value as stamps. What results, if you will, is a perception of "number-value." We know precious little about such perceptual compromises, although we shall be discussing experiments demonstrating their operation.

As for *equivocality,* or ambiguity in the perceptual field, it has generally been supposed that the greater the equivocality the greater the chance for behavioral factors in perception to operate, all other things being equal. Sherif [26] chose the autokinetic phenomenon to work with for this reason. Proshansky and Murphy [23] worked close to threshold illumination with similar intent. Within broad limits, which we shall discuss, the generalization is valid, in so far as equivocality reduces the organizing capacity of autochthonous perceptual determinants. How important this generalization is we, who think so exclusively in terms of the well-controlled dark-room experiment, often forget. For in everyday life, perception is, by and large, a series of quick looks, glances, inattentive listenings, furtive touches. Save for what is at the very focus of interested attention, the world of sense is more equivocal than our textbook writers seem to think.

EMPIRICAL HYPOTHESES

We may turn now to the experiments with which this paper is primarily concerned. Three general hypotheses, growing out of the systematic principles just presented, are under consideration.

1. *The greater the social value of an object, the more will it be susceptible to organization by behavioral determinants.* It will be *selected* perceptually from among alternative perceptual objects, will become *fixated* as a perceptual response tendency, and will become perceptually *accentuated*.

2. *The greater the individual need for a socially valued object, the more marked will be the operation of behavioral determinants.*

3. *Perceptual equivocality will facilitate the operation of behavioral determinants only in so far as equivocality reduces the operation of autochthonous determinants without reducing the effectiveness of behavioral determinants.*

In the experiments reported here, only one aspect of behavioral determination will be treated, what we have called *accentuation* —the tendency for sought-after perceptual objects to become more vivid. Perceptual selectivity and fixation have already been demonstrated in other experiments, though they remain poorly systematized. For purposes of economy of exposition we omit consideration of them here, though they constitute important variables in the broader research project of which the present experiments are a part.

The Subjects and the Apparatus

The subjects were 30 ten-year-old children of normal intelligence, divisible according to certain characteristics to be discussed shortly into three groups, two experimental and one control. The apparatus consisted of a rectangular wooden box (9" x 9" x 18") at one end of which was a 5" square ground-glass screen and a knob at its lower right-hand corner. At the center of the ground-glass screen was an almost circular patch of light (16.2 app. ft. cdls.) cast upon the back of the screen by a 60-watt incandescent light shining through an iris diaphragm which could be varied in diameter from ⅛" to 2" by turning the knob on the front end of the box. All that was visible to the subject was the box with its ground-glass screen and the circle of light whose diameter he could change by turning the knob. The circle was not truly round, containing the familiar nine elliptoid sides found in the Bausch & Lomb iris diaphragm. It was so close to round, however, that subjects had no difficulty making the subjective equations required of them.

Subjects individually sat in a chair in front of the screen on the box with the light circle slightly below eye level. The box rested on a table behind which sat the experimenter. The child was told that this was a game, and that he was to make the circle of light on the box the same size as various objects he was shown or told about. Before beginning judgments, each child, with no urging, was encouraged to see how large and small the circle of light could be made.

The two experimental groups received the same treatment. Two series were run for these groups, comprising 20 of the children in all. First the child was asked to estimate the sizes of coins from a penny through a half dollar from memory. He did the first in ascending order of value, then in descending order, always making two judgments for each coin named, one from the open, the other from the closed position of the iris diaphragm. Four judgments were made for each coin by each child. No inkling was given the child as to how "close" he had come.

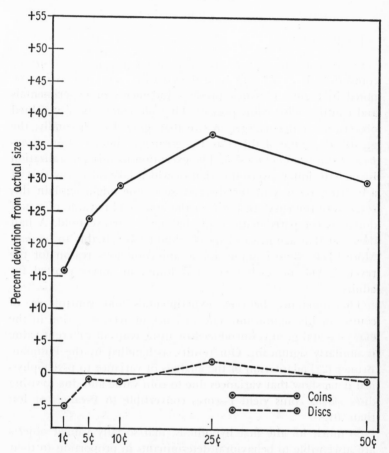

Fig. 1. Size estimations of coins and discs of same size made by ten-year-olds. (Method of average error)

Following the memory series, and using the same order of presentation, a similar series was then run with coins present. Coins, individually, were held close to the center of the palm of the left hand, at a level with the light circle and six inches to its left. The subjects took as much time as suited them.

A control group of ten subjects followed a procedure identical with the one just described. Instead of coins, medium gray cardboard discs of identical size were employed. No mention of money was made to this group.

RESULTS

Let us compare the difference between judgments of size of coins and identically sized cardboard discs. Two things can be noted in Figure 1, which presents judgments of experimentals and controls with coins present. First off, coins, socially valued objects, are judged larger in size than gray discs. Secondly, the greater the value of the coin, the greater is the deviation of *apparent* size from *actual* size. The exception to this generalization is the half dollar, overestimation of which falls off below that of a quarter. By way of the sheerest guess one might explain this reversal of the curve in terms of the lesser reality-value of a half dollar as compared with a quarter for the ten-year-old. A half dollar at that age is, so to speak, almost too valuable to be real! More likely there is some simple autochthonous reason for the reversal. Yet, no such reversal is found in curves plotted for adults.

The difference between experimentals and controls is, of course, highly significant. The variance in overestimation in the experimental groups introduced by using coins of different value is similarly significant. Our results, as handled by the Postman-Bruner [22] adaptation of the analysis of variance to psychophysical data, show that variances due to coin value and due to using discs *versus* coins yield F-scores convertible to P-values of less than .01.[2]

So much for the first hypothesis, that socially valued objects are susceptible to behavioral determinants in proportion to their value. Consider now the second hypothesis, that the greater the

---

2 P-values at the .01 level were also found for constant errors introduced by ascending and descending value orders and for judgments made from the open and closed positions of the diaphragm. Since these parameters were controlled and valanced in the judgment data for the groups discussed, nothing further need be said of them here. They will be discussed in another place. [6] Analysis of variance was carried out both with percentage scores representing deviation of individual judgments from actual size and with raw scores. Necessary corrections suggested by Snedecor [27] were used in the former method. The values presented here are applicable to both raw and percentage scores.

subjective need for a socially valued object, the greater will be the role of behavioral determinants of perception. In the second experimental variation, the experimental group was divided into two component groups. One we call the *rich* group, the other the *poor* group, each comprising ten subjects. Well-to-do subjects were drawn from a progressive school in the Boston area, catering to the sons and daughters of prosperous business and professional people. The poor subjects came from a settlement house in one of Boston's slum areas. The reasonable assumption is made that poor children have a greater subjective need for money than rich ones. When the figures presented in Figure 1 are broken down into scores for rich and poor groups, a striking difference will be noted (Figure 2). The poor group overestimates the size of coins considerably more than does the rich. Again there are some irregularities in the curves. The drop-off for the half dollar we have already sought to explain. As for the dip in the rich group's curve at a dime, the explanation is problematical. All curves which we have plotted for adults—and by now we have collected more than two thousand judgments [6]—show this dip. Perhaps it is due to the discrepancy between the relative size and value of the dime, perhaps to some inherent characteristic of the coin itself.[3]

The difference between rich and poor is highly significant, analysis of variance showing that the source of variance is significant beyond the P level of .01. Our second hypothesis cannot, then, be rejected. It is notable too that the interaction between the parameters of economic status and value of coins yields an F-score convertible to a P-value between .05 and .01 which leads to a secondary hypothesis: given perceptual objects of the same class but varying in value, the effect of need for that class of objects will be to accentuate the most valuable objects most, the least valuable least, etc.

What of ambiguity or perceptual equivocality? We have arbitrarily assumed that a situation in which one is judging size from

---

[3] If the reader is a smoker, let him ask himself whether a dime will cover the hump on the camel which appears as a trademark on Camel cigarettes. Hold the two six inches apart. In spite of the apparently small size of the coin it will cover the camel's hump with margin to spare.

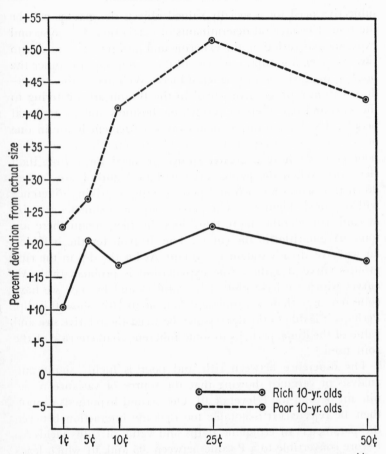

Fig. 2. Size estimations of coins made by well-to-do and poor ten-years-olds.
(Method of average error)

memory is more "equivocal" than one in which the object being judged is in clear view six inches away from the test patch. The assumption is open to serious question, but let us examine what follows from it experimentally. Compare first the judgments of the rich group under conditions like those described: with coin present as compared with coin as a mere memory image. The curves are in Figure 3. It would seem that, for all values below a quarter, equivocality has the effect of making judgments conform more to actual size, aiding, in other words, the operation of autochthonous determinants. For values over a quarter, equivocality favors behavioral factors, making apparent size diverge still more from actual size. For the rich group, with coin *present,* a half dollar is overjudged by 17.4 per cent; with coin *absent,* by 34.7 per cent.

This finding is difficult to interpret by itself. Consider now Figure 4, showing the discrepancy in "absent" and "present" judgments for the poor group. Here there is no crossing. Equivo-

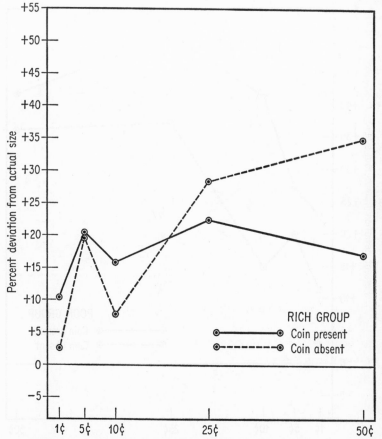

Fig. 3. Size estimations of coins with coins present and from memory by well-to-do ten-year-olds.

(Method of average error)

cality seems, in this group, to have the exclusive effect of bringing judgments down toward actual size. Equivocality even brings out the "dime dip" in the poor group. How account for the difference? Why does equivocality liberate behavioral determinants among the rich children for higher values, and depress these factors for poor children? We can offer nothing but a guess, one which needs confirmation by further research. Some years ago, Oeser [19] reported that in his study of children in Dundee he

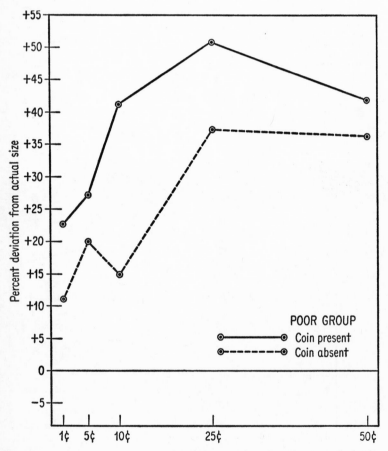

Fig. 4. Size estimations of coins with coins present and from memory by poor ten-year-olds.

(Method of average error)

TABLE 1

PERCENTAGE DEVIATION FROM ACTUAL SIZE OF JUDGMENTS OF COINS
AND DISCS UNDER VARIOUS CONDITIONS

Group and Condition	Penny	Nickel	Dime	Quarter	Half-dollar	Number Judgments per Coin
20 O's coin present	16.5	23.9	29.1	37.0	29.6	80
20 O's coin absent	7.2	19.6	11.6	32.8	35.8	80
10 O's disc present	—5.4	—.9	—1.5	1.8	—.8	40
10 rich O's coin present	10.3	20.4	16.3	22.4	17.4	40
10 rich O's coin absent	2.6	19.8	7.8	28.3	34.7	40
10 poor O's coin present	22.7	27.3	41.8	51.6	42.0	40
10 poor O's coin absent	11.8	19.4	15.4	37.3	36.9	40

found the fantasy life of the children of the unemployed strikingly choked off. Asked what they would like to be when grown, normal children of employed parents gave such glamorous replies as cowboy or film star, while children of the unemployed named the rather lowly occupations traditionally followed by members of their class. In the figures just presented, it is our contention that we are witnessing the same phenomenon. In the case of the poor children, judging coin size from memory, a weakened fantasy is substituted for the compelling presence of a valued coin, while among rich children equivocality has the effect of liberating strong and active fantasy.[4]

Are any other explanations available to account for the shape of the curves we have been concerned with here? Weber's Law

---

[4] The difference between rich and poor children in their size judgments of "absent" and "present" coins as here discussed is statistically significant. The interaction variance for these two parameters (economic status and presence-absence of coins) is at the .01 level of significance.

would predict in all cases a straight line plot parallel to the axis representing actual size. DL should be a constant fraction of the stimulus, whatever its magnitude. If one were to treat the slope of the curves by reference to Hollingworth's central-tendency effect [11], one should find a negative rather than a positive slope. All values smaller than the center of the series should appear larger in size; all larger than the center of the series, smaller. Assuming that the Hollingworth effect is mediated by autochthonous factors, then it represents one more autochthonous factor outweighed by the behavioral determinants discussed in the course of this paper.

In conclusion, only one point need be reiterated. For too long now, perception has been virtually the exclusive domain of the Experimental psychologists with a capital *E*. If we are to reach an understanding of the way in which perception works in everyday life, we social psychologists and students of personality will have to join with the experimental psychologists and reexplore much of this ancient field of perception whose laws for too long have been taken for granted.

⸻▶ **L. Joseph Stone
and Joseph Church**

The Infant's Perception of the World and the Beginning of Self-awareness

From *Childhood and Adolescence*, by L. Joseph Stone and Joseph Church. © Copyright 1957 by Random House Inc. Reprinted and abridged by permission.

HOW THE INFANT PERCEIVES HIS WORLD

The baby's experience of reality is at first global and undifferentiated. It develops, just like embryonic structures and like motor skills, from the general and diffuse to the specific and precise, by a series of differentiations followed by reorganizations and functional subordinations.

Infant and Adult Views of Reality

We can perhaps best make clear the character of infantile experience by contrasting it with the more familiar adult forms. In early, global experience, almost everything is like the adult's perceptual *background*, of which he is almost unaware while he is concentrating on something; out of this only the vaguest objects come and go and melt into each other. For the adult, this kind of experience—background without foreground—is all but unrecapturable except in dream-like states. Central in adult experience is the distinction between "me" and "rest-of-the-world." This distinction does not exist in early infancy; self and environment are one. For the adult, both the "me" and the "rest-of the world" have been still further differentiated. The me of the adult is both a body-me and a person-me which knows about "my" body. The things that happen in the body-me are recognized as "my" aches and pains and pleasures and appetites and needs. The things that happen in the person-me are "my" feelings and ideas and memories and plans. The rest-of-the-world is differentiated into people and not-people; into different kinds of people, into different kinds of things. There is a further differentiation in the adult's world between objects and their settings.

Moreover, when reality becomes differentiated, its newly distinguishable segments become related to each other in new integrations. The adult has a kind of many-dimensioned map or ground plan of the world he moves in, a sense that it exists even if he is not there. For the adult (but not at all for the infant) objects exist in an organized world in which he distinguishes (fairly well) reality and fantasy, as well as up and down and sideways, or past, present, and future. In addition, some objects exist in a social network with countless subtle relationships of blood, respect, duty, affection, envy, role, status, power, etc. Possibly most important for human experience, perceptual reality—and unreality—exists for the adult not only as a theater of action but as something to be talked about and thought about.

In earliest infantile experience, the world is only a diffuse field with objects coming and going but without a fixed framework. To begin with, events or objects come into the baby's awareness in terms of immediate threat or gratification to him. Soon after, there may be connections between things, but the connection is always personal, through the infant. [For example,] orange juice may signify that a bath will follow, but these are related as things that happen to *him* in close succession, and not as events in a world which includes his mother's schedule, too. The baby's experience is *personal*, as we have said, because, after all, it is only his own hunger and wetness and pleasures that he has any knowledge of. But there is no me until a me (the *self*) has emerged as an entity from the total welter of experience. In effect, the whole world is wet and hungry, because "I" and "rest-of-the-world" are, as yet, one. This state of affairs, where all the child's universe is centered upon him, without his being aware of himself at the center, has been named *egocentrism* by Piaget. [21] This term is rather misleading because it implies an *ego*—a self—but it is intended to indicate the infant's isolation within his own experence before he knows of a me or of a world with an existence apart from him. This term has occasioned a great deal of controversy, usually based on a misinterpretation of its meaning.

Perceptual Development

Now that we have seen some of the contrasts between infantile and adult perceptual experience, let us concentrate on the way the baby's experience develops. For the first few weeks of his life, the infant is enclosed within the immediacy of his own body (although, it is now clear, he does not recognize it as his own). His eyes and ears are in good working order—he may stare at things or seem to be listening—but the information they bring him is negligible. As we have said, his experiencing is like the adult's background-of-awareness except when there is a sharp, sudden increase in the intensity of light or sound, producing a startle response. In general, the newborn baby seems to be aware only of considerable disruptions of his equilibrium—hunger, pain, loud noise—that is, his first perceptions are identical with a feeling that something is dreadfully wrong. When he is in equilibrium—when his stomach is comfortably full and his digestion working smoothly, when he is warm and snugly wrapped and supported—his awareness seems to fade out, and he drifts into sleep. As both Bridges and Spitz have pointed out, events are either distressing or neutral. [5]

Beginning at the age of a few weeks, he seems to become aware of the process of gratification of his needs as well as of the needs themselves. His feelings and his perceptions, still intimately linked, are becoming differentiated by one further step: instead of the simple distinction between distress and neutrality that marked his experience as a newborn, he now knows distress, neutrality, and pleasure. At the same time, his awareness of threat (will hunger never end?) and gratification (how wonderful the warm flow in my mouth and insides) begins to expand, including now in an ill-formed way the recognition that it is Person (not *a* person, not *people*) who holds and feeds and fondles him. His awareness of pleasure seems still to be centered in his mouth and stomach, but is enhanced by the movements of rocking, by the things that touch his skin, and, after a couple of months, by the sight of the faces that hover over him, and the sound of voices that murmur reassuringly, and somehow includes all these experiences in the initial person-awareness.

What this says is that the baby *first perceives emotional significances*. At the beginning it is the meaning of threat and gratification, and not body states or external objects, that is perceived. Objectively, a cross and a circle should be easier to tell apart than two human faces, or than a smiling face and a frowning one; but long before the baby can differentiate a cross from a circle, he can tell his mother's face from all other women's faces, and his mother's smiling face from his mother's face wearing a frown, because these have emotional significance for him. It is important to see that *meanings* always precede *objects* in perception. We begin to mobilize our responses to objects before we become aware of the objects themselves, and the way we perceive an object is determined as much by our response (that is, what the object *mean*s to us) as by the object's stimulus properties. In the adult, perceptual processes are highly skilled and almost instantaneous —provided he is not dealing with wholly novel situations—but it can be demonstrated in the laboratory that even adults require a tiny interval of time for their perceptions to take shape from the meaning of an object to the object itself. For instance, adults distinguish the threatening quality of words that have previously been accompanied by an electric shock when these words are again flashed on a screen at speeds too fast to be seen as anything more than a blur. [15] It is as though the baby could not yet go beyond this first stage in adult perception, where only the emotional meanings appear.

The meaning of an object for the baby is defined first of all by what it can do to him; at about three or four months of age, when the baby can grasp and handle objects and bring them to his mouth, objects come to be defined by what he can do with them. In other words, at about the time people often say that the baby is "becoming human," there is a beginning shift from a passive to an active relationship with reality. But it is essential to note that throughout infancy only those objects, and only those aspects of objects, which have some behavioral meaning, some functional relevance, become differentiated for the baby. Infants usually do not discriminate the colors we adults consider vividly obvious. But if six-month-old babies are fed a pleasant-tasting formula from a red bottle and an unpleasant-tasting one from a blue bottle, they quickly learn to accept the red bottle and reject the blue one. [28] In other words, when previously undifferentiated aspects of reality are made functionally important, then they may be differentiated and perceived. That is, the baby perceives only what Werner calls *action-objects* rather than things in themselves. [29] We see the same tendency at work in the preschool child's definition, "a chair is to sit."

In the same way, as the baby becomes able to move around, he comes to inhabit an action-space—differentiated by his activities in it. A stairway is largely meaningless, and essentially nonexistent, to a six-month-old; but for a one-year-old a stairway has strongly appealing action qualities: it is something to be climbed. In other words, with the shift from a passive to an active orientation toward the world, emotional meanings emerge as more elaborate action-meanings, which become as variegated as the behavior of which the baby is capable. The baby is liberated from strictly biological concerns and becomes susceptible to "esthetic" (what does this toy feel like, and sound like, and taste like?) and "intellectual" (what can I do with it) appeals: he becomes curious. Again we see that earlier psychological views of the independence of perception, of action, and of emotion must be questioned. Perception (the perceived world) grows out of emotions, as we have seen; it grows out of behavior, too.

Although the baby becomes active with regard to objects, he still has to rely on the objects to tell him what to do. What they tell him depends on three things: (a) their action possibilities (stairs are to climb); (b) the baby's general readiness for action of the kind suggested by the object (stairs aren't anything at all if I'm too young to climb them); and (c) his momentary state (stairs mean a lot more to me when I'm not hungry; they're not very attractive when I've been on them ten times in a row). But when an object does tell the baby to act, he cannot refuse. This means that he is highly distractible, and if he is exposed to excessive stimulation—too many new toys, too many new people, too much activity—he may be pulled in all directions at once and start to cry in confusion. Goldstein has given the name "stimulus-bound" to this inability to turn away from the solicitation of objects. [18]

It is worth noting that action-objects, although rich in vitality and meaning, are lacking in continuity and solidity. Up to the age of about four months, when an object breaks contact with the baby, it ceases to exist. If the rattle he is watching disappears behind his carriage top, he may stare for a moment at the point where it vanished and then forget about it. If the bottle from which he is being fed goes out of reach and sight, he will shriek with dismay. After four or five months of age, he will be tense with the expectation that the rattle or bottle will reappear, but he will not look for it. By about six months, he will begin to look to see where something has gone. By this time, certain objects have taken on some degree of permanence and reliability, notably his mother and his own body—although these may not be clearly differentiated from each other. He now counts on the bundle of warm sensations and visual patterns that other people see as his mother to continue existing even when she is absent. Although his mother may now exist for him as a stable identity, he still may not recognize her when she is dressed up to go to a party. He is becoming aware that those two tiny hands tugging at each other under his nose, carrying each other to his mouth, belong to the same intimate complex of feelings as the mouth that chews on them, the eyes that look at them, as the feet that rise up over the horizon of his belly and are quickly held captive by the ever-active fingers. A little later, at seven or eight months, perhaps, he is fascinated by the behavior of objects that he bangs together as though sampling their solidity, but he still cannot understand why *it hurts* (him) when he kicks the bars of his crib. It is at about this time that he seems to begin to know what he wants. His awareness of his own distress is becoming more differentiated, and he has a better idea of what behaviors of his and what objects are necessary for gratification. All in all, he is developing a rudimentary *frame of reference*—although still essentially a "self"-centered one. In terms of this frame of reference, he has expectations. For instance, when he is hungry and his mother carries him past the door of the room where he usually eats, he gives a sudden start, becomes tense, and may begin to cry or whimper.

Along with this increased permanence of objects and growing stability of organization of his world, there goes a shift toward the *dominance of visual perception*—a shift that may not reach completion before adulthood. This shift has two aspects. First, there is the shift from a focus on things with which the baby is in bodily contact—his own physiological states, the movements of his body, the nipple in his mouth, the things that touch his skin—to things perceived at a distance through sight and hearing. During the first six months, the *mouth* is the main channel of perception, with touch, manipulation, and vision playing subordinate roles. Thereafter, until the baby can move around freely, *touching* and *handling* seem to take the lead. Once the baby is fully mobile, over-all *body movement* appears to be the central component of his experience. Vision is important in keeping the infant oriented to action-things and action-space, but the reality of things lies in what he can do with them rather than with what they look like. To be able really to *see* an object without touching it or manipulating it is an achievement of a high order.

The second aspect of the visual trend is the shift to a stage where movement is no longer necessary to visual perception. The newborn baby can only perceive things that change. Then, action objects can be perceived in terms of their potential movements. Space is first perceived only in terms of the baby's movements within it. Only much later, perhaps not until the school years, does space become a stable setting for fixed objects with properties and meanings that have little to do with their or the baby's action patterns.

It is important to see that the emergence of action qualities from feeling qualities, and of objective properties from action qualities, does not mean that these earlier components are lost. The meaning of an object always continues to comprise its action qualities and its emotional or esthetic connotations, although adults may be able to resist these or, by intent, exclude them from consideration.

At least during the first six months or so of life, and probably well into toddlerhood, all of the baby's experience is wrapped up in the *present moment*. He has no conception of past or future time. If he has expectations, it is of things that will happen in the present; the present situation points forward, but only as far as the next step, with no intervening ones. Out of this "present future," of course, will emerge the real future of which the toddler starts to be aware. The infant, however, does not remember that the sun set yesterday or anticipate that it will set again today. This does not mean that he does not learn. His past experiences teach him what objects are like, what they can do to him and he to them, but this learning is embedded in the way things exist for him in the new *now*—he also has a "present past"—but he cannot recall the lessons that taught him what he knows. His closest approach to remembering comes, we may speculate, when he is sleeping or near sleep and the attitudes and sensations of past events rise unbidden to awareness; but these are felt as real present experiences and not as recollections. We shall see later how the preschool child attributes to his dreams the same substantial reality as waking events. But although the baby may not see the resemblance between today's sunset and yesterday's, he is not surprised when it occurs, and is able to recognize it as a signal for bedtime; or at a given moment, thanks to internal and external cues, he knows that it is now time to eat.

For the sake of simplicity, we have been talking as though the development of the baby's experience of reality depended solely on his random encounters with the environment. Needless to say, the baby does not meet life alone. Throughout infancy, his feelings are closely tied to the emotional reactions of his parents, which have an immediacy and an impact far transcending the reality of virtually any other experiences, both because of their primacy and because of their importance for him. His experience of himself and of objects, as we have seen, is initially altogether ambiguous, and is shaped to a large extent by what his parents communicate to him about it. The objects he becomes aware of, and how he becomes aware of them, are determined not merely by the action characteristics of the objects and his own readiness to react to them, but also by his parents' reaction or lack of reaction. In addition, of course, the objects the baby does and *does not* meet up with are selected by his parents. Thus, many objects come to be colored with moral and emotional values that for the baby would not have been conveyed by their action qualities. According to signals from the parents, things are exciting, disgusting, mysterious, alarming, pleasant, and so forth. Sometimes, when a baby has been bumped on the head, he does not even know that his head hurts—until he sees and hears and feels his parents' worry. He may be inclined to laugh at his sneezes and hiccups— unless they provoke parental concern. Tension in his mother's manner, a note or anger in her voice, a sudden jerk of the arm in which she holds him, or even strangely loud and prolonged laughter, will set him crying; a word or gesture of affection and reassurance can sometimes transform his discomfort into pleasure.

AWARENESS OF SELF

In discussing infancy, we were forced to make inferences about the baby's *self-awareness*—or lack of it—from his often vocal but nevertheless wordless behavior. In dealing with the toddler, we were somewhat better off, since his behavior repertory included a fair number of words. The preschool child, by contrast, can often tell us directly about his self-experience—although we are still in many cases obliged to infer it from what he says about other things. [1]

It should be remembered that the child's developing self-awareness is almost a special case of his developing awareness of things around him, particularly other people. His awareness both of himself and of the environment increases as he becomes psychologically more differentiated from his surroundings, as he comes to distinguish between external events and internal ones, and as he learns to suspend action in favor of contemplation, thought, and feeling. In one sense, of course, the child's awareness of other people precedes awareness of himself: he is aware of their capacity to gratify or harm him before he knows that *he* is there to be gratified or harmed. But as his experience begins to add up, as he becomes aware of his own boundaries and strengths and vulnerabilities, he becomes ready to see that other people too share, in differing degrees, his strengths and vulnerabilities, his capacities for joy and sorrow and pain. It is a difficult thing to perceive other people in the round. We have already spoken of how the preschool child's feelings of sympathy develop from direct participation in what happens to other children into a more mature sympathy based on a detached understanding. But even though the preschool child soon learns to appreciate the feelings of other children, the feelings of adults present a much greater problem. To the preschool child, adults—even when he consciously or unconsciously mocks their ways—appear as omniscient, omnipotent beings who order other people and things around and do only what they want to do. How can he suspect that these lordly beings have fears and worries and frailties—not to mention constitutions —like his own? But each discovery about himself tells him something about other people, and vice versa.

Fears

The vulnerability that comes with self-awareness is often expressed in a sudden outcropping of new fears at ages four and five [13]. At age four, these seem to have less to do with specific damage to the child's integrity than with a menacing cast in his emotional world. He is learning about the real and imaginary dangers that exist—kidnappers, spooks, burglars, giants—but does not see their explicit relationship to himself. It is not uncommon that four-year-olds will need to have the light left on while they sleep; in a dark or half-dark room, it is too easy for the swaying curtains to take on monstrous aspects, for unnamed terrors to lurk under beds or in closets.

By age five, the child often has a fairly specific sense of the harm he can suffer. Among other things, he may become afraid of dying. This fear is not rooted in a recognition that all men are mortal, and that he himself will some day grow old and die, but simply that people do die and that something could happen to him—not eventually, but now. What "die" means, of course, is likely to be indistinct and variable. In games, death is reversible: "Bang! You're dead! O.K. Now you must be alive again." Children find it very hard to grasp the blank finality of death; one child asks, "If you woke up one morning, and you were dead, would it hurt?"

Adults, particularly in middle-class society, are inclined to shield young children from the knowledge of death. This may even take the form of pretending there has been no death. The child, however, with his acute emotional sensitivity, will rapidly detect that something is seriously wrong. His perception of adult distress, his awareness of mystery and exclusion and of the macabre atmosphere with which our society surrounds death, and his interior elaborations of fragments of knowledge, are likely to lead to fear and bewilderment far greater than would be produced by simple frankness about what has happened and honesty about adult feelings. The tendency to conceal death from the child rests on the same assumption of childish innocence as other tendencies in our society to insulate the child from the hard realities—sex, money, disagreements and animosities between parents, for instance. In all of these areas, in our view, children benefit from being given as many facts as they can understand, rather than inventions and denials that complicate their feelings.

Awareness of Growth and Continuity

A further aspect of self-awareness is the child's increasing knowledge of growth and continuity. Time is beginning to move

—as we are aware, it seems to slip away with ever greater velocity as we grow older—and the child begins to sense the transitory nature of his experience; as one child remarked, his birthday had come and gone and there was nothing left, but he was older. In addition, the child is now learning about the penalties as well as the gratifications of growing. Along with the power and independence of being big come the responsibilities and the loneliness. Such notions, of course, exist only fleetingly and inarticulately for the preschool child, but they may well underlie otherwise unaccountable spells of babyishness, sulkiness, clinging behavior, weeping and whining. Such feelings and such behavior are often precipitated by the birth of a younger brother or sister, when the child may for the first time be aware of the state of passive bliss he has left behind and the self-reliance that is now demanded of him.

The child's emerging awareness of himself does not yet make for a constant *self-image* or *identity*. The child's identity can shift dramatically in emotionally charged circumstances, in dramatic play, or in the course of being an imaginary personality. Biber relates the story (poignantly familiar to nursery school teachers) of the three-year-old who, meeting his well-loved teacher on the street, totally failed to recognize her. In school the next morning, he gave her his usual affectionate hug and then, as though struck by a sudden thought, asked her in some bafflement, "What's your name with your hat on?" [3] It seems that, for the preschool child, identity may shift beyond recognition when removed from a familiar context. Needless to say, adults are somewhat prone to the same instability: we may have difficulty recognizing the corner grocer when we see him away from his customary setting; almost proverbially, the people who made such stimulating cruise companions turn out to be utterly commonplace when we meet them again ashore.

We should mention here Horowitz's study on the *localization of the self* in preschool children. [12] Having ascertained a child's name, he would ask him to point to Johnny. It developed that children would consistently indicate one circumscribed region of the body: a point in the jaw, for instance, or in the abdomen. Horowitz would then point to other parts of the body, asking each time, "Is this Johnny?" Parts other than the one first pointed out were acknowledged as Johnny's, but not as Johnny. This finding might be contrasted with Claparède's observation that for adults the center of being comes to rest in the middle of the skull, just behind the eyes.[1]

It is interesting to note that, although the preschool child is aware of himself and others, he seldom seems able to entertain both awarenesses simultaneously. Asked how many people there are in his family, he forgets, because he is counting them from his standpoint, to count himself. Similarly, if he draws a picture of his family, he himself is not likely to appear in it. Asked if he has a brother, he will (assuming it is so) answer yes. Has his brother a brother? No. Is he his brother's brother? Yes. Has his brother a brother? No. [20]

REFERENCES

1. AMES, LOUISE B., "The Sense of Self of Nursery School Children as Manifested by Their Verbal Behavior," *Journal of Genetic Psychology*, 1952, 81:193–232.

2. ANSBACHER, H., "Perception of Number as Affected by the Monetary Value of the Objects," *Archives of Psychology*, 1937, No. 215.

3. BIBER, BARBARA, personal communication.

4. BINET, A., "La mesure des illusions visuelles chez l'enfant," 1895, 40:11–25.

5. BRIDGES, KATHERINE M. B., "Emotional Development in Early Infancy," in Spitz, Rene A., "Diacritic and Conesthetic Organizations," *Psychoanalytic Review*, 1945, 32:146–162.

6. BRUNER, J. A., & POSTMAN, L., Perception and the Dynamics of Behavior. In preparation.

7. ELLSON, D. G., "Experimental Extinction of an Hallucination Produced by Sensory Conditioning," *Joural of Experimental Psychology*, 1941, 28:350–361.

8. GOLDSTEIN, K., & SCHEERER, M., "Abstract and Concrete Behavior," *Psychological Monographs*, 1941, 53, No. 2, p. 3 and *passim*.

9. HALLOWELL, A. I., *The Role of Conjuring in Saulteaux Society, Publications, Philadelphia Anthropological Society*, Vol. 2, Philadelphia: University of Pennsylvania Press, 1942.

---

[1] Cited by Horowitz (1935). [12]

10. HALLOWELL, A. I., "Some Empirical Aspects of Northern Saulteaux Religion," *American Anthropologist*, 1934, 36:389–404.

11. HOLLINGWORTH, H. L., "The Inaccuracy of Movement," *Archives of Psychology*, 1909, No. 13.

12. HOROWITZ, R. E., "Spatial Localization of the Self," *Journal of Social Psychology*, 1935, 6:379–387.

13. JERSILD, A. R., & HOLMES, FRANCES B., *Children's Fears*, New York: Bureau of Publications, Teachers College, Columbia University, 1935.

14. KRECHEVSKY, I., " 'Hypothesis' Versus 'Chance' in the Presolution Period in Sensory Discrimination Learning," *University of California Publications of Psychology*, 1932, 6:27–44.

15. LAZARUS, R. S., & McCLEARY, R. A., "Autonomic Discrimination Without Awareness: A Study of Subception," *Psychological Review*, 1951, 58:113–122. Some of the theoretical implications of "subception" are brought out sharply in Werner, Heinz, "Microgenesis and Aphasia," *Journal of Abnormal and Social Psychology*, 1956, 52:347–353.

16. LEEPER, R., "A Study of a Neglected Portion of the Field of Learning—The Development of Sensory Organization," *Journal of Genetic Psychology*, 1935, 46:41–75.

17. LEVINE, R., CHEIN, I., & MURPHY, G., "The Relation of the Intensity of a Need to the Amount of Perceptual Distortion: A Preliminary Report," *Journal of Psychology*, 1942, 13:283–293.

18. MacLEOD, R. B., "The Phenomenological Approach to Social Psychology," *Psychological Review*, 1947, 54:205.

19. OESER, O. A., personal communication, 1939.

20. PIAGET, J., *Judgement and Reasoning in the Child*, New York: Harcourt, Brace and World, Inc., 1928.

21. PIAGET, J., *The Construction of Reality in the Child*, New York: Basic Books, Inc., 1954, p. 352.

22. POSTMAN, L., & BRUNER, J. S., "The Reliability of Constant Errors in Psychophysical Measurement," *Journal of Psychology*, 1946, 21: 293–299.

23. PROSHANSKY, H., & MURPHY, G., "The Effects of Reward and Punishment on Perception," *Journal of Psychology*, 1942, 13:295–305.

24. SANFORD, R. N., "The Effect of Abstinence from Food upon Imaginal Processes: A Preliminary Experiment," *Journal of Psychology*, 1936, 2:129–136.

25. ———, "The Effect of Abstinence from Food upon Imaginal Processes: A Further Experiment," *Journal of Psychology*, 1937, 3:145–159.

26. SHERIF, M., "A Study in Some Social Factors in Perception," *Archives of Psychology*, 1935, No. 187.

27. SNEDECOR, D., *Statistical Methods*, Ames, Iowa: The Iowa State College Press, 1940.

28. THURSTONE, L. L., *A Factorial Study of Perception*, Chicago: The University of Chicago Press, 1944.

29. WERNER, HEINZ, *Comparative Psychology of Mental Development*, Chicago: Follett Publishing Company, 1948, p. 100.

30. ———, *Comparative Psychology of Mental Development*, Chicago: Follett Publishing Company, 1948, p. 173.

CHAPTER

SIX

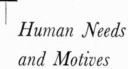

*Human Needs
and Motives*

THE CONCEPT THAT BEHAVIOR IS CAUSED—
is not its own cause—was emphasized in certain of the readings
in Chapter Two. Fundamental to much of human behavior are
basic needs and motives—the *prime movers* that energize and dis-
pose the individual toward certain kinds of behavior.

What exactly do scientists who study human behavior mean
by such terms as "drive," "goal object," "motive," and "motive
pattern"? These are key words in the discussion of motivation.
And the concepts to which they apply are fundamental to our
understanding of people's behavior. The selected pages from a
chapter of Theodore M. Newcomb's *Social Psychology* provide
a very useful introduction to the meaning and significance of
motivation and such related concepts as were just mentioned.
Newcomb is Chairman of the Doctoral Training Program in
Social Psychology at the University of Michigan.

One of the more highly regarded theories of human motivation is that advanced by Abraham H. Maslow. In his paper, Maslow has listed thirteen propositions which he believes must be taken into account by a theory of human motivation for it to be adequate. He then proceeds to a classification and description of basic human needs—a classification which many students have found most helpful. Especially to be noted is his concept of hierarchy of prepotency of human needs. Maslow is Chairman of the Department of Psychology, Brandeis University.

To what extent is a person dependent for his optimum functioning upon a continuing contact with the sights, sounds, and bodily contacts that have become familiar to him? What happens to him motivationally when there is drastic interference with his usual (familiar) exteroceptive stimulations? The reader will find the report by D. O. Hebb highly significant for the understanding of the relationships between perceptual deprivation and motivation and especially as the implications of these relationships bear upon the phenomenon of brainwashing. Hebb is Professor and Chairman of the Department of Psychology at McGill University.

——▶ Theodore M. Newcomb

Human Motivation

From *Social Psychology*, by Theodore M. Newcomb. Copyright, 1950, by Holt, Rinehart and Winston, Inc.; pp. 77–83, 96–97. Reprinted by permission.

Discovering Motives by Observing Direction in Behavior

Most people manage to understand one another's behavior reasonably well, with or without the use of words, most of the time. A simple illustration will point to one thing that makes it possible for them to do so. A mother in her kitchen carries out a series of behaviors including beating eggs, sifting flour, and pouring batter into a pan which she puts into the oven. At the same time her four-year-old son carries out a series of behaviors including building a tower with blocks, beating a drum, looking at a picture book, and talking to his mother while he watches her work. An observer would have no difficulty (if he had any familiarity with American kitchens) in concluding that the mother is baking a cake, but if asked what the boy was doing he would probably say, "just playing." The mother's behavior is easy to understand because it involves a sequence of behaviors which, in connection with the end result (the cake), "makes sense." The boy's behaviors could equally well have been carried out in a different order, and there is no end result to which they can be connected.

The mother's series of behaviors, in this instance, constitutes a single act, whereas the boy's does not. An act (or a motive pattern, as we shall later call it) is defined not as just any motor response, like a single muscle twitch, but as a *sequence* of behavior which has some meaning in terms of a goal or end result. Its meaning to the behaving individual himself depends upon how he relates his own sequence of behaviors to the end results which he anticipates; and its meaning to others depends upon how they relate his sequence of behaviors to the end results which they observe or anticipate. If the observer fails to identify the end result, or if he glimpses the behavior sequence so briefly that he cannot make a judicious guess as to end results, then he will be puzzled by what he sees; it will have dubious meaning. If, for example, you were to look at a photograph showing only the bent knee and raised foot of a man, you would not know whether he was running or kicking. The mere bending of his knee and raising of his foot does not constitute an act. In order to understand his behavior, you must see something of what comes before or after, or both, as you would in a motion picture sequence. The successive behaviors which together constitute an act are "tied together" by a certain *consistency of direction*. The clue to the existence of a motive lies in such consistency of direction.

We understand one another's behavior, then, by observing *sequences* of behavior (not mere isolated responses), and relating them to observed (or anticipated) *end results*. In everyday practice, as a matter of fact, we go beyond this. We assume that the behavior sequence was carried out in order to achieve the end result. We recognize the possibility of mistakes, or unintended results, of course, but nevertheless we attribute to others (as we do to ourselves) the expectation or the hope that a certain behavior sequence will lead to a certain kind of result. And we assume that others, like ourselves, want one kind of result and do not want another. We understand the behavior of others by attributing motives to them.

In doing so, we often make mistakes. (One of the most important areas of social psychology deals with accurate communication with other people as to motives and intentions—both our own and theirs.) We make mistakes, to mention just one reason, because we are forced to rely on rules of thumb. There are no social-psychological slide rules by which we can measure accurately the motives of others. It is the social psychologist's job, however, to approach the accuracy of the slide rule as nearly as he can; he dare not rely merely upon rules of thumb. And so the social psychologist, like the man in the street, makes inferences concerning people's motivations. He does not, of course, rely upon mere hunches or guesswork. He does not take at face value what people have to say about their own motivation but simply includes such statements as part of a sequence of behavior.

Director Behavior and Random Behavior

Directed behavior (from which we infer the existence of motives) is quite different from random behavior. An extreme illustration of the latter is the behavior of a fowl whose head has just been cut off; there is no directionality whatever in its flutterings. Such utter aimlessness probably never occurs under "normal" human conditions. The nearest approach to it seems to be the activities of the newborn infant when in discomfort. He quite literally does everything that he can do; he kicks, drools, cries, thrashes his arms about, twitches, blinks, clenches his fists. Contrast such behavior with that of the commuter who takes the shortest possible route from office to railroad station, where he takes a certain seat on a certain coach on a certain train, gets off at a certain station, unlocks and drives a certain automobile to a certain house which he enters and then seats himself in a certain chair. Every step in this unit of behavior has been so guided and directed as to eventuate in his "getting home and relaxing."

Our wants and desires are expressed sometimes with a low and sometimes with a high degree of directionality. At times we are able to respond to our environment with such selectivity as to attain our end result through our own behavior. At other times, particularly in infancy, our dissatisfactions are so vaguely related to our environment that our behavior shows very little sense of direction. If, under such conditions, dissatisfactions are removed, it is through random behavior rather than behavior directed toward their removal.

The Inner-outer Nature of Motivated Behavior

Motive, like the nontechnical terms "want" and "desire," is a word which points both inward and outward. Such terms refer both to an inner state of dissatisfaction (or unrest, or tension, or disequilibrium) and to something in the environment (like food, mother's presence, or the solution to a puzzle) which serves to remove the state of dissatisfaction. There is both a condition *within* the organism and something *outside* the organism which it wants, toward which its behavior is directed. (The "outsideness" of what is wanted may be only symbolic.) For purposes of psychological analysis it is possible to separate the inner from the outer aspects of wants and desires. For example, if external conditions are held constant, the intensity of a person's desire for water varies directly with the moisture content of his body tissues (his throat membranes, in particular). Conversely, if inner conditions are held constant, a person's desire for water varies with such external factors as the attractiveness or repulsiveness of what there is to be drunk, the sight of other people drinking, or environmental pressures (like a sudden danger which must be avoided) which compete with the need for water.

Needs, wants, or desires are thus variable phenomena, being dependent on changes in both inner and outer stimulation. The more intense the inner stimuli, the lower the threshold for external stimulation: if a man is hungry enough he will want any kind of food. And the less intense the inner stimuli, the higher the threshold for external stimulation: a well-fed man can be tempted only by a special delicacy, and if he is utterly satiated nothing at all will tempt him. Both inner and outer influences (or symbols which stand for them) are always involved.

Definitions

In the light of the distinctions between directed and random behavior and between inner and outer influences, we are able to indicate more exactly what we shall mean by the term "motive," and how it is distinguished from related terms. *Motive,* as here used, refers to a *state of the organism in which bodily energy is mobilized and selectively directed toward parts of the environment.* To understand what this means, we shall have to look at two parts of the definition.

Drive.   First, the "mobilization of bodily energy" referred to in the definition points to the same thing that psychologists mean when they use the word *drive.* Drives are *bodily states felt as restlessness, which initiate tendencies to activity.* In somewhat more technical language, they correspond to regions of more or less concentrated energy potential. The important thing about them is that they function like "motors here and there within the body, each delivering energy to appropriate muscles and glands." [30] Drive states may be sharply localized, like a toothache, or broadly distributed, like over-all fatigue. But even when the original source of the drive is narrowly focused, as in the case of a mosquito bite, there is often a "spread" of drive states; a single mosquito bite may lead a person to "feel itchy all over." Many drives are very diffuse indeed, and nearly all of them tend to become so if not rather soon relieved. This is because every part of the body is directly or indirectly connected with every other part, particularly by way of the blood stream and the nervous system.

Drives are often felt, subjectively, as discomfort. But this is not always or necessarily so. Many states of drive have their origins in obscure chemical changes within the body of which we are not at all aware. They may be sensed only as a need to do something—perhaps something very specific (e.g., telling a funny story of which you have just been reminded) or perhaps just anything (e.g., to the small boy coming out of school, almost any sort of activity is welcome). Such states of drive are not necessarily uncomfortable. It is quite clear, in fact, that tension in and of itself is not necessarily something to be avoided. We read detective stories or ride on roller coasters in order to experience certain kinds of tension. The fact seems to be that drive, or tension, while often uncomfortable in itself, is not necessarily so unless appropriate behavior is prevented. If a state of drive can be relieved only by telling the funny story, or by finishing the detective story, it will be felt as discomfort if these acts are prevented, but the state of wanting to tell it is not in itself uncomfortable.

Psychologists commonly consider drive as something which the organism is impelled to relieve, or remove, and we too shall so consider it—not because it is necessarily uncomfortable but simply because it impels the organism to activity. The ensuing activity usually serves to reduce the drive, whether it was originally uncomfortable or not. We shall therefore use the phrase "drive reducing," which is both traditional and convenient, with less emphasis upon the meaning of "making less uncomfortable" and more upon the meaning of "impelling to activity." It is incidentally true that to be prevented from taking action is felt as discomfort. The important thing, however, is that energy is mobilized and made available for activity.

Goal. The phrase "selected parts of the environment" in the definition refers to the end results of behavior sequences. They are known as *goals*. More exactly, a goal is a *state of affairs toward which behavior is directed,* whether successfully or not. A goal may involve a long-range behavior sequence (earning a college degree), or a short-range sequence (hitting a baseball that has just been pitched), or a sequence of any intermediate length. A goal is something toward which behavior is *directed*.

The use of the word "toward" in the preceding sentence may lead you to wonder about "negative goals"—that is, parts of the environment *away* from which behavior is directed. A pedestrian may have the momentary goal of avoiding a puddle in the side-walk; the goal of an escaped convict is apt to be avoiding de-tection and return to prison. There are often some important differences between behavior which is directed away from and behavior which is directed toward certain things in the environ-ment. Nevertheless, for present purposes, we shall ignore the distinction, because there is no way of avoiding one thing with-out going toward some other thing. The pedestrian avoids the puddles by going toward the dry portions of the sidewalk, and the convict avoids the police by going toward places which he considers safe. We shall therefore refer to goals as including parts of the environment toward which behavior is directed in order to avoid other parts of the environment.

Goals correspond to some state of affairs in the environment, though sometimes only in a rather indirect way. Human beings have a very great capacity to substitute symbols for actual objects and events in the environment. And so it often happens that in-ternal, symbolic events rather than any change in the external environment serve as goals. Examples of such goals might be the "happy ending" to a daydream, or the solution to a problem in mental arithmetic. Such symbolic events come to function as goals because they have come to stand for something in the en-vironment. During a large part of our waking lives, and even during a part of our sleeping lives, we respond to what might be called an internalized environment—like the objects, people, or words which we see or hear in our daydreams. We are con-stantly directing our behavior—especially our verbal behavior, whether the words are spoken aloud or not—toward goals in this internalized environment. In these pages, therefore, when we speak of goals as being in the environment, or of behavior as being directed toward something in the environment, we shall be using the term environment as including both the external and the internalized. Motivated behavior is always an inner-outer affair, if the term "outer" is used to include symbols for things in the environment.

There is one other important thing to remember about goals. They do not exist, as such, in the environment apart from per-sons whose behavior is being directed toward them. A million dollars, a score of 300 in bowling, or a lollipop are goals only in relation to someone who is seeking them as goals. We know about goals only by observing specific sequences of behavior (often including verbal statements of intention) on the part of individuals. Goals, in brief, are inferred from sequences of behavior. The term "goal" is actually no more than a way of referring to the *directional* aspect of behavior, just as "drive" refers to the *energy* aspect of behavior.

Motive as mobilized and directed energy. The concept of motive as defined above, includes both the directional and the energy aspects of behavior. It refers not merely to the energy mobilized by the organism, nor merely to the goal toward which energy is directed, but to a relationship between energy and goal. An organism is motivated when—and only when—it is characterized *both* by a state of drive *and* by a direction of behavior toward some goal which is selected in preference to all other possible goals. Motive, then, is a concept which joins together drive and goal. Without drive or without goal there can be no motive, as the term is here used.

Unfortunately, there is no standard usage of these terms. Many social psychologists—Klineberg [18], for example—use "motive" and "drive" interchangeably. Some psychologists—e.g., Muenzinger [29]—define motive simply as "direction of behavior." Any usage is, of course, permissible so long as it is clear, consistent, and objectively definable. Nevertheless, it is confusing to find different writers using the term "motive" with different meanings. As you read various social-psychological sources, therefore, you should note carefully what each writer means by the term.

Certain implications of our use of the term "motive" should be noted. First, it refers not to a directed sequence of behavior as such but to a *state of the organism* which accounts for the fact that the behavior sequence is characterized by direction. "Motive" refers not to the carrying out of behavior but to a way of being set for directing one's energy toward a certain goal. Such a way of being set is sometimes known as an *orientation*. An orientation which persistently reappears over a period of time is known as an attitude. All these terms refer to inferred conditions, or intervening variables, not to behavior, which is our dependent variable.

Secondly, a restriction concerning the labeling of specific motives should be noted. For social-psychological purposes it is more convenient to label any particular motive according to its goal than according to its state of drive. The principal reason for this preference is that the drives involved in most social behaviors are rather diffuse and usually difficult to isolate. We do not have the means, for example, of distinguishing between the drive states of a given individual when he is motivated to win at poker and when he is motivated to win at tennis. The goals can easily be distinguished, but the drives can not. Hence we shall speak of a *hunger drive* and a *food motive,* but not of a food drive or a hunger motive. The phrase "food motive" does not deny the influence of the hunger drive but stresses the directional aspect of whatever behavior is involved. Likewise, the phrase "hunger drive" does not imply that no food motive is present but simply emphasizes the tension or energy aspect of the behavior.

Finally, the use of the term "motive" is restricted in another way—to situations in which there is some selectivity in arriving at a goal. Thus the term is not ordinarily applied to reflexes, such as hiccoughing, because, by our definition, simple reflex behavior is not motivated. The attempt to inhibit a reflex response, however, like smothering a cough during a church service, is motivated—i.e., it is directed toward the goal of maintaining silence.

MOTIVE PATTERNS

The never-ceasing behaviors which characterize a person's interaction with his environment throughout his life, from conception to death, may be likened to a flowing river. The stream of behavior, like a river, may be studied in many ways. One may examine samples of the river's water for chemical or bacterial content; one may measure its width, depth, and rate of flow at various points; one may discover how these and other factors vary with the seasons, with rainfall, with local topography and vegetation, and with the activities of the human population.

The stream of behavior, like a river, is not static. Its interdependence with its environment is dynamic and is maintained through constant change. One can no more understand behavior by studying a static organism than one can a river from samples of its water or a cross section of its channel. Neither the river nor the living organism exists apart from dynamic, continued interaction with its environment. The analogy of a stream, though only a figure of speech as applied to behavior, serves to stress both the continuity and the change which characterize the living organism.

The entire life of an individual may be thought of as a stream flowing from conception to death, with many twistings, detours, eddies, floods, and quiet pools, but nevertheless with a well-marked course from beginning to end. For most purposes, however, we cannot profitably study the course as a whole; our study of human behavior must be in terms of something intermediate between an entire life stream and a static cross section of a single instant, like one frame of a motion picture film. Such an intermediate unit must be inclusive enough to show continuity, but not so inclusive as to obscure changes and beginnings of new continuities. It must be a unit of continuity, but not of indefinite continuity.

"Motive Pattern" Defined

An act, as a sequence of behaviors dominated by a common motive, is such a unit. The term "act," however, stresses the performance aspect of the sequence of behaviors, whereas the sequence, in fact, includes at least three other important aspects: *perception, thought,* and *affect* (feeling and emotion), as well as *performance,* are all involved. It is the motive that "ties together" all these aspects of behavior and makes of them a single, meaningful unit. The term *motive pattern* (rather than the term "act"), therefore, will be used as meaning a *sequence of behaviors characterized by relative constancy of motivation.*[1]

A motive pattern refers to all of a person's behavior which is "caught up" in the stream while it maintains relative con-

---

[1] I am indebted to Professor Karl F. Muenzinger (1942) for this concept, though not for this exact formulation of it.

stancy of motivation. (The word "all" means simply that no aspect of behavior is deliberately excluded. It is not intended to suggest that behavior can simultaneously be analyzed in all its aspects, or that all of a person's behavior at a given moment is included in a single motive pattern.) To revert to our earlier analogy, a motive pattern is comparable to a section of a river in which the general direction and rate of flow remains about the same. To put the matter in nontechnical language and somewhat oversimply, a motive pattern includes everything an individual notices, does, feels, and thinks in more or less integrated fashion while he is wanting a given thing.

Relative, not absolute, constance characterizes a motive pattern. A man may be hurrying to arrive at the railroad station before the 5:42 train comes in, for example. "What he notices" may include, in succession, his watch, street signs, traffic lights, other people, and passing vehicles. (He may also notice things irrelevant to the motive of catching his train, of course.) "What he does" may shift from running to dodging pedestrians to hailing a taxi. "What he thinks" may include reflections about the wisdom of allowing himself more time, or calculations concerning ways of saving a few seconds. "What he feels" may be chiefly excited anticipation of meeting a friend at the train, or despair lest he miss it. All are part of the motive pattern; all are dominated by the motive of catching the train. All are related to one another by reason of the common motive. Each of them, moreover, shows continuity—until the goal is reached. The motive pattern continues as long as his stream of behavior (noticing-acting-thinking-feeling) is dominated by the concern of reaching the goal. After it is reached, a new motive pattern ensues.

A motive pattern is thus quite different from a motive. The latter, you will recall, does not refer to behavior but to a *state of the organism* inferred from behavior. A motive pattern, however, does refer to behavior. It is *a unit of behavior* which begins and ends with the beginning and ending of behavior directed toward a certain goal. It corresponds to a unit of time measured by behavior rather than by a clock.

Thus defined, a motive pattern is a way of describing the unity of the organism as it relates itself to its environment. It is a unity of the several aspects of behavior (noticing, acting, feeling, thinking) which persists over a period of time—i.e., for the duration of the motive pattern. No one of these aspects occurs alone, but for purposes of analysis it is necessary to treat them singly in order to understand how each of them is related to the others. Although it is by no means complete, there is a considerable body of experimental evidence for the interdependence of noticing, acting, feeling, and thinking, such as we should expect if a motive pattern actually functions as a unit. The interdependence is first indirect, and only secondarily direct. That is, noticing, acting, etc. are primarily related to one another by way of the common motive but, in subsidiary ways, any one of them may be directly determined by any one of the others.

—▶ **A. H. Maslow**

A Theory of Human Motivation

From *Psychological Review*, July, 1943, 50:370–396. Reprinted and abridged by permission.

INTRODUCTION

In a previous paper [23] various propositions were presented which would have to be included in any theory of human motivation that could lay claim to being definitive. These conclusions may be briefly summarized as follows:

1. The integrated wholeness of the organism must be one of the foundation stones of motivation theory.
2. The hunger drive (or any other physiological drive) was rejected as a centering point or model for a definitive theory of motivation. Any drive that is somatically based and localized was shown to be atypical rather than typical in human motivation.
3. Such a theory should stress and center itself upon ultimate or basic goals rather than partial or superficial ones, upon ends rather than means to these ends. Such a stress would imply a

more central place for unconscious than for conscious motivations.

4. There are usually available various cultural paths to the same goal. Therefore conscious, specific, local-cultural desires are not as fundamental in motivation theory as the more basic, unconscious goals.

5. Any motivated behavior, either preparatory or consummatory, must be understood to be a channel through which many basic needs may be simultaneously expressed or satisfied. Typically an act has more than one motivation.

6. Practically all organismic states are to be understood as motivated and as motivating.

7. Human needs arrange themselves in hierarchies of prepotency. That is to say, the appearance of one need usually rests on the prior satisfaction of another, more prepotent need. Man is a perpetually wanting animal. Also every drive is related to the state of satisfaction or dissatisfaction of other drives; no need or drive can be treated as if it were isolated or discrete.

8. Lists of drives will get us nowhere for various theoretical and practical reasons. Furthermore any classification of motivations must deal with the problem of levels of specificity or generalization of the motives to be classified.

9. Classifications of motivations must be based upon goals rather than upon instigating drives or motivated behavior.

10. Motivation theory should be human-centered rather than animal-centered.

11. The situation or the field in which the organism reacts must be taken into account but the field alone can rarely serve as an exclusive explanation for behavior. Furthermore the field itself must be interpreted in terms of the organism. Field theory cannot be a substitute for motivation theory.

12. Not only the integration of the organism must be taken into acount, but also the possibility of isolated, specific, partial, or segmental reactions.

It has since become necessary to add to these another affirmation.

13. Motivation theory is not synonymous with behavior theory. The motivations are only one class of determinants of behavior. While behavior is almost always motivated, it is also almost always biologically, culturally, and situationally determined as well.

The present paper is an attempt to formulate a positive theory of motivation which will satisfy these theoretical demands and at the same time conform to the known facts, clinical and observational as well as experimental. It derives most directly, however, from clinical experience. This theory is, I think, in the functionalist tradition of James and Dewey, and is fused with the holism of Wertheimer [38], Goldstein [11], and Gestalt Psychology, and with the dynamicism of Freud [10] and Adler. [1] This fusion or synthesis may arbitrarily be called a "general-dynamic" theory.

It is far easier to perceive and to criticize the aspects in motivation theory than to remedy them. Mostly this is because of the very serious lack of sound data in this area. I conceive this lack of sound facts to be due primarily to the absence of a valid theory of motivation. The present theory then must be considered to be a suggested program or framework for future research and must stand or fall, not so much on facts available or evidence presented, as upon researches yet to be done, researches suggested, perhaps, by the questions raised in this paper.

THE BASIC NEEDS

The "Physiological" Needs

The needs that are usually taken as the starting point for motivation theory are the so-called physiological drives. Two recent lines of research make it necessary to revise our customary notions about these needs first, the development of the concept of homeostasis, and second, the finding that appetites (preferential choices among foods) are a fairly efficient indication of actual needs or lacks in the body.

Homeostasis refers to the body's automatic efforts to maintain a constant, normal state of the blood stream. Cannon [6] has described this process for (1) the water content of the blood, (2) salt content, (3) sugar content, (4) protein content, (5) fat content, (6) calcium content, (7) oxygen content, (8) constant hydrogen-ion level (acid-base balance), and (9) constant temperature of the blood. Obviously this list can be extended to include other minerals, the hormones, vitamins, etc.

Young in a recent article [39] has summarized the work on

appetite in its relation to body needs. If the body lacks some chemical, the individual will tend to develop a specific appetite or partial hunger for that food element.

Thus, it seems impossible as well as useless to make any list of fundamental physiological needs for they can come to almost any number one might wish, depending on the degree of specificity of description. We cannot identify all physiological needs as homeostatic. That sexual desire, sleepiness, sheer activity, and maternal behavior in animals are homeostatic has not yet been demonstrated. Furthermore, this list would not include the various sensory pleasures (tastes, smells, tickling, stroking) which are probably physiological and which may become the goals of motivated behavior.

In a previous paper [23] it has been pointed out that these physiological drives or needs are to be considered unusual rather than typical because they are isolable, and because they are localizable somatically. That is to say, they are relatively independent of each other, of other motivations, and of the organism as a whole, and secondly, in many cases, it is possible to demonstrate a localized, underlying somatic base for the drive. This is true less generally than has been thought (exceptions are fatigue, sleepiness, maternal responses) but it is still true in the classic instances of hunger, sex, and thirst.

It should be pointed out again that any of the physiological needs and the consummatory behavior involved with them serve as channels for all sorts of other needs as well. That is to say, the person who thinks he is hungry may actually be seeking more for comfort, or dependence, than for vitamins or proteins. Conversely, it is possible to satisfy the hunger needs in part by other activities such as drinking water or smoking cigarettes. In other words, relatively isolable as these physiological needs are, they are not completely so.

Undoubtedly, these physiological needs are the most prepotent of all needs. What this means specifically is that in the human being who is missing everything in life in an extreme fashion, it is most likely that the major motivation would be the physiological needs rather than any others.

If all the needs are unsatisfied, and the organism is then dominated by the physiological needs, all other needs may become simply nonexistent or be pushed into the background. It is then fair to characterize the whole organism by saying simply that it is hungry, for consciousness is almost completely preempted by hunger. All capacities are put into the service of hunger-satisfaction, and the organization of these capacities is almost entirely determined by the one purpose of satisfying hunger.

For the man who is extremely and dangerously hungry, no other interests exist but food. He dreams food, he remembers food, he thinks about food, he emotes only about food, he perceives only food, and he wants only food. The more subtle determinants that ordinarily fuse with the physiological drives in organizing even feeding, drinking, or sexual behavior may now be so completely overwhelmed as to allow us to speak at this time (but *only* at this time) of pure hunger drive and behavior, with the one unqualified aim of relief.

Another peculiar characteristic of the human organism when it is dominated by a certain need is that the whole philosophy of the future tends also to change. For our chronically and extremely hungry man, Utopia can be defined very simply as a place where there is plenty of food. Freedom, love, community feeling, respect, philosophy, may all be waved aside as fripperies which are useless since they fail to fill the stomach. Such a man may fairly be said to live by bread alone.

It cannot possibly be denied that such things are true but their *generality* can be denied. Emergency conditions are, almost by definition, rare in the normally functioning peaceful society. That this truism can be forgotten is due mainly to two reasons. First, rats have few motivations other than physiological ones; and since so much of the research upon motivation has been made with these animals, it is easy to carry the rat-picture over to the human being. Secondly, it is too often not realized that culture itself is an adaptive tool, one of whose main functions is to make the physiological emergencies come less and less often. In most of the known societies, chronic extreme hunger of the emergency type is rare, rather than common.

The average American citizen is experiencing appetite rather than hunger when he says, "I am hungry." He is apt to experience sheer life-and-death hunger only by accident and then only a few times through his entire life.

Obviously, a good way to obscure the "higher" motivations, and to get a lopsided view of human capacities and human nature, is to make the organism extremely and chronically hungry or thirsty. Anyone who attempts to make an emergency picture into a typical one, and who will measure all of man's goals and desires by his behavior during extreme physiological deprivation is certainly being blind to many things. What happens to man's desires when there *is* plenty of bread and when his belly is chronically filled?

At once other (and "higher") needs emerge and these, rather than physiological hungers, dominate the organism. And when these in turn are satisfied, again new (and still "higher") needs emerge and so on. This is what we mean by saying that the basic human needs are organized into a hierarchy of relative prepotency.

One main implication of this phrasing is that gratification becomes as important a concept as deprivation in motivation theory, for it releases the organism from the domination of a relatively more physiological need, permitting thereby the emergence of other more social goals. The physiological needs, along with their partial goals, when chronically gratified cease to exist as active determinants or organizers of behavior. Want that is satisfied is no longer a want. The organism is dominated and its behavior organized only by unsatisfied needs. If hunger is satisfied, it becomes unimportant in the current dynamics of the individual.

This statement is somewhat qualified by a hypothesis to be discussed more fully later; namely, that it is precisely those individuals in whom a certain need has always been satisfied who are best equipped to tolerate deprivation of that need in the future, and that furthermore, those who have been deprived in the past will react differently to current satisfactions than the one who has never been deprived.

The Safety Needs

If the physiological needs are relatively well gratified, there then emerges a new set of needs, which we may categorize roughly as the safety needs. All that has been said of the physiological needs is equally true, although in lesser degree, of these desires. The organism may equally well be wholly dominated by them. They may serve as the almost exclusive organizers of behavior, recruiting all the capacities of the organism in their service, and we may then fairly describe the whole organism as a safety-seeking mechanism. Again we may say of the receptors, the effectors, the intellect, and the other capacities that they are primarily safety-seeking tools.

Although in this paper we are interested primarily in the needs of the adult, we can approach an understanding of his safety needs perhaps more efficiently by observation of infants and children, in whom these needs are much more simple and obvious. One reason for the clearer appearance of the threat or danger reaction in infants is that they do not inhibit this reaction at all, whereas adults in our society have been taught to inhibit it at all costs. Thus, even when adults do feel their safety to be threatened, we may not be able to see this on the surface. Infants will react in a total fashion and as if they were endangered, if they are disturbed or dropped suddenly, startled by loud noises, flashing light, or other unusual sensory stimulation, by rough handling, by general loss of support in the mother's arms, or by inadequate support.[1]

In infants we can also see a much more direct reaction to bodily illnesses of various kinds. Sometimes these illnesses seem to be immediately and *per se* threatening and seem to make the child feel unsafe. For instance, vomiting, colic, or other sharp pains seem to make the child look at the whole world in a different way. At such a moment of pain, it may be postulated that, for the child, the appearance of the whole world suddenly changes from sunniness to darkness, so to speak, and becomes a place in which anything at all might happen, in which previously

---

[1] As the child grows up, sheer knowledge and familiarity as well as better motor development make these "dangers" less and less dangerous and more and more manageable. Throughout life it may be said that one of the main conative functions of education is this neutralizing of apparent dangers through knowledge, e.g., I am not afraid of thunder because I know something about it.

stable things have suddenly become unstable. Thus, a child who because of some bad food is taken ill may, for a day or two, develop fear, nightmares, and a need for protection and reassurance never seen in him before his illness.

Another indication of the child's need for safety is his preference for some kind of undisrupted routine or rhythm. He seems to want a predictable, orderly world. For instance, injustice, unfairness, or inconsistency in the parents seems to make a child feel anxious and unsafe. This attitude may be not so much because this treatment threatens to make the world look unreliable, or unsafe, or unpredictable. Young children seem to thrive better under a system which has at least a skeletal outline of rigidity, in which there is a schedule of a kind, some sort of routine, something that can be counted upon, not only for the present but also far into the future. Perhaps one could express this more accurately by saying that the child needs an organized world rather than an unorganized or unstructured one.

The central role of the parents and the normal family setup are indisputable. Quarreling, physical assault, separation, divorce, or death within the family may be particularly terrifying. Also parental outbursts of rage or threats of punishment directed to the child, calling him names, speaking to him harshly, shaking him, handling him roughly, or actual physical punishment sometimes elicit such total panic and terror in the child that we must assume more is involved than the physical pain alone. While it is true that in some children this terror may represent also a fear of loss of parental love, it can also occur in completely rejected children, who seem to cling to the hating parents more for sheer safety and protection than because of hope of love.

Confronting the average child with new, unfamiliar, strange, unmanageable stimuli or situations will too frequently elicit the danger of terror reaction, as for example, getting lost or even being separated from the parents for a short time, being confronted with new faces, new situations or new tasks, the sight of strange, unfamiliar or uncontrollable objects, illness or death. Particularly at such times, the child's frantic clinging to his parents is eloquent testimony to their role as protectors (quite apart from their roles as food-givers and love-givers).

From these and similar observations, we may generalize and say that the average child in our society generally prefers a safe, orderly, predictable, organized world, which he can count on, and in which unexpected, unmanageable, or other dangerous things do not happen, and in which, in any case, he has all-powerful parents who protect and shield him from harm.

Children who are reared in an unthreatening, loving family do not ordinarily react as we have described above. [31] In such children the danger reactions are apt to come mostly to objects or situations that adults too would consider dangerous.

The healthy, normal, fortunate adult in our culture is largely satisfied in his safety needs. The peaceful, smoothly running, "good" society ordinarily makes its members feel safe enough from wild animals, extremes of temperature, criminals, assault and murder, tyranny, etc. Therefore, in a very real sense, he no longer has any safety needs as active motivators. If we wish to see these needs directly and clearly we must turn to neurotic or near-neurotic individuals, and to the economic and social underdogs. In between these extremes, we can perceive the expressions of safety needs only in such phenomena as, for instance, the common preference for a job with tenure and protection, the desire for a savings account, and for insurance of various kinds (medical, dental, unemployment, disability, old age).

Other broader aspects of the attempt to seek safety and stability in the world are seen in the very common preference for familiar rather than unfamiliar things, or for the known rather than the unknown. The tendency to have some religion or world philosophy that organizes the universe and the men in it into some sort of satisfactorily coherent, meaningful whole is also in part motivated by safety-seeking. Here, too, we may list science and philosophy in general as partially motivated by the safety needs (we shall see later that there are also other motivations to scientific, philosophical, or religious endeavor).

Otherwise the need for safety is seen as an active and dominant mobilizer of the organism's resources only in emergencies, e.g., war, disease, natural catastrophes, crime waves, societal disorganization, neurosis, brain injury, chronically bad situation.

Some neurotic adults in our society are, in many ways, like the unsafe child in their desire for safety, although in the former it takes on a somewhat special appearance. Their reaction is often to unknown, psychological dangers in a world that is perceived to be hostile, overwhelming, and threatening.

The neurotic individual may be described in a slightly different way with some usefulness as a grown-up person who retains his childish attitudes toward the world. It is as if his childish attitudes of fear and threat reaction of a dangerous world had gone underground and, untouched by the growing up and learning processes, were now ready to be called out by any stimulus that would make a child feel endangered and threatened.

The neurosis in which the search for safety takes its clearest form is in the compulsive-obsessive neurosis. Compulsive-obsessives try frantically to order and stabilize the world so that no unmanageable, unexpected, or unfamiliar dangers will ever appear. What we can see only as a none-too-strong preference in the healthy person, e.g., preference for the familiar, becomes a life-and-death necessity in abnormal cases.

The Love Needs

If both the physiological and the safety needs are fairly well gratified, then there will emerge the love and affection and belongingness needs, and the whole cycle already described will repeat itself with this new center. Now the person will feel keenly, as never before, the absence of friends, or a sweetheart, or a wife, or children. He will hunger for affectionate relations with people in general, namely, for a place in his group, and he will strive with great intensity to achieve this goal. He will want to attain such a place more than anything else in the world and may even forget that once, when he was hungry, he sneered at love.

In our society the thwarting of these needs is the most commonly found core in cases of maladjustment and more severe psychopathology. Love and affection, as well as their possible expression in sexuality, are generally looked upon with ambivalence and are customarily hedged about with many restrictions and inhibitions. Practically all theorists of psychopathology have stressed thwarting of the love needs as basic in the picture of maladjustment. Many clinical studies have therefore been made of this need and we know more about it perhaps than any of the other needs except the physiological ones. [24]

One thing that must be stressed at this point is that love is not synonymous with sex. Sex may be studied as a purely physiological need. Ordinarily sexual behavior is multi-determined, that is to say, determined not only by sexual but also by other needs, chief among which are the love and affection needs. Also not to be overlooked is the fact that the love needs involve both giving *and* receiving love.

The Esteem Needs

All people in our society (with a few pathological exceptions) have a need or desire for a stable, firmly based (usually) high evaluation of themselves, for self-respect, or self-esteem, and for the esteem of others. By firmly based self-esteem, we mean that which is soundly based upon real capacity, achievement, and respect from others. These needs may be classified into two subsidiary sets. These are, first, the desire for strength, for achievement, for adequacy, for confidence in the face of the world, and for independence and freedom. Secondly, we have what we may call the desire for reputation or prestige (defining it as respect or esteem from other people), recognition, attention, importance, or appreciation. More and more today, however, there is appearing widespread appreciation of their central importance.

Satisfaction of the self-esteem need leads to feelings of self-confidence, worth, strength, capability, and adequacy of being useful and necessary in the world. But thwarting of these needs produces feelings of inferiority, of weakness, and of helplessness. These feelings in turn give rise to either basic discouragement or else compensatory or neurotic trends. An appreciation of the necessity of basic self-confidence and an understanding of how helpless people are without it can be easily gained from a study of severe traumatic neurosis. [17]

The Need for Self-actualization

Even if all these needs are satisfied, we may still often (if not always) expect that a new discontent and restlessness will soon develop, unless the individual is doing what he is fitted for. A musician must make music, an artist must paint, a poet must write, if he *is* to be ultimately happy. What a man *can* be, he *must* be. This need we may call self-actualization.

This term, first coined by Kurt Goldstein, is being used in this paper in a much more specific and limited fashion. It refers to the desire for self-fulfillment; namely, to the tendency for him to become actualized in what he is potentially. This tendency might be phrased as the desire to become more and more what one is, to become everything that one is capable of becoming.

The specific form that these needs will take will of course vary greatly from person to person. In one individual it may take the form of the desire to be an ideal mother, in another it may be expressed athletically, and in still another it may be expressed in painting pictures or in inventions. It is not necessarily a creative urge although in people who have any capacities for creation it will take this form.

The clear emergence of these needs rests upon prior satisfaction of the physiological, safety, love, and esteem needs. We shall call people who are satisfied in these needs basically satisfied people, and it is from these that we may expect the fullest (and healthiest) creativeness. Since, in our society, basically satisfied people are the exception, we do not know much about self-actualization, either experimentally or clinically. It remains a challenging problem for research.

The Preconditions for the Basic Need Satisfactions

There are certain conditions which are immediate prerequisites for the basic need satisfactions. Danger to these is reacted to almost as if it were a direct danger to the basic needs themselves. Such conditions as freedom to speak, freedom to do what one wishes so long as no harm is done to others, freedom to express one's self, freedom to investigate and seek for information, freedom to defend one's self, justice, fairness, honesty, orderliness in the group are examples of such preconditions for basic need satisfactions. Thwarting in these freedoms will be reacted to with a threat or emergency response. These conditions are defended because without them the basic satisfactions are quite impossible, or at least very severely endangered. If we remember that the cognitive capacities (perceptual, intellectual, learning) are a set of adjustive tools, which have, among other functions, that of satisfaction of our basic needs, then it is clear that any danger to them, any deprivation or blocking of their free use, must also be indirectly threatening to the basic needs themselves. Such a statement is a partial solution of the general problems of curiosity, the search for knowledge, truth and wisdom, and the ever-present urge to solve the cosmic mysteries.

We must therefore introduce another hypothesis and speak of degrees of closeness to the basic needs, for we have already pointed out that any conscious desires (partial goals) are more or less important as they are more or less close to the basic needs. The same statement may be made for various behavior acts. An act is psychologically important if it contributes directly to satisfaction of basic needs.

The Desires to Know and to Understand

So far, we have mentioned the cognitive needs only in passing. Acquiring knowledge and systematizing the universe have been considered as, in part, techniques for the achievement of basic safety in the world, or, for the intelligent man, expressions of self-actualization. Also freedom of inquiry and expression have been discussed as preconditions of satisfactions of the basic needs. True though these formulations may be, they do not constitute definitive answers to the question as to the motivation role of curiosity, learning, philosophizing, experimenting, etc. They are, at best, no more than partial answers.

This question is especially difficult because we know so little about the facts. Curiosity, exploration, desire for the facts, desire to know may certainly be observed easily enough. It may be largely a function of relatively high intelligence. Rather tentatively, then, and largely in the hope of stimulating discussion and research, we shall postulate a basic desire to know, to be aware of reality, to get the facts, to satisfy curiosity, or as Wertheimer phrases it, to see rather than to be blind.

This posulation, however, is not enough. The facts that we acquire, if they are isolated or atomistic, inevitably get theorized about, and either analyzed or organized or both. This process has been phrased by some as the search for "Meaning." We shall then postulate a desire to understand, to systematize, to organize, to look for relations and meanings.

Once these desires are accepted for discussion, we see that they too form themselves into a small hierarchy in which the desire to know is prepotent over the desire to understand. All the characteristics of a hierarchy of prepotency that we have described above seem to hold for this one as well.

We must guard ourselves against the too easy tendency to separate these desires from the basic needs we have discussed above, i.e., to make a sharp dichotomy between "cognitive" and "conative" needs. The desires to know and to understand are themselves conative, i.e., have a striving character, and are as much personality needs as the "basic needs" we have already discussed. [38]

Further Characteristics of the Basic Needs

The Degree of Fixity of the Hierarchy of Basic Needs

We have spoken so far as if this hierarchy were a fixed order, but actually it is not nearly as rigid as we may have implied. It is true that most of the people with whom we have worked have seemed to have these basic needs in about the order that has been indicated. However, there have been a number of exceptions.

1. There are some people in whom, for instance, self-esteem seems to be more important than love. This most common reversal in the hierarchy is usually due to the development of the notion that the person who is most likely to be loved is a strong or powerful person, one who inspires respect or fear, and who is self-confident or aggressive. Therefore, such people who lack love and seek it may try hard to put on a front of aggressive, confident behavior. But essentially they seek high self-esteem and its behavior expressions more as a means-to-an-end than for its own sake; they seek self-assertion for the sake of love rather than for self-esteem itself.

2. There are other, apparently innately creative people in

whom the drive to creativeness seems to be more important than any other counter-determinant. Their creativeness might appear not as self-actualization released by basic satisfaction, but in spite of lack of basic satisfaction.

3. In certain people the level of aspiration may be permanently deadened or lowered. That is to say, the less prepotent goals may simply be lost, and may disappear forever, so that the person who has experienced life at a very low level, i.e., chronic unemployment, may continue to be satisfied for the rest of his life if only he can get enough food.

4. The so-called "psychopathic personality" is another example of permanent loss of the love needs. These are people who, according to the best data available [19], have been starved for love in the earliest months of their lives and have simply lost forever the desire and the ability to give and to receive affection.

5. Another cause of reversal of the hierarchy is that when a need has been satisfied for a long time, this need may be underevaluated. People who have never experienced chronic hunger are apt to underestimate its effects and to look upon food as a rather unimportant thing. If they are dominated by a higher need, this higher need will seem to be the most important of all. A man who has given up his job rather than lose his self-respect, and who then starves for six months or so, may be willing to take his job back even at the price of losing his self-respect.

6. Another partial explanation of *apparent* reversals is seen in the fact that we have been talking about the hierarchy of prepotency in terms of consciously felt wants or desires rather than of behavior. Looking at behavior itself may give us the wrong impression. What we have claimed is that the person will *want* the more basic of two needs when deprived in both. Let us say again that there are many determinants of behavior other than the needs and desires.

7. Perhaps more important than all these exceptions are the ones that involve ideals, high social standards, high values, and the like. With such values people become martyrs; they will give up everything for the sake of a particular ideal, or value. These people may be understood, at least in part, by reference to one basic concept (or hypothesis) which may be called "increased

frustration tolerance through early gratification." People who have been satisfied in their basic needs throughout their lives, particularly in their earlier years, seem to develop exceptional power to withstand present or future thwarting of these needs simply because they have strong, healthy character structure as a result of basic satisfaction.

I say all this in spite of the fact that there is a certain amount of sheer habituation which is also involved in any full discussion of frustration tolerance. For instance, it is likely that those persons who have been accustomed to relative starvation for a long time are partially enabled thereby to withstand food deprivation. What sort of balance must be made between these two tendencies, of habituation on the one hand, and of past satisfaction breeding present frustration tolerance on the other hand, remains to be worked out by further research. In respect to this phenomenon of increased frustration tolerance, it seems probable that the most important gratifications come in the first two years of life.

Degrees of Relative Satisfaction

So far, our theoretical discussion may have given the impression that these five sets of needs are somehow in a step-wise, all-or-none relationship to each other. We have spoken in such terms as the following: "If one need is satisfied, then another emerges." This statement might give the false impression that a need must be satisfied 100 per cent before the next need emerges. In actual fact, most members of our society who are normal are partially satisfied in all their basic needs and partially unsatisfied in all their basic needs at the same time. A more realistic description of the hierarchy would be in terms of decreasing percentages of satisfaction as we go up the hierarchy of prepotency. For instance, if I may assign arbitrary figures for the sake of illustration, it is as if the average citizen is satisfied perhaps 85 per cent in his love needs, 70 per cent in his safety needs, and 10 per cent in his self-actualization needs.

As for the concept of emergence of a new need after satisfaction of the prepotent need, this emergence is not a sudden, saltatory phenomenon but rather a gradual emergence by slow degrees from nothingness. For instance, if prepotent need A is satisfied only 10 per cent then need B may not be visible at all. However, as this need A becomes satisfied 25 per cent, need B may emerge 5 per cent, as need A becomes satisfied 75 per cent, need B may emerge 90 per cent, and so on.

Unconscious Character of Needs

These needs are neither necessarily conscious or unconscious. On the whole, however, in the average person, they are more often unconscious rather than conscious. It is not necessary at this point to overhaul the tremendous mass of evidence which indicates the crucial importance of unconscious motivation. It would by now be expected on *a priori* grounds alone, that unconscious motivations would on the whole be rather more important than the conscious motivations. What we have called the basic needs are very often largely unconscious although they may, with suitable techniques, and with sophisticated people, become conscious.

Cultural Specificity and Generality of Needs

This classification of basic needs makes some attempt to take account of the relative unity behind the superficial differences in specific desires from one culture to another. Certainly in any particular culture an individual's conscious motivational content will usually be extremely different from the conscious motivational content of an individual in another society. However, it is the common experience of anthropologists that people, even in different societies, are much more alike than we would think from our first contact with them, and that as we know them better we seem to find more and more of this commonness. Our classification of basic needs is in part an attempt to account for this unity behind the apparent diversity from culture to culture. No claim is made that it is ultimate or universal for all cultures. The claim is made only that it is relatively more ultimate, more universal, more basic, than the superficial, conscious desires from culture to culture and makes a somewhat closer approach to common-human characteristics. Basic needs are more common-human than superficial desires or behaviors.

Multiple Motivations of Behavior

These needs must be understood not to be *exclusive* or single
determiners of certain kinds of behavior. An example may be
found in any behavior that seems to be physiologically motivated,
such as eating, or sexual play, or the like. The clinical psychologists have long since found that any behavior may be a channel
through which flow various determinants. Or to say it in another
way, most behavior is multi-motivated. Within the sphere of
motivational determinants, any behavior tends to be determined
by several or *all* of the basic needs simultaneously rather than by
only one of them. As an illustration, I may point out that it would
be possible (theoretically if not practically) to analyze a single act
of an individual and see in it the expression of his physiological
needs, his safety needs, his love needs, his esteem needs, and self-
actualization. This contrasts sharply with the more naive brand
of trait psychology in which one trait or one motive accounts for
a certain kind of act, i.e., an aggressive act is traced solely to a
trait of aggressiveness.

Multiple Determinants of Behavior

Not all behavior is determined by the basic needs. We might
even say that not all behavior is motivated. There are many determinants of behavior other than motives. For instance, one
other important class of determinants is the so-called "field" determinants. Theoretically, at least, behavior may be determined
completely by the field, or even by specific isolated external
stimuli, as in association of ideas, or certain conditioned reflexes.
If in response to the stimulus word "table," I immediately perceive a memory image of a table, this response certainly has
nothing to do with my basic needs.

Secondly, we may call attention again to the concept of "degree
of closeness to the basic needs" or "degree of motivation." Some
behavior is highly motivated, other behavior is only weakly motivated. Some is not motivated at all (but all behavior is determined).

Another important point is that there is a basic difference
between expressive behavior and coping behavior (functional

striving, purposive goal seeking). An expressive behavior does not try to do anything; it is simply a reflection of the personality. A stupid man behaves stupidly, not because he wants to, or tries to, or is motivated to, but simply because he *is* what he *is*. Also the *style* in which a man carries out almost all his behavior, motivated as well as unmotivated, is often expressive.

We may then ask, is *all* behavior expressive or reflective of the character structure? The answer is "No." Rote, habitual, automatized, or conventional behavior may or may not be expressive. The same is true for most "stimulus-bound" behaviors.

It is finally necessary to stress that expressiveness of behavior and goal-directedness of behavior are not mutually exclusive categories. Average behavior is usually both.

Goals as Centering Principle in Motivation Theory

It will be observed that the basic principle in our classification has been neither the instigation nor the motivated behavior but rather the functions, effects, purposes, or goals of the behavior. It has been proven sufficiently by various people that this is the most suitable point for centering in any motivation theory.

Animal-and-Human-Centering

This theory starts with the human being rather than any lower and presumably "simpler" animal. Too many of the findings that have been made in animals have been proven to be true for animals but not for the human being. There is no reason whatsoever why we should start with animals in order to study human motivation. The logic or rather illogic behind this general fallacy of "pseudo-simplicity" has been exposed often enough by philosophers ond logicians as well as by scientists in each of the various fields.

We may also reject the old, naive behaviorism which assumed that it was somehow necessary, or at least more "scientific," to judge human beings by animal standards. One consequence of this belief was that the whole notion of purpose and goal was excluded from motivational psychology simply because one could not ask a white rat about his purposes. Tolman [37] has long since proven in animal studies themselves that this exclusion was not necessary.

Motivation and Theory of Psychopathogenesis

The conscious motivational content of everyday life has, according to the foregoing, been conceived to be relatively important or unimportant accordingly as it is more or less closely related to the basic goals. A desire for an ice cream cone might actually be an indirect expression of a desire for love. If it is, then this desire for the ice cream cone becomes extremely important motivation. If, however, the ice cream is simply something to cool the mouth with, or a casual appetitive reaction, then the desire is relatively unimportant. Everyday conscious desires are to be regarded as symptoms, *as surface indicators of more basic needs.*

Thwarting of unimportant desires produces no psychopathological results; thwarting of a basically important need does produce such results. Any theory of psychopathogenesis must then be based on a sound theory of motivation. A conflict or a frustration is not necessarily pathogenic. It becomes so only when it threatens or thwarts the basic needs, or partial needs that are closely related to the basic needs. [22]

The Role of Gratified Needs

It has been pointed out above several times that our needs usually emerge only when more prepotent needs have been gratified. Thus, gratification has an important role in motivation theory. Apart from this, however, needs cease to play an active determining or organizing role as soon as they are gratified.

What this means is that, e.g., a basically satisfied person no longer has the needs for esteem, love, safety, etc. The only sense in which he might be said to have them is in the almost metaphysical sense that a sated man has hunger, or a filled bottle has emptiness. If we are interested in what has, will, or might motivate us, then a satisfied need is not a motivator. It must be considered for all practical purposes simply not to exist, to have disappeared. This point should be emphasized because it has been either overlooked or contradicted in every theory of motivation I know.[2] The perfectly healthy, normal, fortunate man has no sex esteem, except in stray moments of quickly passing threat. If we were to say otherwise, we should have to aver that every man had all the pathological reflexes, e.g., Babinski, etc., because if his nervous system were damaged, these would appear.

It is such considerations as these that suggest the bold postulation that a man who is thwarted in any of his basic needs may fairly be envisaged simply as a sick man. This is a fair parallel to our designation as "sick" of the man who lacks vitamins or minerals. Who is to say that a lack of love is less important than a lack of vitamins? Since we know the pathogenic effects of love starvation, who is to say that we are invoking value-questions in an unscientific or illegitimate way, any more than the physician does who diagnoses and treats pellagra or scurvy? If I were permitted this usage, I should then say simply that a healthy man is primarily motivated by his needs to develop and actualize his fullest potentialities and capacities. If a man has any other basic needs in any active, chronic sense, then he is simply an unhealthy man. He is as surely sick as if he had suddenly developed a strong salt-hunger or calcium hunger.[3]

If this statement seems unusual or paradoxical, the reader may be assured that this is only one among many such paradoxes that will appear as we revise our ways of looking at man's deeper motivations. When we ask what man wants of life, we deal with his very essence.

SUMMARY

1. There are at least five sets of goals, which we may call basic needs. These are briefly physiological, safety, love, esteem, and

[2] Note that acceptance of this theory necessitates basic revision of the Freudian theory.

[3] If we were to use the word "sick" in this way, we should then also have to face squarely the relations of man to his society. One clear implication of our definition would be that (1) since a man is to be called sick who is basically thwarted, and (2) since such basic thwarting is made possible ultimately only by forces outside the individual, then (3) sickness in the individual must come ultimately from a sickness in the society. The "good" or healthy society would then be defined as one that permitted man's highest purpose to emerge by satisfying all his prepotent basic needs.

self-actualization. In addition, we are motivated by the desire to achieve or maintain the various conditions upon which these basic satisfactions rest and by certain more intellectual desires.

2. These basic goals are related to each other, being arranged in a hierarchy of prepotency. This means that the most prepotent goal will monopolize consciousness and will tend of itself to organize the recruitment of the various capacities of the organism. The less prepotent needs are minimized, even forgotten or denied. But when a need is fairly well satisfied, the next prepotent ("higher") need emerges, in turn to dominate the conscious life and to serve as the center of organization of behavior, since gratified needs are not active motivators.

Thus, man is a perpetually wanting animal. Ordinarily the satisfaction of these wants is not altogether mutually exclusive, but only tends to be. The average member of our society is most often partially satisfied and partially unsatisfied in all of his wants. The hierarchy principle is usually empirically observed in terms of increasing percentages of non-satisfaction as we go up the hierarchy. Reversals of the average order of the hierarchy are sometimes observed. Also, it has been observed that an individual may permanently lose the higher wants in the hierarchy under specific conditions. There are not only ordinarily multiple motivations for usual behavior, but in addition many determinants other than motives.

3. Any thwarting or possibility of thwarting of these basic human goals, or danger to the defenses which protect them, or to the conditions upon which they rest, is considered to be a psychological threat. With a few exceptions, all psychopathology may be partially traced to such threats. A basically thwarted man may actually be defined as a "sick" man, if we wish.

4. It is such basic threats which bring about the general emergency reactions.

5. Certain other basic problems have not been dealt with because of limitations of space. Among these are (a) the problem of values in any definitive motivation theory, (b) the relation between appetites, desires, needs, and what is "good" for the organism, (c) the etiology of the basic needs and their possible derivation in early childhood, (d) redefinition of motivational

concepts, i.e., drive, desire, wish, need, goal, (e) implication of our theory for hedonistic theory, (f) the nature of the uncompleted act, of success and failure, and of aspiration-level, (g) the role of association, habit, and conditioning, (h) relation to the theory of inter-personal relations, (i) implications for psychotherapy, (j) implication for theory of society, (k) the theory of selfishness, (l) the relation between needs and cultural patterns, (m) the relation between this theory and Allport's theory of functional autonomy. These as well as certain other less important questions must be considered as motivation theory attempts to become definitive.

——▶ **D. O. Hebb**

The Motivating Effects of Exteroceptive Stimulation

From *American Psychologist*, March, 1958, 13:109–113. Reprinted by permission.

My instructions from the man who cracked the whip—in the role of Chairman of this symposium—were to center my talk about the effects of perceptual deprivation on human motivation and the study of brainwashing made at McGill. It's obvious, no one can *really* deal with my topic in a 20-minute paper and also go on and talk about broad implications. So I'll make no pretence at covering the field. But if I see a chance to make a broad remark, of course, I will.

THE INFANT'S ENVIRONMENT

What we are considering here is the relation of the mammal to his sensory environment. To put this in perspective I shall start with perceptual deficit in infancy, as far as it bears on motivational and emotional problems. As you know, it is now clear that such a deficit also produces intellectual defects at maturity [2, 9, 16], but this I am not directly concerned with, except as it bears incidentally on social intelligence. Also, I am going to restrict this further to the dog, an animal that shows *some* of the complexities of temperament found in the higher species—more so than the rat, certainly. The work I refer to is mainly that of Thompson, Melzack, Heron, and Mahut. [7, 21, 26–28, 33–36] These studies of temperamental variables have shown, like those on intelligence, that the normal development of behavior depends on a normal perceptual environment. The animal reared in isolation is a permanent screwball at maturity: motivationally, socially, intellectually abnormal.

These rearing experiments, of course, relate to the early observations of Spitz [32] concerning "hospitalism" and social deprivation of the hospitalized infant, and to the later observations of Bowlby [5] and others, also on hospitalized children. It is important to mention also such reports of single human subjects, reared in pretty extreme isolation, as those of Davis [8], Hill and Robinson [15], and Mason. [25] But in these human cases, of course, there are a number of uncontrolled variables, making interpretation difficult indeed.

The animal experiments not only have the advantage of experimental control; they also make it possible to observe long-term effects, because the dog grows up in a reasonable period of time. It is quite practical to rear dogs in different ways and test not only at adolescence, so to speak, but also in young middle age. There is a lot of talk in the literature about how to rear the human animal so as to produce the kind of motivations ("personality") you want, at maturity; but the child psychologist sometimes forgets to what a great extent these statements depend on some theoretical formulation or other, and there aren't any theories that we can really trust that much.

There is no evidence whatsoever that shows factually, reliably, the effects of a particular kind of rearing, for the first six years of life, upon personality and so forth when the human subject has grown up. It's a long step from dog to man, of course, and we can't put much trust in this kind of inference either. The ideal subjects for experiment would be the anthropoid apes, but these take almost as long to grow up as man does, so this again is not really practical. Perhaps Harry Harlow will manage the trick in his rearing experiments with rhesus monkeys, but in the end we are going to have to depend on a better development of basic theory, combined with the data of animal experiments.

Anyway, let me summarize the dog-rearing experiments, as far as they bear on motivational questions. One point, first, is most important in the interpretation of the results. The dogs reared in isolation showed none of the physical debility and susceptibility to infection that Spitz reported. They developed exceptionally well: in fact, being nice and stupid, they made excellent show dogs; and William Ponman, who was in charge of the colony, filled a small display cabinet in the laboratory with first-prize ribbons won with our dogs, year after year, in dog shows. This physical vigor should be kept in mind in considering the motivational deviations.

The restricted dogs were markedly atypical in activity measures, exploratory behavior and the search for variety, sharing of food in a single food-dish, social responsiveness to another dog, response to either threatening or friendly persons, and response to pain stimulation.

They were also low in formal problem-solving ability, of course, and this brings me to the question of their "social intelligence." Their behavior suggested repeatedly that the motivational differences, or what seemed motivational differences, were partly due to not perceiving the situation in the same way as the normal dogs and not having acquired normal ways of dealing with others. "Social intelligence" used to be in the literature, along with the abstract and mechanical varieties of intelligence, and one of the things suggested by these experiments is that it ought still to be in the literature.

How do social skills develop? It's no longer possible just to take for granted that your heredity will do it. You don't grow up to be socially perceptive, sensitive to another's attitudes, able to be friendly without overdoing it, able to conceal your own attitudes as need be, and so forth—you don't develop all the social skills that one must have to live with others simply as a matter of heredity and growth. We know, with reasonable certainty, that this aspect of intellectual function, like others, must depend on experience also. But what kind of experience, when, at what age?

This symposium of course is concerned with motivation, not cognitive processes as such; but the point is that motivation is also a function of perceptions and skills. We want to bring up children with "democratic" values; if in fact this is to be so, they must know how to put them satisfyingly into effect. It is hardly realistic for the social scientist to concentrate only on establishing desirable motivations—how long can one expect them to survive, not to extinguish, if the corresponding social skills are missing?

The Environment at Maturity

Now we come closer home, with studies directly concerned with motivation in the adult. The infant-environment work shows that the adult is a product both of his heredity and physical environment (as necessary for growth) and of his perceptual experience during the growth period. Once development is complete, does the organism then become less dependent psychologically on sensory stimulation? When a man's or a woman's character is formed, his or her motivations and personality pattern established, is character or personality an entity that exists so to speak in its own right, no matter where or in what circumstances (assuming physical health and reasonable bodily welfare)?

In the Korean war the Chinese Communists gave us a shocking answer: in the form of brainwashing. The answer is No. Without physical pain, without drugs, the personality can be badly deformed simply by modifying the perceptual environment. It becomes evident that the adult is still a function of his sensory environment in a very general sense, as the child is.

I am not going to ask you to listen again to all the details of the experiments that have been done and are still being done in this country and Canada (though the Canadian experiments are over) to investigate the problem. The work of Heron, Bexton, Scott, and Doane [3, 13, 14] began when the Defence Research Board of Canada asked us in 1952 to find out what we could about the basic phenomena, with the hope that some possibilities for protection against brainwashing might turn up. Now brainwashing, as you know, takes different forms and can involve lack of sleep, fatigue, and hunger; and it makes a lot of use of having the subject write out "confessions" (or whatever you want to call them). Only one aspect was picked out for study: isolation from the environment. The isolation was drastic, but far from complete. Visual perception was completely prevented; auditory perception was cut down, perhaps, to about a quarter of normal; tactual perceptions, to perhaps a tenth of normal (but don't ask how this quantification is done!).

The result, again in brief, was an acute disturbance of the normal personality. (The effect observed by Lilly [20], was apparently even greater than in the McGill studies.) There were great swings of motivation, which alternated between periods of apathy and an intense desire to get back to a normal environment. Any variation of sensory input was welcomed, but with this there was a lack of energy for problem solving; and, after leaving isolation, the subject found it difficult or impossible to get back to his normal work habits for about 24 hours. In addition, there were some handsome visual hallucinations, disturbances of perception of the self, impairment of intelligence test performance, changes in the EEG, and marked visual disturbances on first emerging from isolation.

With the possible exception of the effects of propaganda, the changes were reversible, disappearing in a day or so. For the problem of brainwashing we learned something of value, which should be as widely known as possible, since we do not know who will fall into Communist hands in the future and be subjected to this—appalling, indecent, choose your own adjective—this atrocious procedure; and knowing something about it may mitigate its effects.

First, the occurrence of hallucinations can itself be terrifying to the naive subject and help to break down his resistance. If he knows that hallucinations are "normal" in these circumstances and that the effects are quite reversible, he has at least a little protection.

Second, the subject should know that his critical thinking will be impaired and that he is especially vulnerable to propaganda after being in radical isolation. Knowing this may help to resist propaganda, if the subject can keep reminding himself to make an extra critical effort. Heron's group did not try to investigate means of resistance, but did demonstrate the vulnerability to ridiculous propaganda. The subject was given talks on ghosts, poltergeists, ESP, and so forth, the experimenters deliberately propagandizing and having no truck with scientific detachment or such like. He was told that scientists are biased against psychic phenomena, that there is plenty of evidence to show the existence of ghosts, and so on—the statements being made as persuasive as possible. Control subjects were paid to listen to the same stuff and were influenced by it, but the experimental subjects significantly more. Part of this was no doubt due to the subject's eagerness to *listen*, to almost anything; again, if the prisoner being brainwashed knows in advance that he will have this weakness, he may be able to some extent to guard against it.

The effects of the propaganda were the only ones that showed signs of lasting beyond the experimental period. The groups tested two weeks later were too small to establish the point definitely, in a statistical sense, but the tentative conclusion was reinforced by incidental reports from the subjects. A number of the experimental subjects, unlike the controls, went to the library to borrow books on psychical (*not* psychological) research, mind reading, and so forth; there were spontaneous reports of being afraid of ghosts, late at night, for the first time in the subject's experience; and reports of trying to use ESP in card-playing.

It is hardly necessary to say that the experiment, taken as a whole, was very unsettling to us. Our subjects were of course free to walk out on the experiment at any time they chose (as soon as they felt they could give up the $20 a day pay!), but it would be very different for a man in fear of his life, with no choice in the matter and no termination in sight. It is one thing to hear that the Chinese are brainwashing their prisoners on the other side of the world; it is another to find, in your own laboratory, that merely taking away the usual sights, sounds, and bodily contacts from a healthy university student for a few days can shake him, right down to the base; can disturb his personal identity, so that he is aware of two bodies (one hallucinatory) and can not say which is his own, or perceives his personal self as a vague and ill-defined something *separate from his body*, looking down at where it is lying on the bed; and can disturb his capacity for critical judgment, making him eager to listen to and believe any sort of preposterous nonsense.

Fundamentally, this raises the whole question of the relation of man to his sensory environment, and it bears particularly on research in personality and social processes. There are other aspects of the problem, but for those I refer you to the chapter by Thompson and myself [12] in Lindzey's *Handbook of Social Psychology*. What I want to do now is to bring the discussion closer to everyday living.

The effects I have been talking about can occur in varying degree. Lilly [20] has shown that making isolation more drastic produces motivational and emotional disturbance much more quickly; but he has also shown that the lonely man, in not too abnormal an environment otherwise, may suffer gross disturbances when the social deprivation is long continued. Lilly has reviewed some of the published reports of solitary sailors, Arctic groups in the long polar night, and shipwreck survivors in a small boat. These people, the ones who survive, develop one or other of the symptoms of the mentally ill—and among the many who do not survive, of course, there are those who develop outright psychosis. Mystical feelings of oneness with the universe develop; fears of being insane, or of seeming to be insane, are common. In larger groups, socially closer to normal situations, Boag [4] has described a motivational process that parallels—but on a more extended scale—a puzzling aspect of results found in the McGill experiments. The experimental subjects were always eager to be tested, as a break in the monotony, and then paradoxically lacked the energy to work on problems even of moderate difficulty. Similarly, Boag reports that men in Arctic stations would make extensive plans for spare-time activities, exactly the sort of thing that would protect them against their lack of stimulation, only to slump later into a kind of apathy. There was:

. . . apathy, lack of interest in surroundings, motor retardation, greatly increased hours of sleep, lack of attention to personal appearance and tidiness of quarters, and disinclination to undertake extra work or odd jobs, *in spite of complaints of not having enough to do* [italics added]. An occasional man will spend a whole winter in his quarters without leaving them to visit neighbors half an hour's walk away . . . [4]

Clearly, man's motivation is a function of his exteroceptive stimulation. I don't need to labor this further, but instead draw your attention to another set of phenomena that don't get into the books. These concern the relation of our own work habits to an accustomed environment, and the ease with which motivation is broken down. How many of you, when you get back from these meetings, will be able to go on with your work on the first day, as if you had never been away? How many of you go on vacation with plans for work that do not get carried out—that is, not even to the extent that you carry out plans when you are in your normal work environment? How many of you can write only in a particular setting, after elaborate preparation, with everything just so?

It was Karl Menninger in a personal communication who drew my attention to the similarity of the deficient-environment effects and the phenomenon of not being able to get back to work after being away—I believe it is quite common, but at any rate Menninger and I suffer from it.

Being often my own best subject when it comes to the study of abnormal behavior, I have now finally to report some peculiar behavior of my own bearing on this question of the relation of motivation to the accustomed environment. I do so with the idea that others may have observed similar phenomena and may perhaps have better ideas as to how they are to be understood. The peculiarity, really, is only in certain time relations. I have repeatedly found, when I have been a visiting lecturer or away from my usual habitat in some other similar role, that my ability to write, or do other work that I jokingly call creative, runs down over a two-week period or thereabouts. It can be restored by a short period in my own laboratory setting, and then again runs down. This is presumably a function of homesickness, of what

Hunt, I believe, called cryptic nostalgia—an acute condition, at times, from which I as well as many other persons suffer, though it is not mentioned among adults. (Rather vulgar, one gathers.) I can understand the nostalgia, in the sense that it is part of the whole picture of man's motivation as dependent on an accustomed environment, but I have more trouble understanding why the clock, so to speak, takes so long to run down. There are some problems here for research that have the happy combination of both theoretical and practical interest. I wish someone would tackle them.

REFERENCES

1. ADLER, A., *Social Interest,* London: Faber & Faber, Ltd., 1938.
2. BEACH, F. A., & JAYNES, J., "Effects of Early Experience upon the Behavior of Animals," *Psychological Bulletin,* 1954, 51:239–263.
3. BEXTON, W. H., HERON, W., & SCOTT, T. H., "Effects of Decreased Variation in the Sensory Environment," *Canadian Journal of Psychology,* 1954, 8:70–76.
4. BOAG, T. J., "The White Man in the Arctic: A Preliminary Study of the Problems of Adjustment," *American Journal of Psychiatry,* 1952, 109:444–449.
5. BOWLBY, J., "Maternal Care and Mental Health," *World Health Organization Monographs,* 1941, No. 2.
6. CANNON, W. B., *Wisdom of the Body,* New York: W. W. Norton & Co., Inc., 1932.
7. CLARKE, R. S., HERON, W., FETHERSTONAUGH, M. L., FORGAYS, D. G., & HEBB, D. O., "Individual Differences in Dogs: Preliminary Report on the Effects of Early Experience," *Canadian Journal of Psychology,* 1951, 5:150–156.
8. DAVIS, KATHRYN, "Extreme Social Isolation of a Child," *American Journal of Sociology,* 1940, 45:554–565.
9. FORGAYS, D. G., & FORGAYS, JANET, "The Nature of the Effect of Free-environmental Experience in the Rat," *Journal of Comparative and Physiological Psychology,* 1952, 45:322–328.
10. FREUD, S., *New Introductory Lectures on Psychoanalysis,* New York: W. W. Norton & Co., Inc., 1933.
11. GOLDSTEIN, K., *The Organism,* New York: American Book Company, 1939.

12. HEBB, D. O., & THOMPSON, W. R., "The Social Significance of Animal Studes," in G. Lindzey, ed., *Handbook of Social Psychology*, Cambridge, Mass.: Addison-Wesley Publishing Co., 1954.

13. HERON, W., "The Pathology of Boredom," *Scientific American*, 1957, 196:54–56.

14. ————, Doane, B. K., & SCOTT, T. H., "Visual Disturbances after Prolonged Perceptual Isolation," *Canadian Journal of Psychology*, 1956, 10:13–18.

15. HILL, J. C., & ROBINSON, B., "A Case of Retarded Mental Development Associated with Restricted Movement in Infancy," *British Journal of Medical Psychology*, 1929, 9:268–277.

16. HUMOVITCH, B., "The Effects of Experimental Variations on Problem-solving in the Rat," *Journal of Comparative and Physiological Psychology*, 1952, 45:313–321.

17. KARDINER, A., *The Traumatic Neuroses of War,* New York: Paul B. Hoeber, Inc., 1941.

18. KLINEBERG, O., *Social Psychology*, New York: Holt, Rinehart and Winston, Inc., 1940.

19. LEVY, D. M., "Primary Affect Hunger," *American Journal of Psychiatry*, 1937, 94:643–652.

20. LILLY, J. C., "Mental Effects of Reduction of Ordinary Levels of Physical Stimuli on Intact, Healthy Persons," *Psychiatric Research Reports*, 1956, No. 5.

21. MAHUT, HELEN, "Breed Differences in the Dog's Emotional Behavior," *Canadian Journal of Psychology*, in press.

22. MASLOW, A. H., "Conflict, Frustration, and the Theory of Threat," *Journal of Abnormal and Social Psychology*, 1943, 38:81–86.

23. ————, "A Preface to Motivation Theory," *Psychosomatic Medicine*, 1943, 5:85–92.

24. ————, & MITTELMANN, B., *Principles of Abnormal Psychology*, New York: Harper & Brothers, 1941.

25. MASON, MARIE K., "Learning to Speak after Six and One-half Years of Silence," *Journal of Speech Disorders*, 1942, 7:295–304.

26. MELZACK, R., "The Genesis of Emotional Behavior: An Experimental Study of the Dog," *Journal of Comparative and Physiological Psychology*, 1954, 47:166–168.

27. ————, & SCOTT, T. H., "The Effects of Early Experience on the Response to Pain," *Journal of Comparative and Physiological Psychology*, 1957, 50:155–161.

28. ————, & THOMPSON, W. R., "Effects of Early Experience on Social Behavior," *Canadian Journal of Psychology*, 1956, 10:82–90.

29. MUENZINGER, K. F., *Psychology: The Science of Behavior*, New York: Harper & Brothers, 1942.

30. MURPHY, G., *Personality: A Bio-social Approach to Origins and Structure,* New York: Harper & Brothers, 1947.

31. SHIRLEY, MARY, "Children's Adjustments to a Strange Situation," *Journal of Abnormal and Social Psychology,* 1942, 37:201–217.

32. SPITZ, R. A., "Hospitalism: A Follow-up Report," *Psychoanalytic Study of the Child,* 1946, 2:113–117.

33. THOMPSON, W. R., & HERON, W., "The Effects of Restricting Early Experience on the Problem-solving Capacity of Dogs," *Canadian Journal of Psychology,* 1954, 8:17–31.

34. ———, & ———, "The Effects of Early Restriction on Activity in Dogs," *Journal of Comparative and Physiological Psychology,* 1954, 47:77–82.

35. ———, & MELZACK, R., "Early Environment," *Scientific American,* 1956, 194:38–42.

36. ———, ———, & Scott, T. H., " 'Whirling Behavior' in Dogs as Related to Early Experience," *Science,* 1956, 123:939.

37. TOLMAN, E. C., *Purposive Behavior in Animals and Men,* New York: Appleton-Century-Crofts, Inc., 1932.

38. WERTHEIMER, M., Unpublished Lectures at the New School for Social Research.

39. YOUNG, P. T., "The Experimental Analysis of Appetite," *Psychological Bulletin,* 1941, 38:129–164.

CHAPTER
SEVEN

↑

Feelings and Emotions

FEW PROBLEMS OF PSYCHOLOGY HAVE RE-
ceived as much attention over the years as feelings and emotions.
There is good reason for this. Feelings and emotions enter into
virtually every experience the individual has. Excitement, joy,
love, hope, feelings of security—these are very much a part of a
person's life. So, too, are disappointment, discouragement, fear,
anger, dismay, anxiety, and various other affective reactions.

The emotional and feeling aspects of what an individual experiences enter into his choices, influence his expectations and
plans, and over a period of time profoundly affect the pattern of
his personality. Anything so all-pervading of the individual's behavior and so powerfully related to the kind of life he leads is,
to repeat, deserving of the psychologist's most systematic study.
It is deserving, also, of study by teachers and other professional

workers engaged in helping individuals develop mature personalities.

What are the circumstances that give rise to and accompany
the affective aspects of human behavior? When in the development of the individual do certain kinds of affective expressions
become evident? What generalized explanation of the emotions
do the answers to these questions suggest? The research report
by Katherine M. Banham Bridges is notable for the thoroughness
with which it deals with the emotional behavior of infants and
points the way to a theory about the genesis of the emotions. Few
studies of child growth and development have been cited as frequently by other writers as this research. Bridges is a professor of
psychology at Duke University.

In the second reading included in this chapter, Fritz Redl and
Stanley Jacobson present practical suggestions for helping the
child who is emotionally disturbed. They emphasize that general
prescriptions for relieving children of emotional disturbances are
likely to be of limited value for individual cases since each child's
situation must be considered in the light of factors specific to it.
They do, nevertheless, offer some ideas that teachers will find very
useful as they confront the problems of emotionally troubled
children. Both Redl and Jacobson are psychologists on the staff
of the National Institute of Mental Health; Redl is Chief of the
Child Research Branch.

—→ **Katherine M. Banham Bridges**

Emotional Development
in Early Infancy

From *Child Development*, 1932, 3:324–334. Reprinted and abridged by permission of the author and the Society for Research in Child Development.

The emotional behavior of 62 infants in the Montreal Foundling and Baby Hospital was carefully observed and recorded daily over a period of three or four months. The circumstances attendant upon these reactions were noted, and the whole data was studied from the point of view of development from age to age. A summary of the findings will be presented in the following paragraphs. They will be seen to lend support to the writer's [2, 3] theory of the genesis of the emotions and to add further illuminating detail.

The babies under observation were in separate wards more or less according to age. In different rooms were infants under one month, one to three months, three to six months, six to nine months, nine to twelve months, and twelve to fifteen months. An older group of children between fifteen and twenty-four months of age played together in the nursery.

Table 1 shows the number of children at the different ages whose behavior was observed for this study.

Development in the emotional behavior of the young child comprises 3 main classes of change. From birth onward there is a gradual evolution of the emotions taking place. The earliest emotional reactions are very general and poorly organized responses to one or two general types of situation. As weeks and months go by the responses take on more definite form in relation to more specific situations. It seems to the writer, as already mentioned elsewhere, that in the course of genesis of the emotions there occurs a process of differentiation. Coincident with

TABLE 1

Age, months	Number of Children
Under 1	3
1–3	16
3–6	23
6–9	18
9–12	11
12–15	20
15–18	8
18–21	5
21–24	6
Over 24	2

the partial isolation of certain responses is a combining of the simpler reactions within the unit responses and the formation of bonds of association between these emotional syndromes and detailed aspects of the provoking situations. In this manner slowly appear the well known emotions of anger, disgust, joy, love, and so forth. They are not present at birth in their mature form.

In addition to the progressive evolution of the emotions, there is, going on at the same time, a gradual change in the mode of response of each specific emotion. Muscles are developing, new skills are being learned. So that the anger, for instance, expressed by the eighteen-month-old differs in detail of form from the anger manifested by the ten-month-old baby. A gradual substitution takes place of the situations which prompt the emotions. In the language of the behaviorists, emotional responses become conditioned to fresh stimuli.

Excitement, the Original Emotion

After observing the behavior of babies *under one month* of age, the writer felt more than ever convinced that the infant does not start life with 3 fully matured pattern reactions, such as have been mentioned by behaviorists and named fear, rage and love. Unfortunately the writer was not able to observe the infants within a few hours of birth, but this fact in no way invalidates observations made on children two or three weeks old. And, even if the process of conditioning begins before or immediately upon birth, one may expect the original emotion-producing stimuli to elicit their natural responses at least for two or three weeks after birth.

It was observed in the hospital that, on presentation of certain strong stimuli the infants became agitated, their arm and hand muscles tensed, their breath quickened, and their legs made jerky kicking movements. Their eyes opened, the upper lid arched, and they gazed into the distance. The stimuli producing such agitation or excitement were: bright sun directly in the infant's eyes, sudden picking up and putting down on the bed, pulling the child's arm through his dress sleeve, holding the arms tight to the sides, rapping the baby's knuckles, pressing the bottle nipple into the child's mouth, and the noisy clatter of a small tin basin thrown on to a metal table whence it fell to the radiator and the floor.

Lowering the babies suddenly into their cribs, and in some cases lifting them quickly, also startled and excited them. Sometimes they would cry following upon such a surprise. Rocking a quiet child would cause him to open his eyes attentively. But gently rocking a crying infant would often, though not always, cause him to reduce his activity, stop crying, and eventually become tranquil. Gentle handling, slow patting, wrapping in warm blankets, and nursing easily soothed an agitated or crying infant, making him relax and yawn and become sleepy.

Light pinching of the arm left the three- or four-week-old baby unmoved. Deeper pressure caused him to kick slightly, breathe faster and move his arms. A sharp flick on the hand produced similar agitation, but a second rap resulted in a sudden check to breathing followed by a prolonged cry and other signs of distress. The first exciting experience had been found disagreeable and the second rap produced unmistakable distress.

Time after time on waking suddenly from sleep the infants were observed to wave their arms jerkily, kick, open and close their eyes, flush slightly, and breathe quickly and irregularly. Some grunted, some cried spasmodically for a moment or two, while others cried loudly for several minutes. The combined stimulation of light, of sounds, of damp or restricting bed clothes, and the change from sleeping to waking breathing-rate seemed to produce a temporary agitation and often distress. Waking apparently requires emotional adjustment.

The hungry child before feeding would often show restless activity, waving, squirming, mouthing and crying at intervals. The infant who had been lying in one position for a long time and the tired child before falling asleep would also show emotional agitation. Their breath would come jerkily, uttering staccato cries of "cu-cu-cu-ah," and they would thrust out their arms and legs in irregular movements. At the moment the nipple was put into the hungry baby's mouth he again breathed quickly, occasionally cried, waved the free arm, and kicked in excited agitation.

The emotional reactions of the tiny infant are certainly not highly differentiated. The most common response to highly stimulating situations seems to be one of general agitation or excitement. It is a question which word most aptly describes the behavior. The former perhaps conveys more the idea of general disturbance, although the two words are often used synonymously. This vague emotional response to a large variety of circumstances must surely be one of the original emotions, if not the only one.

A kind of general excitement over new and startling or other highly stimulating circumstances may be seen at any age. The behavior manifestations vary from time to time, but the main characteristics of accelerated response, alertness, slight tension or restlessness remain as constant attributes. In the babies, excitement is frequently manifested in kicking movements. The month-old infants kick jerkily with both feet at random. In another month or so, the kicking becomes more regular, the legs being thrust out alternately. By five or six months the babies express their emotions in combined leg thrusts, kicking with one foot, and in swinging the legs from the hips. At fourteen months when the children can stand they will hold on to a support and "mark time" with their feet or stamp. Stamping, jumping and running express excited agitation at a still later age.

Two- and three-month-old babies may be seen to suck their thumbs or fingers rapidly in moments of stress. At seven months and over, children bite, pull and suck their garments, as well as their fingers. This behavior seems to produce a gradual subsidence of the emotion. Body-rocking accompanied in many instances by rhythmic vocalizations is another expression of mixed emotion. Hungry, annoyed, excited or restless children will sit and rock for minutes on end. The five-month-old baby lies prone and pushes with his knees, or sways when lying dorsally. Seven-month-old infants support themselves on their arms and rock back and forth murmuring "mm-ŭm, mm-ŭm." After nine months they sit up and rock to and fro, or they kneel and bounce up and down holding on to the crib bars. Sometimes they sit and bump their backs against the side of the crib. This kind of behavior was observed in the nursery up to eighteen months of age.

Rhythmical movements were observed not only to be the outcome of emotional excitement or tension, but they were seen to have a soothing and pacifying effect. These must be attempts at adjustment on the part of the organism to reduce tension and restore emotional equilibrium or tranquility. In the light of these observations, it can be easily understood how long walks, games, field sports, singing, dancing, and sea-voyages are found to be so universally health-giving and positively curative for "nervous wrecks."

DISTRESS AND ITS DERIVATIVES

It is a moot question whether "distress" is an original emotion or whether it is a very early differentiated reaction to disagreeably painful and unsatisfying experiences. It may be that it is a part of the general emotional response of excitement which copes more satisfactorily with obnoxious stimuli. Tense muscles resist or remove pressure; activity warms a chilled body and reduces tension; and cries, at first reflex due to the rush of air in and out of the lungs, bring comfort and aid. These responses become differentiated from excitement, associated together and conditioned to the disagreeable stimuli as a result of experience. If such differentiation actually takes place, it must begin immediately after birth. For the two emotions of excitement and distress are already distinguishable in a three-weeks-old infant.

On the other hand, it is possible that there is a native emotional response to pain, particularly muscle pain. The sympathetic branch of the autonomic nervous system is predominantly active and the overt behavior is definitely that of distress. Other stimuli, such as loud sounds and sudden falling merely produce startled excitement. Blanton [1] observed that the infant's cry of colic had a specially shrill character accompanied by rigidity of the abdominal walls. She also noted that infants during the first days of life cried from "(a) hunger; (b) in response to noxious stimuli (including rough handling, circumcision, lancing and care of boils, sores, etc.); and (c) possibly fatigue or lack of exercise." The writer has observed the same phenomena in three-weeks-old babies. But, hunger, rough handling, and fatigue were also noticed on many occasions to produce a restless excitement rather than specific distress.

It is not easy, in the case of the very young infant, to distinguish distress from general agitation. The cry of distress, recognizable in the month-old baby, is irregular. There are short intakes of breath and long cries on expiration. The eyes are "screwed up" tight, the face flushed, the fists often clenched, the arms tense, and the legs still or kicking spasmodically. The mouth is open and square in shape or, more usually kidney-shaped with the corners pulled down. The pitch of the cry is high and somewhat discordant, and sounds something like "ah, cu-ah, cu-ah, cu-ah." The three main causes of distress at this age seemed to be discomfort, pain, and hunger.

Crying from discomfort and on awakening usually developed slowly, and sounded like "cu-cu-cu-cah-ah—." The cry of pain came suddenly, often after a holding of the breath. The sound was a loud shrill prolonged "ă-ă-ă," and lowered in pitch slightly from the first emission. The cries of hunger were rather like those of discomfort. The former came perhaps more in intermittent waves; the intervening moments being taken up with mounting or sucking movements. Occasionally the hungry child would utter a sharp loud cry, as if in pain, and then whine or moan for a time.

Two-month-old babies cry less of the total waking time; but slighter discomforting stimuli seem to cause distress more frequently than in the case of the younger infants.

By *three months* of age a child will cry and show other signs of distress when placed in an unusual position or moved to a strange place. The hospital baby has learned to associate feeding time with the presence of an adult; for, when he is hungry he shows some excitement at the close approach of a person. If no food is forthcoming, he becomes more tense and jerky in his movements and begins to cry. He is distressed at the delay in normal proceedings.

Should the adult remain tantalizingly near for some minutes without either picking up the child or feeding him, his cry increases in intensity, his eyes become moist with tears, he holds his breath longer, and utters prolonged flat "ă-ă-ă" sound reminiscent of an older child's "paddy" or temper cry. The infant's motor responses were all set for being picked up and fed, and then he was thwarted and disappointed. His excitement changed into bitter distress with a semblance of angry vexation.

The slight change in vowel sound of the cry, the long holding of breath combined with more than usually vigorous leg thrusts and arm movements, seemed to suggest that the emotion of anger is beginning to evolve from general distress at about this age. Although for the most part the distress shown at discomfort differs almost imperceptibly from distress in response to disappointment, occasionally the latter includes, to a marked degree, those behavior elements peculiar to the emotion of anger. The situations which evoke these demonstrations of temper in the tiny infant are a stop or check in the progressive satisfaction of a physical need. Lack of even the first sign of a need being satisfied merely produces vague distress.

A *four-month-old* baby shows distress at the same general sort of situation that troubles the younger child. He is, however, less frequently disturbed by bodily discomfort. He moves about sufficiently to relieve tired muscles and local pressures, and to eliminate gas from his stomach. He cries vigorously at delay in the feeding process and may show decided temper on such occasions. He is getting very fond of attention at this age, and will show distress and often anger when a person leaves the room or ceases to pay attention and play with him.

At *five months,* the baby's interest in small objects, such as rattles, stuffed animals and, of course, his milk bottle, causes him to be distressed when these objects are removed. He may express his displeasure as formerly by crying, squirming, waving and kicking, but he may also be heard merely to call out in a protesting tone of voice, "ah aye," without the half-closing of the eyes and the accompanying tensions of crying.

By this age the child may show slight revulsion for certain foods, coughing, spluttering, frowning and crying while he is being fed. A genuine emotional revulsion did not appear till five months or later. Perhaps this is the beginning of the emotion of disgust. Revulsion at nauseating sights and smells, the adult form of disgust, apparently does not develop until two or more years of age.

Several of the babies in the hospital *between six and eighteen months* were observed to splutter and choke, and refuse to swallow spinach more than other vegetables. The mouthfuls that were rejected were usually, though not always, those containing large or stringy pieces of spinach. When the latter was chopped fine it was swallowed a little more easily; but only when it was mixed with other vegetables was it eaten without any protest. There must be factors other than consistency and size of morsel to account for this objection to spinach.

It seemed to the writer that some cans of spinach tasted more bitter than others and were less palatable on that account. In order to find how the children would react to a bitter taste, two teaspoonfuls each of unsweetened grapefruit juice were given to nine children in the nursery. Four of them pursed or curled their lips, 1 turned his head away, and 1 frowned. The others sat still and solemn, and kept tasting their lips attentively for some time. There were certainly individually different reactions to this bitter-sour, astringent taste. Several of the children definitely disliked it and none of them seemed to like it. It is possible then that there is a bitter taste to spinach which may in part account for children's aversion to it. Another factor, that of the dark green colour of spinach may influence older children's and adult's feeling reaction towards it. One two-year-old in the hospital on turning away and refusing to eat the vegetable was seen to point to it and say "dirty."

The *six-month-old* baby's attention is usually arrested by the presence of a stranger. His movements are inhibited and he watches the newcomer intently. He is not pleased and one could hardly say he is afraid. But he seems diffident and uncertain what to do, or utterly unable to move for a few moments. At seven months he reacts in the same way to the approach of a stranger, though the general inhibition of movement is greater and lasts longer. After a few moments or several seconds of tension he may begin to cry slowly, or burst suddenly into tears. The whole body is usually rigid and inactive. The eyes, previously wide open, close tight and the head bends. Should the stranger touch the child he will probably turn or draw away. Here is the emotion of fear already differentiated. Frightened distress results when the child through inhibition, ignorance, or inability finds himself unable to respond at all adequately to the situation.

At *seven months* of age an infant calls out protestingly when a familiar person ceases to attend to him, instead of crying distressfully like a four-month-old. If he fails to attain his objective he may give up and cry in helpless distress, or he may just grunt in protestation.

A *nine-month-old* child will struggle longer and make more varied attempts to reach the object of his desire. Should he fail to do so after putting forth considerable effort he may become tense and red in the face with anger. He will kick and scream and look for assistance, while tears flow copiously. The cry at this age is becoming exceedingly loud, and tears flow more readily than at the earlier ages. Prolonged crying at four or five months is accompanied by slight lacrimal secretion, but after six months of age tears often flow down the child's cheeks as he cries, especially after an adult's attention has been attracted.

Strangers are still quite terrifying to the nine-month-old baby. His movements are more completely arrested by the unfamiliar presence than those of the six-month-old. At ten months of age he may even be so frightened as to flop down suddenly on the bed and scream loudly. Then follows prolonged and tearful crying.

When children of *ten months* and over are hungry, uncomfortable, tired, or fretful and unwell, they will set up a whine or cry as the result of suggestion when another child cries. They do not, however, ordinarily imitate crying when they are occupied and happy. Small objects which can be manipulated interest them so intensely that they can be distracted from a distressing trouble fairly easily at this age. These objects need not necessarily be new so long as they are freshly presented. *Year-old* babies often cry suddenly when they feel themselves falling, or when they lose their grip while climbing. If they miss the assistance of a helping hand they will also sit down and cry loudly. Sometimes their emotion is anger at the thwarting or failure of their endeavors. They scream, flush, and tremble in rage. At other times they sit motionless in fright and look for aid or comforting sympathy. When strangers approach the *twelve- or thirteen-month-old* baby he may hold his hand behind his ear in a withdrawing motion and stare apprehensively. He may actually hide his eyes behind his hands or look away so as not to see the awe-inspiring or annoying intruder.

At *fourteen months or* thereabouts we may see the real temper tantrum. At least, that is the age when it became noticeable in the hospital. If a child is not given his food or a coveted toy exactly when he wants it he may respond by throwing himself suddenly on the bed or floor. He then screams, holds his breath, trembles, turns red, kicks or thrusts his feet out together. Tears flow and he will wave away anything that is not the desired object. These outbursts may occur frequently for a few weeks, or only spasmodically for another year or eighteen months.

Distressful crying becomes less common as the months go by. Extreme hunger and weariness after a long day or great activity may be accompanied by whining and intermittent outbursts of tears. Anger is expressed more in protesting shouts, pushing and kicking, but less in tearful screaming. So long as adults are present, however, the interference and rough handling of another child may bring forth cries and tears. A *fifteen-month-old* may show his annoyance by hitting a child who has taken his toy or who is holding on to the thing he most wants. He may even bite him or pull his hair without a preliminary scream or shout.

The attention of familiar and interested adults is much sought by children of *fifteen to eighteen months*. If such attention is given to another child there may be signs of deep distress. The neglected one may stiffen, stand motionless, bend his head and burst into tears. Here is perhaps the beginning of jealousy, distress at the loss of, or failure to receive, expected attention and affection.

A *twenty-one-month-old* child will show less mistrust of strangers than will a younger infant. He may, however, run away and watch the newcomer for a time at a safe distance. After eighteen months he shows anger at adult interference by obstinate refusal to comply with their requests. He may shake his head and refuse either to be fed or to feed himself. At two he will play with his food, throwing it about instead of eating it, as a spite against some offending or scolding adult. Distress is shown chiefly at pain and acute discomfort, though the child will cry miserably at much less discomfort if a sympathetic adult is close at hand.

The children in the nursery group, *between fifteen and twenty-four months,* were more or less unconcerned when being undressed for the annual physical examination. This part of the procedure was familiar and not unpleasant. Several of the children cried and stiffened somewhat when placed on the table in the examining room. One or two continued to show distress throughout the examination. The most distressing events were when a flashlight was thrown into the eyes, and when the throat and ears were examined with the aid of the usual tongue-depresser and otoscope. The children had to be held firmly and their movements curbed during these operations.

It was patent to the observer that the children were undergoing rather different emotions according to their fast-developing individual idiosyncracies. Some were mainly startled and afraid, their movements were paralyzed. Some seemed to be just generally distressed at the unusual proceeding and the discomfort; while others were chiefly annoyed at the interference with their freedom. Several children showed signs of all three emotions. These individual differences have their foundation in variants in the physical constitutions of the children, both hereditary and acquired. They are certainly very much determined by the particular experiences the infants have gone through since their birth. A continuous study of behavior week by week reveals the actual differentiation and consolidation of individual traits of temperament.

Two or three of the nursery children over fourteen months developed fears for specific objects or persons. Toy animals that squeaked frightened one or two, causing them to draw away, stare wide-eyed and perhaps cry. This squeak could hardly be called a "loud low sound" such as Watson [4] describes as one of the original fear-producing stimuli. The sound is, however, rather unusual and comes at first as a surprise to the babies.

Parents often remark how their children may suddenly show fear of some surprisingly trivial and inoffensive object. The answer to this may be found in certain partial associations with disturbing events of the past. It may also be found in the particular mental set of the child's mind and body when he came in contact with the object. Still another phenomenon may account for the peculiar fears and objections of children. Timid behavior may be actually learned and preserved as a social asset, one of the numerous means of drawing attention.

The nursery child who cried and crawled away after touching the rough-haired, stuffed animal was flattered with the attention of all the adults in the room. A nurse brought the dog up to the child, smiling and saying "nice doggie." He looked up at her face, saw her kindly smile, then bent his head and began to whimper again. He was having a delightful time out of his apparent fear.

DELIGHT AND ITS DERIVATIVES

Delight is much later in becoming differentiated from general excitement than distress. The baby under a month old is either excited or quiescent. Gentle stroking, swaying and patting soothe him and make him sleepy. When satisfied after a meal he is no longer excited nor even distressed by hunger. And yet he is not positively delighted. He is just unemotionally content, and either tranquil or busy mouthing and staring at distant objects. When he is *over two weeks old* he will sometimes give a faint reflex smile upon light tapping at the corners of his mouth. This is hardly an emotional response.

One- and two-month old babies cry and kick from hunger before they are fed, rather than show delight on presentation of the much desired food. They become calm, however, immediately when given their milk, but not at the mere approach of the adult who brings it. At two months infants will give fleeting smiles upon being nursed, patted, wrapped warmly, spoken to, tickled, or gently rocked. Perhaps this is the beginning of the emotion of delight.

By *three months* of age the emotion of delight is becoming more clearly differentiated from agitated excitement on the one hand and non-emotional quiescence or passivity on the other. The child kicks, opens his mouth, breathes faster, and tries to raise his head upon sight of his bottle. He gives little crooning sounds when being fed, nursed or rocked. He smiles when an adult comes near and talks to him; and he will even stop crying momentarily at the sound of a person's voice. He may also show delight in distant moving objects.

The chief characteristics of delight are: free as against restrained movement; open eyes and expansion of the face in a smile as contrasted with the puckering of the forehead and closing of the eyes in distress; body movements or muscle tension of incipient approach rather than withdrawal; audible inspirations and quickened breathing; soft, lower pitched vocalizations than those of distress or excitement; more or less rhythmic arm and leg movements; prolonged attention to the object of interest; and cessation of crying. Although behavior varies in detail from child to child at successive ages, delight is always recognizable from certain general types of response. Free and rhythmic movements, welcoming and approaching gestures, smiles and vocalizations of middle pitch are most common features.

A *four-month old* baby laughs aloud when some person smiles and frolics with him. Food, though sometimes welcomed eagerly, is often neglected for the more interesting attendant who talks and smiles at him.

At *five months* a child vocalizes his delight in sounds of "uh-uh-ung" in addition to waving, laughing, kicking and wriggling around. He shows special interest in small objects that he can handle and explore. Musical or noisy rattles are popular at this age. When hungry he kicks, breathes fast, and calls out eagerly at the first sign of the person who brings his food. His smiles are more transient, however, and his movements less vigorous on approach of a stranger.

By _six months_ of age a child will reach towards a familiar person but will lie still and observe a stranger dubiously. He crows and coos frequently, taking pleasure in his own movements and sounds.

A _seven-month-old_ baby is becoming increasingly interested in small objects and in the act of reaching and grasping those close at hand. He will even struggle to attain things somewhat out of his reach. When his efforts meet with success he often smiles, takes a deep breath and expresses his satisfaction in a sort of grunt. After a moment or two spent in examination and manipulation of the object, he goes exploring again with fresh vigor. Possibly this is the beginning of the emotion of elation, exhilarating pleasure in personal accomplishments.

At _eight months_ of age the child seems to take more delight than ever in self-initiated purposeful activity. He babbles and splutters and laughs to himself. Especially does he seem delighted with the noise he makes by banging spoons or other playthings on the table. He waves, pats, and coos, drawing in long breaths, when familiar adults swing him or talk to him. He will watch the person who nurses him attentively, exploring her, patting gently, and often smiling. Here are perhaps the earliest demonstrations of affection. The child will also pat and smile at his own mirror image. But his behavior is rather more aggressive and inquisitive than really affectionate.

A _nine-month-old_ baby is very popular with adults. He laughs frequently, bounces up and down and tries to mimic their playful actions. He pats other babies exploratively but does not show particular affection for them. Strange adults may frighten him at first. but, after studying them for some time in the distance, he will smile responsively and join in play with them. By _ten months_ of age the child is taking more interest in other babies. He will mimic their calls and even their laughter. The hospital babies of this age would pat and bang and laugh in imitation of each other.

An *eleven-month-old* baby takes great delight in laughter, not only his own but that of another. He will laugh in order to make another child laugh, then jump and vocalize and laugh again in response. At twelve months of age he will repeat any little action that causes laughter. He is becoming increasingly affectionate. He puts his arms around the familiar adult's neck, and strokes and pats her face. Sometimes he will actually bring his lips close to her face in an incipient kissing movement. He looks eagerly for attention; and may stand holding a support and changing weight from one foot to the other in rhythmic motion, as a solace when neglected.

Between *twelve and fifteen months* a child usually learns to walk with a little help. This performance, though often accompanied by panting and tense effort, causes great delight and even elation when a few steps have been accomplished. The child calls out, smiles and waves ecstatically (i.e. rapidly or jerkily). When attentive adults are too enthusiastic in their appreciation, the little one may become positively tense with excitement. His efforts may consequently meet with less success, and then he cries in vexatious disappointment.

There is already a noticeable difference between the responsiveness of different *fifteen-month-old* children to demonstrated affection. Some children come readily to be nursed and petted, others require a little coaxing. One or two will kiss back when kissed, while others merely cling closely to the adult caressing them. At this age the children begin to show definite affection for each other.

Variations in affection no doubt have a number of causal factors. They depend upon the child's physical constitution and his condition of health at the moment. Whether a child is affectionate or not also depends upon the nature of his dominant interest at the moment. Affection for a grown person depends upon the child's attitude towards adults in general; and that again is largely a matter of the amount of fondling or scolding the child has received. Affection for other children is considerably determined by the agreeable or exasperating nature of chance contacts.

Between *fifteen and twenty-one months* the children find increasing enjoyment in walking and running about. They chase each other laughingly and enjoy snatching one another's toys. They come back again and again to adults to be lifted high or swung round. The nursery slide is very popular at this age. One or two of the hospital children pulled away and watched apprehensively in the distance after the first slide. A little encouragement from the nurses and the eager shouts of the other children soon overcame their fear, and they joined the sliding group again.

Gramophone music was listened to intently by almost all the nursery children. Some of them responded by swaying or nodding motions to time. Variations in appreciative interest in things and activities may be the precursors of the more mature emotion of joy.

Most of the eighteen-month-olds in the hospital were anxious to attract attention. They called out or came running to greet an adult. They would smile and hold out their arms to a familiar nurse in expectation of being lifted. A stranger they would watch solemnly for a while. Then they would approach slowly, touch and explore her clothes, or hit and watch for the effect. The children seemed to recognize their nurses at this age, whether the latter appeared in uniform or not. Babies of seven to twelve months, however, would sometimes turn away in fear or hostility when the nurses approached them wearing outdoor clothes.

Slight preferences for certain nurses were noticed as early as six months, but definitely affectionate attachments were observed chiefly between the ages of twelve and twenty-four months. One or two youngsters of eighteen months showed preferences for certain playmates. Some children were friendly with almost everybody including strange visitors. Others showed more specific and decided likes and dislikes. When a terrifying stranger was present, some times a child would show more than usual affection for his familiar nurse, but at other times he would be restrained and aloof from everybody. Similarly when a beloved parent was nursing a child on visiting day he might be hostile to anyone else; but more often he would smile agreeably at everybody including awe-inspiring strangers.

A specific "like" does not necessarily enhance a specific "dislike" by force of contrast, though this does sometimes happen. If the disliked object threatens the satisfaction or enjoyment of the object preferred then the dislike becomes stronger. Similarly a preferred object may be enjoyed with greater intensity in the presence of, or following upon, something disliked. It is a comforting relief from distress. This effect of contrast is perhaps what Freud terms "ambivalence." There are situations, however, where it has no noticeable effect. Strong emotions may thus have a decided "halo" effect.

Although children between *eighteen months and two years* of age tease and hit each other frequently, they show more affection for one another than younger infants. They not only pat and stroke fondly, but they will kiss and hug each other on occasion. The older children in the nursery group were seen to direct the younger ones' activities and point out their errors by gesture and exclamation. There was no evidence, however, of the parental affection and almost self-sacrificing care shown by four-year-olds for their much younger playmates.

Noisy activities delighted the eighteen- to twenty-four-month old youngsters. They took pleasure in tearing and pulling things to pieces and in lifting large but portable objects, such as their own chairs. They jabbered happily to each other at table. When the children received new toys in the hospital they would cling to them and guard them jealously from the other children. But they would hold them out for the nurses to share in their appreciation. Here is a mark of trusting friendship for their kindly guardians such as the children had not yet developed for one another. They would always rather share the other child's plaything than give up or share their own.

Affection, thus, begins as delight in being fondled and comforted by an elder. It becomes differentiated from general delight and manifested in tender caressing responses at about eight months of age. This earliest affection is essentially reciprocal in nature. Spontaneous affection for adults may be seen, however, by eleven or twelve months of age. Both reciprocal and spontaneous affection for other children make their appearance around fifteen months, but they are not as strong as affection for adults.

Specific affection for the grown-ups who give special attention may be manifested as early as demonstrative affection itself, i.e. eight or nine months. Attachments between two children were not observed in the hospital till after fifteen months of age. They were usually very temporary, lasting only for a few hours or days. The behavior of a child-friend is so much more erratic and less dependable than that of an adult. Friendships between eighteen- to twenty-four-month-old children would sometimes last, however, for several weeks. There seemed to be no preference in these attachments either for the same or the opposite sex.

Summary and Conclusion

The emotional behavior of young infants as observed in the Montreal Foundling and Baby Hospital seemed to lend support to the writer's theory of the genesis of the emotions. Emotional development was found to take place in three ways. The different emotions gradually evolved from the vague and undifferentiated emotion of excitement. The form of behavior response in each specific emotion changed slowly with developing skills and habits. Different particular situations would arouse emotional response at succeeding age-levels, although these situations would always be of the same general type for the same emotions.

The one-month-old baby showed excitement in accelerated movement and breathing, upon any excessive stimulation. He exhibited distress by crying, reddening of the face and tense jerky movements at painful and other disagreeable stimulations. But he was more or less passive and quiescent when agreeably stimulated.

By three months of age the child was seen to exhibit delight in smiles, deep inspirations and somewhat rhythmic movements when his bodily needs were being satisfied. Between three and four months angry screaming and vigorous leg-thrusts, in response to delay in anticipated feeding, were observed. A few weeks later anger was aroused when an adult's playful attention was withdrawn.

Distress and delight came to be expressed more in specific vocalizations with increasing age. General body movements gave place to precise responses to details of a situation. A four-month-old baby would laugh aloud with delight and cry tearfully when distressed. A child of five months was seen to cough and reject foods of a certain taste and consistency in incipient disgust. He would reach towards objects that caused him delight. By six months of age he showed definite fear when a stranger approached. He remained motionless and rigid, his eyes wide and staring. It is possible that "non-institutional" children might show fear in response to other unusual or unexpected events a little earlier than this. There was little variation in the daily routine of the children under observation, and fear was a rare occurrence.

By seven months of age the child showed positive elation, and renewed his activity as a result of success in his own endeavours. At eight months he began to show reciprocal affection for adults, and by twelve months spontaneous affection. Delight was manifested in much laughter, bouncing up and down, and banging with the hand.

Between nine and twelve months of age the hospital babies would hide their heads, like ostriches, upon the approach of a relatively unfamiliar person. They would scream and become flushed with anger when their efforts or desires were thwarted; and they would cry out in fear and sit motionless after perceiving themselves falling.

It was observed that a child learns to kiss soon after twelve months of age, and by fifteen months he expresses his affection for other children. Anger over disappointment becomes more dramatic in its manifestation. The true temper-tantrum makes its appearance roughly about fourteen months of age. By eighteen months anger at adults is expressed in obstinate behavior; and annoyance at interfering children is manifested in hitting, pulling and squealing.

Eighteen-month-olds would constantly seek the attention of adults, and take great delight in running about and making noises. One or two children of this age showed depressed, and others angry, jealousy when another child received the coveted attention. A few specific fears were noticed; and several children developed particular affectionate attachments.

Thus it seems that in the course of development, emotional behavior becomes more and more specific, both as regards arousing stimuli and form of response. Distress, though more readily aroused, comes to find adequate expression in a variety of actions, and delight becomes sensitive appreciation and joy in numerous pursuits. The emotions evolve slowly, and the exact age of differentiation is difficult to determine.

A diagram showing the approximate ages of the appearance of the different emotions, as observed in the Montreal Foundling Hospital, is given in Figure 1. Study of a number of children in

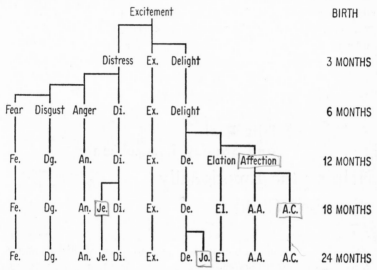

Fig. 1. Showing the approximate ages of differentiation of the various emotions during the first two years of life.

Key: A.A. = Affection for adults, A.C. = Affection for children, An. = Anger, De. = Delight, Dg. = Disgust, Di. = Distress, El. = Elation, Ex. = Excitement, Fe. = Fear, Je. = Jealousy, Jo. = Joy.

private homes might suggest a somewhat different age arrangement. Readers of the Journal of Genetic Psychology will note that a greater number of different emotions are attributed to the two year level than were suggested in a previously published diagram [3], based on a study of nursery school children.

Emotional behavior and development are very much determined by particular events and experiences and the routine of living. It is, therefore, to be expected that "institution babies" will show some deviations in their reactions from those of children at home. The former will probably exhibit fear of a larger number of things than other children, due to their very limited experience. On the other hand, they may show greater tolerance of interference, as a result of much practice in self-control in the nursery. They may also be more affectionate with other children, in consequence of the many happy play-hours spent together.

The daily round of feeding, washing, dressing and sleeping, however, has so many factors in common for all babies, that the observations made on the emotional development of a few hospital children, and the suggested inferences presented above, may have at least some general significance for infants brought up under other circumstances.

──▶ **Fritz Redl
and Stanley I. Jacobson**

Helping the Emotionally Disturbed Child

From *N. E. A. Journal,* December, 1958, 609–611. Reprinted by permission.

It isn't easy to become *an emotionally disturbed child.* We don't mean that it isn't easy to have an emotional disturbance—that's the easiest and most natural thing in the world. All of us have to meet the frustrations and disappointments that are standard procedure in living, and all of us react with more or less disturbance.

We feel hurt or angry or anxious or depressed or some subtle variation of some unnamed emotion. We behave in ways we wouldn't approve of—hopefully not for long and with minimum damage to ourselves or others. Then we get over the disturbance, and maybe we even learn from it so that the next time we face the frustration we aren't thrown quite so fast or far.

For children, especially, this process is as regular as meals, only more frequent. And with good reason. Children are still busy learning to recognize feelings and urges that are an old story to us. To learn to cope with those emotions is one important job of the growing child, and to make it doubly hard, he can't do it alone. He has to depend on us to help him. We expect the process to be punctuated by an occasional "disturbance," just as we expect a healthy child to suffer an occasional cold.

Because school is a natural focus for so much of the growing, school is also bound to be the scene of some of the disturbances. We learn to recognize the symptoms—a sudden change from typical behavior, more fighting or more crying or more absence or less concentration. Six-year-old Johnny suddenly refuses to come to school. Twelve-year-old Bobby cries when he sees the "C" in math on his report card. Teen-age Sally, an "A" student, suddenly stops trying.

As we probe behind this behavior with parent, child, or school counselor, we find there is a reason:

"Ever since the baby came, Johnny hangs around me all the time."

"My father said he'd buy me a bike if I got an 'A,' and now he won't buy it."

"If I can't go away to college, I'm not going to do anything."

Then we apply the first aid that is usually all that is required. Johnny and his mother get some counseling about the meaning of the new baby. Bobby's father begins to look at his son's ability realistically. Sally learns the economic facts of life, and her parents learn about adolescent independency striving. And all is fixed.

But to become an *emotionally disturbed child* is another matter. For one thing, transient disturbances like the ones we mentioned above must have been repeatedly ignored, misjudged, or badly handled earlier in the game, before the child reached school age as well as afterward, so that anger or distrust or despair, a feeling of badness or wrongness in himself or in the world has already begun to look like a permanent fixture in the personality.

By then, no one-sided, one-step remedy will work. By then, it isn't *simply* the chemistry of the glands or the focus of the eyes or the level of the IQ or what Papa said just before Johnny left for school this morning. By then, warmth and caring are not enough.

What is an emotionally disturbed child like? First of all, the term itself is much too broad. It covers illnesses as simple as measles and as serious as cancer, as different as tonsillitis and a broken arm.

For example, if little Johnny's screaming and vomiting and refusal to come to school continue even after ample demonstration that he is loved and appreciated as fully as the newly arrived infant, chances are that the baby is not the source of the problem, but only the last straw.

Johnny and his mother may need guidance deeper in focus and longer in duration. Mother may need to take an unsettling new look at her child-rearing attitudes, and Johnny may have to let off considerable steam in the safety of a therapist's office before he can take the risk of growing up.

There may be another Johnny in the same first-grade class who comes to school obediently day after day and goes robot-like through his classroom paces; but his teacher notices a mask-like quality about him, a pseudo-understanding. He's in another world.

Now it *may* be that this Johnny is by inheritance an especially slow child, as yet unequipped for the rigors of first-grade life. Or perhaps he is one of those unfortunate children so badly hurt by early experiences that his thinking is twisted, and he really *cannot* understand the world as we do. Both are certainly disturbed, but they are as different from each other as they are from our first Johnny.

As a fourth variety of disturbance, take the kind of child we have been studying at the National Institute of Mental Health. In the first grade, this Johnny would probably have the teacher threatening to resign, for he's the boy whose hand is quicker than his head, who wants but cannot share, who acts as if yesterday never happened and tomorrow's an eternity away. He's the acting-out boy, long on aggression and short on self-control.

All these children, and many more varieties, are emotionally disturbed. We could have added at least a fifth child—the wonderfully co-operative one whose private life is an anxious striving to meet self-imposed, perfectionistic goals—but we are not trying to list all the kinds of disturbance. That would be impossible in any case. Our point is that the term *emotionally disturbed* is too broad to have any practical meaning.

To say a child is emotionally disturbed is like saying that he has a fever: Both statements merely point out that something is wrong without indicating the nature of the illness, how serious it is, or what remedies are indicated to effect a cure. Notice too, that there is a difference between *disturbed* and *disturbing*. The child who causes us most trouble may happen to be the most deeply troubled child in the room; but sometimes he is a normal child engaged in a temporary campaign—perhaps to overcome immigrant status in a new community or to prove he's "somebody" to the girl across the room. The opposite child, the quiet oasis of calm in a too easily distracted group, often needs our attention more, even though he does nothing to force it.

It is no doubt clear by now that emotional disturbances defy generalization. On the face of it, symptoms know no logic. Every situation requires its own analysis, every illness its own cure.

This means that general prescriptions for handling disturbed children in the classroom will have limited relevance for individual cases. It does not mean, however, that there are no guides for thinking about what to do. These there are, and many of them are already familiar to you. Here are only a few we would like to suggest:

A teacher is to teach. Children bring their emotional problems to the classroom, and the teacher has to find ways of helping them to cope with the problems while they are in school. When the emotional disturbances become entangled with classroom and learning situations, it is the teacher's job to try to disentangle them for the duration. It is not the classroom teacher's job to solve the child's difficulties for good and all.

Disturbances are real. It may be true that a particular child "could" do the work if he "wanted" to, but this doesn't mean he isn't really disturbed. It only means that the trouble lies in the motivational machinery instead of in the cognitive machinery. We may call him stubborn, negative, resistant, or withholding; but whatever we call him, chances are the condition is beyond his control and as real a disturbance in its way as faulty vision.

This is also true of the child who promises but can't deliver, the one who has to keep his eye on everything but his assignment, and many others who try our patience day after day.

It isn't personal.   Not only are disturbances real; they also run deeper than the events of the day, as we have tried to indicate. The boy who continues his nasty disruptions in spite of your efforts to contain him probably has nothing against you personally, nor have you created the problem by failing to smile his way in the morning. You may symbolize all the adults who "do nothing but boss me around all the time," or you may be an innocent casualty in a battle to win prestige in the gang.

The exceptional child is an exception.   Although many disturbed children can be helped in a regular classroom, the fact remains that the disturbed child is exceptional, and the techniques that provide stimulating learning experiences for most normal children may only stimulate the disturbed child's pathology.

If a promising activities program leads to chaos in the classroom, the trouble may lie in one or two children with faulty control systems and not in the technique itself. Even in a very small class, with more than one teacher, some children cannot manage a program which depends on inner controls and self-maintained task-centeredness. On the other hand, one can see the very same activities producing significant learning in large classes of relatively normal children.

Is the answer to assign disturbed children to separate groups? Perhaps, but not for all of them. Some disturbed children need special classes or special schools and some cannot manage school at all, but the majority need the presence of a normal group in order to develop an image of constructive social behavior.

For these children, the answer lies in the kind of flexible planning that many schools are finding easier to achieve than they had imagined. Children are going to school part time, moving to different rooms and grades as their needs require it, staying home on bad days—and the schools are seeing the programs bear fruit.

What is right for any disturbed child still depends on an analysis of that case alone, but there are plenty of alternatives if a school is willing to be imaginative.

You can't go it alone. What we have just said is not meant to imply that a teacher has to find a way to teach every child on the class roster. In the first place, some *disturbing* children are unmanageable (and therefore unteachable) even if they are not seriously *disturbed*. Others who might be reached are all too frequently lost because of special school conditions.

When the teacher is hamstrung by a rigid curriculum, a dearth of special facilities, ragged equipment, and short supplies, he can only choose the path of sanity and admit his limitations. Too many teachers still stand like martyrs, alone and unprovided with necessary tools, struggling to accomplish a task which requires artistry even under the best of circumstances.

Refer it. Tell somebody. The guidance counselor, the principal, the pupil personnel worker, the school social worker, the school psychologist—tell whichever person in your school has the job of knowing the resources for the troubled child and how to get child and resource together. And if the child you refer is lucky enough to arrive at the scource of help, remember, specialists in helping troubled people can't go it alone either.

To be a specialist means to have special knowledge and skill in a specific area. It also means having less knowledge and skill in other areas. Psychiatrists, psychologists, and social workers may know as little about the classroom as teachers may know about the clinic. The helping specialist will depend on information from you to help him understand the case and plan the treatment *outside* the school.

As for the classroom program, that remains your area of specialty, and it will be up to you to translate findings about the child's personality and needs into classroom action. Education has perhaps done too little to develop specific educational techniques for the emotionally disturbed child, but that gap is being filled by a growing catalogue of literature and course work on the subject, and we urge you to take advantage of it.

Speak up. Disturbed children need special services, not only in the school but in the recreation, health, and welfare fields as well. For too many years, teachers have tried to provide services beyond their scope because those services were not available elsewhere in the community. It is time the teachers shoved back— not to get even, but because it is hard enough to be what classroom teachers are trained to be without also trying to be social workers, psychologists, and psychiatrists. Only if we speak up can the community understand the need and begin to meet it.

REFERENCES

1. BLANTON, MARGARET G., "The Behavior of the Human Infant During the First Thirty Days of Life," *Psychological Review*, 1917, 24:456–483.
2. BRIDGES, KATHERINE M. B., "The Social and Emotional Development of the Pre-school Child," London: Kegan Paul, Trench, Trubner & Co., p. 277.
3. ————, "A Genetic Theory of the Emotions," *Journal of Genetic Psychology*, 1930, 37:514–527.
4. WATSON, J. B., "Experimental Studies on the Growth of the Emotions," *Pedagogical Seminary*, 1925, 32:328–348.

CHAPTER
EIGHT

▲

*Social-Cultural Basis
of Behavior*

A HUMAN BEING IS A SOCIAL CREATURE FROM
the moment of his birth. Surrounding him from that moment to
the end of his life is an environment that consists of more than
physical things—an environment that includes ideas, feelings,
expectations, beliefs, and activities related thereto. Such social-
psychological factors, together with the many things that man
has made, are the elements of the culture. They communicate to
the growing, developing individual a way of life that becomes his
way: that make him act, think, and feel in certain fundamental
respects in the same way as the people with whom he is most
closely associated.

What precisely is the culture? *Why* do people who comprise
one social group think and feel and do things differently from
people of another social group? How much of an individual's pat-

317

tern of behavior is attributable to the influence of the culture? Clear answers to such questions as these are given in the selection from *Mirror for Man* by Clyde Kluckhohn. Until his death in 1960 he was for many years Professor of Anthropology at Harvard University.

Growing up in any society involves the learning of certain ways considered "right" by that society for dealing with the more basic problems that the individual encounters. The fundamental *tasks* associated with growing up do not differ greatly in their essentials from one society to another. But each society has its own version of how the tasks are to be accomplished by children and youth. Stephen M. Corey and Virgil E. Herrick, in the second reading, describe and illustrate the developmental tasks that involve children and young people in our society. The concept of *developmental tasks* has much significance for teachers in their improvement of their understanding of human development and behavior. Corey is Professor of Education, Teachers College, Columbia University. Herrick is Professor of Education at the University of Wisconsin.

The third reading in this chapter fixes attention on the influence that home life has on the developing behavior patterns of children. In the article we are given a view of the home as a fundamentally important social agency; even more, we are helped to see the kinds of behavior settings within the home that serve as the effective context for much of the patterning of the life of individual children. The study of *Midwest* on which this report is based has attracted much attention not only for its findings, per se, but also for the evidence in it regarding the effectiveness of the research method employed—a method devised for gathering and interpreting data about how children behave under "the naturally occurring conditions of their lives."

Roger G. Barker and Herbert F. Wright have carried the principal responsibility for the research of the Midwest Psychological Field Station; they are also professors of psychology at the University of Kansas. All the co-authors of the article have been at different times associated with the *Midwest* research.

——▶ Clyde Kluckhohn
Cultural Factors in Personality

Why do the Chinese dislike milk and milk products? Why would the Japanese die willingly in a Banzai charge that seemed senseless to Americans? Why do some nations trace descent through the father, others through the mother, still others through both parents? Not because different peoples have different instincts, not because they were destined by God or Fate to different habits, not because the weather is different in China and Japan and the United States. Sometimes shrewd common sense has an answer that is close to that of the anthropologist: "because they were brought up that way." By "culture" anthropology means the total life way of a people, the social legacy the individual acquires from his group. Or culture can be regarded as that part of the environment that is the creation of man.

This technical term has a wider meaning than the "culture" of history and literature. A humble cooking pot is as much a cultural product as is a Beethoven sonata. In ordinary speech a man of culture is a man who can speak languages other than his own, who is familiar with history, literature, philosophy, or the fine arts. In some cliques that definition is still narrower. The cultured person is one who can talk about James Joyce, Scarlatti, and Picasso. To the anthropologist, however, to be human is to be cultured. There is culture in general, and then there are the specific cultures such as Russian, American, British, Hottentot, Inca. The general abstract notion serves to remind us that we cannot explain acts solely in terms of the biological properties of the people concerned, their individual past experience, and the immediate situation. The past experience of other men in the form of culture enters into almost every event. Each specific culture constitutes a kind of blueprint for all of life's activities.

One of the interesting things about human beings is that they try to understand themselves and their own behavior. While this has been particularly true of Europeans in recent times, there is no group which has not developed a scheme or schemes to explain man's actions. To the insistent human query "why?" the most exciting illumination anthropology has to offer is that of the concept of culture. Its explanatory importance is comparable to categories such as evolution in biology, gravity in physics, disease in medicine. A good deal of human behavior can be understood, and indeed predicted, if we know a people's design for living. Many acts are neither accidental nor due to personal peculiarities nor caused by supernatural forces nor simply mysterious. Even those of us who pride ourselves on our individualism follow most of the time a pattern not of our own making. We brush our teeth on arising. We put on pants—not a loincloth or a grass skirt. We eat three meals a day—not four or five or two. We sleep in a bed—not in a hammock or on a sheep pelt. I do not have to know the individual and his life history to be able to predict these and countless other regularities, including many in the thinking process, of all Americans who are not incarcerated in jails or hospitals for the insane.

To the American woman a system of plural wives seems "instinctively" abhorrent. She cannot understand how any woman can fail to be jealous and uncomfortable if she must share her husband with other women. She feels it "unnatural" to accept such a situation. On the other hand, a Koryak woman of Siberia, for example, would find it hard to understand how a woman could be so selfish and so undesirous of feminine companionship in the home as to wish to restrict her husband to one mate.

Some years ago I met in New York City a young man who did not speak a word of English and was obviously bewildered by American ways. By "blood" he was as American as you or I, for his parents had gone from Indiana to China as missionaries. Orphaned in infancy, he was reared by a Chinese family in a remote village. All who met him found him more Chinese than American. The facts of his blue eyes and light hair were less impressive than a Chinese style of gait, Chinese arm and hand movements, Chinese facial expression, and Chinese modes of thought. The biological heritage was American, but the cultural training had been Chinese. He returned to China. Another example of another kind: I once knew a trader's wife in Arizona who took a somewhat devilish interest in producing a cultural reaction. Guests who came her way were often served delicious sandwiches filled with a meat that seemed to be neither chicken nor tuna fish yet was reminiscent of both. To queries she gave no reply until each had eaten his fill. She then explained that what they had eaten was not chicken, not tuna fish, but the rich, white flesh of freshly killed rattlesnakes. The response was instantaneous—vomiting, often violent vomiting. A biological process is caught in a cultural web.

A highly intelligent teacher with long and successful experience in the public schools of Chicago was finishing her first year in an Indian school. When asked how her Navaho pupils compared in intelligence with Chicago youngsters, she replied, "Well, I just don't know. Sometimes the Indians seem just as bright. At other times they just act like dumb animals. The other night we had a dance in the high school. I saw a boy who is one of the best students in my English class standing off by himself. So I took him over to a pretty girl and told them to dance. But they just stood there with their heads down. They wouldn't even say anything." I inquired if she knew whether or not they were members of the same clan. "What difference would that make?"

"How would you feel about getting into bed with your brother?" The teacher walked off in a huff, but, actually, the two cases were quite comparable in principle. To the Indian the type of bodily contact involved in our social dancing has a directly sexual connotation. The incest taboos between members of the same clan are as severe as between true brothers and sisters. The shame of the Indians at the suggestion that a clan brother and sister should dance and the indignation of the white teacher at the idea that she should share a bed with an adult brother represent equally nonrational responses, culturally standardized unreason.

All this does not mean that there is no such thing as raw human nature. The very fact that certain of the same institutions are found in all known societies indicates that at bottom all human beings are very much alike. The files of the Cross-Cultural Survey at Yale University are organized according to categories such as "marriage ceremonies," "life crisis rites," "incest taboos." At least seventy-five of these categories are representd in every single one of the hundreds of cultures analyzed. This is hardly surprising. The members of all human groups have about the same biological equipment. All men undergo the same poignant life experiences such as birth, helplessness, illness, old age, and death. The biological potentialities of the species are the blocks with which cultures are built. Some patterns of every culture crystallize around focuses provided by the inevitables of biology: the difference between the sexes, the presence of persons of different ages, the varying physical strength and skill of individuals. The facts of nature also limit culture forms. No culture provides patterns for jumping over trees or for eating iron ore.

There is thus no "either-or" between nature and that special form of nurture called culture. Culture determinism is as one-sided as biological determinism. The two factors are interdependent. Culture arises out of human nature, and its forms are restricted both by man's biology and by natural laws. It is equally true that culture channels biological processes—vomiting, weeping, fainting, sneezing, the daily habits of food intake and waste elimination. When a man eats, he is reacting to an internal "drive," namely, hunger contractions consequent upon the lowering of blood sugar, but his precise reaction to these internal stimuli cannot be predicted by physiological knowledge alone. Whether a healthy adult feels hungry twice, three times, or four times a day and the hours at which this feeling recurs is a question of culture. *What* he eats is of course limited by availability, but is also partly regulated by culture. It is a biological fact that some types of berries are poisonous; it is a cultural fact that, a few generations ago, most Americans considered tomatoes to be poisonous and refused to eat them. Such selective, discriminative use of the environment is characteristically cultural. In a still more general sense, too, the process of eating is channeled by culture. Whether a man eats to live, lives to eat, or merely eats and lives is only in part an individual matter, for there are also cultural trends. Emotions are physiological events. Certain situations will evoke fear in people from any culture. But sensations of pleasure, anger, and lust may be stimulated by cultural cues that would leave unmoved someone who has been reared in a different social tradition.

Except in the case of newborn babies and of individuals born with clear-cut structural or functional abnormalities we can observe innate endowments only as modified by cultural training. In a hospital in New Mexico where Zuni Indian, Navaho Indian, and white American babies are born, it is possible to classify the newly arrived infants as unusually active, average, and quiet. Some babies from each "racial" group will fall into each category, though a higher proportion of the white babies will fall into the unusually active class. But if a Navaho baby, a Zuni baby, and a white baby—all classified as unusually active at birth—are again observed at the age of two years, the Zuni baby will no longer seem given to quick and restless activity—*as compared with the white child*—though he may seem so as compared with the other Zunis of the same age. The Navaho child is likely to fall in between as contrasted with the Zuni and the white, though he will probably still seem more active than the average Navaho youngster.

It was remarked by many observers in the Japanese relocation centers that Japanese who were born and brought up in this country, especially those who were reared apart from any large colony of Japanese, resemble in behavior their white neighbors much more closely than they do their own parents who were educated in Japan.

I have said "culture channels biological processes." It is more accurate to say "the biological functioning of individuals is modified if they have been trained in certain ways and not in others." Culture is not a disembodied force. It is created and transmitted by people. However, culture, like well-known concepts of the physical sciences, is a convenient abstraction. One never sees gravity. One sees bodies falling in regular ways. One never sees an electromagnetic field. Yet certain happenings that can be seen may be given a neat abstract formulation by assuming that the electromagnetic field exists. Similarly, one never sees culture as such. What is seen are regularities in the behavior or artifacts of a group that has adhered to a common tradition. The regularities in style and technique of ancient Inca tapestries or stone axes from Melanesian islands are due to the existence of mental blueprints for the group.

Culture is a *way* of thinking, feeling, believing. It is the group's knowledge stored up (in memories of men; in books and objects) for future use. We study the products of this "mental" activity: the overt behavior, the speech and gestures and activities of people, and the tangible results of these things such as tools, houses, cornfields, and what not. It has been customary in lists of "culture traits" to include such things as watches or lawbooks. This is a convenient way of thinking about them, but in the solution of any important problem we must remember that they, in themselves, are nothing but metals, paper, and ink. What is important is that some men know how to make them, others set a value on them, are unhappy without them, direct their activities in relation to them, or disregard them.

It is only a helpful shorthand when we say "The cultural patterns of the Zulu were resistant to Christianization." In the directly observable world of course, it was individual Zulus who resisted. Nevertheless, if we do not forget that we are speaking at a high level of abstraction, it is justifiable to speak of culture as a cause. One may compare the practice of saying "syphilis caused the extinction of the native population of the island." Was it "syphilis" or "syphilis germs" or "human beings who were carriers of syphilis"?

"Culture," then, is "a theory." But if a theory is not contradicted by any relevant fact and if it helps us to understand a mass of otherwise chaotic facts, it is useful. Darwin's contribution was much less the accumulation of new knowledge than the creation of a theory which put in order data already known. An accumulation of facts, however large, is no more a science than a pile of bricks is a house. Anthropology's demonstration that the most weird set of customs has a consistency and an order is comparable to modern psychiatry's showing that there is meaning and purpose in the apparently incoherent talk of the insane. In fact, the inability of the older psychologies and philosophies to account for the strange behavior of madmen and heathens was the principal factor that forced psychiatry and anthropology to develop theories of the unconscious and of culture.

Since culture is an abstraction, it is important not to confuse culture with society. A "society" refers to a group of people who interact more with each other than they do with other individuals—who cooperate with each other for the attainment of certain ends. You can see and indeed count the individuals who make up a society. A "culture" refers to the distinctive ways of life of such a group of people. Not all social events are culturally patterned. New types of circumstances arise for which no cultural solutions have as yet been devised.

A culture constitutes a storehouse of the pooled learning of the group. A rabbit starts life with some innate responses. He can learn from his own experience and perhaps from observing other rabbits. A human infant is born with fewer instincts and greater plasticity. His main task is to learn the answers that persons he will never see, persons long dead, have worked out. Once he has learned the formulas supplied by the culture of his group, most of his behavior becomes almost as automatic and unthinking as if it were instinctive. There is a tremendous amount of intelligence behind the making of a radio, but not much is required to learn to turn it on.

The members of all human societies face some of the same unavoidable dilemmas, posed by biology and other facts of the human situation. This is why the basic categories of all cultures are so similar. Human culture without language is unthinkable. No culture fails to provide for aesthetic expression and aesthetic delight. Every culture supplies standardized orientations toward the deeper problems, such as death. Every culture is designed to perpetuate the group and its solidarity, to meet the demands of individuals for an orderly way of life and for satisfaction of biological needs.

However, the variations on these basic themes are numberless. Some languages are built up out of twenty basic sounds, others out of forty. Nose plugs were considered beautiful by the predynastic Egyptians but are not by the modern French. Puberty is a biological fact. But one culture ignores it, another prescribes informal instructions about sex but no ceremony, a third has impressive rites for girls only, a fourth for boys and girls. In this culture, the first menstruation is welcomed as a happy, natural event; in that culture the atmosphere is full of dread and supernatural threat. Each culture dissects nature according to its own system of categories. The Navaho Indians apply the same word to the color of a robin's egg and to that of grass. A psychologist once assumed that this meant a difference in the sense organs, that Navahos didn't have the physiological equipment to distinguish "green" from "blue." However, when he showed them objects of the two colors and asked them if they were exactly the same colors, they looked at him with astonishment. His dream of discovering a new type of color blindness was shattered.

Every culture must deal with the sexual instinct. Some, however, seek to deny all sexual expression before marriage, whereas a Polynesian adolescent who was not promiscuous would be distinctly abnormal. Some cultures enforce lifelong monogamy, others, like our own, tolerate serial monogamy; in still other cultures, two or more women may be joined to one man or several men to a single woman. Homosexuality has been a permitted pattern in the Greco-Roman world, in parts of Islam, and in various primitive tribes. Large portions of the population of Tibet, and of Christendom at some places and periods, have practiced complete celibacy. To us marriage is first and foremost an arrangement between two individuals. In many more societies marriage is merely one facet of a complicated set of reciprocities, economic and otherwise, between two families or two clans.

The essence of the cultural process is selectivity. The selection is only exceptionally conscious and rational. Cultures are like Topsy. They just grew. Once, however, a way of handling a situation becomes institutionalized, there is ordinarily great resistance to change or deviation. When we speak of "our sacred beliefs," we mean of course that they are beyond criticism and that the person who suggests modification or abandonment must be punished. No person is emotionally indifferent to his culture. Certain cultural premises may become totally out of accord with a new factual situation. Leaders may recognize this and reject the old ways in theory. Yet their emotional loyalty continues in the face of reason because of the intimate conditionings of early child-hood.

A culture is learned by individuals as the result of belonging to some particular group, and it constitutes that part of learned behavior which is shared with others. It is our social legacy, as contrasted with our organic heredity. It is one of the important factors which permits us to live together in an organized society, giving us ready-made solutions to our problems, helping us to predict the behavior of others, and permitting others to know what to expect of us.

Culture regulates our lives at every turn. From the moment we are born until we die there is, whether we are conscious of it or not, constant pressure upon us to follow certain types of behavior that other men have created for us. Some paths we follow willingly, others we follow because we know no other way, still others we deviate from or go back to most unwillingly. Mothers of small children know how unnaturally most of this comes to us—how little regard we have, until we are "cultural-ized," for the "proper" place, time, and manner for certain acts such as eating, excreting, sleeping, getting dirty, and making loud noises. But by more or less adhering to a system of related designs for carrying out all the acts of living, a group of men and women feel themselves linked together by a powerful chain of sentiments. Ruth Benedict gave an almost complete definition of the concept when she said, "Culture is that which binds men together."

It is true any culture is a set of techniques for adjusting both to the external environment and to other men. However, cultures create problems as well as solve them. If the lore of a people states that frogs are dangerous creatures, or that it is not safe to go about at night because of witches or ghosts, threats are posed which do not arise out of the inexorable facts of the external world. Cultures produce needs as well as provide a means of ful-filling them. There exist for every group culturally defined, ac-quired drives that may be more powerful in ordinary daily life than the biologically inborn drives. Many Americans, for ex-ample, will work harder for "success" than they will for sexual satisfaction.

Most groups elaborate certain aspects of their culture far beyond maximum utility or survival value. In other words, not all culture promotes physical survival. At times, indeed, it does exactly the opposite. Aspects of culture which once were adaptive may persist long after they have ceased to be useful. An analysis of any culture will disclose many features which cannot possibly be construed as adaptations to the total environment in which the group now finds itself. However, it is altogether likely that these apparently useless features represent survivals, with modifications through time, of cultural forms which were adaptive in one or another previous situation.

Any cultural practice must be functional or it will disappear before long. That is, it must somehow contribute to the survival of the society or to the adjustment of the individual. However, many cultural functions are not manifest but latent. A cowboy will walk three miles to catch a horse which he then rides one mile to the store. From the point of view of manifest function this is positively irrational. But the act has the latent function of maintaining the cowboy's prestige in the terms of his own subculture. One can instance the buttons on the sleeve of a man's coat, our absurd English spelling, the use of capital letters, and a host of other apparently nonfunctional customs. They serve mainly the latent function of assisting individuals to maintain their security by preserving continuity with the past and by making certain sectors of life familiar and predictable.

Every culture is a precipitate of history. In more than one sense history is a sieve. Each culture embraces those aspects of the past, which, usually in altered form and with altered meanings, live on in the present. Discoveries and inventions, both material and ideological, are constantly being made available to a group through its historical contacts with other peoples or being created by its own members. However, only those that fit the total immediate situation in meeting the group's needs for survival or in promoting the psychological adjustment of individuals will become part of the culture. The process of culture building may be regarded as an addition to man's innate biological capacities, an addition providing instruments which enlarge, or may even substitute for, biological functions, and to a degree compensating for biological limitations—as in ensuring that death does not always result in the loss to humanity of what the deceased has learned.

———▶ **Stephen M. Corey
and Virgil E. Herrick**

The Developmental Tasks of Children and Young People

From *Youth, Communication and Libraries,* American Library Association, 1949, pp. 3–13. Reprinted by permission.

Most human beings constantly struggle with the task of growing up. Our twenty-first birthdays provide no mystic termination of this striving. Throughout our lifetimes we try to become increasingly mature in our intellectual and social behavior, to gain increased recognition from those whose judgments we respect, and to find out more about this person who walks around within our physical body and who responds to our name.

While it is true that adults work constantly at becoming more mature, the problem is particularly critical and dramatic for children and young people. That is why those of us who are interested in the effects of communication upon children and youth, and the extent to which young people can be served by libraries, want to know as much as possible about the way in which boys and girls develop and mature.

DEFINITION OF DEVELOPMENTAL TASKS

It has become increasingly common, especially at the University of Chicago, to study children in terms of what are called their "developmental tasks." This term may be unknown to some, but the concept has proved to be very useful. One generally accepted definition of developmenal tasks is: "a task which arises at or about a certain period in the life of the individual, successful achievement of which leads to his happiness and to success with later tasks, while failure leads to unhappiness in the individual, disapproval by the society, and difficulty with later tasks."[1]

What this definition means is that a young person growing up in any culture, faces more or less constantly certain lessons that he *must* learn. These required lessons result from the interaction between the child's maturing body and the pressures of his social and physical environment. These learnings are essential in the sense that they are necessary for a reasonably adequate life as a person—a life that is happy and that results in effective and satisfying membership in a social group.

This use of the term "developmental tasks" to describe the lessons children learn as they grow up does not mean brand new wine in brand new bottles. The concept is closely related to earlier notions about individual and social needs, interests, and drives. The chief advantage in talking about developmental tasks is that it focuses attention on what the individual is trying to accomplish rather than postulating some inner drive or need which is very difficult to define. The developmental task, too, allows for observation of behavior in a total dynamic context without artificial distinctions between physical, mental, social, and emotional aspects of growth.

It is always necessary, of course, to guard against the possible error of believing that the youngster who is growing up realizes the developmental tasks he is trying to achieve. Frequently the individual himself may not be aware of the task with which he is struggling or which he has recently accomplished. So far, children themselves have not made any study of their own developmental tasks. Everything that has been reported represents the inferences of adults, and it is dangerous for older people to assume that they know the essence of the problems with which younger persons are coping.

---

[1] Robert J. Havighurst, *Human Development and Education,* New York: Longmans, Green and Company, 1953, p. 2.

Some Illustrative Developmental Tasks

The definition of developmental tasks can be considerably clarified by a description of some of the most common tasks that are faced during various periods of growth. The remainder of this paper is devoted to such descriptions and to a brief statement of some general characteristics of all developmental tasks.

One of the important developmental lessons children and youth must learn is the important one of creating for themselves a more infallible system of security. This illustrates a task which is achieved by coping successfully with a whole series of more specific learnings. The young child at first tends to find security in his parents and in other adult relationships. As he extends his social contacts and comes to school, he quickly discovers that his parents are fallible, and that his peers not only fail to provide him with security but many times are actually dangerous to him. He becomes, too, increasingly aware of the degree to which the adults he knows depend for their security upon certain ideas of God, and of right and wrong. The child tries to adapt these ideas to his own life and social behavior, and he has a great deal of difficulty. A youngster's interest in Superman and in all sorts of similar fantasy may be only his efforts to explore a world where social and physical realities are not threatening and where he can with some safety search for rules, ideas, and conceptions of himself which will provide him with a more comfortable and safe existence.

Another developmental task, the importance of which is underestimated, is faced by the child when he first comes to school. All of us have watched some child struggling with this adjustment. Frequently for the first time, he is faced with the problem of finding out how to win his place in a group. He must learn that his personal significance depends on what he is able to do in a relatively impersonal situation. He must accept the fact that school is a place where he has to share his adult world with many other children.

Some boys and girls make this transition from home to school without much difficulty. Others seem to be baffled by what goes on in kindergarten and first grade. They try many bizarre kinds of behavior in an effort to find in this new social environment the same place they had in the circle of the family's affection.

In the primary grades, too, some children first meet the mysterious and ubiquitous written symbol so dear to teachers. Many a child, until he reaches kindergarten, has never been expected to put on his own rubbers and coat, and to refrain from taking things not his own. He must not lie. He must "mind" adults. The school is a place where one has to learn to make specific inferences from such vague generalizations as "keep out of danger when crossing the street."

At about the second grade the child begins to work more intensively at the task of moving from a society primarily adult-centered to a child-centered peer society. Here he becomes engaged in working out his role and status values with his own age mates. Many teachers who follow their children for more than one year become disturbed when they note that children who cultivated them in the first grade in order to find an adult in the school situation who would assume the role of their mother, now are not quite as "nice" as they were the year previous. This developmental task of finding his role in the peer group becomes increasingly complicated as the child adds to it the tasks of seeing more clearly his own sex role in relation to others of his own sex, to the opposite sex, and to his prospective adult life.

Some of the other developmental tasks of early childhood are:

1. Achieving skill and competence in motor control and coordination

   The young child must learn to walk, run, control his bowels and bladder, eat whole foods, and use his fine muscles.

2. Achieving independence in caring for himself as an individual

   Here he must dress and undress himself, feed himself, get and put away his toys, and use the toilet independently.

3. Achieving rhythm of living according to the culture imposed upon him

   In American middle-class culture this means the child must eat three meals a day, sleep at regulated hours, and play at play times.

4. Learning the process of belonging to and becoming a member of the family and the social group

Before he leaves for school, the typical child has learned to recognize himself and recognize other individuals, as adults, siblings, or peers, and to accept his role in the family.

5. Learning to give as well as receive affection
   As he works at this task the child seeks emotional stability and security of mutual expression.

6. Learning communication and symbolization from jargon to words
   The young child learns to progress from words to phrases, phrases to sentences. He increases his ability to understand larger units of language, such as the point to a story.

7. Achieving emotional release through sensory experiences
   Preschool children come to enjoy feeling, seeing, smelling, tasting, and hearing. They begin to develop an aesthetic sense.

8. Learning the realities of the physical and social world
   Small boys and girls learn the names and nature of many inanimate and animate objects, such as pets.

9. Learning to discriminate, to generalize, and to make judgments
   The ability to form concepts to solve one's daily problems, to become a thinking person, has its beginning very early in life.

10. Internalizing and accepting rules; developing a conscience
    In early childhood, boys and girls learn some of the accepted "stop and go" patterns. They make distinctions between right and wrong. They develop some respect for authority, reliance on themselves to follow rules.

11. Identifying self to adults and accepting intellectually and emotionally the fact of sex

Developmental Tasks of Later Childhood

The major developmental tasks of later childhood are in the main extensions of those of the earlier period. To these, however, are added the special "lessons" required by the school. Of critical importance to the child at this stage is the demand for increased competency in the use of language, particularly in the handling of written symbols. It is at this period that books become available to him personally and provide an important means for exploring and testing the ramifications of his world.

Some of the important developmental tasks of later childhood are:

1. Broadening the concept of self
   Prior to the time the child enters school, he has examined his social self only in relation to his family and small play groups. In school he is forced to expand this social consciousness to groups of twenty-five to thirty-five children, organized much more formally and impersonally to achieve definite purposes.

2. Establishing and maintaining a role in the peer group
   The egocentric adult-centered world of early childhood expands to include groups of peers with rules, aspirations, and controls somewhat different from the world directed by his family and teacher.

3. Gaining independence from adults
   As the prestige and power of the peer group grows, the child is also engaged in the process of weaning himself from his dependence on adults. This task is important to his continued success in the first two tasks mentioned.

4. Developing further the sex role and sense of sexual modesty
   The fact that Johnny is a boy and Mary is a girl becomes increasingly important, although in the early periods of the school boy–girl relationships are many and extremely complex. As children move toward adolescence, there are fewer and fewer boy–girl relationships in peer groups and more and more boy–boy, girl–girl contacts. At the same time, even in the fifth and sixth grades, while boys and girls would not be seen with the opposite sex in school, they may have opposite sex friends at home and in the community.

5. Developing further the physical skills
   This period is characterized by rapid increase in motor coordination and the ability to make finer and finer muscular discriminations. Also the general energy output tends to increase.

6. Broadening and deepening of intellectual concepts and value systems
   It is on this task that the most noticeable gains are made during later childhood. The child is developing the elements of his value system, testing out many important concepts of distance, time, quantity, and relationships—concepts which he will continue to expand and develop for the rest of his life.

7. Developing intellectual skills and techniques of communication
Here the skills involved in the arts of language, use of resources, and testing and use of data are developing under the guidance and direction of the school and community. Values as well as the procedures used by the home, school, play groups, and community organizations in aiding the child to move along in his area of development are often in conflict.

Developmental Tasks of Adolescence

Among the more important developmental tasks that adolescents face are the following:

1. Coming to terms with their own bodies
During early adolescence, most young people seem to be very much aware of their own bodies. The reasons for the heightened consciousness of self at this age are numerous. First, it is during late preadolescence that changes occur in proportion, structure, and functions of the human body that are oft times startling. Second, personal appearance is of great significance in adolescent society. Young people learn quickly that the way their bodies look does have significance not only for courtship and the eventual selection of a mate, which is a bit far off for adolescents, but also in connection with many other types of social achievement.

2. Learning new relationships to their age mates
Adolescents must acquire many new attitudes, skills, and understandings as they work out a new sort of social relationship to their age mates of both sexes. Few things are more important than acceptance by their group. The isolates are excruciatingly unhappy, at least until some adjustment is worked out which usually involves escape to books or movies or hobbies or adult society. Preadolescent groups are usually single sex groups with boys and girls somewhat contemptuous of one another. It is during adolescence that young people must learn how to be attractive to the opposite sex. In middle-class society, this problem is a difficult one. A large number of boys and girls in high school spend most of their time working at it.

3. Achieving independence from parents
This task probably causes parents even more difficulty than it does their sons and daughters. The fact is, though, that chil-

dren must learn a new relationship to their fathers and mothers
if they are to achieve complete adulthood. This new relationship
is one which involves mutual affection and respect *without
dependence*. In some cultures the adolescent's experience as he
breaks away from his family is less traumatic. In a modern
industrial society, however, social change is so rapid that the
new generation usually has quite different standards of acceptable behavior from those that govern its parents.

4. Achieving adult social and economic status
   The obligation of our young people to behave like adults and
   eventually to accept the social and economic responsibilities of
   adults defines a developmental task that baffles many of them.
   This adjustment gets complicated at regular intervals by our
   economic system.

5. Acquiring self-confidence and a system of values
   To have self-confidence and the attendant self-respect is of
   great importance to adolescents. Consequently, they are constantly testing themselves out. The boys want to find out if
   they have courage and resourcefulness. Girls also seek adventure, not only to test the limits of their environment, but to
   find out what they can do successfully.

This quick description of the developmental tasks for the
various growth periods should emphasize their continuity. Many
tasks are common to more than one period, such as developing a
concept of self, learning sex roles, learning to get along with
age mates, achieving independence from parents and adults, developing more infallible bases for security, developing intellectual
skills and techniques of communication, and broadening and
deepening intellectual concepts while the general task remains
relatively constant.

The specific manifestations of these general developmental
tasks and the periods of their critical importance to the child
vary widely during the different growth periods of his life. This
accounts for much of the difficulty parents and teachers have in
making good judgments about the relative importance of behavior
which may be greatly annoying to them at that time. The loud
voices, exuberant outbursts of behavior, table manners, unwashed
faces, uncombed hair, and dirty, smudgy papers of preadolescents
are irritating to all who have to work with them.

Another problem involved in the persistence of many of the general developmental tasks is the danger of mistaking each new phase of a given task for an entirely new task. This error is less apt to be made by those who recognize the inherent consistency and continuity of development. One who has watched an adolescent girl trying out her new selves in her mirror and on her long-suffering parents and brothers and sisters, is strongly tempted to conclude that this behavior is unique to the adolescent period. This conclusion does not take into account the girl's more or less continuous attempts to try herself out in the permissive, acceptive environment of her own home and circle of friends. The adolescent girl's antics before the mirror are related both to her previous and future behavior. The girl's success with her past development of self makes the present exploration possible. Her success in dealing with the present will allow her to go on. Many librarians recognize the opportunity literature provides for self-explorations of this kind. We know that this girl has many other means of communication than those customarily learned in school and related to language alone. We know, too, that such means of communication are as important, if not more so, to her future as those involving the written and spoken word.

General Characteristics of Developmental Tasks

This discussion of some of the major developmental tasks of children and youth does not begin to cover everything that young people must learn. It is quite likely, too, that any present list of tasks will be revised extensively in the next few years as more complete information is gained about children and adolescents. For these reasons, it behooves us to give attention to some of the common characteristics of developmental tasks. Each one has much in common with the others.[2]

1. *Developmental Tasks Are Necessary Learnings.*—Each of

---

[2] Stephen M. Corey, "The Developmental Tasks of Youth" in *The American High School,* Eighth Yearbook, John Dewey Society, New York: Harper & Brothers, 1946, pp. 70–99.

the developmental tasks that has been discussed briefly represents a lesson that must be learned at least to some degree of mastery. There is no choice if the individual is to make a relatively normal, wholesome, and acceptable adjustment to his culture. The boy or girl who fails to learn one of these developmental lessons in ways that conform, at least approximately, to the standards of his cultural group, is punished in various ways. The punishment may be calculated and overt, as in the case of persons who learn to engage in unorthodox sex practices, or it may be subjective, like the anxiety of the chronic coward.

The frustrations of a woman who as an adolescent girl and, for one reason or another, later in life did not break away from her mother, but restructured the original child-parent relationship, is one illustration of the consequences of a failure to achieve an important adolescent developmental task. The relationship of an adult daughter to her mother should involve mutual affection and mutual regard, but not constant personal dependence of either party on the other. Our culture places a premium on a relatively well-knit family life. But it also literally forces a family to disintegrate eventually in order that its young members can strike out on their own.

2. *Developmental Tasks Must Be Learned Within Restricted Time Periods.* — Because young people achieve successive stages in their maturity at roughly the same chronological age, and because their culture expects them to learn various developmental lessons at much the same time, educational and social patterns have provided for learning what must be learned during a relatively restricted time interval. This is quite satisfactory in the case of most individuals. Difficulty arises, however, when one person lives through the period when opportunities are provided for particular developmental learnings without having acquired them. He then may find it almost impossible to get the sort of learning experience that he needs.

Through the social life of the high school, or of young people's groups, or of neighborhood groups, adolescents have numerous opportunities to learn the techniques involved in courtship, choosing a mate, and reacting with propriety toward young people of the opposite sex. If a young man, because of parental influence, or because of an unusually high I.Q. and an interest in books and academic things, belittles and tends to avoid these opportunities provided during adolescence for learning court-ship techniques, he is likely to be more or less handicapped in this regard for the rest of his life.

It should be borne in mind that while the sequence of develop-mental tasks is much the same for all children within a given cul-tural group, the time at which certain concerns occupy the atten-tion of specific boys and girls varies. This is due to differences in rate of maturation, and also to differences in the impact of cul-tural influence.

3. *Developmental Tasks Are Interdependent.* — The child is working on more than one developmental task at one time, and there is a high degree of interrelationship existing among all tasks. Many times progress in one is blocked until a different lesson is learned to the point where it is possible for the first to continue. Similarly, progress on one task is frequently accom-panied by progress all along the line.

4. *Developmental Tasks Involve Varied Types of Learning.*— In order for boys and girls to acquire these necessary learnings or achieve these developmental tasks, they must change in many ways. Not only are there numerous facts and skills that must be learned, but many new concepts and generalizations are essential as well. Attitudes must be changed. All these changes, however, are means to an end. And the end is learning the lessons the cul-ture requires—or, in other words, achieving the developmental task. Discerning teachers have learned that when the skills and concepts and attitudes implied by the school curriculum are meaningfully and rationally related in the minds of boys and girls to their developmental tasks, learning is rapid and tends to be permanent.

5. *Their Developmental Tasks Define the Concerns of Chil-dren.*—This fact has been implied above. Men and women who are interested in helping boys and girls grow up need to study and learn more about these required lessons, because working at them takes up most of the time of the children. Whatever is done by boys and girls is related in some fashion to their develop-mental tasks.

IMPLICATIONS FOR TEACHERS AND LIBRARIANS

This fact, that most of their learning in school or out is a consequence of what children and young people feel must be done in order for them to accomplish developmental tasks, is most important. Each of these tasks can be stated in terms of certain goals that are sought by children. For example, the general developmental tasks of working out new relations with age mates of the same sex can be analyzed into a number of immediate goals, such as becoming a member of the play group in the back yard, or being elected to the captaincy of the football team or to the presidency of the high school sorority. Such goals represent a more or less limited objective, which, if achieved, contributes to the accomplishment of the larger tasks.

All that a teacher or librarian can do is to suggest to the child certain experiences, which in her judgment will help him attain the goals he is seeking. When the relationship between these suggested experiences and what the child wants is clear and reasonable in his judgment, he learns rapidly. And because he uses what he learns, he, in the language of the school, remembers.

⟶ **Herbert F. Wright,
Roger G. Barker, William Koppe,
Beverly Meyerson, and Jack Nall**

Children at Home in Midwest[1]

From *Progressive Education,* March 1951, Vol. 28, No. 5, pp. 137–142. Reprinted by permission of the authors and The John Dewey Society.

There are in Midwest, a small town in the middle farm belt of the United States, 133 children below the age of twelve years. Information from field observers indicates that these

---

1 The research upon which this paper is based is being supported by the National Institute of Mental Health, U. S. Public Health Service, and the University of Kansas.

children spend approximately 400,000 waking hours per year in their own homes. How, and in what kind of life situations, do they spend this time?

What does a child of Midwest do at home before, during and right after breakfast? How does he behave when other children come to play, when there are chores or lessons to do, when there is "nothing to do," when it is time for bed? What do his parents say and do to him and how does he react to their words and actions? How often, how, and in what degree, does he meet with frustration, failure, or success? How much of the time is he angry, anxious, sorry, calm, excited, sad or happy?

No one has given reliable answers to questions like these about the behavior and home situations of the children in any community or culture. This places parents and parent educators in a comparatively poor position. The truth is that if you want to raise almost anything but children, you can go for accurate information to scientists who know how it behaves in its natural habitat. If you want to raise corn in Kansas or Vermont, you can get scientific advice from field agronomists who know how corn grows on Kansas or Vermont farms. If you want to raise livestock, run a fish hatchery, or grow flowers, you can go to animal husbandrymen, field ichthiologists, or plant ecologists who know how livestock, fish and flowers behave in a great variety of natural habitats. But if you want to raise children, you have to fall back on novelists, diarists, news reporters, and biographers for information on how children behave under the naturally occurring conditions of their lives.

Questions of vital importance for parent education cannot be answered adequately so long as this is true. Many of these questions will only provoke debate until scientific methods are used to gather reliable descriptive data on the naturally occurring behavior and psychological habitats of children. Children at home present a major case in point.

PROBLEMS FOR A PSYCHOLOGICAL ECOLOGY OF THE HOME

What are the norms of psychological home life, for Midwest and for other communities of other cultures? "John comes from an *average* home." We know from sociology what this means in terms of house construction and utilities, ancestry and educational background, income level, occupational classification, and social-class position. But we do not know from any source what this means in terms of the concrete disciplinary methods of the parents, their social and emotional expansiveness, how protective, coercive or restrictive they are, the wealth or poverty of inviting home activities, and the geniality or hostility of the total, home situation.

What are the characteristics of an *optimum* home environment for children? Parents and teachers have no place to go for adequate, practical answers to this question. The problem is one of identifying the psychological conditions that go with optimum behavior. This cannot be done in laboratories. Even if the psychological conditions of life in particular homes were known, the most skillful and ingenious experimenter could never recreate them in all their richness and complexity. The basic fact of the matter, though, is that these conditions are not known; we are now at the point where they have to be discovered. The task of discovering the prevailing psychological conditions of home life, and of then sorting out the ones that go to make up an optimum home environment, is one that can be done only by ecological, field methods.

Psychologists are not well prepared to supply parent educators with knowledge about the naturally occurring behavior and situations of children at home or anywhere else. They know how children behave in the special situations of psychological tests, clinical procedures, and laboratory experiments, which means that they know in some degree how children are able to behave or will behave *if* like situations occur outside the laboratory or clinic. They know relatively little, however, about the behavior and situations that *do* occur in the daily lives of children. The fact is that psychology has largely neglected the naturalistic, ecological side of its problems; unlike other biological and social sciences, it has never devised adequate techniques of field investigation.

One attempt to develop psychological field methods for the study of children's behavior is now being made in Midwest. The present report on children at home in Midwest presents some of these methods and gives some sample results.

Homes and Other Behavior Settings in Midwest

A home in Midwest is seen by the people of the town, by the children, their parents and the others, as a place where particular kinds of behavior are appropriate. It is seen as a place where, for example, you put on almost anything but a hat, sit in a comfortable chair, and listen to the radio. A church in Midwest is otherwise perceived; it is seen as a place where you wear your best clothes, sit in a pew, and listen to a sermon. This home or that church is a stable and generally recognized center of activity in Midwest in which you commonly do some things, but not others. So are Clifford's Drug Store, the Courthouse Square, Hallowe'en, Thanksgiving, the 4-H Club, and the annual Pioneers' Picnic. All such stable activity centers of a community that are perceived by its people in general as appropriate for particular kinds of behavior, we call *behavior settings*. Two hundred and sixty-three of the behavior settings in Midwest are homes.

The behavior settings of a community are parts of its larger, social and physical milieu. As such, they have smaller parts that are social, like mothers and rules, or physical, like tables and beds. Rather than using up all of the milieu, they leave over a vast residue of parts that are never seen as units and, also, many discriminated parts, such as silver dollars and dollar bills, that are seldom if ever seen as appropriate for different things to do. Behavior settings are by no means neutral scenes of action. They are the seats of social pressures and limiting physical properties and arrangements that impose in some degree certain kinds of psychological situations, with the net result that they tend to *require* certain kinds of behavior.

The 263 homes of Midwest are *unit settings*. What we mean by this is that each of them, like Doctor Emerson's Office or Christmas in Midwest or Scout Troop 92, is a complete, perceived unit that is not seen as a part of any other behavior setting. There were, in all, 453 unit settings of the community in 1949. They pro-

vide in effect a psychological map of the town. How important
for the children of Midwest are the homes on this map?

One measure of the importance of a setting is its *temporal
weight*. This index tells how much time people spend in the setting by a number denoting *hours per year per person*. It can be
used to indicate the importance of a setting for any population
within a community. We have computed the temporal weights of
the current unit settings in Midwest for children under 12 years
of age. How many hours per year per child do all of these children, from the youngest to the oldest, spend in the Matson
home? The answer, 120, gives the temporal weight of this setting
for the whole population of children. Each of the presently assigned weights is an approximation, based upon available records
of attendance, reports of informants, casual observations, and detailed records of children's behavior.

Behavior Setting	Temporal Weight for Children Under 12
School	450
THE CULVER HOME	215
THE HOPE HOME	130
THE MATSON HOME	120
Movie Theatre	70
Sidewalks and Streets	70
HOMES 4–25	60–75
HOMES 26–53	26–50
Methodist Church	30
Presbyterian Church	28
Courthouse Lawn	20
Christmas	18
HOMES 54–77	16–25
Brownie Scouts	12
C's Drug Store	12
G's Grocery Store	12
K's Grocery Store	12

With an eye to the homes of Midwest, let us look at the ninety-
five unit settings in the community with temporal weights above
10.

Consider the figure, 450, for the unit setting, school. It means that an average of 450 hours per year is spent in the school setting by each child of Midwest under 12 years of age.

What this adds up to is that Midwest's homes, as behavior settings, account for 67 *per cent* of its children's waking hours. Parent educators do not have to be told that homes are of great importance in the lives of children. Here, though, is evidence as to how true this is for America's Midwests.

Behavior Settings in Midwest Homes

Most of the unit behavior settings in Midwest include subordinate settings; they contain within themselves stable, clearly limited and commonly recognized centers of activity. Midwest homes are subdivided in this way. We have made an inventory of the subordinate home settings in the community. Also, a temporal weight has been tentatively assigned to each. These weights are for children in their own homes. One could look in a village of England to see what the people there see as appropriate places and times for different kinds of children's behavior at home; one could do the same in an Alpine village, in a suburb of Berlin, in a town of India. We have looked in Midwest and here, with our present estimations of how much time children spend in them, are the home behavior settings of this Mid-American town.

The children of Midwest spend the greatest part of their time at home in an indoor setting which means to them: "This is a place and time for me to play." Our records show that they usually see the home setting, *outdoor activity*, where the next to the greatest number of their home hours are spent, in the same way. These data are in line with more direct observations which indicate that Midwest children enjoy a good deal of freedom in their homes. One hundred and ninety-three hours per year at home in the setting, *radio program!* Perhaps, though, this would not look high in the light of norms for the homes of other cultures. In any case, here is a channel, made by modern technology, through which the currents of American life flow at a high rate to the children of Midwest.[2] Some may find it interesting that these

---

[2] Television came to Midwest only within the past few months. It is gaining rapidly, however, and we are watching it climb with considerable fascination.

| | *Temporal Weight* |
| | *For All Midwest* |
Subordinate Home Setting	*Homes*
Free Play Indoors	1260
Outdoor Activity	705
Radio Program	193
Nap	192
Family Activity	143
Supper	126
"Reading" Period	73
Going-to-bed Time	71
Getting-up Time	54
Breakfast	49
Regular Chore	47
Lunch	43
Infant Feeding	37
Leave-taking Period	17
Music Practice	11
Special Task	11
Homework	
Adult Visit Period	
Party	Approximate
Holiday Celebration	Rank
Television Program	Order
Adult Social Affair	

children spend a relatively high number of their hours at home in the setting, *family activity,* one that means: "This is a place and time to do something with my folks"—to pop corn with them or to fix something or read something or argue or only talk with one or more of them. What is the temporal weight of *family activity* for apartment homes in Chicago? For farm homes in western Kansas? A main point of interest in the 18 remaining settings, aside from their identities, is that they do not differ greatly in temporal weight.

Parent educators can use a definition of a home in terms of its concrete centers for children's behavior and in terms of the way it is seen by those who live in and around it. The ledger sheet, above, on the home settings of Midwest elaborates such a definition for one community and culture.

SETTINGS VERSUS SITUATIONS AND BEHAVIOR

Roy Eddy, age seven, is at home in Midwest on the evening of February 22, 1949. He is in the smaller behavior setting, *going-to-bed time*. This tells us something. It places Roy on the psychological map of Midwest. It points to a very generally familiar time and place. It even says in a broad way what Roy is doing. But the fact that Roy Eddy is in this behavior setting leaves us without information of the kind that parent educators need most. It tells us nothing about the particular parts of the setting as Roy sees them. Nor does it tell us at all concretely what he is doing or *how* he is behaving. One way to get information of this kind about children is to record their behavior and life situations in the behavior settings of a community. That is what we have done in the instance at hand.

At one minute past eight, Roy's mother stepped out of his bedroom, leaving the door ajar. She seated herself in the adjoining room. Then:

In a pleading, self-pitying tone of voice, Roy called, "Mommy, my back hurts."

His mother laughed a little and said simply, "Well, rub it."

"No, it hurts too bad," Roy answered in a plaintive way.

Mrs. Eddy again laughed softly and asked, "Is there anything mother can do for you?"

Roy did not answer.

After a quiet interlude, he called, "My stomach hurts."

His mother answered quickly, raising her voice some, "Well, rub it, too." She laughed merrily. Then, in a more firm, very serious tone she said, "Now, son, you lie still and just think about the things you did in school today. Think of little memory pieces and say them over and over to yourself till you go to sleep." She asked pleasantly, "Do you think you could sleep better if I closed the door?" Roy answered, "Yes," in a matter-of-fact way. His mother walked over and shut the bedroom door.

This unit of behavior linked with a situation is one of several thousand like units or *episodes* that we have collected in Midwest.

It is taken from a continuous, narrative record covering all of the time from 7:06 in the morning, when Roy was awakened by his mother, until 8:31, when he quieted down to go to sleep at night. The record was made by eight trained observers who took turns in watching and reporting what Roy did and said and what or who he saw, heard, approached, avoided or interacted with in other ways. A number of these day records, and many shorter accounts of the same kind, have been made in Midwest.[3]

Episodes of behavior are the basic population units of ecological research in psychology. We believe that the ones in our *specimen records* tell more than other kinds of available materials about the naturally occurring behavior and psychological habitat of children. Four more episodes, from the life streams of different Midwest children, are set forth below. Each is taken from a day record, to illustrate the behavior and psychological situation of a child in a particular home setting.

Ben in the Setting, *Free Play Outdoors*

When Ben Hutchings, age 6, came home from school on November 23, 1948, he and his classmate and good friend, Morris Bryan, got a saw apiece and went out to the back yard to saw off the limb of a tree. They sawed away for 25 minutes with only negligible results. At last, they climbed down from the tree and started toward the house, carrying the saws.

Time, 4:08 After Ben had gone only four or five steps, he spied a pear. He swished his saw down at the pear and happened to slice it right through the center. Quite surprised at this turn of events, he stepped back and said, "Look what I did."

Morris, noting Ben's "achievement," picked up another pear and stopped to saw off parts of it. He said, "I'm sawing the head and the feet off."

Ben glanced back briefly to see what Morris was doing. Then he continued on his way toward the house. He said with determination, "That's what I'm going to do." He began to hit at several

---

[3] A complete record of a day in the life of a Midwest child is now in press (Harper) under the title, *One Boy's Day*. Our methods in making and analyzing records of this kind are described by the present authors in: Wayne Dennis, *Readings in Child Psychology*, Prentice Hall, Inc., 1951.

pears that were scattered around on the ground. He said, "And that, and that, and that," vehemently and with satisfaction as he chopped one of the pears to bits.

Morris stood admiring the forcefulness of Ben's actions.

Ben walked on toward the back porch, followed by Morris. Noticing a flower pot near the back step, Ben gave it a gentle, exploratory push with the tip of his saw, chipping off a piece of the pot. Then he hit it a little harder.

Morris caught up with him and stopped to watch.

Ben hit the pot hard several times in quick succession, breaking it completely to pieces. Morris said, "You *did* it," in an admiring way, commending Ben for his thoroughness. Without giving the pot a backward glance, Ben walked up the back steps and onto the porch.

Ben in the Setting, *Radio Program*

On the same day, just before supper, Ben Hutchings, his ten-year-old sister, Sarah, and three of their playmates were listening to a radio program, "Cuddles and Tucky." Ben had taken possession of a comfortable chair and was sitting as close to the radio as he could get. At a dramatic moment in the story, all of the children crowded around Ben.

Time, 5:53   Mr. Hutchings came into the room, reached over the back of Ben's chair, and started to manipulate the dial of the radio.

Ben jumped to a standing position on his chair and exclaimed, "Daddy, that's the right place, leave it alone."

Sarah said, very dramatically, "Daddy, now leave it alone. Don't fiddle. We'll lose it!"

Ben bounced up and down in his excitement: he shook his fist in his father's face.

Mr. Hutchings, who looked hurt by this reaction, said, "Well, I was trying to get it to come in better for you." He went over and sat down on the davenport to read his newspaper.

Ben settled back to listen to the conclusion of the story.

Maud in the Setting, *Family Activity*

After supper on the evening of December 1950, Maud Pintner, age 5, was in the living room with her father, who was sitting down to read the evening paper. Mrs. Pintner was busy in the kitchen.

Time, 6:51   Maud walked up to her father and asked, "When are we going down to Mrs. Bellows?"

Mrs. Bellows does the ironing for the Pintners. Earlier in the day Maud had pestered her mother about going to get the ironing.

Mr. Pintner said, "I don't know when we're going." Then he added, "Whenever your mother wants us to."

Maud promptly walked to the kitchen. "Can we go down to Mrs. Bellows?" she asked plaintively.

Her mother said in a matter-of-fact but firm way, "No, not tonight. I think it'll be better if we go tomorrow."

Maud walked back to the living room. She told her father, "She said, 'Yes'."

Mr. Pintner, who had heard his wife's answer, asked pleasantly, "Did she?"

6:53   Maud evidently felt that this tactic hadn't worked. She went back to her mother in the kitchen. In a very reasonable way she asked, "Why don't we go today so we can finish?"

Her mother didn't answer.

Then Maud said, "Are we going?"

"No!" her mother replied decisively.

Maud exclaimed, "We are, too!"

Her mother just said, "No," offering no compromise.

Maud left the kitchen, returned to Mr. Pintner and announced, "She said, 'Yes,' this time."

Her father asked with an indulgent smile, " 'Yes' to what question?"

Maud spent a moment in deliberation.

Then she said, "Yes, we can go tomorrow."

Douglas in the Setting, *Special Task*

As soon as he reached home from school on April 18, 1949, Douglas Crawford, age 9, got his air rifle and rushed to ask his mother for some money, explaining that he needed it to buy some shot.

Time, 3:35   Mrs. Crawford said in a bargaining tone, "Well, I'll tell you what. You go out into the hen house and get some more eggs." She pointed to an egg crate which needed three more eggs to fill out the top dozen.

Douglas peered hastily into the crate.

His mother continued, "You carry the eggs down and you can take enough for the bee-bees out of the egg money.

Douglas scurried to the chicken house. He quickly unhooked the screen door and stepped inside. Hurriedly he flipped the hook of the door so the hens wouldn't get out. Then he went eagerly, almost impatiently, to look for the eggs. He found two right away. After just peeking into the remaining nests, he opened the screen door and stepped outside. With a swift motion, he fastened the hook. Then he bounded across the porch and through the door chortling, "Cluck, cluck, cluck" with satisfaction. Swaggering into the kitchen, he said, "I got two eggs."

His mother laughed. She was surprised, I took it, that Douglas had come back in such a rush with only two eggs.

Douglas looked at his mother hopefully, as if he expected her to tell him to put the two eggs with the others and go on downtown.

Instead she just looked into the crate and went on with her work.

Douglas was flustered. He stood with uncertainty and impatience. Then he said in a babyish way, as though to cover up his uncertainty, "Shall I take them on anyway?" "'Yes, go ahead," his mother answered, yielding.

Showing relief, Douglas hastily stowed the two eggs. He picked up the heavy crate with a vigorous sweep and slung the attached leather strap around his neck. Then he hurried out of the kitchen and set out for the store.

Habitat and Behavior at Home in Midwest

These episodes and the others of our collection tell their own stories. Yet they leave unfilled a need for systematic description. To meet this need we have developed a method of analyzing the sample of behavior and situation preserved for study in an episode. Ratings or judgments are made on various aspects of both the behavior and the situation. The method cannot be expounded here; but we would like to illustrate how we are using it to un-ravel the skeins of children's behavior and psychological habitat that wind through the homes and other behavior settings of Mid-west by presenting very briefly some sample results from an analysis of the episodes that occurred during one day in the life of one boy.

Raymond Birch behaved in 712 episodes on April 16, 1949. Ninety-two of these occurred in the behavior settings of his home. One hundred and sixty-six of them occurred in the unit setting, *school*. Our data show, as the reader will remember, that any one of the homes in Midwest is outranked in temporal weight only by the school. Here are the two behavior settings of greatest sig-nificance for parent education. With our attention fixed on Ray-mond's life situation and behavior, let us compare the 92 episodes

Per Cent of Episodes in which Raymond's Habitat in the Setting:	Home	School
was generally beneficent	88	51
was cognitively clear	74	50
created strong needs in R	27	16
created ego needs in R	5	11
provided end-in-itself activity	39	35
presented means-to-end activity	50	33
promised reward from authority	0	0
threatened punishment by author-ity	1	1
imposed direct social pressure	10	31
was frustrating	16	27
made conflicting demands	12	22
included associate(s)*	82	78
included associate(s) seen by R as		
warm and friendly	92	49
appreciative	14	1
openly approving	5	8
openly disapproving	13	18
dominating	20	54
hindering	17	39
helping	15	5

* Person(s) who interacted with Raymond.

of his life at home with the 166 episodes of his life in this other very important behavior setting.

First, what were the characteristics of Raymond's psychological habitat at home and at school? Part of our answer to this question is given on page 352: the *per cent* of the episodes from each setting in which the situation was found to have certain characteristics.

Now, how about Raymond's behavior at home and at school? How did he react to the conditions indicated above? In part, like this:

Per Cent of Episodes in which Raymond's Behavior in the Setting:	Home	School
was high in intensity	32	36
was high in efficiency	14	22
was *minimum* in creativity	1	21
showed curiosity	20	27
showed exhibition	10	15
showed deference to someone	10	14
showed avoidance of blame	5	16
showed friendly affiliation	11	5
was predominantly gross motor	41	40
was predominantly verbal	40	14
was predominantly perceptual (as listening)	29	15
involved competition with someone	12	11
involved cooperation with someone	82	78
involved an attempt to change another's behavior	39	10
by opposing the person	15	5
by helping the person	19	3
was directed toward something	80	75
was directed away from something	9	11
led to attainment or success	88	79
led to non-attainment or failure	2	8
yielded dissatisfaction	7	16
yielded satisfaction	76	53

Look under *home;* look at the situation, then at the behavior. Now, look under *school;* look at the situation, then at the behavior. The possibility of linking certain features of Raymond's behavior at home, or at school, with particular characteristics of his psychological habitat in either behavior setting at once suggests itself. In the light of common sense, laboratory experiments, or psychological theory, one is not surprised to find that Raymond's behavior at home was relatively creative, successful and satisfying after noting that his psychological habitat at home was relatively beneficent, clear, friendly, and free of social pressure, frustration and conflict. Actually, we do not feel very confident in deducing behavior from habitat on the basis of our present data. This explanatory step can be taken safely only after the task of building good operational definitions for our habitat characteristics, on the one hand, and the behavior characteristics, on the other, is further advanced. But the possibilities along the line of understanding what Midwest children do, at home or elsewhere, by describing their psychological habitats now appears to be promising.

ANOTHER LOOK AT SETTINGS AND SITUATIONS

Statistical analyses indicate that the differences in behavior and habitat between the episodes at home and those at school are reliable and stable. This takes us back to the earlier consideration that certain kinds of psychological situations and, therefore, particular sorts of behavior are imposed in some degree by a behavior setting. But in what degree is this true? Knowing a setting, and knowing that a child is in it, can one say with much accuracy what the psychological world of that child is like and predict with any precision what he will do? Below, in answer, are some ratings of the situation and the behavior of Raymond Birch in four consecutive episodes which took place within a period of only three minutes in the one, single, subordinate setting, *lunch,* of Raymond's home.

Our earlier evidence has indicated that Raymond's home as a behavior setting did affect his psychological habitat so that he was made to behave at home in certain ways; and the same ap-

CONSECUTIVE EPISODES IN LUNCH SETTING

Characteristics of Raymond's Situation and Behavior	Joking with Mother	Balancing on Chair	Arguing with Mother	Eating Marshmallow
Kind of Action by Associate	appreciativeness	none	dominance	acquiescence
Power Role of Associate	jollifier	none	rule maker	permission granter
Warmth of Associate	medium	none	low	medium
Centrality of Needs	medium	very low	high	medium
Kind of Action	affiliation, exhibition	expansiveness	blame avoidance	nutriance, deference
Direction of Action	going toward	enjoying	going away from	going toward, enjoying
Intensity of Action	medium	medium	medium	high

peared to be true for his school. The findings above show none-theless that, from moment to moment, the situation and behavior of a child in a particular behavior setting can vary greatly. The relationship between behavior setting and psychological habitat, in other words, is not a simple, binding one, such that one can say: In *this* setting *that* situation and, consequently *that* kind of behavior will occur. In ecological studies of what children do, then, there can be no substitute for description of momentary life situations. More can be said. Parents in homes and teachers in schools and the educators of parents and teachers can find no substitute for knowledge about and diagnosis of momentary, life situations.

We have looked at children at home in Midwest through three lenses, each sharper than the last. We saw the homes of Midwest and other important behavior settings of this mid-American town through the first lens. We saw the behavior settings within the homes of Midwest through the second. The third brought into focus the behavior and life situations at home of individual Midwest children. These three perspectives may have demon-strated the advantages for parent education in the sort of informa-titon about children that ecological science has gathered about corn, livestock, fish, and flowers.

PART

THREE

▲
|

Development
and Adjustment

The readings in the chapters of Part Three serve two main functions. One of these is to clarify through the findings of research certain of the more important aspects of human growth and development. Principles of physical, mental, social, and communicative development will be presented and illustrated.

The other function is to clarify problems of adjustment that relate to the growth of children and youth. This latter is not a separate topic having limited connection with growth and development. On the contrary if we are to understand the problems of adjustment that involve children and young people, we will study them in the context of the best available knowledge of human growth and development.

CHAPTER

NINE

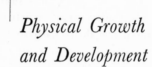

*Physical Growth
and Development*

THE MOST EVIDENT ASPECTS OF HUMAN
growth and development are those we identify as physical. The
size and shape of an individual's body, the coordination of his
movements, his physical strength, his facial features: these and
other aspects of his physical make-up are not only relatively observable but also (possibly because they are so observable) matters of considerable concern to us all and especially to older
children and youth.

Observable as such aspects of growth are, it would be a mistake
to assume that our knowledge related thereto is reasonably
complete and satisfactory. Numerous systematic studies of physical growth—especially those of a longitudinal nature—have
shown (1) that the factors involved are highly complex, (2) that
much of what was assumed to be true in the past on the basis of

359

cross-sectional studies has limited value for our understanding of the growth of *individuals*, and (3) that there are profoundly important relationships (formerly not recognized) between the physical and other aspects of human development.

What are some of the major objectives of researchers who are concerned with how human beings grow and develop physically? Few persons have written as extensively and as well about the problems of human growth as Howard V. Meredith, Professor of Physical Growth, the State University of Iowa. His discussion in the first selection of this chapter provides a good orientation to this important area of study.

Some of the questions so often raised about the influence of fetal environment, the relationship of emotional factors and nutrition, the influence on adjustment of irregularities in rates of maturation and growth are dealt with in the article by L. W. Sontag, M.D., and are answered in the light of scientific research. Dr. Sontag is Director, the Fels Research Institute, Antioch, Ohio.

How do late maturity and early maturity, respectively, influence the personal and social adjustment of youth? More specifically, how does late versus early maturity relate to a youth's underlying motivations, his self-assessment, and his interpersonal attitudes? Authoritative answers to such questions are greatly needed by teachers, school counselors, and other persons responsible for the wise guidance of boys and girls. The report by Paul H. Mussen and Mary Cover Jones is a highly significant addition to the mounting body of knowledge concerned with the psychology of growing up. It will be advantageous to the reader to examine a comparable report by the same authors concerning early- and late-maturing girls.[1]

Mussen is a professor in the Department of Psychology, Uni-

---

[1] Mary Cover Jones, and Paul Henry Mussen, "Self-conceptions, Motivations, and Inter-personal Attitudes of Early- and Late-maturing Girls," *Child Development*, December, 1958, Vol. 29, No. 4.

versity of California. Jones is professor of Education, University of California.

———→ **Howard V. Meredith**

Why Physical Growth Is Studied

From *The Encyclopedia Americana*, 1960, Vol. 13, pp. 500–502a. Reprinted by permission.

Scientists engage in the study of physical growth to attain certain objectives. An examination of the studies on human physical growth reveals that these objectives include (1) describing sequences of morphologic change, (2) systematizing the sequences obtained, (3) discovering what factors modify physical growth, (4) supplying standards to meet clinical and manufacturing needs, (5) investigating the relationships between physical growth and other aspects of ontogenetic development, (6) comparing the physical growth of human beings with that of other animal organisms, and (7) contributing to a fuller understanding of the attributes of desirable human growth and the conditions which produce it.

The purpose of many investigations is *to describe a particular sequence of change*. The investigator selects a morphologic item for study and proceeds to trace its ontogenetic history or a portion thereof. There have been descriptions of the trunk with reference to the appearance of different *kinds* of tissues and organs; descriptions of the mouth with reference to the *number* of erupted teeth; descriptions of the limbs with reference to their *size* at successive ages; descriptions of ontogenetic modifications in *shape* of the nose and ears, in *position* of the abdominal viscera, in *texture* of bone and *pigmentation* of the skin. Sequences vary greatly in the period over which they extend. The period from emergence to submergence of the external tail does not exceed two months, the period from differentiation to discard of the umbilical cord is less than a year, the period from formation to loss of the deciduous front teeth lies within a decade, while the intervals over which changes may be traced for the liver or femur (thigh bone) are only one to two months shorter than the entire life span.

Some investigators have been interested in assembling descriptions of specific growth sequences, comparing them, and endeavoring to find meaningful ways of classifying them. Their aim has been *to discover similarities and differences among growth sequences* and thereby arrive at broad generalizations or growth principles. One of the generalizations discovered by students of prenatal growth is known as the principle of developmental direction. This principle epitomizes numerous findings showing that (a) tissues and organs toward the head end of the organism tend to develop earlier than those toward the abdominal end, and (b) those portions of the limbs nearest the trunk (upper arm and thigh) tend to differentiate earlier than the portions farthest away from the trunk (fingers and toes). For the period from birth to early adulthood, certain patterns of growth in size have been found with sufficient frequency to be termed growth-pattern classes. One class comprises all of the sequences obtained for growth of the head, brain, spinal cord, and eye; its course is rapid increase during infancy followed by fairly abrupt transition to very small year-by-year gains throughout childhood and adolescence. In a second class are such items as weight of the prostate gland and testes, length of the penis, and size of the ovaries and mammary glands; here there is slight increment in early infancy, practically no change between late infancy and late childhood, rapid increase during the years around puberty, and slow gain in late adolescence. Another class represents growth in length of arms and legs, width of shoulders and hips, girth of chest and abdomen, weight of liver and kidneys, and such overall items as height, weight, and surface area of the body; its pattern is one of rapid gain in infancy, moderately slow gain throughout childhood, moderately rapid gain around puberty, and slow gain in late adolescence.

A third objective in studying physical growth is to *identify and investigate the factors that modify growth.* Literally hundreds of investigators have been interested in exploring the various conditions under which growth is retarded or accelerated, and ascertaining how influential each ingredient is at different ages, in different individuals, and on different parts of the body. A partial list of the factors studied includes diet and health care, activity and rest, illness and injury, disaster and economic depression, housing and sanitation, climate and season, birth order and sex, social class and race, gene constellation and endocrine function. Illustrative of the many findings obtained are those in infancy on bone growth in relation to intake of calcium and vitamin D, and those during childhood and adolescence on sex differences. One of the best established relationships between diet and growth is the finding from infancy studies that, in addition to adequate milk intake, children must receive a daily vitamin D supplement if bone growth is to be optimal. Compared with the growth in height of infants receiving sufficient milk but no supplementary D, infants given adequate milk plus a teaspoonful of cod liver oil daily are, on the average, taller by ½ inch at 1 year of age. Sex differences are many and diverse. Over the childhood and adolescent years, it has been found that on the average males exceed females in width of head and girth of chest, while females exceed males in girth of thighs and thickness of adipose tissue on the arms. Height and weight averages show males to be larger than females up to age 10 years, females to be larger than males between 11 and 14 years, and males to surpass females after age 15 years. The deciduous dentition erupts slightly earlier in males than females, and the permanent dentition earlier in females than males.

One of the most practical or "applied" reasons for studying physical growth is *to obtain normative materials.* The clinician cannot appraise a child's growth as satisfactory or unsatisfactory unless standards have been developed for this purpose. The investigator cannot determine the extent to which a special diet or activity program influences growth unless he has access to norms for growth under nonexperimental conditions. The manufacturer cannot adequately produce fitted garments, or clothing patterns, or equipment such as tricycles and children's chairs lacking information on age changes and individual variations in the size of different parts of the body and the ratio of one part to another. Even lay interest in knowing whether a child is tall or short for his age, whether growth is unusually rapid or slow, or whether a particular tooth is erupting "on time," presupposes the existence of reference material for normal children on body size, growth rates, and eruption ages. Many studies have been concerned with the construction of normative tables and charts. Norms for height and weight, eruption of the teeth, and growth of the wrist bone have received greatest attention. Pediatricians have shown special interest in norms for head size, orthodontists in norms for size of the dental arches, orthopedists in norms for length of the thigh and leg bones, counselors of youth in norms pertaining to the timing of the growth accelerations and marked sexual changes that occur around puberty. Recently there has developed an appreciable interest in norms for body shape, ratio of muscle to bone, and amount of adipose tissue.

A fifth objective is *to discover relationships between physical growth and other aspects of ontogenetic development*. The relation of different phases of physical growth to aspects of physiologic, mental, motor, and personality development has attracted the interest of scores of scientists. The largest number of studies has dealt with the association between morphology and intelligence. In the early 1880's, height and weight comparisons were made for public school children and children in institutions for the feebleminded. There followed studies of body size in relation to grade placement in school, teachers' ratings of mental ability, school marks, and standardized tests of intelligence. Overlapping this cumulative work were investigations of head size, forehead width, head shape, trunk and limb proportions, hair color, tooth eruption, and bone development in relation to intelligence and personality traits. During the period 1925 to 1940, the focus shifted from the school ages to infancy and preschool years. One of the major outcomes at these younger ages was the finding that there is no relationship between the size or stockiness of the child and the age at which he sits, stands, or walks. At all ages (infancy to adulthood) the most conclusive and consistent finding was that, except under conditions of extreme pathology, little or no relationship exists between physique and intelligence. Problems on which further experimentation is needed include (1) the influence of limb structure on such motor skills as throwing and running, (2) the relation of rate of physical growth to motor coordination and emotional control, (3) the influence of body size and physical features on individual and group attitudes, and (4) the relation of morphologic asymmetries to personality idiosyncrasies.

Another purpose in studying physical growth is *to compare developmental morphology in man and other animals*. Interest in the similarities and differences between human physical growth and the physical growth of infrahuman species (especially mammals) is one of the oldest interests in biologic science. Space precludes reference to more than a few of the findings obtained. Items which represent likenesses are: (1) ontogeny begins in a similar way in all mammals, that is, a small zygote approximately 1/200 inch in diameter is formed and this, by cleavage, becomes successively a 2-, 4-, and 8-cell organism; (2) mammalian embryos all show early predominant development of the head, and later development of the limbs; and (3) in the prenatal period all primates are characterized by high shoulders, a prominent chest, an external tail, a broad low-bridged nose, fingers and toes similarly arranged, and a covering of fine body hair. Dissimilarities occur (1) in length of the prenatal period—20 days for the mouse, 9 weeks for the cat and dog, 9 months for man and the cow, 20 months for the elephant; (2) in rates of growth—during the first 30 days of life the rabbit reaches a body weight of 38 grams and the child a body weight of less than 1/100 gram, during postnatal life the lower limbs are accentuated in the child and the upper limbs in the great apes; and (3) in patterns of growth—growth in body weight for man and the chimpanzee is rapid in infancy, slower in childhood, moderately rapid around puberty, and slow in late adolescence, whereas weight growth for the rat, pigeon, pig, sheep, and horse is rapid in infancy and slow thereafter. Fndings on human growth in comparison with the adult morphology of other animals are: (1) the heart is at first like the 2-chamber heart of a fish, then like the 3-chamber heart of an amphibian, and finally like the 4-chamber heart of mammals; (2) the vertebral column consists first of bars of cartilage as in the lamprey, then of cartilaginous vertebrae as in the shark, and finally of osseous vertebrae as in the anthropoid apes; and (3) kidney stages are from a pronephros as in lower fishes, through a mesonephros as in amphibians, to a metanephros as in reptiles, birds, and mammals.

The broadest and most far-reaching objective in the study of physical growth can be stated as the effort *to discover the attributes of desirable growth and the conditions that produce it.* Sufficient knowledge to be able to specify what is optimum, and sufficient grasp of control to know what must be brought together for its realization, these are the ultimate goals. To achieve them is a threefold task. First there must be a formulation of the values that are to serve as criteria of "desirable." For animals bred and reared to fulfill narrowly restricted purposes, such criteria are used as quantity of milk, ratio of muscle to bone, or grade of pelt. With human beings the formulation is a more complex matter; "desirable" encompasses low incidence of developmental defects, high resistance to infection, low susceptibility to fatigue, high resistance to impairment and deterioration of organs, and certain standards of physical vigor, intellectual competence, emotional stamina, motor efficiency, longevity, and phylogenetic adaptability. The second step is the study of morphologic traits in relation to these criteria and identification of attributes of desirable growth. This is a large order. It requires exploration into what is desirable growth during the prenatal period, in infancy, during childhood, in adolescence, during adulthood, and in old age. It requires intensive investigation of desirable growth in both sexes, in different races, under varying climatic conditions, and with respect to different human pursuits. The final step relates to the discovery of the constellations of factors that will yield optimal growth. Here answers must be sought to such comprehensive questions as: By what procedures can physical growth be controlled and directed in the best interests of the individual and the species? How much is it possible to accomplish through eugenics? What can be done at different ages through diet, health care, activity programs, and so forth? Clearly, the development of this objective is sufficiently vast and important to challenge the research efforts of students of physical growth for generations ahead.

—→ **Lester W. Sontag**

Some Psychosomatic Aspects
of Childhood

From *Nervous Child*, 1946, 5:296–304. Reprinted and abridged by permission.

A discussion of the psychosomatic and somatopsychic aspects of childhood really should include every aspect of the behavior, health, growth, nutrition, and care of children, for certainly the child's body, his emotions, and his environment are even less divisible than are those of an adult. There is almost no aspect of any of them which may be considered separately from and without regard to the others. A paper on the psychosomatics of childhood might, therefore, assume the proportions of a text integrating the various aspects of the child and his world into a significant whole. Infancy and childhood are the periods of rapid change—change in body size and maturity of structure; expansion in experience, in breadth of social contact and adaptation, in the acquiring of new knowledge and concepts [16]; interpreting and understanding of the world [16]; and adoption by the child of attitudes toward it. The child's physiological functions are developing a more adequate homeostatis, but they are, nevertheless, in a relatively immature state. No one of these changes is a unit in itself. Each is a part of a total developmental pattern and does not vary independently. Impingement upon the organism from any point distorts the shape of the whole, just as surely as will pressure on one point of a water-filled rubber balloon. Perhaps the same statement might be made about the adult as a mind-body-environment unit. Yet, the processes of growth, social adaptation, and many other features of childhood and infancy can perhaps most profitably become a discussion of some of the more important points of environmental pressure and vulnerability of this whole organism, the child, and which are, to a greater or lesser degree, peculiar to that period.

Since the birth of the child or the beginning of his postnatal life follows immediately the termination of his intra-uterine life, the young infant may be subject to a unique source of psychosomatic disturbance, one resulting from a disturbed fetal environment. A modification of a new born infant's overt behavior pattern, together with a disturbance of his various body functions, may arise from disturbances of his mother's emotional or metabolic processes. There are, of course, no communicating fibres between the mother's and the fetus's nervous systems; therefore the fetus cannot experience an emotional episode of the mother in the usual sense. The fetus is, nevertheless, an intimate part of a total psychosomatic organism. To the degree that the mother's somatized anxieties or fears modify the function of her endocrine organs, cell metabolism, etc., and therefore change the composition of the blood momentarily or over longer periods, the fetus is able to experience certain aspects of this emotional state. [16, 17]

Such "blood borne" anxieties or stimulations may, and in certain instances do, prove irritating to the fetus as evidenced by his immediate increase in bodily activity. A fetus subject to repeated stimuli of this sort may maintain throughout his later intra-uterine life a state of irritability and hyper-activity. As a newborn infant his muscular activity level is high, as is the level of certain other of his physiological functions. He is the infant who is prone to have an exaggerated bowel activity and a higher fluctuation of heart rate. Such disturbances of somatic function may include cardiospasm. Infants who do not tolerate their feedings, regurgitating them or passing them as undigested curds, often have a history of such disturbing prenatal environment.

There are many other aspects of antenatal environment which may or may not be of importance in a similar way. Excessive fatigue of the mother, exposure to loud and prolonged noise and vibration, the possibility of the development of fetal allergies are all factors of problematical importance. For example, one woman recently complained of her fetus's violent reaction to the vibration of the washing machine motor which was transmitted directly from the apparatus to her abdomen on those days when she was working in the laundry.

This whole problem of fetal environment offers, then, the possibility of lessening the adaptability of the infant to his new environment at birth, rendering him less able to utilize food successfully. In addition, his behavior may be further modified by causing him to be an irritable, nervous, and crying infant, a less desirable child in the eyes of the new mother.

The physical immaturity of infancy and early childhood is in itself a factor somewhat unique to the psychosomatics of that period. A newborn infant is limited in his ability to maintain in a fairly stable state his various physiological processes. He will have a normal body temperature so long as he is in a room the temperature of which is not much above or below that of his own, but the degree of differential necessary to destroy this stability of temperature control is much less during infancy than during later life. Disturbances of and motor control of the bowels and of the peristalsis of the stomach are much more readily accomplished during infancy than later, when maturational processes have established more resistance or stability of the gastrointestinal tract. This same immaturity of homeostasis is a part of the picture of every physiological function of infancy, almost any of which may be more readily disturbed during childhood than in later life. There is a greater somatic component of anxiety during infancy when even mild environmental stress situations will produce significant degrees of somatic dysfunction.

The process of acquiring and utilizing food necessary for growth and energy has psychosomatic implications peculiar to the period of early childhood. Nutrition during infancy and childhood is of course not merely a matter of an individual selecting for himself what he needs or wants to satisfy his appetite or his concepts of what his body needs in terms of vitamins, proteins, etc. It involves rather a combination of the appetites and desires for food and emotional needs of the infant plus the anxieties and concern of his parents for his proper nutrition and welfare. Such anxieties are to a degree an expression of the parents' desire for the child to grow into a strong and beautiful creature, reflecting the virtues and beauties of the parents themselves. The child's failure to cooperate with his parents in this process of gratifying the parents' ego is, of course, a parental frustration and a source of tension to the infant. The somatic effect of this psychosomatic situation may be important both in terms of the child's optimum processes of growth and in the maintenance of a maximum level of energy with which to meet competitive situations and to adjust to the various environmental impacts on his expanding social world. Here again, the particular and peculiar circular aspects of certain of the processes of the child's reaction to his environment are important. Limitations on growth and energy level as a result of poor nutrition increase the mother's anxiety which in turn further disturbs the child and makes him less satisfactory to his parents.

One of the aspects of the psychosomatics of infancy and childhood which deserves mention is the limited social environment of the child. The adult is the product of an adjustment process in which the social group in which he moves has been enlarged from one which at birth may have had only two important components, father and mother, to one which includes innumerable people in vocational, social, and family groups. The intensity of this interpersonal relationship of the infant and immaturity of social adaptation is in itself a hazard. The growth of an anxiety or resentment on the part of either parent for the child leaves little opportunity for compensation or amelioration through identification with others. A situation in which the mother rejects the child leaves him without resource for substituting other relationships for this maternal affection which he so badly needs. Furthermore, the intensity of his relationship to parents is such as to provide opportunity for anxieties and resentments from types and degrees of emotional exchange which might be unimportant at a later age. The child tends to respond to every fluctuation in this intensive emotional interplay between him and his parents in terms of changes in overt behavior and, organically, as changes in the motor and secretory functions of the gastrointestinal tract, vasomotor control, and other body functions. It is an example of a somatopsychic situation in which a child's physical peculiarities or lack of conformity to certain physical standards modify his environment which in turn modifies his social-emotional adjustment and is a potent factor in the final delineation of his personality.

The use of attention-getting devices by infants and children has psychosomatic aspects peculiar to their early age level. As mentioned above, the high degree of dependence of an infant upon one individual as a source of his emotional gratification and need leads to an intensity of relationship between mother and child, or child and other members of the immediate household. Therefore, if a child's emotional needs are not being adequately or properly met by this relationship, he is left to adopt measures or find devices of his own with which to secure the attention and concern which he desires. In addition to the fact that this very close emotional relationship exists, the child has, as indicated above, more labile physiological function in almost every respect than has the adult. As a result, he may adopt as an attention-getting device any one of several disturbances of organ function which have been proven to elicit anxiety from his adult contacts. The mother who overemphasizes toilet training and the necessity of adequate bowel movement at regular intervals may, if the child feels the need for more attention from her, find that he has become constipated through the simple process of retaining his feces. Her resulting anxiety, together with the manipulation involved in the use of suppositories or an enema, may confirm in the child's mind the desirability of this somatic pattern of function. Vomiting as an attention-getting device and perhaps, in some instances, as an aggressive behavior response is a condition seen not infrequently. The conventional breath-holding temper tantrum pattern as an aggressive response to frustration or as an attention-getting device may involve fairly profound changes in somatic function such as anoxia, rise in blood pressure, increased heart rate, etc., and may be chosen by a child because he possesses a particular type of psychosomatic constitution.

Growth and maturation, while they are processes extending beyond infancy and young childhood, have psychosomatic implications peculiar to early childhood. It is common for various growth and maturational factors to progress independently of each other in any individual child. Any combination of acceleration and retardation in growth in height, weight, intelligence, maturation of emotional processes, or sexual maturation may occur. The child may even be relatively mature or immature in his homeostatic characteristics. This irregularity of rates of maturation and growth of various aspects of structure, function, social adaptation, and intelligence, has many psychosomatic implications. A child with the body of a six-year-old may be socially unacceptable to a class of eight-year-olds even though his chronological age is eight years. He is certain to be aware of his physical inadequacy both from the attitudes of his classmates and from the limitation his small size puts upon his ability to compete in all kinds of physical endeavor. The immaturity of his body in size, therefore, has a profound effect upon his social adjustment, his sense of personal adequacy and very probably upon the development of drives and motivation. Similar problems of social adjustment and adaptation are presented to the child who is overlarge for his age or obese or markedly underweight. A so-called gifted child, a child whose intellectual growth is outstripping his physiological maturity, must face certain problems of group adaptation which would not be present if other aspects of his structure and function kept pace with the growth of his intelligence. The environmental forms into which the child is thrust are almost as unyielding and as disregarding of the disunities of physiological, physical, emotional growth, and maturation as are the dimensions of a man's ready-made suit, which disregards unusual stature, shoulder breadth, or other characteristics.

One aspect of somatopsychics which is peculiar to the period of childhood is the nature of the social group in which the child moves. I refer to what might be called the unconscious cruelty of children in their uninhibited and unthinking treatment of physical defects and deficiencies of their fellows. "Fatty," "skinny," and "stumpy," nicknames implying physical differences, are indicative of the readiness with which children call attention even in their nicknames to the physical differences and deformities of their fellows. This emphasis on lack of physical attractiveness or even physical deformity comes at a time when it can be most important in terms of permanent personality delineation and emotional adjustment.

The state of bodily attractiveness of the child to the mother has considerable somatopsychic significance. As suggested above, the child may represent to the mother an accomplishment. Through him she has acquired a sense of validity for her daily existence. He may be a part of her reason for existence and she may place in him a hope for many of the accomplishments she has failed to attain. As she becomes less attractive physically, she is apt to be increasingly concerned with the attractiveness and the beauty of her child. The effect, therefore, of an extensive facial eczema is to change greatly the relationship of the child to mother. There may be conscious or unconscious disappointment on the part of the mother, often a repressed resentment. Her child is something to hide, not to display proudly, and while she cannot give in to such feelings, of course, and express them overtly, the change in her attitude is often apparent to the child. Congenital defects such as club foot, hare lip, or hypospadias act similarly. Eneuresis, occasionally the result of a congenital defect of the genitourinary tract, may have a similar effect. Here again the child's physical state helps to shape his environment which in turn involves his emotional processes.

Since training to conformity with accepted social custom is an integral part of the maturation of the child, the various pressures of such a program offer many opportunities for rebellion both in overt behavior pattern and in terms of somatic function. The withholding of feces mentioned above may be, as indicated, an attention-getting device, or it may be an expression of aggression toward the training program of an overzealous parent. Resentment of this enshrouding process of teaching and enforcing social conformity may be expressed in a variety of forms of antisocial behavior, some of them, such as eneuresis, psychic vomiting, and disturbance of gastrointestinal motor control, somatic. Socialization viewed as a process of maturation involves the application of successive pressures impinging upon the ego of the child. These pressures applied upon the child by the parents, may be applied with or without skill and without insight into his need for self-approval. They may be applied with or without understanding of his drives and constitutional ease of conformity or psychosomatic constitution. As a result, they may or may not produce a significant rebellion expressed in psychosomatic behavior.

The energy level of a child is extremely important in determining the pattern of behavioral and personality response to an expanding environment. Every individual is endowed with certain hereditarily determined or constitutional characteristics of physical and mental vigor. These qualities, perhaps with others not so easily defined, determine his potential resistive or reactive response to environmental pressures. The strong, highly active, mentally alert child may respond to a restrictive parent with open rebellion. Furthermore, he may be able to compensate in part for what he interprets as rejection by his mother, by identifying somewhat with others. The child with a lower energy level, with less toughness and vitality, may make a passive adjustment to his mother's restrictive attitude. His pattern of behavior becomes a conforming one with a tendency to withdraw from new or anxiety-producing situations rather than to meet them aggressively.

While every individual is born with an inherited potential vitality or energy level, that energy level is, of course, subject to constant modification through nutrition, disease, and environmental pressures. Such modification of energy level, and therefore of behavior, is not limited to the period of childhood. The adult with a nutritional or thyroid deficiency reacts differently to an environmental impact than he would have in a state of excellent health; however, in childhood, the processes of growth-limited homeostasis make for much more dynamic and drastic changes in energy level in response to nutritional deficiencies or illness. Furthermore, childhood is the period of personality formation—the time when the individual is most rapidly expanding his social sphere. He is for the first time meeting and competing with fellow humans of a comparable age and physique. Rachitic bones and flabby muscles with their limitation upon a child's ability to compete in a nursery school situation have a quite different significance than would a few months of lowered vitality from a nutritional deficiency or other cause thirty years later. The state of a child's physical well-being, then, is a dynamic factor in the whole process of his social adjustment and emerging personality. The primary tubercular infection of infancy which usually goes unrecognized can, and often does, produce a period of poor weight gain, lessened endurance and increased apathy. Environmental pressures elicit a different and usually less adequate and resistive response during such a period. Childhood is, more than any other segment of life, a period of fluctuating adequacy of the whole organism to resist and successfully adjust to an expanding parade of environmental encroachments.

The health of the child has another psychosomatic implication in addition to modifying his aggressive resistance to environmental impact. Severe illness can change that environment and the position of the child in it. Illness causes withdrawal of the child from his normal social situation and from contact and competition with others of his own age. Again he spends his hours in a quiescent state, often flat in bed. He is waited upon solicitously, perhaps even fed, by a mother as anxious and solicitous as during his early infancy. Illness for him means a regression or retreat to infancy, its limited family circle, and extreme state of helplessness. Illness is, then, in many ways a desirable state, and he is most apt not to give up all of its advantages readily. If the episode is prolonged, he is likely to emerge with a lapse in toilet training, food fussiness or other attention-getting devices as compensations. His modified behavior patterns and the regression of his process of socialization are somatopsychic aspects of illness.

A discussion of the ways in which the psychosomatic factors of childhood differ from those during later periods of life would not be complete without mention of the so-called psychosomatic diseases. Hypertension and peptic ulcer are rarely seen during childhood. Reynaud's disease, mucous colitis and ulcerative colitis rarely appear before adolescence. Eczema and asthma—allergies which certainly in many instances at least have an emotional component—do appear often in early infancy. Just why these allergies should occur in childhood while organic lesions resulting from derangements of function (arteriosclerosis and peptic ulcer) should not, is not clear. Perhaps in certain organ systems the immaturity of the tissue is responsible for a resiliency of resistence to real tissue damage, while in others that factor is unimportant. At any rate there is a very real difference in the organic changes resulting from organ dysfunction of emotional origin between infancy and adulthood.

SUMMARY

Here then are some of the ways in which the psychosomatics of childhood are peculiar to that period of life. The most important of them are:

1. Certain aspects of behavior and body function may be modified through result of modification of fetal environment.

2. Immaturity of the child's homeostatic processes makes for a larger somatic component of response to environmental impact.

3. Many emotional factors may influence nutrition and therefore its dual role of providing not only for body maintenance but also for growth.

4. Limited social environment of infancy may lead to a heightened emotional relationship with parents, fluctuations of which are readily expressed as changes in behavior and somatic function.

5. Changes in somatic function may be adopted as means for heightening parental anxiety and securing more attention.

6. Irregularity in the rates of maturation and growth of various aspects of the individual may make for difficulties in adjustment.

7. The unconscious cruelty of children toward any one of them whose body does not conform to theirs in size, form, and function may be an important factor in the emotional adjustment of children lacking this conformity.

8. Lessened attractiveness of the child from severe eczema or other cause may change the mother's emotions toward him and thus his own behavior and adjustment.

9. The child's program of training to conform with social custom may, if not skillfully administered, result in rebellions sometimes expressed somatically.

10. A child's energy level or "constitutional vitality" may be very important in determining his response to what he interprets as a hostile environment.

11. Physical illness produces an abrupt change in social status and environment and may be responsible for prolonged behavior and somatic functional changes.

12. Most of the common psychosomatic diseases of the adult do not often occur in infancy, perhaps because of the resiliency of young tissue.

——▸ **Paul H. Mussen
and Mary Cover Jones**

Self-conceptions, Motivations, and Interpersonal Attitudes of Late- and Early-Maturing Boys[1]

From *Child Development*, June, 1957, 28:243–256. Reprinted and abridged by permission of the authors and the Society for Research in Child Development.

While many intensive case studies show that personal and social adjustment during adolescence may be profoundly influenced by rate of physical maturation, there is a scarcity of systematic data on the relationship between the adolescent's physical status and his underlying motivations, self-conceptions and interpersonal attitudes. There is, however, a small body of evidence which demonstrates that greater physical maturity is associated with greater maturity of interest among girls [21] and that early-maturing boys differ from their late-maturing peers in both overt behavior and reputational status. In one study [10] in which a staff of trained observers assessed a large group of adolescents on a number of personality variables, boys who were consistently retarded in physical development were rated lower than those who were consistently accelerated, in physical attractiveness, grooming, and matter-of-factness; and higher in sociability, social

---

[1] The TAT data for this study were obtained by Harold E. Jones in connection with a test program at the Institute of Child Welfare.

initiative (often of a childish, attention-getting sort), and eagerness. Reputation Test [22] data indicated that classmates regarded the late-maturing boys as more attention-getting, more restless, more bossy, less grown-up and less good-looking than those who were physically accelerated.

On the basis of these findings, it may be inferred that adult and peer attitudes toward the adolescent, as well as their treatment and acceptance of him, are related to his physical status. This means that the socio-psychological environment to which late-maturers are subjected—and consequently the social learning situations they encounter—may be significantly different from that of their early-maturing peers. As a consequence, according to the ratings summarized above, they acquire different patterns of overt social behavior. It seems reasonable to hypothesize that groups differing in physical status will also differ in more covert aspects of behavior and personality.

Indirect evidence relevant to this hypothesis comes from investigation of the long-term consequences of physical acceleration or retardation during adolescence. Jones [8] found that group differences in physique had practically disappeared by the time her early- and late-maturing subjects reached their early thirties. Nevertheless, young adults who had been physically retarded adolescents differed from those who had been accelerated in several important psychological characteristics. In general, it appeared that the adult subjects could be described much as they had been during adolescence.

The present study was designed to investigate the relationship between maturational status and certain important, covert aspects of personality during late adolescence. Personality structure was assessed by means of the Thematic Apperception Test (TAT) which seems to be the most appropriate and sensitive instrument for this purpose. More specifically, on the basis of the literature reviewed above and other general works on the psychology of adolescence [3, 6, 7], we formulated and tested a series of propositions relating to differences between the physically retarded and the accelerated in self-conceptions, underlying motivations, and basic interpersonal attitudes. These variables were translated into TAT categories—needs (n), press (p), and descriptions (defined briefly in Table 1)—and the scores of early- and late-maturers in each of these categories were compared. The propositions and the rationale underlying them, together with the TAT variables involved, follow.

1. In view of their obvious physical retardation, relatively unfavorable reputations and disadvantageous competitive position in many activities, the late-maturing boys are more likely to have feelings of inadequacy. Hence, more boys in this group than in the early-maturing group are likely to have negative self-conceptions (TAT category: *negative characteristics*).

2. The adolescent in our culture generally desires some independence and adult status. This may be the source of a major problem for the late-maturer, however, since he is often regarded and treated as a small boy by adults and peers and is not likely to be granted independence as early as physically accelerated boys. Therefore, it may be anticipated that more late- than early-maturers regard adults, particularly their parents, as dominating, forcing them to do things they don't want to or preventing them from doing things they want to do (high scores in *p Dominance*). Moreover, the parental treatment these boys experience and parental refusal to grant them independent status may be interpreted as personal rejection. Hence, we predicted that more late-maturing boys would score high in *p Rejection*.

3. These feelings of being dominated and rejected may result in attitudes of rebellion against the family and in feelings of hostility. We therefore expected that more of the late-maturing group would reveal strong aggressive needs (high scores in *n Aggression*) and desires to escape from (*n Autonomy—leaving parents*), or to defy, the family (*n Autonomy—defying parents*).

4. On the basis of the data indicating that slow-maturers showed a great deal of social interest (although often of an immature kind), we hypothesized that more members of this, than of the early-maturing group would reveal strong interests in friendly, intimate interpersonal relationships (high scores in *n Affiliation*).

5. Assuming that, as Jones and Bayley [10] suggest, the social initiative and attention-getting devices of the late-maturers are of a compensatory nature, we would expect this group to be basically

dependent and to have strong needs for support from others. These should be manifest by higher scores in TAT *n Succorance* and *p Nurturance*. The latter may be considered a more indirect measure of dependence, a kind of wish-fulfilling view of the world as helpful and friendly.

6. The early-maturer, being regarded and treated as more adult, is more likely to become self-confident, and to acquire high status goals. For these reasons, we predicted that more of the physically accelerated would give evidence of high achievement goals (high scores in *n Achievement*) and concern with personal recognition (high scores in *n Recognition*).

7. Late-maturing boys in our culture probably face more problems of personal adjustment than do their early-maturing peers. As a result of this, they may become more aware of their problems, and, as the high degree of flexibility of young adults who had been retarded in maturing suggests, more insightful. Hence we predicted that they would be more willing and able than early-maturers to face their own feelings and emotions (low scores in the TAT variable *denial of feeling*).

In summary, we attempted to test seven propositions related to differences in the personalities of early- and late-maturing boys. It was hypothesized that more late-maturers would score high in variables relating to negative self-conceptions, dependence, aggression, affiliation, rebelliousness, and feelings of being dominated and rejected. More early-maturers, on the other hand, were expected to reveal strong achievement and recognition needs, feelings of personal success, and tendencies toward denial of feelings.

Procedure

The 33 seventeen-year-old male subjects of this investigation were members of the Adolescent Growth Study which included a normal sample of boys in an urban public school system. [5] The subjects of the present investigation represented two contrasting groups, selected on the basis of their physical maturity status: 16 of them had been among the most consistently accelerated throughout the adolescent period; the other 17 had been among the most consistently retarded.[2] All of them took the Thematic Apperception Test, which provides the basic data of this study, at age 17.

The TAT consisted of 18 pictures: nine from the Murray set which is now standard (cards 1, 5, 6, 7BM, 10, 11, 14, 15, 17); five pictures from the set generally used in 1938 when these data were collected (a man and woman seated on a park bench; a bearded old man writing in an open book; a thin, sullen, young man standing behind a well-dressed older man; a tea table and two chairs; an abstract drawing of two bearded men); and four designed especially for this investigation (the nave of a large church; a madonna and child; a dramatic view of mountains; a boy gazing at a cross which is wreathed in clouds).

As we noted earlier, each of the personality variables involved in the seven propositions was translated into a TAT scoring category. The scoring scheme involved counting the relevant needs, press, and descriptions of the heroes of the stories, the assumption being that the storyteller has identified with the hero: the hero's needs are the same as the boy's; the press that impinge upon the hero are the ones that affect the boy telling the story. A total of 20 needs, press, and descriptive categories, each defined as specifically as possible, was developed in the analysis of the protocols. A score for each subject for each TAT category was derived by counting the number of stories in which it appeared. A list of the categories used, together with brief descriptions of them, is found in Table 1.

To test the reliability of this analysis, one of the authors (PM) and another psychologist[3] independently scored 15 complete protocols (300 stories). The percentage of interrater agreement was

---

[2] The present sample includes 27 of Jones and Bayley's [10] 32 subjects (the 16 most consistently retarded and 16 most consistently accelerated boys in the study). The other five boys had not taken the TAT at age 17. The six subjects who were in the present study but not in Jones and Bayley's study are the three "runners-up" from each end of the physical maturity distribution, i.e., the three who were closest to the 16 most accelerated cases and the three cases next to the 16 most retarded.

[3] We are indebted to Dr. Virginia B. Ware for her participation in this aspect of the study.

TABLE 1

NUMBER OF EARLY- AND LATE-MATURERS SCORING HIGH
IN TAT VARIABLES

TAT Variable	Definition of Variable	High Early-Maturers	High Late-Maturers	Chi Square Value	p
Proposition 1 Negative Characteristics . . .	H is described in negative terms (e.g., imbecile, weakling, fanatic)	5	13	6.80	<.01
Proposition 2 p Dominance 1 . .	H forced by parents to do something he doesn't want to	4	8	1.73	.09
p Dominance 2 . .	H prevented by parents from doing something he wants to	6	8	.31	>.30
p Dominance 3 . .	Total instances of H's being forced by parents to do something and/or prevented from doing something	7	11	1.46	.11
p Rejection	H rejected, scorned, or disapproved of by parents or authorities	5	11	3.69	.03
Proposition 3 n Aggression 1 . .	H is aggressive in physical, asocial way	8	3	3.88	.02
n Aggression 2 . .	H is mad at someone, argues	7	4	1.52	.10
n Aggression 3 . .	Total of all H's aggressive actions	11	8	1.26	.10
n Autonomy 1 . .	H leaves home	7	10	.75	.20
n Autonomy 2 . .	H disobeys or defies parents	7	11	1.46	.11

TABLE 1 (continued)

TAT Variable	Definition of Variable	High Early-Maturers	High Late-Maturers	Chi Square Value	p
n Autonomy 3 ..	Total of instances in which hero leaves and/or defies his parents	3	9	4.16	.02
Proposition 4					
n Affiliation 1 ..	H establishes good relations with his parents	8	8	.00	>.50
n Affiliation 2 ..	H falls in love, has a romance, marries	9	14	2.66	.05
n Affiliation 3 ..	Total instances in which H establishes and/or maintains friendly relations	8	12	1.46	.11
Proposition 5					
n Succorance	H feels helpless, seeks aid or sympathy	7	12	2.43	.06
p Nurturance 1 ..	He is helped, encouraged, or given something by parents	5	8	.93	.18
p Nurturance 2 ..	H is helped, encouraged, or given something by someone else (not parents)	8	14	3.88	.02
Proposition 6					
n Achievement ...	H attempts to attain a high goal or to do something creditable	9	10	.02	>.50
n Recognition ...	H seeks fame and/ or high prestige status	9	8	.28	>.30
Proposition 7					
Denial of Feeling .	S states that picture elicits no thoughts or feelings	9	5	2.43	.06

90, computed by the usual formula (number of agreements divided by number of agreements plus number of disagreements).

In order to eliminate bias, the scoring used in the present study was done "blind," that is, independently of knowledge of the subject's maturational status.

RESULTS

Frequency distributions of the scores of all subjects were made for all the TAT variables. Each distribution was then dichotomized at the point which most nearly enabled the placing of half of the 33 subjects above, and half of them below, the dividing point. Subjects having scores above this point were considered high in this particular variable; those with scores below this point were considered low in this variable. Chi square tests were used to test the seven propositions, i.e., to ascertain whether or not high scores in certain TAT variables were in fact more characteristic of one group (late- or early-maturers) than of the other.

Table 1 lists the TAT variables, the number of late- and early-maturers with high scores in the variable, the chi square value obtained and the level of significance. It should be noted that the hypotheses tested were one-sided hypotheses, while the chi square value is in terms of a two-sided hypothesis. When chi square has only one degree of freedom, the square root of chi square has a distribution which is the right hand half of a normal distribution. In order to test a one-sided hypothesis, the chi square test must be converted into the equivalent value in terms of a unit normal deviate. [4] The levels of significance reported in Table 1 were evaluated in these terms.

Table 1 shows that, as had been predicted, more late-maturing than early-maturing boys revealed feelings of inadequacy and negative self-concepts, i.e., scored high in the TAT variable *negative characteristics*. Hence proposition 1 was confirmed. This finding is consistent with the frequently made clinical observation that retardation in physical maturation may be an important source of personal maladjustment and attitudes of inferiority.

Proposition 2 stated that more late-maturers regard their parents as highly dominating and rejecting. The evidence summarized in Table 1 substantially supported this proposition. While the difference was not statistically significant, more late- than early-maturers scored high in *p Dominance by parents* (total). There was a marked difference between the groups in the variable which involves parental domination by forcing the child to do something he does not want to do (*p Dominance by parents, forcing*). However, examination of the data with respect to the variable *p Dominance by parents (prevention)* makes it necessary to reject that part of the proposition which maintains that late-maturers are more likely to view their parents as highly restrictive of their activities.

That aspect of proposition 2 which deals with feelings of rejection was confirmed by our data. Compared with the early-maturing group, a significantly greater proportion of the late-maturers told stories in which the hero was rejected by parents or authority figures. These feelings of rejection may stem from different sources. In some cases, the parents' behavior may make it clear that they are disappointed in their physically retarded son whom they regard as immature. The boy, perceiving this attitude, may interpret it as rejection. In other cases, parental reluctance to allow the late-maturing boy to establish his independence may lead to considerable tension in the family and the boy's feelings of rejection may simply reflect the ongoing parent-child conflict.

It is possible that earlier in their teens, soon after the physical changes of adolescence became apparent, many of the early-maturing boys also experienced conflicts with their parents, arising from difficulties in establishing their independence or in handling emerging heterosexual interests. At that time they too may have felt dominated or rejected. However, by the age of 17, when these data were collected, these boys were ordinarily treated as adults and granted more freedom. Hence, they were more likely to have resolved many of their conflicts with their parents and to feel accepted and independent.

The hypothesis (part of proposition 3) that more late-maturers would be highly aggressive was rejected on the basis of the evidence given in Table 1. In fact, the differences between the two groups on all the TAT aggression variables were in the opposite direction from the prediction. High scores in the variables relat-

ing to aggession of the most overt and violent type were significantly more frequent among the early-maturers, and more members of this group also scored high in measures of milder (verbal)
aggression and of total aggression. While late-maturers may experience more problems of adjustment and greater frustrations
than their early-maturing peers, they apparently do not manifest
greater aggressive motivation. It may be that their own feelings
of inadequacy or fears of retaliation and punishment for aggression inhibit their expression of hostile feelings, even in fantasy.
On the other hand, the early-maturers who feel more secure personally, and recognize their own relatively advantageous physical
and social status, may feel freer to express their aggressive needs.
Since aggression is a culturally stereotyped masculine trait, it
seems possible that the physically accelerated, being accepted as
mature and identifying readily with adult males, are more likely
to acquire this characteristic. In any case, the finding that early-
maturers express higher aggressive motivation during late adolescence seems consistent with Jones' finding that, as young adults,
they score high on the dominance scale of the Edwards Personal
Preference test. [8] Perhaps the relatively strong aggressive motivation of the early-maturer, or the mature sex-role identification
it may imply, serves as a basis for the development of later qualities of leadership and persuasiveness. [9]

As Table 1 indicates, the other aspect of proposition 3 was confirmed: a significantly greater proportion of late- than of early-
maturers displayed strong motivations to escape from, or defy,
their parents. These may be essentially aggressive reactions, stemming from feelings of prenatal domination and rejection, or they
may reflect the late-maturer's awareness of their strife with their
parents whom they perceive as blocking their drives for independence. These strong needs for escape and defiance may also be
considered evidence of a generally immature way of handling
parent-child conflicts. Perhaps, by the age of 17, the early-maturers
have already resolved many of their conflicts with their families
and/or have learned to handle these in less rebellious and in more
direct and mature ways.

Proposition 4 stated that, compared with their early-maturing
peers, more late-maturers would manifest strong needs for estab-

lishing close social contacts with others. While there was some confirmatory evidence, the results were not clear-cut. When all affiliative needs were considered together (score for n *Affiliation— total*), the group differences were in the predicted direction, but not statistically significant. Examination of the protocols revealed that almost all instances of affiliation concerned either parents or the opposite sex; there were very few stories involving close, friendly associations between like-sexed peers. The two major types of affiliation were scored separately. As Table 1 shows, late-maturers did not differ from early-maturers with respect to need for affiliation with parents, but a significantly greater proportion of the former group displayed strong motivation for heterosexual affiliation.

In view of the late-maturers' strong feelings of inadequacy and dependent needs (see below), it is surprising that a greater proportion of this group did not exhibit strong needs to establish and maintain close bonds with their parents. This may be due to the late-maturers' more intense conflicts with their parents at this age (17 years), their fears of being rejected and dominated by them, and their generally defiant attitudes which prevent them from admitting, even in fantasy, their strong underlying needs to form close contacts with them.

The significant difference between the groups in n *Affiliation* (*love, romance, marriage*) is subject to several possible interpretations. For one thing, this category may refer to general needs to establish close relations with others (with peers or adults other than parents) and not merely to desire for contact with the opposite sex. The set of stimulus cards may not have been adequate to elicit responses indicative of more general affiliative needs; hence, these were expressed through responses in the heterosexual affiliation category. If this is true, proposition 4 was confirmed, and the late-maturers' high scores in this variable indicate their greater general interest in establishing and maintaining friendly relationships.

It is also possible that the late-maturers' strong affiliative needs are actually directed only toward members of the opposite sex, i.e., that n *Affiliation* (*love, romance, marriage*) measures specifically heterosexual interests. Assuming that this is true, there is another plausible explanation for the discovered difference. As we saw earlier, the late-maturer may be afraid to admit that he desires close associations with his parents. He may also feel that his immaturity and poor reputational status prevent him from establishing successful social relationships with like-sexed peers. Hence, he may "displace" his affiliative needs to members of the opposite sex, who, in his fantasies, may seem more responsive.

A third possible explanation of the difference is based on Jones and Bayley's findings that the late-maturers show less overt interest in girls and are regarded as less good-looking. [10] From these data, it may be inferred that the physically retarded probably do not have successful and rewarding experiences with girls. Hence their heightened need for affiliation with the opposite sex, expressed in the TAT, may reflect their attempts to satisfy in fantasy needs which they cannot satisfy adequately in reality.

The data were generally supportive of proposition 5 which stated that late-maturers are likely to have strong underlying dependent needs. A higher proportion of this group than of their early-maturing peers scored high in n Succorance, the difference between the two groups approaching statistical significance ($p = .06$). Furthermore, high scores in the category involving receiving help and support from others (not including parents) (p Nurturance—non-parents)—an indirect measure of dependent needs—were significantly more characteristic of the physically retarded than of the physically accelerated. In view of the late-maturers' attitudes toward their parents, discussed above, it is not surprising to find that perceptions of parents as kindly and supportive (high scores in p Nurturance-parents) were not significantly more common in this group than in the early-maturing group.

On the basis of the data involving the TAT variables n Achievement and n Recognition, we rejected proposition 6 which stated that more early-maturers would be self-confident and have high needs for achievement and personal recognition. In our culture there is strong pressure to develop needs for achievement and personal recognition, and, according to our results, these needs and feelings may become intense regardless of—or perhaps in spite of—the child's maturational status, feelings of personal adequacy, dependency, and adjustment to parents.

Proposition 7, which stated that relatively few of the physically retarded boys are unwilling or unable to face their own feelings and emotions, received some support from the TAT data summarized in Table 1. A smaller proportion of the members of this group than of the physically accelerated group specifically denied that the pictures evoked any feelings or emotions (e.g. "It doesn't make me think of anything"). While this variable may not adequately measure *denial of feeling* as a major defense mechanism, this result seems to indicate that late-maturers are more sensitive to their own feelings and more ready to admit and face them openly. Since these qualities are basic to the development of psychological insight, it may be inferred that late-maturers, as a group, are more likely to become insightful individuals.

Discussion

The results of the study support the general hypothesis that, in our culture, the boy whose physical development is retarded is exposed to a sociopsychological environment which may have adverse effects on his personality development. Apparently, being in a disadvantageous competitive position in athletic activities, as well as being regarded and treated as immature by others, may lead to negative self-conceptions, heightened feelings of rejection by others, prolonged dependent needs, and rebellious attitudes toward parents. Hence, the physically retarded boy is more likely than his early-maturing peer to be personally and socially maladjusted during late adolescence. Moreover, some of his attitudes are likely to interfere with the process of identification with his parents, which is generally based on perceptions of them as warm and accepting. [12] This, in turn, may inhibit or delay the acquisition of mature characteristics and attitudes which are ordinarily established through identification with parents. Fortunately for the late-maturers' subsequent adjustments, they seem more willing and able to face their feelings and emotions. This may be a result of their awareness of others' attitudes toward their immaturity or their feelings of personal inadequacy and dependency.

The physically accelerated boys, on the other hand, are likely to experience environmental circumstances which are much more conducive to good psychological adjustments. Hence, their psychological picture, as reflected in their TAT stories, is much more favorable. By the time they were 17, relatively few early-maturers harbored strong feelings of inadequacy, perceived themselves as rejected or dominated by parents or authorities, or felt rebellious toward their families. As a group, they appeared to have acquired more self-confidence and had probably made stronger identifications with mature adults. Hence, they perceived themselves as more mature individuals, less dependent and in need of help, and more capable of playing an adult male role in interpersonal relationships.

These findings assume additional, probably greater, importance when they are considered in the light of Jones' findings on the early adult (age 33) adjustments of boys who had been retarded or accelerated in physical maturing. [8] It should be recalled that by this age physical differences between the two groups had practically disappeared. Certain important psychological differences were noted, however, and these were consistent with the differences at age 17, reported in the present study. For example, the responses of the early-maturing group to two paper-and-pencil tests revealed that, as young adults, they were more dominant, more able to make a good impression and more likely to be turned to for advice and reassurance; more self-controlled; and more willing and able to carry social responsibility. In short, they present a general picture of psychological maturity. Moreover, more of the early-maturers seemed to have made succesful vocational adjustments. In contrast to this, when the late-maturers became adults, they tended to be highly dependent individuals who could be described, on the basis of their test responses, as tending to be rebellious, touchy, impulsive, self-indulgent, and insightful. Most of these characteristics are indicative of poor adjustment and psychological immaturity. Fewer members of this group had made good vocational adjustments.

The striking correspondence between the two descriptions of the groups, derived from different kinds of tests and collected at widely separated periods of time, lends further support to Jones' conclusion that "the adolescent handicaps and advantages associated with late- or early-maturing appear to carry over into adulthood to some extent." [8] It seems clear that many attributes of adolescent personality (patterns of motivation, self-conceptions, and attitudes toward others) characteristic of late- and early-maturing boys are relatively stable and durable rather than situational and transitory. This may be attributable to the fact that in our culture adolescence is generally a critical and difficult period of adjustment. Within a relatively brief interval of time, the child must work out numerous complex and vitally important personal problems—e.g., adaptation to his changed biological and social status, establishment of independence, vocational adjustment. In dealing with these problems, he may acquire new behaviors and personality attributes which have broad ramifications, not only on his current adjustment, but also on his subsequent development. If the adolescent can cope with his problems without too much inner stress and turmoil, his self-esteem, feelings of adequacy, and consequently his subsequent adjustment, are likely to be enhanced. On the other hand, if his problems induce great tension and anxiety, he is likely to feel frustrated and inadequate, and, if these feelings are maintained, to adjust less satisfactorily as an adult.

Insofar as our results permit generalization, they suggest that some important aspects of motivation, such as needs for achievement and personal recognition, are not significantly affected by maturational status. It may be that among subjects whose achievements are strongly encouraged and rewarded from early childhood, the need to achieve becomes powerful and resistant to change even in the face of feelings of helplessness and inadequacy. The latter may inhibit the achievement-oriented overt behavior of some late-maturers, but the underlying motivation to achieve seems as strong in this group as it is among the physically accelerated.

In conclusion, it should be noted that, although rate of maturing and associated factors may affect personality development, the relationship between physical status and psychological characteristics is by no means simple. A vast number of complex, interacting factors, including rate of maturation, determine each adolescent's unique personality structure. Hence, in any specific instance, the *group* findings of the present study may not be directly applicable, for other physical, psychological, or social factors may attenuate the effects of late- or early-maturing. For example, an adolescent boy who is fundamentally secure and has warm, accepting parents and generally rewarding social relationships may not develop strong feelings of inadequacy even if he matures slowly. Analogously, the early-maturing boy who has deep feelings of insecurity, for whatever reasons, will probably not gain self-confidence simply because he matures early. In summary, in understanding any individal case, generalizations based on the data of the present study must be particularized in the light of the individual's past history and present circumstances.

SUMMARY

The present investigation was designed to test propositions concerning the relationship between rate of physical maturation and important aspects of personality structure, specifically, self-conceptions, underlying motivations, and basic interpersonal attitudes. The TAT protocols of 33 seventeen-year-old boys—16 who had been consistently physically accelerated throughout adolescence and 17 who had been consistently retarded—were analyzed according to a scoring schema involving 20 needs, press, and descriptive categories. The scores of early- and late-maturers in each of the categories were compared.

An earlier study [10] demonstrated that late-maturing boys are more likely than their early-maturing peers to encounter a generally unfavorable sociopsychological environment. Analysis of the data of the present study indicates that this situation may have adverse effects on the personalities of the physically retarded. These boys are more likely to have negative self-conceptions, feelings of inadequacy, strong feelings of being rejected and dominated, prolonged dependency needs, and rebellious attitudes toward parents. In contrast, the early-maturing boys present a much more favorable psychological picture during adolescence. Relatively few of them felt inadequate, rejected, dominated, or rebellious toward their families. More of them appeared to be self-confident, independent, and capable of playing an adult role in interpersonal relationships. Early- and late-maturing groups did not differ significantly from each other in needs for achievement or personal recognition.

These findings make it clear that rate of physical maturing may affect personality development in crucially important ways. However, it is important to note that in any particular case the effects of early- or late-maturing may be significantly modified by the individual's psychological history and present circumstances.

REFERENCES

1. BAYLEY, NANCY, "Size and Body Build of Adolescents in Relation to Rate of Skeletal Maturing," *Child Development*, 1943, 14:47–90.

2. ESPENSCHADE, ANN, "Motor Performance in Adolescence." *Monographs of the Society for Research in Child Development*, 1940, 5:126.

3. FARNHAM, MARYNIA F., *The Adolescent*, New York: Harper & Brothers, 1951.

4. FISHER, R. A., *Statistical Methods for Research Workers*, 7th ed., Edinburgh: Oliver & Boyd, Ltd., 1938.

5. JONES, H. E., "Observational Methods in the Study of Individual Development," *Journal of Consulting Psychology*, 1940, 4:234–238.

6. ———, *Development in Adolescence*, New York: Appleton-Century-Crofts, Inc., 1943.

7. ———, "Adolescence in Our Society," in *The Family in a Democratic Society, Anniversary Papers of the Community Service Society of New York*, New York: Columbia University Press, 1949, pp. 70–82.

8. JONES, MARY C., "The Later Careers of Boys Who Were Early- or Late-maturing," *Child Development*, 1957, 28:113–128.

9. ———, A Study of Socialization at the High School Level. In preparation.

10. ———, & BAYLEY, NANCY, "Physical Maturing Among Boys as Related to Behavior," *Journal of Educational Psychology*, 1950, 41:129–148.

11. NEWMAN, F. B., "The Adolescent in Social Groups," *Applied Psychology Monographs*, 1946, No. 9, p. 94.

12. RICHEY, H. G., "The Relation of Accelerated, Normal and Retarded Puberty to the Height and Weight of School Children," *Monographs of the Society for Research in Child Development*, 1936, 1:141.

13. SHUTTLEWORTH, F. K., *The Adolescent Period: A Graphic and Pictorial Atlas*, Monographs of the Society for Research in Child Development, Vol. III, No. 3. Washington: National Research Council, 1938.

14. ————, "The Physical and Mental Growth of Girls and Boys Age Six to Nineteen in Relation to Age at Maximum Growth," *Monographs of the Society for Research in Child Development*, 1939, 4:291.

15. SIMMONS, K., "The Brush Foundation Study of Child Growth and Development. II: Physical Growth and Development." *Monographs of the Society for Research in Child Development*, 1944, 9:87.

16. SONTAG, L. W., "Effect of Fetal Activity on the Nutritional State of the Infant at Birth," *American Journal of Diseases of Children*, 1940, 60:621–630.

17. ————, "The Significance of Fetal Environmental Differences," *American Journal of Obstetrics and Gynecology*, 1941, 42:906–1003.

18. STOLZ, H. R., "Shorty Comes to Terms with Himself," *Progressive Education*, October, 1940, 17:405–412.

19. ————, *Summary of Material Presented to the Collaboration Center on Child Development October 15 to December 11, 1939*, Chicago: Division on Child Development and Teacher Personnel, Chicago University, May 1940. Mimeographed.

20. ————, *University of California Study of Adolescents: A Condensed Description of the Data and the Findings Concerning Some Physical Aspects of Development*, Chicago: Division on Child Development and Teacher Personnel, Chicago University, December, 1939. Mimeographed.

21. STONE, C. P., & BARKER, R. G., "The Attitudes and Interests of Premenarcheal and Postmenarcheal Girls," *Journal of Genetic Psychology*, 1939, 54:27–71.

22. TRYON, CAROLINE M., "Evaluation of Adolescent Personality by Adolescents," *Monographs of the Society for Research in Child Development*, 1939, Vol. 4, No. 4.

CHAPTER

TEN

↑

Mental Development

FEW TOPICS IN PSYCHOLOGY HAVE BEEN accorded as much attention over the years as mental ability. Theories regarding the nature of intelligence have been developed, vigorously debated, and sometimes considerably modified in the light of new evidence. What is intelligence? How does it develop and what conditions influence its development? Do intelligence quotients ever *really* change? Do most children and youth tend to maintain a fairly constant rate of mental growth? Do the bright stay bright—possibly grow even brighter? Do the dull stay dull—or possibly grow duller? These are some of the kinds of questions for which researchers, teachers, and people in many other walks of life would like sound answers.

One of the very difficult questions to answer about intelligence is whether it consists of a number of relatively separate abilities, a very few separate, basic abilities, or essentially only one general ability that is manifested in a number of specific aptitudes. Closely interlocked with this question of the nature and number of the abilities that are identifiable is the problem of how best to measure them. Among the most active investigators of intelligence and its measurability is J. P. Guilford, of the University of Southern California. His Walter V. Bingham Memorial Lecture is a searching analysis of the kinds of problems just mentioned.

Another persistent and often warmly contested issue is the constancy or lack of constancy in the rate of mental growth. Where there is some evidence of variability in mental growth rate for certain individuals, to what conditions may the variability be attributed? The importance of the longtitudinal growth study presented by Lester W. Sontag, M.D., Director of the Fels Research Institute, and his associates, Charles T. Baker and Virginia L. Nelson, cannot be overemphasized. Students of psychology would do well to secure the monograph and read it in its entirety.

One of the truly great contributions to the literature of psychology is the series of reports known as the "Genetic Studies of Genius," to which in 1959 was added the fifth volume, *The Gifted Group at Mid-Life*. Begun in 1921 by Lewis M. Terman as an inquiry into the traits that characterize mentally gifted individuals, the investigation grew into a long-range follow-up study. It is a study which, in the words of Melita H. Oden, "stands as a landmark in the identification of superior mental ability and the factors that make for its effective utilization." Mrs. Oden, of Stanford University, who prepared the resumé of *The Gifted Group at Mid-Life*, was associated with Terman in much of the research and writing of the "Genetic Studies of Genius."

The fourth reading in this chapter deals with some of the persistent and important questions related to the kinds of adjustments persons of limited mental ability are able to make. Don Charles, of Iowa State University, presents findings based on a long-term follow-up study of a group of persons, now adults, who were first identified as mentally deficient when they were of elementary school age. The article by Charles was based on an address given by him at a meeting in London of the International Association of Applied Psychology in July 1955.

——▶ **J. P. Guilford**

Three Faces of Intellect[1]

From *The American Psychologist*, August, 1959, 14:469–479. Reprinted by permission.

My subject is in the area of human intelligence, in connection with which the names of Terman and Stanford have become known the world over. The Stanford Revision of the Binet intelligence scale has been the standard against which all other instruments for the measurement of intelligence have been compared. The term IQ or intelligence quotient has become a household word in this country. This is illustrated by two brief stories.

A few years ago, one of my neighbors came home from a PTA meeting, remarking: "That Mrs. So-And-So, thinks she knows so much. She kept talking about the 'intelligence *quota*' of the children; 'intelligence *quota*'; imagine. Why, everybody knows that IQ stands for 'intelligence *quiz*.'"

The other story comes from a little comic strip in a Los Angeles morning newspaper, called "Junior Grade." In the first picture a little boy meets a little girl, both apparently about the first-grade level. The little girl remarks, "I have a high IQ." The little boy, puzzled, said, "You have a what?" The little girl repeated, "I have a high IQ," then went on her way. The little boy, looking thoughtful, said, "And she looks like such a nice little girl, too."

---

[1] The Walter V. Bingham Memorial Lecture given at Stanford University on April 13, 1959.

It is my purpose to speak about the analysis of this thing called human intelligence into its components. I do not believe that either Binet or Terman, if they were still with us, would object to the idea of a searching and detailed study of intelligence, aimed toward a better understanding of its nature. Preceding the development of his intelligence scale, Binet had done much research on different kinds of thinking activities and apparently recognized that intelligence has a number of aspects. It is to the lasting credit of both Binet and Terman that they introduced such a great variety of tasks into their intelligence scales.

Two related events of very recent history make it imperative that we learn all we can regarding the nature of intelligence. I am referring to the advent of the artificial satellites and planets and to the crisis in education that has arisen in part as a consequence. The preservation of our way of life and our future security depend upon our most important national resources: our intellectual abilities and, more particularly, our creative abilities. It is time, then, that we learn all we can about those resources.

Our knowledge of the components of human intelligence has come about mostly within the last 25 years. The major sources of this information in this country have been L. L. Thurstone and his associates, the wartime research of psychologists in the United States Air Force, and more recently the Aptitudes Project[2] at the University of Southern California, now in its tenth year of research on cognitive and thinking abilities. The results from the Aptitudes Project that have gained perhaps the most attention have pertained to creative-thinking abilities. These are mostly novel findings. But to me, the most significant outcome has been the development of a unified theory of human intellect, which organizes the known, unique or primary intellectual abilities into a single system called the "structure of intellect." It is to this system that I shall devote the major part of my remarks, with very brief mentions of some of the implications for the psychology of thinking and problem solving, for vocational testing, and for education.

---

2 Under Contract N6onr-23810 with the Office of Naval Research (Personnel and Training Branch).

The discovery of the components of intelligence has been by means of the experimental application of the method of factor analysis. It is not necessary for you to know anything about the theory or method of factor analysis in order to follow the discussion of the components. I should like to say, however, that factor analysis has no connection with or resemblance to psychoanalysis. A positive statement would be more helpful, so I will say that each intellectual component or factor is a unique ability that is needed to do well in a certain class of tasks or tests. As a general principle we find that certain individuals do well in the tests of a certain class, but they may do poorly in the tests of another class. We conclude that a factor has certain properties from the features that the tests of a class have in common. I shall give you very soon a number of examples of tests, each representing a factor.

THE STRUCTURE OF INTELLECT

Although each factor is sufficiently distinct to be detected by factor analysis, in very recent years it has become apparent that the factors themselves can be classified because they resemble one another in certain ways. One basis of classification is according to the basic kind of process or operation performed. This kind of classification gives us five major groups of intellectual abilities: factors of cognition, memory, convergent thinking, divergent thinking, and evaluation.

Cognition means discovery or rediscovery or recognition. Memory means retention of what is cognized. Two kinds of productive thinking operations generate new information from known information and remembered information. In divergent-thinking operations we think in different directions, sometimes searching, sometimes seeking variety. In convergent thinking the information leads to one right answer or to a recognized best or conventional answer. In evaluation we reach decisions as to goodness, correctness, suitability, or adequacy of what we know, what we remember, and what we produce in productive thinking.

A second way of classifying the intellectual factors is according to the kind of material or content involved. The factors known thus far involve three kinds of material or content: the content may be figural, symbolic, or semantic. Figural content is concrete material such as is perceived through the senses. It does not represent anything except itself. Visual material has properties such as size, form, color, location, or texture. Things we hear or feel provide other examples of figural material. Symbolic content is composed of letters, digits, and other conventional signs, usually organized in general systems, such as the alphabet or the number system. Semantic content is in the form of verbal meanings or ideas, for which no examples are necessary.

When a certain operation is applied to a certain kind of content, as many as six general kinds of products may be involved. There is enough evidence available to suggest that, regardless of the combinations of operations and content, the same six kinds of products may be found associated. The six kinds of products are: units, classes, relations, systems, transformations, and implications. So far as we have determined from factor analysis, these are the only fundamental kinds of products that we can know. As such, they may serve as basic classes into which one might fit all kinds of information psychologically.

The three kinds of classifications of the factors of intellect can be represented by means of a single solid model, shown in Figure 1. In this model, which we call the "structure of intellect," each dimension represents one of the modes of variation of the factors.[3] Along one dimension are found the various kinds of operations, along a second one are the various kinds of products, and along the third are various kinds of content. Along the dimension of content a fourth category has been added, its kind of content being designated as "behavioral." This category has been added on a purely theoretical basis to represent the general area sometimes called "social intelligence." More will be said about this section of the model later.

In order to provide a better basis for understanding the model and a better basis for accepting it as a picture of human intellect, I shall do some exploring of it with you systematically, giving

───────────

3 For an earlier presentation of the concept, see Guilford. [6]

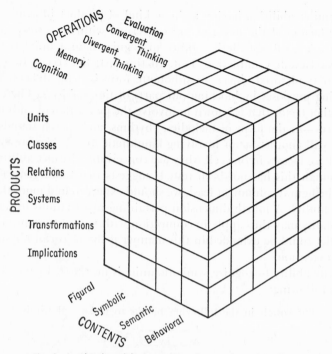

Fig. 1. A cubical model representing the structure of intellect.

some examples of tests. Each cell in the model calls for a certain kind of ability that can be described in terms of operation, content, and product, for each cell is at the intersection of a unique combination of kinds of operation, content, and product. A test for that ability would have the same three properties. In our exploration of the model, we shall take one vertical layer at a time, beginning with the front face. The first layer provides us with a matrix of 18 cells (if we ignore the behavioral column for which there are as yet no known factors) each of which should contain a cognitive ability.

The Cognitive Abilities

We know at present the unique abilities that fit logically into 15 of the 18 cells for cognitive abilities. Each row presents a triad of similar abilities, having a single kind of product in common. The factors of the first row are concerned with the knowing of units. A good test of the ability to cognize figural units is the Street Gestalt Completion Test. In this test, the recognition of familiar pictured objects in silhouette form is made difficult for testing purposes by blocking out parts of those objects. There is another factor that is known to involve the perception of auditory figures—in the form of melodies, rhythms, and speech sounds— and still another factor involving kinesthetic forms. The presence of three factors in one cell (they are conceivably distinct abilities, although this has not been tested) suggests that more generally, in the figural column, at least, we should expect to find more than one ability. A fourth dimension pertaining to variations in sense modality may thus apply in connection with figural content. The model could be extended in this manner if the facts call for such an extension.

The ability to cognize symbolic units is measured by tests like the following:

Put vowels in the following blanks to make real words:

P____W____R
M____RV____L
C____RT____N

Rearrange the letters to make real words:

R A C I H
T V O E S
K L C C O

The first of these two tests is called Disemvoweled Words, and the second Scrambled Words.

The ability to cognize semantic units is the well-known factor of verbal comprehension, which is best measured by means of a vocabulary test, with items such as:

GRAVITY means _____
CIRCUS means _____
VIRTUE means _____

From the comparison of these two factors it is obvious that recognizing familiar words as letter structures and knowing what words mean depend upon quite different abilities.

For testing the abilities to know classes of units, we may present the following kinds of items, one with symbolic content and one with semantic content:

Which letter group does not belong?

XECM   PVAA   QXIN   VTRO

Which object does not belong?

clam   tree   oven   rose

A figural test is constructed in a completely parallel form, presenting in each item four figures, three of which have a property in common and the fourth lacking that property.

The three abilities to see relationships are also readily measured by a common kind of test, differing only in terms of content. The well-known analogies test is applicable, two items in symbolic and semantic form being:

JIRE : KIRE : : FORA : KORE KORA LIRE GORA GIRE

poetry : prose : : dance : music walk sing talk jump

Such tests usually involve more than the ability to cognize relations, but we are not concerned with this problem at this point.

The three factors for cognizing systems do not at present appear in tests so closely resembling one another as in the case of the examples just given. There is nevertheless an underlying common core of logical similarity. Ordinary space tests, such as Thurstone's Flags, Figures, and Cards or Part V (Spatial Orientation) of the Guilford-Zimmerman Aptitude Survey (GZAS), serve in the figural column. The system involved is an order or arrangement of objects in space. A system that uses symbolic elements is illustrated by the Letter Triangle Test, a sample item of which is:

d ‾‾‾

b   e   ‾‾‾

a   c   f   ?

‾‾‾

What letter belongs at the place of the question mark?

The ability to understand a semantic system has been known for some time as the factor called general reasoning. One of its most faithful indicators is a test composed of arithmetic-reasoning items. That the phase of understanding only is important for measuring this ability is shown by the fact that such a test works even if the examinee is not asked to give a complete solution; he need only show that he structures the problem properly. For example, an item from the test Necessary Arithmetical Operations simply asks what operations are needed to solve the problem:

A city lot 48 feet wide and 149 feet deep costs $79,432. What is the cost per square foot?

A. add and multiply
B. multiply and divide
C. subtract and divide
D. add and subtract
E. divide and add

Placing the factor of general reasoning in this cell of the structure of intellect gives us some new conceptions of its nature. It should be a broad ability to grasp all kinds of systems that are conceived in terms of verbal concepts, not restricted to the understanding of problems of an arithmetical type.

Transformations are changes of various kinds, including modifications in arrangement, organization, or meaning. In the figural column for the transformations row, we find the factor known as visualization. Common measuring instruments for this factor are the surface-development tests, and an example of a different kind is Part VI (Spatial Visualization) of the GZAS. A test of the ability to make transformations of meaning, for the factor in the semantic column, is called Similarities. The examinee is asked to state several ways in which two objects, such as an apple and an orange, are alike. Only by shifting the meanings of both is the examinee able to give many responses to such an item.

In the set of abilities having to do with the cognition of implications, we find that the individual goes beyond the information given, but not to the extent of what might be called drawing conclusions. We may say that he extrapolates. From the given information he expects or foresees certain consequences, for example. The two factors found in this row of the cognition matrix were first called "foresight" factors. Foresight in connection with figural material can be tested by means of paper-and-pencil mazes. Foresight in connection with ideas, those pertaining to events, for example, is indicated by a test such as Pertinent Questions:

In planning to open a new hamburger stand in a certain community, what four questions should be considered in deciding upon its location?

The more questions the examinee asks in response to a list of such problems, the more he evidently foresees contingencies.

The Memory Abilities

The area of memory abilities has been explored less than some of the other areas of operation, and only seven of the potential cells of the memory matrix have known factors in them. These cells are restricted to three rows: for units, relations, and systems. The first cell in the memory matrix is now occupied by two factors, parallel to two in the corresponding cognition matrix: visual memory and auditory memory. Memory for series of letters or numbers, as in memory span tests, conforms to the conception of memory for symbolic units. Memory for the ideas in a paragraph conforms to the conception of memory for semantic units.

The formation of associations between units, such as visual forms, syllables, and meaningful words, as in the method of paired associates, would seem to represent three abilities to remember relationships involving three kinds of content. We know of two such abilities, for the symbolic and semantic columns. The memory for known systems is represented by two abilities very recently discovered. [5] Remembering the arrangement of objects in space is the nature of an ability in the figural column, and remembering a sequence of events is the nature of a corresponding ability in the semantic column. The differentation between these two abilities implies that a person may be able to say where he saw an object on a page, but he might not be able to say on which of several pages he saw it after leafing through several pages that included the right one. Considering the blank rows in the memory matrix, we should expect to find abilities also to remember classes, transformations, and implications, as well as units, relations, and systems.

The Divergent-Thinking Abilities

The unique feature of divergent production is that a *variety* of responses is produced. The product is not completely determined by the given information. This is not to say that divergent thinking does not come into play in the total process of reaching a unique conclusion, for it comes into play wherever there is trial-and-error thinking.

The well-known ability of word fluency is tested by asking the examinee to list words satisfying a specified letter requirement, such as words beginning with the letter "s" or words ending in "-tion." This ability is now regarded as a facility in divergent production of symbolic units. The parallel semantic ability has been known as ideational fluency. A typical test item calls for listing objects that are round and edible. Winston Churchill must have possessed this ability to a high degree. Clement Attlee is reported to have said about him recently that, no matter what problem came up, Churchill always seemed to have about ten ideas. The trouble was, Attlee continued, he did not know which was the good one. The last comment implies some weakness in one or more of the evaluative abilities.

The divergent production of class ideas is believed to be the unique feature of a factor called "spontaneous flexibility." A typical test instructs the examinee to list all the uses he can think of for a common brick, and he is given eight minutes. If his responses are: build a house, build a barn, build a garage, build a school, build a church, build a chimney, build a walk, and build a barbecue, he would earn a fairly high score for ideational fluency but a very low score for spontaneous flexibility, because all these uses fall into the same class. If another person said: make a door stop, make a paper weight, throw it at a dog, make a bookcase, drown a cat, drive a nail, make a red powder, and use for baseball bases, he would also receive a high score for flexibility. He has gone frequently from one class to another.

A current study of unknown but predicted divergent-production abilities includes testing whether there are also figural and symbolic abilities to produce multiple classes. An experimental figural test presents a number of figures that can be classified in groups of three in various ways, each figure being usable in more than one class. An experimental symbolic test presents a few numbers that are also to be classified in multiple ways.

A unique ability involving relations is called "associational fluency." It calls for the production of a variety of things related in a specified way to a given thing. For example, the examinee is asked to list words meaning about the same as "good" or to list words meaning about the opposite of "hard." In these instances the response produced is to complete a relationship, and semantic content is involved. Some of our present experimental tests call for the production of varieties of relations, as such, and involve figural and symbolic content also. For example, given four small digits, in how many ways can they be related in order to produce a sum of eight?

One factor pertaining to the production of systems is known as expressional fluency. The rapid formation of phrases or sentences is the essence of certain tests of this factor. For example, given the initial letters:

W_____ c_____ e_____ n_____

with different sentences to be produced, the examinee might write "We can eat nuts" or "Whence came Eve Newton?" In interpreting the factor, we regard the sentence as a symbolic system. By analogy, a figural system would be some kind of organization of lines and other elements, and a semantic system would be in the form of a verbally stated problem or perhaps something as complex as a theory.

In the row of the divergent-production matrix devoted to transformations, we find some very interesting factors. The one called "adaptive flexibility" is now recognized as belonging in the figural column. A faithful test of it has been Match Problems. This is based upon the common game that uses squares, the sides of which are formed by match sticks. The examinee is told to take away a given number of matches to leave a stated number of squares with nothing left over. Nothing is said about the sizes of the squares to be left. If the examinee imposes upon himself the restriction that the squares that he leaves must be of the same size, he will fail in his attempts to do items like that in Figure 2. Other odd kinds of solutions are introduced in other items, such as overlapping squares and squares within squares, and so on. In another variation of Match Problems the examinee is told to produce two or more solutions for each problem.

A factor that has been called "originality" is now recognized as adaptive flexibility with semantic material, where there must be a shifting of meanings. The examinee must produce the shifts

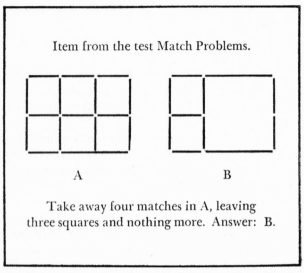

Fig. 2. A sample item from the test Match Problems. The problem in this item is to take away four matches and leave three squares. The solution is given.

or changes in meaning and so come up with novel, unusual, clever, or farfetched ideas. The Plot Titles Test presents a short story, the examinee being told to list as many appropriate titles as he can to head the story. One story is about a missionary who has been captured by cannibals in Africa. He is in the pot and about to be boiled when a princess of the tribe obtains a promise for his release if he will become her mate. He refuses and is boiled to death.

In scoring the test, we separate the responses into two categories, clever and nonclever. Examples of nonclever responses are: African Death, Defeat of a Princess, Eaten by Savages, The Princess, The African Missionary, In Darkest Africa, and Boiled by Savages. These titles are appropriate but commonplace. The number of such responses serves as a score for ideational fluency. Examples of clever responses are: Pot's Plot, Potluck Dinner, Stewed Parson, Goil or Boil, A Mate Worse Than Death, He Left a Dish for a Pot, Chaste in Haste, and A Hot Price for Freedom. The number of clever responses given by an examinee

is his score for originality, or the divergent production of semantic transformations.

Another test of originality presents a very novel task so that
any acceptable response is unusual for the individual. In the
Symbol Production Test the examinee is to produce a simple
symbol to stand for a noun or a verb in each short sentence, in other words to invent something like pictographic symbols. Still another test of originality asks for writing the "punch
lines" for cartoons, a task that almost automatically challenges
the examinee to be clever. Thus, quite a variety of tests offer approaches to the measurement of originality, including one or two
others that I have not mentioned.

Abilities to produce a variety of implications are assessed by
tests calling for elaboration of given information. A figural test
of this type provides the examinee with a line or two, to which
he is to add other lines to produce an object. The more lines he
adds, the greater his score. A semantic test gives the examinee
the outlines of a plan to which he is to respond by stating all
the details he can think of to make the plan work. A new test
we are trying out in the symbolic area presents two simple equations such as $B - C = D$ and $z = A + D$. The examinee is to
make as many other equations as he can from this information.

The Convergent-Production Abilities

Of the 18 convergent-production abilities expected in the three
content columns, 12 are now recognized. In the first row, pertaining to units, we have an ability to name figural properties
(forms or colors) and an ability to name abstractions (classes,
relations, and so on). It may be that the ability in common to
the speed of naming forms and the speed of naming colors is not
appropriately placed in the convergent-thinking matrix. One
might expect that the thing to be produced in a test of the convergent production of figural units would be in the form of figures
rather than words. A better test of such an ability might somehow
specify the need for one particular object, the examinee to furnish the object.

A test for the convergent production of classes (Word Group-
ing) presents a list of 12 words that are to be classified in four,

and only four, meaningful groups, no word to appear in more than one group. A parallel test (Figure Concepts Test) presents 20 pictured real objects that are to be grouped in meaningful classes of two or more each.

Convergent production having to do with relationships is represented by three known factors, all involving the "education of correlates," as Spearman called it. The given information includes one unit and a stated relation, the examinee to supply the other unit. Analogies tests that call for completion rather than a choice between alternative answers emphasize this kind of ability. With symbolic content such an item might read:

pots   stop   bard   drab   rats   <u> ? </u>

A semantic item that measures education of correlates is:

The absence of sound is _____.

Incidentally, the latter item is from a vocabulary-completion test, and its relation to the factor of ability to produce correlates indicates how, by change of form, a vocabulary test may indicate an ability other than that for which vocabulary tests are usually intended, namely, the factor of verbal comprehension.

Only one factor for convergent production of systems is known, and it is in the semantic column. It is measured by a class of tests that may be called ordering tests. The examinee may be presented with a number of events that ordinarily have a best or most logical order, the events being presented in scrambled order. The presentation may be pictorial, as in the Picture Arrangement Test, or verbal. The pictures may be taken from a cartoon strip. The verbally presented events may be in the form of the various steps needed to plant a new lawn. There are undoubtedly other kinds of systems than temporal order that could be utilized for testing abilities in this row of the convergent-production matrix.

In the way of producing transformations of a unique variety, we have three recognized factors, known as redefinition abilities. In each case, redefinition involves the changing of functions or uses of parts of one unit and giving them new functions or uses in some new unit. For testing the ability of figural redefinition, a task based upon the Gottschaldt figures is suitable. Figure 3

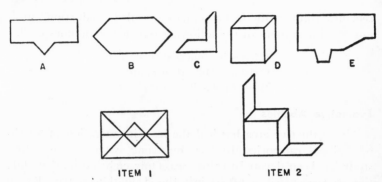

Fig. 3. Sample items from a test Hidden Figures, based upon the Gottschaldt figures. Which of the simpler figures is concealed within each of the two more complex figures?

shows the kind of item for such a test. In recognizing the simpler figure within the structure of a more complex figure, certain lines must take on new roles.

In terms of symbolic material, the following sample items will illustrate how groups of letters in given words must be readapted to use in other words. In the test Camouflaged Words, each sentence contains the name of a sport or game:

> I did not know that he was ailing.
> To beat the Hun, tin goes a long way.

For the factor of semantic redefinition, the Gestalt Transformation Test may be used. A sample item reads:

> From which object could you most likely make a needle?
>> A. a cabbage
>> B. a splice
>> C. a steak
>> D. a paper box
>> E. a fish

The convergent production of implications means the drawing of fully determined conclusions from given information. The well-known factor of numerical facility belongs in the symbolic column. For the parallel ability in the figural column, we have a test known as Form Reasoning, in which rigorously defined operations with figures are used. For the parallel ability in the semantic column, the factor sometimes called "deduction" probably qualifies. Items of the following type are sometimes used.

> Charles is younger than Robert
> Charles is older than Frank
> Who is older Robert or Frank?

Evaluative Abilities

The evaluative area has had the least investigation of all the operational categories. In fact, only one systematic analytical study has been devoted to this area. Only eight evaluative abilities are recognized as fitting into the evaluation matrix. But at least five rows have one or more factors each, and also three of the usual columns or content categories. In each case, evaluation involves reaching decisions as to the accuracy, goodness, suitability, or workability of information. In each row, for the particular kind of product of that row, some kind of criterion or standard of judgment is involved.

In the first row, for the evaluation of units, the important decision to be made pertains to the identity of a unit. Is this unit identical with that one? In the figural column we find the factor long known as "perceptual speed." Tests of this factor invariably call for decisions of identity, for example, Part IV (Perceptual Speed) of the GZAS or Thurstone's Identical Forms. I think it has been generally wrongly thought that the ability involved is that of cognition of visual forms. But we have seen that another factor is a more suitable candidate for this definition and for being in the very first cell of the cognitive matrix. It is parallel to this evaluative ability but does not require the judgment of identity as one of its properties.

In the symbolic column is an ability to judge identity of symbolic units, in the form of series of letters or numbers or of names of individuals.

> Are members of the following pairs identical or not:
> 825170493_____825176493
> dkeltvmpa_____dkeltvmpa
> C. S. Meyerson_____C. E. Meyerson

Such items are common in tests of clerical aptitude.

There should be a parallel ability to decide whether two ideas are identical or different. Is the idea expressed in this sentence the same as the idea expressed in that one? Do these two proverbs express essentially the same idea? Such tests exist and will be used to test the hypothesis that such an ability can be demonstrated.

No evaluative abilities pertaining to classes have as yet been recognized. The abilities having to do with evaluation where relations are concerned must meet the criterion of logical consistency. Syllogistic-type tests involving letter symbols indicate a different ability than the same type of test involving verbal statements. In the figural column we might expect that tests incorporating geometric reasoning or proof would indicate a parallel ability to sense the soundness of conclusions regarding figural relationships.

The evaluation of systems seems to be concerned with the internal consistency of those systems, so far as we can tell from the knowledge of one such factor. The factor has been called "experiential evaluation," and its representative test presents items like that in Figure 4 asking "What is wrong with this picture?" The things wrong are often internal inconsistencies.

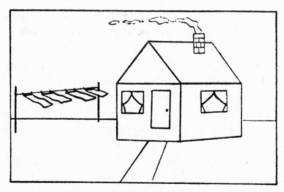

Fig. 4. A sample item from the test Unusual Details. What two things are wrong with this picture?

A semantic ability for evaluating transformations is thought to be that known for some time as "judgment." In typical judgment tests, the examinee is asked to tell which of five solutions to a practical problem is most adequate or wise. The solutions frequently involve improvisations, in other words, adaptations of familiar objects to unusual uses. In this way the items present redefinitions to be evaluated.

A factor known first as "sensitivity to problems" has become recognized as an evaluative ability having to do with implications. One test of the factor, the Apparatus Test, asks for two needed improvements with respect to each of several common devices, such as the telephone or the toaster. The Social Institutions Test, a measure of the same factor, asks what things are wrong with each of several institutions, such as tipping or national elections. We may say that defects or deficiencies are implications of an evaluative kind. Another interpretation would be that seeing defects and deficiencies are evaluations of implications to the effect that the various aspects of something are all right.[4]

Some Implications of the Structure of Intellect

For Psychological Theory

Although factor analysis as generally employed is best designed to investigate ways in which individuals differ from one another, in other words, to discover traits, the results also tell us much about how individuals are alike. Consequently, information regarding the factors and their interrelationships gives us understanding of functioning individuals. The five kinds of intellectual abilities in terms of operations may be said to represent five ways of functioning. The kinds of intellectual abilities distinguished according to varieties of test content and the kinds of abilities distinguished according to varieties of products suggest a classification of basic forms of information or knowledge. The kind of organism suggested by this way of looking at intellect is that of an agency for dealing with information of various kinds in various ways. The concepts provided by the distinctions among the intellectual abilities and by their classifications may be very useful in our future investigations of learning, memory, problem

---

[4] For further details concerning the intellectual factors, illustrative tests, and the place of the factors in the structure of intellect, see Guilford. [7]

solving, invention, and decision making, by whatever method we choose to approach those problems.

For Vocational Testing

With about 50 intellectual factors already known, we may say that there are at least 50 ways of being intelligent. It has been facetiously suggested that there seem to be a great many more ways of being stupid, unfortunately. The structure of intellect is a theoretical model that predicts as many as 120 distinct abilities, if every cell of the model contains a factor. Already we know that two cells contain two or more factors each, and there probably are actually other cells of this type. Since the model was first conceived, 12 factors predicted by it have found places in it. There is consequently hope of filling many of the other vacancies, and we may eventually end up with more than 120 abilities.

The major implication for the assessment of intelligence is that to know an individual's intellectual resources thoroughly we shall need a surprisingly large number of scores. It is expected that many of the factors are intercorrelated, so there is some possibility that by appropriate sampling we shall be able to cover the important abilities with a more limited number of tests. At any rate, a multiple-score approach to the assessment of intelligence is definitely indicated in connection with future vocational operations.

Considering the kinds of abilities classified as to content, we may speak roughly of four kinds of intelligence. The abilities involving the use of figural information may be regarded as "concrete" intelligence. The people who depend most upon these abilities deal with concrete things and their properties. Among these people are mechanics, operators of machines, engineers (in some aspects of their work), artists, and musicians.

In the abilities pertaining to symbolic and semantic content, we have two kinds of "abstract" intelligence. Symbolic abilities should be important in learning to recognize words, to spell, and to operate with numbers. Language and mathematics should depend very much upon them, except that in mathematics some aspects, such as geometry, have strong figural involvement. Semantic intelligence is important for understanding things in terms of verbal concepts and hence is important in all courses where the learning of facts and ideas is essential.

In the hypothesized behavioral column of the structure of intellect, which may be roughly described as "social" intelligence, we have some of the most interesting possibilities. Understanding the behavior of others and of ourselves is largely nonverbal in character. The theory suggests as many as 30 abilities in this area, some having to do with understanding, some with productive thinking about behavior, and some with the evaluation of behavior. The theory also suggests that information regarding behavior is also in the form of the six kinds of products that apply elsewhere in the structure of intellect, including units, relations, systems, and so on. The abilities in the area of social intelligence, whatever they prove to be, will possess considerable importance in connection with all those individuals who deal most with other people: teachers, law officials, social workers, therapists, politicians, statesmen, and leaders of other kinds.

For Education

The implications for education are numerous, and I have time just to mention a very few. The most fundamental implication is that we might well undergo transformations with respect to our conception of the learner and of the process of learning. Under the prevailing conception, the learner is a kind of stimulus-response device, much on the order of a vending machine. You put in a coin, and something comes out. The machine learns what reaction to put out when a certain coin is put in. If, instead, we think of the learner as an agent for dealing with information, where information is defined very broadly, we have something more analogous to an electronic computer. We feed a computer information; it stores that information; it uses that information for generating new information, either by way of divergent or convergent thinking; and it evaluates its own results. Advantages that a human learner has over a computer include the step of seeking and discovering new information from sources outside itself and the step of programing itself. Perhaps even these steps will be added to computors, if this has not already been done in some cases.

At any rate, this conception of the learner leads us to the idea that learning is discovery of information, not merely the formation of associations, particularly associations in the form of stimulus-response connections. I am aware of the fact that my proposal is rank heresy. But if we are to make significant progress in our understanding of human learning and particularly our understanding of the so-called higher mental processes of thinking, problem solving, and creative thinking, some drastic modifications are due in our theory.

The idea that education is a matter of training the mind or of training the intellect has been rather unpopular, wherever the prevailing psychological doctrines have been followed. In theory, at least, the emphasis has been upon the learning of rather specific habits or skills. If we take our cue from factor theory, however, we recognize that most learning probably has both specific and general aspects or components. The general aspects may be along the lines of the factors of intellect. This is not to say that the individual's status in each factor is entirely determined by learning. We do not know to what extent each factor is determined by heredity and to what extent by learning. The best position for educators to take is that possibly every intellectual factor can be developed in individuals at least to some extent by learning.

If education has the general objective of developing the intellects of students, it can be suggested that each intellectual factor provides a particular goal at which to aim. Defined by a certain combination of content, operation, and product, each goal ability then calls for certain kinds of practice in order to achieve improvement in it. This implies choice of curriculum and the choice or invention of teaching methods that will most likely accomplish the desired results.

Considering the very great variety of abilities revealed by the factorial exploration of intellect, we are in a better position to ask whether any general intellectual skills are now being neglected in education and whether appropriate balances are being observed. It is often observed these days that we have fallen down in the way of producing resourceful, creative graduates. How true this is, in comparison with other times, I do not know. Perhaps the deficit is noticed because the demands for inventiveness are so much greater at this time. At any rate, realization that the more conspicuously creative abilities appear to be concentrated in the divergent-thinking category, and also to some extent in the transformation category, we now ask whether we have been giving these skills appropriate exercise. It is probable that we need a better balance of training in the divergent-thinking area as compared with training in convergent thinking and in critical thinking or evaluation.

The structure of intellect as I have presented it to you may or may not stand the test of time. Even if the general form persists, there are likely to be some modifications. Possibly some different kind of model will be invented. Be that as it may, the fact of a multiplicity of intellectual abilities seems well established.

There are many individuals who long for the good old days of simplicity, when we got along with one unanalyzed intelligence. Simplicity certainly has its appeal. But human nature is exceedingly complex, and we may as well face that fact. The rapidly moving events of the world in which we live have forced upon us the need for knowing human intelligence thoroughly. Humanity's peaceful pursuit of happiness depends upon our control of nature and of our own behavior; and this, in turn, depends upon understanding ourselves, including our intellectual resources.

──▶ **Lester W. Sontag, Charles T. Baker, and Virginia L. Nelson**

Mental Growth and Personality Development: A Longitudinal Study

From "Individual and Group Differences in the Longitudinal Measurement of Change in Mental Ability," *Monographs of the Society for Research in Child Development*, 1958, No. 2, 23:13–15; 51–53; 119–120; 135–139. Reprinted and abridged by permission.

Some problems in child development research can be approached only by the longitudinal method. One such problem is the study of individual differences in mental growth rate, or individual patterns of change in measured intelligence in children. The fact that significant changes in intelligence quotients (IQs) do occur among many children has been documented by data from nearly every research organization using longitudinal techniques. One of our purposes in this monograph is to present the data on IQ change among Fels children in a more complete way than has been presented before.

Our main interest, however, lies beyond the psychometric implications of the data on IQ change. For some time the director of the Institute has been interested in the relationship between IQ change and the personality structure of the child. He has watched the Fels children as they grew older and observed that shifts in relative mental ability over a period of years seemed to be associated with broader aspects of the children's individual pattern of adjustment in life. The development of personality patterns of adjustment in children with progressively increasing IQs appeared to be different from those of children with decreasing IQs.

A formal program of research was initiated with the purpose of investigating the relationship between IQ change and personality factors. Our interest expanded to include other variables of children's total life situations in our investigation.

The present research is based on the study of 140 Fels children. These children were selected from the total group of Fels children for only one reason. They alone had a relatively complete series of Stanford-Binet Intelligence Tests and other longitudinal records from infancy through at least 10 years of age. There are 89 different families in this group. In some cases all of the children of a family were members of the Fels program; in other cases only one or few of the children participated in the program although incidental information may have been recorded about the non-Fels siblings. The children used as subjects are, at the time of this writing, all over 12 years of age. The longitudinal records of their complete childhood are the extensive data which will be used in this study.

The data descriptive of the IQ performance of the entire group was much like data of other comparable longitudinal studies. The mean IQ of our group was near 120 at all ages. The standard deviations of the IQ distributions at different ages were similar to those found in both longitudinal and cross-sectional studies. The variability of the standard deviation with age also followed a pattern similar to that found in both cross-sectional and longitudinal studies. The total group was broken down into a number of subgroups for purposes of studying sampling differences within the total Fels sample, and also for purposes of studying differences in performance on different forms of the Stanford-Binet. Losses and gains in the mean IQ at different ages were similar to previously reported studies.

The pattern of retest correlation of IQs at one age with IQs at other ages was similar to the pattern found in other studies in the literature. Correlations decreased as the age interval between the two tests was lengthened and increased as the child grew older if the interval between the two tests was held constant. However, the inter-age correlations in the preschool period were slightly higher than those previously reported in the literature, suggesting the possibility that the correlations during the preschool period may have been somewhat underestimated in the past.

The study of individual differences in IQ change began with plotting an individual's IQ scores obtained at each age during his childhood. A technique of smoothing was adopted in order to minimize the error of measurement found in any one single test. The smoothed trend lines obtained from this procedure became the basis for many of our analyses regarding the nature and extent of change in IQ. A study of the variability of the actual raw scores about this trend line was made. The preschool tests were found to be only slightly more variable about this trend line than the tests administered during the elementary school years. The smoothed trend lines were assumed to represent a better picture of actual change in mental growth rate than the curves based on the raw scores. The amount of variability about these smoothed trend lines was relatively small in comparison to the larger amounts of change found in the smoother trend lines themselves.

An analysis of the amount of change in smoothed IQ trend lines showed that there were larger increments of change during the preschool years than during the school years. In this sense the preschool tests may be considered as unreliable for prediction of future status in IQ because of the nature of changes in mental growth found in a group rather than from the standpoint of unreliabiltiy due to error of measurement.

One of the characteristics noted in the individual curves of smoothed IQ was the idiosyncratic nature of the patterns of change which were found. Some individuals had periods of loss in IQ followed by a gain, other cases had periods of gain in IQ followed by a period of relatively little change, and others had still differing patterns of change. _T·Q·_

When various aspects of the group data are viewed in relation to the individual differences found in these smoothed IQ curves, it may be seen that some of the group statistics reflect these individual curves. For example, the constriction of the standard deviation found in many studies may be shown to be a function of the combined effects of the individual curves. The age of 5 in our sample happens to be the age of more homogeneity in group performance due to the characteristics of the curves themselves. One part of this is due to the fact that many of the cases showing decelerative trends started out at a relatively high level of IQ, and the smooth trend lines of the acceleratory group and deceleratory group cross at about this age. The pattern of inter-age retest correlations found in other studies may also be interpreted with reference to the pattern of smooth trend lines occurring among the individuals in our sample.

It may be noted that it is impossible to speak of the amount or nature of IQ change found during childhood without reference to the idiosyncratic nature of the curves themselves. In terms of individual differences it would appear to be relatively meaningless for some of our purposes to pick two ages at random and attempt to specify the amount of IQ change found. Rather, an analysis was made of the ages of the inflection points in various individual curves in order to determine the most appropriate ages for studying the phenomenon of acceleration and deceleration in mental growth as related to other factors. This analysis and other pertinent information indicated that the age periods 4 to 6 and 6 to 10 were the best ones to use for this purpose. During these age intervals the least amount of distortion of the individual profiles occurred; the homogeneity of the linearity of patterns during these periods was maximized.

The criterion using these ages appeared to be the most appropriate one for the study (to be reported in Part II of this monograph) dealing with personality and other factors associated with IQ change. In order to specify the greatest change which can occur in individual profiles, another criterion seemed more appropriate; this was based on the lowest point and highest point in the individual graphs. Viewing the individual profiles of IQ change in this manner, it would appear that the extent of IQ change found during childhood has been previously underestimated. (The median amount of change in this instance was 17.9 IQ points.) Sixty-two per cent of the children changed more than 15 IQ points sometime during the course of mental development from the age of 3 to age 10. The greatest amount of change to be found in any individual graph curve of smoothed IQ was approximately 58 smoothed IQ points. Significantly more boys than girls were found to have accelerative patterns in their trend lines, particularly during the school years.

A number of analyses pertaining to artifacts and other methodological considerations necessary in order to draw conclusions about IQ change were made. The evaluation of the effects of serial testing on individuals was shown to be ultimately dependent upon longitudinal information available over a more representative sample. Through comparison of changes in mean IQ found in our total group, observation of practice effect on the standard deviation, and consideration of other factors, it would appear that the effects of practice were a minor consideration when adequate provision was made in the selection of criterion groups (such as used in Part II of this monograph). The extent of artificial increases in IQ due to the use of different forms of the Binet was also considered, and provisions were made for correcting this error.

An extensive analysis of performance on individual items of the Binet test was made in order to evaluate the relationship between change in IQ and competence in special areas of ability. It has been supposed that changes in IQ during childhood could occur as a result of test construction artifact in which the changing ratio of verbal to performance types of items could result in children with special competence in verbal areas accelerating over a period of years and children with relatively more competence in performance areas tending to decelerate. Accelerative and decelerative rates of mental growth did not appear to be related to any specific areas of ability as measured by the differences in performances on the different types of items. Rather, there appeared to be a general acceleratory-deceleratory factor present regardless of a child's area of special competence.

From the description of the nature and amount of change in IQ and from the analysis of possible artifacts in our data, we may conclude that real changes in relative mental ability do occur in childhood. It would appear that, by choosing extreme groups who accelerate or decelerate in IQ, we are relatively sure of having also selected accelerative or decelerative groups who change in actual mental growth. Lastly, accelerative and decelerative rates of mental growth do not appear to be related to any specific areas of abilities as measured by the differences in performance on different types of items found in the Stanford-Binet. Rather, there appears to be a general acceleratory-deceleratory factor present during the preschool years and thereafter. . . .

Our findings regarding the development of personality as related to the development of intellectual ability would appear to be consistent with an increasingly prevalent attitude toward problems of child development. We may regard intelligence as but one aspect of the total personality. The general motives for behavior which characterize the child's adjustment to many life situations may appropriately serve as a conceptual framework for viewing intelligence and other aspects of personality.

We have restricted our study to the childhood years and therefore can only speculate about the future development of our subjects. It would seem logical to assume that the children who have shown a high need for achievement during the elementary school years, and who had increased in IQ during these years, will show greater achievement in the academic area during the ensuing years. As a group, we think they would reach higher educational and vocational levels than the subjects of corresponding IQ levels who showed little change in mental ability or declined during the elementary school years. This hypothesis has already been considered, not from a predictive approach, but in an investigation of the antecedent IQ careers of persons who achieved various educational levels. Husén [8] found that the children of a Swedish town who had remained in school for the longest periods of time tended to be those subjects who had shown the most gain in IQ during adolescent years. Husén investigated this hypothesis from the standpoint of influence of schooling upon the IQ. He concluded that schooling subsequent to leaving primary school considerably increases intellectual level. A logical extension of our findings would lead rather to suppose that personality variables such as need for achievement could explain subjects' decisions regarding continuation of schooling, as well as explaining changes in IQ.

It would likewise appear that the controversy of the Iowa studies [e.g., 11] regarding the influence of nursery school attendance upon the IQ may be, in part, clarified by future research. Although there appear to be many methodological problems [10] involved in the work of the Iowa group, the clinical acumen and perceptiveness of the research workers themselves need not be questioned. It is conceivable that nursery school experience can serve as training in emotional independence for some children. The insights which led to the Iowa workers' hypotheses might well have arisen from such observations. All of the children of our sample attended the experimental nursery school at Fels. A pilot study of the nursery school reports of a small number of these subjects would seem to indicate that some children made significant learnings during this period in their relationships with peers. These sorts of learnings could conceivably start the child on new paths of adjustment. These learnings could contribute toward the development of independent modes of behavior leading to increased motivation and increasingly better performance on mental tasks . . .

The major portion of Part II of this monograph reports an investigation conducted at the Fels Research Institute, studying the relationship between personality development and change in mental growth rate. The study of personality development made use of most of the longitudinal information gathered on the children in this study from birth through the age of ten years. Test data and narrative information were obtained during visits by parents and children to the Institute, and from visits made to homes and schools by trained observers. Fourteen rating scales were developed using dimensions which permitted quantification of the extensive data on each subject.

The scales which were used to rate personality during the pre-school years were as follows: Emotional Dependence upon Parents, Aggressiveness in Peer Relationships, Self-Initiated Behavior, Socialization, Friendliness, Problem-Solving Behavior, Anticipation of Reward, General Competitiveness, Femininity (used only to rate girls), Sibling Rivalry, and Anxiety. In addition to the above scales, three other dimensions were used in rating personality during the elementary school years. These were: Scholastic Competition, Independence in Scholastic Achievement, and Parental Emphasis on School Achievement. A seven-point rating scale was used in rating each dimension. Each scale was named for the trait suggested by the high rating. Referent behaviors for each scale were developed during the initial phases of the research. It was assumed that the rating scales would identify some gross aspects of various types of behavior patterns used by children during these years.

It was hypothesized that children who gained most in IQ would be those children who entered learning situations with behavior patterns which would be characterized by a high rating on each of the scales except Femininity. (Actually, the latter was expected to be associated with a decline in IQ in girls). For example, we expected the child with relatively strong emotional dependence on parents to approach learning situations in a different manner from that of a child of the same age whose dominant traits of personality were emotional independence, self-reliance, or competitiveness in peer situations. It was hypothesized that differences such as these in characteristic modes of adjustment, and in the different learning histories and types of motivation characterized by these modes of adjustment, should presumably influence the child's performance on tests such as the Stanford-Binet. Performance on the test was presumed to be affected by personality characteristics not only in the immediate motivation in the test situation, but also in the achievement of the child prior to the test and in the acquisition of the ability to learn. It was hypothesized, therefore, that personality factors play an important role in "learning to learn," which was assumed to be the basis of acquisition of intellectual ability during childhood under normal environmental conditions. Children who were judged emotionally dependent on parents, or otherwise lacking in modes of behavior suggesting readiness to make contact with and to interact successfully with new aspects of their environment, were expected to show deceleration in IQ. . . .

Ordinarily, conclusions are drawn on the basis of the statistical probability that obtained differences between groups represent real differences. In this study this was not the case. Because of certain uncontrolled factors in the study, such as the raters' prior knowledge of sex differences in IQ change and the use of different forms of the Binet, a more rigorous criterion for judging significance was used. Probability levels obtained from different quartile groups at each age period were determined to be interpretable only if they met with such other criteria as internal cross-validation, statistical probability of discrimination within sex groups and within groups having data based on the 1937 form versus those having data based on the 1916 form of the Binet, and when IQ level was not involved.

An analysis of the ratings made at age 6 of those children who gained the most and of those who lost the most in IQ during the preschool period resulted in the Emotional Independence from Parents scale being significant in the over-all analysis and in the various subanalyses. The analyses of the ratings made at age 10 resulted in a larger number of scales discriminating significantly between subjects who gained and subjects who lost in IQ during the elementary school years. Independence, Aggressiveness, Self-Initiation, Problem-Solving, Anticipation, Competitiveness, and the two scales having to do with scholastic competition all appeared to be related clearly to an accelerated pattern of IQ change during this period. The ratings made on the basis of these significant scales were all highly inter-correlated, suggesting that a common dimension of personality could explain the results obtained at this age. The referent behaviors of these scales suggested the achievement motive as a common dimension. The use of an achievement motive concept would therefore appear to be more economical than the use of separate scales in understanding the mental development of children during the elementary school years.

A predictive analysis was also made, using the ratings at age 6 of those children who were extreme ascenders or descenders during the following four years of their lives. When the age 6 ratings were analyzed for differences between ascending and descending groups, only Aggressiveness, Self-Initiation, and Competitiveness were judged to be significant predictors of future IQ change.

From the various analyses made of preschool and elementary school behavior, it would appear that our major hypotheses about the relationship between personality factors and differences in mental growth rate were essentially substantiated in the broad aspects involved in the hypotheses. Our findings would seem to warrant some generalizations regarding variables to be used in predicting a child's mental growth rate and in understanding something of the basic nature of underlying processes involved in the acquisition of the ability to learn and profit from experience.

It would appear that the theoretical construct of intelligence is somewhat artificial in nature, reflecting not only motivational aspects of content learning, but also reflecting another level of learning which has been termed "learning to learn." Some types of learning appear to be necessary to other types of learning in the acquisition of various types of skills and achievements. We believe that performance on tests of intelligence also reflects different levels of learning. We have speculated about the order of events which may lead to individual differences in measured intelligence throughout childhood. It seems reasonable to suppose that learnings during the first few years of life are relatively more dependent upon physiological and maturational factors. This period of life was not included in the scope of the present study. However, the model of reinforcement theory suggests that functioning structure must be present before the first behaviors can be reinforced and established. From the years of 3 to 6 it would appear that the learning of broad patterns of behavior in relation to parents is of primary importance in establishing a foundation for later interaction with the environment. The child who is emotionally dependent upon his parents during these years would appear to be establishing a mode of behavior which is not conducive to "learning to learn" during this time. However, if the child is learning to meet some of his needs through appropriate aggressive behavior, competitiveness, or individual problem-solving, it would appear that he is laying a groundwork for the kind of motivation characterized in need for achievement, which may operate as a motive in learning experiences. During the elementary school years it is therefore not surprising to see a high need for achievement being related to an accelerated mental growth rate.

A number of limitations of the present study have been discussed previously. Our generalizations are most appropriate to children in the higher range of measured intelligence. However, it would appear that the principles of mental growth which have been suggested would be applicable over the entire range of normal intelligence. In the opinion of the authors, relevant variables necessary to understand mental deficiency would seem to lie more in the first three years of life than thereafter. The present study was, of necessity, based on extreme quartiles of IQ change and on some of the more gross aspects of personality development. It is hoped that the findings from the present study will provide guideposts for setting up of experimental studies of personality as re-related to learning in children.

Our findings may be of benefit to workers in the field of applied child psychology. It would seem that whenever prediction of future intellectual status is an important consideration in making decisions, such as in the placement of children for adoption and grade level placement in school, modes of personality adjustment must be considered along with an estimate of present intellectual functioning. Consideration of emotional dependence on parents during the preschool years appears to be useful in the prediction of mental growth rate during these years. Prediction of future intellectual functioning at the time the child enters school may possibly be aided through consideration of the referent behaviors used in the scales of Aggressiveness, Self-Initiation, and Competitiveness. During the school years an appraisal of need for achievement may prove helpful in similar problems of prediction. Future studies at the Fels Research Institute are contemplated which will bear on later scholastic and vocational achievement as related not only to IQ level but to accelerated and decelerated mental growth rate.

——▶ Melita H. Oden

The Gifted Group at Mid-Life[1]

The Gifted Group at Mid-Life is the fifth volume in the "Genetic Studies of Genius" series and the fourth concerned with the longitudinal study of gifted children initiated by Lewis M. Terman in 1921. As this report is being completed in the summer of 1958, more than 35 years have elapsed since the investigation was undertaken, and more than one and one-half years have passed since the death of Dr. Terman.

His imagination and vision, his fortitude and perseverance, his persuasiveness and charm—all these enabled him to follow the careers of this same group of subjects continuously for three and one-half decades until his death. It was due, in large measure, to the human qualities of Dr. Terman that his study of gifted children grew into a very close relationship that has been main-

---

[1] This resumé of the study reported in the book, *The Gifted Group at Mid-Life*, was prepared by Mrs. Oden from an address which she delivered at a conference on the gifted child held at Stanford University, April 13, 1957, in honor of the late Professor Lewis M. Terman.

tained throughout the years. Always active in the research, he was able, after his retirement as head of the Psychology Department in 1942, to give it his full attention. His affection for the group is shown in the warm and personal tone of the follow-up letters, even the form letters, which bore the salutation *To My Gifted "Children,"* the quotation marks added in recognition of their adult status. It happens that the gifted children turned out, in one way or another, to be gifted adults, but if they had not, Dr. Terman's affection for them would have been no less. He repeatedly expressed, and not infrequently was called on to prove, his deep personal interest in each subject. As one of his letters accompanying a questionnaire put it, "although the published reports will be largely statistical, I want you to know that each of you is to me a real person and not just another statistic."

This study is unique in a number of ways: the many years it has continued, the vast amount of immensely valuable data collected, the zeal with which the inviolability of the records has been safeguarded and the confidences of the subjects respected, the enduring friendship and loyalty of the group, and their unparalleled cooperation. The fact that 95 percent of the group are still actively participating in the study, a striking manifestation of the rapport between investigator and subjects, strengthens the validity of the findings. The debt of gratitude owed the subjects and their parents can never be adequately expressed.

The research has yielded documentary evidence that the gifted child is far more apt to become the intellectually superior, vocationally successful, well-adjusted adult than will the average. These findings have tremendous importance for education and it is a source of satisfaction to know that this study has contributed to the present interest in better educational provisions for gifted children everywhere. Dr. Terman's work stands as a landmark in the identification of superior mental ability and the factors that make for its effective utilization.

The purpose of the study was two-fold; first, to find out what physical, mental, and personality traits characterize children of high intelligence, and secondly, to find out by means of long-range follow-up how such children develop, what kinds of adults they become, and as far as possible what factors influence their later achievements. And this ambitious goal was realized, for Dr. Terman lived to see his "children" reach mid-life.

The study grew out of Dr. Terman's early interest in individual differences. After the publication of his revision of the Binet-Simon Intelligence Scale in 1916 he began to make plans for his long-dreamed-of study of superior intelligence. The project got under way in the 1921–22 school year when he and his assistants canvassed a public school population of nearly a quarter million in the urban and semi-urban areas of California in order to locate a thousand or more of highest IQ. The standard set was an IQ of 140 or higher; this was purely arbitrary and intended merely to insure that all would be in the top 1 percent of the school population. The total number selected for study was 1528. Their average IQ was 151, with 83 testing at IQ 170 or higher. The average age of the group was close to 11 years. They ranged in age from 3 to 18 years with only a small number below 5 or above 17 years of age. It was estimated that not more than 10 percent of those in the areas canvassed who could have qualified were missed. This sample of 90 percent insured that whatever traits were typical of these children would be typical of high-testing children in general.

To summarize briefly what the group was like when first located: physical measurements, health histories, and medical examinations showed the typical gifted child to be a better physical specimen than the average. His interests covered a wide range, were avidly pursued, and revealed a maturity about 2 or 3 years above the age norm. A battery of character tests, personality tests, and trait ratings all placed him above a control group of corresponding age.

Tests of school achievement showed that in mastery of school subject matter the typical gifted child rated about 2 grades beyond the one in which he was enrolled, and some rated as much as 3 or 4 grades beyond. Moreover, the ability of the gifted as measured by these tests was so general as to refute completely the traditional belief that gifted children are one-sided. There was no evidence of any law of compensation whereby intellectual superiority is offset by inferiority along non-intellectual lines.

Such are the outstanding traits of gifted children expressed in composite portraiture. Actually, of course, there was a wide range of variability within the group. Among these children one could find individual examples of personality defects, behavior problems, and physical frailty, but the incidence of unfavorable deviations was well below that in the general population.

But what kind of adults do gifted children become? That is the question the most recent data have tried to answer. Since the original survey there have been three full-scale field follow-ups at approximately 12-year intervals supplemented by intervening follow-ups by mail. The latest field study was in 1951–52 and the information secured then was brought up to date through an additional questionnaire mailed in 1955. By now it is possible to give a fairly good picture of the gifted at mid-life. The average age in 1955 was just under 45 years and the group ranged in age from 35 to 55 years. However, the great majority were in their forties with only about 10 per cent under 40 and 10 percent over 49.

By 1955 the number of deaths in the group totaled 104; this figure is about four-fifths of the normal expectancy for their age. The gifted as adults, just as in childhood and youth, appear for the most part to have good health. Self-ratings on general health obtained in 1951 and in 1955 indicated that the incidence of ill health was low. Less than 2 percent of men and about 3 percent of women reported poor or very poor health, while 91 percent of men and 88 percent of women rated their health as good or very good.

In the matter of mental health the record is also good. Less than 10 percent have had serious problems involving nervous or emotional difficulties and only 3 percent have had mental disorders serious enough to require hospitalization, and that only briefly in most cases. Comparison with the generality in the area of mental health is difficult to make; however, on the basis of the record to date it seems unlikely that the gifted will exceed—if they even equal—the estimated 5 percent of the general population that will at some time in their lives be hospitalized for mental disorder. The incidence of crime and delinquency is especially low. One man has served a prison term and three boys had youthful records of delinquency that resulted in their being sent to a juvenile reformatory. All four of these are married, employed, and fulfilling their duties as responsible citizens.

But if the gifted are not prone to die young or become invalids or suffer from mental disorder or go to jail, there still remains the question as to how their intelligence holds up—whether many regress to the average. So far there has been no such case. In order to measure their intelligence as adults, our very difficult Concept Mastery test was administered to the group in 1940 and again in 1951–52. At both testings the majority of subjects rated about as superior in comparison with adults as they had rated in childhood comparison with other children. In other words, 30 years after their selection as gifted children the group still fell in the top 1 or 2 percent of the generality in intellectual ability. There were, of course, a few exceptions but in the overall picture the intellectually superior child had become the intellectually superior adult.

For comparative purposes the Concept Mastery test was given to several other groups. These included graduate and undergraduate students as well as a group of scientists and a group of Army Air Force Officers. The average score for the gifted, regardless of amount of schooling, was far above the average of every other group tested. To cite one example, the 146 gifted subjects who did not go to college at all averaged exactly the same on the Concept Mastery test as a group of Ph.D. candidates at a leading university.

Moreover, a comparison of the Concept Mastery scores of 1940 with those made 12 years later showed a significant gain in scores at the second testing. The increase occurred on all educational and occupational levels, in all grades of ability, and at all ages represented. From our data it appears that not only do the mentally superior hold their own but there is strong evidence that the type of intelligence tested by the Concept Mastery continues to increase at least through age 50.

Now that we have established the fact that the group still outranks not only the generality but also highly selected university students in intelligence as measured by tests, let us consider what they have done with their abilities. First of all they equipped themselves with a good education. Close to 90 percent entered college and close to 70 percent graduated, each figure being about 8 times the corresponding figure for the general population of their generation. About 40 per cent graduated with honors of one kind or another. Approximately two-thirds of the college graduates continued for one or more years of graduate work. One or more graduate degrees were taken by 56 percent of the men and one-third of the women. Of these 80 men and 17 women took a Ph.D. But good as these educational records are, the fact remains that although all were potentially superior college material, more than 10 percent never entered college and 30 percent did not graduate. In a few cases college attendance was prevented by the necessity of helping to support the family; in many more cases the high schools either failed to recognize the gifted student's potentialities or failed to give the needed encouragement and intellectual stimulation.

In the discussion of occupation, it becomes necessary to treat the gifted men and women separately since their careers, just as is the case with men and women in general, follow such different patterns. First, let us look at the vocational status and achievements of the men in 1955 when the majority are at the mid-point of their careers. With such a large proportion preparing for the professional and management fields, it is not surprising to find that 46 percent are engaged in one or another of the professions and 40 percent in the higher business and semi-professional occupations. The representation in the professions and higher echelons of business is about 8 or 9 times their proportionate share. About 12 percent are in small businesses, clerical work, or skilled trades, and 2 percent are engaged in farming or ranching.

The achievement of the gifted men is best illustrated by a few examples. Among the notable scientists are three members of the National Academy of Science, and some 70 others are listed in American Men of Science. At least 4 men are in top level atomic energy research, one is an eminent physiologist, several are leaders in the fields of medicine, psychology, engineering, and the social sciences. Nor are all the achievements in the field of science. There are 25 or 30 men who are presidents or executive officers of corporations or other large-scale business or industrial enterprises. Two men are vice-presidents of top-ranking universities and one is the president of a small college. Another is a vice-president and director of a division of one of the largest philanthropic foundations. One is a Brigadier General in the U.S. Army, and 3 are high officials in the diplomatic service. There are at least 3 career writers of fiction who have achieved wide recognition. Four men hold judicial positions, including both Superior Court and Appellate Court judgeships. One highly successful farmer is a member of various state and federal boards and has served as consultant to the U. S. Department of Agriculture. Among others who have won wide recognition are a landscape architect, a playwright who has achieved great success on Broadway, and a motion picture director whose pictures have been given many awards and who himself has won an Oscar.

There are 31 men listed in *Who's Who in America,* and many more appear in various regional and professional *Who's Who* listings. The group has published 70 books including 30 to 35 volumes of fiction, and close to 2000 scientific, professional, and technical articles as well as several hundred short stories and miscellaneous articles. In addition they have taken out more than 200 patents.

These are examples of conspicuous achievement and could be multiplied several times. The great majority, though not all so outstanding as those I have mentioned, have been highly successful in terms of professional and business accomplishment as measured by responsibility and importance of position, prestige, and income. There is, however, considerable range of achievement within the group and in an attempt to get at some of the nonintellectual factors affecting life success a comparison was made of the 150 most successful and the 150 least successful men. A number of interesting differences in the two sub-groups were brought out; however, the four traits on which they differed most widely were: persistence in accomplishment of ends, integration toward goals, self-confidence, and freedom from inferiority feelings. In the total picture the greatest contrast in the two groups of men was in drive to achieve and in all-round mental and social adjustment. It should be remembered, however, that "success" is a relative term and the records of our "under-achievers" (as defined by gifted standards) when compared with the generality, show few failures in the absolute sense. Actually the less successful 20 percent among the gifted men compare favorably with the average college graduate population.

The gifted women for the most part have not gone in for professional or business careers. Of the married women 60 percent are housewives with no employment outside the home. About two-thirds of those employed are in the professions and semi-professions and the remainder in office and business occupations. School teaching, including elementary and secondary administrative and supervisory positions, is the most frequent occupation, accounting for almost one-fourth of the employed women. In second place are the secretaries, bookkeepers and similar office workers with about one-fifth of the total employed. The women on college faculties and in the higher professions (physicians, lawyers, economists, psychologists, etc.) account for 11 percent and the remainder are distributed over a number of occupations, each with less than 10 percent representation. A number of the "career" women have achieved considerable success and recognition. Among the more distinguished are 8 scientists who are listed in *American Men of Science,* a well-known poet, a biochemist who was one of the team of scientists who made possible the Salk vaccine, a highly successful magazine writer, and a prominent college administrator.

Marriage and marital adjustments are important factors in the total picture of life success and happiness and a comparison of the gifted subjects with the generality of men and women is of interest. By 1955 the proportion of the gifted who had married was 93 percent of the men and 89 percent of the women. This incidence is about the same as for the total U. S. population of corresponding age. In other words, being highly intelligent has not been an impediment to marriage in the case of either sex. Actually the marriage rate for women of the gifted group who graduated from college is considerably higher than for women college graduates in general of whom less than 70 percent marry, according to a recent survey.

The incidence of divorce in the gifted group appears to be somewhat better than that estimated for the total population. To date a fifth of those who married have been divorced. Recent estimates of marital failures in the generality of marriages place the figure at one-fourth to one-third of the marriages formed.

When a gifted subject marries, our interest has extended to include the spouses and the children. The gifted have shown considerable selectivity in their choice of spouses. More than half the husbands and almost half of the wives are college graduates and another 20 to 25 percent of the spouses have had some college education. The Concept Mastery test scores indicate the superior mental ability of the spouses. Their average score, though lower than that for the gifted, is approximately the same as the average for college graduates at top ranking universities. Many of the spouses could easily have qualified for the gifted group itself if they had been tested in childhood.

And now we turn for a moment to the next generation. The group by 1955 had produced more than 2500 children. The average number of offspring of those who married is slightly under 2, and the typical family with children has 2.4 children. There are 40 families with 5 or more children including one with 7 and another with 8. Furthermore, the group now has more than 100 grandchildren to their credit.

As part of the follow-up procedures, Stanford-Binet tests have been given to all the children of suitable age in the areas reached by the field workers. Slightly more than 1500 children have been tested. The average IQ for the boys and girls was exactly the same, namely, 133. However, there was a wide range, the lowest IQ among those tested being 70 and the highest, 200. One-third of the offspring tested at IQ 140 or above.

But more has been learned about the gifted than that they are well educated, hold positions that are important and responsible as well as remunerative, that they have married well and have produced superior children. They also are responsible citizens and active participants in community life. Nearly half of the men and two-thirds of the women are engaged in some form of community service or welfare activities. Such youth programs as PTA, Scouts, YMCA, etc., are the most frequent interest with both men and women. A number have served on boards of education, city councils, planning commissions and various appointive civic committees. Other activities have included committee work with the Red Cross, Community Chest, hospital boards, and many similar projects. Additional evidence of awareness of community responsibility is shown in the large number of memberships in various cultural and civic organizations. Recognition of such activities has come in the form of many awards and citations. Some of these are: Man (or Woman) of the Year, Distinguished Service Award, Community Service Plaque, Outstanding Citizen Award.

The gifted has also shown his interest and responsibility to our democratic society in his voting record: 94 percent of the men and 98 percent of the women report that they always or nearly always vote at national elections. The record is almost as good for state and local elections (91% and 95%). The figures at every level are far superior to the voting record of the population at large.

One of the most interesting and valuable sources of information has been an autobiographical questionnaire filled out in the 1951–52 follow-up when the group averaged about 41 years of age. From that point in their lives they reviewed their childhood and youth and the factors that had influenced their early years, and also evaluated their adult attitudes, goals, and values. As might be expected in this predominantly college trained group, four-fifths of the men and nearly three-fourths of the women felt that they had had sufficient schooling. Half of the men and more than half of the women reported deep satisfaction in their jobs. Only 6 percent of the men and 3 percent of the women expressed serious vocational discontent. As a corollary to the general vocational satisfaction was the opinion of an overwhelming majority that their lives offered satisfactory outlets for their mental abilities.

When asked to indicate from a list of 10 which factors had contributed most to their life accomplishment to date, both men and women put "adequate education" in first place and "mental stability" second. Other important contributing factors for half or more of the men were superior mental ability, good health, good personality, and persistence in working toward a goal. The other important factors in life accomplishment for a majority of the women were good social adjustment, good personality, and superior mental ability—in that order.

Additional light is shed on the character of the gifted in their sources of satisfaction. Their work itself is in first place for men, being mentioned by more than three-fourths of those responding. It is followed closely by marriage and by children as sources of satisfaction. Men put recognition for their accomplishments in fourth place and their avocational interests and hobbies in fifth. The women, after their children and their marriage, most often find their satisfactions in social contacts, avocational interests, and in community service activities. Income is in sixth place with men (mentioned by 38%) and in ninth place for women with only 15 percent mentioning it.

The final question in the biographical data blank asked the subjects to give their opinion on what constitutes success in life. There was a wide range of responses to this query and we have classified the definitions into 15 categories. For the gifted men, success in life most often means a happy home, successful marriage, and bringing up a family satisfactorily. The next most frequent definition of success is an adequate income for comfortable living, and the third ranking category defines success in life as making a contribution to society, and doing something positive to improve the world.

The women, perhaps more altruistic than the men, give as their most frequent definition of success in life making a contribution to society, helping others, and doing something positive to improve the world. Almost as frequent, however, was the definition of success as a happy home, successful marriage, and bringing up a family satisfactorily. The third most frequent definition of success for women was in terms of realization of goals, living up to one's abilities, and self-expression.

We would agree with the subjects that vocational achievement is not the only—perhaps not even the most important—aspect of life success. To many, the most important achievement in life is happiness, contentment, emotional maturity, integrity. Even failure to rise above the lowest rungs of the occupational ladder does not necessarily mean that success in the truest sense has been trivial. There may have been heroic sacrifices, uncommon judgment in handling the little things of daily life, count-less acts of kindness, loyal friendships won, and conscientious discharge of social and civic responsibilities. If we sometimes get discouraged at the rate society progresses, we might take com-fort in the thought that some of the small jobs, as well as the larger ones, are being done by gifted people.

⟶ **Don C. Charles**

Adult Adjustment of Some
Deficient American Children

From *American Journal of Mental Deficiency*, September, 1957, 62:300–304. Reprinted by permission.

As Alan Clarke has pointed out, our perception of the potential adjustment and performance of mentally handi-capped persons has undergone a marked change, especially in the last decade. Evidence is accumulating which gives us ground for a much more optimistic view of the future of deficient per-sons than was once the case. Some of this evidence will be pre-sented here, together with comments on some agencies involved in the care and training of mentally deficient persons in the United States.

There are regional and national differences in the terminology of mental deficiency. Therefore, Leo Kanner's descriptive termi-nology would appear to be useful. Kanner [9] classifies types of mental deficiency into these groups.

1. *Absolute:* persons who are markedly deficient in every sphere of mentation and who continue life-long to need custodial care. (In the United States this group would be called the idiot and imbecile population.)

2. *Relative:* persons whose limitations are related to the standards of society around them. They can become successful farm hands, factory workers, miners, waitresses, char-women. These are not

truly feeble-minded or mentally deficient; their inability is with demands of our society—reading, mathematics, etc. Their deficiency is an ethnologically determined phenomenon of "intellectual inadequacy." (We refer to this level as "moron" in the United States; in England it is the "feeble-minded" level.)

3. *Apparent or pseudo:* persons whose defects are visual, hearing, word deafness, specific reading, writing or numerical disability, negativism, emotional blocking, petit mal, withdrawal, etc.

Considerable evidence has been amassed relative to all three categories. Much of this evidence is in the form of surveys and clinical studies of individuals or of small groups. In such investigations controls may be carefully exercised and rather complete data obtained. Some fine researches of this type have been reported recently by Clark, Gordon, O'Connor, Tizard and others. The results of these and other studies demonstrate a most promising capacity for good adjustment in persons of low abilities.

Another source of evidence is the longitudinal study of individuals and groups. Such investigations are primarily descriptive and may lack the wealth of data and the rigorous controls of experimental studies. The longitudinal method, however, provides knowledge of the behavior patterns of individuals over a number of years. From the study of lives in progress we may learn to predict and plan for deficient persons with greater confidence than without such knowledge.

One such long–term investigation has been carried on in the United States by Warren Baller, of the University of Nebraska, and by myself.

The subjects were 206 persons among whom all three of Kanner's categories of deficiency were found. Baller first reported their characteristics in 1936. [1] They were chosen for the research on the basis of three criteria: 1916 Stanford–Binet IQ's below seventy, demonstrated inability satisfactorily to perform the usual elementary school work, and training in the opportunity rooms of the Lincoln, Nebraska schools. (The "opportunity rooms" are special classrooms where individualized attention can be given children who do not fit into the regular school program.) At the time of his report, Baller found them to be more successful than had been anticipated.

I studied this group in the late 1940's and early 1950's. At this time their ages ranged from thirty-six to fifty, with a mean age of forty-two. It seems reasonable to suppose that by this age, their adult patterns of behavior would be fairly clear and well-established.

It was possible to locate 151, or three-fourths of the original group. These subjects did not appear to differ from the original total population in any significant way. The term "located" includes twenty-four subjects known to be deceased, leaving 127 living subjects. The present status of these surviving subjects offers some insight into the possible future of apparently deficient children. [2]

1. *Health and vitality.* It is generally accepted that persons of low intelligence do not live as long as their more intelligent fellows. The death rate for this group was about fifteen per cent, somewhat higher than average. Accidents were a remarkably frequent cause of death. The general health of the non-institutionalized subjects appeared to be good.

2. *Institutionalization.* Only about five per cent of the subjects were institutionalized in 1950. These were in institutions for the mentally deficient, hospitals for the insane and in reformatories. Another ten per cent had been institutionalized earlier but had been released.

3. *Family status.* About eighty per cent were married; this figure is somewhat below average for this age group. Divorce data in the United States are somewhat unreliable, but records of this group did not appear to differ much from the available national figures.

4. *Children.* The number and characteristics of children produced by these persons is a matter of considerable concern to society. The general impression seems to be that persons of low intelligence produce hordes of feeble-minded offspring. Such was not the case with this group. They averaged slightly more than two children per family. This was slightly less than the national average for this age-group. Intelligence test scores were secured for a sample of the children. The evidence obtained was encouraging, for the mean of these scores was in the low-average range of abilities. Only two were institutionalized, and only two others required special school training.

5. *Homes.* A considerable range in type and characteristics of homes was observed, but most lived in small one-family houses. In general, they seemed to be adequate, and typical of their socio-economic level.

6. *Employment.* To what extent are persons of low intelligence employable? The answers to this question are increasingly optimistic. Recent work in England shows that, with training and assistance, far more of them are employable than once seemed possible. Of the population of this study, more than eighty per cent were employable and were usually employed. Almost half had been steadily employed at the same jobs for periods of three to twenty years. Most of the rest followed one or two general lines of work and worked at whichever was in demand.

A surprisingly wide range of occupations was found. The majority of males of course were in various labor categories while most of the females were housewives or were in service occupations. However, some workers were found in each of managerial, clerical and sales, service and agriculture categories, as well as the various levels of skilled work. There were carpenters, plasterers, cement finishers, lens-grinders, machine-operators, welders, etc. Most of the latter skilled and semi-skilled workers had been earning quite good wages since the early 1940's.

7. *Law conformity.* Police and court records were studied for the subjects who were residents of Lincoln and vicinity. A substantial proportion of the males had been involved in some infraction of the law. Excluding traffic violations, about half of the male resident subjects had been arrested and prosecuted for some law violation. The females had few clashes with the law.

Despite the high percentage of violations, a look at the *kinds* of law infractions does not suggest that this is a dangerous criminal population. Drunkenness was the commonest complaint, complicated by unnecessary noise, assault, trespass, etc. The rest of the offenses included wife and child abandonment, stealing, disturbing the peace, failure to license dogs, and the like. Many of these offenses are perhaps as suggestive of low socio-economic class behavior as they are of low intelligence.

The fact remains, however, that the men were often, in some way, in conflict with society.

8. *Self-support.* A comment not infrequently heard about per-

sons of low intelligence is that they spend their entire lives dependent on someone, family or public, for their support. Records of public relief and assistance were studied for all but seven subjects who were living with parents and nine subjects who were institutionalized. The picture was one of decreasing public relief with advancing years. In the depression years of the 1930's less than half got along without any relief and about a fourth needed considerable help to survive. In the post-war years, only about eight per cent needed considerable assistance and two-thirds required no help at all. It is apparent that as economic conditions improved, few of the subjects required relief at all, and those who did received progressively less.

We do not have time to discuss the stability of intelligence here, but a few comments about the present abilities of the group may be useful.

Intelligence tests and personal observations of behavior suggested that about twenty per cent had given evidence of life-long absolute deficiency, another ten per cent still tested deficient but had adjusted to society, about sixty-five per cent gave evidence of being dull-normal or average, and about five per cent had afflictions suggesting pseudo-deficiency. [3]

From the available data it is possible to draw some general conclusions concerning this group of persons who were classified as mentally deficient in their early years [4]:

1. Certain encouraging circumstances are apparent. While there was a wide range of individual variation, the subjects did not appear to be unlike the general population in many ways; their types of dwellings and per cent of ownership were average. Their divorce rates were close to the national average. The great majority of their children proceeded through school with little or no retardation and the mean of the children's intelligence test scores was in the average range. Very few of the children required opportunity room training as their parents did.

The institutionalized subjects of course affect some of these data: they were not included in the housing figures, they had not married or produced children. This latter circumstance undoubtedly contributed to the over-all quality of the group of children.

2. They showed considerable improvement, as a group, from their 1935 status. The dullest subjects were institutionalized early and remained so, but many others were released from institutions and adjusted well enough to remain outside. They were able to take advantage of improving economic conditions; a greater percentage was employed regularly than was the case in 1935, and the percentage requiring relief decreased steadily, as did the amount of assistance required by those unable to subsist on their own earnings.

3. They continued to differ from the general population in certain ways. A lower percentage was married than was typical of their age group, even excluding the life-long institutionalized group. The married subjects had slightly fewer children than average. Their death rate was somewhat greater than average, and the rate of violent death much greater than average. A very large percentage of the males failed to conform to the laws of their community. Also, some members of the group were unable at any time to be self-supporting, contributing members of society and required care from their families or institutions, or assistance from public relief agencies.

In general, this group of what one might describe as "typical" mentally deficient children has fared better, as a group, than early prognoses indicated that they might.

To me, the most striking and the most impressive result of this study is the evidence of such great differences among the members of the group. The great variation in the present abilities and achievements of the subjects should dispel any notion that persons who give evidence of low ability in childhood develop and perform according to a rigid stereotype. We may gain encouragement in the knowledge that many children whose test scores and academic performance suggest mental deficiency develop into self-sufficient and desirable citizens as adults.

Since we know that such development is possible, our major concern now must be how best to aid these persons.

In the United States, a number of agencies participate in the care and training of deficient persons.

Frequently the first agency to identify and help a dull child is the public school. Since American schools are supported by state and local taxes, and are governed by community school boards (usually with some state supervision) there is no uniform technique or approach used. Probably the most common is the "opportunity room" or "opportunity school" in the larger city. Children who find the usual classroom work difficult, for physical, mental or emotional reasons, find individual help and guidance here. The subjects described earlier had at least some training in such classes. The teachers in these classes vary greatly in training and experience, but the standards appear to be rising in most communities.

A second source of help is Federal and State vocational training agencies. These agencies help train handicapped persons of all types, and place them in jobs. This aid is most likely to be extended to persons in late adolescence and early adulthood. Most of the hospitals and training institutions for the mentally deficient are operated by the various states. In the past, many of these have been primarily housekeeping institutions for institutionalized defectives. Today, however, many of them are expanding their training facilities and preparing their charges for independent life in society. Most of these institutions are understaffed and are lacking in adequately trained personnel.

Some of our larger cities operate institutions much like the state-supported ones. These differ essentially only in their source of tax support. In addition to institutions, many cities are now providing social and recreational facilities for persons of limited intelligence, and aiding them with job placement services, family counseling, legal advice and in general, functioning in a paternal fashion.

Finally, there are many private and religious organizations which provide a variety of services ranging from hospitals to individual counseling services.

We have in the United States then a variety of agencies designed to aid persons of limited intelligence. We have a constantly-growing supply of trained workers. Our greatest need, and I believe it is a great need everywhere, is probably for increased public support.

Those of us who work with deficient persons in clinics or hospitals, who study them or teach others about them have an opportunity to gain this support. The lay public still stereotypes mentally deficient persons as hopeless creatures to be incarcerated, cared for and forgotten. The public should be made aware of what we know—that many persons of low intelligence can, with help, become desirable and productive members of society.

REFERENCES

1. BALLER, W. R., "A Study of the Present Social Status of a Group of Adults Who, When They Were in Elementary Schools, Were Classified as Mentally Deficient," *Genetic Psychology Monographs*, 1936, Vol. 18, No. 3.

2. CHARLES, D. C., "Ability and Accomplishment of Persons Earlier Judged Mentally Deficient," *Genetic Psychology Monographs*, 1953, 47:27–45.

3. ———, "Ability and Accomplishment of Persons Earlier Judged Mentally Deficient," *Genetic Psychology Monographs*, 1953, 47:47–53.

4. ———, "Ability and Accomplishment of Persons Earlier Judged Mentally Deficient," *Genetic Psychology Monographs*, 1953, 47:66–67.

5. CHRISTAL, R. E., "Factor Analytic Study of Visual Memory," *Psychological Monographs*, 1958, Vol. 72, No. 13 (Whole No. 466).

6. GUILFORD, J. P., "The Structure of Intellect," *Psychological Bulletin*, 1956, 53:267–293.

7. ———, *Personality*, New York: McGraw-Hill Book Company, Inc., 1959.

8. HUSEN, T., "The Influence of Schooling upon IQ," *Theoria*, 1951, 12:61–88.

9. KANNER, L., "Feeble-mindedness, Absolute, Relative, and Apparent," *Nervous Child*, 1948, 7:365–397.

10. McNEMAR, Q., "A Critical Examination of the University of Iowa Studies of Environmental Influences upon the IQ," *Psychological Bulletin*, 1940, 37:63–92.

11. WELLMAN, BETH L., & McCANDLESS, B. V., "Factors Associated with Binet IQ Changes of Preschool Children," *Psychological Monographs*, 1946, Vol. 60, No. 2 (Whole No. 278).

CHAPTER

ELEVEN

↑

Communication and Behavior

THE ABILITY TO GENERALIZE EXPERIENCES and represent them with symbols which can be manipulated mentally is a characteristic in which man differs markedly from lower animals. Language is more than just audible sounds: it is a system used by a society for classifying, preserving, and transmitting its knowledge, skills, beliefs, and values to all its members. Considered somewhat differently, language consists of a set of symbols accepted by all the members of a society with which to represent the total of the experiences and activities of that society.

In such terms has John E. Anderson in the opening selection of this chapter described certain of the principal functions of language. He emphasizes the fact that language makes it possible for each new human being to pick up quickly where his elders leave off the accumulating fund of knowledge. This Anderson calls *time bending*.

Anderson's discussion of language as a system of symbols, his explanation of the manner in which symbols facilitate experience and the control of behavior, and his emphasis upon the relationship of language to the quality of an individual's life provide an excellent orientation to this important area of the psychology of human development. From 1925 to 1954 Anderson was Director of the Institute of Child Development and Welfare at the University of Minnesota, and since then he has continued as Professor in the Institute.

Many researchers have traced the appearance and development in the child of vowels, consonants, words, and sentences. Few have so clearly pointed out relationships between language development and the general developmental processes as Dorothea McCarthy. Especially noteworthy in her article in this chapter is the observation that research in the field of language development has been predominantly descriptive and normative, and that the urgent need now is for studies aimed at learning the dynamic factors that influence language development. "We need to know," she says, "why language develops in a particular way and what factors seem to accelerate or retard its development." McCarthy is Professor of Psychology at Fordham University and Research Consultant at Rutgers University.

The majority of children experience a normal development of language, beginning with the use of isolated vowel sounds, the connecting of these sounds into "babbling," and the progression toward the use of conventional words and the awareness that sounds have meanings. Some children, however, as is shown by Nancy E. Wood, are unable to master the use of symbols for communication because of physiological, mental, emotional, or nervous impairments.

A considerable part of Wood's article consists of a very helpful description of aphasia. The main impact of the discussion, however, is the emphasis upon the need for more adequate services in the schools and related clinics for children with various language disorders. Wood is Consultant on Speech and Hearing Disorders in the Department of Health, Education, and Welfare, Washington, D.C.

—▶ **John E. Anderson**

The Development of Language and Symbolic Skill

From *The Psychology of Development and Personal Adjustment,* by John E. Anderson. Copyright, 1949, by Holt, Rinehart and Winston, Inc. Reprinted and abridged by permission.

In the modern world a man has at his disposal many means for communicating his wishes and needs to others. He can speak directly or use the telephone; he may make gestures or use the Morse code; he may write or send a telegram. If, as a student, he seeks additional spending money from home, he will communicate with his parents. If, as a politician, he seeks re-election, he will make speeches or send out circulars and leaflets. Many types of symbols (such as pictures, music, and diagrams) are used to influence other persons. But the primary and basic mode of communication in human society is speech. It is difficult to imagine a human society without means of intercommunication; even in the most primitive societies there are sign languages and simple speech.

Language is not only a device for communicating with one's fellows, it also is a device by means of which man preserves knowledge and skill and hands it on in some symbolic form through his colleagues and descendants. This characteristic of human action has been called *time-binding*. In a very real sense, the young human being starts where his elders leave off, because he finds the knowledge and skill worked out by previous human beings preserved in symbols and available for his own use.

Language has still an additional function besides the transmission of knowledge. Through it the human being can represent his experiences in shorthand or in symbols that can easily be manipulated. By moving words and symbols around and by working out their interrelations, man can think and solve problems without having the actual materials or objects before him. Although many persons regard thinking as a mysterious process, careful investigation suggests that most thinking takes on a verbal form both during waking and sleeping hours. Whether or not the person is talking aloud, there seems to be much implicit speech activity. What is called daydreaming, imagination, and thinking involves the use of symbols quite as much as does the actual expression that makes symbols available to others. In a very real sense, language is the most useful tool that human beings have available for social living. Communication between persons is essential to society: each interacts on the other. Language makes society possible; society in turn gives the chief impetus and form to the development of language.

LANGUAGE AS A SYSTEM OF SYMBOLS

In using language, a sign or symbol is substituted for an action or experience. The *language symbol* is usually a sound (produced by a throat movement) which stands either for experiences or for the concepts developed about experience or movements. This definition covers the description of a sunset you have just witnessed, or the series of equations necessary to derive a formula. In using this capacity to represent complex experiences or action by moving the throat, the person increases tremendously his control over the environment. If someone asked a person without language the way to a downtown hotel, he would find it necessary to walk to the hotel and make the complete movements in order to answer him. But if he has language, by flicking his throat muscles he can give the questioner a series of directions for arriving there. By the substitution of a brief movement for a great mass of movements, much time and energy has been saved. Notice too that even the stranger's question is itself in the form of symbols—to imagine living in a world without symbols is almost beyond us. The outstanding characteristic of a symbolic system is the substitution of responses of one modality for experiences or actions in another. In learning motor skills, movements are selected, simplified, and coordinated within their own modality; in language or speech, throat movements take the place of bodily movements. The ape and the dog by learning can simplify movements. But the human being also has, in the easily manipulable process of language, an additional means of securing amazing control over the world.

A clear distinction between the *symbol* and the *meaning* is necessary. By a *symbol* we mean any one of the series of movements of the throat which can stand for or take the place of an experience or activity. The *meaning* is that for which the symbol stands; it consists of the experience or activities for which the symbol is substituted. There is no inherent or necessary connection between a symbol and what it represents. Thus, while the word corresponding to the letters DOG causes an American or Englishman to think of a four-legged creature, the Frenchman says CHIEN and the German says HUND for the same creature and does not understand DOG at all. All these symbols refer to a four-legged animal which emits an explosive noise, is larger than a mouse but smaller than a cow, and eats meat and gnaws bones but refuses sawdust and rocks. The English word is neither more nor less correct than the French or German word. Through social convention, symbols become attached to meanings.

There are many symbol systems in the world. One can represent the same material by speech, by printing on a page, by writing letters on a blackboard, by dots and dashes, by wig-wagging with flags and in many other ways. The same basic experience can be represented by many different symbols, each of which, however, refers back to a common "tag" or symbol. Writing, telegraphing, and wig-wagging go back to speech for their primary symbols. Why does speech become so important? Several reasons have been advanced by investigators. The primary one is that the extraordinary flexibility and adaptability of the human vocal mechanism permits sounds of an almost infinite variety. But speech has other advantages. It is a relatively useless activity that can go on parallel to or alongside the actions of the hands and arms or legs, without interference. If the arms and fingers are used for symbols, whatever activity is going forward must be interrupted. Further, speech can be carried on independently of light or, within limits, of space, and thus can be heard around corners and in the dark.

Although the system of symbols used by the person depends on the particular society in which he grows up (the English child learns English, the French child learns French), meanings depend upon the particular experiences of the individual. If each reader of this book described what the symbol DOG means to him, almost as many different statements would appear as there are readers. But all would have some common elements, even if one person thought of a cocker spaniel, another of a bulldog, or another of a setter. If words are studied and defined, it soon appears that each has a common quality of meaning which can be set down and that each also has a number of meanings which vary. This is the distinction between what a word *denotes* and what it *connotes*. A word denotes what it specifically covers; a word connotes all that it implies.

For the sake of simple and clear presentataion, the previous discussion has emphasized the attachment of meaning to the specified word or symbol. Actually, it is more accurate to view a language as a system of symbols, many of which are interchangeable, and to realize that much of the meaning is carried by the context in which the word is used. There is a parlor game called "Shedding light," in which one contestant makes statements about a word without using it, while the others try to guess what the word is. This game is perhaps more like what language is. For almost every word, we look to the context to clarify the meanings. For example, in the sentence "She ate toast while the speaker proposed a toast," the meaning of the word "toast" depends on the context. Even dictionary makers use context when they append to definitions of words examples of how they are used.

SYMBOLS FACILITATE EXPERIENCE AND CONTROL

Just as experiences determine the meanings represented by symbols, so in turn do symbols facilitate experience. Thus, a botanist will point out the characteristics of many plants in walking through the woods, while the ordinary person merely distinguishes bushes and grass from trees. When his attention is called to them, he sees differences in leaves, bark, and structure, but without the symbols attached to these differences, they do not register very well in memory or thought. Trained and untrained observers coming back from the same series of events give very different accounts. For example, the botanist after his walk through the woods can talk at great length about what he has seen both because he has seen, heard, and felt, and more because he has the symbols with which to tag his experiences for retention.

Each person brings to a particular experience a series of symbols out of his past. A very large portion of the instruction in any human activity, whether it be trade, profession or hobby, centers on the vocabulary of the field. For example, a carpenter learns what a "shim" is, an electrician what a "loom" is, and a statistician what a "standard deviation" is. In each instance, the word or symbol facilitates thought and action, and enables the worker to remember and keep distinct many different processes.

Speech the Primary Means of Social Communication

Too much emphasis cannot be given to the importance of symbols as the primary means of communication with other persons. From the very beginning of life, the child hears words used to control him, quiet him, encourage him, and stimulate him. His parents and older children talk to him, sing to him, and play simple verbal games with him. When he begins to talk, he receives much encouragement and praise and quickly learns that speech is the most convenient and easy method for attracting the attention of other persons and of getting them to do what he wishes. Moreover, whatever he says takes place in a sequence or current of speech rather than as an isolated act. When he asks questions, answers are made; when he relates his experiences, others relate theirs. If he speaks incorrectly, he may be corrected.

This circular process in which first the child speaks, then others speak, the child speaks, others speak, or the one in which first others speak, then the child speaks, others speak goes on continuously, whenever the child is with older persons or other children. The extensiveness and the amount of practice received in speech is revealed in several studies. In one it was found that the four-year-old speaks some 10,000 words a day and the five-year-old some 12,000 words a day. The longest period of quietness (without audible speech) was 19 minutes; the average length of periods of linguistic inactivity, which were relatively few, was 4 minutes. Thus, the child not only receives an enormous amount of practice (if 10,000 a day is multiplied by 365 the number of words for one year is in the millions), but if we think of what is going on in other children and adults who are the child's companions, the child is seen to be bathed in linguistic stimulation. This is quite different from the ordinary point of view or the impression gained from any texts that language consists of short responses in single situations. Instead, language is an almost continuous process, which is corrected, modified, and changed by what the child hears and by his observation of the effects of what he says on others.

THE DEVELOPMENT OF TALKING

The human being makes sounds as naturally as he moves his arms and legs. From birth onward, the infant tries out his vocal apparatus and experiments with many sounds. In contrast to the chimpanzee, which is limited to a few grunts and makes almost no sounds spontaneously in play, the human being not only can produce a wide range of sound, with almost infinite shadings of individual sounds, but also can tie them together in patterns and sequences. Man has invented thousands of languages and an endless variety of dialects within languages.

In developing speech, the infant begins with single vowel sounds, often produced as cries or wails in order to bring his mother to him. Soon he uses his lips while emitting the wail and thus forms an initial consonant, which results in a sound such as "mah," which reiterated becomes "mama," a sound closely related to crying. In time, because his mother responds to his cries, "mama" becomes attached to the mother as a symbol or name and is used to call her. In some primitive groups "mama" is attached to the father and "dada," another early sound, is attached to the mother. Thus, even though "mama" stands for mother in our society, there is no inherent connection between it and its meaning. The next step it taken when the infant adds final consonants to vowels, as when he says "at." For many months he repeats and plays vocally with simple syllables.

At about six or seven months, he strings syllables together into patterns that resemble speech. Apparently this "babbling" is very pleasant, for the infant keeps at it much of the time. It is not true language, however, since these vocal reflexes and habits become language habits only when they are used as symbols. Although it is difficult to determine the exact age at which the infant moves from making sounds spontaneously for pleasure to using them as "words" or symbols, it is generally found that the first "word" comes somewhere between nine and fifteen months.

After the child first uses a sound pattern as a symbol, he acquires new symbols very slowly and adds only five or six words in the next six months. Apparently these words are learned by conditioning. The mother hands the child a ball and says "ball"; the child says "bah" and the mother hands him the ball, repeating the word "ball" and thus reinforcing the response. Gradually the child corrects his pronunciation to include the "l" sound. At about eighteen months one of the most interesting events in the whole developmental process occurs. It is both difficult to explain and to understand, even though most of us take it for granted. Suddenly the infant becomes aware that sounds have meanings and he begins to hunt out objects and asks for their names.

A dramatic description of this process is given in Helen Keller's autobiography. Her teachers tried a system of instruction in which, through pressures and touches on her hands and arms, they attempted to convey meanings to her. As water ran from a pump onto one of her hands, they traced signs on the palm of her other hand, with no response. Just as they were about to give up, she suddenly made the connection between running water and the sign. Thereafter she actively sought the signs for many objects and made rapid progress.

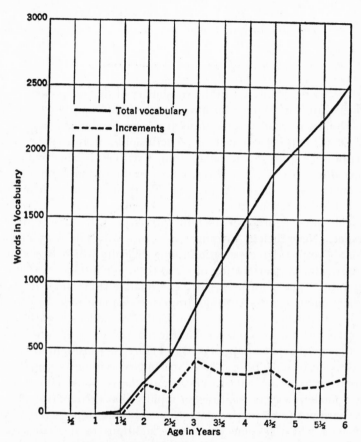

Fig. 1. *Vocabulary and Age in Young Children*
The upper curve shows the total vocabulary of the child. Note the sharp rise after the age of 1–1/2 years. The bottom curve shows the increment or amount added to the vocabulary in each six-month period. Note the fairly uniform rate of acquisition after the age of 3–1/2 years. (Drawn by permission from Smith, M. E., "An Investigation of the Development of the Sentence and the Extent of Vocabulary in Young Children." *University of Iowa Studies in Child Welfare*, Vol. 3. No. 5, 1926. Table 8.)

Within a few weeks after the child gains "insight" into the relation between objects and names, the rate of acquiring new words jumps enormously. He runs about the house pointing to objects and saying "What's that?" At three years of age, he is acquiring new words at the rate of 300 words every six months, and although his rate of learning is uneven, by the age of six years has a total vocabulary of some 2,500 words. Figure 1, based upon the study by Smith, shows the rapid rates at which vocabulary develops in the preschool period.

There is wide interest in the vocabulary of the high-school and college student. Many who have heard of Shakespeare's reputed vocabulary of 20,000 words think it a large vocabulary, but compared with the vocabulary of modern adults it is a small one. Because the study of vocabulary from 6 years on is beset by many difficulties, there is some disagreement in the various studies and estimates made. Figure 2 presents the results from one of the recent investigations which covered vocabulary from 6 to 19 years.

The large figures revealed in this chart will surprise most readers. Nevertheless, investigators consistently find vocabulary size above popular expectations. One difficulty which besets the investigator is the counting of derivatives. For instance, we have aircraft, airplane, airspeed, airline, airmail, airfoil, and a host of other similar words. All come from one common root, to which in most instances a familiar word has been added. Is each one word or two words? Do you count the root only once or every time it appears? In the data presented in Figure 2 a consistent attempt was made to separate the basic vocabulary (without derivatives) from the total vocabulary. The size of the vocabulary available in a modern society increases so rapidly that dictionary makers are hard put to keep up to date. New words are coined every day, some of which become permanent additions to the language. Shakespeare's vocabulary was large for his day; if he were alive now, with all the new words that have become a part of our language, his vocabulary would be many times as large.

LANGUAGE AND LIFE

So far, concern has been with the content and articulation of language and the factors affecting its development. What are the functions which language fulfills in the life of the inividual, and how well are they carried out at different ages? Language is a series of symbols used to represent life experiences and to modify

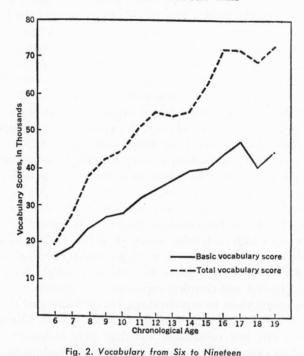

Fig. 2. *Vocabulary from Six to Nineteen*
The upper curve represents the total vocabulary and the lower
the basic vocabulary. Notice that increases are very consistent
from year to year and that both measures of vocabulary increase during the entire period of growth. The 6-year-olds in this
chart are superior to those in Fig. 1. because they had been in
school for almost a year and because the vocabulary was obtained by a different method. (Adapted by permission from Smith,
K., "Measurement of the Size of the General English Vocabulary
in the Elementary Grades and High School." *Genetic Psychology
Monographs,* 24:311–45, 1941. Figures 3 and 4.)

or change the behavior of other persons. What is the relation between what is related in symbols and what happens in the world
of reality?

Suppose a mother asks a five-year-old just home from kindergarten to tell what happened in school that morning. No matter
how much he is pressed, the child will be unable to describe his
experiences in connected and logical action. By piecing together
the bits of information which the child gives at odd times during

the afternoon, the mother may be able to reconstruct the kindergarten events, much as a jig-saw puzzle is put together. A child lacks the capacity to organize and relate his experiences in logical or connected fashion and if forced by an overinsistent mother will tell a false story to keep her quiet. Not until he is nine or ten years old can a child give a reasonably accurate account of what happened within a definite period of time. Since a child is not considered a good witness in court, his evidence is admitted only under sharp limitations. Even many adults cannot give logical accounts of their experiences, as you will learn from anyone who has listened to a legal trial, where an attempt is made to get basic facts from a number of witnesses.

An outstanding series of investigations of the functions that language fulfills has been made by Piaget, who recorded children's conversations with each other and with adults. He also recorded their answers to questions such as "What makes the wind blow?" and "What makes an airplane fly?" He gave simple demonstrations of physical and chemical experiments to children of various ages and asked them to explain them. He then analyzed the comments and answers of these children in terms of their function as language. His first conclusion was that early language is self-centered or egocentric and that as children grow older language becomes more *socialized*, or in other words, more adapted to circumstances of time and place.

Second, Piaget found that the associations made by young children tend to be largely *accidental* or *syncretic*, as he calls it. Anything can be connected with anything else in the child's mind, whereas the associations of the older child and adult tend to become more and more logical with growth. Thus, a child says that an airplane flies because it is blue, associating the color (which is incidental) with support of the plane, whereas an older child will mention that the plane is supported by the air moved by the propeller or under the wing surface. Third, Piaget found that the explanations given by children tend to be *mystical* and *animistic*, whereas the explanations of older children and adults tend to be more causal and scientific. For example, children will explain the movements of clouds by saying that they are alive or that people in the sky make them move.

From this analysis, it is clear that a characteristic of development is the steady increase in the capacity to represent experience in abstract or symbolic terms and to give scientific or logical explanations of experience. Language, then, is a curious device which can either be closely connected with what it represents or be far dissociated from it. It can be used either to hide meaning or to show meaning. The use of language to show *what is* and *what is not* depends both on an awareness of the representative capacity of language and symbolic systems, and on discrimination and honesty in their use. The modern man not only needs to know how words can be slanted to give any impression speakers or writers desire but also needs a conscience to keep him from using his knowledge of language processes to exploit others.

How well and how accurately language is used is of great importance in an age in which new devices for spreading information by word-of-mouth affect the behavior of countless persons. In a world of propaganda, the only refuge of the individual lies in building up a critical faculty that enables him to discriminate between those occasions in which language is used to falsify and those in which it is used to represent experience accurately.

In actual life, a person would not get far if he told the truth literally and absolutely on every occasion. He would soon lose his friends if he told them they were homely rather than beautiful and were wearing unattractive rather than good-looking clothes. He would be impolite on social occasions. Much polite language is essentially language to facilitate human intercourse, to make it easier for people to live together, without being in the truth-falsity continuum. There are many advantages in politeness and good form. But no matter how polite a person may be, he should discriminate between that language which has no other purpose than helping people adjust to each other, and that language which seeks to represent experience and move people.

In everyday life, language is used for three purposes: to convey information and represent relations, to convey feeling, and to incite people to action. The first of these is in the truth-falsity continuum in which accuracy is at a premium. The second is important but need not be accurate. Thus, we say "Good morning" to our neighbor on mornings which are not good, when it is snowing, blowing, or hailing. The "good morning" expresses our feeling, not the truth of the situation with respect to the weather.

The third use of language—to incite to action—is one in which the listener has to be on his guard. The politician makes a speech to lead the listener to vote for the candidate, the advertiser tries to sell him goods, and the solicitor wants a donation for a supposedly good cause. Whenever action is sought, the listener should cut behind the expressed symbols and examine the meanings critically, in order that he may make up his own mind and not be rushed into an action that he may regret later. And in his own use of symbols, he should have not only a clear understanding of what language is, but also high moral standards in its use. It is not easy to rear a child in a framework in which language is looked upon as relative to the situation it symbolizes. But it does prepare him more effectively for later adjustment in a world of words, which requires a sense of fair play and essential honesty in human relationships.

CONCLUSION

In language, the human being has an extraordinarily facile tool with which to initiate and maintain his relations with other persons; he lives in a world in which symbols are constantly present and are used to express needs and wishes. Language is not only the primary basis for social intercommunication. It is also the device by means of which the lore of the race is handed on to the young and progress in material and social relations is made possible. It is also a mechanism by means of which the phases of experience can be short-circuited and combined and recombined in various ways to solve problems and gain control over the world. The symbolic process develops with great rapidity in infancy and early childhood, largely because the child practices it in extraordinary amounts and because he desires to express his wants and to communicate with others. Spoken language develops well ahead of the written language, and actually is quite a different language when examined in detail. Similarly, the language of understanding is far wider than the language of use. The development of this instrument for social adjustment and inter-communication is facilitated in an atmosphere of good linguistic example and practice.

The problem of the relation between symbols and reality has become of major import in this day of propaganda. For the individual, awareness of the nature of symbols, and of the necessity for care and honesty in their use, offers some hope for good adjustment.

⟶ Dorothea A. McCarthy

Language Development

From "Language Development and Language Disorders: A Compendium of Lectures," Nancy E. Wood, editor, *Monographs of the Society for Research in Child Development*, 1960, 25, No. 3, 5–14. Reprinted by permission.

You who have been specializing in the study and improvement of speech are already aware of the vital importance of clear speech and effective communication. You have seen the educational cripples who have resulted from inadequate development of language skills and you also realize the heights to which a person with effective language skills can rise in his ability to communicate with and influence others. Let us ask ourselves, then, how do these tremendous individual differences come about? How can we promote good verbal skills in children and what can be done to avoid speech defects and other language disabilities?

In order to answer such questions, we must examine the developmental process from the beginning and try to discover the environmental factors that facilitate language development, and what factors seem to be present in the case histories of those who suffer from the various language disorders. Many people think that language development begins when the child uses his first word, but there are many things which happen in a child's prelinguistic babblings long before true speech is heard which have important developmental significance. The newborn infant sleeps most of the time when he is not eating. He is basically mute, except for crying sounds, which communicate his physical distress to those who care for him. At this time, his entire respiratory system is very much occupied with the establishment of breathing patterns and with the taking of food, essential for the survival of the infant. During the few waking moments before and after each feeding, the infant hears the voices of other members of the household as they speak to him and about him, or to each other. He uses his own voice, not only in his cries of hunger and discomfort, but in eager anticipation of being fed, as well as in little grunts and gurgles of satisfaction after having been fed. His language experience is beginning during the early listening process in which the mother is the child's first language teacher and in which he soon begins to echo back her voice in vocal play, cooing, and in babbling.

Reports from major infant studies record children's babbling in rather crude terms, but all the studies report infants as responding to the human voice and engaging in spontaneous cooing sometime between the second and fourth months of life. A variety of syllables are heard between the fourth and sixth months of life, and by the tenth month most babies begin to imitate the sounds and voices of others. The studies by Irwin [16, 17, 18] and his associates at Iowa have developed techniques for the more detailed study of early infant babblings. The earliest noncrying speech sounds are vowels with about four different vowels heard during the first two months, and thereafter, about one more vowel is added every two months for the first year of life. The rest of the vowels are added to the repertoire more slowly during the second year of life. These data are based on Irwin's investigations in which 95 infants were studied at bimonthly intervals for the first 30 months. It is also of interest to note that the number of different consonants exceeds the number of different vowels at about one year, and this is approximately the age at which normal babies speak their first word. There are many more consonants in the language to be learned than vowels, and only about two or three of them are used in the first months of life. They, too, increase rapidly at first and then more slowly until about 15 different ones, or about half the total that are to be acquired, are uttered by two and one-half years of age. One of the most interesting and significant measures is the ratio of the total number of consonants to the total number of vowels. In the first two months, babies use about one consonant for every four vowels. By one year, they use about one consonant for every two vowels, and by two years of age they are using about an equal number of vowels and consonants. They are then able to form simple syllables for all of their utterances.

Turning our attention from the quantitative aspects of vowel-consonant development to the more qualitative aspects, some interesting trends in vowel development are noted. Irwin's [16] data indicate that in the earliest months the vowels are predominantly those made with the front part of the oral cavity and that these vowels show a relative decrease with age in the first two and one-half years. However, vowels made with the back part of the oral cavity are very few in the earliest months and show a marked relative increase with age. Consonants, on the other hand, yield a developmental curve just the reverse of that for vowels. The consonants made with the back parts of the oral cavity (the glottal and velar sounds) are predominant in the vocalizations of six-month-old infants, whereas records made by Voelker [36] show the consonants made with the front part of the oral cavity (labials, labio-dentals and post-dentals) are predominant in the speech of adults.

Consonant sounds made with the front part of the oral cavity, especially the labials, labio-dentals and post-dentals, increase markedly with age in infants. It must be remembered that these changes in the development of speech sounds are occurring in a very complex organism, which is also developing very rapidly in a variety of other ways. In making these sounds, the child is using extremely complex and delicate groups of organs which serve not only the speech function, but also the two other basic functions of breathing and eating.

The child does not engage in playful cooing and babbling until after the more basic functions of breathing and eating are well established. Following the age when most babies have experience with solid food, which affords exercise and helps to develop the speech mechanisms, much more variety in the utterances is heard. In Irwin's data, 50 per cent of all sounds uttered by newborn babies and 97 per cent of all consonants heard in this early stage were the aspirate *h* sound which is undoubtedly associated with the infant's early gasping for breath in the state of "oxygen hunger" which has been described by Ribble. [29] It is interesting to note in this connection that Webster gives the Greek origin of the letter *h* as meaning "rough breathing." Some writers have made the point that, by the time the baby makes the cooing sounds characteristic of the second month of life, it is a sign that respiration is well established and that the child has breath to spare for other than emergency uses. Much of the neonatal waking time is concerned with the second important physiological function of the organs of speech, in which he develops skill in sucking and swallowing. Practically no non-crying speech sounds are heard until after breathing, sucking, and swallowing are well established. Shohara [32], working at Michigan, claimed that all movements involved in speech are first used for, and are virtually identical with, movements of swallowing, chewing, and mastication. It appears that the gross movements of opening the oral cavity and changes in the elevation of the dorsum, or root, of the tongue are all that are needed for this early phase of vowel production which is the sound stream or the raw material for speech.

The finer motor control of the blade and tip of the tongue needed to produce consonant sounds comes later, after the child has had considerable exercise in swallowing, chewing, etc. It is these modifications of the sound stream to form recognizable syllables which seem to be the most significant in the child's development of true speech. The earliest consonants, then, are the back consonants *k* and *g* which are primarily associated with swallowing or belching in the feeding situation.

Certain developmental changes seem to be associated with the infant's gain in postural control. Vocalizing in response to social stimulation is reported to occur in about the second and third months, when most babies are learning to hold their heads erect.

The so-called "babbling stage" has its onset at about seven months of age, which coincides approximately with the age at which the average baby learns to sit up; and the appearance of the first real words corresponds quite well to the average age of standing. No nasal sounds occur in the first four months, which is the period when the child lies down all of the time in either the supine or prone position. There is, however, a gradual rise in the percentage of nasal sounds as the child sits up more of the time, and nasal sounds constitute only about 10 per cent of the child's consonants from the age of sitting up at about seven months to about 15 months. Another spurt in the curve for the development of nasal sounds occurs between 18 and 24 months as the child enters the runabout period.

Several writers [7, 31] have pointed out that there seems to be a cyclical relationship between the child's development of motor skills and his progress in vocalization. While babies are concentrating on the new skill of sitting up, they may be relatively silent and babble freely only *after* the skill of sitting is mastered. Even reaching and grasping are often deferred until the more basic postural skill of sitting is accomplished.

Similarly, another type of plateau occurs in vocabulary building when babies are concentrating on learning to walk, usually between 15 and 18 months. The absence of nasal sounds when the child is lying down is quite understandable, when the mechanisms involved are considered, for the force of gravity pulls the velum in such a way as to close off the nasal passages, so that it would be practically impossible to make nasal sounds while lying down. X-ray studies indicate that even a 20-degree shift in the head tilt of adults does change their pronunciation of vowels. Therefore, it seems quite reasonable to assume that postural changes in the infant are related to the development of vocalization. It should also be noted that the naso-pharyngeal cavity doubles in height during the first few months when the sucking drive is very strong. Babbling occurs not only at the same age at which most babies sit up, but it also coincides quite closely with the period when most infants are given spoon and cup feeding and begin to have experiences with solid food which affords exercise and the development of many speech mechanisms.

Gesell and Ilg [12] report that most solid foods are taken well by 10 months of age, which is the age at which most students of speech report syllabic utterances due to anticipation of the feeding situation. Possibly these syllables are the child's first words, for it is indeed in just such situations that sounds take on meaning and become real words when used consistently in the same situations.

At about one year of age, when the average child has a speaking vocabulary of about three words, he gains considerable independence not only in self feeding, but also in getting about from place to place. Immediately thereafter, most babies show a rapid increase in vocabulary which is no doubt related to their broadening experience with more places and things. When the infant is in the earliest stage, in which most of his sounds are of a vowel character, he has no front teeth to form the front wall of the oral cavity. It is interesting to note, however, that there is a marked increase in the occurrence of front consonant or post dental sounds between six and 28 months which is the normal dentition period.

Having examined, briefly, the structural and physiological correlates of infancy, let us now consider some of the psychological factors and some problems of individual differences in the development of vocalization. The mother is normally the child's first language teacher in our culture, and it is she who furnishes the example for the baby to imitate. It is her voice that he echoes back in his babbling and her smile and fondling which most often elicit his cooing and other prelinguistic utterances.

Evidence that the amount of contact with the mother is significant for language growth comes from the fact that only children talk earlier and better than children with brothers and sisters [9] and that twins and other multiple-birth children, who always have to share the mother, are usually retarded in language development. [5, 10, 15]

Studies indicate that it is not merely the amount of contact with the mother which is important, but also that the quality of the mother-child relationship has a significant influence on the acquisition of language. This factor is difficult to measure, but it is necessary to understand what the qualitative differences are and to learn how to measure and evaluate them. The mother reflects her own personality in the kind of nurture she gives her baby. The very way she approaches motherhood is significant. Whether she welcomes or dreads the child's arrival; whether she feels adequate to care for him; whether she is tense, worried, and uncertain in everything she does for him; whether she is happy and talks to him as she goes about her tasks or pushes the baby carriage; whether she is silent and preoccupied while giving mere physical care, or is impersonal and allows the child to vegetate most of the time are the kinds of things which are important in determining whether his language development will thrive, or be stunted and distorted in some unfortunate way. The mother is the child's primary love object, as Wyatt [37, 38, 39] has pointed out, who unavoidably gratifies and frustrates the child in the process of socialization and training. Wyatt [38] suggests that it is almost inevitable that the child feel ambivalent toward his mother, and she cites Melanie Klein [21] who claims that an optimum amount of anxiety, as well as sufficient capacity of the emerging ego to tolerate anxiety, is necessary for the beginning of symbol formation or the onset of true language. Wyatt [37] states, as her main thesis, that satisfactory interpersonal relations, in particular, the relationship between mother and child, at the prelinguistic as well as at the linguistic level, are prerequisite to the development of symbol formation and for the successful acquisition of language. The vicissitudes of the mother-child relationship she says have a determining effect on the nature and outcome of the process of language training, and further, that the learning of the mother's speech is a deeply emotional experience for the young child and, like other learning, is achieved through the process of unconscious identification. Learning to speak, like all other primary learning, will therefore be influenced by the child's relationship to the mother.

Agreeing with the work of Baker [2], Wyatt [37] states that the mechanism of reciprocal identification emerges as a core mechanism in all language behavior. Geber [11] reports a fascinating cross-cultural study, showing the effects of maternal behavior on the psychological development of African children during the first year. In the particular population which was sampled, the children were not malnourished, as many African babies are. Among these people, the author states, the arrival of a baby is always looked forward to with great pleasure, and sterility is regarded as a calamity. Pregnancy is not a source of anxiety for the future. The mother is placid, not at all upset by her pregnancy, and is active up to the time of delivery. The unborn child is her chief interest in life and she accepts motherhood happily. She believes that any other interest at this time may have a deleterious effect on the baby. As soon as he is born, he is her constant companion and he is carried on her back as she goes about her various activities. She sleeps with him, feeds him on demand, forbids him nothing, and never chides him. Such a regime obviously reduces the ambivalence we were discussing previously. Geber [11] goes on to state that the baby in the culture studied is continually being stimulated by seeing the mother at her various occupations and hearing her "interminable conversations," and, because he is with her, his world is described as relatively extensive.

Children reared in this fashion, when tested with the Gesell schedule and other infant tests which have been standardized in western culture, were found to be well in advance of European and American standards in psychomotor development. For example, these children were able to hold their heads erect on the first day; were sitting up at seven weeks; and standing, with support, at five months. Geber [11] states: "their interest was lively and their personal-social relations excellent. They made very good contact with the tester, turning and 'talking' to her, smiling at her, and trying in every way to communicate with her" (p. 186). The development was not homogenous in all sections of the tests, for up to the fifth month the motor precocity was remarkable. Between the fifth and seventh months, adaptivity, *language,* and personal social relations, however, came to equal this motor development. The level was that of European children two or three months older. One wishes this study were reported in more quantitative form, with due regard for variability and individual differences. However, the writer claims that the behavior of the babies was almost strikingly like that of European babies whose mothers had a very strong desire to become mothers and who had learned the relaxation techniques advocated by Dr. Grantly Dick Read [28] of "Natural Childbirth" fame. She also notes that the babies of more sophisticated African parents, who left their infants in cribs much of the time and fed them on regular schedules in imitation of the European mores, were not showing the same precocity in motor development and were later inclined to be "quiet and subdued." The African babies studied by Geber [11], however, are usually weaned suddenly and then manifest extremely clinging behavior, their development showing a marked change for the worse following the abrupt weaning. These observations would lend support, then, to the theories of Wyatt [37] and others which emphasize the crucial role of maternal attitudes in the language development of children.

Myklebust [24] has described the genetic development of language by stating that, functionally, language can be divided into three types: inner, receptive, and expressive which are aquired in that order. Inner language is described as that which the child uses to talk to himself in an autistic fashion and manifests itself during the first eight or nine months of life. Receptive language, involving the comprehension of the language of others, appears usually from eight or nine months to 12 or 13 months. This is followed by the onset of expressive language or the ability to make oneself understood. The expressive use of language, Myklebust [24] claims, can occur only after both inner and receptive language have been partially established. He states that it is apparent that much of the language process, in terms of language acquisition, has preceded the specific occurrence of being able to use words expressively.

The same author states that normal language development assumes the integrity of the organism. Not only must the sensory, motor, and central nervous systems be intact, but the organism must possess "psychological integrity." Myklebust [24] says normal language development may be interfered with by sensory involvement such as deafness or blindness and by central nervous system damage such as aphasia, cerebral palsy, or mental deficiency. It can also be obstructed by any interference with the process of integration such as childhood schizophrenia, infantile autism, and even severe anxieties. Any of the above may impair the normal integrative processes and impede the development of the first stage, namely, inner language. In other words, if a baby develops under conditions of severe tension and anxiety, he may not be psychologically well integrated and may develop one or more forms of language disorder.

Mowrer [23] has pointed out that the psychological processes which are directly related to language acquisition are identification, internalization, and imitation. He cites Sullivan who stressed the importance of the role of anxiety in early infancy with reference to language development. Many authorities agree, therefore, as to the necessity of what Myklebust calls *psychological integrity* in order for normal language development to occur.

The relationship between language development and intelligence is a question of perennial interest. It is safe to say that mentally defective children are always delayed in the onset of speech, and their articulation and sentence structure are usually of poor quality. All children who speak late are not, however, mentally retarded, for there are many other reasons for delay in talking, and even some very bright children have not talked until three or three and one-half years of age. However, intellectually gifted children are usually early and efficient speakers and early speech is a very good index of future mental precocity.

The major reason why the age of onset of speech is so important is that, once children have begun to talk in sentences, they talk much of their waking day and practice their speech almost incessantly in a normal environment. Estimates based on records of all-day conversations [3, 6, 26] and on the work of Smith [33] indicate that children between three and four years of age use approximately 15,000 words per day or about 5,500,000 words in a year. Thus, a great deal of practice in oral language occurs in the preschool period, and a delay of six months or a year in its onset can seriously handicap a child for entrance into the verbal competition of the classroom. Just when this practice in oral expression is in its ascendency, the traditional type school represses talking as part of the socialization process and frustrates the child in the practice of oral language. Yet a good foundation in oral expression is the best preparation a child can have for learning the tool subjects which will lead to success in the academic situation.

Results of studies of infant language are being applied in the development of infant intelligence tests. Although the best single intelligence test is a measure of vocabulary, most of the infant tests have, in the past, concentrated on psychomotor development and have more or less neglected the infant speech area. Because various instruments for measuring infant intelligence have proved disappointing for long-term prediction, there has been a decided lag in the attempts to measure intelligence at the earliest levels. Griffiths [13] has developed a test which includes a speech and hearing scale within the total battery which should prove useful as a research and clinical tool. Since Spiker and Irwin [34] and Catalano and McCarthy [8] have found substantial correlations between such measures as consonant-type frequency and the consonant-vowel ratio in infancy with IQs obtained on the Kuhlmann and the Stanford-Binet tests, it appears that measures of infantile language do have promise and should be used in further attempts to measure the verbal factor in infancy. Griffiths [13] says, when a child is backward in learning to speak, or has a speech disorder, he is in danger of being regarded as a generally backward or even a defective child. This tendency to regard delayed speech development as an indication of general mental retardation is sometimes applied when there is evidence of normal progress in other directions. If it can be demonstrated with a new method of assessment in certain of these cases that the defect is specific and not general, then the disability can be regarded less fatalistically and as something to be treated and alleviated.

The future of research in the field of language development appears to be primarily a matter of the team approach involving experts in a wide variety of disciplines including electronic engineers, developmental psychologists, speech pathologists, linguists, and anthropologists. With regard to sampling, too much of our research on children's language has been based on the white preschool child of the middle western United States. With our rapidly shrinking world we must broaden our outlook to include cross-cultural studies which could indicate how children's language develops in different societies and in different racial and cultural groups. Most of the research in the field of language development has been primarily descriptive, aimed at determining norms and describing how the child's language develops. More dynamically oriented studies are attempting to determine why language develops in a particular way and what factors seem to accelerate or retard its development. Infant studies, which have shown clearly the importance of early personal contact for normal language development, have had a marked influence in stimulating a tremendous interest in research on family relations. With these facts in mind, it is my prediction that, if we are to make real progress in this area, some way of teaching phonetics to larger groups of research investigators in the field must be found, and greater cooperation between linguists and developmental psychologists and speech therapists must be achieved.

——▶ Nancy E. Wood
Language Disorders in Children

From "Language Development and Language Disorders: A Compendium of Lectures," Nancy E. Wood, editor, *Monographs of the Society for Research in Child Development*, 1960, 25, No. 3, 15–23. Reprinted by permission.

Numerous factors can impede or delay the normal acquisition of language. Children with deafness or hearing loss will not develop language normally because of their inability to hear sounds or words; the mentally retarded child will usually develop language in direct relationship to his mental age; the child with emotional disturbance may ignore sounds and words, withdrawing from all language stimuli around him. A thorough report of studies concerned with language development and the many factors that can impede this development has been made by McCarthy. [22]

Delay in language development can also be caused by central nervous system impairment which results in the limitation or inability of the child to use symbols for communication. A *symbol* can be defined as an abstraction which represents a concrete object, person, or thing. For example, the word *cat* is a symbol for an animal; *mother* a symbol for a person; *pencil* a symbol for a writing tool.

Language disorders caused by central nervous system impairment vary not only in type but in degree of involvement. The three terms most frequently used to refer to specific types of language disorders are aphasia, alexia, and agraphia. Sometimes, dysphasia, dyslexia, or dysgraphia are used to indicate that, although the problem in the use of symbols exists, it is a partial, rather than a total problem.

DELINEATION OF APHASIA

The term *aphasia* or *dysphasia* is described classically as a disorder of spoken language either in its reception or expression. Although the symptom of aphasia is the limited ability to understand or produce the spoken word, the problem cannot be considered one of speech production alone. Aphasia refers to a limitation in the reception or expression of spoken words because of a basic inability to receive stimuli or classify symbols. For example, the word *book* may not be understood by the aphasic child since he may not be able to associate the name of the object, which is a symbol, with the actual object itself. Because he does not comprehend the word and because he cannot apply it to the object, he is then unable to express himself adequately using this word.

There is still controversy surrounding the subject of aphasia in children. In essence, much of this controversy is based upon semantic and clinical confusion. At times, the term aphasia is confused with terms that describe other types of language disorders. More frequently, the symptoms of cerebral pathology and mental retardation are confused with the symptoms of aphasia.

As it has been stated previously, a language disorder refers to the inability or limited ability of the child to use symbols for communication. Aphasia refers to *one type* of language disorder that is concerned exclusively with an inability to receive or express spoken symbols. Conversely, aphasia does not refer to disorders in the reception or expression of *written* symbols. We have other terms for those problems. For example, *alexia* is used to indicate a problem in the *reception* of written symbols; alexia, then, is a disorder of reading. *Agraphia* is used to refer to a problem in the expression of written symbols; therefore, agraphia is a disorder of writing. There are other terms used also to denote other types of language disorders, such as *acalculia*—an inability to comprehend numbers; *amusica*—a disorder in the use of music symbols, etc. Unless a basic delineation is made between the meaning of the term *aphasia* and those terms used to describe other types of language disorders, more confusion is added to an already complex disorder. Therefore, it must be clear that aphasia is a disorder of the reception or the expression of the *spoken word* because of an inability to comprehend or use the symbol of speech.

Karlin [19] has pointed out that aphasia in children is caused by cerebral pathology—more specifically, injury to or lack of development of the cortex. It should also be emphasized that, although aphasia is caused by cerebral pathology, all cerebral pathology does not result in aphasia. Unfortunately, a diagnosis of aphasia is often made on the basis of clinical clues that should be used *only* to give hints that aphasia may be present. For example, the child with aphasia may have a generalized motor impairment. He may have a problem in balance, gait, or cerebral dominance. He may have a fine motor disorder with problems in prehension, grasp, or grip. There also may be evidence of tremors, asteriognosis, or overflow. But these factors support *only* the probability that a central nervous system disorder exists and the presumption that aphasia *might* exist, but they do not delineate the problem of aphasia.

In sensory reception the child with aphasia may have a visual perceptual disorder with figure-ground disturbances, difficulty in Gestalt closure, and visual perseveration. But in these children such behavioral responses are also related to cerebral pathology and must not be confused with aphasia.

The auditory system of the child with aphasia may also be

impaired so that he cannot comprehend auditory symbols. But the fine differentiation between acuity and comprehension, such as those discussed by Hardy [14], must be made before the presumption for aphasia is accurate.

The child with aphasia may have demonstrated certain behavioral symptoms, such as distractibility, disinhibition, perseveration, and catastrophic reactions. These behavior symptoms have been discussed by Strauss and Lehtinen. [35] However, these emotional and social deviations are, again, related to cerebral pathology and must not be confused with the diagnosis of aphasia.

Differentiating Aphasia from Mental Retardation

One of the most difficult decisions the examiner must make in the diagnosis of aphasia is the separation of this problem from that of mental retardation. This, of course, depends upon how the term *mental retardation* is defined. If we assume that the term mental retardation refers to a reduced mental capacity in all functions that are basic to learning, then we should be able to select some specific capacities in which the aphasic child *does not* operate adequately while, at the same time, he is able to function at a normal or near normal level in all other capacities. These normal capacities should make it possible for him to compensate for his speech deficiency and inability to use symbols, so that he can operate in some, or many, or nearly all ways like a normal child in terms of interaction with his environment. In other words, the child with aphasia must be considered different in kind rather than degree, whereas the mentally retarded child is different in degree rather than kind. The major difference between the two problems is that the aphasic child can plan in a nonsymbolic or object-oriented situation and he can learn from past experience in nonsymbolic situations.

If we were to compare the performance of a mentally retarded child with that of a child with aphasia and if we were to assign values to these performances so that they could be plotted on a chart, the mentally retarded child would show, predominantly, a straight line graph. On the other hand, a child with aphasia would be represented graphically by a chart having many points at normal, near normal, or even above normal level. The low points on the graph would be fairly extreme, showing a jagged profile, and the low points of performance would represent activities that require the use of symbols, abstractions, and judgment.

In fact, one major area of breakdown in the aphasic child seems to occur when he is required to make a judgment on a verbal level which requires the use of symbols. For example, he may have difficulty judging differences in size, distance, direction, weight, volume, speed, length, time, or height, unless he has a referent within his immediate environment. Stated differently, when he is asked to do any assortment of nonverbal performances, he may score well, but, if he is asked to make a judgment on a purely abstract level, he may be unable to perform.

This inability to judge relationships was a major differentiating factor in a recent experiment involving 50 children known to have language disorders, including aphasia. This was one major criterion used to differentiate the problem of aphasia from mental retardation in 90 Ss in a sample of over 500. These data resulted from a project supported by funds obtained from the Beaumont Foundation and the Department of Health, Education, and Welfare, and a complete report of this study is scheduled for June, 1960. However, cursory inspection of these data suggested that the inability of the child to make judgments on a symbolic level while, at the same time, he is able to function fairly adequately on a nonsymbolic level is possible the crux of aphasia in children. Clinically speaking, it seems that the child with aphasia is unable to make such judgments of relationships on a symbolic level because he is unable to deal with abstractions. From an operational standpoint, aphasia in children can be considered a disorder in the reception or expression of spoken symbols due to an inability to deal with abstractions for which there is no referent in the immediate environment.

THERAPEUTIC PROCEDURES FOR APHASIA

But it is not enough to define or describe aphasia unless we can make some suggestions as to what to do about it. As one would suppose, what you do about the problem depends upon the type of aphasia which is present, the degree to which it exists, and the age at which therapy is begun. No one method of procedure serves all aspects of the problem. However, one major trend appeared in our study of aphasia in children; that is, if a child's problem is primarily a receptive disorder, he may learn to react to stimuli with behavioral patterns that are almost identical with those of the deaf child. Our method of approach to this type of problem is similar to that described by Kleffner [20], which stresses the production of individual speech sounds with each sound associated with its written letter symbol. This method seems to be successful with a child with a primary receptive problem.

Conversely, we found that, if the child's language disorder is primarily that of expression, he tends to become so frustrated that his behavioral responses assume many of the characteristics observed in emotionally disturbed children. These children tended to respond better to an approach which stresses the whole word concept such as those procedures described by Myklebust. [25] With these children we allow more permissiveness in our therapeutic sessions, and our aim is to provide a stimulating language environment for the child and introduce him to whole word concepts.

We also found that, if the child has severe limitations in both receiving and expressing language symbols, language development is severely impeded and he is unable to perform adequately on any test requiring the use of symbols. As he becomes older and as tests require increased use of symbols, he becomes, almost in fact, mentally retarded. However, since he is retarded in *kind* rather than *degree,* our approach combines sound units, whole word concepts, and a wide-based educationally oriented approach.

It should not be assumed that we believe that such procedures are able to be packaged this neatly but we have observed children with receptive aphasia, expressive aphasia, and mixed aphasia during a four-year study. The apparent trend that the child with receptive aphasia becomes more like the deaf child, the child with expressive aphasia becomes more like the emotionally disturbed child, and the child with mixed aphasia becomes more like the mentally retarded child as they grow older suggests that this so-called *associative adjustment* may be one type of behavioral compensation that a child may assume because of the basic aphasic condition. The problems of deafness, emotional disturbance, and mental retardation are difficult to diagnose in any child but, in the child with aphasia, these problems are even more difficult to differentiate. This suggests that the majority of children with aphasia, due to the nature of the case, which is cerebral pathology, will probably have multiple problems. Thus, all types of therapy—whether the approach is concerned with isolated sounds, whole word concepts, or a wide-based educational approach—all methods are needed in a complete training program. This also suggests that perhaps many of the differences in diagnostic opinion that occur in reports from various examiners may be due to the fact that the child himself has changed from one test session to another, rather than a basic clinical disagreement among examiners. For this reason, it is extremely important to stress that, as the child becomes older, it is increasingly difficult to untangle the many factors as they become superimposed, one upon another, and that the child's problem may be entirely different from year to year.

Early Diagnosis Indicated

This brings us to the question of how early we can detect the problem of aphasia in children. If additional problems are to be prevented, it becomes apparent that earlier diagnosis of aphasia is indicated. By the time the child reaches three or four years of age, he may have so many other problems superimposed upon the aphasia that the differentiation of aphasia becomes increasingly difficult. Therefore, in a child under three years of age, we must watch for symptoms such as failure of speech development, failure of auditory comprehension, and additional clues as central nervous system involvement which adds to the presumption for aphasia. These symptoms would be especially significant if there were relatively normal development in other areas. Although early detection of aphasia in children will depend upon the increased awareness on the part of the examiner of these symptoms, the actual diagnosis of aphasia must be delayed until the child reaches the chronological age when we could expect him, maturationally, to be using verbal symbols and making judgments. In other words, we cannot diagnose aphasia until the child fails to perform adequately on the criterion we use for diagnosing aphasia, namely, the inability to use speech symbolically at a judgment level.

DELINEATION OF ALEXIA AND AGRAPHIA

Most discussions of aphasia in children are limited to the diagnosis and treatment of young children who have not developed speech. But some children, for reasons not entirely clear, apparently learn speech patterns and will talk fluently. Yet, careful consideration of their speech gives evidence of *word finding* problems or *speech circumlocution*. Usually, this child is not identified in the early grades and remains unrecognized until he is found to have a learning disorder. Learning disorders are more frequently identified when the child is unable to read or write even though psychological assessment of his mental capacities indicates that he should be able to master these performances. Orton [27] pointed this out over two decades ago. This inability to read or write may be diagnosed as problems in alexia or agraphia.

The term *alexia* or *dyslexia* refers to the inability or limited ability of the child to receive, understand, and associate *written* words with an object or an experience. This is related possibly to his inability to "revisualize" or "reauditorize" the symbol so that the visual or auditory image of the word is not retained for a sufficient period of time. This results in a reading disorder. He may reverse entire words, reading *saw* for *was*, or *ton* for *not*. He may omit initial or final sounds. Primarily, alexia refers to a problem in silent reading. The major symptom is the inability of the child to relate verbally what he has read. Bender [4] and Schilder [30] have discussed alexia in more detail.

The terms *agraphia* or *dysgraphia* usually describe the inability or limitations of the child to expressively associate written words with an object or an experience. This, then, is a writing disorder. Agraphia and alexia are interassociated, since they are both concerned with written symbols and since it is necessary to be able to read before one is able to write.

Tentative Research Findings

A number of children now attending public school are unable to function adequately in reading, writing, or arithmetic because they are unable to understand or comprehend symbols. A portion of these children show little or no absolute evidence of problems in speech production; yet their speech may consist of severe hesitations, circumlocution, and word finding, *or* they may show significant delay in comprehending speech concepts.

As stated previously, the data from our entire study of children with language disorders are being treated currently and a detailed report of findings will be available soon. However, for this discussion, 100 consecutively selected case histories of children between the ages of six and nine years were inspected for trends. A few rather salient points emerged from this initial examination of the data.

Of the 100 histories studied, 69 were males and 31 were females, giving a ratio of approximately 2:1 in favor of the males. This ratio supports previous conclusions that there is a higher incidence of males in handicap populations.

In activities such as writing or drawing, 73 used the left hand exclusively, six were ambidextrous, and 21 were right-handed. Reversals and/or inversions of writing symbols were found in 59 *S*s. This information suggests that problems in cerebral dominance were prevalent in this sample population.

Delayed speech and language development was reported in 72 cases and 20 *S*s had been classified as behavior problems in school, indicating that the histories of these children require careful consideration even though an actual speech disorder seemingly does not exist.

Of the 100 *S*s, 40 were referred for electroencephalographic studies. Of these 40, only 10 electroencephalograms were classified as positive. However, it is important to note that, of the 30 considered *negative,* the term "generalized dysrhythmia" appeared in 17 of these reports. This suggests that in these types of problems further exploration of the neurological findings is indicated.

Psychologic assessment of these Ss gave an IQ range from 86 to 111; yet all of these children were referred for evaluation because of learning disorders in school. They performed poorly on timed tests and less accurately on verbal than performance tests. There was a significant element of defeatism throughout the testing sessions and a tendency to "give up" before the work was completed.

Although none of these children were found to have a hearing loss when tested by routine audiometric screening, a large proportion of these Ss reported that they could not "hear" instructions in the classroom. They showed confusion in spatial orientation and at times were unable to differentiate between directions such as: *up* and *down;* or *left* and *right.* In general, judgment of relationships was poor. The majority of these children had "word finding" difficulties when they were asked to explain or discuss an abstract concept.

Discussions of the problem with the parents most often included descriptions of the child's behavior at home. The words, "daydreamer," "forgetful," "stubborn," "lazy," and "inconsistent," were heard often in these conferences.

Some of these children stated that they were insecure in the school setting and were overly concerned with their inadequate performance. Conversely, a larger segment of this population actually boasted of being superior in the very educational functions in which they were found to be *inadequate.* For example, those who were known to be extremely poor readers often reported that they were "the best reader in the class." Whether or not this unawareness is clearly superficial compensation, or whether they are actually unaware of their inadequate performance, it is apparent that the unawareness itself is a factor that must be considered in the educational planning and general guidance of these children.

EDUCATIONAL NEEDS

It is important to stress that all of these 100 children were attending normal school at the time they were seen for evaluation. It is quite possible that a large number of these children have now been excluded from school because of their inability to learn. It is a startling realization that these children, who give evidence of normal intellectual potential, are unable to receive help for the very problem that forces this type of exclusion. It is understandable why teachers are confused and frustrated by these children, or why parents become irritated with school systems that cannot provide these educational needs.

Education for the deaf child, guidance for the mentally retarded child, and psychotherapy for the emotionally disturbed child may be insufficient at the present time, but at least the needs are recognized and such programs are developing within our communities. In the same way, plans for children with orthopedic handicaps or blindness are materializing and special classes, geared to these specific needs, are being organized. The child with a language disorder appears to stand alone with a learning problem that has no educational provision and their educational deficit remains unrecognized, misdiagnosed, or misunderstood. Specific educational procedures must be initiated if these problems are to be reduced in complexity.

The basic aim of educational procedures for the child with a language disorder is to help him *organize* incoming stimuli so that useful concepts can result. Drill and rote procedures will not serve his purpose. It is not the production of words, nor the rote recognition of them, nor the memorization of arithmetic principles that is of major importance. Rather, it is the understanding and comprehension of the meaning of these principles that are important if they are to become useful entities in communication.

A major portion of the initial detection of language disorders in children will probably continue to be the responsibility of the educator. But the evaluation of the problem must remain the responsibility of specialists trained in this area. Although there are several clinics in this country that offer specialized diagnostic services in language disorders, they cannot begin to provide communities with diagnostic services, let alone undertake the educational needs of these children.

It is no longer enough for us to sit on our academic pedestals and argue as to whether or not these language disorders exist. Neither is it enough for us to hope that sometime in the future an educational program will be designed for children with these problems. Adequate legislation must be obtained to support the introduction or expansion of diagnostic and educational programs in clinics and schools for children with these problems. Universities must train more specialists in diagnostic services that include educational recommendations. Until this is done, the child with a language disorder will continue to be a confusing educational enigma, for a language disorder *is* an educational problem.

REFERENCES

1. ANDERSON, J. E., "An Evaluation of Various Indices of Linguistic Development," *Child Development*, 1937, 8:62–68.

2. BAKER, S. J., "The Theory of Silences," *Journal of Genetic Psychology*, 1955, 53:147–167.

3. BELL, S., "The Significance of Activity in the Child's Life," *Independent*, 1903, 55:911–914.

4. BENDER, L., "Problems in Conceptualization and Communication in Children with Developmental Alexia," in P. H. Hoch & J. Zubin, *Psychopathology of Communication*, New York: John Wiley & Sons, Inc., 1958.

5. BLATZ, W. E., FLETCHER. M. I., & MASON, M., "Early Development in Spoken Language of the Dionne Quintuplets," in W. E. Blatz, *et al., Collected Studies on the Dionne Quintuplets,* University of Toronto Study of Child Development, 1937, No. 16.

6. BRANDENBURG, G. C., & BRANDENBURG, JULIA, "Language Development During the Fourth Year," *Pedagogical Seminary,* 1916, 23:14–29.

7. BRIGANCE, W. N., "The Language Learning of a Child," *Journal of Applied Psychology*, 1934, 18:143–154.

8. CATALANO, F. L., & McCARTHY, DOROTHEA, "Infant Speech as a Possible Predictor of Later Intelligence," *Journal of Psychology*, 1954, 38:203–209.

9. DAVIS, E. A., "The Development of Linguistic Skill in Twins, Singletons with Siblings, and Only Children from Age Five to Ten Years, *University of Minnesota Institute of Child Welfare Monograph,* 1937, No. 14.

10. DAY, E. J., "The Development of Language in Twins: I. A Com-

parison of Twins and Single Children," *Child Development*, 1932, 3:179–199.

11. GEBER, M., "The Psychomotor Development of African Children in the First Year, and the Influence of Maternal Behavior," *Journal of Social Psychology*, 1958, 47:185–195.

12. GESELL, A., & ILG, FRANCES L., *Infant and Child in the Culture of Today*, New York: Harper & Brothers, 1943.

13. GRIFFITHS, R., *The Abilities of Babies*, New York: McGraw-Hill Book Company, Inc., 1954.

14. HARDY, W. G., & PAULS, M. D., "Significance of Problems of Conditioning in GSR Audiometry," *Journal of Speech and Hearing Disorders*, 1959, 24:123–126.

15. HOWARD, R. W., "The Language Development of a Group of Triplets," *Journal of Genetic Psychology*, 1946, 69:181–188.

16. IRWIN, O. C., "Infant Speech: Vowel and Consonant Frequency," *Journal of Speech Disorders*, 1946, 11:123–125.

17. ————, "Infant Speech: Equations for Consonant-vowel Ratios," *Journal of Speech and Hearing Disorders*, 1946, 11:177–180.

18. ————, & CHEN, H. P., "Infant Speech: Vowel and Consonant Types," *Journal of Speech Disorders*, 1946, 11:27–29.

19. KARLIN, I. W., "Aphasia in Children," *American Journal of Diseases of Children*, 1954, 87:752.

20. KLEFFNER, F. R., "Teaching Speech and Language to Aphasic Children," *Volta Review*, 1958, 709.

21. KLEIN, MELANIE, *The Psychoanalysis of Children*, London: The Hogarth Press, Ltd., 1932.

22. McCARTHY, DOROTHEA, "Language Development in Children," in L. Carmichael, ed., *Manual of Child Psychology*, New York: John Wiley & Sons, Inc., 1954.

23. MOWRER, O. H., "Speech Development in the Young Child," *Journal of Speech and Hearing Disorders*, 1952, 17:263–268.

24. MYKLEBUST, H. R., "Language Disorders in Children," *Exceptional Child*, 1956, 22:163–166.

25. ————, "Aphasia in Children–Language Development and Language Pathology," in L. Travis, *Handbook of Speech Pathology*, New York: Appleton-Century-Crofts, Inc., 1957.

26. NICE, M. M., "Concerning All-day Conversations," *Pedagogical Seminary*, 1920, 27, 166–177.

27. ORTON, S. T., *Reading, Writing and Speech Problems in Children*, New York: W. W. Norton & Co., Inc., 1937.

28. READ, G. D., *Children Without Fear*, New York: Harper & Brothers, 1953.

29. RIBBLE, MARGARET, *The Rights of Infants,* New York: Columbia University Press, 1943.

30. SCHILDER, P., "Congenital Alexia and its Relation to Optic Perception," *Journal of Genetic Psychology,* 1944, 65:67.

31. SHIRLEY, MARY M., *The First Two Years: A Study of Twenty-Five Babies: Intellectual Development,* University of Minnesota Institute of Child Welfare Monograph Series No. 7. Minneapolis: University of Minnesota Press, 1933.

32. SHOHARA, H., "A Contribution to the Genesis of Speech Movements and the Etiology of Stuttering," *Journal of Speech Disorders,* 1942, 7:29–32.

33. SMITH, MADORAH E., "A Study of Some Factors Influencing the Development of the Sentence in Preschool Children," *"Journal of Genetic Psychology,* 1935, 46:182–212.

34. SPIKER, C., & IRWIN, O. C., "The Relationship Between I. Q. and Indices of Infant Speech Sound Development," *Journal of Speech and Hearing Disorders,* 1949, 14:335–343.

35. STRAUSS, A., & LEHTINEN, L., *Psychopathology and Education of the Brain Injured Child,* New York: Grune and Stratton, Inc., 1947.

36. VOELKER, C. H., "Technique for a Phonetic Frequency Distribution Count in Formal American Speech," extract from *Archives néerlandaises de phonétique expérimentale,* 1935, 11:69–72.

37. WYATT, GERTRUD L., *Speech and Interpersonal Relations: The Psychodynamics of Language Learning, Object Relations and Language Deviations in Childhood.* Mimeographed. Limited circulation, 1957.

38. ———, *Mother-child Relationships and Stuttering in Children.* Unpublished doctoral dissertation, Boston University, 1958. (University Microfilm, Ann Arbor, Michigan.)

39. ———, "A Developmental Crisis Theory of Stuttering," *Language and Speech,* 1958, 1:250–264.

CHAPTER
TWELVE

↑

*Development of Peer
Relationships*

A CHILD IS AN ACTIVE MEMBER OF A PEER group from the moment of his first contact with other children in his neighborhood. Peers are those with whom an individual associates on terms of approximate equality. A peer group consists, therefore, of individuals who have a great deal in common in certain important respects. Discussions of peer groups where children (or youth) are concerned generally imply a closeness in age. Actually, as will be evident in certain of the readings in this chapter, there are numerous factors besides equality of age that operate in the formation of peer groups and in the behaviors that characterize a particular group.

In the first of the readings in this chapter, Theodore Bienenstok describes the function that the peer group serves in relating the child to the social world outside his home. "Here in groups of their age-mates," says Bienenstok, "boys and girls tend to create a body of customs, standards of behavior and moral values that constitute a distinctive culture." This "subadult" culture exerts "a growing pressure upon the child as he progresses toward maturity." In such statements as these one finds reasons why teachers must be alert to the importance of knowing the psychology of peer group development and behavior and the implications it has for the work of the school. Bienenstok is a member of the staff of the New York State Department of Education.

There are numerous factors and relations among factors that operate in the formation and the functioning of adolescent groups. This conclusion is especially relevant to *informal* groups of adolescents. What are the commonalities that characterize the members of an informal group of adolescents? And what are the things that most strikingly differentiate one group from another? John E. Horrocks, of Ohio State University, and Harold R. Phelps, of Illinois State Normal University, chose to investigate these questions with a particular kind of approach—a nonnormative survey—and to subject their findings to factor analysis. The method and the results of this study deserve careful, thoughtful study on the part of the reader.

Significant shifts occur in the social world of the adolescent. One of the shifts involves the increase of interest in the opposite sex. The study by Raymond G. Kuhlen and Beatrice J. Lee, of Syracuse University, discloses some interesting trends in the relationships of personal traits to social acceptability as youngsters progress from the sixth through the twelfth grade. The study is especially noteworthy for the picture it gives of adolescence as viewed by the adolescents themselves.

The final reading in this chapter provides a good transition to the chapter that follows—the psychology of parent-child relationships. Harris and Tseng examine the factors involved in the shift of attitude on the part of boys and girls toward parents and peers as, with their increasing age, they gain in skills and independence. Are boys more favorable to their own sex as peers than to the opposite sex? What about the attitude of girls in this respect? What trend, if any, is indicated in the attitudes of boys toward their parents as the youngsters' ages increase? Is the trend different for girls? These and other questions of similar importance related to children's attitudes towards peers and parents were explored in this study. The reader will find the conclusions thought-provoking, and he will be interested in the methodology employed in the study. Harris is Professor of Psychology, Pennsylvania State University. Mr. Tseng collaborated in this study while Harris and he were at the University of Minnesota.

——▶ Theodore Bienenstok

The Peer Culture of Youth and the School

From *The Educational Forum*, March, 1954, 18:312–319. Reprinted by permission.

Inevitably, all who care for children come to realize that youth lives in a world of its own. Here in groups of their age-mates, boys and girls tend to create a body of customs, standards of behavior and moral values that constitute a distinctive culture. The requirements of this subadult peer culture exert a growing pressure upon the child as he progresses toward maturity. In fact, a satisfactory adjustment to his group of contemporaries and their demands is one of the major tasks in the child's social development. It is therefore essential that the teacher understand the nature of peer groups, so that their potential value for education may be capitalized, and some of their disadvantageous effects counteracted.

Role of Peer Culture in Transition from Childhood to Adulthood

The formative influence of the peer culture can best be understood if considered in connection with the difficult transition from childhood to adulthood. Conditioned to one set of behavior patterns in childhood, the individual must revise his conduct from almost all points of view as he assumes the role of an adult. Growing up means that new patterns of behavior must be learned, and new adjustments made, in activities, interests and habits.

All societies are faced with the problem of this change and regulate it in various ways. Some try to assure a continuity of conditioning by allowing the child to put into practice forms of behavior essentially the same as those upon which he will rely as an adult, but graded to his physical and mental capacity. Other societies which expect, as we do, basically different conduct from a child than from an adult, try to minimize the strain of this change. Either they give new duties and prestige to age groups of young people at each stage of development, or they mark the passage from childhood to adulthood by publicly ritualized steps, the meaning of which is clearly understood and accepted by both the youth and his elders.

In contrast to this, in modern societies of the Western world, while it is expected that young people will become emancipated from parental control and will make their own way in the world, the exact time, manner and meaning of such emancipation remains uncertain, and a subject of dispute and recrimination. Only grudgingly and with reluctance does modern society accord status to growing-up boys and girls. In some situations they are treated like adults and are asked to show maturity of conduct and a sense of responsibility. In other situations they are treated like children incapable of taking responsibility or of making even simple judgments.

Confused about their role and function in society, and lacking a definite place in the scheme of things, young people turn to their own peers, or equals, for guidance, protection and support. The peer culture thus created helps to carry them over the adolescent period of strain and stress. In close personal relations with their contemporaries they can satisfy their needs for security, for belonging, and for status, while gradually trying to free themselves from dependence upon their families.

PEER CULTURE IN CHILDHOOD

As soon as a child begins to play with other children, he ceases to be a member solely of a family group and enters the society of his peers. In the early years of elementary school, of course, parental influences are still predominant, but little by little the standards of age-mates come to the fore. Actions and opinions of play associates increasingly occupy the child's attention, and there is a growing desire for identification with the peer group.

A major factor fostering this tendency today is the impact upon children of mass media of communication. Radio and television programs, comics and movies transmit to the child the values and rules of behavior prevalent in his peer culture. Mass media tell him what other children eat, wear and read, what interests they have, and what particular slang they use in intimate communication. They create for him a picture of what boyhood and girl-hood are like in the culture. Well-known personalities of comics and movies such as Superman, Hopalong Cassidy, Bugs Bunny and a host of others, suggest to a child ideas and images of things and activities which he may share with other children of his age. All this lore is further spread throughout the peer group by way of continuous exchange on playgrounds and in school.

The direction received by a child from his contemporaries and from mass media extends even to the norms of parental behavior. What children of a given age should be allowed to do, how they should be brought up by their parents, how much spending-money they should receive can be learned from these two sources of authority. And such information may be, and actually often is, used successfully by the child to oppose parental commands and prohibitions and to influence parental action.

CHARACTER OF PEER GROUPING IN PREADOLESCENCE

The importance of the peer group increases greatly in the preadolescent period. In contrast to the earlier stage of development, when contacts and associations with age-mates were organized and directed by adults, youngsters now spontaneously seek to form "gangs" and "cliques" removed from adult supervison.

Segregation by sex, which is characteristic of this period, goes together with a differentiation of roles and values along sex lines. Boys disapprove of girls, unless they are nearly like boys. Games and plays are assigned to one sex or the other. Crossing of sex lines is subject to ridicule, when done by boys; it requires a change of behavior, language and appearance, when attempted by girls. Lines of inclusion and exclusion are drawn sharply. Conformity to group norms is enforced by boys through "razzing," raillery and ostracism—quite often in fist fights or other types of physical aggression. Girls assure conformity primarily by the method of exclusion.

THE EFFECT OF PEER GROUPS ON PREADOLESCENT BOYS

Play groups of preadolescent boys often tend to develop a rather closely knit organization, with a more or less formal leadership. These so-called "gangs" perform a vital function in the process of socialization. In collective undertakings conducted by the peer group, boys learn and practice the social virtues of co-operation, self-sacrifice and loyalty to the group, while outdoor activities such as roaming neighborhoods and streets, camping out, playing Indians and cowboys, cops and robbers, offer many opportunities for the exercise of daring, resourcefulness, self-reliance and initiative. The free life led by the "gang" satisfies the boys' deep desire for adventure, excitement and novelty. The very fact that all these experiences are taking place in an atmosphere of intimate fellowship and freedom from adult supervision apparently makes them more effective in molding character and personality than the conventional training in a classroom situation.

Due to the rising desire for independence from adult pressure, "gangs" are more thoroughly enjoyed if they are somewhat on the "subversive" side in terms of adult standards. This does not mean that generally accepted social norms are totally rejected, but only that some adult-fashioned values are abrogated or prohibited by the preadolescent peer code of behavior. Thus, studying too much may expose one to the suspicion of being a sissy, while paying strict obedience to the wishes of adults may be looked upon with disfavor by the peer group. Even in a not too delinquent "gang," a child may be expected to lie in order to protect a pal from punishment, and sometimes stealing may be encouraged—either for fun or to display one's courage.

"Cliques" of Preadolescent Girls

Organized "gangs" composed entirely of girls are very rare. Girls are more inclined to form smaller "cliques" of friends, which are strongly exclusive and normally have little formal organization or leadership. On the whole, information regarding such "cliques" is scanty. Apparently there is no system of mutual obligations between members in such groups and little, if any, deepseated loyalty to the group. Girls, being more carefully supervised than boys, tend also toward more conventional patterns of behavior and interests.

Change of Grouping in Adolescence

In adolescence a change takes place in the pattern of juvenile groupings. Social activities in company with the opposite sex become the focus of interest, and this in turn leads to the breaking up of one-sex groups of boys or girls into a two-sex pattern of "dating." There is some evidence suggesting that at present this change occurs even as early as the sixth or seventh grade level; though boys, maturing more slowly than girls, may show little inclination for such activities and are almost pushed into them by dancing classes organized in schools.

The "Dating" Pattern

A "dating" relationship is highly patterned by norms of peer culture. "Dating" starts as an invitation by a boy to a girl for an evening's public entertainment. Food and drink to be consumed on this occasion, place and type of entertainment are to be proposed by the boy; clothes to be worn and favors to be accorded by the girl to her escort are clearly prescribed or understood in advance. On the whole, "dating" is largely dominated by the quest for thrill and is regarded mostly as an amusement, but frequently it develops into serious courtship. In those cases where partners are emotionally uninvolved, the elements of competition and building of prestige play an important role. Boys and girls evaluate each other as desirable "dates" in accordance with a rating of popularity assigned by the peer group. On the other hand, a person's status and prestige will be greatly influenced by the rating of the person with whom he or she dates. Under these conditions, rivalry and competition for desirable "dates" is keen, and this in turn introduces a good deal of suspicion and antagonism into the "dating" relationship. The anxiety accompanying the competitive process of being accepted in "dating," and the associated standards of desirability—phrased in terms of good clothes, physical appearance, "smooth" manners and ability to entertain and dance well—bring to a number of young people strong feelings of humiliation, frustration and failure.

Demand for Conformity in Peer Culture

Peer culture is essentially intolerant of deviation. It demands almost complete conformity to the dominant concerns and standards of the group. Except for those who have already won high prestige in the group, only slight leeway is given for individual variation from the accepted pattern. There seems to be a distinct tendency on the part of contemporaries to suppress any idiosyncratic qualities among themselves. Any claim to independent judgment, taste, personal behavior or opinion must be surrendered. "He thinks he is big," or "He thinks he is somebody" are often heard in the peer groups. The fear, even among the very young, of standing out in any direction, combined with the fantasy enjoyment of such achievement, is illustrated by the following interview reported by Wolfe and Fiske in "Children Talk About Comics":

A. I like Superman better than others, because they can't do everything Superman can do. Batman can't fly and that is very important.

Q. Would you like to be able to fly?

A. I would like to be able to fly if everybody else did, but otherwise I would be kind of conspicuous.[1]

Since norms of peer culture cover so many aspects of personal and social life of young people, strenuous efforts are made to appear and behave like the group and to do what the group does. This is not an easy task, however. Standards of behavior and qualifications for status in the peer group undergo many changes between childhood and maturity.

VALUES PROMOTED BY PEER CULTURE

The limited number of studies at present available shedding light on children's and youth's value systems seem to indicate that the most admired qualities in the preadolescent boys are competence and leadership in group games, fearlessness and daring. To win the approval of the peer group it is better to be aggressive, boisterous and not too tidy, than to be submissive, extremely reserved or too clean. Boys who are enthusiastic, happy, fun-loving and "good sports" are preferred to those who are sulky, shy and timid, impudent, and hard to get along with. Interestingly enough, many characteristics which constitute a problem for the teacher, such as restlessness, talkativeness and attention-getting, are often associated in preadolescence with traits highly admired by the peer group.

In adolescence the value system of boys still places great stress on physical prowess, skill in athletics and self-assertiveness, but in this period such qualities as ease and poise, personableness and

---

[1] Communications Research 1948–1949, edited by Paul Lazarsfeld and Frank Stanton, New York: Harper & Brothers, 1949, pp. 26–27.

grooming (all particularly effective with the opposite sex) become equally important.

For girls the problem of adjustment to the changing values of the peer culture is more difficult than for boys. In preadolescence it is desirable to be friendly, pretty, tidy and quietly gracious. Enthusiasm, good humor and docility are also approved of. On the other hand, aggressive and boisterous behavior is disapproved of strongly by girls. A partial reversal of values occurs in adolescence. The "ladylike" design for status among peers is replaced by new patterns. One constellation is a somewhat aggressive, buoyant "good fellowship" with both boys and girls, in which dominating tendencies, previously frowned upon, now become desirable. Another constellation of traits, this one particularly attractive to boys, but not always appreciated by other girls, is the "glamor" type of a well-groomed, attractive, self-possessed and sophisticated personality.

There is at present little indication as to how certain intellectual, volitional and emotional qualities, such as imagination, aesthetic sensitivity, creativeness, etc., are rated by the peer group. What is known about the peer culture suggests that it favors the normal as against the unusual personality, the attractive as against the outstanding, the likeable and pleasant as against the strong-willed and independent. Since participation in group life is expected, while withdrawal on any grounds arouses suspicion and is an offense in the eyes of the peers, sociability appears to rank higher than individuality. In this situation, not a few youngsters whose personality characteristics and conduct go beyond the tolerance level of the peer group are likely to suffer social neglect and isolation.

PARENTS' AND TEACHERS' ATTITUDES TOWARD PEER CULTURE

The difficulties confronting youth in trying to meet the exacting demands of the peer culture are intensified by the failure of adults to understand the complexity of this adolescent problem. Attitudes of parents toward the peer group and its culture alternate between approval and alarm. Parents want their children to be popular and accepted by other children, and they show the keenest interest in the way the child manages his peer relations. Many parents tend even to regard the success of their children in the peer group as a true measure of their own success in the parental role. Along with this, however, goes a certain anxiety that some of the apparently irresponsible "good time" activities of youth may lead them to forsake the more serious interests, and the obligations to do satisfactory work in school.

There are also other reasons why peer culture is likely to result in conflicts between parent and child. While parents often urge the adolescent to stand on his own feet, to assume greater responsibility for his actions and to demonstrate his independence, they become irritated when in seeking self-direction a child defies parental authority, or turns away from parental ideas, beliefs, and sometimes ways of living, to gain acceptance by his peer group. Furthermore, some parents are at a loss to understand the vacillating behavior of the rebellious child who, while he takes most of his cues from his peers, will still at times seek parental advice, protection and reassurance. Finally, many parents, bewildered by new ideas on how to bring up children, and confused by the incongruity of their own habits and beliefs in a rapidly changing society, are too often apt to be intolerant of changing attitudes and standards in their offspring.

Teachers, also, fail frequently to grasp the complexity of peer relations. Sociometric studies have shown that teachers tend to confuse the social adjustment between children with the social adjustment between children and adults. It was found that children most liked in class by teachers are not always highly regarded by their peers, while pupils teachers prefer least are often popular with their peers. Indicative of the lack of orientation in peer values is the known fact that teachers' judgments of the social adjustment of pupils show a declining accuracy from kindergarten to the seventh grade.

Educational Implications of Peer Culture

The implications of the material just presented confirm the desirability and soundness of many accepted educational practices such as school assemblies, student councils, social clubs, social parties, etc. All of these activities offer opportunities for children to gain acceptance and status in the peer group. If anything, such activities should be more widely spread and regarded as an integral part of the school curriculum and not as extra.

But in dealing with peer groups it is worth remembering that they are not an unmixed blessing, for they carry potentialities for both good and bad influence. The school will do well to use the powerful group forces in fostering among young boys and girls socially desirable habits, attitudes and relations. Yet, at the same time, the school has the responsibility to counteract the ill effects of complete submission to peer pressure, whenever independent judgment, conduct and action on the part of an individual child is warranted.

Experience of various schools has shown that peer groups can be effectively used in combatting juvenile delinquency. Similarly it was found that codes of behavior cooperatively drawn up by parents, faculty members and teen-agers are faithfully observed by the boys and girls when such norms become accepted as peer group standards. It is perhaps not too far-fetched to assume, for instance, that the pressure of peer groups could be mobilized against irresponsible driving of cars. Some states are already making extensive use of student schoolbus drivers with highly satisfactory results. As reported, these student drivers have maintained an enviable safety record.

Peer groups frequently tend to favor aggressive, shocking and irresponsible behavior. Turning a corner in a car on two wheels, or staying out late at night, or being impudent to parents and teachers is often a required practice. Yet these same peer groups, once they have accepted different standards, will with equal success teach boys and girls habits of responsible and socially desirable conduct.

The challenge to the teachers, then, is to recognize the power of the peer group over its members and to harness that power for educationally useful purposes. At times this may require injecting new and more desirable values into the peer culture. But if this attempt is successful, forceful pressures stemming from the peer group will support educational efforts to change the behavior of individual boys and girls.

——▶ **Raymond G. Kuhlen
and Beatrice J. Lee**

Personality Characteristics
and Social Acceptability
in Adolescence[1]

From *Psychological Studies of Human Development,* edited by Raymond G. Kuhlen and George G. Thompson. Copyright, 1952, Appleton-Century-Crofts, Inc. Reprinted by permission of the publishers and Warwick & York, Inc.

It is evident that at any age an acceptable social status is an important requisite for satisfactory personal and social adjustment. Lack of such status frequently makes for misery and unhappiness; whereas attainment of status once lacking may produce marked changes in an individual's personality and feelings of well-being. Inasmuch as emerging interest in social relationships, especially heterosexual relationships, seems particularly characteristic of adolescence, problems of attaining and maintaining social status may be of greater importance at that age.

The purpose of the present study was to obtain measures of social acceptability at different ages through the adolescent period, and also to get judgments from the associates of the subjects as to their personal characteristics. By examination of these data, it was hoped that some new insights into social development in adolescence might be gained, and some evidence obtained as to what particular personal characteristics are associated with, and hence might conceivably foster, social acceptability at these ages.

---

1 Adapted and abridged from R. G. Kuhlen and Beatrice J. Lee, "Personality Characteristics and Social Acceptability in Adolescence," *Journal of Educational Psychology,* 1943, Vol. 34, pp. 321–340. (With permission of the publisher, Warwick & York.)

PROCEDURE

In obtaining the data two instruments were used. The first was a "Guess Who" test. Its purpose was to obtain information regarding the personalities of the children, and contained some forty items asking for nominations of children who fit particular desriptions, such as "Here is someone who is always cheerful, jolly and good-natured, laughs and smiles a good deal." Descriptions were always in pairs representing polar traits. Thus the mate to the above sample item was: "Here is someone who always seems rather sad, worried or unhappy, who hardly ever laughs or smiles." Similar descriptive statements were presented representing the twenty pairs of characteristics listed below:[2]

Restless—Quiet

Talkative—Silent

Active in games—Not active in games

Enjoys jokes—Does not enjoy jokes

Friendly—Not friendly

Sociable—Not sociable

Initiates games and activities—Follows in activities

Enjoys a fight—Does not enjoy a fight

Willing to take a chance—Unwilling to take a chance

Neat—Unkempt

Girl likes opposite sex—Girl avoids opposite sex

Boy likes opposite sex—Boy avoids opposite sex

Enjoys jokes on self—Does not enjoy jokes on self

Acts older than age—Acts younger than age

Seeks attention—Does not seek attention

Popular with others—Unpopular with others

Cheerful and happy—Sad and unhappy

Goodlooking—Not goodlooking

Enthusiastic—Listless

Always bossing others—Does not mind being bossed

The second instrument was devised for the purpose of determining social acceptability. This blank contained directions asking each child to indicate first and second choices of companions for: (1) occupying the next seat in the classroom, (2) attending

---

[2] Such tests can be "scored," but the comparisons reported in this paper concerned only the percentages of various groups receiving *any mention at all* for a given trait.

the movies, (3) going for a walk, (4) going skating, (5) making things as model boats, dresses, etc., (6) playing outdoor games, (7) playing indoor games, (8) studying school work, (9) reading for fun. The only restriction was that the choices must be made from the subject's own grade, not necessarily his own classroom. Any individual could be chosen as many times as desired. An "acceptability" score for each individual was arrived at by weighting first choices 2, second choices 1, and dividing their sum by the number of potential raters. Several mentions of a particular child by the same person received the same weight as an equal number of mentions by different children.[3] As used in this report "social acceptability" means social acceptability among one's own sex. Scores were determined in this manner, because it was observed that a certain individual might be exceedingly popular with his own sex but be chosen by none of the opposite sex. In other instances, indivduals were popular with both sexes. It was deemed better to have the scores mean the same thing in the case of each individual, hence the restriction to popularity among one's own sex.

Subjects

Seven hundred children were studied—over one hundred of each sex in each of grades VI, IX, and XII. The sample included all of the sixth-, ninth-, and twelfth-graders in four centralized schools and the twelfth-graders in two similar schools, all in central New York. The mean ages in years of the three grade groups studied were as follows: Boys, 11.9, 14.7, 17.4; Girls, 11.6, 14.3, 17.3.

Social Acceptability at Grades VI, IX, and XII

One of the most striking trends evident in the data is the increase in heterosexual relationships as age increases. Among the

---

[3] Reliability of such measures of social acceptability seems good. C. W. Hunnicutt, of Syracuse University, for example, used a very similar blank and found that for five groups of sixth-graders, about thirty children to a group, the reliability coefficients based on tests ten days apart were .88, .86, .89, .85, and .92, respectively.

sixth-graders less than a third are chosen by members of the opposite sex, but by the twelfth grade almost two-thirds are so chosen. A count was also made of those who chose members of the opposite sex. Forty-five per cent of boys and 39 per cent of girls at the sixth-grade level chose members of the opposite sex, and by the twelfth grade 75 and 63 per cent of boys and girls respectively chose opposite sex companions. Most of this increase occurred between grades six and nine. Sex differences are also apparent, the boys choosing the opposite sex more frequently. Inasmuch as this finding differs from what might be expected in view of data on comparative age of sexual maturing of the sexes, it should be pointed out that the subjects had been asked to restrict their choices to their own grade levels. Since girls tend to prefer older associates, while boys prefer associates of their own ages, the girls may have chosen boys less frequently under the conditions of this study than would have been the case if they had had unrestricted choice. That this is the case is suggested by the fact that girls, but not boys, frequently made notations, such as "He's not in this grade," or "Not a sixth-grader," on their response blanks. Also girls may be more reticent than boys in recording opposite sex choices.

The emerging interest in the opposite sex thus demonstrated can be put into proper developmental perspective if viewed in the light of other facts regarding social relationships. Moreno found that first-graders, but not sixth-graders, chose the opposite sex with fair frequency; the trend from the first to the sixth grade was one of decreasing choice of the opposite sex. Data of other investigators have called attention to the so-called "gang age" which seems to occur typically just prior to pubescence. At this age youngsters tend to associate primarily with their own sex. Thus the general picture of development through the school years is one of association with the opposite sex in early childhood, a gradual withdrawal from opposite-sex contacts in late childhood, and then an emerging interest in heterosexual relationships as development proceeds into adolescence. It is noteworthy that heterosexual adjustment is far from general even in the twelfth grade. Under the conditions of this study, over 35 per cent were chosen by none of the opposite sex and over 25 per cent made no choice of the opposite sex. A somewhat different picture might be obtained if no restrictions were placed on choices.

Though most children are chosen by some one of their classmates for some activity, in every grade there are individual instances which amount to social tragedy. Each child was asked to choose individuals for nine activities, actually to make eighteen choices, yet from 2 to 5 per cent of these children were chosen by no one. Undoubtedly these children, and others chosen only infrequently, represent cases in serious need of attention if social adjustment is to be fostered.

CHANGES IN PERSONALITY DURING ADOLESCENCE

The basic data to be considered here are judgments of youngsters by their associates. Sixth-graders rated sixth-graders; ninth-graders rated ninth-graders; and personality characteristics of twelfth-graders were judged by twelfth-graders. This is an important fact to keep in mind because rating devices measure the raters as well as ratees. Some of the differences to be pointed out below may be due to differences in sensitivity of the age groups to various traits as well as to differences in the degree to which a given trait is present at any age. Since a trait can have no great social significance unless associates can recognize it and respond to it, the differences to be presented likely represent genuine personality differences between age groups, whether the characteristics are inherent in the rater or in the ratee.

Perhaps the simplest way of portraying the age trends and sex differences that exist in the present data is to indicate the percentage of each group mentioned as evidencing a particular characteristic. Since the forty items were in polar pairs, this can be accomplished by indicating the percentages evidencing one characteristic of each of the pairs. Instead, for example, of presenting the data for both "Restless" and "Quiet" (the first pair of items), we have chosen for convenience to give only the facts for "Restless," and in the tables have indicated the percentage of each group who received *any mention at all*[4] as evidencing that characteristic.

Table 1 contains the essential findings in this phase of the study. Boys appear to have changed a statistically significant[5] degree in five characteristics. As the age of the groups increases, boys are more frequently mentioned as liking the opposite sex, enjoying jokes on self, being popular with others, being willing to take a chance, and as being enthusiastic. Increasing sensitivity to social situations and increasing social activity are implied in these trends. Girls gained in judged interest in the opposite sex; but beyond this, they showed only slight or no change in those characteristics which changed reliably for boys. Girls apparently became less interested in active games with development into adolescence.

In the last three columns of Table 1, the results have been presented in such a way as to focus attention upon sex differences. At all ages, boys were judged more frequently than girls to be restless, talkative, active in games, to enjoy a joke, to enjoy fighting, to be willing to take a chance, and to seek attention. Conversely, girls were either mentioned more frequently than boys for the opposite extreme of these characteristics, or tended not to be mentioned at all. At each grade level girls were judged more frequently than boys to act older than their ages. This last point is interesting in connection with the usual view of the earlier emotional and social maturity of girls. Interestingly enough, in spite of this finding, girls are not judged to show greater and earlier interest in the opposite sex, though one analysis of the data did suggest this to be true.

Certain interesting trends are apparent in the sex differences. With increased age there is increasing divergence between the sexes with respect to activity in games and willingness to take a chance, boys showing increasingly greater activity and greater

---

[4] Unless counterbalanced by an equal or greater number of mentions for the other extreme of the pair.

[5] CR's of 2.0 or more, indicating chances of a true difference existing to be some ninety-eight out of one hundred in repetitions of the study with similar populations, have been taken in this investigation as indicative of statistical reliability.

TABLE 1

CHANGES IN PERSONAL CHARACTERISTICS DURING ADOLESCENCE AS
INDICATED BY THE PERCENTAGE OF EACH GRADE GROUP WHO WERE
JUDGED BY THEIR ASSOCIATES AS EVIDENCING CERTAIN CHARACTERISTICS

	Boys				Girls				Sex Differences*		
	VI	IX	XII	CR 6–12	VI	IX	XII	CR 6–12	VI	IX	XII
Restless	50	50	42	1.3	30	21	23	1.3	20*	29*	19*
Talkative	50	48	58	1.2	33	32	37	0.4	17	16	21*
Active in Games ..	57	51	53	0.6	43	32	28	2.5	14	19*	25*
Enjoys Jokes	58	57	64	0.9	37	40	39	0.3	21*	17	25*
Friendly	50	51	56	0.7	53	60	55	0.2	−3	−9	1
Sociable	51	47	48	0.5	49	62	52	0.5	3	−15	−4
Initiates Games and Activities	36	31	44	1.2	36	41	27	1.4	0	−10	17
Enjoys a Fight	61	51	52	1.3	22	21	26	0.8	39*	30*	26*
Willing to Take a Chance	43	53	65	2.8	37	42	34	0.5	9	11	31*
Neat and Clean	41	52	50	1.1	66	61	61	0.8	−15	−9	−11
Likes Opposite Sex	30	36	53	3.5	27	40	55	4.5	3	−4	−2
Enjoys Joke on Self	37	43	57	3.1	35	48	45	1.5	2	−5	12
Acts Older than Age	22	28	32	1.7	39	45	47	1.2	−17	−17	−15
Seeks Attention	39	38	40	0.1	27	26	28	0.2	12	12	12
Popular with Others	41	52	65	3.6	48	52	49	0.2	−7	0	16
Cheerful and Happy	50	58	60	1.5	53	60	50	0.4	−3	−2	10
Good-looking	33	38	36	0.5	38	50	39	0.1	−5	−12	−3
Enthusiastic	47	53	60	2.0	48	52	53	0.8	−1	1	7
Bosses Others	25	43	30	0.8	42	37	35	1.0	−17	6	−5
No. of Cases	109	120	108	...	120	124	119				

* Numbers represent difference between sex-pairs of columns in the table. A minus
value indicates girls were more frequently mentioned than boys for a particular trait.
Differences marked with an asterisk are three or more times their standard errors; differences printed in italics are between two and three times their standard errors.

daring as compared with girls as age increases. The data also suggest that as age increases boys take over domination of the adolescent social scene. While at the sixth-grade level girls receive

more mention than do boys as being popular with others, at the twelfth-grade level the boys are mentioned much more often than are girls. Further interesting evidences of a sex shift in social initiative with increased age are apparent. At the sixth grade, the sexes are mentioned with equal frequency as "Initiating games and activities"; at the ninth grade the girls are more frequently mentioned (CR 1.7); but at the twelfth grade boys seem to have taken over social initiative with a sex difference that is statistically reliable. Also at the ninth grade, girls are judged (reliably) more frequently to be "sociable," but at the other grades no sex difference exists. This seems to bear out the earlier suggestion that with progress through adolescence boys gradually become the dominant sex socially. The superiority of girls in sociability and in social initiative at the ninth grade may be associated with their earlier pubescence. At this age girls tend to be taller and more fully developed than boys, who on the average reach pubescence later than the ninth grade.

Personality Characteristics and Social Acceptability

A third aspect of the study has to do with the relationship between personality characteristics and social acceptability. What personality characteristics are the most popular individuals judged to have, and what are deemed to be the characteristics of the least popular? When interpreting the data here presented it should be pointed out that judgments of characteristics were obtained first, and after these papers were collected choices were made as to desirable companions. A reversal of this procedure might have created a greater "halo effect" than probably already exists. Also, it should be remembered that here "social acceptability" means social acceptability among one's own sex.

The plan in this phase of the study was to set up for each sex and grade two groups composed of the 25 per cent most popular and the 25 per cent least popular subjects from each school, and to contrast these extreme groups in terms of the characteristics on which judgments had been obtained. The figures in Table 2 represent, for the two sexes, the difference between the percentage of the highly acceptable group and the percentage of the least acceptable group who received some mention by their associates as evidencing various selected characteristics. Thus, for the sixth grade boys the 28 represents the difference between 32 per cent of the best-liked boys and 60 per cent of the least-liked who were rated as being restless. This difference is 2.1 times its standard error and thus is starred. The remainder of the Table is to be read in similar fashion.

TABLE 2

DIFFERENCES BETWEEN PERCENTAGE OF SOCIALLY ACCEPTED AND SOCIALLY UNACCEPTED CHILDREN IN VARIOUS GRADES WHO WERE THOUGHT BY THEIR CLASSMATES TO POSSESS VARIOUS TRAITS. MINUS DIFFERENCES SHOW TRAITS TO BE MORE CHARACTERISTIC OF UNACCEPTED; PLUS DIFFERENCES SHOW TRAITS TO CHARACTERIZE THE ACCEPTED. NOTE TRENDS THROUGH ADOLESCENT PERIOD.

Traits	Boys' Grades			Girls' Grades		
	6	9	12	6	9	12
Restless	−28*	0	+19	−31*	−14	+25*
Talkative	− 4	+14	+50	− 3	+23	+31*
Acts Older Than Age	+12	+20	+ 4	+17	+17	−25
Good Looking	+80*	+50*	+54*	+73*	+53*	+42*
Enthusiastic	+92*	+76	+77*	+80*	+60*	+69*
Active in Games	+76*	+50*	+38*	+45*	+40*	+52*
Bosses Others	0	+ 3	+19	0	+17	+31
Enjoys Jokes	+44*	+47*	+50*	+42*	+53*	+65*
Enjoys Joke on Self	+76*	+50*	+62*	+65*	+37*	+62*
Number of cases in each extreme group	25	30	26	29	30	29

* Asterisks mark differences larger than two times their standard error.

It will be noted that in spite of the few cases in the extreme groups, most differences are strikingly large and highly reliable statistically. To use as examples those traits that show greatest differentiation for both sexes and at all grades (all traits mentioned are not listed in the table), it is apparent that the highly accepted person is one who is judged to be popular with others, to be cheerful and happy, to be enthusiastic, to be friendly, to enjoy jokes, and to initiate games and activities. It is also interesting to note that at all ages those who are highly accepted by their own sex, were judged also to like the opposite sex.

A number of writers have recently emphasized the importance in adjustment through adolescence of changing values as to what traits are socially important. At one age a person may have those characteristics that make for popularity at that age and be very popular, but a year or more later may show a marked loss in popularity because new traits have assumed importance in the eyes of his age mates—traits which that person may not then possess. Thus age trends, such as are apparent in the present data, may assume considerable importance. Among items showing such trends are "talkative," "seeking attention," "bossing others," and "restless." Of these the first three do not differentiate between the highly acceptable and those not accepted at the sixth grade, but do differentiate at the twelfth grade. The agreement between the sexes adds to the degree of confidence that can be placed in the statistical reliability of these trends. In the case of restlessness, it is noteworthy that a reversal has occurred. At the sixth-grade level a reliably larger proportion of the socially "unaccepted" group were judged to be restless, but by the twelfth-grade level the "popular" group were more often judged to be restless. Again, the same trends are apparent in both sex groups. It would seem from these findings that at the twelfth-grade level, more than at the sixth-grade, the highly accepted adolescent tends to be the active, socially aggressive extrovert.

Other age trends are apparent in the data, though only these characteristics differentiate reliably at all ages. For both sexes, good looks seem less markedly associated with acceptability as age increases. For boys, activity in games does not differentiate between the acceptable and those not accepted as well at the twelfth-grade as at the sixth-grade level. On the other hand, liking the opposite sex seemed to bear a closer relationship at adolescence than earlier. For girls, enjoying a joke and being sociable are associated with acceptability at all ages, but more clearly later in adolescence. Again, the increased importance in adolescence of active social participation and greater social sensitivity, such as responding to humor, is suggested.

——▶ **Harold R. Phelps
and John E. Horrocks**

Factors Influencing Informal Groups of Adolescents

From *Child Development*, March, 1958, No. 1, 29:69–86. Reprinted by permission of the authors and the Society for Research in Child Development.

It has been the purpose of this study to investigate attitudes and activities that lead to the formation of informal adolescent groups. A large portion of adolescent social life is organized around small informal groups. Such groups are the proving ground for the teen-ager's widening perception of his social role and the exploration of techniques to implement that role. The informal group plays a much more important part in the life of the adolescent than do formally organized groups and may be thought of as a focal area of experience in the process of coming of age. Observation of informal adolescent groups leads to the conclusion that while the group is more or less ephemeral in its membership and continuity it does center around certain commonalities possessed by its members. Membership is usually exclusive in that some youth are excluded or are made to feel uncomfortable when participating in the group's activities. An understanding of adolescent behavior would be advanced by an analysis of the kinds of activities and attitudes important in the formation and perpetuation of such groups with particular reference to those things which contrast one group to another as well as to the commonalities which bind them all together as part of the larger adolescent age peer society.

SUBJECTS

The 200 subjects for the present study were obtained from the 800 children enrolled in grades 7 through 12 in the public and parochial schools of a central Ohio community of approximately 9,500 persons. The 200 comprised a sample drawn randomly from among 726 children, stratified according to grade, who filled out the questionnaire on which this study was partly based and for whom comprehensive personal information was available. Most of the youth in the study lived in the city although a few commuted to school from the surrounding rural area.

PROCEDURE

All 800 children in grades 7 through 12 were administered a questionnaire entitled *Recreation in Your Community*. Of the 800 questionnaires given to students, 726 were returned. The questionnaire was omnibus in type. Six major areas of information were investigated as follows: (a) identification of the children by name, age, sex, grade in school, address, and other data of similar nature; (b) location and identification of informal adolescent groups by asking each subject to give names and other identifying characteristics of his favorite group or groups; (c) information concerning group attitudes, such as inclusiveness and exclusiveness, group ideals, and estimated group reactions toward samples of typical adolescent behavior; (d) measurement of the subject's feelings toward his own group and toward other groups with which he was acquainted; (e) naming of the activities and meeting places of the groups identified; (f) measurement of each subject's satisfaction with his groups and their activities.

In its final form the questionnaire[1] consisted of six sections named as follows: (a) What you would like to do for recreation,

---

[1] A detailed discussion of the questionnaire and its construction will be presented in a forthcoming article by Horrocks and Bowlus.

(b) Your group, (c) How do you feel about your group? (d) Whom you like in your group, (e) What your group does, and (f) Where your group goes.

Wherever possible check type questions were used. Considerable effort was made to make the questionnaire interesting to those who were asked to fill it out. Among other devices intended to achieve interest, the questionnaire was illustrated with line drawings. Every effort was made to refer to the respondent as an individual and to make him feel that the study was really interested in, and highly valued, his opinions. This was done, in part, by directing the questions to the individual, by using personal pronouns, and by heading each group of questions by personal reference statements such as "Your Group." With the cooperation of community authorities it was also possible to promise children who answered the questionnaire that recreational needs revealed by their answers would, whenever possible, be incorporated in the recreational programs of the schools and other community agencies.[2] Questionnaires were filled in and left in the local school offices in envelopes marked "confidential." Subjects were assured that their questionnaires would be available to no one in their community.

In addition to the information obtained by the questionnaire the following data on each subject were available: (a) socioeconomic status based on Warner's Index of Status Characteristics [12], and (b) intelligence as recorded in the local school records.

Analysis of the Data

Of major concern in designing this study was the selection of a technique of statistical analysis which would allow all data equal opportunity of influencing the final outcome of the study. Multiple factor analysis appeared the best technique to meet this criterion. However, from the questionnaire and socioeconomic

---

[2] At the end of the study, through cooperation with the City Recreation Commission and the public schools, a number of the children's desires as revealed by the questionnaire were taken into consideration in planning the community's recreational program.

data of the present study there were 168 items to be treated as separate variables. This would have made it necessary to start the analysis with 14,028 correlation coefficients in the factor matrix. Under the circumstances it was decided to use the Wherry-Gaylord [13] method of obtaining oblique factors by iteration utilizing easily computed tetrachoric correlation coefficients.[3]

One hundred and fourteen variables concerning attitudes and activities were subjected to the Wherry-Gaylord method of analysis. To make computation of the tetrachoric correlations simpler, 200 cases of the original 726 were selected randomly, stratified according to grade in school. In this way simple frequencies could be read as percentages in the calculation of the tetrachoric coefficients of correlation. From this analysis emerged 10 oblique factors. Loadings on each of the 10 oblique factors were computed for the variables which had not been included in the first analysis.

By means of a modification[4] of the Doolittle solution for solving simultaneous equations, the oblique factors were rotated to orthogonality. Loadings for all variables on the newly obtained orthogonal factors were computed. These orthogonal factors were rotated visually, attempting (a) to maximize the loadings of variables on the factor to which they appeared to belong, and (b) to minimize their loadings on all other factors. Ultimately, however, the criterion for rotation was meaningfulness. It was believed that mathematically neater categories are of little value if they do not make sense psychologically.

INTERPRETATION OF FACTORS

Ten factors emerged from the factor analysis and were labeled I through X. Although loadings of .20 or more were significant at the 1 per cent level of confidence, none below .25 was included

---

[3] The tables for this study were so extensive that it was impractical to include them in the present publication. They have been mimeographed and may be obtained by writing either of the authors.

[4] Obtained from Dr. Robert J. Wherry, The Ohio State University.

in the interpretation. Loadings lower than .25 were omitted because it was believed that their inclusion would interfere with interpretation to a greater degree than the amount they might add to the meaning of a factor. Since all variables were treated as dichotomies their names were changed in the interpretation so that most loadings on the factor being considered were positive. Such positive loadings made interpretation of the factors less complicated and more meaningful.

Factor I

Factor I depended to a very considerable extent on having automobile transportation available, being able to get around freely in the community, and going a considerable distance outside the small city in which the present study was carried out. Adolescents scoring high on Factor I liked riding around in cars (.75),[5] preferred people who had cars (.56), frequently went to a large city (.62) about 25 miles distant, and expressed a desire to leave town to have a good time (.52, .54).[6] A water gym (.36) with picnic grounds attached where there was considerably less supervision than at the city swimming pool was patronized. This recreational facility was located about three miles from the small city. Walking around town (.48) and window shopping (.62) were popular activities. The bowling alley (.69) was a favorite meeting place.

Much activitiy involved going to various establishments serving food. Enjoyment of eating in restaurants (.65) was expressed, but this was by no means the only reason for patronizing them since sitting or talking in restaurants (.49) was frequently listed as an activity. Drive-in type restaurants were preferred (.79, .70), and one about three quarters of a mile outside of town (.53) was frequently mentioned. Four ordinary eating places (.57, 51, .51, .42) any several dairy bars (.53, .43, .42, .37) were also named.

---

[5] Numbers with decimal points in front of them enclosed in parentheses are factor loadings of the variable immediately preceding them on the factor being discussed.

[6] Two items expressed essentially the same idea.

Having dates (.70) was important to young people scoring high on Factor I. They preferred people in their group who liked to date (.57) and were not likely to disapprove of people in the group who "neck" (.29) and "park" (.29). They liked to go to a drive-in theatre (.58) about one and a half miles outside the city. They also liked to go to regular movie theatres (.43). Most often the favorite group named was heterosexual in its make-up (.64). The groups sometimes went to an old, abandoned slate pit (.34). Most frequent time of meeting was on Sundays (.38) and at night (.28).

Activities appealing to adolescents scoring high on Factor I were playing cards (.26), listening to the radio (.42), watching television (.29), and having parties (.26). They liked to play baseball (.32). It did not seem to matter much to them if members of the group smoked (.40) or were not of the same age (.28), but they tended to prefer that members of the group not be colored (.28).

Young people influenced by Factor I were likely to be 17 years of age or older (.57) and to be no younger than 14 (.56). They were for the most part members of grades 11 and 12 (.53), and there was some tendency for seventh graders (.38) *not* to show the influence of the factor. There was some evidence that adolescents of IQ 111 or better (.28) whose fathers were in the upper occupations (.28) and whose families were of upper socioeconomic status (.26) were *not* likely to name a group influenced by the factor.

The satisfaction of heterosexual interests and a desire for peer-group activities not associated with the home were important pressures in this factor. None of the activities named was home-centered or home-influenced to any great degree. Associated with extra-home interests appeared a need for ranging about and going some distance from the community for social participation. It seems reasonable to assume that the forces underlying Factor I are a combination of pressures leading to the assumption of an adult role. Certainly, getting away from the influence of the home and ranging over territory farther and farther away from home and community are important aspects of becoming an adult in the American culture. Of equal importance in becoming an adult are the physiological and social pressures which culminate in sexual mating.

It is of interest that lower socioeconomic status and lower intelligence were somewhat associated with Factor I. One expects adolescents whose parents have limited financial resources to assume the adult role sooner than those whose parents are more comfortably fixed. Previous studies have established that earlier emancipation from home, earlier assumptions of the adult role, and greater sex activity are associated to some degree with lower socioeconomic status.

It is proposed that the present factor be described as a: *Pattern of pressures leading to assumption of the adult role, emancipation from the home, and satisfaction of heterosexual interests.*

Factor II

One variable stood out markedly in this factor. People who sometimes cheat to get by (.86) were not acceptable to groups influenced by Factor II. There were many behaviors which were thought to be inappropriate for group members. People who gamble (.57), smoke (.57), tell off-color jokes (.44), "park" (.44), "neck" (.43), ride motorcycles (.40), are noisy (.38), swear (.32), and race cars (.31) were not acceptable. It was preferred that members of the group be persons of about the same age (.30), who have a good reputation (.36), nearly always agree (.34), and think good manners are important (.32). They thought that it was important for members to go to church (.30) but it was *not* important whether they went to churches other than their own (.30). Playing cards (.28) tended to be a rejected activity. There was a tendency to reject those who lived in the best part of town (.28).

There was much evidence that both home and school were forces in producing Factor II. Adolescents were preferred in the group who did not get in trouble with teachers (.57), did not quit school (.42), and were good students (.33). In relation to family matters, they expressed a preference for people who "stick-up" for their families (.48) and usually mind their parents (.28). The groups frequently met at places which were either part of the school or sponsored by the school. The assembly at high school (.54), noon movies at school (.52), and the high school stadium

(.27) were favored places to go. They went to school athletic events (.34) together. One of the elementary school grounds (.42) located in a better part of town was a meeting place, and they patronized a recreation center (.31) sponsored by the school and located in one of the elementary school buildings.

Groups influenced by Factor II frequently went to the city swimming pool (.53) and liked to go swimming together (.28). They went together to movie theatres (.51), but tended to avoid the drive-in theatre (.31) so popular with adolescent groups identified with Factor I. Bicycle riding (.45) and hiking (.27) were favored physical activities, but it was likely that groups influenced by the factor would not play baseball (.25). They sometimes watched television (.26).

They patronized a hamburger "joint" (.40) in the business district, but tended to avoid a dairy bar (.39) also avoided by adolescent groups influenced by Factors III and V. One of the best restaurants in town (.26) most popular with adolescents of high socioeconomic status influenced by Factor V and avoided by those of low socioeconomic status reacting to the pressures of Factor IV was a meeting place for the Factor II group. They expressed a mild interest in sitting in restaurants and talking (.26).

Adolescents naming groups scoring high on Factor II were likely to be in the eighth grade (.38) and to come from families who obtained high, composite, socioeconomic ratings (.31). Their fathers tended to be employed in an upper socioeconomic occupation (.26).

With the high concentration of variables indicating disapproval for behavior and attitudes which are generally considered to be socially unacceptable, it may be hypothesized that Factor II has to do with a moralistic point of view or a need to conform to certain social standards. The fact that many of the activities were connected with school, that there was a moderately high loading on identification with persons and activities having upper socioeconomic status, and an emphasis upon family loyalty suggests that the pressures behind this factor may be largely those induced by an upper socioeconomic home and school companions from homes of such status. One inconsistency was the appearance of a loading, however small, on the rejection variable for those who live in the best part of town. Such inconsistency might possibly be explained as a simple stereotype and expression of the belief that one should not overtly choose one's friends on the basis of their living in the best part of town. Although loadings on this factor were relatively low on variables having to do with church, there is some reason to believe that Factor II may be fostered by religious background since many of the values held by young people scoring high in this factor are characteristic of numerous religious groups.

Factor II is designated as follows: *Pattern of pressures assuming the form of a moral code approved by the school and upper socio-economic home.*

Factor III

Very prominent in Factor III were variables having to do with going to business establishments where ice cream and other dairy bar products might be purchased. Going to three dairy parlors had loadings in the .60's. Two of the dairy bars had no provision for remaining after the purchase had been made. For some reason which the writers were unable to determine, one dairy bar was rejected with a negative loading of .33.

Noticeable were variables related to school life such as going to school affairs (.46), studying together (.52), going to the public library (.48), to school lunch room (.39), and assembly at the high school (.39).

There were many activities included in the factor. Those with highest loadings were having picnics (.61), listening to the radio (.59) and records (.57), bicycle riding (.57), making candy (.56), playing cards (.59), roller skating (.55), and playing volley ball (52). Having parties, watching television, walking around town, swimming and tennis had loadings in the .40's. Only one activity was rejected and that was playing baseball with a negative loading of .32.

Groups scoring high on Factor III were likely to have seven or more adolescents in them (.35) and tended to be named more often by girls (.37). Young people naming groups high in this factor were likely to be in the eighth grade (.27), preferred the group they named (.28), and have fathers in the middle occupational classification (.26). Whether or not the person lived in the best part of town (.29) or wanted to quit school (.36) did not seem to matter.

It is very likely that this factor represents a cluster of activities around which some informal groups are organized. Most of the activities are ones which would generally be approved by teachers and parents. In contrast with Factor I all of the activities are ones which can be carried on within a relatively short radius of the home. In fact, all could be done within the small community in which the study was carried out.

Perhaps Factor III is the result of supervision exercised by the family forcing the adolescent to engage in activities which may be carried out not too far distant from home or under the surveillance of responsible adults. This would appear to be a logical conclusion particularly since girls who are supervised much more closely in our culture had a relatively large loading (.37) on this factor. It is therefore proposed that Factor III be named: *Non-emancipated, home, school, and community centered activity pattern.*

Factor IV

Adolescents preferring a group characterized by behaviors and characteristics associated with Factor IV were most likely to be of low socioeconomic status. Their families very often received a composite, socioeconomic rating (.38) placing them in the lowest category. They lived in the poorest housing (.40) located in the poorest sections of the city (.31). It was quite unlikely that any of their fathers were to be found in occupations rated among those in the highest category (.41) utilized in the present study. There was a trend for them to have an IQ on group tests of intelligence less than 89 (.25).

They appeared to make discriminations concerning group membership along socioeconomic lines. It was preferred that group members' fathers be laborers (.89) and they were likely to reject people who lived in the best part of town (.69) and had more money than most (.50). Persons who lived in the same neighborhood (.75) and were about the same age (.34) were preferred. They liked people who had high aspirations expressing a preference for those who wanted to go to college (.74) and worked after school (.60). Strength was important to them (.84).

It was important that group members go to church a lot (.50) and go to other churches (.85). What was meant by going to other churches is difficult to understand. Perhaps it was not particularly important what churches their group members attended, but that they go a lot to whatever church they preferred.

They thought that it was important that members of their group be in early at night (.56). Some value was placed on good looks (.29) and having a car (.25). People who were always kidding (.55) and nearly always agreed (.32) were liked. Colored young people were sometimes acceptable in their groups (.29). Frequently they made candy (.50) when they were together and went to an abandoned slate quarry (.43) located in a poorer section of the city. Roller skating (.41) was a popular activity, but there was a tendency for them not to go to movie theatres (.30) as a group.

One restaurant (.38) of very poor appearance, located in the business district, was popular. It was also popular with the adolescents of Factor I. Three dairy bars (.33, .30, .28) were sometimes patronized, one of which was popular with adolescents of Factors I and III, but avoided by those influenced by Factor V. One of the drive-in type was also popular with people influenced by Factor I. The remaining dairy-bar was popular in both Factors I and III.

Some restaurants were avoided. One (.40) of very modern appearance located in the business district and specializing in fancy candies was not patronized by young people influenced by this factor but was found desirable by the young people of Factors I, III, and V. The restaurant (.34) which was possibly the finest in the city and very popular with the upper socioeconomic adolescents of Factor V was also avoided.

Without question Factor IV was the result of socioeconomic differences which are reflected in the nature of the activities and attitudes finding their places in this category. There appeared to be identification with their socioeconomic peers and a rejection of others in more fortunate circumstances. Perhaps they sensed the social and economic differences between themselves and other adolescents and were trying to make up for them by having higher ideals as manifested by their attitude toward church attendance and their somewhat unrealistic aspiration of going to college. Lack of financial means must not have been the sole determiner of the kinds of activities they participated in for they were able to patronize several restaurants and dairy bars. It was significant, however, that they avoided to some extent places popular with young people of upper socioeconomic status.

It is proposed that Factor IV be considered a: *Pattern of activities and social values deriving from a very low socioeconomic status.*

Factor V

Groups influenced by Factor V were more often named by girls (.41) who did *not* live in the poorer sections of the community (.48) or whose fathers were *not* engaged in low status occupations (.43). They were more likely to have fathers in the highest status occupations (.34) and to live in the best part of town (.32). As a matter of fact, several of the socioeconomic variables had loadings ranging from .26 to .48, rather clearly indicating that adolescents scoring high on Factor V tended to come from upper socioeconomic homes and *not* from the lowest group in the community. There were no significant loadings on the middle group.

Adolescents scoring high on Factor V named groups with seven or more in them (.56). The activities most favored were having slumber parties (.78), going to two higher quality restaurants downtown (.75, .73), and one about three-fourths mile outside the community (.58) which required some kind of transportation to reach it. In general, they liked to eat (.39) and talk (.34) in restaurants but were likely to shun certain establishments serving dairy products (.40, .30, .25) which were popular with groups scoring high in Factors I and III.

They liked to dance (.53), make candy (.41), listen to records (.40), have parties (.66) and picnics (.53), and date (.50). Physical activities engaged in were tennis (.60), swimming (.44), and baseball (.35), but they tended *not* to participate in basketball (.32), hunting (.30), and football (.26). It was their preference that members of the group recognize the importance of good manners (.35) and like to date (.28). The groups named were likely to be of heterosexual composition (.29) and to some extent participate in the activities of riding in cars (.29), going out of town to have a good time (.27), and walking around town (.26). They were more likely to meet at night (.31) or in the afternoon (.25).

Many of their activities were related to the school. They studied together (.54), went to school affairs (.46), met in the hallways of the high school (.45), attended school athletics (.44), went to a school sponsored recreation center (.43), and met at the public library (.42). They preferred that their group members be of the type which would not quit school (.41). The adolescents naming this type of group were likely to be in grades 11 and 12 (.32) and to have IQ's above 111 (.32) and not below 89 (.34). Also, at school they attended movies together (.39) and met outside the school building (.35).

Dominant in this factor were socioeconomic variables. Many of the activities depended upon the adolescent's being a member of a family in average or better economic circumstances. There was a definite trend for adolescents from low socioeconomic level families *not* to designate this type of informal group as their favorite.

In Factor V there are evidences of a need to satisfy heterosexual interests and a need to participate in activities away from the home and community. However, many of the activities, such as having slumber parties, listening to records, having picnics, etc., suggest that approval of the family and ability of the parents to provide certain facilities were important influences. Worth noting is the fact that much activity involved the school.

Apparently Factor V involved a somewhat complex set of social relationships characteristic of upper socioeconomic adolescents in the last two grades of high school. Girls appeared to be most sensitive to the pattern of pressures resulting in Factor V.

It is proposed that this factor be briefly described as follows: *Pattern of pressures leading to the assumption of an upper socioeconomic, quasi-adult social role.*

Factor VI

Social conformity and a concern for appearances are central to Factor VI. Adolescents' groups influenced by this factor rejected people who ride motorcycles (.61), "park" (.52), make wisecracks (.48), desire to quit school (.38), and are noisy (.35). They tended to reject other adolescents who race cars (.29), smoke (.29) and "neck" (.25). A strong preference was expressed for persons who are good-looking (.55), are good students (.42), work after school (.39), and are of about the same age (.31). It was important that others in the group not be afraid of being different (.30). There was a tendency for them to like people who stick up for their family (.28), nearly always agree (.27), and dress neatly (.25).

Adolescents in groups scoring high on Factor VI went places together mostly associated with the school (.48, .29, .27) and a small dairy bar (.27). They participated in only two activities, volleyball (.39) and tennis (.26).

A concern for good appearance and the rejection of a noisy, show-off type of social role seems to typify Factor VI. Undoubtedly, pressures from the school and the home have much to do with the type of social conformity expressed by this factor. At first glance, the fact that a positive value was placed on "not afraid to be different" seems a contradiction. However, it is not uncommon for adults trying to produce conformity in adolescents to point out that if one wishes to amount to anything he must not be afraid of being different from other people.

It is therefore proposed that this factor be characterized as: *Pressures toward social conformity manifested by a concern for good appearances and rejection of a noisy, "show-off" type behavior.*

Factor VII

Groups scoring high on Factor VII frequented a water gym (.66) with picnicking facilities located about three miles outside the city and the city swimming pool (.26). They also liked to go to a partially abandoned amusement park (.61) at which a miniature golf course was still in operation. Restaurants (.54) were favorite places for congregating and they liked to sit and talk in them (.28). A dairy bar (.30) favored by adolescents scoring high on Factors I and III, but to some extent rejected by those scoring high on Factor V, was mildly popular. Groups of this type were most likely to be named by boys (.58).

As groups they participated in the sports of golf (.58), football (.57), basketball (.43), swimming (.34), tennis (.32), and wrestling (.25). They went fishing (52), hiking (47), and hunting (.44) together. They sometimes played pool (.47), but tended to reject the activity of making candy (.26).

There was some evidence that groups scoring high on this factor may have been influenced to some extent by the school. They preferred that their group members be popular in school (.60). A recreation center (.53) housed in a school was a popular meeting place and they sometimes met outside the high school building (.41). It is not clear whether they played together at the high school stadium (.43) or went there to view athletic events.

They liked members of their group to be good looking (.37), and to work after school (.30), but they did not care if they swore (.37), would fight (.29), or got in trouble with teachers (.27). Members were acceptable who were always "kidding" (.28), who "necked" (.26), and sometimes cheated (.26). It was not necessary that they dress neatly (.26).

The fact that groups influenced by Factor VII were most frequently named by boys and many of the activities engaged in by the groups are usually considered to be primarily of interest to males suggests that this factor may be largely the result of pressures involved in playing a masculine role. Many of the activities required that the adolescent have the freedom to move about and freedom from adult supervision frequently denied girls in our culture.

It is interesting that the groups named by adolescents scoring high on this factor were not necessarily unisexual in their composition. As a matter of fact, there was a 50-50 chance that the groups named were made up of both boys and girls. This suggests that some females may have been involved in this factor who were perhaps having difficulty in establishing their roles as feminine members of society. Worth noting also is the fact that no socioeconomic variables were related significantly to Factor VII. If this factor is an expression of the male role, apparently socioeconomic status has much less meaning for boys than it does for girls.

Factor VII gave some evidence of being positively related to the school, but some activities and values deemed quite important by the adolescents influenced by Factor II had negative loadings on Factor VII. Apparently, the adolescent male is allowed to hold some values contrary to those held by the school and upper socioeconomic families. Or perhaps, this is a manifestation of his rebellion against the restriction of such a moral code.

It is proposed that Factor VII be considered: *Pattern of pressures and needs involved in playing a masculine role.*

Factor VIII

Some kind of conformity seemed to be important in this factor. It was apparently necessary that members of the group strive to please parents and teachers. They preferred that their friends be good students (.43), plan on going to college (.36), and stay out of trouble with their teachers (.38). It was important that group members mind their parents (.40) and be in early at night (.32).

What other people thought of them appeared to be important to young people scoring high in this category. They liked people who had a good reputation (.42) and believed that good manners are important (.32). A preference was expressed for people who were not afraid to be different (.43). Apparently they were willing to maintain these standards at the expense of sometimes being considered a little "queer." Or perhaps, adults in seeking to control them explained that individuals who wish to amount to anything can not be concerned about appearing to be different from the general run of people.

They avoided the slate pit (.34) and the old county fair grounds (.35) which was a large wood lot at the edge of town. It was unlikely that they would make candy (.31) when they got together. Their groups met at school movies (.35) and outside the high school building (.30), but to some extent avoided the school cafeteria (.26). Adolescents most frequently naming this type of group were in the ninth and tenth grades (.34).

It is somewhat difficult to interpret Factor VIII; however, it seems fairly apparent that adolescents under the influence of this factor must have been convinced of the importance of pleasing their parents and certain teachers. On the other hand, one can hardly resist conjecturing what the effect of living by such a code might have had on peer relationships, particularly at the ninth and tenth grade level. Could the adolescents influenced by this factor have been isolates because their standards made it difficult for them to establish satisfactory peer relationships? Only further, more definitive research can answer this question. In the meantime, it is tentatively suggested that Factor VIII be considered a: *Pattern of pressures resulting from adult domination and lack of emancipation from the home.*

Factor IX

Good appearances seemed very important in Factor IX. A strong preference was expressed for people who dress neatly (.68), have a good reputation (.62) and think manners to be important (.56). Frequent church attendance (.33) was desirable. Persons were likely to be rejected from their groups who told off-color jokes (.57), swore (.49), made wisecracks (.32), would fight (.49), or would gamble (.47). They preferred that members of their group be white (.66) and were likely to reject colored young people (.56). A high value was placed on minding parents (.61), and there was a tendency to prefer people who got in early at night (.27). It was important to avoid appearing as if one always had to win (.59) presumably in various kinds of games or discussions. Racing cars (.40) was frowned on.

Factor IX almost took on the appearance of being an expression of a feminine role. Perhaps it is an expression of a particular type of female role. Many of the activities important in Factor VII which appeared to be dominated by masculine interests were rejected. Adolescents of the present factor did not wrestle (.63) or play basketball (.61) and football (.55). Hunting (.53) and fishing (.45) were not at all popular. Playing pool (.53) was frowned on. Baseball (.29) and roller-skating (.27) were the only physical activities in which they engaged to any extent. They liked to go on picnics (.26).

Young people naming groups rated high on this factor came from families receiving a composite socioeconomic rating in the middle group (.40) for the community. Their fathers tended to be employed in occupations falling in the middle (.26) of the classification employed in the present study. Seventh graders (.37) were not likely to be found among those naming groups high in Factor IX.

Apparently the questionnaire failed to include any places that groups of this kind liked to go; however, they appeared to avoid some which were listed. The playground of an elementary school (.49) located in the better part of town, school movies (.41), and the cafeteria at high school (.26) were not acceptable meeting places. The slate pit (.48) and the old fair grounds (.33) were not approved places to be seen. A dairy bar (.26) popular with adolescents of Factors I and III and avoided by those of V was to some extent avoided by young people scoring high on Factor IX.

The moving force behind Factor IX appeared to be a need for approval and status. Apparently this need found its expression in maintaining the very best of appearances, having good intentions, associating with the right people and avoiding activities which might mark one as an uncouth or perhaps unladylike person. Since groups scoring high on the present factor were most frequently named by middle-class girls, it is perhaps to some extent the manifestation of a middle class, feminine role. Apparently it does not become an issue until after the seventh grade.

Factor IX may suggest that the most frequent means for the middle class girl to climb the socioeconomic ladder is through a program of appearing to be highly virtuous, having the very best of intentions, and avoiding any activity which would detract from her femininity. On the other hand, such a pattern of activities, attitudes, and values might be an attempt to maintain status by appearing to be as different as possible from those in a lower socioeconomic classification.

It is significant to note that the school does not play a role to any extent in this factor, in spite of the fact that many of the values related positively to this factor were important in Factor II which was so closely allied to the school. There was, however, some indication that the home plays a part in the formation of the factor.

It is proposed that Factor IX be characterized as a: *Need for approval and status growing out of pressures applied by the middle class family.*

Factor X

After a thorough consideration of the variables which emerged in Factor X the meaning was so unclear that it did not seem wise to attempt an interpretation. It was the last and weakest factor to emerge from the analysis.

DISCUSSION AND CONCLUSIONS

Many of the variables in the present study had loadings on more than one factor. While an attempt is made in multiple factor analysis by means of rotation to maximize loadings on one factor and minimize them on all other factors, there are limits imposed by the very nature of the data under consideration. This is true because some activities and attitudes have varied meanings to adolescents and are used by them in different ways. As an example, dancing, with a loading on Factor I, appeared to be a means of assuming the adult role and to a considerable degree a means of satisfying heterosexual interests. In Factors III and V it appeared to take on the meaning of an activity by means of which relatively uncomplicated social needs are satisfied. Making candy in Factor III appeared to be an activity which is done around home and which in all probability requires the cooperation of parents. In Factor IV it appeared to be one of the few activities which can be done at the home of adolescents who are of very low socioeconomic status, while in Factors III and V making candy was one of many activities characteristic of upper socioeconomic social groups. In Factors III, V, and VII, making candy appeared to be a more feminine than masculine activity. In Factor VIII it took on the possible meaning of an activity which is refused children in a family exercising undue control. While the analyses just made of the two activities may be subject to a great deal or error, they are examples of the kinds of hypotheses which might be proposed on the basis of the present type of study.

Adolescent girls tended to mention groups that were typical of factors showing a considerable amount of association with socioeconomic status. This fact may indicate that girls tend to make distinctions along socioeconomic lines more often than do boys. Or perhaps it may be accounted for by the fact that girls tend to be under more strict adult supervision. Closer supervision and closer home ties may produce in girls a greater consciousness of status and values held by the family than is found in boys.

Noticeable is a tendency for the upper socioeconomic factors to be associated with activities centered in the school. This suggests that the school tends to encourage attitudes and standards that are characteristically upper socioeconomic in nature. "Upper socioeconomic" in this small Ohio city probably means what one would ordinarily speak of as "middle class" for the United States as a whole. In this city there was a very small "upper" class insofar as one existed at all. In the socioeconomic typing there were no houses that could be rated "1," using Warner's method. It was most difficult to make clear-cut distinctions as to the quality of the various neighborhoods.

Intelligence tended to be related to the same factors upon which socioeconomic measures were loaded, thus bearing out the considerable amount of research that shows a positive relationship between intelligence as measured by the traditional mental test and socioeconomic status. There is no evidence in the present study to throw light on the nature of the relationship between measured intelligence and socioeconomic status.

There was a tendency for factors loaded on upper socioeconomic status to be loaded also on the variable "seven or more in a group," indicating perhaps that adolescents of higher socioeconomic status tended to associate with larger peer groups than did the adolescents of lower socioeconomic status. Apparently, adolescents of high socioeconomic level tended to make more social contacts and to be involved in more interpersonal relationships than those of a lower socioeconomic level. This fact may be of significance in the area of social skills. The upper socioeconomic status adolescent has much greater opportunity to practice the skills of social intercourse. As a result, he is likely to have a great advantage over his peers of lower socioeconomic status when it comes to effectively relating himself to others in the competitive situation which is characteristic of his social milieu.

While the naming of factors in the preceding section of the present study is in a real sense a statement of conclusions, it seems worthwhile to set forth several generalizations which grew out of the study as a whole.

1. The present study has demonstrated that in the area of psychosocial research multiple factor analysis can be a useful statistical method in the development of hypotheses and categories from empirical data all of which have had equal opportunity to influence the final outcome.

2. While socioeconomic status is significantly related to many areas of adolescent informal group attitudes and activities, it does not appear to be the dominant factor.

3. In her informal group activities and attitudes the adolescent girl is influenced to a greater degree by socioeconomic status than are boys.

4. Identical activities and attitudes may be used by adolescents to satisfy widely divergent needs.

5. Degree of emancipation from adult control appears to be a most important influence in the formation of patterns of informal adolescent group activities and attitudes.

6. The public school as a social institution tends to re-enforce upper socioeconomic values and is used to a considerably greater extent to satisfy social needs by upper-socioeconomic young people than by those of lower status.

Summary

In the present study the area of adolescence was considered through the investigation of adolescents' reports concerning activities and standards of social acceptability of informal groups with which they claimed most frequent association.

A small city in Ohio was selected in which to conduct the research project. A questionnaire was developed and administered to students in grades 7 through 12 of the public and parochial schools. In addition to data gathered in the questionnaire, intelligence quotients and socioeconomic ratings were obtained for each subject.

An adaptation of multiple factor analysis was selected as the statistical tool best suited for analyzing the data. Ten factors emerged from the analysis, nine of which were tentatively identified.

——▶ **Dale B. Harris
and Sing Chu Tseng**

Children's Attitudes toward Peers and Parents as Revealed by Sentence Completions[1]

From *Child Development*, December, 1957, No. 4, 28:401–411. Reprinted by permission of the senior author and the Society for Research in Child Development.

Students of child behavior generally believe that a child builds attachments to his parents as a result of their ministrations to him, and that he builds favorable attachments to other children in terms of pleasant and reinforcing experiences had with them. Observational studies of social behavior have sketched some detail within this general picture. Young children play together freely and select best friends regardless of sex. As children grow older there arises an increasing tendency to regard with favor one's own sex peers and with disdain, if not enmity, members of the opposite sex. This trend breaks down only during adolescence when both biological drives and the social setting favor heterosexuality. This period of increasing interest in and association with members of the opposite sex merges with the period of courtship and mate selection which society has institutionalized in various ways.

Along with the growing interest in the peer group and as the child develops skills and independence, there is a waning of

[1] This investigation was supported in part by a research grant (M-690) from the National Institute of Mental Health, U. S. Public Health Service, and in part from funds supplied by the Institute of Child Welfare, University of Minnesota. Dr. Tseng, a Junior Scientist on this project staff, analyzed the data on the sentence completion test and originally suggested the project set forth in this paper.

interest in the parent figures. This is said to be particularly noticeable in early adolescence, when a period of antagonism or, indeed, outright conflict with parents occurs. This conflict is resolved by parents readjusting their expectations of the children and according more freedom. Evidence from various studies asking children to name their preferred parent or best friend has been used to support these trends. Such methodology has been criticized as too direct, yielding only socially approved results.

Theoretically, these phenomena have been explained by psychoanalysis in terms of cathection of the libido, and by learning theorists in terms of secondary drives built upon physiological appetites and extended by a process of conditioning to many persons in the environment. By modification of this latter viewpoint, changes in pattern of the child's affective attachments to others are represented as a complex process, in which the child's "role" as perceived by himself and by others modifies with his increasing maturity. Consequently his attachments to others reflect this changing "role." Data accumulated by a sentence completion test given to some 3000 children from the third grade through high school[2] yield some interesting observations on this general picture of social development.

Procedure

From a series of 32 sentences first developed by Wilson [14], some 10 sentences were selected by an empirical procedure for inclusion in a battery of instruments designed to assess general adjustment. [3] These sentences were "scored" by the simple expedient of evaluating the completions in terms of the positive, negative, or neutral affect of the response. Using a guide list of typical responses, scorers independently classifying responses at-

---

[2] The total school population, public and parochial, in grades 3 through 12 of a county seat town of 8000 in rural Minnesota is included in this analysis. Grade groups ranged in size from 221 in the fourth grade to 123 in the tenth grade and were about evenly divided as to sex. The test was given as one item in a comprehensive program which included 12 instruments.

tained the agreement expressed by correlation coefficients of +.89 to +.96 in several check samples.

Four sentences evoked attitudes toward parents and toward other children. These sentences were "Most boys ———," "Most girls ———," "My father ———," and "My mother ———."

This method of analysis makes no particular "projective" assumptions about hidden affect in sentence completions. Rather, the manifest affect as conveyed by the vernacular is taken as the basis for inferring "positive," "negative," or "neutral" attitudes. However, the technique is indirect; the sentences do not expressly call for an attitude toward parents or toward peers. These sentences, furthermore, are embedded among other sentences referring to school and to other common childhood experiences.

The items "Most boys ———," and "Most girls ———," can be treated as follows: A child may answer both items positively; an example would be "Most boys are nice," and "Most girls are pretty." He might answer both items negatively, as "Most boys are mean," and "Most girls are dumb." He can answer the items in such a way as to be neutral in both: "Most boys are tall," and "Most girls go to school." A child may answer an item positively for boys, but neutrally for girls, such as "Most boys are nice," and "Most girls are small." For any child there are nine possibilities with respect to completing the sentences.

A child may answer the item referring to parents positively for both, for example: "My mother is the best mother in the world," and "My father is the best father in the world." He may answer them negatively, as "My mother yells at me," "My father is mean." A child may answer both items neutrally, as "My mother is a housewife," "My father is a farmer." He may answer neutrally for his mother but positively for father, "My mother is a teacher," "My father is a wonderful man." His responses may be negative for mother but positive for father, as: "My mother scolds me," and "My father is a nice guy" and so on for the nine various combinations of the three grades of responses to both sentences. It is clear that for a particular child a so-called "neutral" response might have positive or negative affect; we are limiting our interpretation to the usual semantic value of the words used.

RESULTS

By combining percentages of boys and girls in each school grade who give responses of a particular affect classification, it is possible to draw curves expressing certain trends in attitude change. Figure 1 depicts boys' attitudes toward other boys and

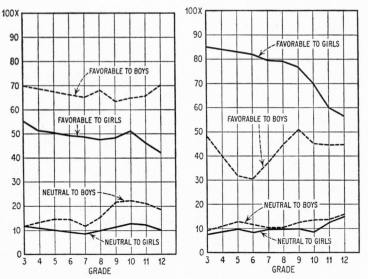

Fig. 1. Boys' attitudes toward peers.   Fig. 2. Girls' attitudes toward peers.

girls. In this figure are plotted the percentage of responses positive or "favorable" to other boys and to girls,[3] smoothed by the

---

3 To the percentage of boys giving favorable responses to both boys and girls are added the percentage of boys giving favorable responses to boys but neutral responses to girls, plus the percentage giving favorable responses to boys but unfavorable to girls. Data for the curve, "Neutral responses to boys" were obtained by combining the percentage of boys giving a neutral response to both boys and girls with the percentage giving a neutral response to boys but unfavorable to girls, and the percentage giving a neutral response to boys but favorable to girls. Similar combinations of percentages were made for Figures 2, 3, and 4a & b.

three-point moving average method. Similar data are plotted for neutral attitudes. Curves showing negative or "unfavorable" responses are omitted because their plots complicate the graph visually, and their character is fully determined by the data shown in the favorable and neutral curves. Figure 2 shows girls' attitudes toward other girls and boys.

Figure 3 reports curves redrawn from Figures 1 and 2 to compare like-sex attitudes. Boys' positive responses toward boys are compared with girls' positive responses toward girls. On this chart negative responses are also plotted, neutral responses being omitted for sake of simplicity. Similarly, Figure 4 depicts cross-sex attitudes by plotting boys' *positive* responses toward girls and girls' *positive* responses toward boys. Negative responses are not plotted because the points would fall close to the percentage points for favorable categories and would complicate the diagram.

The figures speak for themselves but a few comments may be in order. Approximately 65 to 70 per cent of the boys give posi-

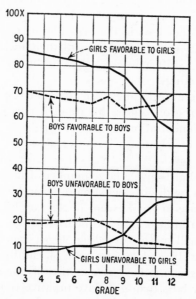

Fig. 3. Attitudes towards peers of like sex.

tive responses to other boys at all grade levels. Boys are more positive to boys than to girls in all grades. In general, taking into account the proportion of neutral attitudes, boys in the intermediate grades are more favorably than unfavorably disposed to girls, judged by the affect tone of their sentence completions. By grade 8, about the same proportion of boys give favorable as give unfavorable responses to girls. Indeed, this general decline in favorable or positive attitude toward girls is counteracted only slightly in the tenth grade, and continues noticeably thereafter. This finding does not bear out the general expectation of boys' heterosexual attitudes in adolescence. It may be that, for older adolescent boys, a positive attitude toward girls is limited to *particular* girls. At any rate, there appears to be a fair proportion of boys throughout adolescence who give a negative completion to the general stimulus "Most girls ———."

A noteworthy trend in girls' attitudes is the noticeable increase in negative responses to other girls following the ninth grade. Perhaps this change expresses an increased competitiveness among females in the adolescent years! Paralleling this trend is the slight but noticeable increase in number of boys showing neutral attitudes toward other boys in the high school years. Perhaps girls personalize their feelings more toward their own sex in adolescence, while boys shift more toward neutrality, and do not move into negative feelings.

In general, there is a falling off in favorable responses extended peers as children grow older; this trend is partly accounted for by an increase in neutral responses. Only in girls is there evidence for an increase of negative response, and these are directed toward their own sex.

Both boys and girls give a large number of favorable responses to their own sex, with girls being more favorable to girls in general than boys are to boys, except in the late high school years. In general, both unfavorable and neutral responses given to the same sex are small, never exceeding 30 per cent, and involving usually between 10 and 20 per cent of children in all grade groups. Below grade 9 boys give noticeably more negative responses to other boys than girls give negative responses to other girls. Possibly the rough and tumble to which boys of this age are prone is not enjoyed by a fair portion of the group. Or possibly a percentage have "interiorized" the social disapproval often visited on the social behavior of boys in this age group.

When cross-sex attitudes are compared, it is interesting to note that more boys are favorable to girls in the intermediate grades than the proportion of girls which express themselves as favorable to boys. This difference increases through the intermediate grades, reaching a maximum around grade 6; then the curves

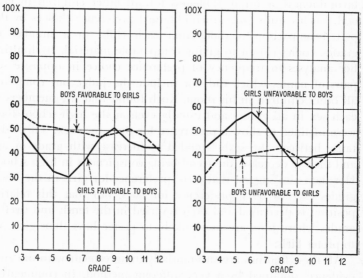

Fig. 4a. Attitudes toward opposite sex.   Fig. 4b. Attitudes toward opposite sex.

tend to come back together. The suggestion is that the boy-girl antipathy in the intermediate grades is more a product of girls changing their attitudes toward boys than it is of boys changing their attitudes toward girls. The impatience of girls aged 10 to 12 with the boisterous conduct of boys is a familiar phenomenon in any family or school room.

These data strongly suggest that girls, in general, are more "emotional" in their attitudes toward peers than are boys. Despite their changing attitudes, girls generally give more positive responses than boys. Generally speaking, boys extend more neutral attitudes than girls. Both sexes give more negative responses to opposite sex than to own sex, and the difference is particularly noticeable in girls. The proportions of negative responses given by either sex to other childen (boys and girls combined) are approximately the same. These percentages tend to be under 10 or 15 per cent.

There are not many other studies of peer attitudes which are comparable. Studies of friendships cast little light on children's favorableness or unfavorableness toward other children in general. Koch's study [6], which obtained preference choices by the paired-comparison method from each child in a number of grades, comes closest to giving comparable material. By limiting her analyses to frequency of preference choice in opposite sex pairs of names which did not include the judge but compared all other children in his room, Koch found that the members of each sex in all grades and usually even at the high school level were inclined to show a preference for their own sex. This, "distance between the sexes" tended to increase with grade or age and then to decrease, the trend being conspicuous in high school. Her data also suggest that girls' preference for girls in the lower grades exceeds boys' preference for boys, but that this relative position is decreased and even reversed in the tenth and twelfth grades where boys are more likely to prefer boys than girls are to prefer girls.

All these findings are substantially in agreement with our own evidence, obtained by a very different method. In commenting on the decline in girls' preference for girls in bi-sex pairs of names in high school, Koch wonders whether older boys and men ultimately reduce their bias in favor of their own sex, as women do. The data of this study, using a quite different method, suggest that this "reduction of bias toward own sex" actually may be characterized in girls as an increase in negative attitude rather than as an increase in neutral attitude. This study, of course, sheds no light on Koch's speculation concerning men. Koch also suggests from indirect evidence in her data that there may be "more hostility to boys in the sex bias of girls than loyalty to girls." Our method, which evaluates the elicited affect toward the other sex in general, supports this conjecture, insofar as attitudes toward boys are concerned. Although Koch believes "girls reject boys more than girls prefer girls," our data do not show that the percentage of girls showing unfavorable affect toward boys ever approximates the proportion expressing favorable attitudes to other girls.

Campbell's study of social-sex attitudes [4] in children was based on observations of same-sex and cross-sex contact in a co-educational club program. Actual contacts were not counted; rather, the character and quality of contacts were described in a systematic, but general manner for each child participating. Her descriptions of typical patterns of behavior support the general finding of like-sex preference in the grades, with girls showing a shift toward greater interest in boys by mid-teens, somewhat sooner than a comparable shift occurs in boys. She notes no behavior which would reflect the sharp increase we found in girls' unfavorable attitudes toward boys in the fifth, sixth, and seventh grades, nor the decline in favorable attitudes toward other girls in the high school years. Campbell records no behavior in boys which is inconsistent with the data of this study. Of the 14- to 17-year-old boy, she states that he "shys away from girls in a group but may be less shy when only one girl is to be considered." This observation is perhaps not incompatible with the data in Figure 1.

The data of our study are congruent with other findings, though not perhaps with the impression that boys go through an anti-girl phase in the elementary grades, followed by an increasing interest in girls in general in high school. This cycle of events does appear to characterize girls. Boys change their affect less as they grow older and incline more than girls to neutral attitudes in peer relationships. In general, children are cordial rather than antipathetic or neutral in their attitudes toward peers.

Figure 5 depicts boys' positively toned responses toward mother and father. Negatively toned responses are also plotted, but not "neutral" responses, which constitute a generous proportion. Figure 6 gives similar data for girls' attitudes toward mothers and fathers. Figure 7 shows the percentage of children expressing preference for mother, or liking parents equally well.[4]

Young boys are more favorable to their mothers than to their fathers, and the sharp drop in favorableness to both parents between grades 3 and 5 is noteworthy. Neutral attitudes toward both father and mother rise sharply from grades 3 to 4 and remain largely unchanged until late high school years, when there is some shift back toward positive attitudes. Unfavorable attitudes toward parents remain close to 5 per cent in all samples. Young girls also show a sharp drop in favorable responses toward both parents between grades 3 and 5, with a corresponding rise in neutral attitudes. In both boys and girls there appears to be a shift away from the young child's uncritical fondness for parents to a more objective judgment which expresses itself in the greater proportion of neutrally toned, matter-of-fact completions. Unfavorable responses for girls, as for boys, constitute about 5 per cent or less for both father and mother, but girls' unfavorable responses, unlike boys', tend to rise slightly after about grade eight.

When we infer attitudes from sentence completions, we find no evidence for hostility to parents in early or mid-adolescence. Such feeling, if it occurs in many young people, either does not find expression in sentence completions or is so variously placed in the teen years and of such short duration that it cannot appear in cross-sectional data. The percentages of boys and girls giving

---

4 The percentage of children preferring the father was obtained in each grade group by combining the percentage giving a neutral response to mother but a favorable response to father with the percentage giving an unfavorable response to mother, but a neutral response to father, and with the percentage giving an unfavorable response to mother, but a favorable response to father. In every case the affect tone of the completion to the stimulus "My father——" was relatively more favorable than the affect tone given by the completion of the stimulus "My mother ——." The percentage "Like equally well" is found in Figure 7 by plotting only those giving a *favorable response to both*. The small percentage of children giving an unfavorable response to both parents (never over 4 per cent in any grade group) is omitted, as well as the fairly high percentage of responses which are neutral to both parents (this runs roughly between 25 and 35 per cent for most grade groups), even though both of these groups in a sense may be said to like their parents "equally well."

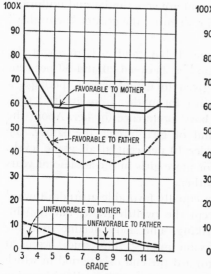

Fig. 5. Boys' attitudes toward parents.

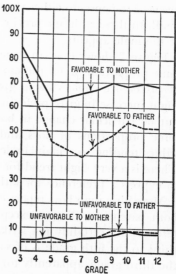

Fig. 6. Girls' attitudes toward parents.

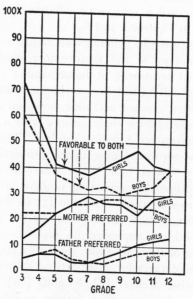

Fig. 7. Children's parent preferences.

negative responses to either parent are very similar and uniformly small. In these, as in the previous figures, the greater "neutrality" of the male appears.

Figure 7 shows that, in general, boys and girls in about the same proportion prefer the mother, between 20 and 30 per cent of preference choices being given to her. There is, perhaps, a slight increase in girls' preference for mother from grades 3 to 7, but no particular change in boys' preference for her. About the same proportions of boys and of girls prefer the father, the values tending to remain under 10 per cent at all grade levels. There is a very slight trend for more girls in the adolescent years to express a preference for fathers.

More girls than boys report equally favorable attitudes toward both parents at all ages except the twelfth grade, but the differences are certainly not striking. The sharp decline from the third to the fifth grade is of some interest. This study begins at the third grade, apparently toward the end of a period in which children give equally to both parents general, undiscriminating and positive attitudes. This trend coincides with and expresses the movement toward a greater proportion of neutrally toned responses noted in Figures 5 and 6.

These findings agree in general with results of other studies. Using a combination of the picture-story method, questions about preferential treatment at home, and a direct question about whom the child liked best at home, Simpson [10] concluded that between ages five and nine, boys and girls alike show a decreasing preference for their fathers, with a very slight increase in the percentage favoring mothers. There was a pronounced increase up to age nine in the proportion of children stating that they "prefer both," which may be compared with the decreasing proportion reporting positive attitudes to both parents in the present study. Anderson [2] in the White House Conference report of 1936 showed that by the mothers' report a majority of children expressed no preference between their parents, and that of those who did, the larger group favored the mother. The percentages for these attitudes changed very little with age. Likewise, Meltzer [8], Stogdill [11], and Mott [9] found mothers more likely than fathers to be designated the favorite parent at all ages. None of these studies showed any trend comparable to the upswing in positive attitude toward parents during mid-adolescence which appears, particularly for boys, in the present study. These data offer a picture of increasing objectivity in later childhood, in part expressed by the increased proportion of children (particularly of boys) who use neutral expressions in their sentence completions, both towards peers and parents.

Summary

A sentence completion technique, used to infer attitudes toward peers and parents, leads to the following conclusions:

1. Boys and girls are predominantly favorable to their peers, and at every age positive attitudes to own sex peers exceed those to opposite sex peers.

2. Boys somewhat more than girls express neutral attitudes. Girls clearly express more negative attitudes to their own sex as they grow older.

3. The so-called boy-girl antipathy of the intermediate grades is more a product of girls changing their attitudes toward boys than vice-versa. Boys show a slight over-all decrease in favorable attitudes toward girls, even in the later high school years.

4. Toward both mother and father, boys and girls extend more favorable than unfavorable attitudes, though there is a noticeable increase in neutral affect in the intermediate grades. Both sexes extend positive attitudes more frequently to mother than to father.

5. Boys in high school years show a slight rise in positive attitudes toward each parent; girls show a more pronounced increase in positive attitude toward father than toward mother in these same years.

6. The small proportions of boys showing negative attitudes toward mother and/or father decrease steadily through childhood and adolescence. The correspondingly small proportions of girls showing negative attitudes increase steadily through childhood and adolescence.

7. When a difference exists in the attitudes a boy or girl extends to his parents, he or she more often prefers the mother

than the father. A larger group, however, extends similar (and positive) attitudes to both parents. There is a slight rise in girls' preference for father during the high school years.

REFERENCES

1. ANDERSON, H. H., & ANDERSON, GLADYS L., "Social Development," in L. Carmichael, ed., Manual of Child Psychology, 2nd ed., New York: John Wiley & Sons, Inc., 1954, pp. 1162–1215.

2. ANDERSON, J. E., The Young Child in the Home, New York: Appleton-Century-Crofts, Inc., 1936.

3. ———, BEILIN, H., HARRIS, D. E., & TSENG, SING CHU, Unpublished work accomplished in 1953 on the Nobles County Project, Institute of Child Welfare, University of Minnesota.

4. CAMPBELL, ELISE H., "The Social-Sex Development of Children," Genetic Psychology Monographs, 1939, 21:461–552.

5. JONES, H. E., "The Environment and Mental Development," in L. Carmichael, ed., Manual of Child Psychology, 2nd ed., New York: John Wiley & Sons, Inc., 1954, pp. 631–696.

6. KOCH, HELEN L., "A Study of Some Factors Conditioning the Social Distance Between the Sexes," Journal of Social Psychology, 1944, 20:79–107.

7. McCANDLESS, B., "Environment and Intelligence," American Journal of Mental Deficiency, 1952, 56:674–691.

8. MELTZER, H., "Children's Attitudes Toward Parents," American Journal of Orthopsychiatry, 1935, 5:244–265.

9. MOTT, SINA M., "Mother-Father Preference," Character and Personality, 1937, 5:302–304.

10. SIMPSON, MARGARETE, Parent Preferences of Young Children, New York: Teachers College, Columbia University, 1935.

11. STOGDILL, R. M., "Survey of Experiments of Children's Attitudes Toward Parents: 1894–1936," Journal of Genetic Psychology, 1937, 51:293–303.

12. WARNER, W. L., & MEEKER, MARCIA, Social Class in America: A Manual of Procedure for the Measurement of Social Status, Chicago: Science Research Associates, 1949.

13. WHERRY, R. J., & GAYLORD, R. H., "The Concept of Test and Item Reliability in Relation to Factor Pattern," Psychometrika, 1943, 8:247–264.

14. WILSON, ISABELLE, "The Use of a Sentence Completion Test in Differentiating Between Well-adjusted and Maladjusted Secondary School Pupils," Journal of Consulting Psychology, 1949, 13:400–403.

CHAPTER
THIRTEEN

↑

Child-Family Relationship

IN THIS CHAPTER ATTENTION IS GIVEN TO factors in parent-child relationships that influence the pattern of behavior of the growing individual. How do the experiences of the individual as infant and child, living under this or that kind of parental influence, shape his personality? How do child-rearing concepts and practices differ from one social group to another? Where do parents get their ideas about how best to rear their children? Such questions as these have been studied systematically in recent years; the researches reported in this chapter give evidence of the significance of advances being made on this relatively new frontier of science.

Though the reading from the research report by Sears, Maccoby and Levin is a very limited selection from a book of more than 500 pages, it is to be hoped that it will, nevertheless, give the reader some idea of the kind of task that was undertaken in the study and its great importance for better understanding of the relationship between child-rearing practices and the personality characteristics of the child. Robert R. Sears and Eleanor E. Maccoby are faculty members of the Department of Psychology, Stanford University. Sears is Executive Head of the Department. Harry Levin is on the faculty in psychology at Cornell University.

What are the differences in the personality patterns of children brought up in good, loving, but strictly disciplined homes as compared with children brought up in good, loving homes but with a high degree of permissiveness? The question has for years led to much speculation and much debate. But little research of any consequence has been aimed at getting an answer. Goodwin Watson of Teachers College, Columbia University, is one person who has tried systematically to investigate the problem of strict versus permissive discipline of children. His article is thought-provoking both for the methods employed in the study and for the importance of the findings.

To what extent does personality derive from responses that the individual makes to his basic social groups? Conversely, how much of the individual's personality consists of responses or response patterns that are individual or "private," that originate in organic and chance factors and in training that deviates from the cultural standard for his group? The questions point to the need for systematic inquiries along each of two lines of investigation. One of these, that pertaining to the cultural impact on children's personality development, was undertaken in the study reported by Havighurst and Davis. Specifically, the study was concerned with the differences in the *cultural training* of children whose families differed in social and cultural status. The authors, Allison Davis and Robert J. Havighurst, are professors of Education at the University of Chicago.

———▶ **Robert R. Sears,**
Eleanor E. Maccoby,
and Harry Levin

A Study of Child Rearing

The process of child rearing, in spite of its proverbial importance as a determinant of adult character, has not been much investigated by scientific procedures. In the history of Western science, the study of man came late. Newtonian physics was a part of history before more than the crudest of scientific observations of normal human social behavior had been made. Although educators and social philosopsers had long speculated on the kinds and amount of influence that childhood experiences might have on social and intellectual functioning, empirical study of the problem did not begin much before the twentieth century.

Why science remained so long at arm's length from human behavior can be a matter only for speculation. Doubtless the philosophic assumptions underlying Western thought were partly responsible. To many, human behavior has never seemed a proper subject for science, man himself being considered as an essentially lawless event in an otherwise lawful universe. Perhaps, too, in the case of child rearing, the fact that science was a male preoccupation was relevant. Men have always tended to dissociate themselves from female functions. Even today, those scientific and medical specialities pertaining to children attract fewer than their share of male practitioners. In any case, whatever the causes for its late arrival among scientific problems, child rearing has become in recent years a matter of considerable interest to behavior science.

There are good reasons for this interest. Clinical studies of disturbed children, as well as experimental observations of normal ones, have shown a number of important causal relationships between mothers' child-rearing practices and the behavior of their children. Some personality characteristics of adults, too, appear to be extensions of the effects of early experiences. This is particularly true of those qualities that involve personal relationships such as love, dependency, jealousy, and competition. Since a child's earliest interpersonal experiences are with his family, and particularly with his mother, there is good reason for examining the mother's behavior to see whether there are consistent consequences of different practices.

If personality is partly a product of childhood experiences, then there seems some likelihood, too, that the forms of behavior which characterize a whole society may be partly explicable on the same basis. Recent anthropological studies have shown, for example, that the kinds of folk tales a culture transmits are consistently related to certain aspects of child training in that culture. [19] Any process that can help to explain both the development of personality and the transmission of culture is important to the behavior sciences, for these two problems are the focal points for the study of man as a social organism.

FROM "EXPERTS" TO RESEARCHERS

From the beginning of time, no doubt, there have been mothers who were driven to distraction by the problems of controlling and training their children. Such pangs and puzzlement left little imprint in written records, however, until the general literacy of the nineteenth century made women as articulate as men. Then various things happened together that, more than metaphorically, left a baby in the lap of twentieth-century science.

There was a great growth spurt of humanitarian values. The time for shrugging off human misery and indignities had passed. The poor, the ill, the young, the underprivileged became suffering equals who needed help and understanding. Care and protection of those who had not reached their place in the sun became a matter of public morality and private ideals. Humanitarian motives had become values that could be invoked in support of nearly any action.

What actions came to be supported depended on another development. This was the astonishing nineteenth-century success of science and engineering as instruments for improving man's control of his environment. The mid-century application of steam to transportation improved the distribution of material goods and tremendously increased the mobility of enterprising people. The development of electricity as a source of power eliminated the time-barrier in communication. And late in the century the application of scientific methods to the control of disease gave man a sense of mastery over the most tragic of all the forces arrayed against him. Solution of problems by rational means replaced reliance on tradition, personal experience, and the self-arrogated wisdom of those who had decision-making power.

These changes did not all come at once. "Wise men" gave up their power reluctantly. The rational problem-solving of science was accepted grudgingly and only in those material matters where financial rewards or improvement in health gave blunt demonstration of the worthwhileness of scientific methods. But the growing absorption of humane values pressed the battlefield into more and more corners where human welfare could still stand improvement. Divorce, criminality, mental disease, and other behavioral sources of human waste and anguish began to be looked upon as social *ills*. The most vigorous champions of humane values and of rational problem-solving began to demand attack on these problems as well as on the more material ones.

So it came about, near the turn of the century, that some people began to concern themselves with the welfare of mothers and children. Many of the problems that caused waste and misery seemed to stem directly from maternal and child labor conditions, and these matters were given first attention. But one wise and courageous woman in Iowa—Mrs. Cora Bussey Hillis—saw farther into the sources of social troubles. She urged the scientific study of the whole process of child growth and rearing. In 1917, she and her co-workers persuaded the Iowa Legislature to establish the Child Welfare Research Station at the State University of Iowa. Thus was launched the massive scientific attack on problems of child development that has characterized the last four decades.

Science is slow, however, and by and large it is cautious. Through the twenties, researchers picked their ways among questions of method and measurement, charting carefully the behavior of this new object of study—the human child. The greatest advances in knowledge were with respect to physical growth, nutrition, and childhood diseases. In psychological matters, only intelligence was widely explored. Not until the thirties did children's motives and personalities receive much attention, and the intensive study of child-training practices came still later.

But what about the parents? The measured progress of *Science* may be useful to an impersonal *Society,* but mothers of young children need answers in a hurry. Toward the end of the nineteenth century, the women's magazines recognized this need and began to print columns of advice. At first, following the lead of medical research, they emphasized problems of feeding especially, drawing on what bits and pieces of information became available. This was not enough. Gradually the list of topics was expanded, and the popular magazines undertook guidance on every phase of child rearing.

Thus was the "expert" born. Properly speaking, an expert in child development is one who knows a great deal of what is known about the subject and has had wide experience in applying his knowledge. When research data were nonexistent, a few pediatricians, psychiatrists, social workers, and teachers filled this role. The treatment of parents and children in trouble provided the most fruitful experience for these advisers. In clinics, schools, courts, and welfare agencies, the new concern for social ills forced practitioners to search for causes, and to reach decisions as to what practices were helpful in forming better personalities. Tentative theoretical formulations grew from clinical practice and from a few early experiments. The challenging observations of Freud offered the greatest stimulation in this respect, and as we move gradually from the era of expert opinion to that of research findings, psychoanalytic theory remains one of the most vital sources of our hypotheses.

During the past half century we have had many writers giving advice to mothers. Some have been truly expert, and have relied heavily on the growing body of child development research. Others have followed fads and prejudices and have probably done more harm than good. Even the wisest and most scientifically oriented have shown notable changes of opinion from time to time. In any case, it is high time for the behavioral sciences to use research methods to replace common sense (or nonsense) fancies with demonstrable facts.

The present report is a step in this direction. It describes the findings of a study that was based on standardized interviews with 379 mothers of five-year-old children. In these recorded interviews, the mothers reported in detail their feelings about motherhood and their families; they described their child-rearing practices from the child's birth until he was five years old; and they gave enough reports about the child's own behavior that we could determine some of the effects of these practices. The chapter headings indicate the general scope of the information obtained.

THE THREE RESEARCH PROBLEMS

There are three kinds of questions that can be asked about child-rearing practices and values. The *first,* and simplest, wants a purely descriptive answer: How *do* parents rear children? The *second* goes deeper and asks what effects different kinds of training have on children. The *third* relates to the mothers themselves: What leads a mother to use one method rather than another?

In pursuing the *first* of these questions, we discovered there is surprisingly little information about what American parents believe or what they do with their youngsters. Do most mothers breast-feed their babies? Do they spank them for being sassy? Are chores and responsibilities a part of most children's lives? Do very many mothers let their three-year-olds run around naked in the house? How serious do mothers think it is when a child strikes a parent? Do any mothers ever actually encourage children to fight the neighbor children? The answers to these questions, and to many others like them, are needed not only to give a frame of reference within which a particular practice can be viewed, but to permit any one mother to gain perspective on her own practices by comparing or contrasting her characteristic ways of treating her child with those of other mothers.

Curiously enough, anthropologists have secured more complete information about child rearing in at least seventy other cultures than they have about child rearing in the United States. [17, 8] With the exception of a few recent studies, the source of most of our knowledge about American child-rearing behavior is inferential, deriving in the main from the books, pamphlets, and magazine articles that give advice to parents. These sources are scarcely data, in the sense of being reports about actual practices, but in certain instances their popularity suggests that a good many people may have found them attractive and may have followed the advice.

One series of pamphlets has provided a unique opportunity to observe changes in what may be called the "official" child-rearing culture of the United States. These are the ten successive editions of *Infant Care,* published by the U. S. Children's Bureau; the first appeared in 1914 and the latest in 1955. This small book provides a great deal of useful information for the young mother. Much of the material is factual, well geared to American economy and conditions of life. But some has to do with methods of child rearing, and it is in this connection that one can see secular changes in attitudes and values.

Dr. Martha Wolfenstein [18] has studied these variations in advice through the first nine editions (1914–1951) with respect to the handling of five problems: Thumb-sucking, weaning, masturbation, bowel and bladder training. We call these "problems" because each refers to a form of child behavior that is *change-worthy,* that is, a kind of action either to be inhibited as much as possible or to be replaced by new behavior of a more mature kind. Such control and training can be done with different degrees of severity. The mother can be highly punitive and refuse to tolerate any lapses whatever, or she can be gentle in her urging of new actions and ignore accidental reversions to the changeworthy ones. Most observers of young children believe this dimension of *severity of training* has important effects on children's personalities, though there is little direct evidence as to just what the effects may be.

Dr. Wolfenstein's evaluation of the degree of severity of training recommended by the authors of the different editions of *Infant Care* shows that there have been substantial changes over the more than forty years spanned. Interestingly enough, changes have been quite different for the five training problems. In 1914, both masturbation and thumb-sucking were to be treated very severely indeed: masturbation, which would "wreck" a child for life, was to be stopped by tying the child's legs to opposite sides of the crib; and thumb-sucking also was to be treated by mechanical restraint. In subsequent editions there was a fairly continuous decline in the degree of severity recommended, the 1951 edition treating the two changeworthy behaviors as rather petty nuisances that might be ignored. Along with this permissiveness there was a distinct devaluing of the satisfactions a child gets from such stimulation.

The other three training problems had quite different histories. There was a steady increase to 1929 in the severity with which weaning was to be done, and there was no noticeable decrease until 1938. Bowel training had a similar development, although severity began to drop off a little earlier. Bladder training severity also increased at first, but there has been a steady decrease since 1921.

These changing patterns of advice are a part of the child-rearing values of their times. What relation there may have been between the values—the "what ought to be"—and the actual practices of mothers cannot now be discovered. The practices of forty years ago are irretrievably buried in mothers' memories, and their only monuments are the personality structures of children who have grown to middle age themselves.

It would be a mistake, of course, to assume that there is any one pattern of child rearing that can be called "The American pattern." The United States contains a rich variety of subcultures. In spite of thirty-six million distributed copies of *Infant Care,* there is no dread uniformity of child-rearing practices. Differences of religion, of ethnic origin, of socio-economic status, and of family size all contribute to the great variety of values and practices.

As an illustration we may cite some comparative findings from three different communities in which we secured information about child rearing. One, called Homestead, is a small New Mexican village with a population originating mainly in the dustbowl areas of Texas and Oklahoma. A second, Rimrock, is just a few miles away, but its population is of Old American stock with Mormon traditions. The third is the suburban metropolitan area in New England from which the information for this present book was obtained. Our interviewers secured reports from about twenty mothers in each of the two villages, and from 379 mothers in the New England area.

Three items exemplify the extraordinary differences that can be found within our national borders. The first is the age at which mothers weaned their children. In Homestead, for instance, 50 per cent had completed weaning before the child was eight months old, while in Rimrock none had. In the New England sample, 37 per cent had. A second item relates to who, in the family, had the chief responsibility for deciding on child-rearing policies. In Homestead, 22 per cent of the mothers said the father was the chief policy-maker; in Rimrock, 67 per cent said the father; and in the New England group, only 8 per cent reported the father. Or consider the degree to which physical punishment was used as a frequent and major method of discipline. In Homestead, 39 per cent of the families used it; in Rimrock, only 5 per cent; and in New England, 20 per cent.

In child rearing, as in so many other things, America is the very archetype of diversity. In Chapters Eleven and Twelve [of *A Study of Child Rearing*] we will describe some of the differences that are related to sex of the child being reared, his ordinal position in the family, and the age and education and socio-economic status of his parents. But our task, first, will be to describe the variations—and their commonness or uncommonness—in the whole population of mothers we interviewed. This will give a provisional answer to the question: How *do* mothers rear their children during the first five years?

The *second* type of question leads to an inquiry about the

effects of training on the child. Does self-demand feeding make children more dependent? Does punishment for bed-wetting just make the matter worse? Does early insistence on complete modesty make children more curious than ever about sex? Does spanking insure the development of a good strong conscience? Answers to such cause-and-effect questions as these will eventually provide some help to parents in making decisions about how to rear children. If a mother knows the effect of a particular practice, she can decide whether to use it or not. She can base her judgment on a knowledge of what product she will get.

Clincal observations, and theories developed from them, have suggested a number of hypotheses about the relation between certain kinds of child rearing and the personality qualities produced by them. Ideally, to test these notions, the measures of mother and child behavior should be entirely independent of one another. The present study, relying entirely on the mothers' interview reports for measuring both, is not ideal for answering all such cause-and-effect questions. However, there are a few kinds of child behavior that a mother can probably describe about as objectively as could an independent observer. Where we have been able to get such measures from the interviews, we will report their child-rearing antecedents. The most successful examples will be found in the chapters on feeding, toilet training, dependency, aggression, techniques of training, and conscience.

Third, and finally, one can ask what leads a mother to use one method rather than another. Child-rearing beliefs and values and practices do not just appear out of the blue. They are products of the mother's own personality, her values and attitudes. She may feel, for example, that she has reasoned herself quite objectively to an answer as to how she *should* handle her child's quarreling, but the extent to which she *can* tolerate open fighting influences her decision. All reasoning rests on assumptions that, in turn, rest on the values and attitudes the mother has developed throughout her own life. Her own upbringing has influenced these, and of course the nature of the family situation at any one time helps dictate a decision as to how to treat the children. Hence it will not prove surprising to find that there are substantial differences in mothers' values and practices depending on the satisfactoriness of her relations with her husband, on her self-esteem, and on certain of her own pervasive moral values, such as her attitudes toward sex and aggression.

To put the matter most succinctly, child-rearing practices can be viewed as both causes and effects. They are responsible, in some degree, for the personality characteristics of the child, and they are themselves the products of cultural factors operating in the life of the mother. We will not attempt to untangle these reciprocal relationships, but will present our findings with respect to the three main problems outlined above.

—→ **Goodwin Watson**

Some Personality Differences in Children Related to Strict or Permissive Parental Discipline[1]

From *Journal of Psychology*, 1957, 44:227–249. Reprinted by permission.

A. INTRODUCTION

In controversies over parental discipline of children, few of the arguments advanced for more permissiveness or for more strict adult control have yet been empirically tested. Does early indulgence "spoil" children or does it give them a foundation of "security" to meet life's stress and strain? Does firm and consistent discipline by the parents create in children inner hostilities, anxieties, and self-rejection or does it relieve anxiety and foster

[1] This study was made possible by a grant from the Columbia University Council for Research in the Social Sciences.

more successful self-discipline? Psychologists, psychoanalysts, teachers, parents, grandparents have often spoken with strong conviction on one or the other side of these issues, but the evidence has usually come from personal experience, clinical cases, plausible theories, or unconscious bias.

A generation ago this writer made a first effort at empirical study of this problem, comparing the self-reports of 230 graduate students who rated their home discipline during childhood along a continuum from the most strict to the most lenient. Those who came from the strictest quartile of homes reported: (a) more hatred for and constraint in relation to parents: (b) more rejection of teachers; (c) poorer relations with classmates, more quarrels, and shyness; (d) more broken engagements and unsatisfactory love affairs; (e) more worry, anxiety and guilt feeling; (f) more unhappiness and crying; (g) more dependence on parents; but (h) better school grades and stronger ambition. [16]² Two cogent criticisms should be made of this study. First, the "strict" category included homes where there was severe punishment and quite possible rejection. The "lax" category included possible indifference and neglect along with genuine concern for freedom. Second, since all data came from the student's self-reports, a generally negative or optimistic outlook may have permeated both the reports on home discipline and the present self-evaluation.

A few years later (1938) Carpenter and Eisenberg [4] reported findings leading to similar conclusions. Among 500 college women, the 50 rated as most "dominant" reported a childhood in which their own "freedom" and "individuality" had been stressed. The more "submissive," like the shy, dependent, anxious students in our 1929 study, came almost entirely from adult-dominated homes. Those who "had to have parents' permission to do practically everything" turned out at college age to be "submissives" (21 %) rather than "dominants" (2%).

Studies attempting to relate specific early child-rearing prac-

---

² Results reported to the 10th International Congress of Psychology in 1929 and later published in G. Watson, "A comparison of the effects of lax versus strict home training." *Journal of Social Psychology*, 1934, 5, 102–105. A popular version appeared in *Parents Magazine*, 1934, 9, 13–20.

tices (e.g., breast feeding, self-demand feeding, method of toilet training, etc.) to child personality seem to have been inconclusive (Cf. Sewell [13] and review by Orlansky [11]). Those which center upon the general social climate in the home, on the other hand, reveal marked and generally consistent differences. One exception is Myers [10] who, in 1935, reported that a pupil adjustment questionnaire and high school teacher ratings on quality of personality adjustment were unrelated to strictness of home discipline.

Hattwick [6, 7] in 1936 found that "over-attentive" homes which "favor" the child or "revolve around" the child were positively correlated (.20 to .40) with tendencies of nursery school pupils to be babyish in such matters as "cries easily," "asks unnecessary help," and "avoids risk." On the other hand, these same over-indulged children were less likely to take the property of others or to mistreat animals.

Ayer and Bernreuter [2] in 1951 reported on another study of the personality traits of nursery school children in relation to their home discipline. Significant correlations appeared between physical punishment at home and a tendency of children not to face reality $(r = .35)$ and between permissiveness of parents (letting children learn from the natural consequences of their acts) and a more "attractive" personality in the child $(r = .33)$.

Symonds [15] matched 28 parents who "dominated" their children in an authoritative way with 28 who permitted the child much freedom and who usually acceded to child wishes. He found the children from stricter homes more courteous, obedient, and neat, but also more shy, timid, withdrawing, docile, and troubled. The more permissive parents brought up children who were more aggressive, more disobedient, and who had more eating problems, but who also were more self-confident, better at self-expression, freer, and more independent.

Anderson [1] identified a group of junior high school pupils who had been brought up with warm affection but little adult dominance. He found these children marked by a high degree of maturity, poise, cheerfulness, coöperation, obedience, and responsibility.

Lafore [9], using techniques of direct, on-the-scene observation, made two half-hour visits in the homes of 21 nursery school children, and reported that:

> Parents who presented the largest number of instances of dictating (to) and interfering with their children, received the largest number of expressions of hostility from their children. . . .
>
> Parents who showed large numbers of instances of blaming, hurrying, punishing, threatening and interfering had children who presented large numbers of crying. . . .
>
> Children who were frequently threatened scored high on fearfulness. . . .
>
> Children who were cautioned most often scored low on resourcefulness.

Radke's study [12] is in some ways closest to the one to be reported here. She studied 43 children of nursery school or kindergarten age, giving the parents a questionnaire and observing the children in free-play and picture-interpretation test situations. Children from more restrictive and autocratic home discipline showed less aggressiveness, less rivalry, were more passive, more colorless, and less popular. They did not get along so well with other children. The children from homes with freer discipline were more active, showed more rivalry, and were more popular. Radke found that parents who were "democratic' 'in their disciplinary methods, giving more respect to the youngsters, fostered children who themselves showed more consideration for others.

Baldwin [3] in 1948, reported on a study of 64 four-year olds, showing that parents who were strict and undemocratic in their methods of control were likely to have children who were quiet, well-behaved, unaggressive, but restricted in curiosity, originality, and imagination.

Shoben [14] found that when parents of "problem children" (defined as: referred for clinical help, or brought into custody of juvenile authorities at least twice) were given an attitude scale they were more apt than were parents of non-problem children to agree with statements approving strict discipline and demand for obedience. Bi-serial correlation was .80 on the orginal group and .62 on a validating group for this variable which Shoben called "Dominating."

There is considerable convergence among the findings of these studies. There seems to be reason to suppose that firm, strict adult domination will produce the conforming, obedient child but will handicap him in initiative and probably burden him with shyness and a sense of inadequacy. More permissive treatment seems, in these studies, to result in more independence and aggressiveness on the part of the child. These children are less docile but in some studies appear to be more popular and more considerate of others. Shoben's results challenge a popular belief that juvenile delinquency is associated with lack of punishment by parents.

B. SELECTION OF SUBJECTS

This study was conducted under the auspices of The Guidance Center, a child-guidance clinic in New Rochelle. Associated with the Guidance Center was a positive program of education in mental health and of community service, reaching hundreds of parents of "normal" children in the eastern part of Westchester County. Subjects for this study were limited to normal children in school from kindergarten through sixth grade. Only "good" homes where children were wanted, loved, and well cared for were included. Any children who had ever been referred for psychological or psychiatric treatment were excluded. Nominations were sought from parents, teachers, and social workers, to find good homes that were known to be clearly "strict" or "permissive."

During a preliminary period, social workers visited the recommended homes and talked with these parents about their practices in child-raising. On the basis of the interviews a multiple-answer questionnaire was constructed and printed under the title, *How I Am Bringing Up My Child*. The instrument asked about parental reaction to each of 35 fairly common situations, such as children's eating, sleeping, toilet training, dressing, keeping clean, caring for toys, quarreling, anger at parents, sex curiosity, attendance at school and church, choice of television programs, friends, etc. Each situation was followed by three kinds of possible response: (*a*) a clearly permissive reaction, (*b*) a middle-of-the-road or "sometimes this and sometimes that" answer, and (c) a reply characteristic of the parent who sets standards and enforces strict obedience. The responses were assigned weights of 5 for the most permissive, 3 for the neutral, and 1 for the strict reaction. There was opportunity for parents to write in a response to each situation in their own words if none of the proposed answers seemed to fit well enough. If a parent's qualified answer fell between "strict" and "middle-of-the-road" it was given 2 points; if it fell between "middle-of-the-road" and "permissive" it was given 4 points. Consistent choice of the "strict" responses would result in a score of 35; consistent "middle-of-the-road" responses would give a total of 105; consistent "permissiveness" would bring a total score of 175. The actual range was from 55 to 158.

A range of 20 points on either side of the neutral point of 105 was arbitrarily set as representing the area of common practice— strict about some things at some times and more lenient on other matters or at other times. Although we had made special efforts to reach the more extreme groups—the permissive parents with scores of 125 or over, and the strict parents with scores of 85 or less—more than half (53%) of our responses fell in the 40 point middle range and were not used in this study.

The home discipline for 34 of the children was rated by fathers independently of the mother's rating. Fathers usually reported a less permissive attitude than did mothers. For these cases, fathers averaged a score of 105 and mothers 115. In only seven instances did the mother's report indicate a stricter attitude than that of the father. Correlation between mother's rating and father's was .61. For the sake of consistency, since mother's rating was available in all cases and since in suburban communities today the mother is more directly and more frequently responsible for discipline in the type of situation listed, our classification into strict or permissive is based only on the mother's report. In no instance would a child's classification have moved from one extreme category to the other if the father's questionnaire had been used instead of the mother's.

C. Procedure

Parents whose questionnaire score was extreme, falling under 86 (strict) or over 124 (permissive), were visited by a trained social worker[3] who conducted an interview designed to check both directly and indirectly on the reported attitudes and practices, to evaluate the general climate of the home, and to obtain the parents' perception of their child's strength and weaknesses. The social workers were not informed as to whether the home to be visited had been reported as permissive or as strict but the differences were so marked that this was seldom in doubt. In the few instances in which the social worker felt that the questionnaire classification was questionable because the home really belonged in the middle-of-the-road category rather than at the extreme, the case was not included in our comparative study. Thus every case which was included met both the criteria: extreme score on the questionnaire, and confirming judgment of a social worker who had independently observed parent and child in the home.

We endeavored to get school behavior ratings for all the children, but this proved impossible in some cases. Wherever they coöperated, teachers or school guidance officers rated the children on a scale which provided intervals from 1 to 5 on: (a) level of activity; (b) initiative; (c) independence, spontaneity, self-reliance; (d) confidence, good adjustment; (e) friendliness and popularity; (f) coöperation; (g) self-control; and (h) persistence. In the case of 16 of 36 children rated by teachers a trained worker from the Guidance Center made an independent appraisal using the same scale. Agreement of the teacher and the outside observer is represented by a correlation of .77. Of 121 parallel judgments, 59 per cent agreed exactly; 31 per cent differed by only one scale step; and 10 per cent were two steps apart. Thus 90 per cent assigned the same or an adjoining category.

---

[3] The writer wishes to acknowledge indebtedness to Mrs. Helen Service and Mrs. Seth Solomon who contributed significantly to this study.

D. RESULTS

1. Permissiveness Is Rare

The first surprise of the study was our difficulty in finding parents who were fairly consistently permissive. Perhaps this should have been anticipated.

Whiting and Child [17] have estimated the over-all indulgence or severity of child training in 47 societies studied by competent anthropological observers. The aspects of discipline which they included in their index were: (a) earliness and severity of weaning; (b) toilet training; (c) repression of sexual activity; (d) repression of aggression; and (e) effort toward child's independence. They found only two of the 47 cultures as severe on the younger child as is the typical American middle-class white family described by Davis and Havighurst. No culture in the records is less permissive with children than we are. The short-shrift given to "progressive education" in this country might further have warned us.

We had been led to believe, however, that in certain sub-cultures of the United States the ideal of respecting the child and of permitting him great freedom to mature in his own way and at his own good time had taken root. We knew that psychoanalytic concepts were commonly heard in upper-middle-class Westchester child-study groups and that "mental hygiene" was looked upon as favorably as Divine Grace once had been. Some teachers complained that children were being given too much freedom at home and writers in popular journals freely listed lack of firm parental discipline as a major cause of juvenile delinquency. It was easy to find citizens who thought that some of their neighbors were overly-permissive parents.

We set the modest goal of 50 cases—25 boys and 25 girls—from child-centered, permissive homes. After strenuous search, with the coöperation of the Guidance Center, the Child Study Association, the Mental Hygiene Association, social workers, clergymen, teachers, pediatricians and P.T.A.'s; and after extending our quest for an extra year and modifying our qualifying scores a step or two downward toward the middle; we eventually located

38 permissively brought-up children—21 boys and 17 girls. (Four of these could not be included in the later testing.) The distribution of our questionnaire returns is shown in Table 1. We em-

TABLE 1

DISTRIBUTION OF SCORES ON "HOW I AM BRINGING UP MY CHILD"

Score	No. of Boys	No. of Girls	Both	Per cent of Total
"Permissive" Extreme				(12%)
145 and over	3	5	8	
135–144	5	4	9	
125–134	13	8	21	
"Middle-of-the-Road"				(53%)
115–124	13	14	27	
105–114	30	39	69	
95–104	31	48	79	
"Strict" Extreme				(35%)
85–94	33	41	74	
75–84	20	8	28	
74 and below	9	4	13	
	157	171	328	(100%)

phasize again that this is not a normal cross-section. We were not interested in "middle-of-the-road" cases for this particular comparison. The point of the table is that with much less effort, we found three times as many "strict" as "permissive" homes in the most "liberal" section of an upper-middle class suburban community. The obtained median score of 101 is below (i.e., more strict than) the arbitrary neutral score of 105.

2. Age, Sex, and Discipline

Demands for conformity to adult standards become stronger as a child grows older. Babies are not expected, except by pathological parents, to "behave" themselves. Many cultures treat young children very indulgently, only later expecting them to exercise mature levels of self-control. Pearl Buck reports that in the China she knew, children were usually treated very permissively until about the age of seven. Their demands were gratified whenever possible. But after seven, they were expected to behave like proper adults, and they did so.

Our data from 328 children in Eastern Westchester county, reported in Table 2, show no clear and consistent age trend.

TABLE 2

AGE AND SEX OF CHILD IN RELATION TO PERMISSIVENESS OF HOME DISCIPLINE

(Higher scores are more permissive)

Age	Boys		Girls	
	No.	Median Score	No.	Median Score
5	11	102	13	101
6	32	105	27	112
7	34	98.5	32	98.5
8	19	96	23	102
9	25	97.5	31	99
10	13	87	27	103
11	17	111	13	100
12	6	104	5	110
All	157	100.3	171	101.7

The anticipated transition from infant indulgence to mature demands does not appear in this cross-sectional survey. Longitudinal studies of qualitative changes in the same child-parent relationship might reveal that tolerance for some kinds of childish misbehavior is decreasing, but that with advancing age children are treated with increased freedom which offsets these restrictions.

3. The Two Groups Compared

Table 3 shows that although our two groups of children, one from exceptionally "permissive" and the other from very "strict" homes, are far apart on Home Discipline score, they are not sig-

TABLE 3

Comparison of "Strict" Group and "Permissive" Group on Age, on Sex, and Intelligence Scores

Home Discipline Scores			Age			Intelligence Scores		
	No. of strict	No. of permissive	Age	No. of strict	No. of permissive	Vocabulary IQ	Strict	Permissive
145 and over	0	7	11	3	3	150–159	1	4
135–144	0	7	10	3	3	140–149	2	4
125–134	0	17	9	9	2	130–139	8	5
120–124	0	3	8	10	7	120–129	5	2
			7	11	7	110–119	3	1
91–120	0	0	6	8	12	Below 110	0	0
81– 90	19	0	Total	44	34		19	16
71– 80	17	0	Mean	7.9	7.6			
61– 70	6	0				Estimate from Rorschach		
51– 60	2	0	Sex					
Total	44	34		Strict	Permissive		Strict	Permissive
Median	79.8	133.3	Boys	25	21	Superior	10	13
			Girls	19	13	Above Aver.	25	12
			Total	44	34	Average	9	9
						Below Aver.	0	0
							44	34

nificantly different in proportion of boys (57 per cent and 62 per cent), or in age. The distributions of intelligence, as estimated from Rorschach or quite independently from a vocabulary test, show relatively a few more top-level *IQ*'s from the permissive homes, but this difference is not large enough to be statistically significant. It is noteworthy that all children in this study have *IQ*'s of 110 or higher as estimated from their vocabulary.

4. Plan of Personality Study

Children who are strictly brought up will be compared with children who are treated much more permissively, on each of nine dimensions of personality as follows:

Overt Behavior
1. Independence—dependence.
2. Socialization—ego-centrism.
3. Persistence—easy discouragement.
4. Self-control—disintegration.
5. Energy—passivity.

Inner Feelings
6. Creativity—stereotyping.
7. Friendliness—hostility.
8. Security—anxiety.
9. Happiness—sadness.

In each instance the null hypothesis—that there is no significant difference between the two groups—will be statistically tested.

a. Independence—Dependence. *Hypothesis 1. Is there no difference between children from strict and those from permissive homes in the personality dimension of independence—dependence?*

Five measures bearing upon this hypothesis have been combined to give an index of independence. One is a rating by the psychologist of the child's behavior as he was brought into the playroom, shown the toys, games, puzzles, craft materials, etc., and told he might play with them in any way he chose. A rating of "5" is assigned to those children who promptly sized up the situation and went to work on their own responsibility with no further demands on the adult. The low extreme of the scale, a rating of "1," is assigned to those children who were unable to get going despite repeated instruction and reassurance. This rating correlates .70 with the composite index.

The second measure is a rating of the child's evident need for adult attention during the later activities of the testing period. Those children who independently judged their own performance with little reference to cues from the psychologist are at the high (5) end of the scale; those who were so dependent on adult approval that without definite reassurance their behavior was disrupted are given a rating of 1. This measures correlates .71 with the composite.

The third rating is based on a period of free play with doll figures representing a family. If the examiner was asked to make decisions for the child, the rating is low; high ratings represent independent, self-reliant structuring of the interpersonal play. This measure has the highest correlation (.76) with the composite index.

The fourth measure is based on the story interpretations which the child assigned to several *TAT* and *CAT* pictures. If the figures with whom the child seemed to identify most were self-reliant, acting on their own responsibility, the rating is 5. The lowest rating, 1, means that the identification figures were generally passive, helpless, or dependent. This correlates only .51 with the composite.

Our fifth rating is derived from Rorschach responses. Whether M (movement) responses were active and extensor or passive and flexor, or absent; whether the balance of C, CF, and FC tended toward or away from control, and the content of food and adult-child relationships were all taken into account. The Rorschach estimate correlates .67 with the composite.

TABLE 4

Differences in Independence—Dependence

	Boys		Girls		All	
	Strict	Permis-sive	Strict	Permis-sive	Strict	Permis-sive
High independence (20–23)	1	7	1	3	2	10
Above average (17–19)	9	6	6	4	15	10
Below average (13–16)	10	7	8	5	18	12
Very dependent (9–12)	5	1	4	1	9	2
Total	25	21	19	13	44	34

$\chi^2 = 20.95$. P < .01.

The reliability of the total index is estimated (Spearman-Brown) at .80. Theoretically scores might range from 5 to 25; the actual range is from 9 (very dependent) to 23 (highly independent). Distributions shown in Table 4 find some children from each type of home at every level of independence but the null hypothesis—that no real difference will be found—must be rejected. Differences (based on χ^2 with Yates' correction) are significant at better than the .01 level. [5] The highly independent children include 29 per cent of our permissive sample, but only 5 per cent of the strictly disciplined children. The very dependent children represent 6 per cent of those from permissive homes and 21 per cent of those from strict homes. We find, therefore, a *marked tendency for greater freedom in the home to show itself in greater independence in the child's behavior outside the home.*

TABLE 5

TEACHER RATINGS ON INITIATIVE AND INDEPENDENCE

Rating	Boys		Girls		All	
	Strict	Permissive	Strict	Permissive	Strict	Permissive
9–10	6	2	5	4	11	6
5– 8	5	3	3	2	8	5
1– 4	4	3	1	0	5	3
	15	8	9	6	24	14

No significant difference.

A study of teacher-ratings on "initiative" and "independence," available for only 38 of our 78 cases, yields no significant difference. The distributions are shown in Table 5. A possible explanation for the apparent disagreement between these ratings and those based on our tests may be the teacher's preference for the kind of initiative which is in close conformity to classroom demands. This seems especially plausible when we note that very low ratings on initiative and independence have been given by the teachers to seven boys but to only one girl.

b. Socialization—Ego-centrism. *Hypothesis 2. Is there no difference between children from strict and those from permissive homes in the personality dimension of socialization—ego-centrism?*

Our index combines four separate ratings: (a) verbal negativism (or overcompliance) versus coöperative consideration of the child's own wishes and the adult requests; (b) behavioral negativism (or over-compliance) versus "positive but differentiated coöperation"; (c) stories told in response to several *TAT* and *CAT* pictures, rated for quality of parent-child relations from resistance to friendly interaction; and (d) responses to Card IV of Rorschach. Average intercorrelation of these ratings on socially integrative responses is .52, yielding a predicted reliability, for the four combined, of .81.

TABLE 6

DIFFERENCES IN SOCIALIZATION—EGO-CENTRISM

	Boys		Girls		All	
	Strict	Permissive	Strict	Permissive	Strict	Permissive
Well socialized, coöperative (15–18)	2	7	2	4	4	11
Above average (12–14)	7	6	2	6	9	12
Below average (10–11)	10	6	9	1	19	7
Negativistic or over-compliant (7–9)	6	2	6	2	12	4
Totals	25	21	19	13	44	34

$\chi^2 = 15.14$. P $< .01$.

Differences, reported in Table 6, show markedly better coöperation by children from permissive homes. Differences are statistically significant, being large enough to have a probability of chance occurrence, less than .01. The highest level of mature coöperation is found among 32 per cent of the children from permissive homes but only 9 per cent of the children strictly disciplined. The null hypothesis must be rejected and so also must the "spoiled child" or "little monster" tradition. *Exceptionally permissive discipline seems on the whole to be associated with better socialization and more effective coöperation with others.* At the same time, it should be remembered that children from each type of home can be found at every step of the socialization scale.

This study does not demonstrate that the higher average level of independence reported earlier, or of coöperation reported here, is produced by the permissive discipline. It may be true—and the data on freedom from hostility to be reported later make this plausible—that the more relaxed home atmosphere is responsible for the observed differences in personality. Alternative explanations cannot, however, be excluded. Perhaps the kind of parents who choose the permissive rôle transmit, via heredity or via associated cultural influences, a different temperament or pattern of living. It should not be assumed that if parents who have heretofore practiced strict discipline were simply to change over to great permissiveness, their children would thereby become more independent or coöperative. They might, or might not. A correlational study cannot satisfactorily answer questions of causation.

Table 7 reports teacher-ratings for 38 of our children on coöperation and popularity in the classroom. The number of cases

TABLE 7

DIFFERENCES IN SOCIALIZATION AS RATED BY TEACHERS ($N = 38$)

	Boys		Girls		All	
	Strict	Permissive	Strict	Permissive	Strict	Permissive
A. Coöperation in classroom						
Coöperative (4–5)	8	4	6	5	14	9
Average (3)	5	2	3	0	8	2
Uncoöperative (1–2)	2	2	0	1	2	3
Total	15	8	9	6	24	14
(Differences not statistically significant.)						
B. Popularity with other children						
Popular (4–5)	8	3	7	5	15	8
Average (3)	4	5	1	1	5	6
Less well liked (1–2)	3	0	1	0	4	0
Total	15	8	9	6	24	14
(Differences not statistically significant.)						

is small and differences are without statistical significance. The most impressive fact in this little sample is that no child from a permissive home was rated below average in friendliness or popularity with other children.

c. Persistence—Easy Discouragement. *Hypothesis 3. Is there no difference between children from strict and those from permissive homes in the personality dimension of persistence versus being easily discouraged?*

All subjects were given the Alexander Passalong test which begins with easy problems in block movement and arrangement but proceeds to those which, although they seem workable, are impossibly difficult. The psychologist noted how long the child persisted at the task and also the effect of increasing difficulty and frustration upon personality organization and ability to make intelligent use of experience.

Table 8 is in accord with the null hypothesis, since the two groups cannot confidently be regarded as from different statistical distributions. The null hypothesis is likewise supported by teacher ratings (for 38 cases) on persistence at school tasks which showed similar distributions for children from strict and from permissive homes.

If our hypothesis were revised to state that permissive discipline is associated with a moderate degree of persistence, while strict

TABLE 8

DIFFERENCES IN PERSISTENCE—EASY DISCOURAGEMENT*

Rating	Boys		Girls		All	
	Strict	Permis- sive	Strict	Permis- sive	Strict	Permis- sive
4 Very persistent	13	6	8	3	21	9
3 Moderate	3	7	4	9	7	16
1–2 Evade, give up	9	7	7	1	16	8
Total	25	20	19	13	44	33

* Distributions not statistically significant, but association of permissive discipline with moderate rather than high or low persistence is significant ($\chi^2 = 12.49$) at better than the .01 level of confidence.

discipline is associated with either unusually persistent or easily discouraged behavior, this *post hoc* revised hypothesis would be supported by the psychological test data of Table 8 at better than the .01 level of significance. The revised hypothesis makes good psychological sense. Since we already know that the children from permissive homes are more inclined to act independently and on their own initiative, we might expect them to make a try at a very difficult problem, but to use their own judgment in giving it up when no progress is made. In contrast, the children accustomed to firm adult control might more readily feel helpless, or, if instructed to keep on trying, persist in their vain efforts. The data on intellectual quality of the continued effort will be helpful in assessing this expectation.

TABLE 9

DIFFERENCES IN EFFECT OF FRUSTRATION ON LEARNING

	Boys		Girls		All	
	Strict	Permis-sive	Strict	Permis-sive	Strict	Permis-sive
3 = Improves despite frustration	8	11	6	9	14	20
2 = No marked effect	7	8	7	3	14	11
1 = Deterioration from frustration	7	1	6	1	13	2
Totals	22	20	19	13	41	33

$\chi^2 = 6.73$. Differences significant at .02 to .05 level.

As the task grew more difficult, some children became frustrated and deteriorated in their learning process. Others continued to study the problem, did not repeat errors, and evidenced growing insight into the difficulty. Type of home discipline does seem to be related to quality of behavior under difficulties, as reported in Table 9. Serious deterioration in intellectual quality of response was found in 13 (32 per cent) of the children with strict up-bringing, but in only 2 (6 per cent) of the children given greater freedom.

The hypothesis that home discipline is unrelated to persistence-discouragement should probably be rejected. The observed differences certainly do not sustain the popular fear that children who are allowed their own way much of the time at home will collapse when faced by difficult tasks. Apparently—with due allowance, again, for the fact that some children from each type of home can be found at every level—there is some tendency for *permissive discipline to foster the type of personality which makes a reasonable effort, continues effective intellectual attack upon problems, but is unlikely to persist indefinitely against odds.* Differences in school work are not significant.

d. Self-control—Emotional Disintegration. *Hypothesis 4. Is there no difference between children from strict and those from permissive homes in the personality dimensions of self-control versus emotional disintegration?*

Closely related to the quality of intellectual attack upon a difficult problem is the emotional response during frustration. The data in Table 10 come from the psychologist's rating of the child's emotional reactions as the Passalong test became too difficult for him. The null hypothesis is acceptable; observed differences are not statistically significant. A further test of the hypothesis may be made, using teacher's ratings for 37 of the children. Again, as shown in Table 11, differences fall within what might well be expected by chance.

Our data do not support the view that children given firm control at home are better able to withstand frustration; neither do they support those who argue that strict parental control interferes with the development of the child's self-control.

e. Energy—Passivity. *Hypothesis 5. Is there no difference between children from strict and those from permissive homes in the dimension of energetic versus passive personality?*

Three ratings are applicable to testing of this hypothesis. One is a rating by the psychologist of the apparent energy level of the child. Scores range from 1 for "inert, uninvolved" manner during play and testing, through 2 for subdued activity, to 5 for very lively participation. This variable refers to focused personality energy, not to merely physical, muscular activity.

TABLE 10

DIFFERENCES IN SELF-CONTROL DURING FRUSTRATION TEST

	Boys		Girls		All	
	Strict	Permis-sive	Strict	Permis-sive	Strict	Permis-sive
Undisturbed	10	12	8	6	18	18
Moderate impatience	10	7	9	5	19	12
Extremely upset	4	1	2	2	6	3
Total	24	20	19	13	43	33

Differences not statistically significant.

TABLE 11

TEACHER RATING ON SELF-CONTROL

Rating	Boys		Girls		All	
	Strict	Permis-sive	Strict	Permis-sive	Strict	Permis-sive
Well balanced; not easily upset	5	2	6	6	11	8
About average	3	2	2	0	5	2
Loses temper, cries, easily upset	7	3	1	0	8	3
Totals	15	7	9	6	24	13

Differences not statistically significant.

The second rating is derived wholly from the Rorschach performance, taking account of total number of responses, number of content categories, number of wholes, and amount of movement.

The third estimate is based on an exercise in which the child drew a man, a woman, and himself.

Average intercorrelation of the three ratings is .46; predicted reliability for the three combined is .72.

As shown in Table 12, the differences between groups are not significant and the null hypothesis is acceptable.

TABLE 12

DIFFERENCES IN ENERGY—PASSIVITY

	Boys		Girls		All	
	Strict	Permissive	Strict	Permissive	Strict	Permissive
Energetic, active productive (13–15)	3	4	3	4	6	8
Above average (11–12)	10	4	8	5	18	9
Average (9–10)	10	3	3	4	13	7
Inert, passive (5–8)	2	9	5	0	7	9
Total	25	20	19	13	44	33

Differences not statistically significant.

"Activity level" has also been rated by the teachers of 38 of our children. Results are reported in Table 13. High (4 or 5) ratings are given to 15 (63 per cent) of 24 children from strict homes as compared with only 5 of 14 children (36 per cent) from permissive homes. Differences between the two distributions are significant at a probability level between $P = .02$ and $P = .05$, with higher

TABLE 13

DIFFERENCES IN ACTIVITY LEVEL AS RATED BY TEACHERS

	Boys		Girls		All	
	Strict	Permissive	Strict	Permissive	Strict	Permissive
Active, energetic 4–5	8	2	7	3	15	5
Average 3	6	3	1	2	7	5
Quiet, inert 1–2	1	3	1	1	2	4
Total	15	8	9	6	24	14

$\chi^2 = 4.20$. P between .02 and .05.

ratings for the children from stricter homes. That pupils from strictly disciplined homes are seen by teachers as more energetic and active may be related to their more ready acceptance of teacher direction. This point came out earlier in connection with teacher ratings on "independence." The sex difference again raises a question about what the typical teacher means by "energetic." High ratings on activity and energy were assigned to 67 per cent of the girls but to only 43 per cent of the boys.

Neither the data from the psychological tests nor those from the classroom would support the view that strict home discipline typically represses impulses to such an extent as to make children inactive. In the test situation no difference is apparent, at school the well-disciplined children appear, on the whole, more active along approved lines.

f. Creativity—Conformity. *Hypothesis 6. Is there no difference between children from strict and those from permissive homes in the personality dimension of creativity versus conformity?*

Five measures of this variable are available. One is based on the child's behavior, ranging from free and imaginative to stereotyped and monotonous, during a free play period. A second has been similarly observed during a period of play with a full family of

TABLE 14

DIFFERENCES IN CREATIVITY—CONFORMITY

	Boys		Girls		All	
	Strict	Permissive	Strict	Permissive	Strict	Permissive
Highly creative, imaginative, spontaneous, original	1	6	1	5	2	11
Above average	12	5	6	1	18	6
Below average	8	4	8	7	16	11
Stereotyped, conventional, restricted	4	6	4	0	8	6
	25	21	19	13	44	34

$\chi^2 = 29.35$. P $<$ .01.

dolls. The third estimates originality and imagination in stories composed as responses to *CAT* and *TAT* pictures. The fourth comes from Rorschach responses and the fifth from human figure-drawing. The average intercorrelation of these measures is .53 and the predicted reliability for the combined rating is .85.

The differences shown in Table 14 are the most impressive of any in our comparisons, and compel rejection of the null hypothesis. *High creativity characterizes 11 (33 per cent) of the children brought up with unusual freedom, but only 2 (5 per cent) of those from strict homes.* The more firmly disciplined children are most apt to be found near the middle of the range in this variable.

g. Friendliness—Hostility.   *Hypothesis 7. Is there no difference between children from strict and those from permissive homes along the dimension of friendly versus hostile feelings toward others?*

Our psychological testing yields four projective indications of inner hostility. One is based on observation of free play with dolls. Hostile contacts or avoidance of contacts is rated 1; friendly interaction is rated 5.

The second is based on the *TAT* and *CAT* stories. The low end of the scale (rating 1) is assigned to stories of violent conflict, death, and destruction. High scores represent stories of friendly interaction.

The third rating is based on such Rorschach signs as content items interpreted as aggressive weapons, mutilated human or animal bodies, and aggressive or hostile M or FM.

The fourth has been drawn from analysis of the figure-drawing test and responses during the drawing.

Intercorrelations among these tests range from .50 to .74, averaging .60; the predicted reliability for the four combined is .87—the highest of any of our measures.

Hostility versus friendliness scores of the two groups are compared in Table 15. The null hypothesis should be rejected. *More hostility is evident in those children who have been strictly disciplined; more positive feelings toward others are expressed by children whose parents have been permissive;* these differences are consistent through the distribution and are statistically significant. At the same time, it should be remembered that neither

TABLE 15

DIFFERENCES IN FRIENDLINESS—HOSTILITY

	Boys		Girls		All	
	Strict	Permis-sive	Strict	Permis-sive	Strict	Permis-sive
High friendliness, little hostility (16 and over)	1	2	0	4	1	6
Above average friend-liness; below average hostility (Scores 13–15)	5	8	8	6	13	14
Above average hostility (Scores 10–12)	12	8	10	1	22	9
High degree of aggressive hostility (Scores 9 and lower)	7	4	1	1	8	5
	25	22	19	12	44	34

$\chi^2 = 10.64$ (Yates correction). $P < .02$.

group has a complete monopoly on positive, friendly feelings toward others or on inner hostility.

Reactions to frustration on the Passalong Test make possible another rating which has in it a high component of hostility for some children. Half of the *TAT* story-completion test was administered before the frustrating experience of failure on the too-difficult block test. The other half was given immediately after the somewhat annoying defeat. For a few children, the consequence was that the stories in the latter part of the test were briefer, the child was less coöperative and gave more evidence of hostility. This behavior characterized six (15 per cent) of the 41 children from strict homes; but only one (3 per cent) of the 32 children from permissive homes. This difference is not statistically significant, but its direction is in accord with the evidence from Table 15 indicating that strict discipline does leave a residue of inner hostility.

h. Security—Anxiety. *Hypothesis 8. Is there no difference between children from strict and those from permissive homes in the personality dimension security—anxiety?*

Five different ratings compose our measure of anxiety. One is the psychologist's impression of the overtly confident or insecure behavior of the child. Three are based on projective tests: one on Card 9 of the *CAT*, one on the Rorschach, and one on the figure drawing test. The fifth measure is the anxiety evident during failure on the Passalong test. These five measures have an average intercorrelation of .33; the combined index would have a predicted reliability of .71 which is not high but would suffice if the groups turn out to be markedly different.

TABLE 16

DIFFERENCES IN SECURITY—ANXIETY

	Boys		Girls		All	
	Strict	Permissive	Strict	Permissive	Strict	Permissive
Secure, relaxed (16–19)	1	4	4	3	5	7
Less than average anxiety (14–15)	10	6	5	7	15	13
More than average anxiety (12–13)	8	7	7	1	15	8
Anxious, tense (7–11)	6	4	3	2	9	6
	25	21	19	13	44	34

$\chi^2 = 1.81$. Differences not significant.

As shown in Table 16 the two groups are not clearly distinguished. The null hypothesis is acceptable. Half a dozen children from each type of discipline show marked evidence of anxiety—another half-dozen from each category behave in an easy, secure manner. What makes for anxiety in a child must be something other than unusually strict or unusually lax parental control.

i. Happiness—Sadness. *Hypothesis 9. Is there no difference between children from strict and those from permissive homes in the personality dimension of happiness versus sadness?*

Three measures are related to general level of happiness. One is a rating of the overt manner and apparent mood of the child during his play and testing periods. Scores range from 5 for the most euphoric to 1 for the most depressed. A second measure is derived by analysis of the imaginative stories given in response to *CAT* and *TAT* pictures. Predominantly optimistic and enjoyable events result in high ratings; stories in which distress, sadness, and unhappiness come to the leading figures result in a low score. The third measure is based upon Rorschach test responses. Predominant use of black, and perception of figures as torn and broken, are used as indicators of depression.

Intercorrelations among the several indices (except for overt behavior and the Rorschach which correlate .54) are low, averaging .28 and giving a combined predictive reliability of .54.[4]

TABLE 17

DIFFERENCES IN HAPPINESS—SADNESS

	Boys		Girls		All	
	Strict	Permissive	Strict	Permissive	Strict	Permissive
Unusually happy, optimistic, cheerful, buoyant	2	6	4	3	6	9
Average or above	18	7	11	8	29	15
Below average; sad, depressed, melancholy	5	8	4	2	9	10
Total	25	21	19	13	44	34

Differences not statistically significant.

Results, shown in Table 17, conform to the null hypothesis. While our data show a slightly larger proportion of permissive

[4] This reliability might have been increased slightly by omission of the picture-story rating, but it seemed better to include all available indications of euphoria or sadness. One test might bring out a response different from the others but still pertinent to an estimate of general level of euphoria.

discipline subjects in both the "happy" and the "unhappy" categories, the differences are unreliable.

E. SUMMARY

Forty-four children brought up in good, loving, but strictly disciplined homes are compared with 34 children from the same community and also brought up in good, loving homes but with an extraordinary degree of permissiveness. Two periods of psychological testing, supplemented (in 38 cases) by teacher ratings, have yielded measures of nine dimensions of personality. On three of the nine, no statistically significant difference is found: these are the dimensions of self-control, inner security, and happiness. Factors making for anxiety, emotional disorganization, and unhappiness are found about equally often under either type of home discipline. No difference in activity and energy level was observed during the psychological testing, but teacher ratings indicate higher activity level of an approved sort, at school for the children accustomed to stricter discipline.

On persistence, teachers observe no differences, but on a psychological test children from strict homes are more apt to fall in extreme categories, being either unusually persistent or very easily discouraged. A moderate persistence is more characteristic of the children from permissive homes. These children maintain a better quality of intellectual activity under difficulty than do the children from strict homes.

On the four remaining variables (which are also those most reliably measured, with predicted r's from .80 to .87) significant differences in each instance are in favor of the children from permissive homes. Greater freedom for the child is clearly associated with: (*a*) more initiative and independence (except, perhaps, at school tasks); (*b*) better socialization and coöperation; (*c*) less inner hostility and more friendly feelings toward others; and (*d*) a higher level of spontaneity, originality, and creativity.

None of the personality differences applies to all cases; some children from strict and some from permissive homes may be found at every level on every characteristic tested. It is impressive, however, to find no clear personality advantage associated in general with strict discipline in a good home. Where differences do emerge, these are consistently to the credit of the more permissive upbringing. This study cannot distinguish the extent to which the advantages associated with permissiveness are due to that procedure alone and the extent to which more permissive parents may convey hereditary or cultural assets with which the permissive attitudes happen to be correlated.

——▶ **Allison Davis
and Robert J. Havighurst**

Social Class and Color
Differences in Child Rearing

From *American Sociological Review*, 1946, 11:698–710. Reprinted and abridged by permission.

In recent years, cultural anthropologists and social psychologists have made intensive studies of the relationships between personality and socialization. They have arrived at a methodological distinction which has proved helpful in the analysis of personality. In the light of their comparative data on the socialization of individual children in different societies, they have set up the operational principle that personality can best be studied in terms of two basic interacting systems of behavior.

One system of actions, feelings, and thoughts is (a) cultural. It is learned by the individual from his basic social groups: his family, his age groups, his sex group, his social class group, and so on. The other system of responses is (b) individual, or "idiosyncratic" or "private." It derives in part from genetic factors and in part from learning. These learned individual traits are responses to organic, affectional and chance factors, and likewise to the particular deviations of a child's training from the standard cultural training for his group. The research whose findings will be summarized below is concerned primarily with the cultural aspects of personality.

DISCUSSION OF THE FINDINGS OF THE STUDY

The answer is clear to the principal question which this study was designed to answer. There are considerable social class differences in child-rearing practices, and these differences are greater than the differences between Negroes and whites of the same social class.

Personality Implications of Social Class Differences in Child-Rearing

Middle-class families are more rigorous than lower-class families in their training of children for feeding and cleanliness habits. They generally begin training earlier. Furthermore, middle-class families place more emphasis on the early assumption of responsibility for the self and on individual achievement. Finally, middle-class families are less permissive than lower-class families in their regimen. They require their children to take naps at a later age, to be in the house at night earlier, and, in general, permit less free play of the impulses of their children.

Generalizing from the evidence of this study, we would say that middle-class children are subjected earlier and more consistently to the influences which make a child an orderly, conscientious, responsible, and tame person. In the course of this training middle-class children probably suffer more frustration of their impulses.

In the light of these findings, the data with respect to thumb-sucking are interesting. Three times as many white middle-class children are reported to suck their thumbs as white lower-class children, and almost twice as many Negro middle-class children do likewise. Thumb-sucking is generally thought of as a response to frustration of the hunger drive, or of the drive to seek pleasure through sucking. Since middle-class children are fed less frequently and are weaned earlier, the higher incidence of thumb-sucking would be expected. The Negro middle-class children are treated much more permissively than the white middle-class children with respect to feeding and weaning, but much more rigorously with respect to toilet-training. Yet the proportion of Negro middle-class children reported as sucking their thumb is almost the same as the proportion of white middle-class children so reported. *Perhaps thumb-sucking is a response to frustration of any sort, rather than to frustration in the feeding area alone.*

The data with respect to masturbation are also of interest in this connection. Three times as many white middle-class as compared with lower-class children are reported as masturbating. Twice as many Negro middle-class children as compared with Negro lower-class children are reported as masturbating. The meaning of these findings is obscured by the possibility that some lower-class mothers may not have understood the question. Or it may be that some of them did not watch as carefully for masturbation as middle-class mothers do, or some lower-class mothers may have been more hesitant than middle-class mothers, in admitting that their children followed this practice. Yet none of these explanations seems probable, and perhaps the data should be taken at their face value. Perhaps masturbation is much more common among middle-class infants than among lower-class infants. If this is true, it might be explained in terms of the hypothesis that masturbation is in part a palliative to frustration. Children who are frustrated more would masturbate more, according to the hypothesis.

It is a surprising fact that the middle-class mothers, in general, expected their children to assume responsibility earlier in the home, to help with the younger children, and to cook and sew at an earlier age. For it seems obvious that there is more actual need of the children's help in lower-class families, where the work of children to be cared for is greater and the mother has very little help with the housework. The explanation probably lies in a tendency on the part of middle-class people to train their children early for achievement and responsibility, while lower-class people train their children to take responsibility only after the child is old enough to make the effort of training pay substantial returns in the work the child will do.

In addition to training their children to take responsibility early and to adopt attitudes favorable to self-achievement, middle-class families attempt to curb those impulses of the child which would lead to poor health, waste of time, and bad moral habits, according to middle-class views. Therefore they require their children to take daytime naps longer and to come into the house at night earlier; they do not permit their children to go alone to movies at an early age. Nevertheless, they encourage their children to be venturesome in the more "constructive" activities, from the middle-class point of view, of going downtown alone to museums, department stores, dancing lessons and the like.

Personality Implications of Color Differences in Child-Rearing

The striking thing about this study is that Negro and white middle-class families are so much alike, and that white and Negro lower-class families are so much alike. The likenesses hold for such characteristics as number of children, ages of parents when married, as well as child-rearing practices and expectations of children.

There are, however, some very interesting color differences. The major color differences are found in the areas of feeding and cleanliness training.

Negroes are much more permissive than whites in the feeding and weaning of their children. The difference is greater in the middle class. Negro babies have a markedly different feeding and weaning experience from white babies.

The situation is reversed with respect to toilet training. Here the Negro parents are much stricter than white parents, both in middle- and lower-class circles. For example, 87 per cent of Negro middle-class mothers said they commence bowel training at six months or earlier, compared with 49 per cent of white middle-class mothers; the comparable figures for bladder training are 40 and 18 per cent.

There is another noticeable color difference. Negroes of both classes tend to give their girls an earlier training for responsibility in washing dishes, going to the store, and dressing themselves. This is probably traceable to the fact that Negroes of both classes have less outside help in the home than whites do and consequently the help of the girls is more urgently needed.

It is noticeable, also, that middle-class Negro girls are not allowed to play across the street or to go to the movies alone as
early as white middle-class girls. This may be due to the fact
that most middle-class Negroes are forced to live in much less
desirable neighborhoods, from their point of view, than those
in which middle-class whites live.

Personality Implications of Intrafamily Differences

The questionnaire was designed to get information on personality characteristics of children as they might be related to
birth order, training experience, and kinds of discipline used.
Very few pronounced relationships appeared. This may have
been due to several factors. Perhaps the interview method as we
used it is not suited to getting information on individual personality characteristics. Again, perhaps such relations as exist are
too complicated to be seen clearly in a study like this with a relatively small number of subjects. Nevertheless, there were a few
interesting intrafamily relationships.

For instance, the relation of "activity when young" to other
characteristics is of considerable importance, since the degree of
physical activity when young may be taken as an index of native
vitality and of whatever inborn drive there may be for exploration or for physical activity. As we should expect, those "most
active when young" were reported as most frequently punished,
and as most active now. They were also reported as fighting most
now, and as least neat. They were reported as happiest, except
in the case of the white middle class. In general, it appears that
various types of expressive, impulse behavior tend to go together, and to characterize the happy child. An exception must
be made of the white middle class, where happiness is reported
by the mothers as associated with quietness rather than activity
in the young child.

The data on birth order in relation to personality characteristics show some interesting trends. The first child in middle-
class families of two children tends to be more jealous and more
selfish than the second child. They may be taken as evidence in
favor of the hypothesis of downward sibling rivalry as strongly
influential in personality formation. Still, it is well to remember

that mothers of young children, when there are only two in the family, may report the older as more jealous and selfish merely because the older is bigger and more able to assert himself. The second child was reported as happier and more generous, and also as more punished.

SUMMARY

This study has given clear evidence of the following things:

1. There are significant differences in child-rearing practices between the middle and lower social classes in a large city. The same type of differences exist between middle- and lower-class Negroes as between middle- and lower-class whites.

2. Middle-class parents are more rigorous than lower-class parents in their training of children for feeding and cleanliness habits. They also expect their children to take responsibility for themselves earlier than lower-class parents do. Middle-class parents place their children under a stricter regime, with more frustration of their impulses, than do lower-class parents.

3. In addition to these social class differences, there are some differences between Negroes and whites in their child-rearing practices. Negroes are more permissive than whites in the feeding and weaning of their children, but they are much more rigorous than whites in toilet training.

4. Thus there are *cultural differences* in the personality formation of middle-class compared with lower-class people, *regardless of color,* due to their early training. And for the same reason there should be further but less marked cultural differences between Negroes and whites of the same social class.

5. In addition to the cultural differences between individuals due to early training experience, there are individual personality differences between children in the same family. These are probably due to physiological differences and to differences in emotional relationships with other members of the family.

REFERENCES

1. ANDERSON, J. P., *The Relationships between Certain Aspects of Parental Behavior and Attitudes of Junior High School Pupils,* New York: Teachers College, Columbia University, 1940.

2. AYER, M. E., & BERNREUTER, R., "A Study of the Relationship Between Discipline and Personality Traits in Young Children, *Journal of Genetic Psychology,* 1937, 50:165–170.

3. BALDWIN, A. L., "Socialization and the Parent-Child Relationship," *Child Development,* 1948, 19:127–136.

4. CARPENTER, J., & EISENBERG, P., "Some Relationships between Family Background and Personality," *Journal of Psychology,* 1938, 6:115–136.

5. FISHER, R. A., *Statistical Methods for Research Workers,* 7th ed., Edinburgh: Oliver & Boyd, Ltd., 1938.

6. HATTWICK, BERTA W., "Interrelations between the Preschool Child's Behavior and Certain Factors in the Home, *Child Development,* 1936, 7:200–226.

7. HATTWICK, BERTA W., & STOWELL, MARGARET, "The Relation of Parental Over-attentiveness to Children's Work Habits and Social Adjustment in Kindergarten and the First Six Grades of School, *Journal of Educational Research,* 1936, 30:162–176.

8. HEINICKE, C., & WHITING, B. B., *Bibliographies on Personality and Social Development of the Child,* New York: Social Science Research Council Pamphlet No. 10, 1953.

9. LAFORE, GERTRUDE, "Practices of Parents in Dealing with Preschool Children," *Child Development Monographs,* 1945, 31:3–150.

10. MYERS, T. R., *Intrafamily Relationships and Pupil Adjustment,* New York: Teachers College, Columbia University, 1935.

11. ORLANSKY, H., "Infant Care and Personality," *Psychological Bulletin,* 1949, 46:1–48.

12. RADKE, MARIAN J., *The Relation of Parental Authority to Children's Behavior and Attitudes,* Minneapolis: University of Minnesota Press, 1946.

13. SEWELL, W. H., "Infant Training and the Personality of the Child," *American Journal of Sociology,* 1952, 58:150–157.

14. SHOBEN, E. J., JR., "The Assessment of Parental Attitudes in Relation to Child Adjustment," *Genetic Psychology Monographs,* 1949, 39:101–148.

15. SYMONDS, P. M., *Psychology of Parent-Child Relationships,* New York: Appleton-Century-Crofts, Inc., 1939.

16. WATSON, G., "A Comparison of the Effects of Lax versus Strict Home Discipline," *Journal of Social Psychology*, 1934, 5:102–105.

17. WHITING, J. W. M., & CHILD, I. L., *Child Training and Personality*, New Haven: Yale University Press, 1953.

18. WOLFENSTEIN, MARTHA, "Trends in Infant Care," *American Journal of Orthopsychiatry*, 1953, 33:120–130.

19. WRIGHT, G. O., "Projection and Displacement: A Cross-Cultural Study of Folktale Aggression," *Journal of Abnormal and Social Psychology*, 1954, 49:523–528.

PART
FOUR
↑

Personality
and the School's Role
in Its Development

The readings in the final two chapters of this book have the following functions to perform. First, they are to indicate what is meant by personality, the nature of factors involved in its development, and the central place that the self-concept occupies in personality.

Second, the readings—especially those in the final chapter—are to give us an idea of how today's teachers are faring in their efforts to apply the concepts of child and adolescent psychology as well as knowledge from other behavioral sciences to the practical affairs of the classroom.

In a very real sense, Part Four represents a culmination of all that has preceded it in this book. A main objective of the book has been to underscore the importance in the psychology of human development of keeping *persons* (children and youth, especially) always in view. Part Four should help the reader determine to what extent the *Readings* have made persons more understandable to him.

CHAPTER
FOURTEEN

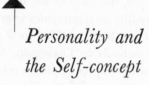

*Personality and
the Self-concept*

PROBABLY NO TOPIC IN PSYCHOLOGY IS MORE
indicative of the important and still to be mastered frontiers of
the study of man than the topic of personality. Admittedly this
area of psychology is still quite indistinctly charted; even so
there is enough now known about it to make it a highly profitable
one for study by teachers and others concerned with children
and youth.

Each reading in this chapter deals with one or more of the
currently challenging problems of personality and its development. Symond's discussion in the first article not only supplies
a helpful orientation to what psychologists mean by *personality*,
but also deals effectively with the question of the extent to which
continuity characterizes personality development and the related
question of the influence of infant and early-childhood experi-

ences upon personality. The article concludes with strong emphasis upon the role of the teacher in personality development.

From 1924 until his death in 1960, Percival M. Symonds was Professor of Education and Psychology in Teachers College, Columbia University. His contributions to the literature of psychology and education are numerous and highly regarded.

A classic study of personality development was published in 1933 by Mary M. Shirley (Reference 73 in this chapter) descriptive of the personality of twenty-five babies during their first two years. Fifteen years after the original study Patricia (Neilon) Naka conducted a follow-up study of the personality of these same individuals. The findings, as presented in the second reading, have clear bearing on the question of the degree to which there is continuity of personality characteristics over a relatively long time-span. Mrs. Naka has been working as a psychologist since 1955 with the Public Schools in Lexington, Massachusetts.

The title of the present chapter implies a relationship between personality and the self-concept. Increasing attention has been given in recent years to the evidence of this relationship and its importance. Among psychologists who have strongly emphasized the role of the self-concept in personality and personal adjustment is Arthur T. Jersild of Teachers College, Columbia University. Surely there will be much agreement with Jersild's statement, "The most important psychological facts in a child's life are his relationships with others and his relationship to himself." Doubtless there will also be considerable agreement with the conclusion, "Learning which pertains to anything so crucial should properly be part of the child's planned education."

——▶ **Percival M. Symonds**

Origins of Personality[1]

From *Teachers College Record*, March, 1960, 61:301–317. Reprinted and abridged by permission.

It is the purpose of this discussion to review some of the findings of psychology that deal with the origin and development of personality, to discuss their implications for education, and to suggest some of the practical steps that may be taken by teachers, if the conclusion is reached that education has some responsibility for the development of personality.

Before we get involved in the subject, it is necessary to clarify what is meant by personality. Freud, in one of his letters to Karl Abraham, wrote, "Personality is a rather indefinite expression taken from surface psychology, and it doesn't contribute much to our understanding of the real processes. Only one can easily believe that by using it one has said something substantial."[2] Personality is approached from the point of view of surface rather than depth psychology in this discussion, and its indefiniteness is quite acceptable. Personality refers to those personal characteristics which define the individual. It may be seen from a number of points of view. It refers to behavior which may be observed by another person (cooperative, boorish, systematic, untidy) or to the ways in which a person experiences himself (I feel uncomfortable in the presence of those whom I recognize as my superiors, I feel confident, I am discouraged, I am successful). These different observations may not agree, but they all must

---

[1] Articles VII and VIII in this series were published in the October and November 1959 issues of *Teachers College Record*. The first six articles are available in a pamphlet published by the Bureau of Publications, Teachers College, Columbia University, New York, N.Y.

[2] Sigmund Freud in a letter to Karl Abraham, October 21, 1907, quoted in Ernest Jones, *The Life and Works of Sigmund Freud*, Volume II, New York: Basic Books, Inc., 1955, p. 438.

be taken into account in defining the complex of characteristics which is personality. Personality refers to the behavior, thoughts and feelings, motives, fantasies, defenses, and self-concepts of an individual.[3]

Attention of psychologists to personality is distinctly a modern phenomenon. Galton may be looked upon as the father of the psychology of personality, for in 1884 he published an article on the "Measurement of Character," but it was not until many decades later that psychologists developed methods for the study of personality along lines suggested by Galton. [21]

James's only references to personality concerned highly pathological aberrations, always fascinating to him, which he classifies under three headings: insane delusions, alternating selves, and mediumships or possessions. [39] Thorndike does not deal with personality as such, but many of his illustrations in discussing instinct deal with personality, and one gathers that he would consider personality as largely a matter of original nature or inheritance. MacDougall discussed personality under the heading of "sentiments." The beginnings of a scientific approach to the study of personality may be dated at 1918, when Woodworth constructed his "Personal Data Sheet," a questionnaire for studying neurotic tendencies in soldiers in World War I.

The first large-scale study of personality was undertaken by the Character Education Inquiry under the direction of Hartshorne and May from 1922 to 1930. [32] The main emphasis in these studies was on the measurement of character looking toward a description of its organization, and little attention was paid to the formation of character. This emphasis on measure-

---

3 Some years ago one of the writer's students undertook to assess what the average person thinks of when he uses the term personality. He went about asking taxicab drivers, elevator operators, waitresses, and others what personality meant to them. He received such answers as: "Personality? Gee, you have it or you don't. Sure, I recognize differences. Some people are 'stinkers' and some are O.K. The rest are just 'blah.' " And again, "The most important thing a person can have. Some people have it, some don't." Or, "The way a person looks at you and talks with you. I guess you might say there are three classes: pleasant people with lots of it, unpleasant people who don't have it, and the ordinary with just a little." All of these comments describe personality in quantitative terms—something that is had in varying degrees—what I should call the Hollywood conception of personality.

ment and the organization of personality persists to the present day, witness two recent comprehensive treatises by Cattell [10] and Guilford. [31] Psychologists have been more interested in the problem of selection than in the formation and modification of personality. Accordingly, most of our information about the development of personality has come from clinical workers and the observations made by students of child development.

Every clinical worker becomes impressed with the persistence of personality. A client mentions some personality trend that is bothering him; for example, he is unable to hold a job for any length of time. Things seem at first to be going satisfactorily, and then he finds that he is being taken advantage of by his employer, who does not trust him and gives preference to others in his office. Matters become intolerable until he is forced to quit in a huff. But as he reviews his life, it appears that he reacted the same way toward one of his college instructors, although he had not previously noticed the similarity. And then sometime later it is revealed that as a boy he had similar thoughts toward his stepfather, who favored his stepbrother. There seems to be a persistence of personality trends extending back not just weeks and months, but apparently over much of the life span.

Recently, evidence of a more systematic nature that verifies such clinical observations has been supplied by psychologists. Madorah Smith [75], reporting from the University of Hawaii, had access to a journal kept by a missionary mother of six children which enabled Dr. Smith to compare ratings of character traits judged from entries in the journal with ratings made of these same individuals fifty years later by persons who knew them all well. Seventy per cent of the ratings differed by not more than one step on the five-step rating scale used, indicating a high degree of stability in the personality traits studied. E. L. Kelly [47] made a follow-up study of individuals twenty years after he had originally studied them as engaged couples. He found considerable consistency in personality test scores and self-ratings represented by correlations in the neighborhood of .30 to .60. He is careful to point out that these correlations also indicate an important amount of change in these same personality traits, even allowing for the unreliability of the measures.

The writer (with A. F. Jensen) has had the privilege of studying, after an interval of thirteen years, 28 out of the original 40 adolescents who were subjects in an investigation of adolescent fantasy. [87] In the initial study the subjects were from thirteen to seventeen years of age; in the follow-up study they were from twenty-six to thirty. We found that there is considerable persistence of observed characteristics of personality as well as of fantasy, but shifts in personality and fantasy were noted which have been related to experiences in the intervening years. [88]

McKinnon reported that ten children who were first seen by her when they were three years old showed the same dominant personality characteristics at age eight or nine that they had exhibited at the earlier age. [51]

Shirley [73] in 1933 reported on an intensive study of twenty-five babies who had been seen at frequent intervals from birth through the first two years. She was able to conclude that "each baby exhibits a characteristic pattern of personality traits that changes little with age."

Fifteen years later Neilon [56] was able to prepare personality sketches of 15 adolescents who had originally been among the 25 babies studied by Shirley. These were matched against Shirley's original sketches, and it was found that the matching could be accomplished well above chance expectancy, more successfully with certain subjects than with others, which made Neilon willing to conclude "personality similarities in an individual persist over a period of time."

It should be pointed out that the prediction of personality was not perfect in Smith's six cases; that Kelly's correlations leave much room for shifts in personality; that in my thirteen-year follow-up of 28 adolescents into adulthood, changes in personality were noted; that McKinnon did find changes in her children followed from age three to age eight or nine; and that Neilon noted changes in the adolescents who were babies in Shirley's study. But these shifts in personality in childhood, adolescent, and adult years do not alter the main fact that there is a pronounced consistency in personality in most individuals throughout life.

The evidence which is available points not only to the persistence of traits of personality throughout life but also to the great resistance of personality traits to change. The evidence for this comes largely from the experience of clinical workers who find that after months and even years of concentrated efforts to change personality in clients, basic personality patterns remain unchanged.

Both the clinical evidence and reports of longitudinal studies by psychologists point to the unescapable conclusion that for the majority of persons and for the majority of characteristics, the dominant characteristics of personality persist throughout life from infancy to old age.

The conclusion reached by Galton from his study of twins was that personality is inherited. He made inquiry of eighty pairs of twins who were "extremely similar" and twenty pairs who were "extremely dissimilar" and reached the conclusion that "man is so educable an animal that it is difficult to distinguish between that part of his character which has been acquired through education and circumstance, and that which was in the original grain of his constitution." [22] Also "In solution of the question whether a continual improvement in education might not compensate for a stationary or even retrograde condition of natural gifts, I made inquiry into the life history of twins, which resulted in proving the vastly preponderating effects of nature over nurture." [23] Again, "There is no escape from the conclusion that nature prevails enormously over nurture when the differences of nurture do not exceed what is commonly to be found among persons of the same rank of society and in the same country." [24]

Coming down from the past, then, were two main theories of personality development. One, and the most popular (the Judean-Christian), held that personality was formed through influences in the family and the church, but this took place through discipline and instruction after the years of understanding and the rational powers had been reached. The other, growing out of the biological-scientific position of the nineteenth century, held that personality is largely inherited.

It seemed utter heresy, then, for Freud to announce that the basic elements of character are formed before the end of the fifth year of life in most instances.

Freud's original statement concerned the development of

sexual impulses. However, his emphasis on the early appearance
of sexual behavior has been interpreted to include the development of all aspects of personality, as the following quotations
from Ernest Jones indicates:

> [Freud] regards the mental processes, and particularly the wishes,
> of early childhood life as the permanent basis for all later develop-
> ment. . . . Freud looks upon the whole of a subject's life as a
> continuity, as a series of associated trends. . . . These views natu-
> rally have great importance in their bearing on education, for it is
> substantially maintained that the main traits of character are per-
> manently determined for good or ill before the end of the fifth
> year of life. Freud holds in general that, owing to our ignorance
> of the most important mental processes of early childhood, and our
> own personal amnesia for this period, the significance for later
> life of these early trends is vastly underestimated. [45]

It is difficult for us to capture the trend of thinking at the beginning of the century, but Freud's position that the "main traits
of character are permanently determined before the end of the
fifth year of life" before powers of reason have developed seemed
utterly inconceivable when he announced it. This is particularly
true because Freud's evidence was gathered from recaptured
memories of adult patients and by "reconstructions" based on
psychoanalytic theory. A psychoanalyst even goes so far as to talk
and think about his adult client's behavior as though it were the
behavior of an infant nursing with its mother or resisting its
mother's attempts to train it in toilet cleanliness. So this Freudian
point of view was discounted for many years and still is by many
persons.

An early study that electrified the psychological world by
demonstrating how emotional responses could be learned in infancy was reported by the behaviorist John B. Watson. Watson
and his wife were able to demonstrate that it was possible to
condition fear in an eleven-month-old infant by "showing him a
rat as soon as he reached for it and touched it to strike a heavy
steel bar behind him." At the eighth presentation "the instant
the rat was shown the baby began to cry. Almost instantly he
turned strongly to the left, fell over, raised himself on all fours
and began to crawl away so rapidly that he was caught with difficulty before he reached the edge of the table." [95]

But it was not until two decades later that empirical evidence was reported that bore more closely on the influence of infantile experiences on personality formation. One of the early objective studies of the influence of parental attitudes on personality formation was made by the writer. [84] I was able to secure data on the personalities of 31 so-called accepted children and 31 rejected children. Each clinical worker who contributed a pair of cases was requested to send in data for an accepted child who was as nearly as possible like the rejected child selected for the study in age, sex, school grade, social background, and intelligence level. A comparison of the two groups showed striking differences in personality, the rejected children exhibiting more emotional instability, an excess of activity and restlessness, and antagonism against society and its institutions.

Spitz [77], a psychoanalyst, spent much time in hospitals observing and photographing babies. He described a state which he called "hospitalism" in infants that were placed in an institutional setting separated from their mothers during the first year of life, a state which is characterized by severe retardation in personality development. Similar findings have been reported by Durfee and Wolf in Austria [14], and by several other investigators in this country.

Spitz and Wolf [79] also found that if the deprivation of the mother starts at a later date, a condition will result which greatly resembles depression in the adult. These same authors [80] studied a group of 153 mothers who showed periodic mood swings, and found that their children showed strange, disturbed personalities, many of them indulging in fecal play. Other mothers, whose personalities were described as infantile, had children who were "retarded in social responses and manipulative ability expressing a diminished capacity to relate to human beings or to manipulate inanimate objects."

In spite of the fact that Spitz has given inadequate statistical treatment to his data, the results have not been controverted. Spitz concludes from his studies that "the mother or her substitute transmits literally every experience to the infant. Barring starvation, disease or actual physical injury, no other factor is capable of so influencing the child's development in every field as its relation to its mother." [78]

Goldfarb was able to compare institutionally reared children with children reared in foster homes from age three to twelve. He concluded that "infant deprivation results in a basic defect in total personality." [28]

Another psychiatrist who has made close observations of infants is Margaret Ribble. [59] Although Ribble presents no data, she states her conclusions are based on the observation of some 600 healthy infants. She also reported studying mentally ill adult patients in Vienna of whom "the earliest upbringing of the individual as well as something of the parents were known, in order to determine, if possible, what part these factors played in the evolution of the mental illness." She concludes that "invariably the child who is deprived of individual mothering shows disordered behavior, with a compensatory retardation in general alertness." [60] And again,

> Poor relationships with the parents result in reactions in the infant which tend to become the basis of adult personality disorders. The most important asset of the baby as he begins life is two emotionally healthy parents. His deepest need by far is the understanding care of one consistent individual—his mother. Perhaps in time we shall recognize the danger of the emotionally unhealthy personality and shall see that emotional disturbance in the parents is as damaging to the baby as is tuberculosis or syphilis. If this sounds shocking to any reader, let it be taken to heart. [61]

Two psychologists, Orlansky and Pinneau, have reacted strongly against Ribble's assertions, in scholarly and highly documented articles. [57, 58]

Orlansky says,

> It is unfortunate that such an influential writer has not attempted to draw a line between her empirical findings and her personal opinions. There is so much panegyric and so little satisfactory evidence in her writing that it is difficult for an impartial critic to evaluate many of her statements objectively.

If the foregoing studies are not convincing, particularly Ribble's (perhaps hers should not be called a study at all), because of the paucity of data and the subjective way in which the conclusions were arrived at, it may be helpful if better controlled studies are reported. Shirley, whose earlier study of twenty-five babies has been referred to, some years later reported a study that attempted to trace some of the factors which may have accounted for differences in the way in which two-year-old children reacted to being taken for an all-day visit to a center for research on child health and development. Some of the children adjusted well to the strange situation; others were much upset. Shirley eliminated such factors as age, sex, illness, and finally concluded that

> . . . a child's level of adjustment depends little upon the extrinsic features of the day, and little even upon his health. It depends much more upon the wholesomeness of his upbringing in the home, and the security and confidence and affection given him by his parents. A secure and wholesomely loved child goes forth to meet new experience in a spirit of adventure and comes out triumphant in his encounters with new places, new materials, and new friends, young and old. A child that is oversheltered and underloved goes forth from home with misgivings and doubts, and gives an impression of inadequacy and immaturity in his encounter with new experiences that makes him unwelcome either in the society of adults or children. [74]

Sears, Maccoby, and Levin have assembled a report of their researches in this field. [66] Sears and his associates were able to question 379 American mothers about their methods of bringing up their children from birth to kindergarten age. These authors say, "[It is] our opinion that child-rearing practices are important determiners [of personality]." [67] "Every interaction between two people has an effect both on their present actions and on their potentialities for future action." [68] "Every moment of a child's life that he spends in contact with his parents has some effect on both his present behavior and his potentialities for future action." [69]

The essence of parent-child relations lies more in how a parent feels than in what a parent does or says. This point of view has been difficult for many to understand and accept because a child can react only to parental behavior in the broad sense and not to unexpressed feeling. But any behavior may mean different things according to its context and concomitant expression. A parent may keep a child in the house on a rainy afternoon out of concern for a child's health, but also as a form of punishment. A child reacts to the parental response in terms of what it means to him rather than arbitrarily and blindly as a response to a stimulus.

From my recent studies of adolescent fantasy and its impact on changes in personality in subsequent years, it has become clear that fantasy is a factor in the determination of later overt trends in personality. [89] What a person yearns and strives for he may later work out in actual living. Personality is, then, in part, a precipitate of fantasy. As I have previously stated, "Behavior or personality is not wholly a direct response to the accepting or rejecting situation, but is also a response to the inner attitude of the child." [85] This is as true, no doubt, in the formation of the earliest trends of personality in infancy as it is in childhood and adolescence. Always accompanying or preceding actual behavior are inner urges, strivings, promptings that determine the direction that personality will take. Very early, as Sullivan [82] suggests, personality takes the character that coincides with one's concept of oneself.

Personality is formed by the infant's reactions to situations long before he develops conscious awareness of his reactions. By the time the child has acquired the language and concepts with which to understand his personality it has been formed so firmly that there is little that he can do to direct or modify it.

Because personality in all its ramifications is learned, we hold that the formation of personality is the task and responsibility of education. Only too often education is made synonymous with schooling. But if education is concerned with learning, then much of education must take place before the school years and in the home. Again, education is often thought of as a process of instruction, largely through language. But much of learning, and most of learning in infancy, takes place without benefit of instruction or language.

The contributions of heredity and experience have never been determined, and a precise answer to this issue is extremely difficult to establish. The point of view generally held today is that there are hereditary-constitutional determinants of personality, but that these are broad and general.

What are the constitutional elements of personality? Newborn babies and babies seen shortly after birth have been observed to differ in a number of characteristics which may represent hereditary differences or differences that originate during the gestation period, and which are presumed to be the basis for fundamental personality differences in later life. The most outstanding of these differences is what has been termed *activity level*. This was noted by a New York psychoanalyst, Fries [18], who not only reported her findings in the literature but also recorded her observations in very convincing motion pictures. Newborn babies will differ in the amount of kicking and thrashing about and in particular in the vigor with which they nurse.

After following these same children (who had been observed periodically from the moment of birth) for five years, it was found that the activity pattern of the so-called normal child can be modified, but only within certain limits; and that the most important factor responsible for modifying it (excluding organic pathology) is the parents' emotional adjustment, their relations to each other and to the child. [19]

Neonates also differ, according to observations by Bergman and Escalona, in their sensitivity to various sensory modalities, and they have been observed to respond differently to colors, bright lights, noises, unusual sounds, qualities of material, experiences of equilibrium, taste, smell, and temperature. [8] In the same report these authors also note that infants differ in their ability to protect themselves by inattention and lowered response to stimuli as "protective barriers against stimuli." This seems to be related to the capacity to tolerate frustration and delay in having their wants satisfied. In another report, Escalona mentioned a related characteristic which she has noted in babies in earliest infancy—"the capacity to focus and channel energies upon a given task." [15]

To this list of possible constitutional factors which are observable in the first weeks of life may be added "social responsiveness," that is, the capacity and tendency of the infant to respond to the mother who nurses it. [26]

What are some of the characteristics that are learned in the early months and years? Some of the characteristics of personality that are formed in the first year of life can best be stated in the form of dichotomies—being a boy or girl, being active or passive, socially responsive or self-centered, assertive or receptive, aggressive or submissive, independent or dependent, spontaneous or repressed. It will be noted that each of these seems to be a variant of the general constitutional tendency to be active or passive. But the precise uniqueness of the personality in the earliest years depends on the reactions of the individual to the mother and other individuals who are with it. It is on the basis of these fundamental trends that the later differentiations of personality take place.

In the first year of life the infant is more or less helpless and dependent on others for the gratification of his needs, and his reaction to this state of helplessness becomes the origin of many personality trends such as passivity, a fatalistic attitude, submissiveness. But if the infant strives to overcome his helpless position, he may develop characteristic modes of behavior which serve as the roots for later ambition, competition, envy, jealousy, rivalry, courage, and optimism. The Freudians have called this the oral stage of development. [1] As the need for parental control arises in the second year, when the infant has greater powers of locomotion, such traits as stubbornness, obstinacy, cooperation, independence, responsibility, and the unwillingness to submit and conform have their beginnings. In this period the so-called authoritarian personality finds its first roots. [3] In connection with toilet training, such traits as cleanliness, stinginess and generosity, reticence and openness appear. [16, 2]

Infancy is the time when attitudes toward sex behavior are formed. The infant may find sex pleasurable, or if it is punished because of autoerotic acts—thumbsucking or play with the genitals—then sexual pleasure may be repressed. The objects or persons that one seeks for satisfaction in later life are determined in infancy, and it is during this period that essential heterosexual or homosexual orientations are formed. [17]

An important aspect of personality is found in the attitudes of an individual as well as in his behavior. Of particular importance is the self-concept. Even in the first year the first mental processes of the infant are concerned with the reactions of others toward him, and out of these reactions of others he builds his concept of himself. The self-concept typically reflects the characteristics that he is forming or, at least, the way in which these characteristics impress others. This phenomenological aspect of personality is fully as important as the more objective impressions that a person makes on others. In fact, the self-concept interacts with the behavioral aspects of personality. One's behavioral tendencies help in a roundabout way to form the self-concept and the self-concept helps to guide and control behavior.

Finally an important aspect of personality that has its origin in infancy is what is called by the psychoanalysts "ego strength." This somewhat vague and ill-defined concept refers principally to the capacity to govern one's actions by reason. Of course this capacity is not fully formed until reason has developed, and this takes place gradually throughout childhood. Ego strength also refers to the capacity to postpone action, the roots of which are laid down early. Ego strength enables the individual to meet crises, threats, deprivations, and traumatic experiences with equanimity, but low ego strength makes the individual susceptible to neurotic adjustment.

If the foundations of personality are laid in infancy, one may well ask what part of its development takes place after the first five or six years of life. Observation reveals that throughout the growth period there is a differentiation of personality along the lines determined by the early formations. The precise direction that personality will take, the persons toward whom it will be directed, the objects and activities that will give personality its unique flavor for each individual are determined by the environment and experiences of an individual. One can teach a child manners, rules of conduct, and etiquette, but the way in which these are expressed is determined by the basic personality.

Aggressive trends are laid down in infancy, but whether they will lead to delinquency and criminality or to socially constructive efforts is determined not only by infantile experiences but also by the influences of later years. A person with strong repressive trends, easily made anxious, and with low ego strength becomes an easy prey to neurotic adjustments in later life, but if he lives in a protected environment and is not subjected to stress, and strain he may be able to work out tolerably satisfactory adjustments.

These facts about the early formation of personality are very difficult for many persons to accept and assimilate into their thinking. This is seen most clearly when some problem involving personality comes to a crisis and steps must be taken to meet the situation. When such circumstances arise many, if not most, persons will tend to decry the possibility that personality has been learned.

It is only natural in such circumstances to turn to other possible explanations. Many persons will search for a physical basis for a personality difficulty. Seeking medical assistance relieves one of the sense of responsibility for one's troubles, for what is physical seems so inexorable. So a person with a personality difficulty may have a physical examination and with hope clutch at the possibility that his troubles may be eased by vitamins, allergy treatment, building up the blood, tranquilizers, electric shock, or even by surgery. Belief in the hereditary basis for personality persists in part because people can evade responsibility for their behavior if they believe that it is inherited. The assertions of Sheldon [70] that morphology (relating to the form and structure of the human body) and temperament correlate in the neighborhood of .80 have attracted much more attention than the facts warrant, for it is obvious that in spite of the well-known temperamental differences between endomorphs (fleshy individuals), mesomorphs (muscular individuals), and ectomorphs (lean individuals), these differences in physical structure cannot begin to account for the differences in personality. Likewise, assertions that glands exert an influence on personality always receive hopeful attention, even though such an authority as Hoskins has said,

Some things we know regarding the direct influence of the hormones upon the personality. By and large, however, the problem remains mostly for future solution. Even in broad outline, the picture is somewhat indeterminate and, in detail, is definitely confused. [38]

Out of these facts follow important and far-reaching implications. The main responsibility for the development of personality falls on parents. The personality of the child develops out of the interaction of parent and infant. As facts concerning parent-child relations become better known, mothers in the future can become more sensitive to the influence that their behavior has on the personality of the child.

Schools may be listed as one of the precipitating factors in the determination of the direction that personality will take, but they must work with the basic personalities of the children who come to them—they cannot hope to modify these basic personalities. If strength is there, education can help the individual grow in worth-while directions; it cannot overcome weakness in the basic personality structure.

And what is the function of the teacher in the development of personality? Teachers are, in part, responsible for the development of character; that is, the direction that personality should take in order that boys and girls may become responsible and moral members of society. This is done, in some measure, by the teaching of ideals. But the psychologist believes that more important than precept are the relations between teachers and pupils. Pupils will identify with teachers whom they like and admire. The teacher wields influence by what she *is* and *does;* that is, by what she stands for, what she approves of, what she holds valuable and honorable. Children need more freedom for spontaneous expression and, in particular, opportunities to express emotions. To make this possible, teachers must cultivate attitudes of greater acceptingness, yet at the same time they should continue to exercise strictness and firmness in control, but without punishment. Pupils need more encouragement and greater satisfaction when their behavior meets with approval. [86]

In summary, while there is evidence that the roots of personality are constitutional, the structure of personality, particularly as it is expressed in human relationships, is the result of learning—learning which begins shortly after birth and continues through infancy and early childhood. The basic patterns of personality are formed in the first five or six years of life. These facts place a great responsibility on parents, for personality is formed largely through parent-child relationships.

——▶ **Patricia Neilon**

Shirley's Babies after
Fifteen Years: A Personality Study

From *Journal of Genetic Psychology*, 1948, 73:175–186. Reprinted by permission.

Although mothers, nurses, and other observers of children have often been convinced that there is some continuity of "characteristicness," or general personality pattern in developing individuals, this continuity has been elusive of objective psychological measurement. That individuality exists in early infancy has been demonstrated by several investigators. That it also exists in adulthood is, of course, accepted, and differences are measured. That the pattern of personality shown in infancy continues through life, or that it changes its form of expression as growth and development proceed has, however, never been established. Just as manifestations of brightness change with age, manifestations of individuality might change with development, while leaving the child in the same relative place in his group at successive measurements. Even assuming continuity of personality patterns, the individual who cries a great deal as an infant would not necessarily be expected to cry a great deal as an adult. The personality characteristic which caused the excessive crying in infancy might persist though, and be expressed in a different manner in adulthood. We do not know merely from the infant's crying, however, what form of expression this characteristic might take later. The infant who cries a great deal might babble a great deal as a toddler, and be talkative as an adult. Or, the same infant who cries a great deal might be subject to severe temper tantrums at preschool age, and have an inclination to impulsiveness or emotionality in adulthood. The entire personality pattern, including emphases and details might continue from infancy with changes in expression to adulthood. Or, perhaps, some elements of individuality might be retained while others disappeared with development and experience. Or, there is a third possibility that differences which existed in infancy, perhaps due to differences in age at birth, physical and physiological conditions. Although these and other more complex possibilities unquestionably exist, they have not been investigated. In part this is due to the difficulties of measurement in the field of personality, and in part to the lack of attempts at measurement of the same individuals after long intervals of time have elapsed. Moreover, measurements which are suitable for infants or children are inapplicable to adults and vice versa, so that continuity of measurements is impossible. As a result, most students of child personality have used the cross-sectional approach to investigate age and sex differences in a certain trait, or to produce experimental modifications. Rarely have they attempted to measure continuity in the natural environment.

Early biographers seem to have believed in the emergence of individuality in infancy. Shinn [71], for example, says: "Our baby showed temperament and luckily of the easy-going and cheerful kind from her first day (though we could hardly see this except by looking back afterward)." Hogan [33] refers to the child's "early inclination to know what was going on about him," which continued, as did his seeming "happiest when he was let alone." In 1925, Woolley [97] described the development of "Agnes, a Dominant Personality in the Making," on the basis of teachers' reports of the child while attending the Merrill Palmer School. This little girl, a sample case, remained the same in her basic personality pattern of aggressive dominant behavior from ages two to five.

In the more recent literature, evidence concerning continuity of individuality is given firstly in studies of certain personality traits, secondly in studies using personality tests and rating scales, and thirdly in studies which aim at total personality investigation, usually by use of a descriptive technique. The individual's characteristic modes of response have tended to persist in the areas of perseveration, which was investigated by Cushing [13], smiling, which was investigated by Washburn [94], laughter, which was investigated by Brackett, and crying, which was investigated by Bayley. [7] After studying "problem" behavior in a large and representative sample, however, Macfarlane [49] concluded that "transitoriness" tended to be the rule rather than "persistence." Using time sampling techniques in studying preschool children, individual consistency has been found by Green [30] in "frequency of group play," by Loomis [46] in the ratio of number of contacts initiated to those received," and by Jersild and Markey [42] in conflict behavior in two observation periods separated by a year's time interval. Because they demonstrate some degree of stability in personality, reports of continuity of such traits or behavior items are valuable. The question of the continuity of total personality pattern, however, is far more complex. While the above reports are objective, they are, for our purposes, limited in scope. Attempts to investigate "total personality," on the other hand, often sacrifice objectivity to completeness.

Halfway between studies of single traits and studies using descriptive methods to investigate total personality are studies of the continuity of individuality which use standard personality tests and rating scales as measuring devices. Test-retest techniques used by Jones and Burks [46] and Tryon [90] have shown that children tend to say the same sorts of things about themselves on two tests separated in time. While personality tests are the most objective of the measures available, such studies cannot adequately demonstrate the continuity or lack of continuity of individuality. In the first place, test-retest reliability, deliberately made a part of the test, might insure measured continuity. To many, in the second place, a person's impression of himself is not so important an aspect of personality as is the impression of him gained by others, which is not measured by a personality test. Finally, a test is also limiting, and totality is again sacrificed to objectivity. The rating scale, which is a semi-objective measure, has also been applied to this problem. Bonham and Sargent [55] used the method on 38 children from birth to two and one-half years finding no consistently positive relationships in ratings except for good looks. Using the same method on 140 preschool children for three consecutive years, Stutsman [81] found constancy in ratings and in profile patterns based on ratings suggesting personality types. Besides evidence from studies of separate personality traits and studies using personality tests and rating scales, the third type of evidence concerning continuity of individuality is from studies of total personality. In *Biographies of Child Development,* for instance, Gesell *et al.* [25] conclude:

> Our data [from ten years of study at the Yale clinic] do not lend support to the concept of a relatively standard pattern of infancy. Nor are the findings of embryology in harmony with such a concept. From the standpoint of embryology the infant is already far advanced in the cycle of life. He is already stamped with individuality rather than with a standard pattern. . . . This perpetuation of characteristicness is not incompatible with morphogenesis and maturing. It is, however, inconsistent with the idea that individual differences at birth are slight and increase with age, or that the period of infancy is in any sense neutral or generic when compared with later periods of the life cycle.

There seemed to have been persistent temperamental differences in twins *T* and *C* [27], and Johnny and Jimmy. [50] After a series of studies of the same group of children for five years at Columbia University [41, 51], "consistency," it was concluded, "rather than inconsistency is characteristic of development." Also using a descriptive technique, Allport [5] studied his own son. Here personality predictions made by the parents when the boy was four months old were compared with records of parents at two later ages and with records of four different teachers at succeeding age levels. "The prognosis at the age of four months," Allport declares, "is borne out in most respects . . . two of the initially dominant characteristics have shifted their emphasis. . . . But on the whole the schedule is consistent throughout." From this material, Allport advances the hypothesis that "from early infancy there is a consistency in the development of personality." Roberts and Fleming [62] with data from 25 women at pre-college, college, and post-college levels found that the ratio of persisting to fluctuating traits was 3:2.

Elimination of the experimenter's bias, which is a factor in all biographical studies, is achieved by Gesell. [25] Movies of five children at ages one and five were used. From the movies, a trained observer who was unacquainted with the children ranked them on 15 behavior traits including energy, demeanor, dependence, social responsiveness, and the like. Out of 75 rankings, 48 coincided, 21 were displaced by one rank order, five were displaced by two rank orders, and one was displaced by three rank orders. "Our periodic cinema records," Gesell writes, "clearly show prophetic characters in behavior traits in the first year."

In the investigation of continuity of individuality, in summary, positive findings are more conclusive than negative ones. An impression of continuity was reported by early biographers. Continuity is likewise found in certain separate traits and behavior items. Investigators of "total personality" have been unable to retain both completeness and objectivity, between which a balance must be struck. Since a breaking down of "totality" has usually given negative results, it would seem that strict quantitative measurement of behavior must be discarded in this area. The method of the Gesell study [25] provides another sort of objectivity. The matching method advocated by Vernon [91, 92, 93] allows the use of total personality, but eliminates the strong effect which the bias of the single experimenter exerts upon the results in the case study of descriptive method. In one study reported by Vernon [91], character sketches of 25 subjects were written by each of three experimenters on the basis of the behavior of the subjects during performance tests. Each experimenter then tried to identify the sketches of the other two. This method applied to growing children should provide evidence about the continuity of individuality.

This is essentially the method adopted in this study. Extensive personality data on infants were presented by Dr. Mary Shirley in her *The First Two Years: a Study of Twenty-Five Babies.* [73] After two years of standardized observations of the children as well as two years acquaintance with them and their families, Dr. Shirley wrote personality sketches. These sketches and later sketches of the same children prepared by the writer were used in a matching procedure to investigate the continuity of individuality.

The plan for the personality follow-up of the 25 babies, which was begun 15 years after the original study, included the objective measurements of the subjects who would be available for study, and the writing of new personality sketches which were to be matched with the original sketches written by Dr. Shirley. The writer did not consult the Shirley sketches after the study was begun, and did not know the pseudonyms used by Shirley until the follow-up sketches were completed. Two formal personality tests were used in the follow-up, the Goodenough *Speed of Association Test* [29] and the Rundquist-Sletto *Minnesota Survey of Opinions*. [64]. In addition to these formally developed scales of personality measurement, a five-point rating scale of 23 traits, and a scale of six special abilities were also used. The *Speed of Association Test, the Minnesota Survey of Opinions,* and the scale for self-rating were administered to the subject in this order. Following this was a more or less standardized interview concerning the subject's interests, in which a general impression of his personality picture could be gained. An interview was also held with each of the mothers. During this interview, the mother rated her child on the 23 traits and six special abilities. She was also encouraged to talk about the child, and to state why she placed him in each of the rating categories. Many anecdotes illustrating the various characteristics of the child were related, and his place in the family group was estimated. Each mother was also asked whether or not she believed the child to have changed in such respects as were referred to on the rating scale or in his general behavior pattern. Rating scales and special ability scales were mailed to the fathers. All of the objective data were interpreted in the light of the short interviews with the subjects and mothers, and personality sketches were written of the children as they seemed to be at the age of 17.

The original group of 25 babies was above average in socioeconomic status, education, and intelligence. Such a superior sample was originally chosen by Dr. Shirley because it was felt that better coöperation of parents could be obtained than would have been the case if a sample more representative of the population at large had been chosen. At the end of two years, Shirley had 19 of her original 25 subjects. Fifteen years later, it was possible to gather partial data on all of these, and full data on 16.

The finished adolescent sketches were two to four typewritten pages in length. To the Shirley infant sketches proper, material was added from her sections of "Incidental Reactions" and "Personality as Revealed in Speech." This made the infant sketches comparable in length to the adolescent sketches. Since sex was readily determined in all sketches, the sexes were separated for the matching procedure. There were five sketches of adolescent girls to be matched with six infant sketches, and 10 sketches of adolescent boys to be matched with 13 infant sketches. One of the adolescent boy sketches had to be thrown out because there was no comparable infant sketch. Keeping the extra infant sketches made matching more difficult by eliminating the possibility of automatically matching the last sketch in either series. Because of the length of the sketches, the matching task was a difficult one. It was performed by graduate students and staff members at the Institute of Child Welfare, University of Minnesota, who carefully read and reread the material, weighed and re-evaluated the evidence. Ten judges matched the sketches of girls (five versus six cases), and five judges matched the sketches of boys (10 versus 13 cases). Although statistically the chances for success are approximately equal for both tasks, the matching of 10 versus 13 cases is psychologically far more difficult. The greater number of cases necessitated more than twice the amount of reading, and made an almost impossible demand upon the memories of the judges. With 10 personality sketches and 10 pictures Vernon [93] found matching "almost impossible" for judges, even though this would involve less reading than the matching of two sets of sketches.

Chances of successful choice are both reduced and increased by the limitations of the matching process. Taking the simpler five versus six matching as an example, the chances that the first adolescent girl's sketch would be correctly matched would be one in six. Assuming this first match to be correct, the chances that the second sketch would be correctly matched would be reduced to one in five. And assuming the first two to be correctly matched, there would be one chance in four that a third would also be successfully matched, and so on, the task being made easier by process of elimination after every successful matching.

The chances of matching all sketches successfully, therefore, would be 1/6! When there are incorrect matches, however, the problem becomes more complex. If the first adolescent girl's sketch were incorrectly matched, it might be matched with either the sixth infant sketch, which has no mate, or with any of the four others. In the latter case, two incorrect matches would automatically come about. If the first two adolescent girls' sketches were incorrectly matched, there would automatically be at least three, and quite possibly four, errors.

Chapman [11, 12] has given formulae for the solution of this rather complex problem which are based on the possible permutations of the cases. In matching five versus six sketches, a total of 720 (6!) permutations are possible, but only one of these arrangements allows for the correct matching of all sketches. When there are four correct matches, and one error, there are five possible permutations, that is the sixth or extra infant sketch might be matched with any one of the five adolescent sketches. The chances of making one error, then, would be 5/720. Other probabilities can be worked out by Chapman's formula. Table 1

TABLE 1

PROBABILITIES OF THE CHANCE SUCCESS OF ONE JUDGE IN MATCHING
PERSONALITY SKETCHES

| | Probable Chances in 100 | |
Number of Successes	5 vs. 6 Cases	10 vs. 13 Cases
0	43	46
1	37	36
2	15	14
3	4	3
4	0.07	0.06
5	0.01	0.008

shows the probabilities of the chance success of one judge in matching five versus six and 10 versus 13 cases worked out by this formula. It must be emphasized that these figures apply only to the chances of successful matching by one judge. The highest number of successful matchings obtained by any judge for the five versus six cases was four, and for the 10 versus 13 cases, five.

The results of 10 judges in matching the five adolescent sketches and six infant sketches of girls are shown in Table 2.

TABLE 2

SUCCESSES OF TEN JUDGES IN MATCHING PERSONALITY SKETCHES OF GIRLS
(5 VS. 6 CASES)

Number of Correct Judgments	Probability Level	Number of Judges
0	43%	0
1	37	0
2	15	1
3	4	6
4	0.07	3
5	0.01	0
		10 Total

The majority of the judges succeeded at the 4 per cent level of probability, three succeeded at the .07 per cent level, and one at the 15 per cent level. The mean number of successes for all of the judges is 3.2. The significance of this figure can be calculated by another special method. According to Chapman [11] the mean of random matchings is, by sampling theory, t/u (t = the smaller number of items to be matched; u = the larger number of items to be matched). This agrees with Zubin's [98] discussion of the problem of matching equal numbers of items, in which the mean of random matchings is one, and the standard deviation is also one. For the more general case, which can apply with either equal or unequal numbers, Chapman gives the formula for the standard deviation. He gives also a formula for calculating the skewness of the distribution of random matchings which becomes more leptokurtic and more skewed as the difference between the numbers to be matched increases. The distribution takes the shape of Pearson's Type III Curve. Tables, which are correct to six places, have been worked out by Salvosa [65] for this function.

Area under the Type III curve above the obtained mean value in terms of the standard deviation can be determined from these tables. Using this procedure, it was found that there is less than one chance in 1,000,000 that the mean of 10 judges in matching five versus six cases would equal or exceed 3.2.

TABLE 3

SUCCESSES OF FIVE JUDGES IN MATCHING PERSONALITY SKETCHES OF BOYS
(10 vs. 13 CASES)

Number of Correct Judgments	Probability Level	Number of Judges
0	46%	0
1	36	1
2	14	2
3	3	1
4	0.06	0
5	0.008	1
		5 Total

The results of five judges in matching the 10 adolescent sketches of boys with 13 infant sketches, which are less clear cut, are shown in Table 3. These results are less clear cut probably because of the difficulty of the task, and the difficulty of obtaining judges for the task. One judge did succeed, however, at the .008 per cent level. The mean number of successes for all of the judges in this case is 2.6. Applying Chapman's formula to this figure, there are only 25 chances in 100,000 that the mean of five judges in matching 10 versus 13 cases would equal or exceed 2.6.

The successes of individual judges as well as the high mean numbers of successes for both tasks as compared to chance demonstrate some common element in the sketches at both levels. Since the writer was not familiar with the earlier sketches nor with the pseudonyms used for the children at the time of preparing the later sketches, and since similarity existed in the sketches of the two-year-olds which were based on subjective thorough acquaintance, and the sketches of the same children at

17 which were based on objective tests and rating material, we conclude that personality similarities exist.

Taking the subject rather than the judge as the unit may shed more light on the results. Table 4 shows that one of the girls,

DISTRIBUTION OF TEN MATCHINGS OF INFANT AND ADOLESCENT
PERSONALITY SKETCHES OF GIRLS

Adolescent Sketch	Times out of 10 Matched with Following Infant Sketch					
	Winnie	Va. Ruth	Sibyl	Judy	Patty	Carol
Winnie	10*					
Va. Ruth		9*				1
Sibyl			7*	3		
Judy			2	*	3	5
Patty				3	6*	

Winnie, was always matched correctly by the 10 judges, while Judy was never matched correctly. It seems possible, in other words, to rank the subjects according to ease of matching: Winnie, whom 10 out of 10 judges matched correctly; Virginia Ruth, matched correctly by nine judges; Sibyl by seven; Patty by six; and Judy who was never matched correctly. In considering the problem of the probability of repeated successes in matching the same adolescent sketch, the only method of attack seems to be in considering the matching of each adolescent sketch as a separate task independent of other matching. This, of course, is not the case. As stated above, the chances of matching the first case are one in six, while after one sketch is correctly matched, the probability that a second will be correctly matched is one in five and so on. Considering each matching as a simple choice of one of six sketches also ignores the fact that the correct match for any given sketch may already be incorrectly matched elsewhere. For calculating the probability of repeated successes, nevertheless, the simplest method is one in which each adolescent sketch is considered separately, or as if it were the first to be matched.

The probability that one sketch would be matched correctly by all judges, using this line of reasoning, is $1/6^n$ while other prob-

TABLE 5

PROBABILITY OF REPEATED SUCCESSES IN TEN MATCHINGS OF
PERSONALITY SKETCHES

Adolescent Sketch	Number of Correct Matches	Probability Level
Winnie	10	0.00000165%
Virginia Ruth	9	0.0000828
Sibyl	6	0.00217
Judy	0	0.1615
Patty	7	0.000248

abilities are worked out through use of the binominal expansion. This trend of difference between subjects in matchability was less definite for the boys on account of the small number of judges used. Fred and Harvey seemed to be most frequently matched, however. It is possible to interpret the trend in three ways. Ease of matching could be attributable, firstly, to the greater degree of similarity in personality in some cases. Perhaps, secondly, it might be due to more adequate description of some cases, at one or both levels. Allied with this is the third possibility that some individuals are more outstanding, and therefore can be matched more successfully than the generality even though the degree of similarity or dissimilarity between early and later status is similar for all.

SUMMARY

Personality sketches of 19 children written by Shirley [73] on the basis of observations during the first two years of life were matched with personality sketches of 15 of the same children prepared by the writer on the basis of test and rating material. Later sketches were prepared without acquaintance with the earlier ones. Five judges matched 10 sketches of adolescent boys, and 10 judges matched five sketches of adolescent girls. Both the results of the individual judges and the mean scores of all judges in matching were significant as compared to chance. Following are the conclusions of the investigation.

1. Personality similarities in an individual persist over a period of time.

2. Some individuals are more readily indentifiable after a period of time, presumably due to greater uniqueness of personality pattern.

3. The matching technique, utilizing total impression, allows for the demonstration of similarities in personality pattern in the same individual over a period of time.

——▶ **Arthur T. Jersild**

Self-understanding in Childhood and Adolescence[1]

From *American Psychologist,* 1951, 6:122–126. Reprinted by permission.

Historically the psychology of childhood and adolescence has been a science which some psychologists try to teach to other psychologists and to college students. My theme today is that we have held too restricted a conception of what child psychology is and what it might be. The proper study for all human beings from the earliest possible age is the human being himself.

Every child is actually or potentially a child psychologist. From an early age, without being deliberate about it, he acquires ideas and attitudes about himself and others. These are woven into the

[1] Adapted from a presidential address given before the Division of Childhood and Adolescence, American Psychological Association, State College, Pennsylvania, September 7, 1950.

pattern of his life. They may be true or false, healthy or morbid. Their development is left largely to chance. This is not as it should be, in my judgment. I propose that the study of child psychology, designed to promote understanding and acceptance of self and understanding of others, should be a planned feature of the education children receive from nursery school onward.

NEED FOR UNDERSTANDING

There is one gloomy fact about children who now are growing up which underscores, as I see it, the need for such a program. A large proportion of children will move into adulthood troubled and unhappy about many things. Many will be afflicted by irrational fears which do not represent dangers in the external environment but unresolved problems within themselves. Many, as adults, will suffer from attitudes of hostility, vindictiveness, and defensiveness which are not a response to hostile forces in the outside world but represent attitudes carried over from unresolved childhood struggles. Many persons similarly will acquire persisting feelings of inferiority or other unhealthy attitudes regarding their personal worth which represent either an irrational estimate of themselves or a failure to accept themselves realistically as they are.

In numerous ways there is a vast carry-over of unhealthy attitudes regarding self and others from childhood and adolescence into adult life.

Is so much distress inevitable? I do not think we have to assume that it is. But I do not think the picture can be changed substantially if we simply try to extend the special services we now provide. These services are good, and need to be continued. But the answer cannot be found simply by offering more psychological counseling, psychoanalysis, or other forms of treatment of the kind now provided for severely disturbed people after they already are on the rocks. A bolder measure is needed for the benefit of the population at large. This measure, I maintain, must involve a vastly enhanced conception of the social functions of research in child psychology and of the role that child psychology might play in the education of children.

THE UNDERLYING HYPOTHESIS

There is a general hypothesis underlying this proposal and it is this: human beings, from an early age, have more capacity for learning to face and to understand and to deal constructively with the realities of life than we have hitherto assumed in our psychological theories or in our educational practices.

CURRENT EVASION AND NEGLECT OF SELF-UNDERSTANDING

It is a curious thing that the subject of self-understanding has been so neglected when we consider how eager we are to teach other things. Childen learn to bound the states of the Union and they memorize the names and dates of bygone wars; they study the habits of beavers, learn about the distant stars, and the antics of Mother Goose. But the subject of human behavior, human motives, and the inner life of man has been pretty much ignored.

Much of what we do in education is an evasion rather than a way of facing problems that occur in the lives of children and adolescents. I have recently been involved in a study of children's interests in which several thousand youngsters in various parts of this country participated. [51] This study emphasizes, as some other studies have emphasized, that the interests children are induced to acquire often are superficial, stereotyped, and fail to lead the child on a road toward facing his real problems. However, we also found in this study that many of the older children expressed a desire to learn more about themselves and others, even though little was done in some of the schools they attended to encourage such a desire or to suggest that it might be fulfilled. What I propose is that we encourage this desire and try to fill it by developing a program to promote wholesome understanding of self and others as a basic feature of the general education of all children.

IMPLICATIONS OF SELF-UNDERSTANDING

I have used expressions such as "self-understanding" and "self-acceptance" in describing my position. These particular words are not, in my judgment, as important as the intention and purpose which I am trying to express. But the concept of the self, especially as it has developed in recent literature in psychology[2] and in some of the newer theoretical formulations in psychiatry and psychoanalysis,[3] is a fruitful one in this connection. I believe this to be true even though in the present state of our knowledge the meaning of "the self" can be defined only in arbitrary and tentative terms.

When we speak of "the self" we mean, among other things, a system of ideas, attitudes, appraisals and commitments pertaining to one's own person. The person experiences these as distinctly belonging to him and all of them together constitute the person's awareness of his individual existence and his conception of who and what he is. These attitudes and ideas are, of course, influenced by learning. This is an obvious but very crucial fact.

The self has been defined as a perceiver and a thing perceived, a knower and a thing that is known. Probably the self can best be studied if viewed as a composite.

I shall not try to list all the features of the composite. But I will mention some of the things which children and adolescents themselves report when they describe themselves. Recently my colleagues and I have gathered compositions from several hundred children from the fourth grade through high school on "What I like about myself" and "What I don't like about myself" and other themes pertaining to self-description or self-evaluation. [43]

When evaluating and describing themselves, many children think, in part, of specific physical characteristics, including stature, facial features, posture, and bearing. (In passing I will mention that some of our preliminary data suggest that there is a

---

2 There is not space to properly acknowledge these contributions, but I would mention especially William James [40], and the later works of Mead [52], Murphy [53], Lecky [48], Rogers [63], and Snygg and Combs. [76]

3 I refer especially to the works of Horney [see, e.g., 34 and 35], Harry Stack Sullivan [82], Allen [4], and Fromm. [20] (A more comprehensive statement of Karen Horney's position was published after this address was written. See K. Horney, *Neurosis and Human Growth*, New York: W. W. Norton & Co., Inc., 1950.)

great deal of irrational overrating, often in the form of self-disparagement, of physical characteristics during childhood.)

A very large proportion of children at all ages describe or appraise themselves favorably and unfavorably in terms of social criteria—their relations with people, their feelings about them, the attitudes others have toward them, and the attitudes they have toward others. Many children also assess their worth or worthlessness in terms of their relationship with their parents. Here again, as in connection with the development of other forms of self-appraisal, it appears that there are many possibilities for misinterpretation and irrational self-disparagement.

Also in the picture, according to our data, there may be attitudes which a person has concerning his inner resources, his talents, powers and abilities, his weaknesses, his defects, shortcomings, past misdeeds, present impulses and temptations, his role or roles in life, and his responsibilities, and (mainly at older levels) his anticipation of the future.

Some children emphasize awareness of religious affiliation and of moral obligations, and some mention commitment to values, goals, causes, which, as recognized by them, give content or direction to their individual ways of life.

Selfhood, in the literature, is often described by using "self" as part of a compound expression with modifiers which highlight one aspect or another of what the term denotes.

In the present context there are some modifiers that are particularly meaningful. We can distinguish, for example, between self-appraisal and appraisal by others and note that a person's self-estimation may be true or false or realistic or unrealistic when judged by group standards or by objective criteria. We can roughly distinguish between self-acceptance and self-rejection, as in the case of the person who lives comfortably with himself, or, by contrast, disparages himself or is ashamed of features in his past life or of his family background or is frightened by his present habits and impulses.

And to do a thorough job we would also have to try to distinguish between the "real self" and idealized or distorted versions of the self.

NEEDED RESEARCH

To carry out the program I am proposing we would need a vast amount of new research.

We especially need to study self-development from a genetic point of view, with attention to normal trends and the influence of various experiences on this development. We need to find out what is the nature of the growing child's perception of himself and of others. What concepts pertaining to understanding of self or others is he able to learn to use meaningfully and to apply? By what means it is possible to communicate with him? What are early symptoms and signs of false or morbid self-evaluation? These are only a few of the questions.

By way of an illustration or two; what is the approximate phase or level of deveolpment at which a child can appreciate the fact, say, that children who bully him are not simply unpleasant persons but troubled persons whose reproaches and adverse opinions should not lower his own self-eteem? At what juncture in his development might the child have the capacity for making allowances for others (or for himself) when they are peevish or irritable, or the ability to "see through" some of the arts and dodges, masquerades, concealments and camouflages of human motives, including his own?

Another research need is for finding out how children can be helped to use their capacity for self-discovery and for understanding others. In the literature there already are some promising leads.

PROFESSIONAL AND PRACTICAL RAMIFICATIONS

The subject I am dealing with raises questions that have a bearing on the definition of what our Division stands for and on our professional affiliations within the APA. There is a crisscrossing here of what we normally think of as matters belonging to several divisions.

Usually we think of something in the teaching field as belonging primarily to educational psychology. But the basic research here required is definitely in the field of genetic and developmental psychology—that is, in our Division.

Much of the information we now have concerning the kinds of problems children face and their capacity for coping with them has come from case work in the branches of psychology and psychiatry which deal with psychotherapy and psychological counseling. But the scope of what would be involved in my proposal goes far beyond the population now reached by these professional groups and involves research that goes beyond the conception which some mental hygienists have concerning the nature of their work, although we will still need to retain special psychotherapeutic services for deeply disturbed children.

The aim in clinical psychology and psychiatry has largely been to help individuals who have failed to make a comfortable adjustment to the conditions of life. The aim in the program I propose is to help the growing person while he is in the process of adjusting to these conditions, including conditions within himself. The aim in psychotherapy, according to one school of thought, is to bring conscious processes to bear upon hidden or unconscious sources of conflict. The aim in the program here proposed would be to try to discover and apply ways of reducing the hiatus between conscious or unconscious factors in the growing person's experience, by trying to help him to develop to the fullest whatever capacity he may have for understanding and interpreting the events of life as they befall, his ability to deal as forthrightly and knowingly as possible with his own feelings and impulses as these come into play, his capacity for discovering his potentialities, for acquiring a realistic appreciation of his assets and limitations, and his capacity for developing goals that might enable him to be true to himself rather than seeking to conform to standards that are out of harmony with what he is or ever could hope to be.

UNANSWERED QUESTIONS

I am sure all of you have thought of questions or misgivings regarding this proposal. Perhaps the greatest skepticism concerning the capacity of children to gain psychological understanding through everyday educational experience, as distinct from special professional treatment, will be found among psychologists themselves.

One misgiving may be phrased in the claim that the business of facing reality in a happy way is more an emotional by-product than a job that can be achieved by a studied approach. People don't make themselves happy by studying how to be happy. We might also phrase a misgiving as follows: If a child already is unhappy or anxious, would it not be impossible for him, while in such a mood, to gain in self-understanding by way of anything the school might offer? And if he is quite happy and free from anxiety, is there any reason why he should try to understand himself? Does it not follow then that the proposal in the first instance is hopeless and, in the second instance, needless? Again, someone might claim that the intellect can do little at the adult level to influence basic attitudes and it perhaps is even more powerless at the childhood level.

I agree that the learning of psychology on an academic level alone is not likely to make much difference, if any. A person can possess a vast knowledge of psychological facts and principles and still be an unhappy neurotic. Yet I do believe that a discovery about self that is first perceived on an intellectual level can sometimes initiate a chain of reactions that have profound emotional consequences in a person's life. And, besides, what I here propose is not just an intellectual or academic approach. In attempting this program we would have to recognize that the process of developing self-understanding involves all of the growing person's faculties for feeling and thinking.

The program would probably make much use of group projects as an aid to self-discovery and self-acceptance.

It would mean a greatly enhanced conception of the psychological possibilities inherent in a calculated use of present features of the school's program such as what is offered, for example, in physical education.

It would mean that each subject that is retained in the curriculum would be used, as far as feasible, as a vehicle for increased understanding of self or others. There is a rich psychological content, for example, in history and in the study of current events.

If these subjects are properly scaled to the pupil's maturity level and if they are treated in realistic terms they give play to a wide range of human motives, hopes, conflicts and perplexities which the pupil can relate to some of the happenings in his own life.

While the program would definitely not be confined to academic learning, intellectual processes would certainly come into the picture. It is true that there are people in psychology who take a dim view of what the intellect can accomplish. Even those who have attached great importance to intelligence have sometimes underestimated the possibilities of intellectual growth. Actually, I don't believe we have begun to fathom what the human intellect can do.

In passing, I would add that, on the basis of limited observations, I have a hunch that the ability which enables a person to be wise to himself does not necessarily show a very high correlation with the kind of ability we measure by means of our common intelligence tests. From everyday observation it appears that a person can have a very high IQ and still thoroughly fool himself and that people with modest IQ's sometimes achieve a very canny and healthy picture of themselves.

One can overrate rational processes, it is true, but it is also absurd to belittle the role intellectual or cognitive processes may play in giving structure to experiences as they occur in life and in modifying or reconstructing the effects of experiences that have occurred. A crucial feature in many of the emotional experiences that might influence a child's self-evaluation is the child's perception of what is happening—a perception which leads him to react to an event as a form of success or failure, as a threat or an affront or a source of joy.

The question as to ways in which rational processes and emotional reactions interact in the course of self-development and in the process of self-discovery, and the question as to the interplay between a person's intellectual insights and the attitudes which govern his life, would constitute an important feature of the research demanded by the hypothesis I set forth early in this paper. Certainly at the present stage of our knowledge it would be ill-timed to settle this question by concluding in advance that understanding and insight occur only as incidental by-products.

Another question is, assuming that we could learn in theory how to do all this, where could we find parents or teachers who could put the theory into practice? That is not easily answered. But I believe that this question represents a problem of research and education rather than a theoretical obstruction that dooms the idea in advance.

To carry out the program it would, of course, be necessary to give careful attention to the selection and training of teachers. Moreover, child study would be a crucial feature of the teacher's job and a very important consideration in the school budget.

We might also ask, is it really possible for parents and teachers and children to establish the kind of relationship out of which mutual understanding and self-understanding might develop? The parent or teacher is a disciplinarian, we are told. He holds authority. He can not permit conditions from which understanding such as here described might evolve. But this view may be questioned. This question should be raised as a problem for study, not as a problem regarded in advance as one that either can't be solved or is bound to yield a negative answer.

It might also be maintained that it is dangerous for teachers, or parents, to dabble with psychology. They might damage a child's mind just as an amateur surgeon might damage a child's body. This point certainly deserves attention. But let us be realistic. Every hour, every day, millions of parents and thousands of teachers practice psychology and, in effect, teach psychology in their dealings with children whether they know it or not. They are involved in situations in which children meet success or failure, acceptance or rejection, and countless other circumstances in which children are discovering themselves and developing attitudes regarding themselves for better or for worse.

This does not mean that we must try to get parents and teachers to take over the functions which psychiatrists and clinical psychologists are now responsible for. At best, there will always be a limit to what a parent and teacher, no matter how well-trained, can do in dealing with problems that arise in their relations with children who are in their immediate care from day to day. Actually, we need to learn more concerning the overlapping and the distinctive and exclusive roles of the parent and teacher, on the one hand, and the specialist in psychology or psychiatry, on the other. Among other matters, we also need more light on the question as to how, in the *education* of children, we might achieve some of the things which the psychological specialist tries to achieve in the *re-education* of his patients.

So I say, let us as far as possible bring the forces which now operate in darkness out into the light. Let us recognize that the most important psychological facts in a child's life are his relationships with others and his relationship to himself. These relationships are constantly in the process of development and are constantly involved in the learning that goes with the business of living. Learning which pertains to anything so crucial should properly be part of the child's planned education and indeed should, in my judgment, be regarded as the most important part of the educational program.

Each child is a student of human nature within the limits of his maturity level and what he has had an opportunity to learn. The home, the classroom, the playground, and other situations are psychological laboratories in which he is now a subject and now an observer. Child psychology will fully come into its own when it discovers the capacities children have for learning from these laboratories and explores the conditions under which these capacities can best be developed.

REFERENCES

1. ABRAHAM, K., "The Influence of Oral Emotions on Character Formation," in *Collected Papers,* The International Psychoanalytical Library, No. 13, London: The Hogarth Press, Ltd., 1927, pp. 393–406.

2. ———, "Contributions to the Theory of the Anal Character," *Collected Papers,* The International Psychoanalytical Library, No. 13, London: The Hogarth Press, Ltd., 1927, pp. 370–392.

3. ADORNO, T. W., *et al., The Authoritarian Personality,* New York: Harper & Brothers, 1950.

4. ALLEN, F., *Psychotherapy with Children,* New York: W. W. Norton & Co., Inc., 1942.

5. ALLPORT, G. W., *Personality: A Psychological Interpretation,* New York: Holt, Rinehart and Winston, Inc., 1937.

6. ———, "The Ego in Contemporary Psychology," *Psychological Review,* 1943, 50:451–478.

7. BAYLEY, NANCY, "A Study of the Crying of Infants During Mental and Physical Tests," *Journal of Genetic Psychology,* 1932, 40:306–329.

8. BERGMAN, P., & ESCALONA, SIBYLLE K., "Unusual Sensitivities in Very Young Children," in *The Psychoanalytic Study of the Child,* New York: International Universities Press, 1949, Vols. 3, 4:333–352.

9. BRACKETT, C. W., "Laughing and Crying of Preschool Children," *Journal of Experimental Education,* 1933, 2:119–126.

10. CATTELL, R. B., *Personality and Motivation: Structure and Measurement,* New York: Harcourt, Brace & World, Inc., 1957.

11. CHAPMAN, D. W., "The Generalized Problem of Correct Matching," *Annals of Mathematical Statistics,* 1935, 6:85–95.

12. ———, "The Significance of Matching with Unequal Series," *American Journal of Psychology,* 1936, 48:167–169.

13. CUSHING, H. M., "A Perseverative Tendency in Preschool Children: A Study of Personality Differences," *Archives of Psychology,* 1929, No. 108.

14. DURFEE, H., & WOLF, K., "Abstaltspflege und Entwicklung im Ersten Lebenjähr," *Zeitschrift für Kinderforschung,* 1933, 42:3.

15. ESCALONA, SIBYLLE K., "The Use of Infant Tests for Predictive Purposes," *Bulletin of the Menninger Clinic,* 1950, 14:117–128.

16. FREUD, S., "Character and Anal Erotism," in *Collected Papers,* Vol. II, The International Psychoanalytical Library, No. 8, London: The Hogarth Press, Ltd., 1924, pp. 45–50.

17. ———, *Three Contributions to the Theory of Sex.* Nervous and Mental Disease Monograph Series, No. 7, New York: Nervous and Mental Disease Publishing Company, 1910; first published in German in 1905. Also reprinted in *The Basic Writings of Sigmund Freud,* New York: The Modern Library, Inc., 1938, Book III, pp. 553–620.

18. FRIES, M. E., "Interrelated Factors in Character Development, Neuroses, Psychoses, and Delinquency," *American Journal of Orthopsychiatry,* 1937, 7:142–181.

19. ———, "Psychosomatic Relationships between Mother and Child," *Psychosomatic Medicine,* 1944, 6:159–162.

20. FROMM, ERICH, *Man for Himself,* New York: Holt, Rinehart and Winston, Inc., 1947.

21. GALTON, F., "Measurement of Character," *Fortnightly Review*, 1884, 42:179–185.

22. ———, *Inquiries into Human Faculty and Its Development*, New York: E. P. Dutton and Company, 1883, 1907, Everyman's Library No. 263, p. 128.

23. ———, *Op. cit.*, pp. 216–217.

24. ———, *Op. cit.*, p. 172.

25. GESELL, A., *et. al.*, *Biographies of Child Development*, New York: Harper & Brothers, 1939, p. 304.

26. GESELL, A., & AMES, LOUISE B., "Early Evidences of Individuality in the Human Infant," *Scientific Monthly*, 1937, 45:217–225.

27. ———, & THOMPSON, HELEN, "Twins T and C from Infancy to Adolescence," *Genetic Psychology Monographs*, 1941, 25:3–121.

28. GOLDFARB, W., "Psychological Privation in Infancy and Subsequent Adjustment," *American Journal of Orthopsychiatry*, 1945, 15:247–255.

29. GOODENOUGH, FLORENCE L., "The Use of Free Association in the Objective Measurement of Personality," in Q. McNemar, and Maude A. Merrill, eds., *Studies in Personality*, New York: McGraw-Hill, 1942, pp. 87–103.

30. GREEN, E. H., "Friendships and Quarrels among Preschool Children," *Child Development*, 1933, 4:237–252.

31. GUILFORD, J. P., *Personality*, New York: McGraw-Hill Book Company, Inc., 1959.

32. HARTSHORNE, H., MAY, M. A., MALLER, J. B., & SHUTTLEWORTH, F. K., *Studies in the Nature of Character:* "Studies in Deceit," Vol. I; "Studies in Service and Self-control," Vol. II; "Studies in the Organization of Character," Vol. III, New York: The Macmillan Company, 1928, 1929, 1930.

33. HOGAN, L., *A Study of a Child*, New York: Harper & Brothers, 1900, p. 15.

34. HORNEY, KAREN, *The Neurotic Personality of Our Time*, New York: W. W. Norton & Co., Inc., 1937.

35. ———, *Our Inner Conflicts*, New York: W. W. Norton & Co., Inc., 1945.

36. ———, *Neurosis and Human Growth*, New York: W. W. Norton & Co., Inc., 1950.

37. HOROWITZ, E. L., "Spatial Localization of the Self," *Journal of Social Psychology*, 1935, 6:379–387.

38. HOSKINS, R. G., *Endocrinology*, New York: W. W. Norton & Co., Inc., 1941, p. 364.

39. JAMES, W., *Psychology*, Vol. 1, New York: Holt, Rinehart & Winston, Inc., 1890, pp. 375–400.

40. ————, *Principles of Psychology,* New York: Holt, Rinehart & Winston, Inc., 1890.

41. JERSILD, A. T., "The Constancy of Certain Behavior Patterns in Young Children," *American Journal of Psychology,* 1933, 45:125–129.

42. ————, *Child Psychology,* rev. ed., Englewood Cliffs, N.J.: Prentice-Hall, Inc., 1942.

43. ————, *Self-evaluation during Childhood and Adolescence: A Preliminary Study,* Unpublished.

44. ————, & TASCH, RUTH, *Children's Interests,* New York: Bureau of Publications, Teachers College, Columbia University, 1949.

45. JONES, E., "Freud's Psychology," *Psychological Bulletin,* 1911, 7:109–128.

46. JONES, MARY C., & BURKS, BARBARA S., "Personality Development in Childhood: A Survey of Problems, Methods, and Experimental Findings," *Monographs of the Society for Research of Child Development,* 1936, 1:No. 4.

47. KELLY, E. L., "Consistency of the Adult Personality," *The American Psychologist,* 1955, 10:659–681.

48. LECKY, P., *Self-consistency,* New York: Island Press, 1945.

49. MACFARLANE, JEAN W., "The Guidance Study," *Sociometry,* 1939, 2:1–23.

50. MCGRAW, MYRTLE B., "Later Development of Children Specially Trained," *Child Development,* 1939, 10:1–19.

51. MCKINNON, KATHERN M., *Consistency and Change in Behavior Manifestations,* Child Development Monographs, No. 30, New York: Bureau of Publications, Teachers College, Columbia University, 1942.

52. MEAD, G., *Mind, Self, and Society,* Chicago: University of Chicago Press, 1934.

53. MURPHY, G., *Personality,* New York: Harper & Brothers, 1947.

54. ————, *Personality: A Biosocial Approach to Origin and Structure,* New York: Harper & Brothers, 1947.

55. ————, MURPHY, LOIS B., & NEWCOMB, T. M., *Experimental Social Psychology,* New York: Harper & Brothers, 1937.

56. NEILON (NAKA), PATRICIA, "Shirley's Babies after Fifteen Years: A Personality Study," *Journal of Genetic Psychology,* 1948, 73:175–186.

57. ORLANSKY, H., "Infant Care and Personality," *Psychological Bulletin,* 1949, 46:1–48.

58. PINNEAU, S. R., "A Critique of the Articles by Margaret Ribble," *Child Development,* 1950, 21:203–228.

59. RIBBLE, MARGARET, *The Rights of Infants,* New York: Columbia University Press, 1943.

60. ———, *Op. cit.,* p. 82.

61. ———, *Op. cit.,* pp. 109–110.

62. ROBERTS, K. E., & FLEMING, V. V., "Persistence and Change in Personality Patterns," *Monographs of the Society for Research in Child Development,* 1943, 8:No. 3.

63. ROGERS, C., *Counseling and Psychotherapy,* Boston: Houghton Mifflin Company, 1942.

64. RUNDQUIST, E. A., & SLETTO, R. E., *Personality in the Depression: A Study in the Measurement of Attitudes,* Minneapolis: University of Minnesota Press, 1936.

65. SALVOSA, L. R., "Tables of Pearson's Type III Function," *Annals of Mathematical Statistics,* 1930, 1:191–198.

66. SEARS, R. R., MACCOBY, ELEANOR E., & LEVIN, H., *Patterns of Child Rearing,* Evanston, Illinois: Row, Peterson and Company, 1957.

67. ———, *Op. cit.,* p. 452.

68. ———, *Op. cit.,* p. 458.

69. ———, *Op. cit.,* p. 466.

70. SHELDON, W. H., *The Varieties of Temperament,* New York: Harper & Brothers, 1942.

71. SHINN, M., *The Biography of a Baby,* Boston: Houghton Mifflin Company, 1900, p. 55.

72. SHIRLEY, MARY M., *The First Two Years: A Study of Twenty-five Babies,* Vol. I, Minneapolis: University of Minnesota Press, 1931.

73. ———, *The First Two Years: A Study of Twenty-five Babies,* Vol. III, Minneapolis: University of Minnesota Press, 1933.

74. ———, "Children's Adjustment to a Strange Situation," *Child Development,* 1942, 37:201–217.

75. SMITH, MADORAH E., "A Comparison of Certain Personality Traits as Rated on the Same Individuals in Childhood and Fifty Years Later," *Child Development,* 1952, 23:159–180.

76. SNYGG, D., & COMBS, A. W., *Individual Behavior,* New York: Harper & Brothers, 1949.

77. SPITZ, R. A., "Hospitalism" in *The Psychoanalytic Study of the Child,* Vol. 1, New York: International Universities Press, 1945, pp. 53–74.

78. ———, "The Role of Ecological Factors in Emotional Development in Infancy," *Child Development,* 1949, 20:145–155.

79. ———, & WOLF, KATHERINE M., "Anaclitic Depression. An Inquiry into the Genesis of Psychiatric Conditions in Early Childhood," *The Psychoanalytic Study of the Child,* Vol. 2, New York: International Universities Press, 1946, pp. 313–342.

80. ———, & WOLF, KATHERINE M., "Autoerotism, Some Empirical Findings and Hypotheses on Three of its Manifestations in the First Year of Life," *The Psychoanalytic Study of the Child,* Vols. 3, 4, New York: International Universities Press, 1949, pp. 85–129.

81. STUTSMAN, RACHAEL, "Constancy in Personality Trends," *Psychology Bulletin,* 1935, 32:701–702. Abstract.

82. SULLIVAN, H. S., "Conceptions of Modern Psychiatry," *Psychiatry,* 1940, 3:1–117.

83. ———, *Concepts of Modern Psychiatry,* Washington, D.C.: The William A. White Psychiatric Foundation, 1947.

84. SYMONDS, P. M., *The Psychology of Parent-Child Relationships,* New York: D. Appleton-Century-Crofts, Inc., 1939.

85. ———, *Op. cit.,* p. 94.

86. ———, "Education for the Development of Personality," *Teachers College Record,* 1948, 50:163–169.

87. ———, *Adolescent Fantasy,* New York: Columbia University Press, 1949.

88. ———, & JENSEN, A. F., *Out of Adolescence into Maturity,* to be published by the Columbia University Press.

89. ———, *Op. cit.*

90. TRYON, CAROLINE M., "Constancy and Generality of Emotional Adjustment in Adolescents as Measured by a Questionnaire," *Psychological Bulletin,* 1934, 31:585–586.

91. VERNON, P. E., "Can the 'Total Personality' Be Studied Objectively?" *Character and Personality,* 1935, 4:1–10.

92. ———, "The Evaluation of Matching Method," *Journal of Educational Psychology,* 1936, 27:1–17.

93. ———, "The Matching Method Applied to Investigations of Personality," *Psychological Bulletin,* 1936, 33:149–177.

94. WASHBURN, R. W., "A Study of the Smiling and Laughing of Infants in the First Year of Life," *Genetic Psychology Monographs,* 1929, 6:403–537.

95. WATSON, J. B., & WATSON, R. R., "Studies in Infant Psychology," *Scientific Monthly,* 1921, 13:493–515.

96. WILE, I. S., NEARY, L., MACE, L., & DAVIES, R., "The Continuity of the Neurotic Processes," *American Journal of Orthopsychiatry,* 1934, 4:49–72.

97. WOOLLEY, HELEN T., "Agnes: A Dominant Personality in the Making," *Journal of Genetic Psychology,* 1925, 32:569–598.

98. ZUBIN, J., "The Chance Element in Matching," *Journal of Educational Psychology,* 1933, 24:674–681.

CHAPTER
FIFTEEN

↑

Psychology of Teacher-Pupil Relationships

WHAT A CHILD LEARNS IN SCHOOL, CONSIST-ing of knowledge, skills, attitudes, beliefs, and purposes, depends in part upon the objectives of curriculum makers and instructors. But there is more to the learning situation for the child than the assignments which are required of him by his school. For him a learning experience consists of the total scheme of circumstances of which he is aware at that moment. He may be aware, for example, of the nod of approval which his efforts receive from his teacher. He may, on the other hand, be painfully conscious of what he perceives as his teacher's rejection of him as a person. He may feel that what he likes and what he aspires to are valued also by his teacher, or he may sense a considerable variance between his values and purposes and those acceptable to his teacher.

The psychological conditions that are conducive to desirable learning and development in school have been studied by many researchers from many different approaches. Much has been revealed by such studies about the ideas which teachers have regarding children's motivations, their problems, and their responsiveness to various kinds of direction and control. Much has been learned also about the influence which teachers' ideas and practices have on the psychological climate of the school —a climate which, as certain of the studies show, has definite and long-lasting influences on learning and personality development.

Extensive investigations have been conducted by Celia B. Stendler into the kinds of understandings teachers have of child behavior and into the relationships between their understandings and the kinds of preparation they received for teaching. It should prove interesting to the reader to relate Stendler's findings to the concepts and practices that are discussed in the other four readings in this chapter. She is Professor of Education at the University of Illinois.

What do today's teachers consider to be important problems of child behavior? The question is one to which much attention has been given since the classic study by Wickman three decades ago comparing teachers' ideas of pupil problems with the ideas of mental hygienists. How do the ideas of teachers today compare with those of teachers a generation or more ago? How do such factors as training, professional experience, and social background influence a teacher's ideas about pupil problems? E. C. Hunter's article provides a very comprehensive answer to questions of these kinds. Hunter is Dean of Education at Tulane University.

Certainly no circumstance is of more concern to the teacher than that of classroom discipline. Concepts of discipline have undergone important changes over the years, and there are definite reasons for these changes. This will be evident from a reading of the article by Percival M. Symonds.

A report on the relationship between pupil growth and teachers' understanding of pupil behavior would appear to be highly appropriate as the the closing selection in this book. The article by Ralph H. Ojemann (Director of the Preventive Psychiatry Research Program, State University of Iowa) and Francis R. Wilkinson deals with a study they made of this relationship. It is not enough, they state, where personality development is the goal, for teachers to be concerned only with "problem children." To be effective guides for children's learning, teachers must know all their pupils, and they must know them "not as entities in the classroom but as living personalities with ambitions, attitudes, conflicts, and problems, coming from environments that vary greatly in the encouragement or discouragement effected."

Thus, with the Ojemann-Wilkinson emphasis upon the importance of a teacher's knowledge of pupils as living personalities, this book concludes on the theme with which it began. The theme is that psychology for teachers must be a psychology of *persons*.

—▶ **Celia B. Stendler**

How Well Do Elementary School Teachers Understand Child Behavior?

From *Journal of Educational Psychology*, 1949, 40:489–498. Reprinted by permission of the author and Warwick & York, Inc.

To the elementary school each year come children with many kinds of problems. Teachers have to deal with children who fight and children who are afraid to fight; children who do too much work and children who don't do enough work; children who lie and children who steal; children who daydream and children who clown; children who are suspicious and children who are withdrawn. The kind of insight into such problems which elementary teachers have is very important. It is a vital factor in determining whether children will be treated in ways conducive to good mental health, or in ways which will further poor adjustment.

What kind of insight do teachers have into child behavior? Wickman's [24] study, completed as far back as 1928, showed that teachers and clinical psychologists differed considerably in their rating of the seriousness of various kinds of behavior. The clinical psychologists listed unsocialness, suspiciousness, unhappiness, resentfulness and the like as being very important problems from the standpoint of adjustment. These were not considered as serious by teachers who placed, instead, such practices as heterosexual activity, stealing, masturbation, or "toilet talk" high on the list of problem behavior. The implication from the study would seem to be that teachers do not always recognize the kinds of behavior which are indicative of poor adjustment.

A study by W. Drayton Lewis [10] contributes additional information about teachers' insight into child behavior. Teachers were asked to select children in their classrooms whom they considered to be retarded, geniuses, or problems. An analysis of the problem group showed that teachers considered as serious cases those who were upsetting to classroom routine. Lack of tidiness or resistance to teacher authority were mentioned as problems, rather than extreme shyness or withdrawal which the clinician would regard as serious.

It has been pointed out, however, that the discrepancy between teachers' and clinicians' judgments as to what constitutes serious behavior may not be as damning to the teacher as appears at first glance. Actually, the difference in opinion as to what constitutes problem behavior may be due to the fact that teachers and clinicians are looking at children from different points of view. The teacher may look upon suspiciousness as important from the standpoint of personal adjustment, but may find aggressiveness or obscene talk much more serious from the standpoint of classroom management.

The approach in the present study to the problem of teacher insight into child behavior had a different emphasis. As part of a comprehensive school survey an attempt was made to find out how teachers thought certain kinds of behavior problems should be handled. By asking a teacher to describe what he considered to be the best way to handle a particular behavior problem, it was hoped that the teacher's insight into that particular problem might be revealed.

METHOD

The procedure, used to disclose teacher insight into child behavior was a test containing twenty-five free response statements describing various behavior patterns in children. Teachers were asked to complete these by describing what they thought was the best way of treating each particular problem. This test was presented to all elementary teachers (one hundred fifty-seven) in a midwestern community. All tests were unsigned and no effort was made to identify the person answering the test. The teachers were part of a fine public school system and had had the advantage of an in-service training program for many years. It was expected, then, that as a group they would deal with behavior more constructively than the average classroom teacher.

The test follows:

PROBLEMS OF CHILD BEHAVIOR

Here are some statements about children which are not complete. Each statement describes a particular kind of behavior problem. For example, the first statement says, "I think the child who never finishes on time should." You are to finish the statement by describing what you think would be the best way of treating his particular problem.

1. I think the child who never finishes on time should
2. I think the child who continually fights with other children should
3. I think the child who continually steals should
4. I think the child who bites his fingernails should
5. I think the child who daydreams most of the time should

6. I think the child who relies on the teacher too much should
7. I think the child who does his work over and over until it is just right should
8. I think the child who never works up to his capacity should
9. I think the child who never pays attention should
10. I think the child who is always late should
11. I think the child who always lies should
12. I think the child who always talks back to the teacher should
13. I think the child who is easily discouraged should
14. I think the child who continually shows off in class should
15. I think the child who always feels everyone is picking on him should
16. I think the child who loses his temper when he doesn't get his way should
17. I think the child who uses vulgar language should
18. I think the child who tries to cheat on exams should
19. I think the child who is always unhappy and moody should
20. I think the child who continually plays truant should
21. I think the child who is a bully should
22. I think the child who wastes school materials should
23. I think the child who continually disobeys should
24. I think the child who is disliked by other children should
25. I think the child who is timid and shy should

Answers to the test describing how teachers thought certain behavior problems should be handled were classified under six categories:

1. Take punitive measures. This category included all answers which recommended punishment of any kind.
2. Talk to him, moralize. Answers which indicated that the child should be talked to and the error of his ways pointed out to him were classified under this category.
3. Send him to a doctor.
4. Adjust the work. This category included teachers' answers recommending that the amount of work be decreased or increased, or recommending a particular kind of project as a way of handling the behavior problem.
5. Praise or encourage him.
6. Study him to find the cause of behavior and plan a course of action accordingly.

Three experts in the field of mental hygiene also completed the sentences on the test. These experts were in agreement that the best answer for all twenty-five items was Category 6. In other words, regardless of what the problem was, these experts would agree that the cause of the behavior should be sought and action planned in the light of the cause.

RESULTS

Table 1 shows the percentage of teacher responses falling under each category. It is interesting to note that teachers in this

TABLE 1

PERCENTAGE OF RESPONSES FOR SIX CATEGORIES ON TWENTY-FIVE
ITEMS DESCRIBING PUPIL BEHAVIOR MADE BY 157 ELEMENTARY
TEACHERS IN A MIDWESTERN PUBLIC SCHOOL SYSTEM

Category	Per Cent of Responses
1. Take punitive measures	13.9
2. Talk to the child	33.4
3. Send him to a doctor	2.7
4. Adjust the work	22.5
5. Praise or encourage	9.1
6. Study him to find cause of behavior	14.6
7. No answer	3.8

modern school system are beyond the stage of attributing behavior to physical causes. Not so long ago it was popular practice with parents and doctors as well as teachers to look to diseased tonsils, infected teeth, and overactive or sluggish glands for an explanation of any kind of behavior pattern. Whenever a child showed any signs of being a problem child, it was immediately suggested that he see a doctor. Only 2.7 per cent of the teachers suggested Category 3 as a remedy. Item 4 on fingernail biting, as Table 2 indicates, was the only item which more teachers answered by referring the child to a doctor than by using some other technique. Thirty-four per cent of the teachers completed the statement in that manner. Seven per

PERCENTAGE OF RESPONSES IN EACH OF SIX CATEGORIES FOR 25 ITEMS ON A PROBLEMS OF CHILD BEHAVIOR TEST TAKEN BY 157 ELEMENTARY TEACHERS IN A MIDWESTERN PUBLIC SCHOOL SYSTEM

	Categories						
	1. Take Punitive Measures	2. Talk to Him; Moralize	3. Send Him to a Doctor	4. Adjust the Work	5. Praise or Encourage	6. Study to Find Cause of Behavior	7. No Answer
1. I think the child who never finishes on time should	12.1	13.4	1.3	44.0	17.2	10.8	1.3
2. I think the child who fights with other children should	15.9	42.7	2.6	10.8	.64	26.8	.64
3. I think the child who steals should	7.0	49.0	1.3	3.2	0	38.2	1.3
4. I think the child who bites his fingers should	1.9	16.6	34.4	18.5	3.2	22.3	3.2
5. I think the child who daydreams should	1.9	17.2	7.6	55.4	2.6	10.8	4.5
6. I think the child who relies on the teacher too much should	3.2	22.9	0	54.8	17.8	.64	.64
7. I think the child who does his work over and over until it is just right should	1.3	49.7	0	17.8	27.4	1.3	2.6
8. I think the child who won't work up to his capacity should	9.6	20.4	3.2	36.9	19.8	8.3	1.9
9. I think the child who doesn't pay attention should	24.2	19.1	7.6	27.4	1.3	8.9	11.5
10. I think the child who is always late should	30.6	22.9	.64	9.6	0	33.8	2.6
11. I think the child who lies should	10.8	58.0	1.3	5.10	0	18.8	6.4
12. I think the child who talks back to the teacher should	14.7	58.0	0	5.10	0	17.2	5.1
13. I think the child who is easily discouraged should	0	7.6	0	33.8	57.3	1.3	0
14. I think the child who shows off in class should	22.3	25.5	0	36.3	.64	7.6	7.6
15. I think the child who feels everyone is picking on him should	1.3	37.6	1.3	15.9	15.3	22.9	5.7
16. I think the child who loses his temper when he doesn't get his way should	29.3	52.9	0	4.5	0	8.3	5.1
17. I think the child who uses vulgar language should	19.1	65.6	0	3.2	0	8.3	3.8
18. I think the child who tries to cheat on exams should	12.7	58.6	0	19.1	0	5.1	4.5
19. I think the child who is unhappy and moody should	0	10.2	6.4	34.4	16.6	29.9	2.6
20. I think the child who plays truant should	12.7	20.4	0	24.8	.64	36.9	4.5
21. I think the child who is a bully should	38.2	25.5	0	22.9	.64	7.6	5.1
22. I think the child who wastes school materials should	38.9	52.9	0	3.8	0	.64	3.8
23. I think the child who disobeys should	38.9	39.5	0	2.6	0	11.5	7.6
24. I think the child who is disliked by other children should	0	46.5	0	15.3	7.6	28.0	2.6
25. I think the child who is timid and shy should	0	2.6	0	56.7	39.6	.64	.64

cent of the teachers thought poor attention and daydreaming were also due to physical causes and children guilty of these practices should see a doctor. Most mental hygienists, however, would agree that fingernail biting, daydreaming and lack of attention would probably indicate emotional difficulty rather than physical.

Categories 4, 5, and 6, which included such remedies as adjusting the work, praising, or encouraging, or studying the child to find causes of behavior, represent constructive ways of dealing with behavior problems. Forty-six per cent of all teachers tested would employ measures such as these in working with children. Adjusting the work was the procedure recommended by 22.5 per cent of the teachers. Forty-four per cent would adjust the work for the child who never finished, fifty-five per cent for the daydreamer, fifty-four per cent for the dependent child, thirty-six per cent for the child who doesn't work hard enough, twenty-seven per cent for the nonattentive child, thirty-six per cent for the show-off, thirty-four per cent for the unhappy child, and fifty-six per cent for the shy, timid child. Techniques for adjusting the work might range from decreasing the load for the child who never finishes to providing jobs which would keep a child busy and out of mischief. Teachers' responses in this category indicated that they accepted the responsibility for changing the environment so that the child might be helped.

Only thirteen per cent of elementary teachers tested recommended punitive measures in dealing with problems of child behavior. Three items in particular were singled out for this kind of treatment: bullying, tardiness and disobedience. More teachers —thirty-eight per cent—would treat bullying by punishment than by any other means. Thirty-eight per cent of the teachers would punish for disobedience, and thirty per cent for tardiness. Favorite punishments were keeping a tardy child after school, shaming the class clown, isolating the disobedient child, and denying "privileges." No teacher recommended corporal punishment.

Although punishment is probably used in classrooms more often than responses would indicate, it must be remembered that teachers in taking the test were asked to describe what they considered "best" methods of dealing with problem behavior.

The fact that only thirteen per cent of the responses recommended punitive measures would seem to indicate that most teachers do not consider punishment a respectable method of dealing with problems of child behavior. This is in line with Mowrer's [16] observation that parents, too, have come to look upon punishment as an undesirable method of handling children and that punishment is, therefore, frequently resorted to with a sense of guilt. This writer is not advocating punitive measures as a method of helping children with the problems listed in the test described in this manuscript, but rather that there needs to be a re-thinking through of the kind of punitive measures used, and the place of these in the elementary-school classroom.

The largest number of responses for any one category was thirty-three per cent for Category 2, Talking to the Child or Moralizing. More teachers tested would use this technique for dealing with children than any other. Responses indicated that teachers would point out to the child the error of his ways, tell him others would not like him if he persisted in such actions, or tell him his parents or his classmates would be ashamed of him. Items of behavior which more teachers would treat by talking to the child rather than any other way including fighting, stealing, doing work over and over, lying, talking back, losing one's temper, being suspicious, swearing, cheating, being unpopular, disobeying and wasting school materials.

While most of the comments teachers would make to pupils do not harm, one might question how effective they are. The cause of lying which persists over a long period of time may be deep-rooted in the emotions, and simply talking to a child about it and telling him it is wrong to lie may do little good. Talking to a child about his behavior as a way of dealing with a problem of behavior assumes that all behavior is dependent upon the will and is rational; a mental hygiene approach assumes that there is more to behavior than will-power and that reasoning with a child may not help him to develop the insight to help himself. This does not rule out talking to a child, but simply says that for serious behavior difficulties it should not be the main approach.

Category 6, Study the Child and Plan Accordingly, was the

response clinicians gave as the best means for changing patterns of child behavior. In other words, clinicians felt the need for more information about the child before prescribing remedies. Only three items of behavior called forth this response with many teachers: stealing, truancy, and tardiness. Thirty-eight per cent of the teachers thought the child who stole should be studied, thirty-six per cent the truant, and thirty-three per cent the tardy child. One might read into this the implication that teachers think these three problems call for facts about the out-of-school life of the child, whereas suspiciousness and withdrawn behavior do not. It also seems to imply that teachers may consider stealing, truancy, and tardiness more serious than other problems of behavior since they warrant additional study.

Summary

As part of a comprehensive school survey, an attempt was made to measure teacher insight into child behavior. The method used was a free response questionnaire consisting of twenty-five items describing problems of child behavior. All elementary teachers in the system surveyed took the test. Three mental hygienists were also asked to take the test and their responses served as a bench mark against which the teachers might be evaluated.

Teachers in the school system being surveyed recognized constructive measures for the most part in dealing with child behavior. They favored such procedures as adjusting the work, praising or encouraging, or studying the child to find causes of behavior. A large percentage of teachers considered talking to the child or moralizing as the best way of treating behavior problems. A smaller percentage of responses favored punitive measures, and very few responses indicated that medical care was necessary to improve behavior.

Results would seem to indicate that the test described in this study might be successfully used by other school systems to evaluate teacher insight into pupil behavior, and that comparisons might be made with the results obtained in the present study.

———▶ **E. C. Hunter**

Changes in Teachers' Attitudes toward Children's Behavior over the Last Thirty Years

From *Mental Hygiene,* January, 1957, 41:3–11. Reprinted and abridged by permission.[1]

That teachers should understand better the social and emotional dynamics of children's behavior is increasingly evident. Effective behavior guidance depends upon properly gauging background factors and carefully appraising misbehavior tendencies. The comparative seriousness of behavior problems in children has now been the subject of systematic study for three decades. Progress has been made in the direction of better appraising misbehavior, but the need for continued study and improvement in this endeavor persists.

In 1926–27 Wickman [24] in his now classic investigation revealed that teachers and mental hygienists differed markedly in their interpretation of children's behavior problems. The teachers rated as most serious transgressions against authority, dishonesty, immoralities, violation of rules, lack of orderliness, and lack of application to school work. In striking contrast, a group of mental hygienists rated the preceding items low in the scale of seriousness, but rated as most serious unsocial, withdrawing, and recessive behavior. They rated as fairly high cruelty, temper tantrums and truancy, each of which was rated low by the teachers. To the teacher in the Wickman study of nearly 30 years ago, profanity, smoking, lack of interest in work, disobedience, de-

---

1 The abridgement of this article involved the omission of the discussion of related research publications: Yourman [25], MacClenathan [13], Laycock [9], Mitchell [15], Stouffer [20], and Sparks [19].

fiance, and writing obscene notes were grave offenses. To the clinicians, excessive suspiciousness, dreaminess, being overcritical of others, sensitiveness and shyness, which were minimized by teachers, were danger signals for trouble in the future.

The present study attempted to answer three questions: What was the relative seriousness of various behavior problems of children as rated by classroom teachers in 1955? How did the 1955 teacher ratings compare with the ratings of the same problems by teachers and mental hygienists in the Wickman study? With regard to attitudes toward behavior problems, how did teachers in 1955 vary with respect to sex, race, marital status, education and teaching experience?

The Wickman list of 50 behavior problems was used in this study. Since it has been established that the ratings of mental hygienists are relatively stable, no new group of clinicians was used in the 1955 study. On the basis of sex, race, educational status, and teaching experience the 308 elementary and secondary school teachers in this study were representative of the teaching force in a large city in the deep south, New Orleans. Nonteaching and administrative personnel were not included. In a questionnaire mailed to their home addresses in February 1955, classroom teachers were asked to rate anonymously the seriousness of each behavior problem on a scale from 0 to 20 (from "no consequence" to "an extremely grave problem") with regard to the child's future adjustment and welfare.

COMPARISON OF RANK-ORDER

Table 1 shows the rank-order arrangement of seriousness assigned to the 50 behavior problems by the 1955 teachers, the Wickman teachers, and the Wickman mental hygienists. Three items in the 1955 teachers' column (inquisitiveness, smoking, and whispering) are juxtaposed with the same items in the mental hygienists' column. Only one item (inquisitiveness) is juxtaposed in the Wickman teachers' column. Five items (cruelty, temper tantrums, slovenly in appearance, thoughtlessness, interrupting) in each of the teacher columns are removed only slightly from one to three ranks, from the same items in the mental hygienists' column.

Further examination of Table 1 reveals that of the ten problems rated most serious in this study eight were rated equally serious by the Wickman teachers. Thus, so far as teachers are concerned, the typical behavior-problem child in 1955, as in 1926, was characterized by annoying, aggressive and irresponsible behavior. The teachers in the present study considered obscene notes and cheating to be much less serious than did Wickman's teachers 29 years earlier. Heterosexual activity and masturbation were ranked 19th and 29th in seriousness by the 1955 teachers; the Wickman teachers ranked these traits 1st and 3rd. The 1955 teachers agreed with the Wickman mental hygienists on two of the ten problems rated most serious (cruelty and unhappiness); the Wickman teachers agreed with the clinicians on only one trait (cruelty).

The teachers in the present study agreed with the Wickman teachers on seven and with the mental hygienists on four of the ten traits rated least serious; the Wickman teachers agreed in only three instances with the mental hygienists' ratings of the ten traits considered least serious.

With respect to the ranks of the ten traits in central position of seriousness (ranks 21 to 30 inclusive), Table I reveals that the 1955 teachers agreed with the Wickman mental hygienists in one case (obscene notes and talk). The Wickman teachers showed no agreement in this portion of the table. Thus there is evidence that the 1955 teachers were closer to the attitudes of mental hygienists than were the teachers in 1926. Studies by Mitchell [15] in 1940 and Stouffer [20] in 1950 showed similar evidence.

Wickman reported a coefficient of correlation of $-.11$ between the rank-order of traits in terms of seriousness as rated by the mental hygienists and by the teachers. In the present study a correlation of $+.22$ was found, indicating a closer agreement between the ratings of the 1955 teachers and the Wickman clinicians than between the latter and the 1926 teachers.

TABLE 1

Rank-Order Comparison of Ratings by Teachers in 1955 and by Teachers and Mental Hygienists in 1926 of the Relative Seriousness of 50 Behavior Problems

308 Teachers (1955) (Hunter)	511 Teachers (1926) (Wickman)	30 Mental Hygienists (1926) (Wickman)
1. Stealing	Heterosexual activity	Unsocial, withdrawn
2. Destroying school materials	Stealing	Suspiciousness
3. Truancy	Masturbation	Unhappy, depressed
4. Cruelty, bullying	Obscene notes, talk	Resentfulness
5. Unhappy, depressed	Untruthfulness	Fearfulness
6. Impertinence, defiance	Truancy	Cruelty, bullying
7. Untruthfulness	Impertinence, defiance	Easily discouraged
8. Unreliableness	Cruelty, bullying	Suggestible
9. Disobedience	Cheating	Overcritical of others
10. Heterosexual activity	Destroying school materials	Sensitiveness
11. Resentfulness	Disobedience	Domineering
12. Impudence, rudeness	Unreliableness	Sullenness
13. Lack of interest in work	Temper tantrums	Stealing
14. Quarrelsomeness	Lack of interest in work	Shyness
15. Easily discouraged	Profanity	Physical cowardice
16. Cheating	Impudence, rudeness	Selfishness
17. Carelessness in work	Laziness	Temper tantrums
18. Temper tantrums	Smoking	Dreaminess
19. Unsocial, withdrawing	Enuresis	Nervousness
20. Selfishness	Nervousness	Stubbornness
21. Laziness	Disorderliness in class	Unreliableness
22. Disorderliness in class	Unhappy, depressed	Truancy

23. Obscene notes, talk	Easily discouraged	Untruthfulness
24. Suggestible	Selfishness	Cheating
25. Domineering	Carelessness in work	Lack of interest in work
26. Inattention	Inattention	Heterosexual activity
27. Nervousness	Quarrelsomeness	Enuresis
28. Masturbation	Suggestible	Obscene notes, talk
29. Profanity	Resentfulness	Tattling
30. Fearfulness	Tardiness	Attracting attention
31. Sullenness	Physical cowardice	Quarrelsomeness
32. Attracting attention	Stubbornness	Impudence, rudeness
33. Stubbornness	Domineering	Imaginative lying
34. Overcritical of others	Slovenly in appearance	Inattention
35. Physical cowardice	Sullenness	Slovenly in appearance
36. Thoughtlessness	Fearfulness	Laziness
37. Tardiness	Suspiciousness	Impertinence
38. Slovenly in appearance	Thoughtlessness	Carelessness in work
39. Sensitiveness	Attracting attention	Thoughtlessness
40. Shyness	Unsocial, withdrawing	Restlessness
41. Suspiciousness	Dreaminess	Masturbation
42. Enuresis	Imaginative lying	Disobedience
43. Interrupting	Interrupting	Tardiness
44. Inquisitiveness	Inquisitiveness	Inquisitiveness
45. Dreaminess	Overcritical of others	Destroying school materials
46. Restlessness	Tattling	Disorderliness in class
47. Tattling	Whispering	Profanity
48. Imaginative lying	Sensitiveness	Interrupting
49. Smoking	Restlessness	Smoking
50. Whispering	Shyness	Whispering

Comparison of Mean Ratings

Table 2 gives the mean ratings for the 1955 study, the Wickman teachers and the Wickman mental hygienists on each of the 20 behavior problems. (It should be remembered that the higher the mean the more serious or undesirable the behavior is considered.) Behavior problems rated substantially (at least two mean points) more serious by the mental hygienists than by the 1955 teachers included suspiciousness, unsocialness, fearfulness, unhappy-depressed, overcritical of others, sensitiveness, shyness, and dreaminess. In addition to these eight items the mental hygienists rated five problems (easily discouraged, suggestible, resentfulness, domineering and sullenness) substantially more serious than did the 1926 teachers. Obviously overt aggressive behavior was rated as more serious by teachers than by mental hygienists, although the differences for the 1955 teachers were not so great as for the 1926 teachers.

Twenty-seven problems were rated substantially more serious by the 1955 teachers than by the mental hygienists: stealing, truancy, impertinence, destroying school materials, disobedience, masturbation, disorderliness in class, unreliableness, untruthfulness, heterosexual activity, lack of interest in work, interrupting, whispering, attracting attention, cheating, obscene notes, quarrelsomeness, impudence, inattention, slovenliness in appearance, laziness, carelessness in work, thoughtlessness, tardiness, inquisitiveness, profanity, and smoking. The same 27 problems were rated substantially more serious by the 1926 teachers than by the mental hygienists. Many of these problems were rated of small consequence by teachers and mental hygienists. For instance, smoking and whispering were ranked 49th and 50th in seriousness by the 1955 teachers and by the clinicians, yet the means differed by five points. In terms of rank, apparently, the differences between teachers and mental hygienists would not seem to be so great as implied by the differences in means.

Fifteen problems were rated about the same by the 1955 teachers and the Wickman clinicians: resentfulness, cruelty-bullying, easily discouraged, suggestible, domineering, sullenness, selfishness, temper tantrums, nervousness, stubbornness, enuresis,

TABLE 2

Comparison of Mean Ratings by Teachers in 1955 and by Teachers and Mental Hygienists in 1926 of the Relative Seriousness of 50 Behavior Problems

	RATING CHART		
Slight Consequence 5.0	Considerable Difficulty 12.0	Extremely Grave Problem 20.0	
Behavior Problems	Teachers (1955) N = 308	Teachers (1926) N = 511	Mental Hygienists (1926) N = 30
1. Stealing	14.9	17.0	12.5
2. Destroying school materials	13.7	14.3	5.1
3. Truancy	13.6	15.6	10.3
4. Cruelty, bullying	13.5	14.8	13.5
5. Unhappy, depressed	13.4	11.5	16.2
6. Impertinence, defiance	13.4	15.0	7.1
7. Untruthfulness	13.3	15.8	10.3
8. Unreliableness	13.3	15.8	10.3
9. Disobedience	13.0	14.1	6.4
10. Heterosexual activity	12.9	17.3	9.9
11. Resentfulness	12.5	10.8	14.1
12. Impudence, rudeness	12.4	12.2	7.6
13. Lack of interest in work	12.1	12.8	9.6
14. Quarrelsomeness	12.0	11.1	8.3
15. Easily discouraged	11.9	11.5	13.4
16. Cheating	11.9	14.7	10.3
17. Carelessness in work	11.8	11.3	7.1
18. Temper tantrums	11.7	13.0	11.7
19. Unsocial, withdrawing	11.6	8.3	17.3
20. Selfishness	11.6	11.3	11.8
21. Laziness	11.6	12.2	7.2
22. Disorderliness in class	11.5	11.7	3.4
23. Obscene notes, talk	11.5	16.6	8.8
24. Suggestible	11.4	11.0	13.3
25. Domineering	11.2	19.3	13.0
26. Inattention	11.1	11.2	7.3
27. Nervousness	11.1	11.7	11.3
28. Masturbation	10.7	16.7	6.4
29. Profanity	10.5	12.3	2.9
30. Fearfulness	10.4	9.7	14.0
31. Sullenness	10.2	9.9	12.6
32. Attracting attention	10.2	8.5	8.5
33. Stubbornness	10.1	10.3	10.9
34. Overcritical of others	9.8	7.9	13.2
35. Physical cowardice	9.8	10.4	12.0
36. Thoughtlessness	9.7	8.7	6.8
37. Tardiness	9.7	10.5	5.6
38. Slovenly in appearance	9.7	10.1	7.2
39. Sensitiveness	9.6	7.0	13.1
40. Shyness	9.5	5.4	12.5
41. Suspiciousnes	9.5	9.1	16.4
42. Enuresis	9.2	11.8	9.2
43. Interrupting	9.0	8.0	2.8
44. Inquisitiveness	8.8	8.0	5.3
45. Dreaminess	8.8	8.3	11.3
46. Restlessness	8.6	6.9	6.4
47. Tattling	8.1	7.5	8.8
48. Imaginative lying	8.0	8.1	7.5
49. Smoking	7.3	12.0	2.3
50. Whispering	6.3	7.5	0.8
Average	10.9	11.3	9.5

tattling, imaginative lying, restlessness, and physical cowardice. The Wickman teachers rated ten of these problems and two others (thoughtlessness and attracting attention) about the same as did the mental hygienists. For five problems (enuresis, suggestible, resentfulness, domineering, and sullenness) the ratings of the 1955 teachers were definitely closer to the mental hygienists' than were the ratings of the 1926 teachers. Four of these problems were characterized by Wickman as describing withdrawing and recessive behavior. Thus it appears that today's teachers are definitely showing more concern about nonaggressive traits and behavior suggesting mental health problems than did the teachers in 1926.

PROBLEMS RELATED TO SEX

In the present study the teachers ranked five behavior problems (cruelty, heterosexual activity, obscene notes, masturbation and enuresis) 4th, 10th, 23rd, 28th, and 42nd in seriousness. The Wickman teachers ranked these problems 8th, 1st, 4th, 3rd and 19th. Among the 1955 teachers these five problems showed the highest standard deviations. Except for enuresis, this was not true for the Wickman teachers. Four of the five problems are associated with sex. The heterogeneity of the 1955 teachers from New Orleans may be attributed in part to various religious backgrounds, ideas, doubts and uncertainties in the realm of sex. The influence of religious training doubtlessly influences the seriousness assigned to problems relating to sex.

Study of the total average means in Table 2 for the three groups further indicates that the 1955 teachers were closer to the mental hygienists in their evaluation of children's problems than were the Wickman teachers in 1926 or the Stouffer teachers in 1950. The total average mean for the Wickman mental hygienists was 9.5, that for the Wickman teachers 11.3, that for the Stouffer teachers 11.2, that for the present group 10.9. On 36 of the 50 problems the 1955 teachers were closer to the evaluations of the clinicians than were the 1926 teachers.

The present study confirms the findings of Sparks [19] that teachers with training beyond the bachelor's degree resembled more closely the mental hygienists' evaluations of behavior problems than did those with less education. In this study teachers without degrees placed much less emphasis on withdrawing types of behavior than did teachers with degrees.

Men and women teachers in the 1955 study gave similar evaluations to overt, aggressive, and attacking behavior. Men teachers definitely considered problems relating to sex to be much less serious than did women teachers, and the latter considered three problems (slovenly in personal appearance, destroying school materials and suggestible) substantially less serious than did men teachers.

Negro teachers in the present study considered tardiness, laziness, and carelessness in work considerably more serious than did the white teachers or mental hygienists. On the other hand, Negro teachers thought that cruelty-bullying, impertinence-defiance, and temper tantrums were definitely less serious than did white teachers.

No significant differences in ratings were found between married and unmarried teachers in this study, confirming one previous study on this point. [4] For 47 of the 50 problems the ratings of married and unmarried teachers did not differ appreciably.

In this study the behavior ratings of teachers with five to ten years of teaching experience more closely resembled those of the mental hygienists than did teachers with less than five or more than 10 years of experience. On 27 of the 50 problems teachers with five to ten years of experience were closer to the evaluations of the mental hygienists than were those with less experience. On 31 problems those with five to ten years of experience were closer to the clinicians than were those with more teaching experience.

Although teachers continue to be concerned with much annoying and aggressive behavior, their understanding of causal factors and of consequences of behavior patterns has expanded and deepened over the last few decades. It can no longer be said that teachers consider only the here and now in dealing with behavior problems, while mental hygienists consider only the future. Teachers today are dealing more effectively with the whole child now and over the long span. The more highly trained teachers especially are better able than teachers were formerly to analyze and interpret the significance of recessive and withdrawing forms of behavior.

At the same time the need for continued effort and more specific training in the study of complicated patterns of behavior is apparent. Through formal and informal means teachers need to be helped to understand the basic patterns of children's lives. Mental hygiene should occupy a larger role in undergraduate and graduate work, in both pre-service and in-service education of teachers. Academic study should be supplemented by abundant observation and realistic experience with children in and out of school. Mutual exchange of ideas and experiences between teachers and mental hygienists with regard to behavior problems should be encouraged. Continued cooperative research in the dynamics of child behavior should be carried on in order to increase our knowledge and understanding of how to deal more effectively with the child and his education.

⟶ Percival M. Symonds

Classroom Discipline

From *Teachers College Record*, 1949, 51:147–158. Reprinted and abridged by permission.

Classroom discipline is important, not only because it is an ever-present concern of teachers but because methods of classroom control are closely related to the whole problem of training for democratic living and action. David Levy, who had an opportunity to study the mentality of anti-Nazis in Germany following the war, reports that the typical Nazi was one who was brought up under strict authoritarian discipline whereas the childhood of the anti-Nazi departed from this typical German pattern. Levy [11] says, "The typical German father is dominating in the family and uses corporal punishment in the discipline of his children. The child is in awe of the father and does not talk to him freely. At the table during mealtime conversation is discouraged." Methods of control in the classroom as well as in the home exert an influence on the growing personality of the children and democratic attitudes formed by them are determined in no small part by the kind of relations set up between teachers and pupils in the classroom.

THE PROBLEM OF CONTROL

Control in and of itself is not an educational aim. Control serves primarily the needs of the teacher. A teacher may attempt to justify his efforts to secure and retain control on the grounds that it is in the interests of education. The statement is frequently made that one must have an orderly classroom if effective learning is to take place, but it has never been demonstrated that learning requires the high degree of order and restraint that is the ideal of many teachers, and the fact remains that effort to secure quiet orderliness serves primarily the need of the teacher to feel secure in his work.

PUNISHMENT

The problem of this discussion, therefore, will be restated as: What forms of teacher-pupil relationships are most conducive to good personality development? Let us get to the heart of the problem and look at the matter of punishment. Is punishment necessary in order to guide behavior of children into acceptable channels? This is a question for psychology to answer. Thorndike [21] originally stated that when a response is followed by an annoying state of affairs the connection between this response and the stimulus which preceded it tends to be weakened. This original statement of the negative law of effect served as a guide for educators for many years. In later experimentation, however, Thorndike discovered that punishment is by no means the opposite of reward and the effect of punishment is by no means so significant in weakening learning as reward is in strengthening learning. In 1932 he states, "A satisfying after-effect which belongs to a connection can be relied on to strengthen the connection. An annoying after-effect under the same conditions has no such uniform weakening effect. . . . There is no evidence that an annoying after-effect takes away strength from the physiological basis of the connection in any way comparable to the way in which a satisfying after-effect adds strength to it." [22] In another place he is even more emphatic: "Rewarding a connection always strengthened it substantially; punishing it weakened it little or not at all." [23]

More recently, Estes [6] working under the direction of Skinner, carried out a thoroughgoing experimental study of punishment in which he concludes, "No evidence has been forthcoming to indicate that punishment exerts a direct weakening effect upon a response comparable to the strengthening produced by a reward."

Many persons find it difficult to accept this conclusion which apparently goes in the face of common sense and everyday observation. The question may well be asked: What does punishment do if it does not result in a decrease of learning?

Perhaps the effect of punishment can best be seen by resorting to a homely illustration. A mother has forbidden her son to play in the street because of the danger of passing automobiles. On one occasion when she sees him run into the street to recover a ball, she speaks sharply to him and gives him a few sharp thwacks. It was noted that after this the boy stayed on the sidewalk and refrained from running into the street. Could it be that the punishment had taught him not to run into the street? The question, however, concerns the strength of the learning. One would have to admit that after the punishment the boy was just as able to run into the street as he was before, and that the inclination to do so when he wished to recover his ball was as strong after the punishment as before. After the punishment, however, he *repressed* his tendency to run into the street and refrained from doing it. In other words, the effect of punishment is to produce an inhibition of behavior, which is quite different from weakening the response or the tendency to make it.

Concomitants to Punishment

Punishment carries with it many undesirable concomitants. For one thing, anxiety may be aroused by the threat of punishment which may cause the effect of punishment to spread to other situations. As Estes [6] says, "An emotional state such as 'anxiety' or 'dread' which has become conditioned to the incipient movements of making the response will be aroused by any stimuli which formerly acted as occasions for the occurrence of the response."

Second, the emotional response and the inhibition may spread to objects or individuals in the neighboring field. It is common knowledge that punishment arouses hate of the punisher and what the punisher stands for, possibly school and learning. When a teacher punishes a child in order to control his behavior he is at the same time fostering feelings of hate and revenge toward himself and possible dislike toward the school and everything connected with it.

Third, since punishment is frequently administered in a spirit of anger, it may arouse in the child who is its recipient tendencies toward counter-aggression. Many children respond to punishment by becoming sulky, revengeful, or obstinate. Punishment may provoke in a child a tendency to struggle and challenge the authority of the person who has administered it.

Fourth, since punishment leads to guilt for the repressed tendencies which on the one hand struggle for expression and on the other hand are blocked from acceptable expression, it eventually leads to a need for punishment to expiate the guilt. This phenomenon explains the tendency which children often show to provoke punishment as a way of paying the penalty for and being absolved from the guilt which they feel for unexpressed tendencies for which on previous occasions they have been punished.

Fifth, the punished child frequently finds it necessary to test the environment in order to discover the extent and severity of punishment to which he is liable and whether this punishment can be tolerated. Frequently, neurotic children, because of their insecurity and their fear of dire consequences of bad behavior, have a need to test the limits of the situation to see whether they can bear the punishment which they will receive. This testing the limits challenges the teacher's patience and self-control where both firmness and restraint of emotions (but not punishment) are called for. This child needs to know that he is understood.

Perhaps the most devastating effect of punishment is the lowering of self-esteem and the arousal of feelings of inferiority that follow in its wake. The punished child feels that he has fallen from the good graces of the punishing person and that as a result he is a person of less value. Snygg and Combs [18] bring out clearly the point that an individual acts in accordance with his conception of himself. If he is made to think of himself as bad, incompetent, worthless, an outcast (as punishment helps him to think of himself), then he will tend to act in accordance with his concept of himself.

Neglect as Discipline

Neglect is another method of discipline which is sometimes advocated. Dr. Hohman [8] professor of neuropsychiatry at Duke University, makes a strong case for this method. The psychological principle involved he describes as follows: "If the reinforcement, which for practical purposes can be called 'rewards' or 'punishment' does not *follow* the desired conditioned response, either the conditioned response is not established or else it is promptly extinguished or abolished. In animals, as well as children, as soon as a conditioned response is not reinforced or rewarded, the pattern begins to disappear. After several trials without reward, there is no longer any conditioned response." Applying Dr. Hohman's point of view, teachers who wish to suppress show-off behavior in the classroom could achieve the results that they desire by ignoring this behavior.

Dr. Hohman is correct in the psychological principle which he adduces and his interpretation of it. He overlooks certain factors, however, which illustrate how dangerous it may be to interpret psychological laws derived from experimentation with animals as applying to human situations. For one thing, the neglect may be looked upon and interpreted by the child as a punishment, and the child may be responding as much to what he considers to be a punishment as to the psychological condition of lack of response. For instance, children are quite frequently punished by being confined alone in a closet, a cellar, or an empty room. Furthermore, this form of control may also have its undesirable concomitants and the resulting insecurity that the child experiences through the parents' failure to respond may be even more traumatic in its consequence than severe punishment. A child may become panic-stricken when he finds himself alone and realizes that his parents will not respond to his cries. Instead of reducing in intensity his behavior may become frenzied.

Both punishment and failure to respond overlook the meaning of the child's original behavior. There is an instructive case in a book by Foster and Anderson [7] which illustrates the point to be made.

Mabel was referred to a clinic at the age of two years and seven months by her mother for a variety of complaints. On the first call to the clinic, the mother complains that the child wets the bed every night, that she refuses to take her nap, is obstinate, does not obey, eats mud, and runs away. Mrs. Miller is advised by the clinic to be more firm, to punish Mabel by isolating her in a room, to allow the child less water to drink in the later afternoon, and to have her wear long cardboard cuffs extending above the elbow so that she will be unable to put her hands in her mouth while playing outdoors.

On the the second visit, the mother reports that these difficulties of Mabel's have cleared up but she now has trouble playing amicably with other children and tells small untruths. Again the mother is given suggestions, and by the next visit the fibbing has disappeared but the child's table manners have become atrocious. On still another visit, it is reported that the table manners have improved, but Mabel has developed show-off behavior. Her mother follows the clinician's advice to ignore the child when she refused to eat, and to put her in a room by herself away from company when she persists in showing off, and at the next visit reports that these difficulties have been overcome but now Mabel whines continually when she cannot have her way. In short, each one of Mabel's problems could be eradicated by a suitable punishment or neglect, but Mabel still remained a problem child.

This case makes it clear that the behavior was a symptom of inner dissatisfaction of a fundamental sort, and when one symptom was stamped out another arose to take its place. In spite of the mother's attempts to control and guide the child, following the directions suggested at the clinic, the child's fundamental problems persisted. This case also illustrated very clearly the point which has been frequently made—that punishment does not get to the root of a child's difficulties and that while punishment may be successful in eradicating undesirable behavior, it does not do anything toward correcting the basic problems. Mabel was a child who needed to be understood. It was interesting in this case that when she went to kindergarten her teacher reported her as very obedient and as doing excellent work, and Mabel apparently enjoyed the kindergarten. Her earlier behavior was a response to the mother's basic rejection and was undoubtedly a persistent attempt on the part of the child to force the mother to pay attention to her and to be good to her. In addition, Mabel's guilt repeatedly forced her to test her mother's evaluation of her and to try out her belief that she was a bad child.

One cannot escape the basic fact that neither punishment nor neglect considers the underlying needs. Much of the undesirable behavior which a child exhibits in the classroom is neurotic—an unsatisfactory attempt to satisfy some underlying need—but neither punishment nor neglect gets to the root of this trouble. It is more important to solve the basic conflict that gives rise to the undesirable behavior than it is to attempt to suppress the behavior directly.

THE INSECURE TEACHER

Within the leeway afforded by the expectations of the principal and the community, variations in teacher-pupil relations in the classroom reflect the security of the individual teacher. An insecure teacher does not dare to relax control for fear that his authority will be irrevocably undermined. He is afraid that he will not be able to handle the hostilities of his pupils as well as his own anger, and he is also afraid of the criticism of his superior officers. The emotionally secure teacher, on the other hand, feeling confident in his own strength, dares to be more informal and natural, and if at the same time he is secure in his position, or is above caring whether he is, he can afford to face possible criticism that he may invoke from his superiors.

The insecure teacher does not dare to let an offense pass unnoticed, but feels that he must deal with it precipitately. The secure teacher, on the other hand, dares to wait. He does not feel the necessity for handling the situation immediately. The secure teacher, because he knows that he has the majority of his class with him, feels that when he must deal with some disciplinary situation he can deal with the individual concerned without undermining his relations with the class as a whole.

In good teaching, problems of discipline seldom arise, because both teacher and pupils are interested in the activities of the class. Apparently the insecure teacher is consigned to being ineffective and the secure teacher, in spite of himself, is effective. Actually, classroom discipline cannot be reduced to a set of rules and principles; it is more a matter of attitude and feeling. The sussessful teacher concentrates on matters other than classroom order and control. He encourages the class to share his interest in the activities and subject matter with which they are concerned, and problems of order do not arise.

The Good Teacher

A good teacher is firm and active. It is important not to confuse firmness with punishment. The two are by no means identical. It is possible to be quietly yet insistently firm without threatening or practicing punishment. A good teacher avoids issuing commands, but he expresses his wishes and his expectations with considerable vigor and, if necessary, persistence. A good teacher does not fail to let his pupils know what he expects of them, and the very clarity with which he expresses his wishes helps to secure good relations.

A good teacher challenges his pupils; he makes them proud of their achievement or ashamed if their work is not up to their best. No teacher can expect to succeed with a pupil whom he dislikes, hence he must find something in every child to like. He must believe that each has possibilities in some direction; he must have faith that each will succeed in some way. A good teacher is patient and tolerant with his pupils; he recognizes that they are children and still have some way to travel to maturity and he is willing to overlook irregularities. But once an irregularity has been condoned, the teacher should not fail to make clear his expectations for them. A good teacher is as honest in telling his pupils when and in what way they please him as in telling them when and in what way they displease him.

Even the best teachers, however, find that disciplinary crises arise on some occasions, but every teacher should recognize that they may arise through no fault of his. Teachers should not expect to be successful with every pupil and it is no threat or defeat for a teacher to find that some pupils do not respond to every effort that he may make to help them succeed. Hostility directed toward a teacher or the classroom situation is in many instances a displacement of hostility which has been aroused in some other situation. The teacher should recognize this and refuse to be drawn into the relationship. The secure teacher does not feel that he must repay rudeness with rudeness or resistance with stubbornness. Some children simply are not ready to accept membership in certain classroom situations and need therapeutic help before they can become acceptable and tolerated members of a group.

DISCIPLINE IN THE NEW SITUATION

Every teacher must decide on the basis of the relationship which he expects to establish with his class. Is it to be a contest of wills or a show of physical superiority or is the relationship going to be pitched on a different level? A secure teacher in a new situation has to be strong enough to decide that the relationship is to be one of reasonableness and interest in the work and not based on dominance and submission. Teachers should be secure enough to be willing to adopt an attitude of take it or leave it with regard to the cooperation of individual pupils, but every teacher must always be ready and able to defend his own person and self-respect. It is one thing to tolerate rebellion and resistance that is expressed verbally and another to be helpless against physical attack and violence. Verbal criticism and attack are not fatal and may actually afford welcome release for a pupil. If disciplinary problems arise, it is essential that the teacher recognize and permit the expression of feeling as Baruch [3] and Axline [2] have so clearly shown. To permit pupils to express their feelings in words need be no threat to the teacher's authority and prestige, and, in fact, may release a good deal of the pent-up emotion which was the occasion of the irregular behavior. When a disciplinary problem arises the successful teacher holds his own feelings in check and deals with the pupil on the basis of reason and an understanding of the motives that lie behind the act. He attempts to guide his pupils into more accepted and preferred modes of behavior with a minimum of emphasis on the mistakes that have been made in the past.

The problem of classroom discipline cannot and should not be thought of in terms of some immediate incident. It is difficult, if not impossible, to tell a teacher how to handle some isolated incident that may arise in the classroom. The problem of discipline is one that requires growth in relationship over a long period of time. Little can be done to help a teacher know how to manage in a given situation. Much can be done to help a teacher work out constructive and growth-producing relationships with his class over a period of weeks and months. Eventually a class must so trust and respect the teacher that he can deal with individuals as occasions arise without disturbing his relationship to the group as a whole.

——▶ **Ralph H. Ojemann
and Francis R. Wilkinson**

The Effect on Pupil Growth
of an Increase in Teacher's
Understanding of Pupil Behavior

From *Journal of Experimental Education*, 1939, 8:143–147.
Reprinted and abridged by permission.

It is clear that effective learning cannot take place unless a strong motive is present. It is equally clear that it is difficult to motivate a child whose energies are spent worrying about in-school or out-of-school situations or whose wants at the moment are of such a character that the work in school does not seem to contribute to his wants. If the teacher does not know that perhaps John is worrying about getting to his street corner on time to sell his papers, or that he does not take part in class discussions because of a feeling of inferiority, or that he is worried about his home, she is not likely to succeed in stimulating John to do his best. On the other hand knowing the child's attitude, conflicts, and purposes should make the teacher a better guide in planning an effective program of work for him.

Furthermore, if the development of personality in its various aspects were closely watched by the teacher it would appear highly probable that the beginnings of behavior difficulties could be detected long before the difficulties emerge as serious behavior problems. Teachers and administrators long ago learned that it is impossible to direct the child's growth in school subjects without careful and frequent checks on the progress the pupil is making.

In the area of personality growth, however, the situation is quite different. The present tendency in schools is to wait until some "maladjustment" or "behavior problem" appears. Then, but usually not before, personality growth becomes a matter of concern. And it is the "problem child" that becomes the center of emphasis. This tendency to wait until the child gets into difficulty before giving attention to personality growth appears analogous to waiting until the pupil has failed on a final examination before giving consideration to his growth in knowledge. Neither course of action is logical. It would seem that if the classroom teacher had at hand information about the child's personality and were trained to follow the development of personality in its several aspects, just as she follows the course of growth in reading, spelling, or history she could detect the beginnings of behavior problems and redirect development long before the deviations become serious. Thinking only in terms of problem children is not adequate for effective guidance.

The foregoing suggestions, namely, that learning becomes more effective and that the development of personality can be more adequately controlled if a careful analysis of behavior is made by the teacher, are in the nature of assumptions. The study reported in this paper was designed to test experimentally the two assumptions.

The general method of the study consisted in selecting an experimental and control group, obtaining measurements of both groups at the beginning of the experimental period, assisting teachers in making an analysis of the motives, attitudes, and environmental conditions of the experimental subjects, and measuring growth again at the close of the experimental period. Underlying the plan of the study is the conception that behavior is determined by such factors as motives, psychological equipment in the form of attitude, emotional control, etc., and the presence or absence of direct restrictions in the environment. It was assumed that to chart the growth of personality data relative to the child's ambitions or motives, attitudes, emotional stability, and the nature of the home and community environment would be needed.

From approximately one hundred thirty-five pupils of the ninth grade of a public school sixty-six subjects for whom various records required in the equating procedure were available were selected and divided into an experimental and control group of thirty-three subjects each. The two groups were equated in terms of chronological age, scores on Otis Group Intelligence Test, and achievement of previous year as measured in grade points. As indicated in Table 1 the two groups were rather closely matched

TABLE 1

	Experimental Group		Control Group	
Factor	Mean	Standard Deviation	Mean	Standard Deviation
Chronological age, years	14.4	.79	13.9	.52
Intelligence	109.7	7.90	108.3	9.09
Achievement, previous year	3.14	.82	3.15	.62

in all three factors.

The comparisons of the experimental and control groups were made in the following areas: school achievement, selected attitudes, personality conflicts, and certain ratings of pupil adjustment. School achievement was determined in terms of grade points. An attitude test including items relative to the pupil's attitude toward his school, his teacher, his home, and toward himself was administered at the beginning and at the close of the experimental period. Personality conflicts were tested by a revision of Luria's [12] method. By the use of this method it seems possible to obtain fairly reliable indications of the extent of personality conflicts, and some indication of their character and of the accompanying mental processes. The method has shown a very satisfactory reliability in a number of studies and also a satisfactory correlation with other indices of personality conflict. [1]

In addition to the data on grade points, attitude, and personality conflicts, teachers' ratings of the general adjustment of pupils at the beginning and at the end of the study were included.

At the beginning of the experimental period personality and environmental data were obtained for the experimental subjects. These data were made available to the teachers who were given rather extended suggestions as to their meaning and use. From the attitude test such items as the nature of the child's ambitions, his satisfaction with various aspects of his home environment, his attitude toward his companions, and the like were obtained. Through a carefully conducted interview with parents data were secured relative to the home environment of the child, the nature of the parental attitudes, and the nature of the child's behavior at home.

With the data for each experimental subject at hand the investigator summarized the important facts in written form and added her interpretations of the situation. An appointment was then made with each teacher who had the subject enrolled in her class. After a satisfactory working relationship had been established between teacher and investigator the analysis was presented, the investigator pointing out the essential facts and making sure that the teacher understood them. Suggestions that seemed helpful in understanding and controlling the pupil's behavior were supplied.

The experiment was begun in the fall and continued through the school year. The necessary measurements were repeated in the spring just before the close of school.

TABLE 2

| Group | Mean | Standard Deviation | | Critical Ratio |
		of Distribution	of Mean	
Experimental	3.21	.63	.10	
Control	2.97	.68	.11	
Difference	.24		.07	3.43

At the close of the experiment the difference in mean grade points between the experimental group and the control group had risen to show a critical ratio of the mean to its standard error of 3.43. An examination of the data in Table 2 will give details.

Thus the experimental group made a significantly greater academic gain. In interpreting this finding it should be pointed out that the teachers were not aware that academic achievement would be used as one measure of comparison.

In the attitude test administered at the beginning and at the end of the experimental period ten items were included dealing with the subject's relation to school and school work. These items were scattered throughout a test which in addition to the attitude toward school included various items relating to the home, the subject's ambitions, and the like. The nature of the attitude test items is indicated by the following samples:

The following directions were given to the subjects:

> Your careful answers to the following questions will help us to help you with your school work. Your answers to the following statements will in no way affect your grades but they will help us to help you. Read each of the following statements carefully. If you feel that the statement is completely or almost completely true, put a circle around 1.
>
> If you feel that it is probably true, or true in large degree, put a circle around 2 or 3.
>
> If you feel that it is quite undecided, an open question, put a circle around 4.
>
> If you feel that it is probably false or false in large degree, put a circle around 5 or 6.
>
> If you feel that the statement is completely or almost completely false, put a circle around 7.

1	2	3	4	5	6	7	Under ordinary circumstances good marks are usually the result of hard studying.
1	2	3	4	5	6	7	The use of lipstick and rouge, if not very noticeable, is permissible for girls of high school age.
1	2	3	4	5	6	7	My school work is easier for me this year than it has been in the past.

An attempt was made to conceal the purpose of the test by including items relating to many areas. It was planned to use only the items relating to school when comparing the growth of the experimental and control groups. Though its purpose was somewhat concealed the attitude test was not as indirect as was desired but was used pending the construction of a good attitude test in this area. [17]

An analysis of the items relating to school revealed that by the close of the study the experimental and control groups differed significantly in their attitude toward school. The experimental group was significantly more willing to ascribe achievement to planned work rather than to chance factors. The experimental group felt that careful work in the long run would bring its reward and that an education can be made worthwhile. The experimental group felt significantly less the need of cheating. They were less willing to be swayed by temporary likes and dislikes in school life. They felt that their work during the experimental year had been more pleasant than that of the preceding year. The experimental group also evidenced a more favorable attitude toward their school companions and gave fewer indications of feelings of inferiority than did the control group. On the whole these data seem to indicate a happier and more logical attitude toward school and school work on the part of the experimental group than the control group.

In the test for personality conflict several types or records were available. These included indications of conflict and types of verbal responses. As indications of conflict, disturbances in the voluntary movements as obtained in the Luria test were used. An analysis of the disturbances shows a significant decrease from fall to spring on the part of the experimental group and a slight but not significant increase on the part of the control group. The critical ratio of the change in the experimental group is 3.45. Thus the experimental group gave a significant reduction in the scores on the voluntary disturbance portion of the mental conflict test. The data are detailed in Table 3.

TABLE 3

	Initial Scores		Final Scores		
Group	Mean Test	Standard Deviation of Mean	Mean Test	Standard Deviation of Mean	Critical Ratio
Experimental	92.3	7.8	61.0	4.6	3.45
Control	70.4	6.0	74.8	5.3	

By analyzing the verbal responses obtained in the course of the conflict test, it is possible to throw some light on the nature of the central processes. The classification of verbal responses used in this investigation is a very simple one. It includes such categories as coadjunction, contrast, predicate relationship, causal dependence, identity, egocentric, and indirect. This classification has been tested under many conditions as to its reliability. The reliability tends to run in the neighborhood of 80 to 85 per cent. [17] An analysis of the verbal responses in this study indicates that both groups tend to change toward a more complex type of response (Table 4). However, the direction of complexity varies

TABLE 4

PER CENT CHANGE IN VERBAL RESPONSES

Category	Per Cent Change	
	Control	Experimental
Coadjunction	−22.92	−8.62
Contrast	−15.51	−25.95
Predicate	50.79	−14.29
Causal dependence	24.44	71.74
Identity	−32.83	15.35
Word-complement	0.00	48.72
Verbal motor forms	28.57	−30.43
Association by sound	28.57	37.50
Indirect association	45.15	−.56
Egocentric	55.81	−47.83
Fault	−26.92	−81.58
Repetition	−33.33	−50.00

with the two groups. In the control group the change takes the form of a more personalized type of response. This is indicated by a comparatively large increase in such categories as egocentric, predicate, and indirect types of response. In the experimental group, however, there is a reduction in the egocentric, predicate and indirect types and a very considerable increase in the category causal dependence. Such an analysis tends to indicate that the subjects making up the control group are finding it relatively more difficult to make adjustments and consequently in their mental life tend to be more occupied with personal difficulties producing a more personalized type of response. The experimental group on the other hand seems to be extending in the direction of more impersonal, objective, and logical type of mental life.

TABLE 5

Group	Initial Scores		Final Scores		Critical Ratio
	Mean Test	Standard Deviation of Mean	Mean Test	Standard Deviation of Mean	
Is He Interested in His School Work?					
Experimental	3.27	.7	2.33	.10	4.94
Control	3.12	.09	2.86	.11	1.94
Is He Apparently Adjusted in the Classroom?					
Experimental	3.45	.13	2.57	.13	4.62
Control	3.03	.10	2.80	.10	1.71

As for the ratings of general adjustment, in this area too the experimental group showed a significant change over the control group. The critical ratio of the difference to its standard error is 4.6 as shown in Table 5. These ratings corroborate the more detailed findings of the attitude and personality conflict tests. It is realized that ratings made by teachers who participated in the study may have a subjective bias. They are included primarily to indicate what the teachers thought of the general adjustment of the student.

Many interesting illustrations could be given as to the changes teachers evidenced in their attitude toward and treatment of pupils after they had gained some insight into the personality of the experimental subjects. One teacher unwittingly gave away this bit of information about one of the subjects:

I welcomed the information concerning H. D. He always appeared to me to be well-mannered but very independent and resentful. So independent in fact that I hadn't bothered very much with him. Naturally I was quite surprised to learn that in reality he was unhappy. At every opportunity that presents itself I am now endeavoring to assure him by my attitude that all of us have a personal interest in his welfare. I am trying to make him feel that he is definitely a part of the group.

Another teacher:

> After your account of L. M. I see her as an unhappy child rather than an insolent one. I find it easier to accept her.

A sewing teacher:

> I was very much interested in the information concerning G. B. I had previously caught myself wishing I knew more about her home life as she always appeared to be undernourished and inclined to be the "mousy" type. After learning that she received so little encouragement at home I endeavor to praise her school work at every opportunity that arises and I notice she beams at every word.

An English teacher:

> After discovering it was shyness and nervousness rather than sulkiness which prevented L. C. from reciting I made a special effort to see what could be done to help him overcome this difficulty. I seated him so he could be centrally located, praised him at every reasonable opportunity, encouraged him not to do things alone but in company with his classmates as asking him along with others to pass paper, and occasionally to read aloud.

These comments show the beginning of more complete understanding of pupil behavior. Shyness, resentment, over-aggression, and indifference are known to be motivated often by conflicts and frustration. They are signals not for neglect or for the drawing of battle lines but for the need of mutual understanding and helpfulness.

The data obtained in this study are consistent in showing that when teachers learn to know their pupils as personalities in their respective environments teachers tend to become more effective guides for learning—the pupils achieve more in academic areas—and teachers also become more effective personality "developers."

What do these findings signify for the school? They indicate that it is not enough to be concerned about "problem children" when it comes to personality development. Teachers to be effective guides for learning must know their pupils not as entities in the classroom but as living personalities with ambitions, attitudes, conflicts, and problems, coming from environments that vary greatly in the encouragement or discouragement effected.

For teacher education data in this study indicate the importance of including training in understanding of child development and interpretation of child behavior. For administration the results signify the importance of devising machinery by which teachers can learn to know their pupils in terms of their ambitions, hopes, and struggles in both in-school and out-of-school environments. The administrative difficulties are not insurmountable and the expense is not great when compared with the many pounds of cure represented by the many ounces of prevention that can be effected by the understanding teacher.

REFERENCES

1. ACKERLY, LOIS, OJEMANN, R. H., NEIL, BERNIECE, & GRANT, EVA, "A Study of the Transferable Elements in Interviews with Parents," *Journal of Experimental Education,* 1936–1937, 5:137–174.

2. AXLINE, VIRGINIA M., *Play Therapy,* Boston: Houghton Mifflin Company, 1947.

3. BARUCH, DOROTHY W., *New Ways in Discipline,* New York: McGraw-Hill Book Company, Inc., 1949.

4. ELLIS, D. B., & MILLER, L. W., "A Study of the Attitudes of Teachers Toward Behavior Problems," *Journal of Educational Psychology,* 1936, 27:501–511.

5. ESTES, W. K., *An Experimental Study of Punishment,* Psychological Monographs, No. 3, 57:36. Whole No. 263, 1944.

6. ————, *An Experimental Study of Punishment,* Psychological Monographs, No. 3, 57:37. Whole No. 263, 1944.

7. FOSTER, J. C., & ANDERSON, J. E., *The Young Child and His Parents: Case II, Mabel Miller,* Minneapolis: University of Minnesota Press, 1930, pp. 49–53.

8. HOHMAN, L. B., "Directive Versus Permissive Techniques in Counseling Children," *Marriage and Family Living,* 1949, 11:66–67.

9. LAYCOCK, S. R., "Teachers' Reactions to Maladjustments of School Children," *British Journal of Educational Psychology,* 1934, 4:11–29.

10. LEWIS, W. D., "Some Characteristics of Children Designated as Mentally Retarded, as Problems and as Geniuses by Teachers," *Journal of Genetic Psychology*, 1947, 70:29–51.

11. LEVY, D. M., "Anti-Nazi: Criteria of Differentiation," *Psychiatry*, 1948, 1:125–167.

12. LURIA, A. R., *The Nature of Human Conflicts: or, Motion Conflict and Will: An Objective Study of Disorganization and Control of Human Behavior*, trans. by W. H. Gantt, New York: Liveright Publishing Corp., 1932.

13. MACCLENATHAN, RUTH H., "Teachers and Parents Study Children's Behavior," *Journal of Educational Sociology*, 1934, 7:325–333.

14. MIRANNE, A. C., JR., *Teachers' Ratings of Children's Behavior Problems*. Unpublished master's thesis, Tulane University, 1955.

15. MITCHELL, J. C., "A Study of Teachers' and Mental Hygienists' Ratings of Certain Behavior Problems of Children," *Journal of Educational Research*, 1942, 36:292–307.

16. MOWRER, O. H., "Discipline and Mental Health," *Harvard Educational Review*, SVII, Fall, 1947.

17. OJEMANN, R. H., "A Revised Method for the Measurement of Attitude," *Psychological Bulletin*, 1937, 34:752.

18. SNYGG, D., & COMBS, A. W., *Individual Behavior*, New York: Harper & Brothers, 1949.

19. SPARKS, J. N., "Teachers' Attitudes Toward the Behavior Problems of Children," *Journal of Educational Psychology*, 1952, 43:382–391.

20. STOUFFER, G. A. W., JR., "Behavior Problems of Children as Viewed by Teachers and Mental Hygienists: A Study of Present Attitudes as Compared with Those Reported by E. K. Wickman," *Mental Hygiene*, 1952, 36:271–285.

21. THORNDIKE, E. L., *The Original Nature of Man*, Bureau of Publications, Teachers College, Columbia University, 1913, p. 172.

22. ———, *The Fundamentals of Learning*, Bureau of Publications, Teachers College, Columbia University, 1932, pp. 311, 313.

23. ———, *Reward and Punishment in Animal Learning*, Comparative Psychology Monographs, No. 4, 8:58, Serial No. 39, 1932.

24. WICKMAN, E. K., *Children's Behavior and Teachers' Attitudes*, New York: Commonwealth Fund, 1928.

25. YOURMAN, J., "Children Identified by Their Teachers as Problems," *Journal of Educational Sociology*, 1932, 5:334–343.

Author Index

Subject Index

Baller   79889